CENSUS OF INDIA 1911

Census of India 1871-1951, 9 Sets In 384 Bindings (9788121258876) Rs. 700000

Census of India 1911, 23 Vols. In 41 Bindings (9788121271271) Rs. 69000

1. India - Report (9788121275071) Rs. 2475 (Vol. I, Pt. 1)
2. India - Tables (9788121275057) Rs. 2225 (Vol. I, Pt. 2)
3. Andaman and Nicobar Islands - Report & Tables (9788121275033) Rs. 900 (Vol. II, Pt. 1 & 2)
4. Assam - Report (9788121275019) Rs. 1000 (Vol. III, Pt. 1)
5. Assam - Tables (9788121274999) Rs. 1300 (Vol. III, Pt. 2)
6. Baluchistan - Report & Tables (9788121274975) Rs. 950 (Vol. IV, Pt. 1 & 2)
7. Bengal, Bihar And Orissa And Sikkim - Report (9788121274951) Rs. 3100 (Vol. V, Pt. 1)
8. Bengal - Tables (9788121274937) Rs. 2250 (Vol. V, Pt. 2)
9. Bihar And Orissa - Tables and Bengal And Sikkim - Chapter I of Administrative Volume (9788121274913) Rs. 1800 (Vol. V, Pt. 3 & 4)
10. City of Calcutta - Report and Tables and Administrative (9788121274876) Rs. 1300 (Vol. VI, Pt. 1 & 2 & 3)
11. Bombay - Report (9788121274814) Rs. 1950 (Vol. VII, Pt. 1)
12. Bombay - Imperial Tables and Administrative Report (9788121274791) Rs. 3300 (Vol. VII, Pt. 2 & 3)
13. Bombay (Town And Island) - Report And Tables (9788121274753) Rs. 1250 (Vol. VIII, Pt. 1 & 2)
14. Burma - Report (9788121274739) Rs. 2250 (Vol. IX, Pt. 1)
15. Burma - Tables (9788121274715) Rs. 1480 (Vol. IX, Pt. 2)
16. Central Provinces And Berar - Report (9788121274692) Rs. 1475 (Vol. X, Pt. 1)
17. Central Provinces And Berar - Tables (9788121274678) Rs. 1900 (Vol. X, Pt. 2)
18. Coorg - Report And Tables Madras - Report (9788121274630) Rs. 1740 (Vol. XI & Vol. XII, Pt. 1)
19. Madras - Imperial And Provincial Tables (9788121274616) Rs. 1500 (Vol. XII, Pt. 2)
20. Madras - Administrative Report and city of Madras (9788121274593) Rs. 630 (Vol. XII, Pt. 3 & 4)
21. North - West Frontier Province - Report & Tables (9788121274579) Rs. 2150 (Vol. XIII, Pt. 1 & 2)
22. Punjab - Report (9788121274555) Rs. 3000 (Vol. XIV, Pt. 1)
23. Punjab - Tables (9788121274531) Rs. 2200 (Vol. XIV, Pt. 2)
24. Punjab - Appendices To The - Imperial Tables (9788121274517) Rs. 950 (Vol. XIV, Pt. 3)
25. United Provinces of Agra And Oudh - Report (9788121274494) Rs. 2225 (Vol. XV, Pt. 1)
26. United Provinces of Agra And Oudh - Tables (9788121274470) Rs. 4000 (Vol. XV, Pt. 2)
27. United Provinces of Agra And Oudh - Provincial Tables And Appendices (9788121274456) Rs. 570 (Vol. XV, Pt. 3)
28. Baroda - Report (9788121274432) Rs. 2000 (Vol. XVI, Pt. 1)
29. Baroda State - The Imperial Tables (9788121274418) Rs. 850 (Vol. XVI, Pt. 2)
30. Central India Agency - Report And Tables (9788121274395) Rs. 1470 (Vol. XVII)
31. Cochin - Report And Imperial Tables (9788121274371) Rs. 1150 (Vol. XVIII, Pt. 1 & 2)
32. Hyderabad State - Report (9788121274357) Rs. 890 (Vol. XIX, Pt. 1)
33. Hyderabad State - Imperial And Provincial Tables (9788121274333) Rs. 1750 (Vol. XIX, Pt. 2)
34. Kashmir - Report (9788121274319) Rs. 1390 (Vol. XX, Pt. 1)
35. Kashmir - Tables (9788121274296) Rs. 1170 (Vol. XX, Pt. 2)
36. Mysore - Report (9788121274272) Rs. 1200 (Vol. XXI, Pt. 1)
37. Mysore - Tables (9788121274258) Rs. 1500 (Vol. XXI, Pt. 2)
38. Rajputana And Ajmer-Merwara - Report (9788121274234) Rs. 1470 (Vol. XXII, Pt. 1)
39. Rajputana And Ajmer-Merwara - Tables (9788121274210) Rs. 1700 (Vol. XXII, Pt. 2)
40. Travancore - Report (9788121274197) Rs. 1870 (Vol. XXIII, Pt. 1)
41. Travancore - Imperial Tables (9788121274173) Rs. 870 (Vol. XXIII, Pt. 2)

Owing to the antiquity and rarity of this book, certain pages are regrettably absent, and readability is compromised due to the blurring of the original text. If you possess any insights regarding the availability of these missing sections, kindly inform us. Your assistance is crucial in ensuring the completion of this significant work for the benefit of future generations.

CENSUS OF INDIA, 1911

VOLUME - XX

KASHMIR

PART II - TABLES

MD. MATIN-UZ-ZAMAN KHAN

GYAN

Published by

GYAN

Gyan Publishing House
5, Ansari Road
Daryaganj, New Delhi-110002
Phone: 011-47034999, 9811692060
E-mail: books@gyanbooks.com

Distribution Network
gyanbooks.com
India, USA, Canada, UK, Australia

ISBN: 978-81-212-7127-1 (Set) 23 Vols. In 41 Bindings

ISBN: 978-81-212-7429-6 (PB) Vol. XX, Pt. II

First Published, 1912

2nd Impression 2024

Printed at: Gyan Press, Delhi.

CENSUS OF INDIA 1911

CENSUS OF INDIA, 1911

VOLUME XX

KASHMIR

PART II
TABLES

BY
MD. MATIN-UZ-ZAMAN KHAN, B. A.
OF THE PROVINCIAL CIVIL SERVICE, UNITED PROVINCES
SUPERINTENDENT OF CENSUS OPERATIONS, JAMMU AND KASHMIR STATE

LUCKNOW
PRINTED AT THE NEWUL KISHORE PRESS
1912

CONTENTS.

CORRIGENDA.

TABLE I.

Page 1,	§ 5, line 2	...	*delete* " Punch and "

TABLE III.

Page	Column	Against		For		Read
.. 6,	No. 9, col. 9...	against Kashmir South	...	*for* 94,530	...	*read* 84,530
.. 6,	,, 12, ,, 3...	,, Gilgit District	...	,, 2,396	...	.. 23,969

TABLE IV.

Page	Column	Against		For		Read
.. 8,	col. 10	against Total cities	...	,, 87,763	...	.. 87,740
.. 8,	,, 12	,, Islamabad	...	,, 8,515	...	,, 5,515
.. 8,	,, 12	,, Punch	...	,, *nil*	...	,, 4.675
.. 8,	,, 9	,, Mirpur	...	,, +613	...	,, − 613
.. 8,	,, 12	,, ,,	...	,, *nil*	...	.. 3,655
.. 8,	,, 12	,, Baramula	...	,, ,,	...	,, 3,003
.. 9,	,, 13	,, Poni	...	,, 474	...	,, 476

TABLE V.

Page	Column	Against		For		Read
.. 14,	,, 5	,, *Total Kashmir Valley*	...	,, 84,409	...	,, 84,499
.. 14,	,, 12	,, Total Gilgit District	...	.. 20	...	.. *nil*
.. 15,	,, 32	,, Srinagar city	...	,, 6	...	,, 60

TABLE VI.

Page	Reference	Against		For		Read
,, 17,	Table below § 7, title page—Under Total, against Basith		...	,, 7,386	...	.. 7,372
,, 17,	,,	,, Females ,, ,,	...	,, 3,782	...	,, 3,768
,, 17,	,,	,, Total ,, Chamiar	...	,, 38,752	...	,, 39,094
,, 17,	,,	,, Males ,, ,,	...	,, 20,386	...	,, 20,459
,, 17,	,,	,, Females ,, ,,	...	,, 18,366	...	,, 18,635
,, 17,	,,	,, Total ,, Dum	...	,, 36,128	...	,, 36,785
,, 17,	,,	,, Males ,, ,,	...	,, 18,734	...	,, 19,391
,, 17,	,,	,, Total ,, Sansi	...	,, 45	...	,, 59
,, 17,	,,	,, Females ,, ,,	...	,, 4	...	.. 18
,, 17,	,,	,, Total ,, Total	...	,, 177,253	...	,, 178,252
,, 17,	,,	,, Males ,, ,,	...	,, 92,434	...	,, 93,164
,, 17,	,,	,, Females ,, ,,	...	,, 84,819	...	,, 85,088

TABLE VII.

Page	Column	Against		For		Read
.. 24,	col. 6	against Musalman (50—55)	...	,, 1,265	...	,, 1,255
,, 25,	,, 9	,, All Religions (Total 0—5)	...	,, 534	...	,, 634
.. 25,	,, 12	,, Hindu Brahmanic (45—50)	...	,, 3,842	...	., 6,842
,, 27,	,, 6	,, Musalman (15—20)	...	,, 38,739	...	,, 36,739
,, 27,	,, 10	,, ,, (30—35)	...	,, 23,353	...	,, 33,353
,, 28,	,, 9	,, All Religions (60—65)	...	,, 19,825	...	,, 19,826
,, 28,	,, 11	,, Sikh (10—15)	...	,, 24	...	,, 224
,, 29,	,, 10	,, Musalman (10—15)	...	,, 5,727	...	,, 5,726
,, 29,	,, 7	,, ,, (70 & over)	...	,, 294	...	,, 298
,, 30,	,, 7	,, All Religions (Total)	...	,, 707,674	...	,, 307,674
,, 30,	,, 9	,, ,, (10—15)	...	,, 23,328	...	,, 23,318
,, 30,	,, 9	,, ,, (20—25)	...	,, 76,913	...	,, 77,913
,, 30,	,, 11	,, ,, (20—25)	...	,, 45,781	...	,, 46,781
,, 30,	,, 10	,, ,, (70 & over)	...	,, 6,841	...	,, 5,841
,, 30,	,, 10	,, Hindu Brahmanic (Total)	...	,, 11,726	...	,, 11,727
,, 31,	,, 6	,, Musalman (Total)	...	,, 487,743	...	,, 487,744
,, 31,	,, 8	,, ,, (Total)	...	,, 200,553	...	,, 200,554
,, 31,	,, 9	,, ,, (10—15)	...	,, 26,887	...	,, 22,387
,, 31,	,, 11	,, ,, (20—25)	...	,, 44,346	...	,, 44,326
,, 31,	,, 10	,, ,, (55—60)	...	,, 4,938	...	,, 4,928
,, 32,	,, 6	,, All Religions (65—70)	...	,, 77	...	,, 127
,, 32,	,, 7	,, ,, (65—70)	...	,, 28	...	,, 78
,, 34,	,, 8	,, ,, (5—10)	...	,, 17,713	...	,, 18,713
,, 34,	,, 10	,, ,, (40—60)	...	,, 22,308	...	,, 22,301
,, 34,	,, 12	,, Musalman (20—40)	...	,, 395	...	,, 3,095
,, 35,	,, 6	,, All Religions (0—5)	...	,, 19,052	...	,, 19,050
,, 35,	,, 7	,, ,, (Total)	...	,, 41,204	...	,, 41,206
,, 36,	,, 7	,, Musalman (40—60)	...	,, 555	...	,, 255
,, 36,	,, 8	,, ,, (40—60)	...	,, 78	...	,, 77
,, 36,	,, 9	,, Hindu Brahmanic (40—60)	...	,, 3,938	...	,, 8,938
.. 37,	,, 4	,, Musalman (15—20)	...	,, 5,678	...	,, 5,478

Page						for		read
Page 37,	col.	5 ...	... against	Musalman	(40—60) ...	7,215	...	7,214
,, 37,	,,	9 ...	... ,,	Hindu Brahmanic	(5—10) ...	247	...	287
,, 38,	,,	12 ...	... ,,	Musalman	(60 & over) ...	8,711	...	8,713
,, 38,	,,	9 ...	... ,,	,,	(10—15) Bhadarwah	286	...	284
,, 40,	,,	5 ...	... ,,	,,	(40—60) ...	4,372	...	25,972
,, 40,	,,	13 ...	... ,,	All Religions	(20—40) ...	4,675	...	4,674
,, 41,	,,	5 ...	... ,,	Hindu Brahmanic	(20—40) ...	532	...	552
,, 42,	,,	9 ...	... ,,	,,	(Total) ...	228	...	218
,, 42,	,,	13 ...	... ,,	Musalman	(Total) Laddakh	2,780	...	2,786
,, 42,	,,	6 ...	... ,,	,,	(15—20) ,,	7,113	...	7,115
,, 43,	,,	7 ...	... ,,	All Religions	(20—40) Gilgit ...	1,164	...	1,144
,, 43,	,,	4 & 10	... ,,	Christian	(40—60) ,, ...	1	...	2
,, 43,	,,	5 & 11	... ,,	,,	(40—60) ,, ...	2	...	1
,, 44,	,,	6 ...	... ,,	Hindu Brahmanic	(10—15) ...	1,773	...	1,373
,, 44,	,,	9 ...	... ,,	,,	(25—30) ...	1,576	...	1,567
,, 45,	,,	5 ...	... ,,	Musalman	(35—40) ...	363	...	263
,, 45,	,,	11 ...	... ,,	,,	(20—25) ...	293	...	393
,, 46,	,,	9 ...	... ,,	Hindu Brahmanic	(Total) ...	2,420	...	12,420
,, 47,	,,	6 ...	... ,,	Musalman	(,,) ...	44,387	...	44,388
,, 47,	,,	8 ...	... ,,	,,	(,,) ...	17,126	...	17,127
,, 48,	,,	10 ...	... ,,	,,	(35—40) ...	2,796	...	2,696
,, 48,	,,	12 ...	... ,,	,,	(30—35) ...	545	...	544

TABLE VIII.

Page						for		read
,, 54,	,,	4 ...	... ,,	Musalman	(20 & over) ...	26,510	...	265,100
,, 54,	,,	8 ...	... ,,	,,	,, ...	568,628	...	568,618
,, 58,	,,	8 ...	... ,,	,,	,, ...	86,338	...	86,387
,, 59,	,,	32 & 34	... ,,	Christian	...	*nil*	...	1
,, 59,	,,	32 & 34	... ,,	,,	,, ...	,,	...	1
,, 60,	,,	8 ...	... ,,	All Religions	,, Jammu Dist.	67,004	...	167,004
,, 60,	,,	4 ...	... ,,	Sikh	(0—10) ,,	344	...	444
,, 62,	,,	9 ...	... ,,	Musalman	(20 & over) ...	9,342	...	9,432
,, 64,	,,	8 ...	... ,,	All Religions	(15—20) Riasi Dist.	17,774	...	17,474
,, 64,	,,	8 ...	... ,,	,,	(20 & over) Mirpur Dist.	16,446	...	164,461
,, 67,	,,	35, 36, 37	... ,,	Christian	...	*nil*	...	7, 6, 1 respectively
,, 68,	,,	3 ...	... ,,	Sikh	(10—15) Punch *Ilaqa*	605	...	665
,, 70,	,,	4 ...	... ,,	Musalman	(15—20) Kashmir North	19,660	...	19,669
,, 72,	,,	4 ...	... ,,	Hindu Brahmanic	(10—15) Muzaffarabad District	203	...	209
,, 72,	,,	15 ...	... ,,	Musalman	(15—20) ,,	10	...	14
,, 72,	,,	10 ...	... ,,	All Religions	(10—15) Laddakh Dist.	9,422	...	8,422
,, 72,	,,	4 ...	... ,,	Hindu Brahmanic	(0—10) ,,	25	...	21
,, 74,	,,	10 ...	... ,,	Musalman	(20 & over) ,,	37,772	...	39,772
,, 74,	,,	11 ...	... ,,	,,	Gilgit Dist.	339	...	239
,, 74,	,,	10 ...	... ,,	,,	(10—15) ,,	1,081	...	1,031
,, 76,	,,	10 ...	... ,,	All Religions	(20 & over) Jammu city	7,234	...	7,238
,, 76,	,,	12 ...	... ,,	,,	Srinagar city	3,528	...	3,428
,, 77,	,,	37 ...	... ,,	,,	,,	56	...	65
,, 77,	,,	21 ...	... ,,	,,	(20 & over) ,,	11	...	18

TABLE X.

Page					for		read
,, 84,	,,	18 ...	... ,,	Punch *Ilaqa* ...	2	...	*nil*
,, 84,	,,	19 ...	... ,,	,, ...	*nil*	...	2
,, 90,	,,	60 ...	... ,,	Total Jammu Province ...	1,059	...	1,049
,, 90,	,,	60 ...	... ,,	Laddakh District ...	32	...	30
,, 90,	,,	61 ...	... ,,	,, ...	*nil*	...	2

TABLE XI.

Page					for		read
,, 94,	line	8 ...	... from the bottom	...	Jallundur	...	Jullundur
,, 94,	col.	3 ...	... against	A. Born in the State ...	1,606,430	...	1,60,6428
,, 94,	,,	3 ...	... ,,	Jammu Province ...	815,694	...	815,692
,, 94,	,,	3 ...	... ,,	Punch *Ilaqa* ...	173,054	...	173.052
,, 94,	,,	4 ...	... ,,	A. Born in the State ...	1,420,286	...	1,420,288
,, 94,	,,	4 ...	... ,,	Jammu Province ...	718,057	...	718,059
,, 94,	,,	4 ...	... ,,	Punch *Ilaqa* ...	160,190	...	160,192
,, 96,	,,	23 ...	... ,,	A. Born in the State ...	332,103	...	332,102
,, 96,	,,	24 ...	... ,,	,, ...	172,035	...	172,033
,, 96,	,,	24 ...	... ,,	Jammu Province ...	171,109	...	171,107
,, 96,	,,	24 ...	... ,,	Punch *Ilaqa* ...	169,061	...	169,059
,, 96,	line	8 ...	... from the bottom	...	Jallundur	...	Jullundur
,, 98,	,,	39 ...	... ,,	...	Haiderabad	,,	Hyderabad
,, 100,	,,	39 ...	... ,,	...	,,	,,	,,

TABLE XII.

Page					for		read
,, 104,	col.	6 ...	... against	40-45 (under Insane) ...	41	...	71
,, 104,	,,	7 ...	... ,,	40-45 ...	71	...	41

TABLE XIII.

INDEX.

Page	Reference			Against		For		Read
Page108,	No. 19	...	...	against	Chamiar ...	*for* 3,999	...	*read* 39,099
,, 108.	,, 46	...	...	,,	Kashmiri Musalman	,, 765,442	...	,, 765,441
,, 108,	,, 80	...	...	,,	Sheikh	,, 10,585	...	,, 105,285
					PART HINDU.			
,, 109,	col. 8	...	...	,,	Total Jammu Province (under Basith)	,, 7,369	...	,, 7,371
,, 109,	,, 10	...	...	,,	,, ,, ,,	,, 3,766	...	,, 3,768
,, 109,	,, 8	...	...	,,	Jammu District ,,	,, 238	...	,, 240
,, 109,	,, 10	...	...	,,	,, ,, ,,	,, 124	...	,, 126

TABLE XV A.

Page	Under		Col.		Against		For		Read
,, 144,	under Entire State	col.	7	,,	Jammu District ...	...	,, 193,041	...	,, 183,041
,, 144,	,, ,,	,,	4	,,	Kashmir North ...	...	,, 96,155	...	,, 96,055
,, 144,	,, Class A	,,	13	,,	Srinagar City ...	...	,, 4,095	...	,, 4,105
,, 144,	,, Sub Class I	,,	19	,,	Jammu District ...	...	,, 117,647	...	,, 117,267
,, 144,	,, ,,	,,	14	,,	Udhampur District ...	...	,, 189,189	...	,, 189,199
,, 144,	,, ,,	,,	19	,,	Srinagar City ...	...	,, 4,095	...	,, 4,105
,, 145,	,, Order 1	,,	25	,,	,, ...	...	,, 3,908	...	,, 3,918
,, 145,	,, ,, 1 (a)	,,	26	,,	Riasi District ...	...	,, 173,918	...	,, 178,918
,, 145,	,, Group (1)	,,	33	,,	Mirpur ...	...	,, 971	...	,, 961
,, 146,	,, ,, (2)	,,	43	,,	Total Kashmir Province...	...	,, 446,805	...	,, 449,485
,, 147,	,, Order 1 (c)	,,	73	,,	Srinagar city	...	,, 538	...	,, 534
,, 147.	,, Group (8)	,,	82	,,	Kashmir South ...	...	,, 38	...	,, 138
,, 148,	,, ,, (10)	,,	98	,,	*Total Kashmir Valley* ...	...	,, *nil*	...	,, 65
,, 148,	,, ,, (10)	,,	99	,,	,, ,, ,, ...	...	,, ,,	...	,, 4
,, 148,	,, ,, (10)	,,	100	,,	,, ,, ,, ...	...	,, ,,	...	,, 13
,, 148,	,, ,, (10)	,,	101	,,	,, ,, ,, ...	...	,, ,,	...	,, 2
,, 148,	,, ,, (10)	,,	103	,,	,, ,, ,, ...	...	,, ,,	...	,, 48
,, 150,	,, Class B	,,	163	,,	Total Kashmir Province...	...	,, 125,871	...	,, 125,876
,, 153,	,, Order 8	,,	236	,,	Srinagar city ...	...	,, 4,315	...	,, 4,319
,, 153,	,, ,, 8	,,	237	,,	,, ,, ...	...	,, 1,407	...	,, 1,408
,, 153,	,, ,, 8	,,	241	,,	,, ,, ...	...	,, 2,685	...	,, 2,688
,, 154,	,, ,, 9	,,	254	,,	,, ,, ...	...	,, 2,546	...	,, 2,549
,, 154,	,, ,, 9	,,	255	,,	,, ,, ...	...	,, 964	...	,, 963
,, 154,	,, ,, 9	,,	256	,,	,, ,, ...	...	,, 4	...	,, 2
,, 155,	,, ,, 10	,,	290	,,	,, ,, ...	...	,, 777	...	,, 833
,, 155,	,, ,, 10	,,	291	,,	,, ,, ...	...	,, 298	...	,, 323
,, 155,	,, ,, 10	,,	295	,,	,, ,, ...	...	,, 406	...	,, 437
,, 156,	,, ,, 11	,,	308	,,	Jammu city ...	...	,, 249	...	,, 251
,, 156,	,, ,, 11	,,	313	,,	,, ,, ...	...	,, 136	...	,, 138
,, 156,	,, ,, 11	,,	308	,,	Srinagar city ...	...	,, 1,203	...	,, 1,207
,, 156,	,, ,, 11	,,	309	,,	,, ...	...	,, 462	...	,, 464
,, 156,	,, ,, 11	,,	313	,,	,, ...	...	,, 712	...	,, 714
,, 157,	,, ,, 12	,,	355	,,	Bhadarwah *Jagir* ...	...	,, 54	...	,, 56
,, 157,	,, ,, 12	,,	350	,,	Total Kashmir Province	...	,, 10,263	...	,, 10,261
,, 157,	,, ,, 12	,,	355	,,	,, ...	...	,, 5,242	...	,, 5,871
,, 159,	,, Group (63)	,,	386	,,	,, ...	...	,, 943	...	,, 993
,, 159,	,, Order 13	,,	398	,,	Jammu city ...	...	,, 2,104	...	,, 2,131
,, 159,	,, ,, 13	,,	399	,,	,, ...	...	,, 938	...	,, 952
,, 159,	,, ,, 13	,,	403	,,	,, ...	...	,, 1,011	...	,, 1,024
,, 159,	,, ,, 13	,,	398	,,	Srinagar city ...	...	,, 13,129	...	,, 13,132
,, 159,	,, ,, 13	,,	400	,,	,, ...	...	,, 213	...	,, 216
,, 162,	,, Group (81)	,,	470	,,	Total Jammu Province...	...	,, 144	...	,, 114
,, 162,	,, ,, (81)	,,	470	,,	Srinagar city ...	...	,, 180	...	,, 131
,, 162,	,, ,, (81)	,,	471	,,	,, ...	...	,, 38	...	,, 84
,, 162,	,, ,, (81)	,,	475	,,	,, ...	...	,, 142	...	,, 47
,, 162,	,, Order 18	,,	493	,,	Total Kashmir Province	...	,, 357	...	,, 3,571
,, 162,	,, ,, 18	,,	488	,,	Srinagar city ...	...	,, 2,637	...	,, 2,640
,, 162,	,, ,, 18	,,	489	,,	,, ...	...	,, 873	...	,, 875
,, 162,	,, ,, 18	,,	493	,,	,, ...	...	,, 1,763	...	,, 1,764
,, 164,	,, ,, 19	,,	541	,,	Total Jammu Province...	...	,, 1,010	...	,, 1,060
,, 164,	,, Group (93)	,,	547	,,	,, ...	...	,, 1,010	...	,, 1,060
,, 168,	,, Sub-class V	,,	645	,,	Jammu Dist. ...	...	,, 61,115	...	,, 6,115
,, 168.	,, Order 24	,,	653	,,	Total Jammu Province	...	,, 223	...	,, 523
,, 168,	,, Group (106)	,,	659	,,	,, ...	...	,, 223	...	,, 523
,, 171,	,, Order 33	,,	716	,,	Jammu city ...	...	,, 2,658	...	,, 2,299
,, 171,	,, ,, 33	,,	717	,,	,, ...	...	,, 1,097	...	,, 963
,, 171,	,, ,, 33	,,	721	,,	,, ...	...	,, 1,546	...	,, 1,321
,, 171,	,, ,, 33	,,	716	,,	Srinagar city ...	...	,, 10,486	...	,, 9,817
,, 171,	,, ,, 33	,,	717	,,	,, ...	...	,, 3,346	...	,, 3,106
,, 171.	,, ,, 33	,,	718	,,	,, ...	...	,, 1,024	...	,, 1,018
,, 171,	,, ,, 33	,,	721	,,	,, ...	...	,, 6,116	...	,, 5,693
,, 172,	,, Group (125)	,,	767	,,	Total Kashmir Province	...	,, *nil*	...	,, 2
,, 172,	,, Order 34	,,	758	,,	Jammu city ...	...	,, 96	...	,, 76
,, 172,	,, Group (125)	,,	764	,,	,, ,, ...	...	,, 96	...	,, 76
,, 175,	,, ,, (131)	,,	831	,,	Total Kashmir Province	...	,, 382	...	,, 380
,, 176,	,, Order 41	,,	863	,,	,, ,, ,, ...	...	,, 98	...	,, 48

Page 177,	Under Class C	col. 891	against	Srinagar city	...	for 6,349	...	read 6,339
,, 178,	,, Group (143)	,, 936	,,	Punch *Ilaqa*	...	,, nil	...	,, 1
,, 179,	,, ,, (145)	,, 959	,,	Jammu District	...	,, 145	...	,, 165
,, 179,	,, ,, (145)	,, 961	,,	Kashmir North	...	,, 543	...	,, 516
,, 179,	,, ,, (145)	,, 961	,,	,, South	...	,, 7,001	...	,, 7,101
,, 179,	,, ,, (145)	,, 956	,,	,, Valley	...	,, 10,328	...	,, 10,338
,, 179,	,, ,, (145)	,, 956	,,	Total Frontier District	...	,, 1,228	...	,, 1,238
,, 179,	,, ,, (145)	,, 961	,,	,, ,, ,,	...	,, 497	...	,, 477
,, 179,	,, ,, (145)	,, 956	,,	Laddakh ,,	...	,, 283	...	,, 282
,, 179,	,, ,, (147)	,, 969	,,	Srinagar city	...	,, 50	...	,, 56
,, 180,	,, Sub-Class VIII	,, 977	,,	Total Kashmir Province	...	,, 444	...	,, 744
,, 180,	,, ,, VIII	,, 974	,,	Jammu city ,,	...	,, 2,240	...	,, 2,440
,, 180,	,, Group (148)	,, 986	,,	Total Jammu ,,	...	,, 2,093	...	,, 3,893
,, 180,	,, ,, (148)	,, 991	,,	Muzaffarabad District	...	,, 44	...	,, 52
,, 181,	,, Order 47	,, 1009	,,	*Total Kashmir Valley*	...	,, 542	...	,, 545
,, 183,	,, Sub-Class IX	,, 1076	,,	,, ,, ,,	...	,, 719	...	,, 714
,, 184,	,, Order 52	,, 1106	,,	Jasrota District	...	,, 9,297	...	,, 2,297
,, 184,	,, ,, 52	,, 1111	,,	Mirpur ,, ,,	...	,, 581	...	,, 981
,, 185,	,, Group (162)	,, 1113	,,	Total Frontier Districts	...	,, 548	...	,, 948
,, 185,	,, Sub-class XI	,, 1129	,,	Kashmir South	...	,, 2,713	...	,, 2,723
,, 185,	,, Order (53)	,, 1135	,,	,,	...	,, 2,713	...	,, 2,723
,, 186,	,, Group (166)	,, 1153	,,	Total State	...	,, 50	...	,, 90
,, 186,	,, ,, (167)	,, 1157	,,	Jammu District	...	,, 109	...	,, 119
,, 186,	,, ,, (167)	,, 1154	,,	Jasrota ,,	...	,, 780	...	,, 790
,, 186,	,, ,, (167)	,, 1156	,,	Kashmir South	...	,, 11	...	,, 14
,, 186,	,, ,, (167)	,, 1155	,,	Muzaffarabad District	...	,, 385	...	,, 285
,, 186,	,, Sub-class XII	,, 1163	,,	Total State	...	,, 1,822	...	,, 1,022
,, 186,	,, ,, XII	,, 1161	,,	Jasrota District	...	,, 793	...	,, 794
,, 186,	,, ,, XII	,, 1160	,,	Punch *Ilaqa*	...	,, 7,310	...	,, 3,310
,, 186,	,, ,, XII	,, 1165	,,	Total Kashmir Province	...	,, 5,330	...	,, 8,330
,, 186,	,, Sub-class XII	,, 1160	,,	Jammu city	...	,, 1,127	...	,, 903
,, 186,	,, ,, XII	,, 1161	,,	,,	...	,, 807	...	,, 593
,, 186,	,, ,, XII	,, 1162	,,	,,	...	,, 139	...	,, 129
,, 187,	,, Group (169)	,, 1187	,,	Mirpur District	...	,, 70	...	,, 90

TABLE XV-B.

Page	col.			Item		for		read
,, 188,	col. 2	...	against	Total State	...	,, 5,385	...	,, 8,385
,, 188,	,, 5	...	,,	Riasi District	...	,, 9	...	,, 19
,, 189,	,, 3	...	,,	Punch *Ilaqa*	...	,, 87,477	...	,, 27,477
,, 189,	,, 6	...	,,	,,	...	,, 3,413	...	,, 7,156
,, 189,	,, 7	...	,,	,,	...	,, 35	...	,, 79
,, 190,	,, 40	...	,,	Total State	...	,, 15,909	...	,, 15,919
,, 190,	,, 27	...	,,	Jammu District	...	,, 24	...	,, 84
,, 191,	,, 2	...	,,	Total Kashmir Province	...	,, 5,434	...	,, 5,433
,, 191,	,, 2	...	,,	Muzaffarabad District	...	,, 749	...	,, 803
,, 191,	,, 3	...	,,	,,	...	,, *nil*	...	,, 475
,, 191,	,, 24	...	,,	Total Frontier Districts	...	,, *nil*	...	,, 1

TABLE XV-D.

Page	col.			Item		for		read
,, 192,	,, 4	...	,,	Order 1—Pasture, &c.	...	*for* 197	...	*read* 199
,, 192,	,, 10	...	,,	,,	...	,, 1,976,203	...	,, 1,976,603
,, 192,	,, 10	...	,,	Order 6—Textiles	...	,, 77,944	...	,, 77,946
,, 194,	,, 3	...	,,	Group 106	...	,, 3,848	...	,, 8,848
,, 195,	,, 8	...	,,	Order 44—Police	...	,, 37	...	,, 137
,, 195,	,, 8	...	,,	Group 143	...	,, 37	...	,, 137
,, 201,	,, 2	...	,,	Order 13—Industries	...	,, 13,129	...	,, 13,132
,, 201,	,, 2	...	,,	Group 81	...	,, 180	...	,, 131

TABLE XVII.

Page	col.			Item		for		read
,, 216,	,, 95	...	,,	Total State	...	,, *nil*	...	,, 1
,, 216,	,, 99	...	,,	,,	...	,, 1	...	,, *nil*
,, 216,	,, 95	...	,,	Total Kashmir Province	...	,, *nil*	...	,, 1
,, 216,	,, 99	...	,,	,,	...	,, 1	...	,, *nil*
,, 216,	,, 95	...	,,	Kashmir South	...	,, *nil*	...	,, 1
,, 216,	,, 99	...	,,	,,	...	,, 1	...	,, *nil*
,, 216,	,, 95	...	,,	Kashmir Valley	...	,, *nil*	...	,, 1
,, 216,	,, 99	...	,,	,,	...	,, 1	...	,, *nil*

PROVINCIAL TABLE I.

Page	col.			Item		for		read
220,	,, 2	...	,,	Tehsil Khas	...	,, } 714	...	,, { 705[illegible]
,, 220,	,, 2	...	,,	Srinagar city	...	,, }	...	,, { 8[illegible]
,, 220,	,, 2	...	,,	Total Tehsil Khas	...	,,	...	,, 714
,, 220,	,, 11	...	,,	Total Frontier Province	...	,, 46·02	...	,, +46·02

TABLE I.

AREA, HOUSES AND POPULATION.

Jammu and Kashmir State Census 1911.

1. The area figures are based on Settlement and Survey records except in case of the Frontier *Ilaqas* and Mansar village of Laddakh District and Bhadarwah *Jagir*. The latter have not been surveyed yet and the figures for them have only been estimated as approximately as possible by the local officers.

2. In Srinagar and certain other smaller towns more than one *Hadbast* villages are included. The town so constituted has been shown as one unit in column 3 but the total number of villages comprised in it have been taken away from the figures of column 4. The total number of *Hadbast* villages is 9127 out of which 178 are uninhabited and 84 are taken up by the towns as above. The uninhabited (*Bechiragh*) villages have not been shown at all in this table.

3. The following is a list of the tracts where enumeration was conducted on special lines with no detail as to age, civil condition, birth-place, mother-tongue, literacy and infirmities. Their figures will, therefore, not be found included in such of the tables as deal with these subjects. They have, however, been incorporated in the first six tables and Tables XIII, XVA, XVII and XVIII :—

Name.	Area in square miles.	POPULATION.		
		Total.	Males.	Females.
(1) *Ilaqa* Punial	1,600	4,423	2,365	2,058
(2) ,, Ishkoman	1,600	2,020	1,075	945
(3) ,, Yasin	1,200	6,310	3,291	3,019
(3) ,, Kuh	480	2,064	1,166	898
(3) ,, Ghizar	1,500	3,637	1,868	1,769
(4) ,, Hunza	3,900	10,126	5,457	4,669
(5) ,, Nagar	1,600	13,347	7,148	6,199
(6) ,, Chilas	2,800	12,508	6,908	5,600
(7) Village Mansar (Laddakh District)	55	190	111	79
TOTAL ...	14,735	54,625	29,389	25,236

4. This table only gives district totals, the figures for Tahsils and smaller units will be found in Provincial Tables I and II at the end of this volume.

5. The figures of the private *jagirs* of His Highness the Maharaja Saheb Bahadur and of the scattered villages and areas of Punch and Bhadarwah are included in the totals of the districts in which they are situate.

I
Area, Houses and Population.

TABLE I.

Area, Houses and Population.

Jammu and Kashmir State Census 1911.

District, Ilaqa or Jagir.	Area in square miles.	Towns.	Villages.	Occupied houses.			Population.								
							Persons.			*Males.*			*Females.*		
				Total.	In towns.	In villages.	Total.	Urban.	Rural.	Total.	Urban.	Rural.	Total.	Urban.	Rural.
1	2	3	4	5	6	7	8	9	10	11	12	13	14	15	16
Total State ...	**84,432**	**61**	**8,865**	**553,124**	**61,866**	**491,238**	**3,158,126**	**300,879**	**2,857,247**	**1,674,367**	**167,028**	**1,507,339**	**1,483,759**	**133,851**	**1,349,908**
I.—Total Jammu Province (including *Jagirs*).	12,439	28	4,525	310,172	22,030	288,142	1,597,865	92,124	1,505,741	846,790	53,685	793,105	751,075	38,439	712,636
1. Jammu District (including city).	1,167	6	1,152	71,412	10,034	61,378	326,691	43,435	283,256	180,691	26,754	153,937	146,000	16,681	129,319
2. Jasrota District ...	989	4	571	31,887	2,346	29,541	151,802	9,986	141,816	81,375	5,569	75,806	70,427	4,417	66,010
3. Udhampur ,, ...	4,399	6	661	39,553	2,065	37,488	215,725	9,032	206,693	113,877	4,927	108,950	101,848	4,105	97,743
4. Riasi ,, ...	1,875	4	652	37,341	1,398	35,943	206,809	5,935	200,874	109,026	3,242	105,784	97,783	2,693	95,090
5. Mirpur ,, ...	1,754	6	709	71,929	3,996	67,933	324,933	13,609	311,324	169,276	7,183	162,093	155,657	6,426	149,231
6. Bhadarwah *Jagir* ...	607	1	294	7,032	601	6,431	37,512	2,563	34,949	18,975	1,348	17,627	18,537	1,215	17,322
7. Punch *Ilaqa* ...	1,648	1	486	51,018	1,590	49,428	334,393	7,564	326,829	173,570	4,662	168,908	160,823	2,902	157,921
II.—Total Kashmir Province (including *Jagirs*).	8,433	21	3,579	197,382	34,763	162,619	1,295,201	188,563	1,106,638	691,780	102,201	589,579	603,421	86,362	517,059
8. Kashmir North (including Langet *Jagir*).	3,553	8	1,376	68,115	4,138	63,977	460,786	23,626	437,160	244,637	12,780	231,857	216,149	10,846	205,303
9. Kashmir South (including city).	2,806	10	1,395	102,232	29,778	72,454	639,210	160,534	478,676	342,835	86,881	255,954	296,375	73,653	222,722
Total Kashmir valley ...	*6,359*	*18*	*2,771*	*170,347*	*33,916*	*136,431*	*1,099,996*	*184,160*	*915,836*	*587,472*	*99,661*	*487,811*	*512,524*	*84,499*	*428,025*
10. Muzaffarabad District (*Wizarat Pahar*).	2,074	3	808	27,035	847	26,188	195,205	4,403	190,802	104,308	2,540	101,768	90,897	1,863	89,034
III.—Total Frontier Districts.	63,560	12	761	45,570	5,093	40,477	265,060	20,192	244,868	135,797	11,142	124,655	129,263	9,050	120,213
11. Laddakh District (including Mansar).	45,762	3	465	33,604	1,431	32,173	186,656	6,407	180,249	93,220	3,354	89,866	93,436	3,053	90,383
12. Gilgit District ...	3,118	2	80	3,558	709	2,849	23,969	4,157	19,812	13,299	2,625	10,674	10,670	1,532	9,138
13. Frontier *Ilaqas* ...	14,680	7	216	8,408	2,953	5,455	54,435	9,628	44,807	29,278	5,163	24,115	25,157	4,465	20,692

TABLE II.

VARIATION IN POPULATION SINCE 1891.

Jammu and Kashmir State Census 1911.

1. The columns relating to the first two regular Indian Censuses have been omitted as this State did not come under those operations. The rough estimate of 1873 is worth no consideration.

2. No comparison could be instituted as regards majority of our districts because of the large territorial changes that have occurred in both the preceding decades and the absence of all village records of the previous enumerations. Full detail of these changes will be found discussed in the Report Volume.

3. The only comparable units are (*a*) Entire State, (*b*) Kashmir Province, (*c*) Kashmir Valley, (*d*) Muzaffarabad and perhaps (*e*) Jasrota Districts and (*f*) Punch and (*g*) Bhadarwah *Jagirs*.

4. For purposes of a rough comparison, however, the figures of the last two censuses have been altered in this way :—In 1901 the present population of Zanskar (persons 4,857, males 2,377 and females 2,480) has been transferred from Jammu Province to Frontier Districts. In 1891 in addition to this change the present population of Frontier *Ilaqas* (persons 54,435, males 29,278 and females 27,157) has been added both to the Frontier District figures and those of the entire State.

5. The comparison of Gilgit figures made in the last Report is wrong as it ignored the fact that the Political *Ilaqas* were not enumerated in 1891 at all. The only comparison possible in regard to this unit is between the figures of the present census and the last which has been made in this Table.

II
Variation in Population.

TABLE II.

VARIATION IN POPULATION SINCE 1891.

Jammu and Kashmir State Census 1911.

District, Ilaqa or Jagir.	Persons.			Males.			Females.			VARIATION. Increase (+) Decrease (—).		Net variation in period 1891—1911 Increase (+) Decrease (—).
	1911.	1901.	1891.	1911.	1901.	1891.	1911.	1901.	1891.	1901 to 1911.	1891 to 1901.	
1	2	3	4	5	6	7	8	9	10	11	12	13
Total State ...	**3,158,126**	**2,905,578**	**2,598,387**	**1,674,367**	**1,542,057**	**1,382,507**	**1,483,759**	**1,363,521**	**1,215,880**	**+252,548**	**+307,191**	**+559,739**
I.—Total Jammu Province (including *Jagirs*).	1,597,865	1,516,450	1,434,686	846,790	805,415	767,864	751,075	711,035	666,822	+81,415	+81,764	+163,179
1. Jammu District (including city)	326,691	...	...	180,691	...	...	146,000	...	...	...	...	...
2. Jasrota District ...	151,802	154,213	151,518	81,375	82,391	81,434	70,427	71,822	70,084	—2,411	+2,695	+284
3. Udhampur ,, ...	215,725	...	...	113,877	...	...	101,848	...	...	...	...	...
4. Riasi ,, ...	206,809	...	...	109,026	...	...	97,783	...	...	...	...	...
5. Mirpur ,, ...	324,933	...	...	169,276	...	...	155,657	...	...	...	...	...
6. Bhadarwah *Jagir* ...	37,512	34,311	32,433	18,975	17,500	16,775	18,537	16,811	15,658	+3,201	+1,878	+5,079
7. Punch *Ilaqa*	334,393	304,488	268,608	173,570	160,679	141,945	160,823	143,809	126,663	+29,905	+35,880	+65,785
II.—Total Kashmir Province (including *Jagirs*).	1,295,201	1,157,394	949,041	691,780	616,887	502,345	603,421	540,507	446,696	+137,807	+208,353	+346,160
8. Kashmir North (including Langet *Jagir*).	460,786	...	...	244,637	...	...	216,149	...	...	...	...	...
9. Kashmir South (including city).	639,210	...	...	342,835	...	...	296,375	...	...	...	...	...
Total Kashmir Valley ...	*1,099,996*	*989,196*	*814,241*	*587,472*	*526,158*	*429,464*	*512,524*	*463,038*	*384,777*	*+110,800*	*+174,955*	*+285,755*
10. Muzaffarabad District (*Wizarat Pahar*).	195,205	168,198	134,800	104,308	90,729	72,881	90,897	77,469	61,919	+27,007	+33,398	+60,405
III.—Total Frontier Districts...	265,060	231,734	214,660	135,797	119,755	112,298	129,263	111,979	102,362	+33,326	+17,074	+50,400
11. Laddakh District (including Mansar).	186,656	...	...	93,220	...	...	93,436	...	...	...	...	...
12. Gilgit District	23,969	60,885	...	13,299	33,778	...	10,670	27,107	...	+17,519	...	...
13. Frontier *Ilaqas*	54,435			29,278			25,157					

TABLE III.

TOWNS AND VILLAGES CLASSIFIED BY POPULATION.

Jammu and Kashmir State, Census 1911.

---

1. The total number of *Hadbast* villages is 9,127. The 178 uninhabited villages have, unlike the last Census, not been shown in the table at all.

2. Towns consisting of more than one village unit have been dealt with as a single unit and their total population has been considered in classifying for this table.

3. The unclassed population is comprised of the following :—

		Population.
(1)	Railway	165
(2)	Water-borne (Boats, house-boats, etc.)	15,451
(3)	Other (encampments, etc.)	1,234
	TOTAL ...	16,850

TABLE III.

Towns and Villages classified by Population.

Jammu and Kashmir State, Census 1911.

District, Ilaqa or Jagir.	Total number of inhabited towns and villages.	Population.	Under 500		500—1,000		1,000—2,000		2,000—5,000		5,000—10,000		10,000—20,000		20,000-50,000		50,000—100,000		100,000 & over		Encampments boat and Railway population unclassed.
			Number.	Population.	Number	Population.	Number.	Population.	Number.	Population.	Number.	Population.	Number.	Population.	Number.	Population.	Number.	Population.	Number.	Population.	
1	2	3	4	5	6	7	8	9	10	11	12	13	14	15	16	17	18	19	20	21	22
Total State ...	**8,926**	**3,158,126**	**7,268**	**1,394,906**	**1,182**	**820.636**	**382**	**514,092**	**84**	**201,195**	**8**	**57,169**	...	...	**1**	**31,726**	...	...	**1**	**121,552**	**16,850**
I.—Total Jammu Province (including *Jagirs*).	4,553	1,597,865	3,683	709,909	596	416,907	213	288,496	56	125,720	4	24,942	...	...	1	31,726	...	...	...	...	165
1. Jammu District (including city).	1,158	326,691	1,034	178,263	90	60,658	23	31,145	10	24,734	...	...	...	...	1	31,726	...	...	...	...	165
2. Jasrota District ...	575	151,802	489	79,824	70	47,591	15	19,147	...	...	1	5,240	...	...	...	...	...	...	...	...	...
3. Udhampur " ...	667	215,725	545	112,108	97	66,622	22	30,184	3	6,811	...	...	...	...	...	...	...	...	...	...	...
4. Riasi " ...	656	206,809	531	106,877	100	61,854	22	29,271	3	8,807	...	...	...	...	...	...	...	...	...	...	...
5. Mirpur " ...	715	324,933	526	105,865	115	81,067	56	79,681	16	46,182	2	12,138	...	...	...	...	...	...	...	...	...
6. Bhadarwah *Jagir* ...	295	37,512	293	34,447	1	502	...	...	1	2,563	...	...	...	...	...	...	...	...	...	...	...
7. Punch *Ilaqa* ...	487	334,393	265	92,525	123	98,613	75	99,068	23	36,623	1	7,564	...	...	...	...	...	...	...	...	...
II.—Total Kashmir Province (including *Jagirs*).	3,600	1,295,201	2,963	562,888	475	329,575	138	181,823	19	51,714	4	32,227	...	...	...	...	...	...	1	121,552	15,422
8. Kashmir North (including Langet *Jagir*).	1,384	460,786	1,130	219,033	183	124,958	62	78,378	7	19,861	2	15,113	...	...	...	...	...	...	...	...	3,443
9. Kashmir South (including city).	1,405	639,210	1,111	221,967	218	155,783	63	94,530	10	26,285	2	17,114	...	...	...	...	...	...	1	121,552	11,979
Total Kashmir Valley ...	*2,789*	*1,099,996*	*2,241*	*441,000*	*401*	*280,741*	*125*	*162,908*	*17*	*46,146*	*4*	*32,227*	...	...	...	...	...	...	*1*	*121,552*	*15,422*
10. Muzaffarabad District (*Wizarat Pahar*). ...	811	195,205	722	121,888	74	48,834	13	18,915	2	5,568	...	...	...	...	...	...	...	...	...	...	...
III.—Frontier Districts ...	773	265,060	622	122,109	111	74,154	31	43,773	9	23,761	...	...	...	...	...	...	...	...	...	...	1,263
11. Laddakh District (including Mansar).	468	186,656	352	76,272	82	54,254	27	38,550	7	17,470	...	...	...	...	...	...	...	...	...	...	110
12. Gilgit District ...	82	2,396	72	13,916	9	5,986	...	...	1	2,914	...	...	...	...	...	...	...	...	...	...	1,153
13. Frontier *Ilaqas* ...	223	54,435	198	31,921	20	13,914	4	5,223	1	3,377	...	...	...	...	...	...	...	...	...	...	...

TABLE IV.

TOWNS CLASSIFIED BY POPULATION WITH VARIATIONS SINCE 1891.

Jammu and Kashmir State, Census 1911.

1. In view of the local conditions and hilly nature of the country, towns and cities have not been determined merely on the basis of the Imperial population standard. Several *abadis* not conforming to the numerical test but having all other characteristics of a town or city have been classed as one or the other and shown in this and the following table.

2. Batala (Vatala) on the other hand which was shown as a town in 1891 with a population of 5,206 has not this time been treated as such, because as a matter of fact it possesses no urban characteristics.

3. The population shown against Gulmarg is delusive. The final Census having come off in winter, the figure shown here represents only the watchmen's population. Gulmarg is the chief summer resort of Kashmir with a large number of European houses and huts, shops, bazar, etc. It swells up to several thousands in summer.

4. The 1911 figures of Jammu city have been compared by deducting 458 persons from the population of 1891 and 1901. This is the population of such portions of the town as have been excluded since the last Census from its limits. The following is their detail :—

	Total.	*Males.*	*Females.*
(*i*) Railway area	*303*	*230*	*73*
(*ii*) Divisional Engineer's bungalow and out-houses	*48*	*35*	*13*
(*iii*) Shops, etc. on Satwari road	*66*	*58*	*8*
(*iv*) Bhattha Gulzari Shah	*36*	*21*	*15*
(*v*) Kunwan Shikar Purian and Segregation camp	*5*	*5*	...
Total ...	*458*	*349*	*109*

These places really form suburbs to Jammu, but they have in 'The Village Tables' been included in the Revenue villages to which they now territorially belong.

5. The towns are arranged in a descending order of population.

TABLE IV.

Towns classified by Population with Variation since 1891.

Jammu and Kashmir State, Census 1911.

Town.	District, Ilaqa or Jagir.	Municipality, Suburbs, Cantonment, etc.	Population.			Variation. Increase (+) Decrease (—)		Variation in period.	Males.			Females.		
			1911.	1901.	1891.	1901 to 1911.	1891 to 1901.	1891 to 1911. Increase (+) Decrease (—)	1911.	1901.	1891.	1911.	1901.	1891.
1	2	3	4	5	6	7	8	9	10	11	12	13	14	15
Total Urban Population,	...	...	**300,879**	**158,290**	**192,079**	**+142,589**	**−33,789**	**+108,800**	**167,028**	**87,414**	**106,124**	**133,851**	**70,876**	**85,955**
Total Cities ...	...	...	158,070	158,290	153,044	−220	+5,246	+5,026	87,763	87,414	84,916	70,330	70,876	68,128
1. Srinagar ...	Kashmir South ...	Total ...	126,344	122,618	118,960	+3,726	+3,658	+7,384	68,378	65,542	62,720	57,966	57,076	56,240
		Municipality ...	124,240	122,618	118,960	+1,622	+3,658	+5,280	66,994	65,542	62,720	57,246	57,076	56,240
		Cantonment ...	2,104	...	...	+2,104	...	+2,104	1,384	...	...	720	...	...
2. Jammu ...	Jammu *wizarat* ...	Total ...	31,726	35,672	34,084	−3,946	+1,588	−2,358	19,362	21,872	22,196	12,364	13,800	11,888
		Municipality ...	29,857	34,421	34,084	−4,564	+337	−4,227	17,712	20,730	22,196	12,145	13,691	11,888
		Cantonment ...	1,869	1,251	...	+618	+1,251	+1,869	1,650	1,142	...	219	109	...
Total Towns ...	...	...	142,809	...	39,035	...	...	+103,774	79,288	...	21,208	63,521	...	17,827
3. Islamabad (Anantnag) ...	Kashmir South ...	...	9,019	...	10,227	...	...	−1,208	4,937	...	8,515	4,082	...	4,712
4. Sopur (Sheopur) ...	,, North ...	...	8,514	...	8,410	...	...	+104	4,465	...	4,360	4,049	...	4,050
5. Zunimar ...	,, South ...	Suburbs to Srinagar.	8,095	...	...	...	...	...	4,369	...	...	3,726	...	...
6. Punch ...	Punch *Ilaqa* ...		7,564	...	7,489	...	...	+75	4,662	...	...	2,902	...	2,814
7. Mirpur ...	Mirpur *wizarat* ...	...	6,640	...	7,253	...	...	+613	3,441	...	...	3,199	...	3,598
8. Baramula ...	Kashmir North ...	...	6,599	...	5,656	...	...	+943	3,586	...	...	3,013	...	2,653
9. Kathua ...	Jasrota ...	...	5,240	...	...	...	...	...	3,008	...	...	2,232	...	...
10. Bijbihara ...	Kashmir South ...	...	4,424	...	...	...	...	...	2,360	...	...	2,064	...	...
11. Gilgit ...	Gilgit *wizarat* ...	...	3,562	...	...	...	...	...	2,301	...	...	1,261	...	...
12. Muzaffarabad ...	Muzaffarabad District...	...	3,462	...	...	...	...	...	2,015	...	...	1,447	...	...
13. Cherar Sharif ...	Kashmir North ...	...	3,380	...	...	...	...	...	1,853	...	...	1,527	...	...
14. Nagar ...	Frontier *Ilaqas* ...	...	3,377	...	...	...	...	...	1,833	...	...	1,544	...	...
15. Pampur ...	Kashmir South ...	...	3,348	...	...	...	...	...	1,851	...	...	1,497	...	...
16. Satwari Cantonment ...	Jammu *wizarat* ...	Cantonment.	3,201	...	...	...	...	...	2,847	...	...	354	...	...
17. Akhnur ...	Do. ...	...	3,033	...	...	...	...	...	1,550	...	...	1,483	...	...
18. Leh ...	Laddakh *wizarat* ...	...	2,895	...	...	...	...	...	1,464	...	...	1,431	...	...
19. Bhadarwah (Naggar *khas*) ...	Bhadarwah *jagir* ...	...	2,563	...	...	...	...	...	1,348	...	...	1,215	...	...
20. Kishtwar ...	Udhampur *wizarat* ...	...	2,378	...	...	...	...	...	1,277	...	...	1,101	...	...
21. Udhampur ...	Do. ...	...	2,360	...	...	...	...	...	1,311	...	...	1,049	...	...
22. Samba ...	Jammu ,, ...	...	2,307	...	...	...	...	...	1,210	...	...	1,097	...	...
23. Doru ...	Kashmir South ...	...	2,202	...	...	...	...	...	1,157	...	...	1,045	...	...
24. Skardu ...	Laddakh *wizarat* ...	...	2,197	...	...	...	...	...	1,137	...	...	1,060	...	...
25. Rampur Rajauri ...	Riasi ,, ...	...	2,192	...	...	...	...	...	1,203	...	...	989	...	...
26. Shopian (Hiragam) ...	Kashmir South ...	...	2,114	...	...	...	...	...	1,161	...	...	953	...	...
27. Verinag ...	Do. ...	...	2,095	...	...	...	...	...	1,063	...	...	1,032	...	...
28. Ramnagar ...	Udhampur *wizarat* ...	...	2,073	...	...	...	...	...	1,107	...	...	966	...	...
29. Manawar ...	Mirpur ,, ...	...	2,057	...	...	...	...	...	1,142	...	...	915	...	...
30. Hunza (Baltat) ...	Frontier *Ilaqas* ...	...	1,971	...	...	...	...	...	1,082	...	...	889	...	...
31. Basohli ...	Jasrota *wizarat* ...	...	1,954	...	...	...	...	...	1,003	...	...	951	...	...
32. Riasi ...	Riasi ,, ...	...	1,905	...	...	...	...	...	1,062	...	...	843	...	...
33. Patan ...	Kashmir North ...	...	1,903	...	...	...	...	...	1,018	...	...	885	...	...

TABLE IV.

Towns classified by Population with Variation since 1898.

Jammu and Cashmir State Census 1911.

Towns.	District, Ilaqa or Jagir.	Municipality, Suburbs, Cantonment, etc.	Population.			Variation Increase (+) Decrease (—)		Variation in period.	Males.			Females.		
			1911.	1901.	1891.	1901 to 1911.	1891 to 1901.	1891 to 1911 Increase(+) Decrease(—)	1911.	1901.	1891.	1911.	1901.	1891.
1	2	3	4	5	6	7	8	9	10	11	12	13	14	15
34. Hamirpur ...	Jammu *wizarat* ...	...	1,832	...	...	...	...	...	1,024	...	...	808	...	...
35. Kulgam ...	Kashmir South ...	...	1,795	...	...	...	...	...	977	...	...	818	...	...
36. Parol ...	Jasrota *wizarat* ...	...	1,678	...	...	...	...	...	917	...	...	761	...	...
37. Kotli ...	Mirpur ,, ...	...	1,584	...	...	...	...	...	825	...	...	759	...	...
38. Bhimbar ...	Do. ...	...	1,438	...	...	...	...	...	777	...	...	661	...	...
39. Sri-Ranbir-Singhpura ...	Jammu *wizarat* ...	...	1,336	...	...	...	...	...	761	...	...	575	...	...
40. Kargil ...	Laddakh ,, ...	...	1,315	...	...	...	...	...	753	...	...	562	...	...
41. Bandipur ...	Kashmir North ...	...	1,303	...	...	...	...	...	757	...	...	546	...	...
42. Yasin ...	Frontier *Ilaqas* ...	...	1,251	...	...	...	...	...	640	...	...	611	...	...
43. Chaumukh ...	Mirpur *wizarat* ...	...	1,198	...	...	...	...	...	621	...	...	577	...	...
44. Jasmirgarh (Hiranagar) ...	Jasrota ,, ...	...	1,114	...	...	...	...	...	641	...	...	473	...	...
45. Awantipura ...	Kashmir South ...	...	1,098	...	...	...	...	...	628	...	...	470	...	...
46. Doda ...	Udhampur *wizarat* ...	...	1,077	...	...	...	...	...	578	...	...	499	...	...
47. Badgam (Sri-Pratap-Singhpura).	Kashmir North ...	...	1,065	...	...	...	...	...	587	...	...	478	...	...
48. Poni ...	Riasi *wizarat* ...	...	1,010	...	...	...	...	...	534	...	...	474	...	...
49. Ghizar ...	Frontier *Ilaqas* ...	...	1,001	...	...	...	...	...	523	...	...	478	...	...
50. Katra ...	Riasi *wizarat* ...	...	828	...	...	...	...	...	443	...	...	385	...	...
51. Chilas ...	Frontier *Ilaqas* ...	...	800	...	...	...	...	...	434	...	...	366	...	...
52. Uttar-Machhipura (Hindwara).	Kashmir North ...	...	792	...	...	...	...	...	444	...	...	348	...	...
53. Naushahra ...	Mirpur *wizarat* ...	...	692	...	...	...	...	...	377	...	...	315	...	...
54. Sherqila ...	Frontier *Ilaqas* ...	...	644	...	...	...	...	...	343	...	...	301	...	...
55. Chaneni ...	Udhampur *wizarat* ...	...	639	...	...	...	...	...	336	...	...	303	...	...
56. Astore (Hasura) ...	Gilgit ,, ...	...	595	...	...	...	...	...	324	...	...	271	...	...
57. Ishkoman ...	Frontier *Ilaqas* ...	...	584	...	...	...	...	...	308	...	...	276	...	...
58. Uri ...	Muzaffarabad *wizarat*...	...	544	...	...	...	...	...	298	...	...	246	...	...
59. Ramban ...	Udhampur ,, ...	...	505	...	...	...	...	...	318	...	...	187	...	...
60. Karnah (Titwal) ...	Muzaffarabad ,, ...	...	397	...	...	...	...	...	227	...	...	170	...	...
61. Gulmarg ...	Kashmir North ...	...	70	...	...	...	...	...	70	...	...	...	...	...

TABLE V.

TOWNS ARRANGED TERRITORIALLY WITH POPULATION BY RELIGION.

Jammu and Kashmir State Census 1911.

Vide remarks on the title page of Table IV *Supra.*

V

Towns arranged territorially and by religion.

TABLE

TOWNS ARRANGED TERRITORIALLY

Jammu and Kashmir

I.—INDO-

District, Ilaqa or Jagir.	Town, Municipality, Suburbs, Cantonment, etc.	TOTAL POPULATION.			A.—HINDU.								
					(a.) *Brahmanic.*			(b) *Arya.*			(c) *Bramho.*		
		Persons.	Males.	Females.	Persons.	Males.	Females.	Persons.	Males.	Females.	Persons.	Males.	Females.
1	2	3	4	5	6	7	8	9	10	11	12	13	14
Total State ...	...	**300,879**	**167,028**	**133,851**	**88,035**	**50,722**	**37,313**	**391**	**250**	**141**	**1**	...	**1**
Total Jammu Province	...	92,124	53,685	38,439	52,713	30,986	21,727	348	224	124	...	...	...
Total Jammu District	...	43,435	26,754	16,681	27,407	17,126	10,281	162	108	54	...	...	...
1. Jammu city ...	Municipality ...	29,857	17,712	12,145	18,532	10,946	7,586	132	87	45	...	...	...
	Cantonment ...	1,869	1,650	219	1,246	1,086	160	...	...	...	...	...	...
	Total ...	31,726	19,362	12,364	19,778	12,032	7,746	132	87	45	...	...	...
2. Satwari ...	Cantonment ...	3,201	2,847	354	2,748	2,481	267	...	...	...	...	...	...
3. Akhnur ...	Town ...	3,033	1,550	1,483	1,609	828	781	...	...	...	...	...	...
4. Hamirpur ...	,,	1,832	1,024	808	1,322	739	583	...	...	...	...	...	...
5. Sri-Ranbir-Singh-Pura	,,	1,336	761	575	583	334	249	13	9	4	...	...	...
6. Samba ...	,,	2,307	1,210	1,097	1,367	712	655	17	12	5	...	...	...
Total Jasrota District	...	9,986	5,569	4,417	6,769	3,738	3,031	42	26	16	...	...	...
7. Kathua ...	,,	5,240	3,008	2,232	3,091	1,781	1,310	42	26	16	...	...	...
8. Parol ...	,,	1,678	917	761	1,221	667	554	...	...	...	...	...	...
9. Jasmergarh ...	,,	1,114	641	473	991	565	426	...	...	...	...	...	...
10. Basohli ...	,,	1,954	1,003	951	1,466	725	741	...	...	...	...	...	...
Total Udhampur District.	...	9,032	4,927	4,105	5,715	3,082	2,633	5	4	1	...	...	...
11. Udhampur ...	,,	2,360	1,311	1,049	1,975	1,069	906	...	...	...	...	...	...
12. Chaneni ...	,,	639	336	303	523	265	258	...	...	...	...	...	...
13. Kishtwar ...	,,	2,378	1,277	1,101	680	379	301	...	...	...	...	...	...
14. Ramban ...	,,	505	318	187	345	195	150	4	3	1	...	...	...
15. Doda ...	,,	1,077	578	499	390	226	164	...	...	...	...	...	...
16. Ramnagar ...	,,	2,073	1,107	966	1,802	948	854	1	1	...	...	...	...
Total Riasi District	...	5,935	3,242	2,693	3,656	1,993	1,663	1	1	...	...	...	...
17. Riasi ...	,,	1,905	1,062	843	1,469	804	665	1	1	...	...	...	...
18. Rampur Rajauri	,,	2,192	1,203	989	785	437	348	...	...	...	...	...	...
19. Poni ...	,,	1,010	534	476	641	347	294	...	...	...	...	...	...
20. Katra ...	,,	828	443	385	761	405	356	...	...	...	...	...	...
Total Mirpur District	...	13,609	7,183	6,426	6,405	3,419	2,986	120	72	48	...	...	...
21. Mirpur ...	,,	6,640	3,441	3,199	2,885	1,554	1,331	106	66	40	...	...	...
22. Chaumukh ...	,,	1,198	621	577	109	65	44	5	2	3	...	...	...
23. Bhimbar ...	,,	1,438	777	661	741	393	348	...	...	...	...	...	...
24. Naushahra ...	,,	692	377	315	427	232	195	...	...	...	...	...	...
25. Manawar ...	,,	2,057	1,142	915	954	510	444	...	...	...	...	...	...
26. Kotli ...	,,	1,584	825	759	1,289	665	624	9	4	5	...	...	...
Total Jagirs ...	,,	10,127	6,010	4,117	2,761	1,628	1,133	18	13	5	...	...	...
27. Bhadarwah ...	,,	2,563	1,348	1,215	771	424	347	...	...	...	...	...	...
28. Punch ...	,,	7,564	4,662	2,902	1,990	1,204	786	18	13	5	...	...	...
Total Kashmir Province.	,,	188,563	102,201	86,362	34,582	19,055	15,527	40	24	16	1	...	1
Total Kashmir North	,,	23,626	12,780	10,846	2,334	1,353	981	...	...	...	...	...	...
29. Badgam (Sri-Pratab Singh-Pura)	,,	1,065	587	478	145	89	56	...	...	...	...	...	...
30. Cherar Sharif ...	,,	3,380	1,853	1,527	3	3	...	...	...	...	...	...	...
31. Baramula ...	,,	6,599	3,586	3,013	1,120	637	483	...	...	...	...	...	...
32. Patan ...	,,	1,903	1,018	885	51	40	11	...	...	...	...	...	...
33. Gulmarg ...	,,	70	70	...	9	9	...	...	...	...	...	...	...
34. Hindwara (Uttarmachhipura). ...	,,	792	444	348	78	60	18	...	...	...	...	...	...
35. Sopur ...	,,	8,514	4,465	4,049	849	446	403	...	...	...	...	...	...
36. Bandipur ...	,,	1,303	757	546	79	69	10	...	...	...	...	...	...
Total Kashmir South	,,	160,534	86,881	73,653	31,357	17,174	14,183	40	24	16	1	...	1
37. Shopian (Hiragam)	,,	2,114	1,161	953	28	20	8	...	...	...	...	...	...
38. Kulgam ...	,,	1,795	977	818	161	109	52	...	...	...	...	...	...
39. Anantnag ...	,,	9,019	4,937	4,082	1,076	602	474	...	...	...	...	...	...
40. Doru ...	,,	2,202	1,157	1,045	29	22	7	...	...	...	...	...	...
41. Verinag ...	,,	2,095	1,063	1,032	311	162	149	...	...	...	...	...	...
42. Bijbihara ...	,,	4,424	2,360	2,064	430	216	214	...	...	...	...	...	...
43. Awantipura ...	,,	1,098	628	470	50	50	...	...	...	...	...	...	...
44. Pampur ...	,,	3,348	1.851	1.497	137	70	67	...	...	...	...	...	...
45. Zunimar ...	,,	8,095	4,369	3,726	396	227	169	...	...	...	...	...	...

V.

WITH POPULATION BY RELIGION.

State Census 1911.

V

Towns arranged territorially and by religion.

ARYAN.									II.—IRANIAN.			III.—SEMITIC.					
B.—Sikh.			C.—Jain.			D.—Budhist.			E.—Zoroastrian.			F.—Musalman.			G.—Christian.		
Persons.	Males.	Females.	Persons.	Males.	Females.	Persons.	Males.	Females.	Persons.	Males.	Females.	Persons.	Males.	Females.	Persons.	Males.	Females.
15	16	17	18	19	20	21	22	23	24	25	26	27	28	29	30	31	32
3,007	**1,741**	**1,266**	**337**	**183**	**154**	**1,649**	**852**	**797**	**31**	**22**	**9**	**206.891**	**112,933**	**93,958**	**537**	**325**	**212**
2,003	1,118	885	337	183	154	2	2	...	5	2	3	36,348	20,930	15,418	368	240	128
790	474	316	334	181	153	...	...	...	5	2	3	14,559	8,758	5,801	178	105	73
693	412	281	334	181	153	...	...	...	2	1	1	10,000	5,991	4,009	164	94	70
2	2	...	...	...	...	...	...	...	3	1	2	618	561	57	...	...	...
695	414	281	334	181	153	...	...	...	5	2	3	10,618	6,552	4,066	164	94	70
16	10	6	...	...	...	...	...	...	...	...	...	423	345	78	14	11	3
51	32	19	...	...	...	...	...	...	...	...	...	1,373	690	683	...	...	...
...	...	...	...	...	...	...	...	...	...	...	...	510	285	225	...	...	...
...	...	...	...	...	...	...	...	...	...	...	...	740	418	322	...	...	...
28	18	10	...	...	...	...	...	...	...	...	...	895	468	427	...	...	...
16	9	7	...	...	...	...	...	...	...	...	...	2,989	1,668	1,321	170	128	42
7	4	3	...	...	...	...	...	...	...	...	...	1,930	1,069	861	170	128	42
7	4	3	...	...	...	...	...	...	...	...	...	450	246	204	...	...	...
...	...	...	...	...	...	...	...	...	...	...	...	123	76	47	...	...	...
2	1	1	...	...	...	...	...	...	...	...	...	486	277	209	...	...	...
41	20	21	3	2	1	...	...	...	...	...	...	3,268	1,819	1,449	...	...	...
11	5	6	...	...	...	...	...	...	...	...	...	374	237	137	...	...	...
...	...	...	...	...	...	...	...	...	...	...	...	116	71	45	...	...	...
6	4	2	3	2	1	...	...	...	...	...	...	1,689	892	797	...	...	...
14	8	6	...	...	...	...	...	...	...	...	...	142	112	30	...	...	...
...	...	...	...	...	...	...	...	...	...	...	...	687	352	335	...	...	...
10	3	7	...	...	...	...	...	...	...	...	...	260	155	105	...	...	...
48	22	26	...	...	...	...	...	...	...	...	...	2,230	1,226	1,004	...	...	...
32	16	16	...	...	...	...	...	...	...	...	...	403	241	162	...	...	...
16	6	10	...	...	...	...	...	...	...	...	...	1,391	760	631	...	...	...
...	...	...	...	...	...	...	...	...	...	...	...	369	187	182	...	...	...
...	...	...	...	...	...	...	...	...	...	...	...	67	38	29	...	...	...
840	435	405	...	...	...	...	...	...	...	...	...	6,244	3,257	2,987	...	...	...
507	247	260	...	...	...	...	...	...	...	...	...	3,142	1,574	1,568	...	...	...
43	21	22	...	...	...	...	...	...	...	...	...	1,041	533	508	...	...	...
84	49	35	...	...	...	...	...	...	...	...	...	613	335	278	...	...	...
16	13	3	...	...	...	...	...	...	...	...	...	249	132	117	...	...	...
168	92	76	...	...	...	...	...	...	...	...	...	935	540	395	...	...	...
22	13	9	...	...	...	...	...	...	...	...	...	264	143	121	...	...	...
268	158	110	...	...	...	2	2	...	...	...	...	7,058	4,202	2,856	20	7	13
...	...	...	...	...	...	1	1	...	...	...	...	1,791	923	868	...	...	...
268	158	110	...	...	...	1	1	...	...	...	...	5,267	3,279	1,988	20	7	13
944	576	368	...	...	...	1	1	...	26	20	6	152,851	82,470	70,381	118	55	63
59	45	14	...	...	...	...	...	...	...	...	...	21,226	11,378	9,848	7	4	3
6	6	...	...	...	...	...	...	...	...	...	...	914	492	422	...	...	...
...	...	...	...	...	...	...	...	...	...	...	...	3,377	1,850	1,527	...	...	...
14	7	7	...	...	...	...	...	...	...	...	...	5,461	2,940	2,521	4	2	2
12	11	1	...	...	...	...	...	...	...	...	...	1,840	967	873	...	...	...
4	4	...	...	...	...	...	...	...	...	...	...	57	57	...	...	...	...
10	6	4	...	...	...	...	...	...	...	...	...	704	378	326	...	...	...
12	10	2	...	...	...	...	...	...	...	...	...	7,653	4,009	3,644	...	...	...
1	1	...	...	...	...	...	...	...	...	...	...	1,220	685	535	3	2	1
517	340	177	...	...	...	...	...	...	26	20	6	128,482	69,272	59,210	111	51	60
1	1	...	...	...	...	...	...	...	...	...	...	2,085	1,140	945	...	...	...
3	3	...	...	...	...	...	...	...	...	...	...	1,631	865	766	...	...	...
10	10	...	...	...	...	...	...	...	...	...	...	7,933	4,325	3,608	...	...	...
...	...	...	...	...	...	...	...	...	...	...	...	2,173	1,135	1,038	...	...	...
...	...	...	...	...	...	...	...	...	...	...	...	1,784	901	883	...	...	...
9	3	6	...	...	...	...	...	...	...	...	...	3,985	2,141	1,844	...	...	...
5	5	...	...	...	...	...	...	...	...	...	...	1,043	573	470	...	...	...
1	1	...	...	...	...	...	...	...	...	...	...	3,210	1,780	1,430	...	...	...
2	1	1	...	...	...	...	...	...	...	...	...	7,697	4,141	3,556	...	...	...

V

Towns arranged territorially and by religion.

TABLE

TOWNS ARRANGED TERRITORIALLY

Jammu and Kashmir

I—INDO-

District, Ilaqa or Jagir.	Town, Municipality, Suburbs, Cantonment, etc.	Total Population.			A.—Hindu. (a) Brahmanic.			(b) Arya.			(c) Bramho.		
		Persons.	Males.	Females.	Persons.	Males.	Females.	Persons.	Males.	Females.	Persons.	Males.	Females.
1	2	3	4	5	6	7	8	9	10	11	12	13	14
46. Srinagar city ...	Municipality ...	124,240	66,994	57,246	28,103	15,188	12,915	40	24	16	1	...	1
	Cantonment ...	2,104	1,384	720	636	508	128	...	...	...	...	...	...
	Total ...	126,344	68,378	57,966	28,739	15,696	13,043	40	24	16	1	...	1
Total Kashmir Valley ...	...	*184,160*	*99,661*	*84,409*	*33,691*	*18,527*	*15,164*	*40*	*24*	*16*	*1*	...	*1*
Total Muzaffarabad District.	...	4,403	2,540	1,863	891	528	363	...	...	...	...	...	...
47. Muzaffarabad ...	Town ...	3,462	2,015	1,447	866	506	360	...	...	...	...	...	...
48. Uri ...	,,	544	298	246	...	...	...	...	...	...	...	...	...
49. Titwal (Karnah)	,,	397	227	170	25	22	3	...	...	...	...	...	...
Total Frontier District	...	20,192	11,142	9,050	740	681	59	3	2	1	...	...	...
Total Laddakh District	...	6,407	3,354	3,053	259	235	24	3	2	1	...	...	...
50. Laddakh ...	,,	2,895	1,464	1,431	32	27	5	...	...	...	...	...	...
51. Kargil ...	,,	1,315	753	562	76	67	9	3	2	1	...	...	...
52. Skardu ...	,,	2,197	1,137	1,060	151	141	10	...	...	...	...	...	...
Total Gilgit District	,,	4,157	2,625	1,532	468	437	31	...	...	...	20	...	...
53. Gilgit ...	,,	3,562	2,301	1,261	453	425	28	...	...	...	...	...	...
54. Astore ...	,,	595	324	271	15	12	3	...	...	...	...	...	...
Total Frontier Ilaqas	,,	9,628	5,163	4,465	13	9	4	...	...	...	...	...	...
55. Yasin ...	,,	1,251	640	611	...	...	...	...	...	...	...	...	...
56. Hunza ...	,,	1,971	1,082	889	...	...	...	...	...	...	...	...	...
57. Nagar ...	,,	3,377	1,833	1,544	...	...	...	...	...	...	...	...	...
58. Sherqila ...	,,	644	343	301	...	...	...	...	...	...	...	...	...
59. Ishkoman ...	,,	584	308	276	...	...	...	...	...	...	...	...	...
60. Chilas ...	,,	800	434	366	13	9	4	...	...	...	...	...	...
61. Ghizar ...	,,	1,001	523	478	...	...	...	...	...	...	...	...	...

V.

WITH POPULATION BY RELIGION.

State Census 1911.

V

Towns arranged territorially and by religion.

ARYAN.									II.—IRANIAN.			III—SEMITIC.					
B.—SIKH.			C.—JAIN.			D.—BUDHIST.			E.—ZOROASTRIAN.			F.—MUSALMAN.			G.—CHRISTIAN.		
Persons.	Males.	Females.	Persons.	Males.	Females.	Persons.	Males.	Females.	Persons.	Males.	Females.	Persons.	Males.	Females.	Persons.	Males.	Females.
15	16	17	18	19	20	21	22	23	24	25	26	27	28	29	30	31	32
396	272	124	...	...	...	...	...	...	26	20	6	95,563	51,439	44,124	111	51	6
90	44	46	...	...	...	...	...	...	...	...	...	1,378	832	546	...	...	...
486	316	170	...	...	...	...	...	...	26	20	6	96,941	52,271	44,670	111	51	60
576	*335*	*191*	...	...	...	...	...	...	*26*	*20*	*6*	*149,708*	*80,650*	*69,058*	*118*	*55*	*63*
368	191	177	...	...	...	1	1	...	...	...	...	3,143	1,820	1,323	...	...	...
308	161	147	...	...	...	1	1	...	...	...	...	2,287	1,347	940	...	...	...
...	...	...	...	...	...	...	...	...	...	...	...	544	298	246	...	...	...
60	30	30	...	...	...	...	...	...	...	...	...	312	175	137	...	...	...
60	47	13	...	...	...	1,646	849	797	...	...	...	17,692	9,533	8,159	51	30	21
25	18	7	...	...	...	1,646	849	797	...	...	...	4,427	2,224	2,203	47	28	21
3	1	2	...	...	...	1,640	843	797	...	...	...	1,173	567	606	47	26	21
13	10	3	...	...	...	4	4	...	...	...	...	1,219	670	549	...	...	...
9	7	2	...	...	...	2	2	...	...	...	...	2,035	987	1,048	...	...	...
20	16	4	...	...	...	...	...	...	...	...	...	3,666	2,169	1,497	3	3	...
20	16	4	...	...	...	...	...	...	...	...	...	3,086	1,857	1,229	3	3	...
...	...	...	...	...	...	...	...	...	...	...	...	580	312	268	...	...	...
15	13	2	...	...	...	...	...	...	...	...	...	9,599	5,140	4,459	1	1	...
...	...	...	...	...	...	...	...	...	...	...	...	1,251	640	611	...	...	...
...	...	...	...	...	...	...	...	...	...	...	...	1,971	1,082	889	...	...	...
...	...	...	...	...	...	...	...	...	...	...	...	3,377	1,833	1,544	...	...	...
...	...	...	...	...	...	...	...	...	...	...	...	644	343	301	...	...	...
...	...	...	...	...	...	...	...	...	...	...	...	584	308	276	...	...	...
15	13	2	...	...	...	...	...	...	...	...	...	771	411	360	1	1	...
...	...	...	...	...	...	...	...	...	...	...	...	1,001	523	478	...	...	...

TABLE VI.

POPULATION BY RELIGION.

Jammu and Kashmir State Census 1911.

1. The religions have been classified and arranged on the plan adopted in the India Volume of the last Census Tables.

2. The Mohamedans have been shown only under two main sects *Sunnis* and *Shias* as per suggestion contained in Government of India $\frac{\text{Home Department}}{\text{Census}}$ No. 104, dated 29th April, 1910, and the consequent orders of H. H. the Maharaja Saheb Bahadur, received with Chief Minister's No. 5023, dated 15th September, 1910.

3. The *Shiah* figures include 24,910 (13,154 Male and 11,756 Female) followers of H. H. Sir Agha Khan, chiefly inhabiting the Political *Ilaqas* of the Gilgit Agency, who are locally called *Mauláis* and whose beliefs are more akin to Shiaism than Sunnism.

4. The Buddhist figures include the population of the Tibetan village, Mansar (Total 190; Male 111, Female 79) that was censused on special lines.

5. The single Bramho returned in the State was a European lady found in Srinagar at the Final Enumeration.

6. Two *Sansis* (a male and a female) and one female Megh in respect of whom the name of caste was entered instead of religion in column 4 have been included in Hindu figures.

7. The following is a list of the tribes which though returned and tabulated as Hindus occupy a "debateable ground" as far as religious status is concerned. Those in Italics are regarded as particularly unclean. The figures given below are only those that have been classed as Hindu (*Brahmanic.*)

Serial No.	Tribe.	Population.		
		Total.	Males.	Females.
1	Barwala (or Batwal)	11,175	6.040	5,135
2	Basith	7,386	3,604	3,782
3	Bawaria	33	20	13
4	Bazigar	121	73	48
5	*Chamiar*	38,752	20,386	18,366
6	*Chuhra*	231	125	106
7	*Dum*	36,128	18,734	17,394
8	Gadri	354	246	108
9	Ghrit	131	71	60
10	Koli	1,784	888	896
11	Megh	74,762	39,000	35,762
12	Ratal	970	531	439
13	Sansi	45	41	4
14	Saryara	2,626	1,330	1,296
15	Thiar (or Dhiar)	2,755	1,345	1,410
	Total ...	177,253	92,434	84,819

TABLE VI.

Population by Religion.

Jammu and Kashmir State Census 1911.

District, Ilaqa or Jagir.	Total Population.			I. Indo-Aryan.														
				A. Hindu.									B. Sikh.			C. Jain.		
				(a) Brahmanic.			(b) Arya.			(c) Brahmo.								
	Persons.	Males.	Females.	Persons.	Males.	Females.	Persons.	Males.	Females.	Persons.	Males.	Females.	Persons.	Males.	Females.	Persons.	Males.	Females.
1	2	3	4	5	6	7	8	9	10	11	12	13	14	15	16	17	18	19
Total State ...	**3,158,126**	**1,674,367**	**1,483,759**	**689,342**	**372,089**	**317,253**	**1,047**	**593**	**454**	**1**	...	**1**	**31,553**	**17,038**	**14,515**	**345**	**191**	**154**
I.—Total Jammu Province (including *Jagirs*).	1,597,865	846,790	751,075	625,456	335,621	289,835	983	554	429	...	...	...	16,659	9,071	7,588	345	191	154
1. Jammu District (including city).	326,691	180,691	146,000	195,470	108,196	87,274	604	310	294	...	...	...	3,156	1,722	1,434	334	181	153
2. Jasrota District ...	151,802	81,375	70,427	116,267	61,994	54,273	72	45	27	...	...	...	108	58	50	...	...	...
3. Udhampur ,, ...	215,725	113,877	101,848	130,748	68,786	61,962	17	12	5	...	...	...	128	61	67	3	2	1
4. Riasi ,, ...	206,809	109,026	97,783	80,886	42,629	38,257	11	10	1	...	...	...	487	265	222	...	...	...
5. Mirpur ,, ...	324,933	169,276	155,657	57,187	30,956	26,231	225	140	85	...	...	...	3,156	1,779	1,377	8	8	...
6. Bhadarwah *Jagir* ...	37,512	18,975	18,537	22,931	11,375	11,556	...	...	...	...	...	...	...	...	...	...	...	...
7. Punch *Ilaqa* ...	334,393	173,570	160,823	21,967	11,685	10,282	54	37	17	...	...	...	9,624	5,186	4,438	...	...	...
II.—Total Kashmir Province (including *Jagirs*).	1,295,201	691,780	603,421	62,368	35,056	27,312	45	27	18	1	...	1	14,772	7,871	6,901	...	...	...
8. Kashmir North (including Langet *Jagir*).	460,786	244,637	216,149	9,917	5,935	3,982	5	3	2	...	...	...	4,575	2,383	2,192	...	...	...
9. Kashmir South (including city).	639,210	342,835	296,375	47,754	26,298	21,456	40	24	16	1	...	1	2,586	1,448	1,138	...	...	...
Total Kashmir Valley ...	*1,099,996*	*587,472*	*512,524*	*57,671*	*32,233*	*25,438*	*45*	*27*	*18*	*1*	...	*1*	*7,161*	*3,831*	*3,330*	...	...	...
10. Muzaffarabad District (*Wizarat Pahar*).	195,205	104,308	90,897	4,697	2,823	1,874	...	...	...	...	...	...	7,611	4,040	3,571	...	...	...
III.—Total Frontier Districts,	265,060	135,797	129,263	1,518	1,412	106	19	12	7	...	...	...	122	96	26	...	...	...
11. Laddakh District (including Mansar).	186,656	93,220	93,436	407	358	49	18	11	7	...	...	...	41	33	8	...	...	...
12. Gilgit District ...	23,969	13,299	10,670	816	770	46	...	...	...	...	...	...	57	41	16	...	...	...
13. Frontier *Ilaqas*	54,435	29,278	25,157	295	284	11	1	1	...	...	...	...	24	22	2	...	...	...

TABLE VI.

Population by Religion.

Jammu and Kashmir State Census 1911.

District, Ilaqa or Jagir.	I. INDO-ARYAN.			II. IRANIAN.			III. SEMITIC.											
	D. Budhist.			*E.* Zoroastrian.			*F.* Musalman.									*G.* Christian.		
							(*a*) *Sunni.*			(*b*) *Shia.*			Total.					
	Persons.	Males.	Females.	Persons.	Males.	Females.	Persons.	Males.	Females.	Persons.	Males.	Females.	Persons.	Males.	Females.	Persons.	Males.	Females.
	20	21	22	23	24	25	26	27	28	29	30	31	32	33	34	35	36	37
Total State ...	**36,512**	**18,281**	**18,231**	**31**	**22**	**9**	**2,194,503**	**1,160,736**	**1,033,767**	**203,817**	**104,799**	**99,018**	**2,398,320**	**1,265,535**	**1,132,785**	**975**	**618**	**357**
I.—Total Jammu Province (including *Jagirs*).	452	211	241	5	2	3	948,258	497,986	450,272	5,035	2,704	2,331	953,293	500,690	452,603	672	450	222
1. Jammu District (including city).	...	...	...	5	2	3	124,823	68,971	55,852	1,836	1,005	831	126,659	69,976	56,683	463	304	159
2. Jasrota District ...	11	4	7	...	...	...	35,014	19,045	15,969	160	101	59	35,174	19,146	16,028	170	128	42
3. Udhampur „ ...	439	205	234	...	...	...	84,277	44,751	39,526	113	60	53	84,390	44,811	39,579	...	...	...
4. Riasi „ ...	...	...	...	...	...	...	125,274	66,014	59,260	150	107	43	125,424	66,121	59,303	1	1	...
5. Mirpur „ ...	...	...	...	...	...	...	262,691	135,534	127,157	1,656	852	804	264,347	136,386	127,961	10	7	3
6. Bhadarwah *Jagir* ...	1	1	...	...	...	...	14,580	7,599	6,981	...	...	...	14,580	7,599	6,981	...	...	...
7. Punch *Ilaqa* ...	1	1	...	...	...	...	301,599	156,072	145,527	1,120	579	541	302,719	156,651	146,068	28	10	18
II.—Total Kashmir Province (including *Jagirs*).	3	3	...	26	20	6	1,174,964	626,395	548,569	42,804	22,290	20,514	1,217,768	648,685	569,063	218	118	100
8. Kashmir North (including Langet *Jagir*).	2	2	...	...	...	...	415,502	220,299	195,203	30,746	15,990	14,756	446,248	236,289	209,959	39	25	14
9. Kashmir South (including city).	...	...	...	26	20	6	576,968	308,876	268,092	11,673	6,089	5,584	588,641	314,965	273,676	162	80	82
Total Kashmir Valley ...	*2*	*2*	...	*26*	*20*	*6*	*992,470*	*529,175*	*463,295*	*42,419*	*22,079*	*20,340*	*1,034,889*	*551,254*	*483,635*	*201*	*105*	*96*
10. Muzaffarabad District (*Wizarat Pahar.*)	1	1	...	...	...	...	182,494	97,220	85,274	385	211	174	182,879	97,431	85,448	17	13	4
III.—Total Frontier Districts.	36,057	18,067	17,990	...	...	...	71,281	36,355	34,926	155,978	79,805	76,173	227,259	116,160	111,099	85	50	35
11. Laddakh District (including Mansar).	36,057	18,067	17,990	...	...	...	43,574	21,158	22,416	106,496	53,561	52,935	150,070	74,719	75,351	63	32	31
12. Gilgit District ...	...	...	...	...	...	...	11,987	6,604	5,383	11,088	5,867	5,221	23,075	12,471	10,604	21	17	4
13. Frontier *Ilaqas* ...	...	...	...	...	...	...	15,720	8,593	7,127	38,394	20,377	18,017	54,114	28,970	25,144	1	1	...

TABLE VII.

AGE, SEX AND CIVIL CONDITION (BY RELIGION).

Jammu and Kashmir State Census 1911.

1. This table is divided into the following parts :—

PART I—Provincial Tables :— (*i*) Entire State, (*ii*) Jammu Province, (*iii*) Kashmir Province, (*iv*) Kashmir Valley, (*v*) Frontier Districts;

PART II—District Tables :— (1) Jammu, (2) Jasrota, (3) Udhampur, (4) Riasi, (5) Mirpur, (6) Bhadarwah, (7) Punch, (8) Kashmir North, (9) Kashmir South, (10) Muzaffarabad, (11) Laddakh, (12) Gilgit ;

PART III—City Tables :— (*a*) Jammu, (*b*) Srinagar.

2. The Provincial and City Tables give all the age periods as prescribed in the Imperial form, but the periods given in the District Tables are only 0-5, 5-10, 10-15, 15-20, 20-40, 40-60, and 60 and over.

3. Details of age and religion having no entries in respect of certain units have been omitted to economise space.

4. The Frontier *Ilaqas* (of Gilgit) and Mansar village (of Laddakh), having been enumerated on special lines without detail of age and civil condition, do not find a place in this table. The following figures should, therefore, be added before making a comparison of it with Table VI or any other in which the total population has been dealt with :—

Locality.	Total population.			RELIGIONS.																		
				HINDU.						Sikh.			Budhist.			Musalman.			Christian.			
				Brahmanic.			*Arya.*															
	Persons.	Males.	Females.	Persons.	Males.	Females.	Persons.	Males.	Females.	Persons.	Males.	Females.	Persons.	Males.	Females.	Persons.	Males.	Females.	Persons.	Males.	Females.
Frontier *Ilaqas* ..	54,435	29,278	25,157	295	284	11	1	1	..	24	22	2	..	..	..	54,114	28,970	25,144	1	1	..
Mansar ..	190	111	79	..	..	..	..	..	..	..	..	..	190	111	79	..	..	..	..	..	..
TOTAL ..	54,625	29,389	25,236	295	284	11	1	1	..	24	22	2	190	111	79	54,114	28,970	25,144	1	1	..

VII
Age, Sex and Civil Condition.

TABLE VII.

Age, Sex and Civil Condition by Religion.

Jammu and Kashmir State Census 1911.

Part I—Provincial Tables.

Religion.	Age.	Population. Persons.	Population. Males.	Population. Females.	Unmarried. Persons.	Unmarried. Males.	Unmarried. Females.	Married. Persons.	Married. Males.	Married. Females.	Widowed. Persons.	Widowed. Males.	Widowed. Females.
1	2	3	4	5	6	7	8	9	10	11	12	13	14
					(i) ENTIRE STATE.								
All Religions.	Total	3,103,501	1,644,978	1,458,523	1,430,936	865,570	565,366	1,406,952	689,990	716,962	265,613	89,418	176,195
	0—1	140,651	71,021	69,630	140,637	71,014	69,623	13	7	6	1	...	1
	1—2	35,648	18,235	17,413	35,642	18,233	17,409	6	2	4	...	...	...
	2—3	86,165	43,482	42,683	86,096	43,468	42,628	68	14	54	1	...	1
	3—4	103,754	52,238	51,516	103,451	52,147	51,304	296	88	208	7	3	4
	4—5	98,026	50,218	47,808	97,678	50,127	47,551	330	89	241	18	2	16
	Total 0—5	464,244	235,194	229,050	463,504	234,989	228,515	713	200	513	27	5	22
	5—10	457,859	237,499	220,360	443,908	234,769	209.139	13.431	2,614	10,817	520	116	404
	10—15	347,154	192,256	154,898	274,855	176,511	98,344	70.721	15,392	55,329	1,578	353	1,225
	15—20	270,870	143,115	127,755	117,959	99,719	18,240	147,914	42,080	105,834	4,997	1,316	3,681
	20—25	265,671	131,613	134,058	58,504	53,657	4,847	197.742	74,581	123,161	9,425	3,375	6,050
	25—30	251,282	129,198	122,084	30,379	28,392	1,987	206,997	95,086	111,911	13,906	5,720	8,186
	30—35	244,218	130,041	114.177	15,418	14,067	1,351	208,380	108,162	100,218	20,420	7,812	12,608
	35—40	165,087	91,287	73,800	6,888	6,274	614	140,243	78,520	61,723	17,956	6,493	11,463
	40—45	187,231	98,037	89,194	6,908	6,154	754	146.556	81,961	64,595	33,767	9,922	23,845
	45—50	95,752	54,395	41,357	2,996	2,702	294	72,607	45,394	27,213	20,149	6,299	13,850
	50—55	130,547	72,463	58,084	3,473	3,088	385	86,733	57,581	29,152	40,341	11,794	28,547
	55—60	37,104	22.292	14,812	1,048	953	95	24,004	17,031	6,973	12,052	4,308	7,744
	60—65	100,869	56,967	43,902	2,596	2,217	379	53,391	40,829	12,562	44,882	13,921	30,961
	65—70	19,383	12,014	7,369	541	456	85	10,551	8,272	2,279	8,291	3,286	5,005
	70 & over	66,230	38,607	27,623	1,959	1,622	337	26,969	22,287	4,682	37,302	14,698	22,604
Hindu (*Brahmanic*).	Total	689,047	371,805	317,242	286,109	190,494	95,615	307,742	152,145	155,597	95,196	29,166	66,030
	0—1	24,980	12,710	12,270	24.980	12,710	12,270	...	...	...	...	...	...
	1—2	7,174	3,686	3,488	7,173	3,686	3,487	1	...	1	...	...	...
	2—3	14,271	7,193	7,078	14.254	7,190	7,064	16	3	13	1	...	1
	3—4	17,592	8,872	8,720	17,520	8,851	8,669	70	19	51	2	2	...
	4—5	17,683	9,011	8,672	17,590	8,995	8,595	83	14	69	10	2	8
	Total 0—5	81,700	41,472	40,228	81,517	41,432	40,085	170	36	134	13	4	9
	5—10	85,762	43,449	42,313	80,716	42,907	37,809	4,825	497	4,328	221	45	176
	10—15	71,020	40,544	30,476	51,860	37,571	14,289	18,488	2,873	15,615	672	100	572
	15—20	57,895	30,716	27.179	24,822	22,862	1,960	31,355	7,547	23,808	1,718	307	1,411
	20—25	58,050	30,282	27,768	15,832	15,410	422	38,827	14,023	24,804	3,391	849	2,542
	25—30	62,877	33,540	29,337	11,140	10,873	267	45,638	20,789	24,849	6,099	1,878	4,221
	30—35	60,146	32,486	27.660	6,554	6,313	241	45,135	23,707	21,428	8,457	2,466	5,991
	35—40	40,207	22,983	17,224	3,482	3,385	97	29,297	17,320	11,977	7,428	2,278	5,150
	40—45	47,812	25,307	22,505	3,400	3,263	137	31,485	18,591	12,894	12,927	3,453	9,474
	45—50	25,461	14,977	10,484	1,633	1,592	41	16,229	11,065	5.164	7,599	2,320	5,279
	50—55	34,490	19,349	15,141	2,004	1,921	83	18,678	13,392	5,286	13,808	4,036	9,772
	55—60	11,532	6,970	4.562	613	594	19	6,224	4,704	1,520	4,695	1,672	3,023
	60—65	27,076	15.116	11,960	1,408	1,328	80	11,635	9,446	2,189	14,033	4,342	9,691
	65—70	6,075	3,722	2,353	247	236	11	2,979	2,352	627	2,849	1,134	1,715
	70 & over	18,944	10,892	8,052	881	807	74	6,777	5,803	974	11,286	4,282	7,004
Hindu (*Arya*).	Total	1,046	592	454	408	280	128	550	271	279	88	41	47
	0—1	41	23	18	41	23	18	...	...	...	...	...	...
	1—2	6	5	1	6	5	1	...	...	...	...	...	...
	2—3	19	11	8	19	11	8	...	...	...	...	...	...
	3—4	29	16	13	28	15	13	...	...	...	1	1	...
	4—5	23	11	12	20	11	9	3	...	3	...	...	...
	Total 0—5	118	66	52	114	65	49	3	...	3	1	1	...
	5—10	108	66	42	107	65	42	1	1	...	...	...	...
	10—15	113	68	45	93	63	30	20	5	15	...	...	...
	15—20	100	50	50	37	32	5	63	18	45	...	...	...
	20—25	125	67	58	34	33	1	89	33	56	2	1	1
	25—30	118	69	49	14	14	...	98	49	49	6	6	...
	30—35	100	57	43	3	3	...	93	51	42	4	3	1
	35—40	59	39	20	1	1	...	52	38	14	6	...	6
	40—45	61	29	32	1	1	...	46	23	23	14	5	9
	45—50	40	30	10	2	2	...	30	21	9	8	7	1
	50—55	34	17	17	...	...	...	17	11	6	17	6	11
	55—60	10	7	3	...	...	...	6	5	1	4	2	2
	60—65	18	13	5	...	...	...	13	10	3	5	3	2
	65—70	10	8	2	1	1	...	4	4	...	5	3	2
	70 & over	32	6	26	1	...	1	15	2	13	16	4	12

TABLE VII.

VII
Age, Sex and Civil Condition.

Age, Sex and Civil Condition by Religion.

Jammu and Kashmir State Census 1911.

Part I—Provincial Tables.

Religion.	Age.	Population.			Unmarried.			Married.			Widowed.		
		Persons.	Males.	Females.	Persons.	Males.	Females.	Persons.	Males.	Females.	Persons.	Males.	Females.
1	2	3	4	5	6	7	8	9	10	11	12	13	14
Hindu (Bramho).	Total	1	...	1	...	...	...	1	...	1	...	...	...
Hindu (Bramho).	25—30	1	...	1	...	...	...	1	...	1	...	...	...
Sikh.	Total	31,529	17,016	14,513	15,363	9,492	5,871	13,690	6,736	6,954	2,476	788	1,688
Sikh.	0—1	1,526	823	703	1,526	823	703	...	...	...	...	...	...
Sikh.	1—2	341	189	152	341	189	152	...	...	...	...	...	...
Sikh.	2—3	892	446	446	889	445	444	3	1	2	...	...	...
Sikh.	3—4	1,060	523	537	1,059	523	536	1	...	1	...	...	...
Sikh.	4—5	1,084	556	528	1,081	555	526	3	1	2	...	...	...
Sikh.	Total 0—5	4,903	2,537	2,366	4,896	2,535	2,361	7	2	5	...	...	...
Sikh.	5—10	5,034	2,641	2,393	4,915	2,621	2,294	113	18	95	6	2	4
Sikh.	10—15	3,648	2,057	1,591	3,001	1,967	1,034	633	86	547	14	4	10
Sikh.	15—20	2,817	1,534	1,283	1,280	1,173	107	1,505	350	1,155	32	11	21
Sikh.	20—25	2,504	1,232	1,272	551	531	20	1,879	686	1,193	74	15	59
Sikh.	25—30	2,582	1,338	1,244	311	303	8	2,153	988	1,165	118	47	71
Sikh.	30—35	2,493	1,304	1,189	127	116	11	2,155	1,115	1,040	211	73	138
Sikh.	35—40	1,612	953	659	79	71	8	1,361	824	537	172	58	114
Sikh.	40—45	1,777	935	842	67	59	8	1,362	790	572	348	86	262
Sikh.	45—50	928	562	366	38	35	3	698	466	232	192	61	131
Sikh.	50—55	1,225	716	509	34	30	4	809	582	227	382	104	278
Sikh.	55—60	376	233	143	14	13	1	219	163	56	143	57	86
Sikh.	60—65	877	509	368	22	16	6	466	381	85	389	112	277
Sikh.	65—70	203	131	72	5	5	...	117	100	17	81	26	55
Sikh.	70 & over	550	334	216	23	17	6	213	185	28	314	132	182
Jain.	Total	345	191	154	178	104	74	119	63	56	48	24	24
Jain.	0—1	14	4	10	14	4	10	...	...	...	...	...	...
Jain.	1—2	4	3	1	4	3	1	...	...	...	...	...	...
Jain.	2—3	11	7	4	11	7	4	...	...	...	...	...	...
Jain.	3—4	8	3	5	8	3	5	...	...	...	...	...	...
Jain.	4—5	16	6	10	16	6	10	...	...	...	...	...	...
Jain.	Total 0—5	53	23	30	53	23	30	...	...	...	...	...	...
Jain.	5—10	42	20	22	40	19	21	2	1	1	...	...	...
Jain.	10—15	42	24	18	41	24	17	1	...	1	...	...	...
Jain.	15—20	29	14	15	20	14	6	8	...	8	1	...	1
Jain.	20—25	39	28	11	16	16	...	21	10	11	2	2	...
Jain.	25—30	28	14	14	3	3	...	19	8	11	6	3	3
Jain.	30—35	22	13	9	2	2	...	15	9	6	5	2	3
Jain.	35—40	20	14	6	3	3	...	13	9	4	4	2	2
Jain.	40—45	13	8	5	...	...	...	9	6	3	4	2	2
Jain.	45—50	14	7	7	...	...	...	10	6	4	4	1	3
Jain.	50—55	18	12	6	...	...	...	9	6	3	9	6	3
Jain.	55—60	9	6	3	...	...	...	5	3	2	4	3	1
Jain.	60—65	5	2	3	...	...	...	4	2	2	1	...	1
Jain.	65—70	7	3	4	...	...	...	2	2	...	5	1	4
Jain.	70 & over	4	3	1	...	...	...	1	1	...	3	2	1
Budhist.	Total	36,322	18,170	18,152	15,667	7,644	8,023	17,564	9,463	8,102	3,090	1,063	2,027
Budhist.	0—1	878	418	460	874	415	459	4	3	1	...	...	...
Budhist.	1—2	385	172	213	384	171	213	1	1	...	...	...	...
Budhist.	2—3	612	284	328	607	280	327	5	4	1	...	...	...
Budhist.	3—4	836	403	433	827	396	431	9	7	2	...	...	...
Budhist.	4—5	753	349	404	740	336	404	13	13	...	...	...	...
Budhist.	Total 0—5	3,464	1,626	1,838	3,432	1,598	1,834	32	28	4	...	...	...
Budhist.	5—10	4,036	2,025	2,011	3,857	1,872	1,985	173	150	23	6	3	3
Budhist.	10—15	3,232	1,633	1,599	2,842	1,332	1,510	381	295	86	9	6	3
Budhist.	15—20	3,122	1,562	1,560	2,027	906	1,121	1,071	642	429	24	14	10
Budhist.	20—25	2,942	1,471	1,471	1,068	465	603	1,787	969	818	87	37	50
Budhist.	25—30	2,927	1,524	1,403	641	339	302	2,175	1,140	1,035	111	45	66
Budhist.	30—35	2,872	1,453	1,419	391	223	168	2,347	1,182	1,165	134	48	86
Budhist.	35—40	2,345	1,180	1,165	260	166	94	1,944	978	966	141	36	105
Budhist.	40—45	2,541	1,236	1,305	270	176	94	2,024	1,000	1,025	246	60	186
Budhist.	45—50	1,977	1,011	966	206	149	57	1,557	803	754	214	59	155
Budhist.	50—55	1,855	896	959	169	102	67	1,300	684	616	386	110	276
Budhist.	55—60	1,148	597	551	119	80	39	809	459	350	220	58	162
Budhist.	60—65	1,677	821	856	149	93	56	992	548	444	536	180	356
Budhist.	65—70	836	435	401	104	65	39	472	267	205	260	103	157
Budhist.	70 & over	1,348	700	648	132	78	54	500	318	182	716	304	412

VII
Age, Sex and Civil Condition.

TABLE VII.

Age, Sex and Civil Condition by Religion.

Jammu and Kashmir State Census 1911.

Part I.—Provincial Tables.

Religion.	Age.	Population.			Unmarried.			Married.			Widowed.		
		Persons.	Males.	Females.	Persons.	Males.	Females.	Persons.	Males.	Females.	Persons.	Males.	Females.
1	2	3	4	5	6	7	8	9	10	11	12	13	14
Zoroastrian.	**Total**	**31**	**22**	**9**	**15**	**11**	**4**	**15**	**10**	**5**	**1**	**1**	...
	0—1	1	1	...	1	1	...	...	...	...	...	...	...
	2—3	1	...	1	1	...	1	...	...	...	...	...	...
	3—4	2	1	1	2	1	1	...	...	...	...	...	...
	Total 0—5	4	2	2	4	2	2	...	...	...	...	...	...
	5—10	6	6	...	6	6	...	...	...	...	...	...	...
	15—20	3	2	1	3	2	1	...	...	...	...	...	...
	20—25	3	1	2	2	1	1	1	...	1	...	...	...
	25—30	1	1	...	...	...	...	1	1	...	...	...	...
	30—35	3	1	2	...	...	...	3	1	2	...	...	...
	35—40	1	...	1	...	...	...	1	...	1	...	...	...
	40—45	5	4	1	...	...	...	5	4	1	...	...	...
	45—50	2	2	...	...	...	...	2	2	...	...	...	...
	50—55	1	1	...	...	...	...	1	1	...	...	...	...
	60—65	1	1	...	...	...	...	1	1	...	...	...	...
	65—70	1	1	...	...	...	...	...	...	...	1	1	...
Musalman.	**Total**	**2,344,206**	**1,236,565**	**1,107,641**	**1,112,693**	**657,248**	**455,445**	**1,066,888**	**521,035**	**545,853**	**164,625**	**58,282**	**106,343**
	0—1	113,167	57,024	56,143	113,157	57,020	56,137	9	4	5	1	...	1
	1—2	27,730	14,175	13,555	27,726	14,174	13,552	4	1	3	...	...	...
	2—3	70,327	35,532	34,795	70,283	35,526	34,757	44	6	38	...	...	...
	3—4	84,197	42,406	41,791	83,977	42,344	41,633	216	62	154	4	...	4
	4—5	78,441	40,265	38,176	78,205	40,204	38,001	228	61	167	8	...	8
	Total 0—5	373,862	189,402	184,460	373,348	189,268	184,080	501	134	367	13	...	13
	5—10	362,751	189,229	173,522	354,147	187,216	166,931	8,317	1,947	6,370	287	66	221
	10—15	269,009	147,868	121,141	216,932	135,496	81,436	51,194	12,129	39,065	883	243	640
	15—20	206,851	109,196	97,655	89,735	74,703	15,032	113,894	33,509	80,385	3,222	984	2,238
	20—25	201,927	98,479	103,448	40,967	37,176	3,791	155,094	58,834	96,260	5,866	2,469	3,397
	25—30	182,640	92,634	90,006	18,239	16,836	1,403	156,841	72,063	84,778	7,560	3,735	3,825
	30—35	178,470	94,655	83,815	8,322	7,398	924	158,544	82,039	76,505	11,604	5,218	6,386
	35—40	120,767	66,076	54,691	3,049	2,639	410	107,521	59,319	48,202	10,197	4,118	6,079
	40—45	134,961	70,476	64,485	3,162	2,651	511	111,586	61,519	50,067	20,213	6,306	13,907
	45—50	67,303	37,781	29,522	1,115	923	192	54,061	33,012	21,049	12,127	3,846	8,281
	50—55	92,878	51,442	41,436	1,265	1,028	227	65,902	42,893	23,009	25,721	7,521	18,200
	55—60	24,015	14,469	9,546	301	265	36	16,735	11,691	5,044	6,979	2,513	4,466
	60—65	71,187	40,483	30,704	1,016	780	236	40,265	30,427	9,838	29,906	9,276	20,630
	65—70	12,245	7,711	4,534	184	149	35	6,975	5,545	1,430	5,086	2,017	3,069
	70 & over	45,340	26,664	18,676	921	720	201	19,458	15,974	3,484	24,961	9,970	14,991
Christian.	**Total**	**974**	**617**	**357**	**503**	**297**	**206**	**382**	**267**	**115**	**89**	**53**	**36**
	0—1	44	18	26	44	18	26	...	...	...	...	...	...
	1—2	8	5	3	8	5	3	...	...	...	...	...	...
	2—3	32	9	23	32	9	23	...	...	...	...	...	...
	3—4	30	14	16	30	14	16	...	...	...	...	...	...
	4—5	26	20	6	26	20	6	...	...	...	...	...	...
	Total 0—5	140	66	74	140	66	74	...	...	...	...	...	...
	5—10	120	63	57	120	63	57	...	...	...	...	...	...
	10—15	90	62	28	86	58	28	4	4	...	...	...	...
	15—20	53	41	12	35	27	8	18	14	4	...	...	...
	20—25	81	53	28	34	25	9	44	26	18	3	2	1
	25—30	108	78	30	31	24	7	71	48	23	6	6	...
	30—35	112	72	40	19	12	7	88	58	30	5	2	3
	35—40	76	42	34	14	9	5	54	32	22	8	1	7
	40—45	61	42	19	8	4	4	38	28	10	15	10	5
	45—50	27	25	2	2	1	1	20	19	1	5	5	...
	50—55	46	30	16	11	7	4	17	12	5	18	11	7
	55—60	14	10	4	1	1	...	6	6	...	7	3	4
	60—65	28	22	6	1	...	1	15	14	1	12	8	4
	65—70	6	3	3	...	...	...	2	2	...	4	1	3
	70 & over	12	8	4	1	...	1	5	4	1	6	4	2

TABLE VII.

Age, Sex and Civil Condition by Religion.

Jammu and Kashmir State Census 1911.

Part I—Provincial Tables.

VII
Age, Sex and Civil Condition.

Religion.	Age.	Population. Persons.	Population. Males.	Population. Females.	Unmarried. Persons.	Unmarried. Males.	Unmarried. Females.	Married. Persons.	Married. Males.	Married. Females.	Widowed. Persons.	Widowed. Males.	Widowed. Females.
1	2	3	4	5	6	7	8	9	10	11	12	13	14
					(ii) JAMMU PROVINCE.								
All Religions.	Total	1,597,865	846,790	751,075	716,513	446,095	270,418	715,130	347,169	367,961	166,222	53,526	112696
	0—1	68,352	34,410	33,942	68,349	34,410	33,939	3	...	3	...	...	...
	1—2	19,828	10,204	9,624	19,824	10,204	9,620	4	...	4	...	...	...
	2—3	38,449	19,602	18,847	38,386	19,592	18,794	62	10	52	1	...	1
	3—4	48,152	24,325	23,827	47,874	24,247	23,627	271	75	196	7	3	4
	4—5	48,571	24,907	23,664	48,259	24,843	23,416	294	62	232	18	2	16
	Total 0—5	223,352	113,448	109,904	222,692	113,296	109,396	534	147	487	26	5	21
	5—10	227,429	117,705	109,724	215,988	115,625	100,363	10,988	1,978	9,010	453	102	351
	10—15	178,646	99,581	79,065	136,808	91,088	45,720	40,736	8,259	32,477	1,102	234	868
	15—20	134,559	69,940	64,619	59,620	50,468	9,152	72,056	18,784	53,272	2,883	688	2,195
	20—25	126,964	62,720	64,244	31,248	28,991	2,257	90,304	32,001	58,303	5,412	1,728	3,684
	25—30	136,354	70,354	66,000	20,775	19,641	1,134	106,103	47,171	58,932	9,476	3,542	5,934
	30—35	133,660	70,486	63,174	10,940	10,173	767	108,814	55,529	53,285	13,906	4,784	9,122
	35—40	84,456	46,785	37,671	4,855	4,528	327	67,644	38,246	29,398	11,957	4,011	7,946
	40—45	100,104	51,827	48,277	4,932	4,494	438	73,264	41,191	32,073	21,908	6,142	15,766
	45—50	50,827	29,259	21,568	1,984	1,841	143	36,055	23,452	12,603	12,788	3,966	8,822
	50—55	72,029	39,914	32,115	2,518	2,292	226	45,134	30,613	14,521	24,377	7,009	17,368
	55—60	21,998	12,874	9,124	675	629	46	13,354	9,547	3,807	7,969	2,698	5,271
	60—65	56,494	31,969	24,525	1,852	1,621	231	28.221	22,284	5,937	26,421	8,064	18,357
	65—70	11,279	6,945	4,334	310	281	29	6,019	4,743	1,276	4,950	1,921	3,029
	70 & over	39,714	22,983	16,731	1,316	1,127	189	15,804	13,224	2,580	22,594	8,632	13,962
Hindu (*Brahmanic*).	Total	625,456	335,621	289,835	255,962	170,184	85,778	281,793	138,700	143,093	87,701	26,737	60,964
	0—1	22,636	11,478	11,158	22,636	11,478	11,158	...	...	...	...	...	...
	1—2	6,740	3,456	3,284	6,739	3,456	3,283	1	...	1	...	...	...
	2—3	12,773	6,465	6,308	12,756	6,462	6,294	16	3	13	1	...	1
	3—4	15,878	8,015	7,863	15,806	7,994	7,812	70	19	51	2	2	...
	4—5	16,044	8,171	7,873	15,952	8,155	7,797	82	14	68	10	2	8
	Total 0—5	74,071	37,585	36,486	73.889	37,545	36,344	169	36	133	13	4	9
	5—10	77,569	39,279	38,290	72.604	38,752	33,852	4,749	482	4,267	216	45	171
	10—15	64,525	36,790	27,735	46,330	34,015	12,315	17,551	2,684	14,867	644	91	553
	15—20	52,511	27,486	25,025	22,131	20,297	1,834	28,747	6,896	21,851	1,633	293	1,340
	20—25	51,874	26,672	25,202	13,689	13,285	404	35,038	12,604	22,434	3,147	783	2,364
	25—30	57,021	30,182	26,839	9,809	9,548	261	41,512	18,884	22,628	5,700	1,750	3,950
	30—35	54,830	29,358	25,472	5,813	5,578	235	41,137	21,487	19,650	7,880	2,293	5,587
	35—40	36,054	20,383	15,671	2,959	2,864	95	26,321	15,459	10,862	6,774	2,060	4,714
	40—45	43,735	23,001	20,734	3,011	2,878	133	28,823	16,950	11,873	11,901	3,173	8,728
	45—50	22,740	13,348	9,392	1,344	1,303	41	14,554	9,963	4,591	3,842	2,082	4,760
	50—55	31,540	17,656	13,884	1,703	1,622	81	17,265	12,370	4,895	12,572	3,664	8,908
	55—60	10,219	6,119	4,100	460	441	19	5,608	4,216	1,392	4,151	1,462	2,689
	60—65	25,048	13,927	11,121	1,218	1,138	80	10,919	8,826	2,093	12.911	3,963	8,948
	65—70	5,552	3,391	2,161	201	190	11	2,813	2,209	604	2,538	992	1,546
	70 & over	18,167	10,444	7,723	801	728	73	6,587	5,634	953	10,779	4,082	6,697
Hindu (*Arya*).	Total	983	554	429	376	260	116	522	256	266	85	38	47
	0—1	37	21	16	37	21	16	...	...	...	...	...	...
	1—2	5	5	...	5	5	...	...	...	...	...	...	...
	2—3	19	11	8	19	11	8	...	...	...	...	...	...
	3—4	27	16	11	26	15	11	...	...	...	1	1	...
	4—5	21	10	11	18	10	8	3	...	3	...	...	...
	Total 0—5	109	63	46	105	62	43	3	...	3	1	1	...
	5—10	96	58	38	95	57	38	1	1	...	...	...	...
	10—15	107	63	44	88	59	29	19	4	15	...	...	...
	15—20	97	48	49	34	30	4	63	18	45	...	...	...
	20—25	114	62	52	32	31	1	80	30	50	2	1	1
	25—30	113	64	49	14	14	...	93	44	49	6	6	...
	30—35	90	51	39	2	2	...	85	47	38	3	2	1
	35—40	57	38	19	1	1	...	50	37	13	6	...	6
	40—45	60	29	31	1	1	...	45	23	22	14	5	9
	45—50	37	28	9	2	2	...	29	21	8	6	5	1
	50—55	33	16	17	...	...	...	16	10	6	17	6	11
	55—60	10	7	3	...	...	...	6	5	1	4	2	2
	60—65	18	13	5	...	...	...	13	10	3	5	3	2
	65—70	10	8	2	1	1	...	4	4	...	5	3	2
	70 & over	32	6	26	1	...	1	15	2	13	16	4	12

VII
Age, Sex and Civil Condition.

TABLE VII.

Age, Sex and Civil Condition by Religion.

Jammu and Kashmir State Census 1911.

Part I—Provincial Tables.

Religion.	Age.	Population.			Unmarried.			Married.			Widowed.		
		Persons.	Males.	Females.	Persons.	Males.	Females.	Persons.	Males.	Females.	Persons.	Males.	Females.
1	2	3	4	5	6	7	8	9	10	11	12	13	14
Sikh.	Total	16,659	9,071	7,588	7,953	5,054	2,899	7,219	3,548	3,671	1,487	469	1,018
	0—1	781	411	370	781	411	370	...	...	...	...	...	...
	1—2	173	97	76	173	97	76	...	...	...	...	...	...
	2—3	414	212	202	411	211	200	3	1	2	...	...	...
	3—4	471	243	228	470	243	227	1	...	1	...	...	...
	4—5	542	265	277	539	264	275	3	1	2	...	...	...
	Total 0—5	2,381	1,228	1,153	2,374	1,226	1,148	7	2	5	...	...	...
	5—10	2,580	1,387	1,193	2,490	1,369	1,121	85	16	69	5	2	3
	10—15	1,995	1,144	851	1,610	1,086	524	377	55	322	8	3	5
	15—20	1,435	792	643	657	599	58	760	186	574	18	7	11
	20—25	1,293	637	656	316	303	13	933	324	609	44	10	34
	25—30	1,354	728	626	219	213	6	1,074	489	585	61	26	35
	30—35	1,335	697	638	94	86	8	1,118	569	549	123	42	81
	35—40	883	515	368	56	53	3	706	423	283	121	39	82
	40—45	989	511	478	45	40	5	722	417	305	222	54	168
	45—50	566	330	236	27	24	3	413	271	142	126	35	91
	50—55	682	405	277	20	19	1	444	326	118	218	60	158
	55—60	236	146	90	12	11	1	134	102	32	90	33	57
	60—65	473	275	198	13	9	4	253	201	52	207	65	142
	65—70	144	91	53	3	3	...	78	67	11	63	21	42
	70 & over	313	185	128	17	13	4	115	100	15	181	72	109
Jain.	Total	345	191	154	178	104	74	119	63	56	48	24	24
	0—1	14	4	10	14	4	10	...	...	...	...	...	...
	1—2	4	3	1	4	3	1	...	...	...	...	...	...
	2—3	11	7	4	11	7	4	...	...	...	...	...	...
	3—4	8	3	5	8	3	5	...	...	...	...	...	...
	4—5	16	6	10	16	6	10	...	...	...	...	...	...
	Total 0—5	53	23	30	53	23	30	...	...	...	...	...	...
	5—10	42	20	22	40	19	21	2	1	1	...	...	...
	10—15	42	24	18	41	24	17	1	...	1	...	...	...
	15—20	29	14	15	20	14	6	8	...	8	1	...	1
	20—25	39	28	11	16	16	...	21	10	11	2	2	...
	25—30	28	14	14	3	3	...	19	8	11	6	3	3
	30—35	22	13	9	2	2	...	15	9	6	5	2	3
	35—40	20	14	6	3	3	...	13	9	4	4	2	2
	40—45	13	8	5	...	...	...	9	6	3	4	2	2
	45—50	14	7	7	...	...	...	10	6	4	4	1	3
	50—55	18	12	6	...	...	...	9	6	3	9	6	3
	55—60	9	6	3	...	...	...	5	3	2	4	3	1
	60—65	5	2	3	...	...	...	4	2	2	1	...	1
	65—70	7	3	4	...	...	...	2	2	...	5	1	4
	70 & over	4	3	1	...	...	...	1	1	...	3	2	1
Budhist.	Total	452	211	241	183	89	94	240	114	126	29	8	21
	0—1	6	2	4	6	2	4	...	...	...	...	...	...
	1—2	3	1	2	3	1	2	...	...	...	...	...	...
	2—3	10	4	6	10	4	6	...	...	...	...	...	...
	3—4	14	7	7	13	6	7	1	1	...	...	...	...
	4—5	12	6	6	12	6	6	...	...	...	...	...	...
	Total 0—5	45	20	25	44	19	25	1	1	...	...	...	...
	5—10	62	29	33	59	26	33	2	2	...	1	1	...
	10—15	46	18	28	37	14	23	9	4	5	...	...	...
	15—20	31	13	18	16	10	6	15	3	12	...	...	...
	20—25	28	11	17	7	6	1	21	5	16	...	...	...
	25—30	46	23	23	5	4	1	41	19	22	...	...	...
	30—35	48	22	26	5	3	2	43	19	24	...	...	...
	35—40	23	12	11	1	1	...	20	10	10	2	1	1
	40—45	34	14	20	3	2	1	26	10	16	5	2	3
	45—50	17	12	5	1	1	...	16	11	5	...	...	...
	50—55	32	13	19	2	1	1	18	10	8	12	2	10
	55—60	4	2	2	1	...	1	3	2	1	...	...	...
	60—65	21	14	7	2	2	...	14	11	3	5	1	4
	65—70	2	...	2	...	...	...	2	...	2	...	...	...
	70 & over	13	8	5	...	...	...	9	7	2	4	1	3

TABLE VII.

VII Age, Sex and Civil Condition.

Age, Sex and Civil Condition by Religion.

Jammu and Kashmir State Census 1911.

Part I —Provincial Tables.

Religion.	Age.	Population. Persons.	Population. Males.	Population. Females.	Unmarried. Persons.	Unmarried. Males.	Unmarried. Females.	Married. Persons.	Married. Males.	Married. Females.	Widowed. Persons.	Widowed. Males.	Widowed. Females.
1	2	3	4	5	6	7	8	9	10	11	12	13	14
Zoroastrian.	Total	5	2	3	1	...	1	4	2	2	...	...	...
	2—3	1	...	1	1	...	1	...	...	...	...	...	...
	Total 0—5	1	...	1	1	...	1	...	...	...	...	...	...
	20—25	1	...	1	...	...	...	1	...	1	...	...	...
	25—30	1	1	...	...	...	...	1	1	...	...	...	...
	40—45	2	1	1	...	...	...	2	1	1	...	...	...
Musalman.	Total	953,293	500,690	452,603	451,512	270,200	181,312	424,974	204,287	220,687	76,807	26,203	50,604
	0—1	44,847	22,483	22,364	44,844	22,483	22,361	3	...	3	...	...	...
	1—2	12,897	6,638	6,259	12,894	6,638	6,256	3	...	3	...	...	...
	2—3	25,191	12,894	12,297	25,148	12,888	12,260	43	6	37	...	...	...
	3—4	31,732	16,032	15,700	31,529	15,977	15,552	199	55	144	4	...	4
	4—5	31,913	16,432	15,481	31,699	16,385	15,314	206	47	159	8	...	8
	Total 0—5	146,580	74,479	72,101	146,114	74,371	71,743	454	108	346	12	...	12
	5—10	146,981	76,880	70,101	140,601	75,350	65,251	6,149	1,476	4,673	231	54	177
	10—15	111,854	61,490	50,364	88,629	55,842	32,787	22,775	5,508	17,267	450	140	310
	15—20	80,417	41,553	38,864	38,739	29,498	7,241	42,447	11,667	30,780	1,231	388	843
	20—25	73,558	35,268	38,290	17,169	15,334	1,835	54,175	19,004	35,171	2,214	930	1,284
	25—30	77,720	39,286	38,434	10,716	9,850	866	63,306	27,684	35,622	3,698	1,752	1,946
	30—35	77,268	40,295	36,973	5,016	4,498	518	66,361	23,353	33,008	5,891	2,444	3,447
	35—40	47,383	25,805	21,578	1,834	1,605	229	40,504	22,292	18,212	5,045	1,908	3,137
	40—45	55,241	28,236	27,005	1,871	1,572	299	43,618	23,768	19,850	9,752	2,896	6,856
	45—50	27,431	15,514	11,917	610	511	99	21,016	13,165	7,851	5,805	1,838	3,967
	50—55	39,698	21,793	17,905	790	647	143	27,374	17,885	9,489	11,534	3,261	8,273
	55—60	11,513	6,590	4,923	202	177	25	7,596	5,217	2,379	3,715	1,196	2,519
	60—65	30,911	17,721	13,190	619	472	147	17,008	13,224	3,784	13,284	4,025	9,259
	65—70	5,561	3,450	2,111	105	87	18	3,119	2,460	659	2,337	903	1,434
	70 & over	21,177	12,330	8,847	497	386	111	9,072	7,476	1,596	11,608	4,468	7,140
Christian.	Total	672	450	222	348	204	144	259	199	60	65	47	18
	0—1	31	11	20	31	11	20	...	...	...	...	...	...
	1—2	6	4	2	6	4	2	...	...	...	...	...	...
	2—3	30	9	21	30	9	21	...	...	...	...	...	...
	3—4	22	9	13	22	9	13	...	...	...	...	...	...
	4—5	23	17	6	23	17	6	...	...	...	...	...	...
	Total 0—5	112	50	62	112	50	62	...	...	...	...	...	...
	5—10	99	52	47	99	52	47	...	...	...	...	...	...
	10—15	77	52	25	73	48	25	4	4	...	...	...	...
	15—20	39	34	5	23	20	3	16	14	2	...	...	...
	20—25	57	42	15	19	16	3	35	24	11	3	2	1
	25—30	71	56	15	9	9	...	57	42	15	5	5	...
	30—35	67	50	17	8	4	4	55	45	10	4	1	3
	35—40	37	18	19	1	1	...	31	16	15	5	1	4
	40—45	30	27	3	1	1	...	19	16	3	10	10	...
	45—50	21	20	1	...	...	...	16	15	1	5	5	...
	50—55	26	19	7	3	3	...	8	6	2	15	10	5
	55—60	7	4	3	...	...	...	2	2	...	5	2	3
	60—65	18	17	1	...	...	...	10	10	...	8	7	1
	65—70	3	2	1	...	...	...	1	1	...	2	1	1
	70 & over	8	7	1	...	...	...	5	4	1	3	3	...
							***(iii)* KASHMIR PROVINCE.**						
All Religions.	Total	1,295,201	691,780	603,421	616,361	365,922	250,439	594,713	294,323	300,390	84,127	31,535	52,592
	0—1	63,657	32,349	31,308	63,657	32,349	31,308	...	...	...	...	...	...
	1—2	12,505	6,426	6,079	12,505	6,426	6,079	...	...	...	...	...	...
	2—3	41,117	20,697	20,420	41,116	20,697	20,419	1	...	1	...	...	...
	3—4	48,430	24,371	24,059	48,425	24,368	24,057	5	3	2	...	...	...
	4—5	43,487	22,450	21,037	43,479	22,445	21,034	8	5	3	...	...	...
	Total 0—5	209,196	106,293	102,903	209,182	106,285	102,897	14	8	6	...	...	...
	5—10	201,054	104,623	96,431	199,132	104,275	94,857	1,878	339	1,539	44	9	35
	10—15	148,131	81,764	66,367	120,727	75,738	44,989	27,011	5,945	21,066	393	81	312
	15—20	118,128	63,427	54,701	48,174	42,628	5,546	68,145	20,292	47,853	1,809	507	1,302
	20—25	115,094	57,718	57,376	21,892	20,874	1,018	90,040	35,553	54,487	3,162	1,291	1,871
	25—30	104,925	53,512	51,413	7,981	7,652	329	92,916	43,868	49,048	4,028	1,992	2,036
	30—35	97,730	52,863	44,867	3,574	3,269	305	88,272	46,831	41,441	5,884	2,763	3,121

VII
Age, Sex and Civil Condition.

TABLE VII.

Age, Sex and Civil Condition by Religion.

Jammu and Kashmir State Census 1911.

Part I—Provincial Tables.

Religion.	Age.	Population.			Unmarried.			Married.			Widowed.		
		Persons.	Males.	Females.	Persons.	Males.	Females.	Persons.	Males.	Females.	Persons.	Males.	Females.
1	2	3	4	5	6	7	8	9	10	11	12	13	14
All Religions. (*Continued*).	35—40	62,429	35,826	26,603	1,435	1,365	70	56,206	32,330	23,876	4,788	2,131	2,657
	40—45	78,050	41,367	36,683	1,534	1,370	164	65,506	36,429	29,077	11,010	3,568	7,442
	45—50	32,971	19,477	13.494	674	642	32	26,929	16.856	10,073	5.368	1,979	3.389
	50—55	52,902	29,514	23,388	743	660	83	37.366	24,395	12.971	14.793	4,459	10,334
	55—60	12,587	7,944	4.643	240	233	7	8.760	6.233	2,527	3,587	1,478	2.109
	60—65	35,645	20,960	14,685	515	453	62	19,825	15,333	4.493	15,304	5,174	10,130
	65—70	5,851	3.795	2,056	104	97	7	3,182	2,608	574	2,565	1,090	1,475
	70 & over	20,508	12,697	7,811	454	381	73	8,662	7,303	1,359	11,392	5,013	6,379
Hindu (*Brahmans*).	Total	62,368	35,056	27,312	29,582	19,786	9,796	25,365	12,915	12,450	7,421	2,355	5,066
	0—1	2,330	1,226	1,104	2.330	1,226	1,104	...	...	...	...	...	...
	1—2	430	227	203	430	227	203	...	...	...	...	...	...
	2—3	1,491	724	767	1.491	724	767	...	...	...	...	...	...
	3—4	1,705	853	852	1.705	853	852	...	...	...	...	...	...
	4—5	1,629	835	794	1,628	835	793	1	...	1	...	...	...
	Total 0—5	7,585	3,865	3,720	7,584	3,865	3,719	1	...	1	...	...	...
	5—10	8,163	4,153	4,010	8,082	4,138	3,944	76	15	61	5	...	5
	10—15	6,469	3,736	2.733	5,509	3,541	1,968	933	187	746	27	8	19
	15—20	5,324	3.178	2,146	2.646	2,520	126	2,593	644	1,949	85	14	71
	20—25	5,864	3,316	2,548	1,949	1,931	18	3,684	1,332	2,352	231	53	178
	25—30	5,553	3,067	2,486	1,202	1,196	6	3,971	1,762	2,209	380	109	271
	30—35	5,129	2,949	2,180	684	678	6	3,879	2,109	1,770	566	162	404
	35—40	4,044	2,494	1,550	503	501	2	2,899	1,787	1,112	642	206	436
	40—45	4,009	2,239	1,770	376	372	4	2,613	1,593	1,020	1,020	274	746
	45—50	2,668	1,577	1,091	281	281	...	1,633	1,061	572	754	235	519
	50—55	2,932	1,675	1,257	297	295	2	1,403	1,012	391	1,232	368	864
	55—60	1,311	849	462	153	153	...	614	486	128	544	210	334
	60—65	2,020	1,181	839	190	190	...	712	616	96	1,118	375	743
	65—70	520	329	191	46	46	...	164	142	22	310	141	169
	70&over	777	448	329	80	79	1	190	169	21	507	200	307
Hindu (*Arya*).	Total	45	27	18	26	16	10	16	8	8	3	3	...
	0—1	2	1	1	2	1	1	...	...	...	...	...	...
	3—4	2	...	2	2	...	2	...	...	...	...	...	...
	4—5	2	1	1	2	1	1	...	...	...	...	...	...
	Total 0—5	6	2	4	6	2	4	...	...	...	...	...	...
	5—10	12	8	4	12	8	4	...	...	...	...	...	...
	10—15	6	5	1	5	4	1	1	1	...	...	...	...
	15—20	3	2	1	3	2	1	...	...	...	...	...	...
	20—25	1	...	1	...	...	...	1	...	1	...	...	...
	25—30	1	1	...	...	...	...	1	1	...	...	...	...
	30—35	9	5	4	...	...	...	8	4	4	1	1	...
	35—40	2	1	1	...	...	...	2	1	1	...	...	...
	40—45	1	...	1	...	...	...	1	...	1	...	...	...
	45—50	3	2	1	...	...	...	1	...	1	2	2	...
	50—55	1	1	...	...	...	...	1	1	...	...	...	...
Hindu (*Brahmo*).	Total	1	...	1	...	...	...	1	...	1	...	...	...
	25—30	1	...	1	...	...	...	1	...	1	...	...	...
Sikh.	Total	14,772	7,871	6,901	7,371	4,410	2,961	6,413	3,143	3,270	983	318	670
	0—1	739	410	329	739	410	329	...	...	...	...	...	...
	1—2	168	92	76	168	92	76	...	...	...	...	...	...
	2—3	477	233	244	477	233	244	...	...	...	...	...	...
	3—4	588	279	309	588	279	309	...	...	...	...	...	...
	4—5	541	290	251	541	290	251	...	...	...	...	...	...
	Total 0—5	2,513	1,304	1,209	2,513	1,304	1,209	...	...	...	...	...	...
	5—10	2,449	1,253	1,196	2,420	1,251	1,169	28	2	26	1	...	1
	10—15	1,648	912	736	1,387	880	507	255	31	24	6	1	5
	15—20	1,369	732	637	615	566	49	740	162	578	14	4	10
	20—25	1,200	585	615	230	223	7	940	357	583	30	5	25
	25—30	1,208	594	614	86	84	2	1,066	490	576	56	20	36

TABLE VII.

Age, Sex and Civil Condition by Religion.

Jammu and Kashmir State Census 1911.

Part I—Provincial Tables.

Religion.	Age.	Population.			Unmarried.			Married.			Widowed.		
		Persons.	Males.	Females.	Persons.	Males.	Females.	Persons.	Males.	Females.	Persons.	Males.	Females.
1	2	3	4	5	6	7	8	9	10	11	12	13	14
Sikh. (Continued).	30—35	1,144	595	549	33	30	3	1,023	534	489	88	31	57
	35—40	720	429	291	21	16	5	648	394	254	51	19	32
	40—45	782	420	362	22	19	3	634	369	265	126	32	94
	45—50	357	227	130	11	11	...	280	190	90	66	26	40
	50—55	543	311	232	14	11	3	365	256	109	164	44	120
	55—60	139	86	53	2	2	...	84	60	24	53	24	29
	60—65	404	234	170	9	7	2	213	180	33	182	47	135
	65—70	59	40	19	2	2	...	39	33	6	18	5	13
	70 & over	237	149	88	6	4	2	98	85	13	133	60	73
Budhist.	Total	3	3	...	2	2	...	1	1	...	...	...	...
	15—20	1	1	...	1	1	...	...	...	...	...	...	...
	20—25	1	1	...	1	1	...	...	...	...	...	...	...
	35—40	1	1	...	...	...	...	1	1	...	...	...	...
Zoroastrian.	Total	26	20	6	14	11	3	11	8	3	1	1	...
	0—1	1	1	...	1	1	...	...	...	...	...	...	...
	3—4	2	1	1	2	1	1	...	...	...	...	...	...
	Total 0—5	3	2	1	3	2	1	...	...	...	...	...	...
	5—10	6	6	...	6	6	...	...	...	...	...	...	...
	15—20	3	2	1	3	2	1	...	...	...	...	...	...
	20—25	2	1	1	2	1	1	...	...	...	...	...	...
	30—35	3	1	2	...	...	...	3	1	2	...	...	...
	35—40	1	...	1	...	...	...	1	...	1	...	...	...
	40—45	3	3	...	...	...	...	3	3	...	...	...	...
	45—50	2	2	...	...	...	...	2	2	...	...	...	...
	50—55	1	1	...	...	...	...	1	1	...	...	...	...
	60—65	1	1	...	...	...	...	1	1	...	...	...	...
	65—70	1	1	...	...	...	...	...	...	...	1	1	...
Musalman.	Total	1,217,768	648,685	569,083	579,258	341,635	237,623	562,818	278,198	284,620	75,692	28,852	46,840
	0—1	60,576	30,704	29,872	60,576	30,704	29,872	...	...	...	...	...	...
	1—2	11,906	6,106	5,800	11,906	6,106	5,800	...	...	...	...	...	...
	2—3	39,147	19,740	19,407	39,146	19,740	19,406	1	...	1	...	...	...
	3—4	46,128	23,234	22,894	46,123	23,231	22,892	5	3	2	...	...	...
	4—5	41,312	21,321	19,991	41,305	21,316	19,989	7	5	2	...	...	...
	Total 0—5	199,069	101,105	97,964	199,056	101,097	97,959	13	8	5	...	...	...
	5—10	190,412	99,199	91,213	188,600	98,868	89,732	1,774	322	1,452	38	9	29
	10—15	140,001	77,106	62,895	113,819	71,308	42,511	25,822	5,727	20,096	360	72	288
	15—20	111,423	59,512	51,911	44,902	39,537	5,365	64,811	19,486	45,325	1,710	489	1,221
	20—25	108,009	53,810	54,199	19,699	18,713	986	85,409	33,864	51,545	2,901	1,233	1,668
	25—30	98,131	49,831	48,300	6,676	6,360	316	87,864	41,609	46,255	3,591	1,862	1,729
	30—35	91,415	49,297	42,118	2,851	2,556	295	83,336	44,173	39,163	5,228	2,568	2,660
	35—40	57,631	32,884	24,747	900	841	59	52,639	30,137	22,502	4,092	1,906	2,186
	40—45	73,232	38,694	34,538	1,129	976	153	62,243	34,456	27,787	9,860	3,262	6,598
	45—50	29,935	17,664	12,271	380	349	31	25,009	15,599	9,410	4,546	1,716	2,830
	50—55	49,408	27,516	21,892	424	350	74	35,590	23,120	12,470	13,394	4,046	9,348
	55—60	11,131	7,004	4,127	84	77	7	8,059	5,684	2,375	2,988	1,243	1,745
	60—65	33,212	19,540	13,672	315	256	59	18,897	14,533	4,364	14,000	4,751	9,249
	65—70	5,268	3,424	1,844	56	49	7	2,978	2,432	546	2,234	943	1,291
	70 & over	19,491	12,099	7,392	367	294	69	8,374	7,049	1,325	10,750	4,752	5,998
Christian.	Total	218	118	100	108	62	46	88	50	38	22	6	16
	0—1	9	7	2	9	7	2	...	...	...	...	...	...
	1—2	1	1	...	1	1	...	...	...	...	...	...	...
	2—3	2	...	2	2	...	2	...	...	...	...	...	...
	3—4	5	4	1	5	4	1	...	...	...	...	...	...
	4—5	3	3	...	3	3	...	...	...	...	...	...	...
	Total 0—5	20	15	5	20	15	5	...	...	...	...	...	...
	5—10	12	4	8	12	4	8	...	...	...	...	...	...
	10—15	7	5	2	7	5	2	...	...	...	...	...	...
	15—20	5	...	5	4	...	4	1	...	1	...	...	...
	20—25	17	5	12	11	5	6	6	...	6	...	...	...
	25—30	31	19	12	17	12	5	13	6	7	1	1	...
	30—35	30	16	14	6	5	1	23	10	13	1	1	...
	35—40	30	17	13	11	7	4	16	10	6	3	...	3
	40—45	23	11	12	7	3	4	12	8	4	4	...	4
	45—50	6	5	1	2	1	1	4	4	...	...	...	...
	50—55	17	10	7	8	4	4	6	5	1	3	1	2
	55—60	6	5	1	1	1	...	3	3	...	2	1	1
	60—65	8	4	4	1	...	1	3	3	...	4	1	3
	65—70	3	1	2	...	...	...	1	1	...	2	...	2
	70 & over	3	1	2	1	...	1	...	...	...	2	1	1

VII
Age, Sex and Civil Condition.

TABLE VII.

Age, Sex and Civil Condition by Religion.

Jammu and Kashmir State Census 1911.

Part I—Provincial Tables.

Religion.	Age.	Population.			Unmarried.			Married.			Widowed.		
		Persons.	Males.	Females.	Persons.	Males.	Females.	Persons.	Males.	Females.	Persons.	Males.	Females.
1	2	3	4	5	6	7	8	9	10	11	12	13	14
					(iv) KASHMIR VALLEY.								
All Religions.	Total	1,099,996	587,472	512,524	518,802	707,674	211,128	508,284	251,911	256,373	72,910	27,887	45,023
	0—1	54,622	27,748	26,874	54,622	27,748	26,874	...	...	...	...	...	...
	1—2	10,544	5,358	5,186	10,544	5,358	5,186	...	...	...	...	...	...
	2—3	34,440	17,289	17,151	34.439	17,289	17,150	1	...	1	...	...	...
	3—4	40,928	20,543	20,385	40.926	20.542	20,384	2	1	1	...	...	...
	4—5	36,178	18,677	17,501	36,174	18,674	17,500	4	3	1	...	...	...
	Total 0—5	176,712	89,615	87,097	176,705	89,611	87,094	7	4	3	...	...	...
	5—10	168,950	87,677	81,273	167,427	87,373	80,054	1,482	295	1,187	41	9	32
	10—15	125,874	69,211	56,663	102,233	63,925	38,308	23,328	5,222	18,096	323	64	259
	15—20	99,945	54,101	45,844	39,840	35,775	4,065	58,541	17,877	40,664	1,564	449	1,115
	20—25	99,119	49,977	49,142	18,458	17,702	756	76,913	31,132	45,781	2,748	1,143	1,605
	25—30	89,123	45,403	43,720	6,409	6,150	259	79,271	37,523	41,748	3,443	1,730	1,713
	30—35	82,959	44,784	38,175	2,914	2,675	239	75,014	39,696	35,319	5,031	2,414	2,617
	35—40	53,914	30,874	23,040	1,221	1,169	52	48,530	27,820	20,710	4,163	1,885	2,278
	40—45	67,133	35,638	31,495	1,266	1,145	121	56,295	31,314	24,981	9,572	3,179	6,393
	45—50	28,850	17,084	11,766	591	563	28	23,479	14,695	8,784	4,780	1,826	2.954
	50—55	45,210	25,323	19,887	630	573	57	31,471	20,733	10,738	13,109	4,017	9,092
	55—60	10,985	6,973	4,012	216	210	6	7,536	5,406	2,130	3,233	1,357	1,876
	60—65	29,078	16,974	12,104	431	390	41	15,741	12,122	3,619	12,906	4,462	8,444
	65—70	5,121	3,311	1,810	92	89	3	2,721	2,232	489	2,308	990	1,318
	70 & over	17,023	10,527	6,496	369	324	45	6,965	6,841	1,124	9,689	4,362	5,327
Hindu (*Brahmanic*).	Total	57,671	32,233	25,438	27,388	18,313	9,075	23,282	11,726	11,555	7,001	2,193	4,808
	0—1	2,136	1,129	1,007	2,136	1,129	1,007	...	...	...	...	...	...
	1—2	402	210	192	402	210	192	...	...	...	...	...	...
	2—3	1,376	666	710	1,376	666	710	...	...	...	...	...	...
	3—4	1,533	769	764	1,533	769	764	...	...	...	...	...	...
	4—5	1,501	763	738	1,500	763	737	1	...	1	...	...	...
	Total 0—5	6,948	3,537	3,411	6,947	3,537	3,410	1	...	1	...	...	...
	5—10	7,536	3,811	3,725	7,476	3,802	3,674	55	9	46	5	...	5
	10—15	5,958	3,434	2,524	5,105	3,262	1,843	828	165	663	25	7	18
	15—20	4,919	2,961	1,958	2.473	2,360	113	2,362	587	1,775	84	14	70
	20—25	5,396	3,032	2,364	1,790	1,773	17	3,390	1,210	2,180	216	49	167
	25—30	5,081	2,753	2,328	1,115	1,111	4	3,615	1,550	2,065	351	92	259
	30—35	4,747	2,707	2,040	651	645	6	3,564	1,914	1,650	532	148	384
	35—40	3,793	2,313	1,480	481	480	1	2,696	1,642	1,054	616	191	425
	40—45	3,712	2,057	1,655	352	348	4	2,408	1,456	952	952	253	699
	45—50	2,484	1,457	1,027	268	268	...	1,510	968	542	706	221	485
	50—55	2,756	1,556	1,200	282	280	2	1,289	923	366	1,185	353	832
	55—60	1,247	793	454	145	145	...	576	448	128	526	200	326
	60—65	1,902	1,104	798	181	181	...	663	572	91	1,058	351	707
	65—70	494	314	180	46	46	...	155	133	22	293	135	158
	70 & over	698	404	294	76	75	1	170	150	20	452	179	273
Hindu (*Arya*).	Total	45	27	18	26	16	10	16	8	8	3	3	...
	0—1	2	1	1	2	1	1	...	...	...	...	...	...
	2—3	2	...	2	2	...	2	...	...	...	...	...	...
	4—5	4	1	3	4	1	3	...	...	...	...	...	...
	Total 0—5	8	2	6	8	2	6	...	...	...	...	...	...
	5—10	10	8	2	10	8	2	...	...	...	...	...	...
	10—15	6	5	1	5	4	1	1	1	...	...	...	...
	15—20	3	2	1	3	2	1	...	...	...	...	...	...
	20—25	1	...	1	...	...	...	1	...	1	...	...	...
	25—30	1	1	...	...	...	...	1	1	...	...	...	...
	30—35	9	5	4	...	...	...	8	4	4	1	1	...
	35—40	2	1	1	...	...	...	2	1	1	...	...	...
	40—45	1	...	1	...	...	...	1	...	1	...	...	...
	45—50	3	2	1	...	...	...	1	...	1	2	2	...
	50—55	1	1	...	...	...	...	1	1	...	...	...	...
Hindu (*Bramho*).	Total	1	...	1	...	...	...	1	...	1	...	...	...
	25—30	1	...	1	...	...	...	1	...	1	...	...	...
Budhist.	Total	2	2	...	1	1	...	1	1	...	...	...	...
	20—25	1	1	...	1	1	...	...	...	...	...	...	...
	35—40	1	1	...	...	...	...	1	1	...	...	...	...

TABLE VII.

Age, Sex and Civil Condition by Religion.

Jammu and Kashmir State Census 1911.

Part I—Provincial Tables.

Religion.	Age.	Population.			Unmarried.			Married.			Widowed.		
		Persons.	Males.	Females.	Persons.	Males.	Females.	Persons.	Males.	Females.	Persons.	Males.	Females.
1	2	3	4	5	6	7	8	9	10	11	12	13	14
Zoroastrian.	Total	26	20	6	14	11	3	11	8	3	1	1	...
	0—1	1	1	...	1	1	...	...	...	...	...	...	...
	3—4	2	1	1	2	1	1	...	...	...	...	...	...
	Total 0—5	3	2	1	3	2	1	...	...	...	...	...	...
	5—10	6	6	...	6	6	...	...	...	...	...	...	...
	15—20	3	2	1	3	2	1	...	...	...	...	...	...
	20—25	2	1	1	2	1	1	...	...	...	...	...	...
	30—35	3	1	2	...	...	...	3	1	2	...	...	...
	35—40	1	...	1	...	...	...	1	...	1	...	...	...
	40—45	3	3	...	...	...	...	3	3	...	...	...	...
	45—50	2	2	...	...	...	...	2	2	...	...	...	...
	50—55	1	1	...	...	...	...	1	1	...	...	...	...
	60—65	1	1	...	...	...	...	1	1	...	...	...	...
	65—70	1	1	...	...	...	...	...	...	...	1	1	...
Musalman.	Total	1,034,889	551,254	483,635	487,743	287,190	200,553	481,645	238,503	243,142	65,500	25,561	39,939
	0—1	52,105	26,406	25,699	52,105	26,406	25,699	...	...	...	...	...	...
	1—2	10,093	5,120	4,973	10,093	5,120	4,973	...	...	...	...	...	...
	2—3	32,830	16,510	16,320	32,829	16,510	16,319	1	...	1	...	...	...
	3—4	39,109	19,635	19,474	39,107	19,634	19,473	2	1	1	...	...	...
	4—5	34,418	17,776	16,642	34,415	17,773	16,642	3	3	...	...	...	...
	Total 0—5	168,555	85,447	83,108	168,549	85,443	83,106	6	4	2	...	...	...
	5—10	160,206	83,252	76,954	158,752	82,959	75,793	1,418	284	1,134	36	9	27
	10—15	119,120	65,333	53,787	96,436	60,236	36,200	26.887	5,040	17,347	297	57	240
	15—20	94,346	50,777	43,569	37,064	33,142	3,922	55,808	17,203	38,605	1,474	432	1,042
	20—25	93,103	46,620	46,483	16,536	15,806	730	74.050	29,724	44,346	2,517	1,090	1,427
	25—30	83,419	42,351	41,068	5.250	5,000	250	75,096	35,719	39,377	3,073	1,632	1,441
	30—35	77,625	41,783	35,842	2,241	2,010	231	70,915	37,516	33,399	4,469	2,257	2,212
	35—40	49,716	28,332	21,384	721	676	45	45,465	25,967	19,498	3,580	1,689	1,841
	40—45	63,005	33,348	29,657	898	787	111	53,529	29,642	23,887	8,578	2,919	5,659
	45—50	26,168	15,496	10,672	315	288	27	21,812	13,617	8,195	4,041	1,591	2,450
	50—55	42,168	23,601	18,567	335	285	50	29,987	19,672	10,315	11,846	3,644	8,202
	55—60	9,666	6,137	3,529	69	63	6	6,915	4,938	1,987	2,682	1,146	1,536
	60—65	26,994	15,756	11,238	244	206	38	14,974	11,465	3,509	11,776	4,085	7,691
	65—70	4,587	2,968	1,619	45	42	3	2,538	2,074	464	2,004	852	1,152
	70 & over	16,211	10,053	6,158	289	247	42	6,745	5,648	1,097	9,177	4,158	5,019
Christian.	Total	201	105	96	100	56	44	82	45	37	19	4	15
	0—1	9	7	2	9	7	2	...	...	...	...	...	...
	1—2	1	1	...	1	1	...	...	...	...	...	...	...
	2—3	2	...	2	2	...	2	...	...	...	...	...	...
	3—4	4	3	1	4	3	1	...	...	...	...	...	...
	4—5	3	3	...	3	3	...	...	...	...	...	...	...
	Total 0—5	19	14	5	19	14	5	...	...	...	...	...	...
	5—10	11	3	8	11	3	8	...	...	...	...	...	...
	10—15	7	5	2	7	5	2	...	...	...	...	...	...
	15—20	5	...	5	4	...	4	1	...	1	...	...	...
	20—25	15	5	10	9	5	4	6	...	6	...	...	...
	25—30	28	16	12	15	10	5	13	6	7	...	...	...
	30—35	28	15	13	6	5	1	21	9	12	1	1	...
	35—40	27	14	13	9	5	4	15	9	6	3	...	3
	40—45	22	10	12	7	3	4	11	7	4	4	...	4
	45—50	6	5	1	2	1	1	4	4	...	...	...	...
	50—55	15	8	7	8	4	4	4	3	1	3	1	2
	55—60	5	4	1	1	1	...	3	3	...	1	...	1
	60—65	7	4	3	1	...	1	3	3	...	3	1	2
	65—70	3	1	2	...	...	...	1	1	...	2	...	2
	70 & over	3	1	2	1	...	1	...	...	...	2	1	1

(v) FRONTIER DISTRICTS.

Religion.	Age.	Population Persons.	Population Males.	Population Females.	Unmarried Persons.	Unmarried Males.	Unmarried Females.	Married Persons.	Married Males.	Married Females.	Widowed Persons.	Widowed Males.	Widowed Females.
All Religions.	Total	210,435	106,408	104,027	98,062	53,553	44,509	97,109	48,498	48,611	15,264	4,357	10,907
	0—1	8,642	4,262	4,380	8,631	4,255	4,376	10	7	3	1	...	1
	1—2	3,315	1,605	1,710	3,313	1,603	1,710	2	2	...	...	...	...
	2—3	6,599	3,183	3,416	6,594	3,179	3,415	5	4	1	...	...	...
	3—4	7,172	3,542	3,630	7,152	3,532	3,620	20	10	10	...	...	...
	4—5	5,968	2,861	3,107	5,940	2,839	3,101	28	22	6	...	...	...

TABLE VII.

Age, Sex and Civil Condition by Religion.

Jammu and Kashmir State Census 1911.

Part I—Provincial Tables.

Religion.	Age.	Population. Persons.	Population. Males.	Population. Females.	Unmarried. Persons.	Unmarried. Males.	Unmarried. Females.	Married. Persons.	Married. Males.	Married. Females.	Widowed. Persons.	Widowed. Males.	Widowed. Females.
1	2	3	4	5	6	7	8	9	10	11	12	13	14
All Religions. (*Continued*).	Total 0—5	31,696	15,453	16,243	31,630	15,408	16,222	65	45	20	1	...	1
	5—10	29,376	15,171	14,205	28,788	14,869	13,919	565	297	268	23	5	18
	10—15	20,377	10,911	9,466	17,320	9,685	7,635	2,974	1,188	1,786	83	38	45
	15—20	18,183	9,748	8,435	10,165	6,623	3,542	7,713	3,004	4,709	305	121	184
	20—25	23,613	11,175	12,438	5,364	3,792	1,572	17,398	7,027	10,371	851	356	495
	25—30	10,003	5,332	4,671	1,623	1,099	524	7,978	4,047	3,931	402	186	216
	30—35	12,828	6,692	6,136	904	625	279	11,294	5,802	5,492	630	265	365
	35—40	18,202	8,676	9,526	598	381	217	16,393	7,944	8,449	1,211	351	860
	40—45	9,077	4,843	4,234	442	290	152	7,786	4,341	3,445	849	212	637
	45—50	11,954	5,659	6,295	338	219	119	9,623	5,086	4,537	1,993	354	1,639
	50—55	5,616	3,035	2,581	212	136	76	4,233	2,573	1,660	1,171	326	845
	55—60	2,519	1,474	1,045	133	91	42	1,890	1,251	639	496	132	364
	60—65	8,730	4,038	4,692	229	143	86	5,344	3,212	2,132	3,157	683	2,474
	65—70	2,253	1,274	979	77	28	49	1,350	921	429	776	275	501
	70 & over	6,008	2,927	3,081	189	114	75	2,503	1,760	743	3,316	1,053	2,263
Hindu (*Brahman*).	Total	1,223	1,128	95	565	524	41	584	530	54	74	74	...
	0—1	14	6	8	14	6	8	...	...	...	...	...	...
	1—2	4	3	1	4	3	1	...	...	...	...	...	...
	2—3	7	4	3	7	4	3	...	...	...	...	...	...
	3—4	9	4	5	9	4	5	...	...	...	...	...	...
	4—5	10	5	5	10	5	5	...	...	...	...	...	...
	Total 0—5	44	22	22	44	22	22	...	...	...	...	...	...
	5—10	30	17	13	30	17	13	...	...	...	...	...	...
	10—15	26	18	8	21	15	6	4	2	2	1	1	...
	15—20	60	52	8	45	45	...	15	7	8	...	...	...
	20—25	312	294	18	194	194	...	105	87	18	13	13	...
	25—30	303	291	12	129	129	...	155	143	12	19	19	...
	30—35	187	179	8	57	57	...	119	111	8	11	11	...
	35—40	109	106	3	20	20	...	77	74	3	12	12	...
	40—45	68	67	1	13	13	...	49	48	1	6	6	...
	45—50	53	52	1	8	8	...	42	41	1	3	3	...
	50—55	18	18	...	4	4	...	10	10	...	4	4	...
	55—60	2	2	...	...	...	...	2	2	...	...	...	...
	60—65	8	8	...	...	...	...	4	4	...	4	4	...
	65—70	3	2	1	...	...	...	2	1	1	1	1	...
Hindu (*Arya*).	Total	18	11	7	6	4	2	12	7	5	...	...	...
	0—1	2	1	1	2	1	1	...	...	...	...	...	...
	1—2	1	...	1	1	...	1	...	...	...	...	...	...
	Total 0—5	3	1	2	3	1	2	...	...	...	...	...	...
	20—25	10	5	5	2	2	...	8	3	5	...	...	...
	25—30	4	4	...	...	...	...	4	4	...	...	...	...
	30—35	1	1	...	1	1	...	...	...	...	...	...	...
Sikh.	Total	98	74	24	39	28	11	58	45	13	1	1	...
	0—1	6	2	4	6	2	4	...	...	...	...	...	...
	2—3	1	1	...	1	1	...	...	...	...	...	...	...
	3—4	1	1	...	1	1	...	...	...	...	...	...	...
	4—5	1	1	...	1	1	...	...	...	...	...	...	...
	Total 0—5	9	5	4	9	5	4	...	...	...	...	...	...
	5—10	5	1	4	5	1	4	...	...	...	...	...	...
	10—15	5	1	4	4	1	3	1	...	1	...	...	...
	15—20	13	10	3	8	8	...	5	2	3	...	...	...
	20—25	11	10	1	5	5	...	6	5	1	...	...	...
	25—30	20	16	4	6	6	...	13	9	4	1	1	...
	30—35	14	12	2	...	...	...	14	12	2	...	...	...
	35—40	9	9	...	2	2	...	7	7	...	...	...	...
	40—45	6	4	2	...	...	...	6	4	2	...	...	...
	45—50	5	5	...	...	...	...	5	5	...	...	...	...
	55—60	1	1	...	...	...	...	1	1	...	...	...	...

TABLE VII.

VII
Age, Sex and Civil Condition.

Age, Sex and Civil Condition by Religion.

Jammu and Kashmir State Census 1911.

Part I—Provincial Tables.

Religion.	Age.	Population.			Unmarried.			Married.			Widowed.		
		Persons.	Males.	Females.	Persons.	Males.	Females.	Persons.	Males.	Females.	Persons.	Males.	Females.
1	2	3	4	5	6	7	8	9	10	11	12	13	14
Buddhist.	**Total**	**35,867**	**17,956**	**17,911**	**15,482**	**7,553**	**7,929**	**17,324**	**7,976**	**9,348**	**3,061**	**1,055**	**2,006**
	0—1	872	416	456	868	413	455	4	1	3	...	...	...
	1—2	382	171	211	381	170	211	1	...	1	...	...	...
	2—3	602	280	322	597	276	321	5	1	4	...	...	...
	3—4	822	396	426	814	390	424	8	2	6	...	...	...
	3—5	741	343	398	728	330	398	13	...	13	...	...	...
	Total 0—5	**3,419**	**1,606**	**1,813**	**3,388**	**1,579**	**1,809**	**31**	**4**	**27**	...	...	...
	5—10	3,974	1,996	1,978	3,798	1,846	1,952	171	23	148	5	2	3
	10—15	3,186	1,615	1,571	2,805	1,318	1,487	372	81	291	9	6	3
	15—20	3,090	1,548	1,542	2,010	895	1,115	1,056	417	639	24	14	10
	20—25	2,913	1,459	1,454	1,060	458	602	1,766	802	964	87	37	50
	25—30	2,881	1,501	1,380	636	335	301	2,134	1,013	1,121	111	45	66
	30—35	2,824	1,431	1,393	386	220	166	2,304	1,141	1,163	134	48	86
	35—40	2,321	1,167	1,154	259	165	94	1,923	956	967	139	35	104
	40—45	2,507	1,222	1,285	267	174	93	1,999	1,009	990	241	58	183
	45—50	1,960	999	961	205	148	57	1,541	749	792	214	59	155
	50—55	1,823	883	940	167	101	66	1,282	608	674	374	108	266
	55—60	1,144	595	549	118	80	38	806	349	457	220	58	162
	60—65	1,656	807	849	147	91	56	978	441	537	531	179	352
	65—70	834	435	399	104	65	39	470	203	267	260	103	157
	70 & over	1,335	692	643	132	78	54	491	180	311	712	303	409
Musalman.	**Total**	**173,145**	**87,190**	**85,955**	**81,923**	**45,413**	**36,510**	**79,096**	**38,550**	**40,546**	**12,126**	**3,227**	**9,899**
	0—1	7,744	3,837	3,907	7,737	3,833	3,904	6	4	2	1	...	1
	1—2	2,927	1,431	1,496	2,926	1,430	1,496	1	1	...	...	...	...
	2—3	5,989	2,898	3,091	5,989	2,898	3,091	...	...	...	...	...	...
	3—4	6,337	3,140	3,197	6,325	3,136	3,189	12	4	8	...	...	...
	4—5	5,216	2,512	2,704	5,201	2,503	2,698	15	9	6	...	...	...
	Total 0—5	**28,213**	**13,818**	**14,395**	**28,178**	**13,800**	**14,378**	**34**	**18**	**16**	1	...	1
	5—10	25,358	13,150	12,208	24,946	12,998	11,948	394	149	245	18	3	15
	10—15	17,154	9,272	9,882	14,484	8,346	6,138	2,597	895	1,702	73	31	42
	15—20	15,011	8,131	6,880	8,094	4,668	2,426	6,636	2,356	4,280	281	107	174
	20—25	20,360	7,601	10,959	4,099	3,129	970	15,510	5,966	9,544	751	306	445
	25—30	6,789	3,517	8,272	847	626	221	5,671	2,770	2,901	271	121	150
	30—35	9,787	5,063	4,724	455	344	111	8,847	4,513	4,334	485	206	279
	35—40	15,754	7,387	8,367	315	193	122	14,352	6,890	7,489	1,060	304	756
	40 45	6,488	3,546	2,942	162	103	59	5,725	3,295	2,430	601	148	453
	45—50	9,936	4,603	5,333	125	63	62	8,035	4,248	3,787	1,776	292	1,485
	50—55	3,772	2,163	1,639	41	31	10'	2,938	1,888	1,050	793	214	579
	55—60	1,371	875	496	15	11	4	1,080	790	290	276	74	202
	60—65	7,064	3,222	3,842	82	52	30	4,360	2,670	1,690	2,622	500	2,122
	65—70	1,416	737	579	23	13	10	878	653	225	515	171	344
	70 & over	4,672	2,235	2,437	57	36	21	2,012	1,449	563	2,603	750	1,853
Christian.	**Total**	**84**	**49**	**35**	**47**	**31**	**16**	**35**	**18**	**17**	**2**	...	**2**
	0—1	4	...	4	4	...	4	...	...	...	...	...	...
	1—2	1	...	1	1	...	1	...	...	...	...	...	...
	2—3	1	1	...	1	1	...	...	...	...	...	...	...
	3—4	2	...	2	2	...	2	...	...	...	...	...	...
	Total 0—5	**8**	**1**	**7**	**8**	**1**	**7**	...	...	...	...	...	...
	5—10	9	7	2	9	7	2	...	...	...	...	...	...
	10—15	6	5	1	6	5	1	...	...	...	...	...	...
	15—20	9	7	2	8	7	1	1	...	1	...	...	...
	20—25	7	6	1	4	4	...	3	2	1	...	...	...
	25—30	6	3	3	5	3	2	1	...	1	...	...	...
	30—35	15	6	9	5	3	2	10	3	7	...	...	...
	35—40	9	7	2	2	1	1	7	6	1	...	...	...
	40—45	8	4	4	...	...	...	7	4	3	1	...	1
	50—55	3	1	2	...	...	...	3	1	2	...	...	...
	55—60	1	1	...	...	...	...	1	1	...	...	...	...
	60—65	2	1	1	...	...	...	2	1	1	...	...	...
	70 & over	1	...	1	...	...	...	...	...	...	1	...	1

VII
Age, Sex and Civil Condition.

TABLE VII.

AGE, SEX AND CIVIL CONDITION BY RELIGION.

Jammu and Kashmir State Census 1911.

Part II—District Tables.

Religion.	Age.	Population.			Unmarried.			Married.			Widowed.		
		Persons.	Males.	Females.	Persons.	Males.	Females.	Persons.	Males.	Females.	Persons.	Males.	Females.
1	2	3	4	5	6	7	8	9	10	11	12	13	14
					(1) JAMMU DISTRICT.								
All Religions.	Total	326,691	180,691	146,000	138,811	90,696	48,115	147,685	74,285	73,400	40,195	15,710	24,485
	0—5	41,216	20,990	20,226	41,079	20,970	20,109	133	20	113	4	...	4
	5—10	44,270	23,290	20,980	41,444	22,731	17,713	2,737	532	2,205	89	27	62
	10—15	36,637	21,368	15,269	26,701	19,217	7,484	9,667	2,090	7,577	269	61	208
	15—20	27,373	15,332	12,041	11,745	10,644	1,101	14,853	4,447	10,406	775	241	534
	20—40	102,383	56,699	45,684	14,951	14,445	506	76,787	37,788	38,999	10,645	4,466	6,179
	40—60	53,917	30,678	23,239	2,234	2,104	130	34,870	22,308	12,569	16,813	6,273	10,540
	60 & over	20,895	12,334	8,561	657	585	72	8,638	7,107	1,531	11,600	4,642	6,958
Hindu (*Brahmanic*).	Total	195,470	108,196	87,274	82,071	55,244	26,827	86,650	43,483	43,167	26,749	9,469	17,280
	0—5	22,757	11,681	11,076	22,735	11,678	11,057	19	3	16	3	...	3
	5—10	24,768	12,948	11,820	23,572	12,843	10,729	1,148	92	1,056	48	13	35
	10—15	21,172	12,640	8,532	15,847	11,824	4,023	5,137	791	4,346	188	25	163
	15—20	16,569	9,308	7,261	7,508	6,823	685	8,482	2,356	6,126	579	129	450
	20—40	63,473	34,890	28,583	10,284	10,036	248	45,738	22,236	23,502	7,451	2,618	4,833
	40—60	33,831	19,143	14,688	1,652	1,595	57	21,012	13,679	7,333	11,167	3,869	7,298
	60 & over	12,900	7,586	5,314	473	445	28	5,114	4,326	788	7,313	2,815	4,498
Hindu (*Arya*).	Total	604	310	294	227	154	73	325	136	189	52	20	32
	0—5	67	39	28	65	39	26	2	...	2	...	...	...
	5—10	57	34	23	56	33	23	1	1	...	...	...	...
	10—15	64	35	29	50	31	19	14	4	10	...	...	...
	15—20	64	33	31	26	23	3	38	10	28	...	...	...
	20—40	212	103	109	26	25	1	180	76	104	6	2	4
	40—60	91	46	45	2	2	...	64	33	31	25	11	14
	60 & over	49	20	29	2	1	1	26	12	14	21	7	14
Sikh.	Total	3,156	1,722	1,434	1,457	909	548	1,417	711	706	282	102	180
	0—5	436	207	229	433	206	227	3	1	2	...	...	...
	5—10	461	246	215	447	241	206	13	4	9	1	1	...
	10—15	364	212	152	294	201	93	70	11	59	...	...	...
	15—20	265	153	112	124	114	10	138	36	102	3	3	...
	20—40	933	500	433	127	121	6	737	348	389	69	31	38
	40—60	535	311	224	27	22	5	381	249	132	127	40	87
	60 & over	162	93	69	5	4	1	75	62	13	82	27	55
Jain.	Total	334	181	153	172	98	74	114	59	55	48	24	24
	0—5	52	22	30	52	22	30	...	...	...	...	...	...
	5—10	41	19	22	39	18	21	2	1	1	...	...	...
	10—15	42	24	18	41	24	17	1	...	1	...	...	...
	15—20	28	13	15	19	13	6	8	...	8	1	...	1
	20—40	102	63	39	21	21	...	64	33	31	17	9	8
	40—60*	53	32	21	...	...	...	32	20	12	21	12	9
	60 & over	16	8	8	...	...	...	7	5	2	9	3	6
Zoroastrian.	Total	5	2	3	1	...	1	4	2	2	...	...	...
	0—5	1	...	1	1	...	1	...	...	...	...	...	...
	20—40	2	1	1	...	...	...	2	1	1	...	...	...
	40—60	2	1	1	...	...	...	2	1	1	...	...	...
Musalman.	Total	126,659	69,976	56,683	54,622	34,137	20,485	59,021	29,778	29,243	13,016	6,061	6,955
	0—5	17,812	8,999	8,813	17,702	8,983	8,719	109	16	93	1	...	1
	5—10	18,869	10,004	8,865	17,256	9,557	7,699	1,573	434	1,139	40	13	27
	10—15	14,940	8,420	6,520	10,414	7,100	3,314	4,445	1,284	3,161	81	36	45
	15—20	10,421	5,803	4,618	4,051	3,656	395	6,178	2,038	4,140	192	109	83
	20—40	37,528	21,049	16,479	4,473	4,225	248	29,960	15,020	14,940	395	1,804	1,291
	40—60	19,343	11,093	8,250	549	481	68	13,352	8,295	5,057	5,442	2,317	3,125
	60 & over	7,746	4,608	3,138	177	135	42	3,404	2,691	713	4,165	1,782	2.383
Christian.	Total	463	304	159	261	154	107	154	116	38	48	34	14
	0—5	91	42	49	91	42	49	...	...	...	...	...	...
	5—10	74	39	35	74	39	35	...	...	...	...	...	...
	10—15	55	37	18	55	37	18	...	...	...	...	...	...
	15—20	26	22	4	17	15	2	9	7	2	...	...	...
	20—40	133	93	40	20	17	3	106	74	32	7	2	5
	40—60	62	52	10	4	4	...	27	24	3	31	24	7
	60 & over	22	19	3	...	...	...	12	11	1	10	8	2

TABLE VII.

Age, Sex and Civil Condition by Religion.

Jammu and Kashmir State Census 1911.

Part II—District Tables.

VII
Age, Sex and Civil Condition.

Religion.	Age.	Population. Persons.	Population. Males.	Population. Females.	Unmarried. Persons.	Unmarried. Males.	Unmarried. Females.	Married. Persons.	Married. Males.	Married. Females.	Widowed. Persons.	Widowed. Males.	Widowed. Females.
1	2	3	4	5	6	7	8	9	10	11	12	13	14
					(2) JASROTA.								
All Religions.	Total	151,802	81,375	70,427	62,239	41,204	21,033	68,989	33,907	35,082	20,574	6,262	14,312
	0—5	19,121	9,745	9,376	19,052	9,740	9,310	66	5	61	5	...	5
	5—10	20,501	10,542	9,959	18,642	10,246	8,396	1,809	281	1,528	50	15	35
	10—15	16,734	9,334	7,400	11,030	8,218	2,812	5,527	1,075	4,452	177	41	136
	15—20	13,563	7,049	6,514	5,116	4,840	276	8,061	2,124	5,937	386	85	301
	20—40	47,251	25,590	21,661	6,676	6,501	175	35,180	17,460	17,720	5,395	1,629	3,766
	40—60	24,255	13,379	10,876	1,360	1,314	46	14,340	9,601	4,739	8,555	2,464	6,091
	60 & over	10,377	5,736	4,641	365	347	18	4,006	3,361	645	6,006	2,028	3,978
Hindu (*Brahmanic*).	Total	116,267	61,994	54,273	47,507	32,098	15,409	51,179	24,930	26,249	17,581	4,966	12,615
	0—5	13,806	7,063	6,743	13,762	7,060	6,702	40	3	37	4	...	4
	5—10	15,070	7,723	7,347	13,976	7,606	6,370	1,048	104	944	46	13	33
	10—15	12,351	7,030	5,321	8,410	6,409	2,001	3,790	597	3,193	151	24	127
	15—20	10,309	5,281	5,028	4,084	3,942	142	5,881	1,280	4,601	344	59	285
	20—40	37,021	19,821	17,200	5,725	5,586	139	26,545	12,970	13,575	4,751	1,265	3,486
	40—60	19,361	10,552	8,809	1,228	1,188	40	10,892	7.430	3,462	7,241	1,934	5,307
	60 & over	8,349	4,524	3,825	322	307	15	2,983	2,546	437	5,044	1,671	3,373
Hindu (*Arya*).	Total	72	45	27	20	12	8	42	28	14	10	5	5
	0—5	3	2	1	3	2	1	...	...	...	...	...	...
	5—10	8	3	5	8	3	5	...	...	...	...	...	...
	10—15	7	5	2	7	5	2	...	...	...	...	...	...
	15—20	5	1	4	...	...	...	5	1	4	...	...	...
	20—40	30	20	10	2	2	...	24	16	8	4	2	2
	40—60	15	12	3	...	...	...	9	9	...	6	3	3
	60 & over	4	2	2	...	...	...	4	2	2	...	...	...
Sikh.	Total	108	58	50	56	34	22	46	24	22	6	...	6
	0—5	16	6	10	16	6	10	...	...	...	...	...	...
	5—10	17	9	8	17	9	8	...	...	...	...	...	...
	10—15	14	11	3	14	11	3	...	...	...	...	...	...
	15—20	6	3	3	2	2	...	4	1	3	...	...	...
	20—40	32	18	14	5	4	1	27	14	13	...	...	...
	40—60	20	9	11	2	2	...	13	7	6	5	...	5
	60 & over	3	2	1	...	...	...	2	2	...	1	...	1
Budhist.	Total	11	4	7	4	...	4	7	4	3	...	...	...
	0—5	1	...	1	1	...	1	...	...	...	...	...	...
	5—10	2	...	2	2	...	2	...	...	...	...	...	...
	10—15	2	1	1	...	...	...	2	1	1	...	...	...
	15—20	1	...	1	1	...	1	...	...	...	...	...	...
	20—40	4	2	2	...	...	...	4	2	2	...	...	...
	40—60	1	1	...	...	...	...	1	1	...	...	...	...
Musalman.	Total	35,174	19,146	16,028	14,587	9,020	5,567	17,626	8,847	8,779	2,961	1,279	1,682
	0—5	5,280	2,668	2.612	5,253	2,666	2,587	26	2	24	1	...	1
	5—10	5,384	2,795	2,589	4,619	2,616	2,003	761	177	584	4	2	2
	10—15	4,340	2,272	2,068	2,583	1,782	801	1,731	473	1,258	26	17	9
	15—20	3,230	1,753	1,477	1,024	892	132	2,164	835	1,329	42	26	16
	20—40	10,084	5,667	4,417	935	900	35	8.519	4,412	4,107	630	355	275
	40—60	4,842	2,790	2,052	130	124	6	3,412	2,141	1,271	1,300	525	775
	60 & over	2,014	1,201	813	43	40	3	1,013	807	206	958	354	604
Christian.	Total	170	128	42	65	42	23	89	74	15	16	12	4
	0—5	15	6	9	15	6	9	...	...	...	...	...	...
	5—10	20	12	8	20	12	8	...	...	...	...	...	...
	10—15	20	15	5	16	11	5	4	4	...	...	...	...
	15—20	12	11	1	5	4	1	7	7	...	...	...	...
	20—40	80	62	18	9	9	...	61	46	15	10	7	3
	40—60	16	15	1	...	...	...	13	13	...	3	2	1
	60 & over	7	7	...	...	...	...	4	4	...	3	3	...
					(3) UDHAMPUR.								
All Religions.	Total	215,725	113,877	101,848	90,576	56,843	33,733	100,449	49,118	51,331	24,700	7,916	16,784
	0—5	29,558	14,905	14,653	29,411	14,833	14,578	139	67	72	8	5	3
	5—10	28,194	14,408	13,786	26,471	14,103	12,368	1,626	292	1,334	97	13	84
	10—15	21,367	11,642	9,725	15,749	10,580	5,169	5.456	1,037	4,419	162	25	137
	15—20	18,089	9,218	8,871	7,207	6,370	837	10,450	2,754	7,696	432	94	338
	20—40	66,204	34,793	31,411	9,107	8,583	524	51,161	24,261	26,900	5,936	1,949	3,987
	40—60	34,530	18,803	15,727	1,818	1,665	153	23,100	14,247	8,853	9,612	2,891	6,721
	60 & over	17.783	10,108	7,675	813	709	104	8,517	6,460	2,057	8,453	2,939	5,514

VII
Age, Sex and Civil Condition.

TABLE VII.

Age, Sex and Civil Condition by Religion.

Jammu and Kashmir State Census 1911.

Part II—District Tables.

Religion.	Age.	Population.			Unmarried.			Married.			Widowed.		
		Persons.	Males.	Females.	Persons.	Males.	Females.	Persons.	Males.	Females.	Persons.	Males.	Females.
1	2	3	4	5	6	7	8	9	10	11	12	13	14
Hindu (*Brahmanic*).	Total	130,748	68,786	61,962	49,748	32,961	16,787	62,180	30,104	32,076	18,820	5,721	13,099
	0—5	15,575	7,869	7,706	15,520	7,842	7,678	50	23	27	5	4	1
	5—10	14,982	7,563	7,419	13,803	7,418	6,385	1,113	135	978	66	10	56
	10—15	11,718	6,343	5,375	7,888	5,777	2,111	3,702	551	3,151	128	15	113
	15—20	10,442	5,217	5,225	3,909	3,690	219	6,231	1,471	4,760	302	56	246
	20—40	41,794	21,792	20,002	6,502	6,229	273	30,496	14,130	16,366	4,796	1,433	3,363
	40—60	23,282	12,712	10,570	1,475	1,402	73	14,542	9,255	5,287	7,265	2,055	5,210
	60 & over	12,955	7,290	5,665	651	603	48	6,046	4,539	1,507	6,258	2,148	4,110
Hindu (*Arya*).	Total	17	12	5	8	6	2	6	3	3	3	3	...
	0—5	3	2	1	2	1	1	...	...	...	1	1	...
	5—10	2	1	1	2	1	1	...	...	...	...	...	...
	20—40	11	8	3	4	4	...	6	3	3	1	1	...
	40—60	1	1	...	...	...	...	...	...	...	1	1	...
Sikh.	Total	128	61	67	55	29	26	54	25	29	19	7	12
	0—5	12	4	8	12	4	8	...	...	...	...	...	...
	5—10	19	7	12	18	7	11	1	...	1	...	...	...
	10—15	16	7	9	14	7	7	2	...	2	...	...	...
	15—20	14	6	8	4	4	...	9	1	8	1	1	...
	20—40	43	20	23	3	3	...	32	14	18	8	3	5
	40—60	19	13	6	4	4	...	8	8	...	7	1	6
	60 & over	5	4	1	...	...	...	2	2	...	3	2	1
Jain.	Total	3	2	1	1	1	...	2	1	1	...	...	...
	0—5	1	1	...	1	1	...	...	...	...	...	...	...
	20—40	2	1	1	...	...	...	2	1	1	...	...	...
Buddhist.	Total	439	205	234	178	88	90	232	109	123	29	8	21
	0—5	44	20	24	43	19	24	1	1	...	...	...	...
	5—10	60	29	31	57	26	31	2	2	...	1	1	...
	10—15	44	17	27	37	14	23	7	3	4	...	...	...
	15—20	30	13	17	15	10	5	15	3	12	...	...	...
	20—40	140	65	75	17	13	4	121	51	70	2	1	1
	40—60	85	39	46	7	4	3	61	31	30	17	4	13
	60 & over	36	22	14	2	2	...	25	18	7	9	2	7
Musalman.	Total	84,390	44,811	39,579	40,586	23,758	16,828	37,975	18,876	19,099	5,829	2,177	3,652
	0—5	13,923	7,009	6,914	13,833	6,966	6,867	88	43	45	2	...	2
	5—10	13,131	6,808	6,323	12,591	6,651	5,940	510	155	355	30	2	28
	10—15	9,589	5,275	4,314	7,810	4,782	3,028	1,745	483	1,262	34	10	24
	15—20	7,603	3,982	3,621	3,279	2,666	613	4,195	1,279	2,916	129	37	92
	20—40	24,214	12,907	11,307	2,581	2,334	247	20,504	10,062	10,442	1,129	511	618
	40—60	11,143	6,038	5,105	332	555	78	8,489	4,953	3,536	2,322	830	1,492
	60 & over	4,787	2,792	1,995	160	104	56	2,444	1,901	543	2,183	787	1,396
					(4) RIASI.								
All Religions.	Total	206,309	109,026	97,783	91,095	56,007	35,088	93,791	46,784	47,007	21,323	6,235	15,688
	0—5	29,275	14,537	14,738	29,190	14,526	14,664	83	11	72	2	...	2
	5—10	28,750	14,244	14,506	26,849	13,965	12,884	1,844	270	1,574	57	9	48
	10—15	22,564	12,052	10,512	16,314	10,829	5,485	6,053	1,196	4,857	197	27	170
	15—20	17,678	8,887	8,791	7,501	6,328	1,173	9,739	2,491	7,248	438	68	370
	20—40	61,084	31,933	29,151	8,833	8,132	701	46,732	22,283	24,449	5,519	1,518	4,001
	40—60	32,075	18,136	13,939	1,738	1,626	112	21,842	14,304	7,538	8,495	2,206	6,289
	60 & over	15,383	9,237	6,146	670	601	69	7,498	6,229	1,269	7,215	2,407	4,808
Hindu (*Brahmanic*).	Total	80,886	42,629	38,257	30,681	20,453	10,228	37,244	18,926	18,318	12,961	3,250	9,711
	0—5	8,740	4,303	4,437	8,693	4,297	4,396	46	6	40	1	...	1
	5—10	8,652	3,784	4,868	7,650	3,704	3,946	966	72	894	36	8	28
	10—15	7,913	4,163	3,750	5,036	3,742	1,294	2,767	410	2,357	110	11	99
	15—20	6,885	3,389	3,496	2,855	2,485	370	3,788	881	2,907	242	23	219
	20—40	25,802	13,752	12,050	4,664	4,546	118	17,573	8,467	9,106	3,565	739	2,826
	40—60	15,433	8,740	6,693	1,276	1,224	52	3,938	6,286	2,652	5,219	1,230	3,989
	60 & over	7,461	4,498	2,963	507	455	52	3,166	2,804	362	3,788	1,239	2,549

TABLE VII.

Age, Sex and Civil Condition by Religion.

Jammu and Kashmir State Census 1911.

Part II— District Tables.

Religion.	Age.	Population.			Unmarried.			Married.			Widowed.		
		Persons.	Males.	Females.	Persons.	Males.	Females.	Persons.	Males.	Females.	Persons.	Males.	Females.
1	2	3	4	5	6	7	8	9	10	11	12	13	14
Hindu (*Arya*).	**Total**	**11**	**10**	**1**	**3**	**3**	...	**4**	**3**	**1**	**4**	**4**	...
	5—10	1	1	...	1	1	...	...	...	...	...	...	...
	15—20	1	1	...	1	1	...	...	...	...	...	...	...
	20—40	6	5	1	1	1	...	4	3	1	1	1	...
	40—60	2	2	...	...	...	...	...	...	...	2	2	...
	60 & over	1	1	...	...	...	...	...	...	...	1	1	...
Sikh.	**Total**	**487**	**265**	**222**	**196**	**129**	**67**	**236**	**114**	**122**	**55**	**22**	**33**
	0—5	60	33	27	60	33	27	...	...	...	...	...	...
	5—10	53	24	29	53	24	29	...	...	...	...	...	...
	10—15	48	27	21	36	25	11	12	2	10	...	...	...
	15—20	43	19	24	17	17	...	25	2	23	1	...	1
	20—40	173	96	77	29	29	...	124	61	63	20	6	14
	40—60	77	45	32	1	1	...	60	35	25	16	9	7
	60 & over	33	21	12	...	...	...	15	14	1	18	7	11
Musalman.	**Total**	**125,424**	**66,121**	**59,303**	**60,215**	**35,422**	**24,793**	**56,306**	**27,740**	**28,566**	**8,903**	**2,959**	**5,944**
	0—5	20,475	10,201	10,274	20,437	10,196	10,241	37	5	32	1	...	1
	5—10	20,044	10,435	9,609	19,145	10,236	8,909	878	198	680	21	1	20
	10—15	14,603	7,862	6,741	11,242	7,062	4,180	3,274	784	2,490	87	16	71
	15—20	10,749	5,678	5,271	4,628	3,825	803	5,926	1,608	4,318	195	45	150
	20—40	35,102	18,079	17,023	4,139	3,556	583	29,030	13,751	15,279	1,933	772	1,161
	40—60	16,563	9,349	7,215	461	401	60	12,844	7,983	4,861	3,258	965	2,293
	60 & over	7,888	4,717	3,171	163	146	17	4,317	3,411	906	3,408	1,160	2,248
Christian.	**Total**	**1**	**1**	...	...	...	...	**1**	**1**	...	...	...	...
	20—40	1	1	...	...	...	...	1	1	...	...	...	...
					(5) MIRPUR.								
All Religions.	**Total**	**324,933**	**169,276**	**155,657**	**152,156**	**93,268**	**58,888**	**141,070**	**66,040**	**75,030**	**31,707**	**9,968**	**21,739**
	0—5	45,011	23,275	21,736	44,874	23,242	21,632	130	33	97	7	...	7
	5—10	47,859	25,252	22,607	46,529	24,979	21,550	1,242	246	996	88	27	61
	10—15	37,287	20,791	16,496	31,015	19,535	11,480	6,142	1,212	4,930	130	44	86
	15—20	25,205	12,824	12,381	12,422	9,809	2,613	12,405	2,925	9,480	378	90	288
	20—40	97,767	48,361	49,406	15,155	13,789	1,366	75,439	32,027	43,412	7,173	2,545	4,628
	40—60	50,483	26,731	23,752	1,690	1,501	189	35,799	21,675	14,124	12,994	3,555	9,439
	60 & over	21,321	12,042	9,279	471	413	58	9,913	7,922	1,991	10,937	3,707	7,230
Hindu (*Brahmanic*).	**Total**	**57,187**	**30,956**	**26,231**	**25,571**	**16,773**	**8,798**	**25,291**	**12,252**	**13,039**	**6,325**	**1,931**	**4,394**
	0—5	7,266	3,787	3,479	7,255	3,786	3,469	11	1	10	...	...	...
	5—10	8,148	4,325	3,823	7,849	4,285	3,564	247	39	248	12	1	11
	10—15	6,337	3,722	2,615	5,000	3,518	1,482	1,287	191	1,096	50	13	37
	15—20	4,640	2,453	2,187	2,085	1,902	183	2,472	537	1,935	83	14	69
	20—40	17,412	9,224	8,188	2,768	2,693	75	13,084	6,058	7,026	1,560	473	1,087
	40—60	9,314	5,176	4,138	480	459	21	6,337	3,958	2,379	2,497	759	1,738
	60 & over	4,070	2,269	1,801	134	130	4	1,813	1,468	345	2,123	671	1,452
Hindu (*Arya*).	**Total**	**225**	**140**	**85**	**96**	**69**	**27**	**118**	**68**	**50**	**11**	**3**	**8**
	0—5	31	17	14	30	17	13	1	...	1	...	...	...
	5—10	21	15	6	21	15	6	...	...	...	...	...	...
	10—15	28	18	10	25	18	7	3	...	3	...	...	...
	15—20	21	8	13	3	2	1	18	6	12	...	...	...
	20—40	96	66	30	16	16	...	78	49	29	2	1	1
	40—60	23	13	10	1	1	...	16	11	5	6	1	5
	60 & over	5	3	2	...	...	...	2	2	...	3	1	2
Sikh.	**Total**	**3,156**	**1,779**	**1,377**	**1,428**	**951**	**477**	**1,387**	**733**	**654**	**341**	**95**	**246**
	0—5	381	203	178	380	202	178	1	1	...	...	...	...
	5—10	416	229	187	407	225	182	7	3	4	2	1	1
	10—15	372	222	150	310	207	103	60	15	45	2	...	2
	15—20	249	136	113	100	93	7	143	43	100	6	...	6
	20—40	970	553	417	177	172	5	732	365	367	61	16	45
	40—60	566	315	251	41	40	1	353	231	122	172	44	128
	60 & over	202	121	81	13	12	1	91	75	16	98	34	64

VII
Age, Sex and Civil Condition.

TABLE VII.

Age, Sex and Civil Condition by Religion.

Jammu and Kashmir State Census 1911.

Part II—District Tables.

Religion.	Age.	Population.			Unmarried.			Married.			Widowed.		
		Persons.	Males.	Females.	Persons.	Males.	Females.	Persons.	Males.	Females.	Persons.	Males.	Females.
1	2	3	4	5	6	7	8	9	10	11	12	13	14
Jain.	**Total**	**8**	**8**	...	**5**	**5**	...	**3**	**3**	...	...	...	...
	5—10	1	1	...	1	1	...	...	...	...	...	...	...
	15—20	1	1	...	1	1	...	...	...	...	...	...	...
	20—40	5	5	...	3	3	...	2	2	...	...	...	...
	40—60	1	1	...	...	...	...	1	1	...	...	...	...
Musalman.	**Total**	**264,347**	**136,336**	**127,961**	**125,050**	**75,466**	**49,584**	**114,267**	**52,981**	**61,286**	**25,030**	**7,939**	**17,091**
	0—5	37,331	19,267	18,064	37,207	19,236	17,971	117	31	86	7	...	7
	5—10	39,272	20,682	18,590	38,250	20,453	17,797	948	204	744	74	25	49
	10—15	30,550	16,829	13,721	25,680	15,792	9,888	4,792	1,006	3,786	78	31	47
	15—20	20,294	10,226	10,068	10,233	7,814	2,422	9,772	2,339	7,433	289	76	213
	20—40	79,278	38,508	40,770	12,188	10,902	1,286	61,540	25,551	35,989	5,550	2,055	3,495
	40—60	40,578	21,225	19,353	1,168	1,001	167	29,091	17,473	11,618	10,319	2,751	7,568
	60 & over	17,044	9,649	7,395	324	271	53	8,007	6,377	1,630	8,711	3,001	5,712
Christian.	**Total**	**10**	**7**	**3**	**6**	**4**	**2**	**4**	**3**	**1**	...	...	...
	0—5	2	1	1	2	1	1	...	...	...	...	...	...
	5—10	1	...	1	1	...	1	...	...	...	...	...	...
	20—40	6	5	1	3	3	...	3	2	1	...	...	...
	40—60	1	1	...	...	...	...	1	1	...	...	...	...
					(6) BHADARWAH.								
All Religions.	**Total**	**37,512**	**18,975**	**18,537**	**16,899**	**10,318**	**6,581**	**16,452**	**7,568**	**8,884**	**4,161**	**1,089**	**3,072**
	0—5	4,984	2,492	2,492	4,982	2,492	2,490	2	...	2	...	...	...
	5—10	5,210	2,657	2,553	5,084	2,619	2,465	124	38	86	2	...	2
	10—15	3,953	2,180	1,773	3,224	2,037	1,187	709	137	572	20	6	14
	15—20	3,179	1,521	1,658	1,389	1,152	237	1,724	359	1,365	66	10	56
	20—40	11,597	5,677	5,920	1,752	1,599	153	8,879	3,816	5,063	966	262	704
	40—60	6,092	3,157	2,935	351	322	29	4,065	2,439	1,626	1,676	396	1,280
	60 & over	2,497	1,291	1,206	117	97	20	949	779	170	1,431	415	1,016
Hindu (*Brahmanic*).	**Total**	**22,931**	**11,375**	**11,556**	**9,803**	**6,051**	**3,752**	**10,189**	**4,614**	**5,575**	**2,939**	**710**	**2,229**
	0—5	2,837	1,391	1,446	2,835	1,391	1,444	2	...	2	...	...	...
	5—10	2,978	1,536	1,442	2,892	1,509	1,383	84	27	57	2	...	2
	10—15	2,302	1,276	1,026	1,867	1,197	670	425	77	348	10	2	8
	15—20	1,826	807	1,019	716	585	131	1,067	219	848	43	3	40
	20—40	7,372	3,509	3,863	1,142	1,050	92	5,539	2,297	3,242	691	162	529
	40—60	3,860	1,989	1,871	262	242	20	2,458	1,487	971	1,140	260	880
	60 & over	1,756	867	889	89	77	12	614	507	107	1,053	283	770
Budhist.	**Total**	**1**	**1**	...	**1**	**1**	...	...	...	...	...	...	...
	20—40	1	1	...	1	1	...	...	...	...	...	...	...
Musalman.	**Total**	**14,580**	**7,599**	**6,981**	**7,095**	**4,266**	**2,829**	**6,263**	**2,954**	**3,309**	**1,222**	**379**	**843**
	0—5	2,147	1,101	1,046	2,147	1,101	1,046	...	...	...	...	...	...
	5—10	2,232	1,121	1,111	2,192	1,110	1,082	40	11	29	...	...	...
	10—15	1,651	904	747	1,357	840	517	286	60	224	10	4	6
	15—20	1,353	714	639	673	567	106	657	140	517	23	7	16
	20—40	4,224	2,167	2,057	609	548	61	3,340	1,519	1,821	275	100	175
	40—60	2,232	1,168	1,064	89	80	9	1,607	952	655	536	136	400
	60 & over	741	424	317	28	20	8	335	272	63	378	132	246
					(7) PUNCH.								
All Religions.	**Total**	**334,393**	**173,570**	**160,823**	**164,737**	**97,757**	**66,990**	**146,694**	**69,467**	**77,227**	**22,962**	**6,346**	**16,616**
	0—5	54,187	27,504	26,683	54,106	27,493	26,613	81	11	70	...	...	...
	5—10	52,645	27,312	25,333	50,969	26,982	23,987	1,606	319	1,287	70	11	59
	10—15	40,104	22,214	17,890	32,775	20,672	12,103	7,182	1,512	5,670	147	30	117
	15—20	29,472	15,109	14,363	14,240	11,325	2,915	14,824	3,684	11,140	408	100	308
	20—40	95,148	47,292	47,856	11,344	10,284	1,060	78,687	35,312	43,375	5,117	1,696	3,421
	40—60	43,606	22,990	20,616	918	724	194	33,791	20,236	13,555	8,897	2,030	6,867
	60 & over	19,231	11,149	8,082	385	277	108	10,523	8,393	2,130	8,323	2,479	5,844

TABLE VII.

Age, Sex and Civil Condition by Religion.

Jammu and Kashmir State Census 1911.

Part II—District Tables.

VII
Age, Sex and Civil Condition.

Religion.	Age.	Population. Persons.	Population. Males.	Population. Females.	Unmarried. Persons.	Unmarried. Males.	Unmarried. Females.	Married. Persons.	Married. Males.	Married. Females.	Widowed. Persons.	Widowed. Males.	Widowed. Females.
1	2	3	4	5	6	7	8	9	10	11	12	13	14
Hindu (*Brahmanic*).	Total	21,967	11,685	10,282	10,581	6,604	3,977	9,060	4,391	4,669	2,326	690	1,636
	0—5	3,090	1,491	1,599	3,089	1,491	1,598	1	...	1	...	...	...
	5—10	2,971	1,400	1,571	2,862	1,387	1,475	103	13	90	6	...	6
	10—15	2,732	1,616	1,116	2,282	1,548	734	443	67	376	7	1	6
	15—20	1,840	1,031	809	974	870	104	826	152	674	40	9	31
	20—40	6,905	3,607	3,298	1,185	1,135	50	5,083	2,276	2,757	687	196	491
	40—60	3,153	1,812	1,341	145	134	11	2,071	1,404	667	937	274	663
	60 & over	1,276	728	548	44	39	5	583	479	104	649	210	439
Hindu (*Arya*).	Total	54	37	17	22	16	6	27	18	9	5	3	2
	0—5	5	3	2	5	3	2	...	...	...	...	...	...
	5—10	7	4	3	7	4	3	...	...	...	...	...	...
	10—15	8	5	3	6	5	1	2	...	2	...	...	...
	15—20	6	5	1	4	4	...	2	1	1	...	...	...
	20—40	19	13	6	...	...	...	16	11	5	3	2	1
	40—60	8	6	2	...	...	...	7	6	1	1	...	1
	60 & over	1	1	...	...	...	...	...	...	...	1	1	...
Sikh.	Total	9,624	5,186	4,438	4,761	3,002	1,759	4,079	1,941	2,138	784	243	541
	0—5	1,476	775	701	1,473	775	698	3	...	3	...	...	...
	5—10	1,614	872	742	1,548	863	685	64	9	55	2	...	2
	10—15	1,181	665	516	942	635	307	233	27	206	6	3	3
	15—20	858	475	383	410	369	41	441	103	338	7	3	4
	20—40	2,714	1,390	1,324	344	326	18	2,179	1,003	1,176	191	61	130
	40—60	1,256	699	557	29	25	4	898	586	312	329	88	241
	60 & over	525	310	215	15	9	6	261	213	48	249	88	161
Budhist.	Total	1	1	...	...	...	...	1	1	...	...	...	...
	40—60	1	1	...	...	...	...	1	1	...	...	...	...
Musalman.	Total	302,719	156,651	146,068	149,357	88,131	61,226	133,516	63,111	70,405	19,846	5,409	14,437
	0—5	49,612	25,234	24,378	49,535	25,223	24,312	77	11	66	...	...	...
	5—10	48,049	25,035	23,014	46,548	24,727	21,821	1,439	297	1,142	62	11	51
	10—15	36,181	19,928	16,253	29,543	18,484	11,059	6,504	1,418	5,086	134	26	108
	15—20	26,767	13,597	13,170	12,851	10,081	2,770	13,555	3,428	10,127	361	88	273
	20—40	85,498	42,277	43,221	9,810	8,822	988	71,452	32,018	39,434	4,236	1,437	2,799
	40—60	39,183	20,470	18,713	744	565	179	30,810	18,238	12,572	7,629	1,667	5,962
	60 & over	17,429	10,110	7,319	326	229	97	9,679	7,701	1,978	7,424	2,180	5,244
Christian.	Total	28	10	18	16	4	12	11	5	6	1	1	...
	0—5	4	1	3	4	1	3	...	...	...	...	...	...
	5—10	4	1	3	4	1	3	...	...	...	...	...	...
	10—15	2	...	2	2	...	2	...	...	...	...	...	...
	15—20	1	1	...	1	1	...	...	...	...	...	...	...
	20—40	12	5	7	5	1	4	7	4	3	...	...	...
	40—60	5	2	3	...	...	...	4	1	3	1	1	...
					(8) KASHMIR NORTH.								
All Religions.	Total	460,786	244,637	216,149	217,618	126,751	90,867	216,171	107,521	108,650	26,997	10,365	16,632
	0—5	76,899	38,815	38,084	76,896	38,813	38,083	3	2	1	...	...	...
	5—10	72,152	37,670	34,482	71,332	37,471	33,861	792	196	596	28	3	25
	10—15	52,681	28,782	23,899	42,714	26,441	16,273	9,815	2,304	7,511	152	37	115
	15—20	43,157	22,978	20,179	16,192	14,313	1,879	26,311	8,461	17,850	654	204	450
	20—40	133,594	69,621	63,973	9,452	8,830	622	118,624	58,293	60,331	5,518	2,498	3,020
	40—60	60,124	33,314	26,810	745	648	97	48,946	29,205	19,741	10,433	3,461	6,972
	60 & over	22,179	13,457	8,722	287	235	52	11,680	9,060	2,620	10,212	4,162	6,050
Hindu (*Brahmanic*).	Total	9,917	5,935	3,982	5,007	3,424	1,583	3,804	2,133	1,671	1,106	378	728
	0—5	1,166	578	588	1,165	578	587	1	...	1	...	...	...
	5—10	1,254	638	616	1,248	637	611	6	1	5	...	...	...
	10—15	1,028	582	446	939	578	361	86	1	85	3	3	...
	15—20	777	486	291	446	427	19	321	56	265	10	3	7
	20—40	3,408	2,196	1,212	897	892	5	2,228	1,225	1,003	283	79	204
	40—60	1,670	1,073	597	233	233	...	966	678	288	471	162	309
	60 & over	614	382	232	79	79	...	196	172	24	339	131	208

VII
Age, Sex and Civil Condition.

TABLE VII.

Age, Sex and Civil Condition by Religion.

Jammu and Kashmir State Census 1911.

Part II—District Tables.

Religion.	Age.	Population. Persons.	Population. Males.	Population. Females.	Unmarried. Persons.	Unmarried. Males.	Unmarried. Females.	Married. Persons.	Married. Males.	Married. Females.	Widowed. Persons.	Widowed. Males.	Widowed. Females.
1	2	3	4	5	6	7	8	9	10	11	12	13	14
Hindu (Arya).	Total	5	3	2	3	2	1	2	1	1	...	...	...
	0—5	1	1	...	1	1	...	...	...	...	...	...	...
	5—10	2	1	1	2	1	1	...	...	...	...	...	...
	20—40	2	1	1	...	...	...	2	1	1	...	...	...
Sikh.	Total	4,575	2,383	2,192	2,241	1,287	954	2,092	1,022	1,070	242	74	168
	0—5	774	393	381	774	393	381	...	...	...	...	...	...
	5—10	747	379	368	743	377	366	4	2	2	...	...	...
	10—15	518	282	236	452	270	182	65	12	53	1	...	1
	15—20	436	217	219	170	154	16	263	62	201	3	1	2
	20—40	1,339	667	672	87	81	6	1,201	573	628	51	13	38
	40—60	552	313	239	9	8	1	447	280	167	96	25	71
	60 & over	209	132	77	6	4	2	112	93	19	91	35	56
Budhist.	Total	2	2	...	1	1	...	1	1	...	...	...	...
	20—40	2	2	...	1	1	...	1	1	...	...	...	...
Musalman.	Total	446,248	236,289	209,959	210,348	122,023	88,325	210,252	104,353	105,899	25,648	9,913	15,735
	0—5	74,955	37,841	37,114	74,953	37,839	37,114	2	2	...	...	...	...
	5—10	70,145	36,650	33,495	69,335	36,454	32,881	782	193	589	28	3	25
	10—15	51,135	27,918	23,217	41,323	25,593	15,730	9,664	2,291	7,373	148	34	114
	15—20	41,944	22,275	19,669	15,576	13,732	1,844	25,727	8,343	17,384	641	200	441
	20—40	128,822	66,742	62,080	8,458	7,848	610	115,180	56,488	58,692	5,184	2,406	2,778
	40—60	57,892	31,920	4,372	501	405	96	47,525	28,241	19,284	9,866	3,274	6,592
	60 & over	21,355	12,943	8,412	202	152	50	11,372	8,795	2,577	9,781	3,996	5,785
Christian.	Total	39	25	14	18	14	4	20	11	9	1	...	1
	0—5	3	2	1	3	2	1	...	...	...	...	...	...
	5—10	4	2	2	4	2	2	...	...	...	...	...	...
	20—40	21	13	8	9	8	1	12	5	7	...	...	...
	40—60	10	8	2	2	2	...	8	6	2	...	...	...
	60 & over	1	...	1	...	...	...	...	...	...	1	...	1
					(9) KASHMIR SOUTH.								
All Religions.	Total	639,210	342,835	296,375	301,184	180,923	120,261	292,113	144,390	147,723	45,913	17,522	28,391
	0—5	99,813	50,800	49,013	99,809	50,798	49,011	4	2	2	...	...	...
	5—10	96,798	50,007	46,791	96,095	49,902	46,193	690	99	591	13	6	7
	10—15	73,193	40,429	32,764	59,519	37,484	22,035	13,503	2,918	10,585	171	27	144
	15—20	56,788	31,123	25,665	23,648	21,462	2,186	32,230	9,416	22,814	910	245	665
	20—40	191,521	101,417	90,104	19,550	18,866	684	162,104	77,877	84,227	9,867	4,675	5,193
	40—60	92,054	51,704	40,350	1,958	1,843	115	69,835	42,943	26,892	[illegible]	6,918	[illegible]
	60 & over	29,043	17,355	11,688	605	568	37	13,747	11,135	2,612	[illegible]	5,652	9,039
Hindu (Brahmanic).	Total	47,754	26,298	21,456	22,381	14,889	7,492	19,478	9,594	9,884	5,895	1,815	4,080
	0—5	5,782	2,959	2,823	5,782	2,959	2,823	...	...	...	...	...	...
	5—10	6,282	3,173	3,109	6,228	3,165	3,063	49	8	41	5	...	5
	10—15	4,930	2,852	2,078	4,166	2,684	1,482	742	164	578	22	4	18
	15—20	4,142	2,475	1,667	2,027	1,933	94	2,041	531	1,510	74	11	63
	20—40	15,609	8,609	7,000	3,140	3,117	23	11,037	5,091	5,946	1,432	401	1,031
	40—60	8,529	4,790	3,739	814	808	6	4,817	3,117	1,700	2,898	865	2,033
	60 & over	2,480	1,440	1,040	224	223	1	792	683	109	1,464	534	930
Hindu (Arya).	Total	40	24	16	23	14	9	14	7	7	3	3	...
	0—5	5	1	4	5	1	4	...	...	...	...	...	...
	5—10	10	7	3	10	7	3	...	...	...	...	...	...
	10—15	6	5	1	5	4	1	1	1	...	...	...	...
	15—20	3	2	1	3	2	1	...	...	...	...	...	...
	20—40	11	6	5	...	...	...	10	5	5	1	1	...
	40—60	5	3	2	...	...	...	3	1	2	2	2	...

TABLE VII.

Age, Sex and Civil Condition by Religion.

Jammu and Kashmir State Census 1911.

Part II—District Tables.

Religion.	Age.	Population. Persons.	Population. Males.	Population. Females.	Unmarried. Persons.	Unmarried. Males.	Unmarried. Females.	Married. Persons.	Married. Males.	Married. Females.	Widowed. Persons.	Widowed. Males.	Widowed. Females.
1	2	3	4	5	6	7	8	9	10	11	12	13	14
Hindu (*Bramho*).	**Total**	**1**	...	**1**	...	...	...	**1**	...	**1**	...	...	...
	20—40	1	...	1	...	...	...	1	...	1	...	...	...
Sikh.	**Total**	**2,586**	**1,448**	**1,133**	**1,288**	**800**	**488**	**1,154**	**597**	**557**	**144**	**51**	**93**
	0—5	407	220	187	407	220	187	...	...	...	...	...	...
	5—10	432	218	214	427	218	209	5	...	5	...	...	...
	10—15	265	152	113	228	148	80	37	4	33	...	...	...
	15—20	233	142	91	123	115	8	107	25	82	3	2	1
	20—40	776	419	357	88	87	1	663	323	340	25	9	16
	40—60	361	224	137	12	10	2	277	190	87	72	24	48
	60 & over	112	73	39	3	2	1	65	55	10	44	16	28
Zoroastrian.	**Total**	**26**	**20**	**6**	**14**	**11**	**3**	**11**	**8**	**3**	**1**	**1**	...
	0—5	3	2	1	3	2	1	...	...	...	...	...	...
	5—10	6	6	...	6	6	...	...	...	...	...	...	...
	15—20	3	2	1	3	2	1	...	...	...	...	...	...
	20—40	6	2	4	2	1	1	4	1	3	...	...	...
	40—60	6	6	...	...	...	...	6	6	...	...	...	...
	60 & over	2	2	...	...	...	...	1	1	...	1	1	...
Musalman.	**Total**	**583,641**	**44,965**	**273,676**	**277,396**	**165,167**	**112,229**	**271,393**	**134,150**	**137,243**	**39,852**	**15,648**	**24,204**
	0—5	93,600	47,606	45,994	93,596	47,604	45,992	4	2	2	...	...	...
	5—10	90,061	46,602	43,459	89,417	46,505	42,912	636	91	545	8	6	2
	10—15	67,985	37,415	30.570	55,113	34,643	20,470	12,723	2.749	9,974	149	23	126
	15—20	52.402	28.502	23.900	21,588	19.410	2,078	30,081	8,860	21,221	833	232	601
	20—40	175,041	92,344	82,697	16,290	15,644	646	150,346	72,438	77,908	8,405	4,262	4,142
	40—60	83,115	46,662	36,453	1,116	1,018	98	64,718	39,618	25,100	17,281	6,026	11,255
	60 & over	26,437	15,834	10,603	376	343	33	12,885	10,392	2,493	13,176	5,099	8,077
Christian.	**Total**	**162**	**80**	**82**	**82**	**42**	**40**	**62**	**34**	**28**	**18**	**4**	**14**
	0—5	16	12	4	16	12	4	...	...	...	...	...	...
	5—10	7	1	6	7	1	6	...	...	...	...	...	...
	10—15	7	5	2	7	5	2	...	...	...	...	...	...
	15—20	5	...	5	4	...	4	1	...	1	...	...	...
	20—40	77	37	40	30	17	13	43	19	24	4	1	3
	40—60	38	19	19	16	7	9	14	11	3	8	1	7
	60 & over	12	6	6	2	...	2	4	4	...	6	2	4
					(10) MUZAFFARABAD.								
All Religions.	**Total**	**195,205**	**104.308**	**90,897**	**97,559**	**58.248**	**39,311**	**86.429**	**42,412**	**44.017**	**11,217**	**3,648**	**7.569**
	0—5	32,484	16.678	15,806	32,477	16,674	15,803	7	4	3	...	...	...
	5—10	32.104	16.946	15,158	31,705	16,902	14,803	396	44	352	3	...	3
	10—15	22,257	12,553	9,704	18,494	11,813	6,681	3,693	723	2,970	70	17	53
	15—20	18,183	9,326	8,857	8.334	6,853	1,481	9.604	2.415	7.189	245	58	187
	20—40	55,063	28.881	26,182	5,880	5,464	416	46,706	22,412	24,294	2.477	1,005	1,472
	40—60	24,332	13,284	11,048	488	414	74	19.780	11,765	8,015	4,064	1,105	2,959
	60 & over	10,782	6,640	4,142	181	128	53	6,243	5,049	1,194	4,358	1,463	2,895
Hindu (*Brahmanic*).	**Total**	**4,697**	**2.823**	**1,874**	**2,194**	**1,473**	**721**	**2,083**	**1,188**	**895**	**420**	**162**	**258**
	0—5	637	328	309	637	328	309	...	...	...	...	...	...
	5—10	627	342	285	606	336	270	21	6	15	...	...	...
	10—15	511	302	209	404	279	125	105	22	83	2	1	1
	15—20	405	217	188	173	160	13	231	57	174	1	...	1
	20—40	1,573	1,021	532	301	297	4	1,168	674	494	104	50	54
	40—60	721	477	244	60	60	...	480	357	123	181	60	121
	60 & over	223	136	87	13	13	...	78	72	6	132	51	81
Sikh.	**Total**	**7.611**	**4.040**	**3,571**	**3,842**	**2,323**	**1,519**	**3,167**	**1,524**	**1,643**	**602**	**193**	**409**
	0—5	1,332	691	641	1.332	691	641	...	...	...	...	...	...
	5—10	1,270	656	614	1,250	656	594	19	...	19	1	...	1
	10—15	865	478	387	707	462	245	153	15	138	5	1	4
	15—20	700	373	327	322	297	25	370	75	295	8	1	7
	20—40	2,157	1,117	1,040	195	185	10	1,813	879	934	149	53	96
	40—60	908	507	401	28	25	3	639	405	234	241	77	164
	60 & over	379	218	161	8	7	1	173	150	23	198	61	137

VII
Age, Sex and Civil Condition.

TABLE VII.

Age, Sex and Civil Condition by Religion.

Jammu and Kashmir State Census 1911.

Part II—District Tables.

Religion.	Age.	Population.			Unmarried.			Married.			Widowed.		
		Persons.	Males.	Females.	Persons.	Males.	Females.	Persons.	Males.	Females.	Persons.	Males.	Females.
1	2	3	4	5	6	7	8	9	10	11	12	13	14
Budhist.	Total	1	1	...	1	1	...	...	...	...	...	...	...
	15—20	1	1	...	1	1	...	...	...	...	...	...	...
Musalman.	Total	182,879	97,431	85,448	91,514	54,445	37,069	81,173	39,695	41,478	10,192	3,291	6.901
	0—5	30.514	15,658	14,856	30.507	15,654	14,853	7	4	3	...	...	...
	5—10	30.206	15,947	14,259	29,848	15,909	13,939	356	38	318	2	...	2
	10—15	20,881	11,773	9.108	17.383	11,072	6.311	3,435	686	2.749	63	15	48
	15—20	17,077	8.735	8.342	7,838	6.395	1,443	9,003	2,283	6,720	236	57	179
	20—40	51,323	26.736	24,587	5,378	4,978	400	43,722	20,857	22,865	2,223	901	1,322
	40—60	22,699	12.296	10.403	400	329	71	18,658	11,000	7,658	3,641	967	2,674
	60 & over	10,179	6,286	3,893	160	108	52	5,992	4,827	1,165	4,027	1,351	2,676
Christian.	Total	17	13	4	8	6	2	6	5	1	3	2	1
	0—5	1	1	...	1	1	...	...	...	...	...	...	...
	5—10	1	1	...	1	1	...	...	...	...	...	...	...
	20—40	10	7	3	6	4	2	3	2	1	1	1	...
	40—60	4	4	...	...	...	...	3	3	...	1	1	...
	60 & over	1	...	1	...	...	...	...	...	...	1	...	1
					(11) LADDAKH.								
All Religions.	Total	186,466	93.109	93,357	86.013	46,384	39,629	86,451	42,853	43,598	14,002	8,872	10,130
	0—5	27.527	13.402	14.125	27.461	13,357	14.104	65	45	20	1	...	1
	5—10	25,759	13,310	12,449	25,225	13,014	12,211	513	291	222	21	5	16
	10—15	18.008	9,584	8.424	15.307	8,434	6.873	2.633	1.114	1,519	68	36	32
	15—20	16,197	8,669	7.528	9,146	5.825	3,321	6.770	2,730	4,040	281	114	167
	20—40	56,652	27,198	29,454	7,282	4.753	2,529	46,619	21,481	25,138	2,751	964	1,787
	40—60	26.428	13,394	13,034	1,058	676	382	21,282	11.804	9,478	4,088	914	3,174
	60 & over	15,895	7.552	8,343	534	325	209	8,569	5,388	3,181	6,792	1,839	4,953
Hindu (*Brahmanic*).	Total	407	358	49	159	137	22	228	191	27	30	30	...
	0—5	22	9	13	22	9	13	...	...	...	...	...	...
	5—10	15	7	8	15	7	8	...	...	...	...	...	...
	10—15	10	9	1	7	6	1	2	2	...	1	1	...
	15—20	13	11	2	8	8	...	5	3	2	...	...	...
	20—40	287	263	24	94	94	...	173	149	24	20	20	...
	40—60	54	54	...	13	13	...	35	35	...	6	6	...
	60 & over	6	5	1	...	...	...	3	2	1	3	3	...
Hindu (*Arya*).	Total	18	11	7	6	4	2	12	7	5	...	...	...
	0—5	3	1	2	3	1	2	...	...	...	...	...	...
	20—40	15	10	5	3	3	...	12	7	5	...	...	...
Sikh.	Total	41	33	8	14	11	3	26	21	5	1	1	...
	0—5	5	2	3	5	2	3	...	...	...	...	...	...
	15—20	8	6	2	5	5	...	3	1	2	...	...	...
	20—40	25	22	3	4	4	...	20	17	3	1	1	...
	40—60	3	3	...	...	...	...	3	3	...	...	...	...
Budhist.	Total	35,867	17,956	17,911	15,482	7,553	7,929	17,324	9,348	7,976	3,061	1,055	2,006
	0—5	3,419	1,606	1,813	3,388	1,579	1,809	31	27	4	...	...	...
	5—10	3,974	1,996	1,978	3,798	1,846	1,952	171	148	23	5	2	3
	10—15	3,186	1.615	1.571	2,805	1,318	1,487	372	291	81	9	6	3
	15—20	3,090	1,548	1,542	2,010	895	1,115	1,056	639	417	24	14	10
	20—40	10,939	5,558	5,381	2,341	1,178	1,163	8,127	4,215	3,912	471	165	306
	40—60	7,434	3.699	3,735	757	503	254	5,628	2.913	2,715	1,049	283	766
	60 & over	3,825	1,934	1,891	383	234	149	1,939	1,115	824	1,503	585	918
Musalman.	Total	150.070	74,719	75,351	70,317	38,659	31,658	68,845	33,274	35,571	10,908	2,780	8,122
	0—5	24.070	11,783	12,287	24,035	11,765	12,270	34	18	16	1	...	1
	5—10	21,763	11,302	10,461	21,405	11,156	10,249	342	143	199	16	3	13
	10—15	14,806	7,955	6,851	12,489	7,105	5,384	2,259	821	1,438	58	29	29
	15—20	13,077	7,097	5,980	7,113	4,910	2,205	5,705	2,087	3,618	257	100	157
	20—40	45,365	21,336	24.029	4,834	3,472	1,362	38,272	17,086	21,186	2,259	778	1,481
	40—60	18,928	9,634	9,294	288	160	128	15,608	8,849	6,759	3,032	625	2,407
	60 & over	12,061	5,612	6,449	151	91	60	6,625	4,270	2,355	5,285	1,251	4,034

TABLE VII.

VII
Age, Sex and Civil Condition.

Age, Sex and Civil Condition by Religion.

Jammu and Kashmir State Census 1911.

Part II.—District Tables.

Religion.	Age.	Population.			Unmarried.			Married.			Widowed.		
		Persons.	Males.	Females.	Persons.	Males.	Females.	Persons.	Males.	Females.	Persons.	Males.	Females.
1	2	3	4	5	6	7	8	9	10	11	12	13	14
Christian.	Total	63	32	31	35	20	15	26	12	14	2	...	2
	0—5	8	1	7	8	1	7	...	...	...	...	...	...
	5—10	7	5	2	7	5	2	...	...	...	...	...	...
	10—15	6	5	1	6	5	1	...	...	...	...	...	...
	15—20	9	7	2	8	7	1	1	...	1	...	...	...
	20—40	21	9	12	6	2	4	15	7	8	...	...	...
	40—60	9	4	5	...	...	...	8	4	4	1	...	1
	60 & over	3	1	2	...	...	...	2	1	1	1	...	1
					(12) GILGIT.								
All Religions.	Total	23,969	13,299	10,670	12,049	7,169	4,880	10,658	5,645	5,013	1,262	485	777
	0—5	4,169	2,051	2,118	4,169	2,051	2,118	...	...	...	...	...	...
	5—10	3,617	1,861	1,756	3,563	1,855	1,708	52	6	46	2	...	2
	10—15	2,369	1,327	1,042	2,013	1,251	762	341	74	267	15	2	13
	15—20	1,986	1,079	907	1,019	798	221	943	274	669	24	7	17
	20—40	7,994	4.677	3,317	1,207	1,164	63	6,444	3,339	3,105	343	194	149
	40—60	2,738	1,617	1,121	67	60	7	2,250	1,447	803	421	110	311
	60 & over	1,096	687	409	11	10	1	628	505	123	457	172	285
Hindu (*Brahmanic*).	Total	816	770	46	406	387	19	366	339	27	44	44	...
	0—5	22	13	9	22	13	9	...	...	...	...	...	...
	5—10	15	10	5	15	10	5	...	...	...	...	...	...
	10—15	16	9	7	14	9	5	2	...	2	...	...	...
	15—20	47	41	6	37	37	...	10	4	6	...	...	...
	20—40	624	607	17	306	306	...	283	266	17	35	35	...
	40—60	87	85	2	12	12	...	68	66	2	7	7	...
	60 & over	5	5	...	...	...	...	3	3	...	2	2	...
Sikh.	Total	57	41	16	25	17	8	32	24	8	...	...	...
	0—5	4	3	1	4	3	1	...	...	...	...	...	...
	5—10	5	1	4	5	1	4	...	...	...	...	...	...
	10—15	5	1	4	4	1	3	1	...	1	...	...	...
	15—20	5	4	1	3	3	...	2	1	1	...	...	...
	20—40	29	25	4	9	9	...	20	16	4	...	...	...
	40—60	9	7	2	...	...	...	9	7	2	...	...	...
Musalman.	Total	23,075	12,471	10,604	11,606	6,754	4,852	10,251	5,276	4,975	1,218	441	777
	0—5	4,143	2,035	2,108	4,143	2,035	2,108	...	...	...	...	...	...
	5—10	3,595	1,848	1,747	3,541	1,842	1,699	52	6	46	2	...	2
	10—15	2,348	1,317	1,031	1,995	1,241	754	338	74	264	15	2	13
	15—20	1,934	1,034	900	979	758	221	931	269	662	24	7	17
	20—40	7,325	4,032	3,293	882	820	62	6,135	3,053	3,082	308	159	149
	40—60	2,639	1,523	1,116	55	48	7	2,170	1,372	798	414	103	311
	60 & over	1,091	682	409	11	10	1	625	502	123	455	170	285
Christian.	Total	21	17	4	12	11	1	9	6	3	...	...	...
	5—10	2	2	...	2	2	...	...	...	...	...	...	...
	20—40	16	13	3	10	9	1	6	4	2	...	...	...
	40—60	3	1	2	...	...	...	3	1	2	...	...	...

VII
Age, Sex and Civil Condition.

TABLE VII.

Age, Sex and Civil Condition by Religion.

Jammu and Kashmir State Census 1911.

Part III—City Tables.

Religion.	Age.	Population.			Unmarried.			Married.			Widowed.		
		Persons.	Males.	Females.	Persons.	Males.	Females.	Persons.	Males.	Females.	Persons.	Males.	Females.
1	2	3	4	5	6	7	8	9	10	11	12	13	14
					(a) JAMMU.								
All Religions.	**Total**	**31,726**	**19,362**	**12,364**	**12,257**	**8,710**	**3,547**	**15,238**	**8,955**	**6,283**	**4,231**	**1,697**	**2,534**
	0—1	802	399	403	802	399	403	...	...	...	...	...	...
	1—2	256	116	140	256	116	140	...	...	...	...	...	...
	2—3	466	262	204	466	262	204	...	...	...	...	...	...
	3—4	505	249	256	505	249	256	...	...	...	...	...	...
	4—5	494	272	222	494	272	222	...	...	...	...	...	...
	Total 0—5	**2,523**	**1,298**	**1,225**	**2,523**	**1,298**	**1,225**	...	...	...	...	...	...
	5—10	3,087	1,645	1,442	3,012	1,631	1,381	75	14	61	...	...	...
	10—15	2,981	1,854	1,127	2,468	1,744	724	499	107	392	14	3	11
	15—20	2,841	1,800	1,041	1,417	1,329	88	1,348	444	904	76	27	49
	20—25	3,461	2,172	1,289	1,113	1,088	25	2,119	991	1,128	229	93	136
	25—30	3,529	2,302	1,227	712	694	18	2,472	1,436	1,036	345	172	173
	30—35	3,438	2,125	1,313	411	382	29	2,576	1,526	1,050	451	217	234
	35—40	1,990	1,360	630	179	151	28	1,448	1,051	397	363	158	205
	40—45	2,894	1,612	1,282	171	158	13	2,005	1,204	801	718	250	468
	45—50	1,262	868	394	68	66	2	858	668	190	336	134	202
	50—55	1,609	1,007	602	85	81	4	881	687	194	643	239	404
	55—60	477	332	145	17	15	2	274	235	39	186	82	104
	60—65	915	528	387	44	39	5	409	336	73	462	153	309
	65—70	204	143	61	4	4	...	83	80	3	117	59	58
	70 & over	515	316	199	33	30	3	191	176	15	291	110	181
Hindu (*Brahmanic*).	**Total**	**19,778**	**12,032**	**7,746**	**7,204**	**5,270**	**1,934**	**9,707**	**5,661**	**4,046**	**2,867**	**1,101**	**1,766**
	0—1	461	218	243	461	218	243	...	...	...	...	...	...
	1—2	153	65	88	153	65	88	...	...	...	...	...	...
	2—3	286	160	126	286	160	126	...	...	...	...	...	...
	3—4	296	146	150	296	146	150	...	...	...	...	...	...
	4—5	278	148	130	278	148	130	...	...	...	...	...	...
	Total 0—5	**1,474**	**737**	**737**	**1,474**	**737**	**737**	...	...	...	...	...	...
	5—10	1,785	941	844	1,737	941	796	48	...	48	...	...	...
	10—15	1,725	1,092	633	1,773	1,020	353	339	70	269	13	2	11
	15—20	1,770	1,132	638	819	801	18	896	316	580	55	15	40
	20—25	2,164	1,356	808	663	655	8	1,315	627	688	186	74	112
	25—30	2,293	1,490	803	473	462	11	1,576	918	649	253	110	143
	30—35	2,205	1,280	925	263	254	9	1,637	901	736	305	125	180
	35—40	1,204	882	322	106	105	1	857	678	179	241	99	142
	40—45	1,966	1,038	928	115	115	...	1,372	765	607	479	158	321
	45—50	818	564	254	53	52	1	532	419	113	233	93	140
	50—55	987	626	361	59	59	...	521	415	106	407	152	255
	55—60	312	217	95	12	12	...	176	152	24	124	53	71
	60—65	602	362	240	31	31	...	262	222	40	309	109	200
	65—70	135	100	35	4	4	...	56	56	...	75	40	35
	70 & over	338	215	123	22	22	...	129	122	7	187	71	116
Hindu (*Arya*).	**Total**	**132**	**87**	**45**	**52**	**41**	**11**	**74**	**43**	**31**	**6**	**3**	**3**
	0—1	2	...	2	2	...	2	...	...	...	...	...	...
	1—2	1	1	...	1	1	...	...	...	...	...	...	...
	2—3	3	1	2	3	1	2	...	...	...	...	...	...
	3—4	5	3	2	5	3	2	...	...	...	...	...	...
	4—5	2	2	...	2	2	...	...	...	...	...	...	...
	Total 0—5	**13**	**7**	**6**	**13**	**7**	**6**	...	...	...	...	...	...
	5—10	12	8	4	12	8	4	...	...	...	...	...	...
	10—15	9	7	2	8	7	1	1	...	1	...	...	...
	15—20	17	15	2	12	12	...	5	3	2	...	...	...
	20—25	23	15	8	6	6	...	16	8	8	1	1	...
	25—30	15	7	8	1	1	...	14	6	8	...	...	...
	30—35	17	8	9	...	...	...	17	8	9	...	...	...
	35—40	10	8	2	...	...	...	9	8	1	1	...	1
	40—45	5	5	...	...	...	...	5	5	...	...	...	...
	45—50	5	4	1	...	...	...	4	3	1	1	1	...
	50—55	1	...	1	...	...	...	...	...	...	1	...	1
	60—65	2	...	2	...	...	...	1	...	1	1	...	1
	65—70	3	3	...	...	...	...	2	2	...	1	1	...

TABLE VII.

Age, Sex and Civil Condition by Religion.

Jammu and Kashmir State Census 1911.

Part III—City Tables.

Religion.	Age.	Population.			Unmarried.			Married.			Widowed.		
		Persons.	Males.	Females.	Persons.	Males.	Females.	Persons.	Males.	Females.	Persons.	Males.	Females.
1	2	3	4	5	6	7	8	9	10	11	12	13	14
Jain.	**Total**	**334**	**181**	**153**	**172**	**98**	**74**	**114**	**59**	**55**	**48**	**24**	**24**
	0—1	14	4	10	14	4	10	...	...	...	...	...	...
	1—2	4	3	1	4	3	1	...	...	...	...	...	...
	2—3	10	6	4	10	6	4	...	...	...	...	...	...
	3—4	8	3	5	8	3	5	...	...	...	...	...	...
	4—5	16	6	10	16	6	10	...	...	...	...	...	...
	Total 0—5	**52**	**22**	**30**	**52**	**22**	**30**	...	...	...	...	...	...
	5—10	41	19	22	39	18	21	2	1	1	...	...	...
	10—15	42	24	18	41	24	17	1	...	1	...	...	...
	15—20	28	13	15	19	13	6	8	...	8	1	...	1
	20—25	34	24	10	14	14	...	18	8	10	2	2	...
	25—30	28	14	14	3	3	...	19	8	11	6	3	3
	30—35	20	11	9	1	1	...	14	8	6	5	2	3
	35—40	20	14	6	3	3	...	13	9	4	4	2	2
	40—45	13	8	5	...	...	...	9	6	3	4	2	2
	45—50	14	7	7	...	...	...	10	6	4	4	1	3
	50—55	17	11	6	...	...	...	8	5	3	9	6	3
	55—60	9	6	3	...	...	...	5	3	2	4	3	1
	60—65	5	2	3	...	...	...	4	2	2	1	...	1
	65—70	7	3	4	...	...	...	2	2	...	5	1	4
	70 & over	4	3	1	...	...	...	1	1	...	3	2	1
Sikh.	**Total**	**695**	**414**	**281**	**299**	**202**	**97**	**330**	**182**	**148**	**66**	**30**	**36**
	0—1	17	8	9	17	8	9	...	...	...	...	...	...
	1—2	8	3	5	8	3	5	...	...	...	...	...	...
	2—3	14	7	7	14	7	7	...	...	...	...	...	...
	3—4	14	7	7	14	7	7	...	...	...	...	...	...
	4—5	11	7	4	11	7	4	...	...	...	...	...	...
	Total 0—5	**64**	**32**	**32**	**64**	**32**	**32**	...	...	...	...	...	...
	5—10	82	45	37	82	45	37	...	...	...	...	...	...
	10—15	80	44	36	68	44	24	12	...	12	...	...	...
	15—20	71	46	25	35	34	1	35	11	24	1	1	...
	20—25	64	38	26	20	20	...	41	17	24	3	1	2
	25—30	64	41	23	13	11	2	47	27	20	4	3	1
	30—35	57	34	23	6	6	...	43	21	22	8	7	1
	35—40	47	22	25	2	2	...	40	19	21	5	1	4
	40—45	65	41	22	3	3	...	46	32	14	14	6	8
	45—50	24	20	4	3	3	...	18	15	3	3	2	1
	50—55	36	25	11	1	...	1	24	20	4	11	5	6
	55—60	17	14	3	...	...	...	14	13	1	3	1	2
	60—65	11	5	6	...	...	...	4	4	...	7	1	6
	65—70	5	2	3	...	...	...	3	1	2	2	1	1
	70 & over	10	5	5	2	2	...	3	2	1	5	1	4
Zoroastrian.	**Total**	**5**	**2**	**3**	**1**	...	**1**	**4**	**2**	**2**	...	...	...
	2—3	1	...	1	1	...	1	...	...	...	...	...	...
	Total 0—5	**1**	...	**1**	**1**	...	**1**	...	...	...	...	...	...
	20—25	1	...	1	...	...	...	1	...	1	...	...	...
	25—30	1	1	...	...	...	...	1	1	...	...	...	...
	40—45	2	1	1	...	...	...	2	1	1	...	...	...
Musalman.	**Total**	**10,618**	**6,552**	**4,066**	**4,451**	**3,050**	**1,401**	**4,943**	**2,970**	**1,973**	**1,224**	**532**	**692**
	0—1	300	165	135	300	165	135	...	...	...	...	...	...
	1—2	87	42	45	87	42	45	...	...	...	...	...	...
	2—3	148	87	61	148	87	61	...	...	...	...	...	...
	3—4	179	90	89	179	90	89	...	...	...	...	...	...
	4—5	182	105	77	182	105	77	...	...	...	...	...	...
	Total 0—5	**896**	**489**	**407**	**896**	**489**	**407**	...	...	...	...	...	...
	5—10	1,149	619	530	1,124	606	518	25	13	12	...	...	...
	10—15	1,101	671	430	954	633	321	146	37	109	1	1	...
	15—20	948	589	359	528	467	61	401	111	290	19	11	8
	20—25	1,164	733	431	407	390	17	721	328	293	36	15	21
	25—30	1,112	737	375	219	214	5	812	468	344	81	55	26
	30—35	1,117	782	335	138	120	18	849	579	270	130	83	47
	35—40	693	430	363	68	41	27	515	334	181	110	55	55
	40—45	836·	512	324	53	40	13	565	391	174	218	81	137

VII
Age, Sex and Civil Condition.

TABLE VII.

Age, Sex and Civil Condition by Religion.

Jammu and Kashmir State Census 1911.

Part III—City Tables.

Religion.	Age.	Population. Persons.	Population. Males.	Population. Females.	Unmarried. Persons.	Unmarried. Males.	Unmarried. Females.	Married. Persons.	Married. Males.	Married. Females.	Widowed. Persons.	Widowed. Males.	Widowed. Females.
1	2	3	4	5	6	7	8	9	10	11	12	13	14
Musalman (*Continued*).	45—50	397	269	128	12	11	1	290	221	69	95	37	58
	50—55	563	343	220	25	22	3	328	247	81	210	74	136
	55—60	136	95	41	5	3	2	79	67	12	52	25	27
	60—65	290	155	135	13	8	5	134	104	30	143	43	100
	65—70	53	35	18	...	...	...	20	19	1	33	16	17
	70 & over	163	93	70	9	6	3	58	51	7	96	36	60
Christian.	Total	164	94	70	78	49	29	66	38	28	20	7	13
	0—1	8	4	4	8	4	4	...	...	...	...	...	...
	1—2	3	2	1	3	2	1	...	...	...	...	...	...
	2—3	4	1	3	4	1	3	...	...	...	...	...	...
	3—4	3	...	3	3	...	3	...	...	...	...	...	...
	4—5	5	4	1	5	4	1	...	...	...	...	...	...
	Total 0—5	23	11	12	23	11	12	...	...	...	...	...	...
	5—10	18	13	5	18	13	5	...	...	...	...	...	...
	10—15	24	16	8	24	16	8	...	...	...	...	...	...
	15—20	7	5	2	4	2	2	3	3	...	...	...	...
	20—25	11	6	5	3	3	...	7	3	4	1	...	1
	25—30	18	12	6	5	3	2	12	8	4	1	1	...
	30—35	20	10	10	1	1	...	16	9	7	3	...	3
	35—40	16	4	12	...	...	...	14	3	11	2	1	1
	40—45	9	7	2	...	...	...	6	4	2	3	3	...
	45—50	4	4	...	...	...	...	4	4	...	...	...	...
	50—55	5	2	3	...	...	...	...	...	...	5	2	3
	55—60	3	...	3	...	...	...	...	...	...	3	...	3
	60—65	5	4	1	...	...	...	4	4	...	1	...	1
	65—70	1	...	1	...	...	...	...	...	...	1	...	1
					(b) SRINAGAR.								
All Religions.	Total	126,344	68,378	57,966	57,391	35,922	21,469	57,065	28,405	28,660	11,888	4,051	7,837
	0—1	4,904	2,506	2,398	4,904	2,506	2,398	...	...	...	...	...	...
	1—2	802	423	379	802	423	379	...	...	...	...	...	...
	2—3	3,224	1,564	1,660	3,224	1,564	1,660	...	...	...	...	...	...
	3—4	3,821	1,845	1,976	3,821	1,845	1,976	...	...	...	...	...	...
	4—5	3,656	1,824	1,832	3,656	1,824	1,832	...	...	...	...	...	...
	Total 0—5	16,407	8,162	8,245	16,407	8,162	8,245	...	...	...	...	...	...
	5—10	16,752	8,384	8,368	16,690	8,370	8,320	59	14	45	3	...	3
	10—15	13,825	8,061	5,764	12,078	7,753	4,325	1,725	304	1,421	22	4	18
	15—20	11,149	6,421	4,728	5,429	5,029	400	5,507	1,334	4,173	213	58	155
	20—25	12,624	6,691	5,933	3,348	3,273	75	8,850	3,250	5,600	426	168	258
	25—30	10,522	5,455	5,067	1,410	1,380	30	8,584	3,838	4,746	528	237	291
	30—35	10,559	5,783	4,776	761	732	29	8,982	4,694	4,288	816	357	459
	35—40	7,206	4,098	3,108	342	336	6	6,071	3,459	2,612	793	303	490
	40—45	8,481	4,644	3,837	320	306	14	6,578	3,842	2,736	1,583	496	1,087
	45—50	4,781	2,823	1,958	198	192	6	3,514	2,275	1,239	1,069	356	713
	50—55	5,852	3,277	2,575	170	162	8	3,473	2,488	985	2,209	627	1,582
	55—60	2,139	1,224	915	78	78	...	1,281	879	402	780	267	513
	60—65	3,696	2,046	1,650	86	84	2	1,602	1,335	267	2,008	627	1,381
	65—70	802	468	334	26	24	2	332	269	63	444	175	269
	70 & over	1,549	841	708	48	41	7	507	424	83	994	376	618
Hindu (*Brahmanic*).	Total	28,739	15,696	13,043	12,692	8,478	4,214	2,420	6,080	6,340	3,627	1,138	2,489
	0—1	939	481	458	939	481	458	...	...	...	...	...	...
	1—2	192	98	94	192	98	94	...	...	...	...	...	...
	2—3	711	345	366	711	345	366	...	...	...	...	...	...
	3—4	728	349	379	728	349	379	...	...	...	...	...	...
	4—5	786	406	380	786	406	380	...	...	...	...	...	...
	Total 0—5	3,356	1,679	1,677	3,356	1,679	1,677	...	...	...	...	...	...
	5—10	3,668	1,832	1,836	3,627	1,826	1,801	38	6	32	3	...	3
	10—15	2,834	1,726	1,108	2,262	1,569	693	553	153	400	19	4	15
	15—20	2,615	1,587	1,028	1,162	1,137	25	1,403	439	964	50	11	39
	20—25	2,816	1,543	1,273	780	775	5	1,918	732	1,186	118	36	82
	25—30	2,530	1,303	1,227	477	475	2	1,891	782	1,109	162	46	116
	30—35	2,447	1,346	1,101	298	293	5	1,881	963	918	268	90	178
	35—40	1,817	1,017	800	191	191	...	1,323	737	586	303	89	214
	40—45	1,878	1,029	849	159	155	4	1,204	726	478	515	148	367
	45—50	1,297	695	602	124	124	...	789	462	327	384	109	275
	50—55	1,417	752	665	104	103	1	666	468	198	647	181	466
	55—60	661	400	261	57	57	...	315	241	74	289	102	187
	60—65	880	481	399	54	54	...	307	262	45	519	165	354
	65—70	216	138	78	17	17	...	62	51	11	137	70	67
	70 & over	307	168	139	24	23	1	70	58	12	213	87	126

TABLE VII.

Age, Sex and Civil Condition by Religion.

Jammu and Kashmir State Census 1911.

Part III—City Tables.

VII
Age, Sex and Civil Condition.

Religion.	Age.	Population. Persons.	Population. Males.	Population. Females.	Unmarried. Persons.	Unmarried. Males.	Unmarried. Females.	Married. Persons.	Married. Males.	Married. Females.	Widowed. Persons.	Widowed. Males.	Widowed. Females.
1	2	3	4	5	6	7	8	9	10	11	12	13	14
Hindu (Arya).	**Total**	**40**	**24**	**16**	**23**	**14**	**9**	**14**	**7**	**7**	**3**	**3**	...
	0—1	1	...	1	1	...	1	...	...	...	...	...	...
	3—4	2	...	2	2	...	2	...	...	...	...	...	...
	4—5	2	1	1	2	1	1	...	...	...	...	...	...
	Total 0—5	5	1	4	5	1	4	...	...	...	...	...	...
	5—10	10	7	3	10	7	3	...	...	...	...	...	...
	10—15	6	5	1	5	4	1	1	1	...	...	...	...
	15—20	3	2	1	3	2	1	...	...	...	...	...	...
	20—25	1	...	1	...	...	...	1	...	1	...	...	...
	25—30	1	1	...	...	...	...	1	1	...	...	...	...
	30—35	7	4	3	...	...	...	6	3	3	1	1	...
	35—40	2	1	1	...	...	...	2	1	1	...	...	...
	40—45	1	...	1	...	...	...	1	...	1	...	...	...
	45—50	3	2	1	...	...	...	1	...	1	2	2	...
	50—55	1	1	...	...	...	...	1	1	...	...	...	...
Hindu (Bramho).	**Total**	**1**	...	**1**	...	...	...	**1**	...	**1**	...	...	...
	25—30	1	...	1	...	...	...	1	...	1	...	...	...
Sikh.	**Total**	**486**	**316**	**170**	**216**	**132**	**84**	**237**	**167**	**70**	**33**	**17**	**16**
	0—1	17	9	8	17	9	8	...	...	...	...	...	...
	1—2	1	...	1	1	...	1	...	...	...	...	...	...
	2—3	6	2	4	6	2	4	...	...	...	...	...	...
	3—4	13	9	4	13	9	4	...	...	...	...	...	...
	4—5	11	3	8	11	3	8	...	...	...	...	...	...
	Total 0—5	48	23	25	48	23	25	...	...	...	...	...	...
	5—10	65	22	43	65	22	43	...	...	...	...	...	...
	10—15	45	31	14	41	29	12	4	2	2	...	...	...
	15—20	47	32	15	33	29	4	14	3	11	...	...	...
	20—25	43	33	10	13	13	...	29	20	9	1	...	1
	25—30	48	33	15	5	5	...	41	27	14	2	1	1
	30—35	49	32	17	5	5	...	42	26	16	2	1	1
	35—40	32	23	9	1	1	...	30	21	9	1	1	...
	40—45	29	24	5	1	1	...	24	21	3	4	2	2
	45—50	26	25	1	1	1	...	22	21	1	3	3	...
	50—55	21	14	7	1	1	...	15	12	3	5	1	4
	55—60	6	4	2	...	...	...	3	2	1	3	2	1
	60—65	16	13	3	1	1	...	6	6	...	9	6	3
	65—70	8	5	3	1	1	...	5	4	1	2	...	2
	70 & over	3	2	1	...	...	...	2	2	...	1	...	1
Zoroastrian.	**Total**	**26**	**20**	**6**	**14**	**11**	**3**	**11**	**8**	**3**	**1**	**1**	...
	0—1	1	1	...	1	1	...	...	...	...	...	...	...
	3—4	2	1	1	2	1	1	...	...	...	...	...	...
	Total 0—5	3	2	1	3	2	1	...	...	...	...	...	...
	5—10	6	6	...	6	6	...	...	...	...	...	...	...
	15—20	3	2	1	3	2	1	...	...	...	...	...	...
	20—25	2	1	1	2	1	1	...	...	...	...	...	...
	30—35	3	1	2	...	...	...	3	1	2	...	...	...
	35—40	1	...	1	...	...	...	1	...	1	...	...	...
	40—45	3	3	...	...	...	...	3	3	...	...	...	...
	45—50	2	2	...	...	...	...	2	2	...	...	...	...
	50—55	1	1	...	...	...	...	1	1	...	...	...	...
	60—65	1	1	...	...	...	...	1	1	...	...	...	...
	65—70	1	1	...	...	...	...	...	...	...	1	1	...
Musalman.	**Total**	**96,941**	**52,271**	**44,670**	**44,387**	**27,261**	**17,126**	**44,341**	**22,120**	**22,221**	**8,212**	**2,890**	**5,322**
	0—1	3,940	2,011	1,929	3,940	2,011	1,929	...	...	...	...	...	...
	1—2	608	324	284	608	324	284	...	...	...	...	...	...
	2—3	2,506	1,217	1,289	2,506	1,217	1,289	...	...	...	...	...	...
	3—4	3,072	1,483	1,589	3,072	1,483	1,589	...	...	...	...	...	...
	4—5	2,856	1,413	1,443	2,856	1,413	1,443	...	...	...	...	...	...

VII
Age, Sex and Civil Condition.

TABLE VII.

Age, Sex and Civil Condition by Religion.

Jammu and Kashmir State Census 1911.

Part III—City Tables.

Religion.	Age.	Population.			Unmarried.			Married.			Widowed.		
		Persons.	Males.	Females.	Persons.	Males.	Females.	Persons.	Males.	Females.	Persons.	Males.	Females.
1	2	3	4	5	6	7	8	9	10	11	12	13	14
Musalman (Continued).	Total 0—5	12,982	6,448	6,534	12,982	6,448	6,534	...	...	...	...	...	...
	5—10	13,000	6,517	6,483	12,979	6.509	6,470	21	8	13	...	...	...
	10—15	10,938	6,298	4,640	9,768	6,150	3,618	1,167	148	1,019	3	...	3
	15—20	8,477	4,798	3.679	4,224	3,859	365	4,090	892	3,198	163	47	116
	20—25	9,755	5,113	4,642	2,549	2,483	66	6,899	2,498	4,401	307	132	175
	25—30	7,924	4,107	3,817	917	893	24	6,643	3,024	3,619	364	190	174
	30—35	8,036	4,391	3,645	456	433	23	7,036	3.694	3,342	545	264	280
	35—40	5,341	3,051	2,290	146	142	4	4,708	2,796	2,012	487	213	274
	40—45	6,559	3,585	2,974	156	149	7	5,343	3,090	2,253	1.060	346	714
	45—50	3,449	2,096	1,353	72	67	5	2.697	1,787	910	680	242	438
	50—55	4,402	2,505	1,897	58	55	3	2,788	2,005	783	1,556	445	1,111
	55—60	1,471	819	652	20	20	...	963	636	327	488	163	325
	60—65	2,795	1,549	1,246	30	29	1	1,287	1,065	222	1,478	455	1,023
	65—70	575	323	252	8	6	2	264	213	51	303	104	199
	70 & over	1,237	671	566	23	18	5	435	364	71	779	289	490
Christian.	Total	111	51	60	58	26	32	41	23	18	12	2	10
	0—1	6	4	2	6	4	2	...	...	...	...	...	...
	1—2	1	1	...	1	1	...	...	...	...	...	...	...
	2—3	1	...	1	1	...	1	...	...	...	...	...	...
	3—4	4	3	1	4	3	1	...	...	...	...	...	...
	4—5	1	1	...	1	1	...	...	...	...	...	...	...
	Total 0—5	13	9	4	13	9	4	...	...	...	...	...	...
	5—10	3	...	3	3	...	3	...	...	...	...	...	...
	10—15	2	1	1	2	1	1	...	...	...	...	...	...
	15—20	4	...	4	4	...	4	...	...	...	...	...	...
	20—25	7	1	6	4	1	3	3	...	3	...	...	...
	25—30	18	11	7	11	7	4	7	4	3	...	...	...
	30—35	17	9	8	2	1	1	14	7	7	1	1	...
	35—40	13	6	7	4	2	2	7	4	3	2	...	2
	40—45	11	3	8	4	1	3	3	2	1	4	...	4
	45—50	4	3	1	1	...	1	3	3	...	...	...	...
	50—55	10	4	6	7	3	4	2	1	1	1	...	1
	55—60	1	1	...	1	1	...	...	...	...	...	...	...
	60—65	4	2	2	1	...	1	1	1	...	2	1	1
	65—70	2	1	1	...	...	...	1	1	...	1	...	1
	70 & over	2	...	2	1	...	1	...	...	...	1	...	1

TABLE VIII.

EDUCATION BY RELIGION AND AGE.

Jammu and Kashmir State Census 1911.

1. The arrangement of this table, both in respect of the territorial sub-divisions and the figures dealt with, is the same as that of table VII (*vide* §§ 1 and 4 of the title-page remarks on that table).

2. Detail has been given in this table only of such languages as are in vogue in the State to any considerable extent. Those with small figures have been grouped together under "others" and they are :—

I. Asiatic.—	Pashto	...	...	...	1
	Sindhi	...	...	...	2
	Bengali	...	...	...	4
	Karnatiki	...	...	...	1
	Gujrati	...	...	...	2
	Lande	...	...	...	323
			Total	...	333
II. European.—	German	...	...	...	1
			GRAND TOTAL	...	334

3. *Gurmukhi* is no *language*. It is only a *character* in which *Panjabi* is written. This script is quite different from *Nagri* or Hindi.

4. *Hindi* is the same as *Dera Nagri*, but its present figures include all the Sanskrit, Shastri, Nagri, totals on the one hand, and Bengali and Lande on the other. Persons literate in Bengali have been returned only 4 although the actual number of Bengalis here is very much larger and the present Lande figures are only 320 as against 2,396 of the last Census.

5. The figures of Arabic and Persian should also be read with caution, as the enumerator here has been quite apt to take the mere ability to read the *Qoran* for a real knowledge of the Arabic language and the people (especially in Kashmir) confound Persian and Urdu most inextricably in common parlance.

6. The figures in this table do not show the whole extent to which each language prevails except in case of English, as only the language best known by each person has been taken into account, although the number of languages known is not unoften more than one. In case of English-knowing persons there is always a second language which has here so far been entirely Urdu. A special table has been prepared in this State which will be found at the end of Education Chapter in the Report Volume showing literacy in each language in its entirety.

7. The figures in this Table include Europeans and Anglo-Indians as well as Native Christians. The details for those who are literate are noted below :—

	Total Literate.			Literate in English.		
	Persons.	Males.	Females.	Persons.	Males.	Females.
European and Anglo-Indian ...	224	117	107	223	117	106
Native Christians	63	46	17	28	21	7

In addition there was 1 European female and 1 Anglo-Indian male both non-Christians who were literate in English.

VIII
Education.

TABLE VIII.

Education by Religion and Age.

Jammu and Kashmir State Census 1911.

Part I—Provincial Tables.

AGE.	POPULATION.									LITERATE IN					
	Total.			Literate.			Illiterate.			Urdu.			Persian.		
	Persons.	Males.	Females.	Persons.	Males.	Females.	Persons.	Males.	Females.	Persons.	Males.	Females.	Persons.	Males.	Females.
1	2	3	4	5	6	7	8	9	10	11	12	13	14	15	16
					(i) ENTIRE STATE.										
All Religions.	3,103,501	1,644,978	1,458,523	64,936	63,251	1,685	3,038,565	1,581,727	1,456,838	22,079	21,829	250	11,612	11,562	50
0—10 ...	922,103	472,693	449,410	835	752	83	921,268	471,941	449,327	471	459	12	53	53	...
10—15 ...	347,154	192,256	154,898	4,565	4,349	216	342,589	187,907	154.682	2,478	2,438	40	355	351	4
15—20 ...	270,870	143,115	127,755	6,188	5,952	236	264,682	137,163	127,519	2.592	2,548	44	696	693	3
20 and over...	1,563,374	836,914	726,460	53,348	52,198	1,150	1,510,026	784,716	725,310	16,538	16,384	154	10,508	10,465	43
Hindu (Brahmanic).	689,047	371,805	317,242	41,753	40,771	982	647,294	331,034	316,260	12,564	12,447	117	5,295	5,273	22
0—10 ...	167,462	84,921	82,541	582	531	51	166,880	84,390	82,490	329	324	5	29	29	...
10—15 ...	71,020	40,544	30,476	3,131	2,989	142	67,889	37,555	30,334	1,638	1,612	26	151	150	1
15—20 ...	57,895	30,716	27,179	3,966	3,815	151	53,929	26,901	27,028	1,500	1.479	21	245	244	1
20 and over ...	392,670	215,624	177,046	34,074	33,436	638	358,596	182,188	176,408	9,097	9,032	65	4,870	4,850	20
Hindu (Arya).	1,046	592	454	258	229	29	788	363	425	102	95	7	3	3	...
0—10 ...	226	132	94	11	9	2	215	123	92	9	8	1	...	...	...
10—15 ...	113	68	45	24	22	2	89	46	43	10	8	2	...	...	...
15—20 ...	100	50	50	26	24	2	74	26	48	3	2	1	...	...	...
20 and over...	607	342	265	197	174	23	410	168	242	80	77	3	3	3	...
Hindu (Bramho).	1	...	1	1	...	1	...	...	...	...	...	...	...	...	...
20 and over...	1	...	1	1	...	1	...	...	...	...	...	...	...	...	...
Sikh.	31,529	17,016	14,513	2,970	2,713	257	28,559	14,303	14,256	621	611	10	26	23	3
0—10 ...	9,937	5,178	4,759	60	46	14	9,877	5,132	4,745	18	18	...	...	...	...
10—15 ...	3,648	2,057	1,591	249	207	42	3,399	1,850	1,549	86	85	1	1	1	...
15—20 ...	2,817	1,534	1,283	322	285	37	2,495	1,249	1,246	93	90	3	4	3	1
20 and over...	15,127	8,247	6,880	2,339	2,175	164	12,788	6,072	6,716	424	418	6	21	19	2
Jain.	345	191	154	76	76	...	269	115	154	9	9	...	...	...	...
0—10 ...	95	43	52	4	4	...	91	39	52	1	1	...	...	...	...
10—15	42	24	18	8	8	...	34	16	18	3	3	...	...	...	...
15—20	29	14	15	7	7	...	22	7	15	2	2	...	...	...	...
20 and over...	179	110	69	57	57	...	122	53	69	3	3	...	...	...	...
Budhist.	36,322	18,170	18,152	1,322	1,283	39	35,000	16,887	18,113	6	6	...	1	1	...
0—10 ...	7,500	3,651	3,849	...	...	...	7,500	3,651	3,849	...	...	...	...	...	...
10—15 ...	3,232	1,633	1,599	28	27	1	3.204	1,606	1,598	...	...	...	...	...	...
15—20 ...	3,122	1,562	1,560	94	93	1	3,028	1,469	1,559	1	1	...	...	...	...
20 and over...	22,468	11,324	11,144	1,200	1,163	37	21,268	10,161	11,107	5	5	...	1	1	...
Zoroastrian.	31	22	9	22	16	6	9	6	3	...	...	...	...	...	...
0—10 ...	10	8	2	3	3	...	7	5	2	...	...	...	...	...	...
15—20 ...	3	2	1	3	2	1	...	...	...	...	...	...	...	...	...
20 and over...	18	12	6	16	11	5	2	1	1	...	...	...	...	...	...
Musalman.	2,344,206	1,236,565	1,107,641	18,247	18.000	247	2,325,959	1,218,565	1,107,394	8,759	8,647	112	6,287	6,262	25
0—10 ...	736.613	378,631	357,982	166	156	10	736,447	378,475	357,972	113	108	5	24	24	...
10—15 ...	269,009	147,868	121,141	1,115	1,091	24	267,894	146,777	121,117	739	728	11	203	200	3
15—20 ...	206,851	109,196	97,655	1,755	1,719	36	205,096	107,477	97,619	990	972	18	447	446	1
20 and over...	1,131,733	600,870	530,863	15,211	15,034	177	1,116,522	585,836	530,686	6,917	6,839	78	5,613	5,592	21
Christian.	974	617	357	287	163	124	687	454	233	18	14	4	...	...	...
0—10 ...	260	129	131	9	3	6	251	126	125	1	...	1	...	...	...
10—15 ...	90	62	28	10	5	5	80	57	23	2	2	...	...	...	...
15—20 ...	53	41	12	15	7	8	38	34	4	3	2	1	...	...	...
20 and over	571	385	186	253	148	105	318	237	81	12	10	2	...	...	...

TABLE VIII.

Education by Religion and Age.

Jammu and Kashmir State Census 1911.

Part I—Provincial Tables.

LITERATE IN

Arabic.			Dogri.			Hindi.			Bodhi.			Gurmukhi.			Others.			English.		
Persons.	Males.	Females.	Persons.	Males.	Females.	Persons.	Males.	Females.	Persons.	Males.	Females.	Persons.	Males.	Females.	Persons.	Males.	Females.	Persons.	Males.	Females.
17	18	19	20	21	22	23	24	25	26	27	28	29	30	31	32	33	34	35	36	37
							(i) ENTIRE STATE.													
2,066	1,963	103	7,741	7,644	97	10,797	10,324	473	1,368	1,323	45	2,807	2,317	490	334	317	17	6,132	5,972	160
22	18	4	26	25	1	111	76	35	...	...	...	52	29	23	1	1	...	99	91	8
109	100	9	158	155	3	482	423	59	31	29	2	205	120	85	11	9	2	736	724	12
158	141	17	370	360	10	772	712	60	96	95	1	263	178	85	29	28	1	1,212	1,197	15
1,777	1,704	73	7,187	7,104	83	9,432	9,113	319	1,241	1,199	42	2,287	1,990	297	293	279	14	4,085	3,960	125
...	...	...	7,448	7,358	90	10,420	9,972	448	...	...	...	924	666	258	284	272	12	4,818	4,783	35
...	...	...	26	25	1	104	71	33	...	...	...	12	2	10	1	1	...	81	79	2
...	...	...	151	149	2	472	414	58	...	...	...	74	27	47	8	7	1	637	630	7
...	...	...	363	353	10	740	683	57	...	...	...	88	33	55	21	21	...	1,009	1,002	7
...	...	...	6,908	6,831	77	9,104	8,804	300	...	...	...	750	604	146	254	243	11	3,091	3,072	19
...	...	...	1	1	...	45	28	17	...	...	...	8	5	3	6	6	...	93	91	2
...	...	...	...	...	...	2	1	1	...	...	...	...	...	...	...	...	...	...	...	...
...	...	...	...	...	...	2	2	...	...	...	...	...	...	...	...	...	...	12	12	...
...	...	...	...	...	...	6	5	1	...	...	...	...	...	...	1	1	...	16	16	...
...	...	...	1	1	...	35	20	15	...	...	...	8	5	3	5	5	...	65	63	2
...	...	...	...	...	...	...	...	...	...	...	...	...	...	...	...	...	...	1	...	1
...	...	...	...	...	...	...	...	...	...	...	...	...	...	...	...	...	...	1	...	1
...	...	...	38	34	4	233	226	7	...	...	...	1,861	1,632	229	12	8	4	179	179	...
...	...	...	...	...	...	2	1	1	...	...	...	40	27	13	...	...	...	...	...	...
...	...	...	2	1	1	7	6	1	...	...	...	131	93	38	2	1	1	20	20	...
...	...	...	1	1	...	25	23	2	...	...	...	175	145	30	3	2	1	21	21	...
...	...	...	35	32	3	199	196	3	...	...	...	1,515	1,367	148	7	5	2	138	138	...
...	...	...	...	...	...	34	34	...	...	...	...	...	...	...	26	26	...	7	7	...
...	...	...	...	...	...	3	3	...	...	...	...	...	...	...	...	...	...	...	...	...
...	...	...	...	...	...	1	1	...	...	...	...	...	...	...	1	1	...	3	3	...
...	...	...	...	...	...	1	1	...	...	...	...	...	...	...	3	3	...	1	1	...
...	...	...	...	...	...	29	29	...	...	...	...	...	...	...	22	22	...	3	3	...
...	...	...	...	...	...	5	5	...	1,309	1,270	39	...	...	...	...	...	...	1	1	...
...	...	...	...	...	...	...	...	...	...	...	...	...	...	...	...	...	...	...	...	...
...	...	...	...	...	...	...	...	...	28	27	1	...	...	...	...	...	...	...	...	...
...	...	...	...	...	...	...	...	...	93	92	1	...	...	...	...	...	...	...	...	...
...	...	...	...	...	...	5	5	...	1,188	1,151	37	...	...	...	...	...	...	1	1	...
...	...	...	...	...	...	...	...	...	...	...	...	...	...	...	...	...	...	22	16	6
...	...	...	...	...	...	...	...	...	...	...	...	...	...	...	...	...	...	3	3	...
...	...	...	...	...	...	...	...	...	...	...	...	...	...	...	...	...	...	3	2	1
...	...	...	...	...	...	...	...	...	...	...	...	...	...	...	...	...	...	16	11	5
2,066	1,963	103	254	251	3	60	59	1	42	42	...	14	14	...	5	5	...	760	757	3
22	18	4	...	...	...	...	...	...	...	...	...	...	...	...	...	...	...	7	6	1
109	100	9	5	5	...	...	...	...	...	...	...	...	...	...	...	...	...	59	58	1
158	141	17	6	6	...	...	...	...	...	...	...	...	...	...	1	1	...	153	153	...
1,777	1,704	73	243	240	3	60	59	1	42	42	...	14	14	...	4	4	...	541	540	1
...	...	...	...	...	...	...	...	...	17	11	6	...	...	...	1	...	1	251	138	113
...	...	...	...	...	...	...	...	...	...	...	...	...	...	...	...	...	...	8	3	5
...	...	...	...	...	...	...	...	...	3	2	1	...	...	...	...	...	...	5	1	4
...	...	...	...	...	...	...	...	...	3	3	...	...	...	...	...	...	...	9	2	7
...	...	...	...	...	...	...	...	...	11	6	5	...	...	...	1	...	1	229	132	97

VIII
Education.

TABLE VIII.

Education by Religion and Age.

Jammu and Kashmir State Census 1911.

Part I—Provincial Tables.

AGE.	POPULATION.									LITERATE IN					
	Total.			Literate.			Illiterate.			Urdu.			Persian.		
	Persons.	Males.	Females.	Persons.	Males.	Females.	Persons.	Males.	Females.	Persons.	Males.	Females.	Persons.	Males.	Females.
1	2	3	4	5	6	7	8	9	10	11	12	13	14	15	16
							(ii) JAMMU PROVINCE.								
All Religions.	1,597,865	846,790	751,075	34,621	33,322	1,299	1,563,244	813,468	749,776	12,379	12,164	215	1,319	1,303	16
0—10	450,781	231,153	219,628	466	400	66	450,315	230,753	219,562	286	275	11	16	16	...
10—15	178,646	99,581	79,065	2,468	2,286	182	176,178	97,295	78,883	1,515	1,481	34	75	75	...
15—20	134,559	69,940	64,619	3,259	3,055	204	131,300	66,885	64,415	1,579	1,538	41	118	117	1
20 and over	833,879	446,116	387,763	28,428	27,581	847	805,451	418,535	386,916	8,999	8,870	129	1,110	1,095	15
Hindu (Brahmanic).	625,456	335,621	289,835	25,149	24,275	874	600,307	311,346	288,961	6,727	6,634	93	493	485	8
0—10 ...	151,640	76,864	74,776	313	267	46	151,327	76,597	74,730	173	169	4	11	11	...
10—15 ...	64,525	36,790	27,735	1,715	1,592	123	62,810	35,198	27,612	969	948	21	42	42	...
15—20 ...	52,511	27,486	25,025	2,285	2,146	139	50,226	25,340	24,886	950	932	18	51	51	...
20 and over...	356,780	194,481	162,299	20,836	20,270	566	335,944	174,211	161,733	4,635	4,585	50	389	381	8
Hindu (Arya).	983	554	429	227	205	22	756	349	407	93	87	6	3	3	...
0—10 ...	205	121	84	10	9	1	195	112	83	9	8	1	...	...	...
10—15 ...	107	63	44	20	18	2	87	45	42	10	8	2	...	...	...
15—20 ...	97	48	49	24	22	2	73	26	47	3	2	1	...	...	...
20 and over ...	574	322	252	173	156	17	401	166	235	71	69	2	3	3	...
Sikh.	16,659	9,071	7,588	1,725	1,527	198	14,934	7,544	7,390	407	398	9	20	17	3
0—10 ...	4,961	2,615	2,346	31	22	9	4,930	2,593	2,337	13	13	...	...	...	...
10—15 ...	1,995	1,144	851	159	122	37	1,836	1,022	814	68	67	1	1	1	...
15—20 ...	1,435	792	643	180	151	29	1,255	641	614	54	51	3	3	2	1
20 and over ...	8,268	4,520	3,748	1,355	1,232	123	6,913	3,288	3,625	272	267	5	16	14	2
Jain.	345	191	154	76	76	...	269	115	154	9	9	...	...	...	...
0—10 ...	95	43	52	4	4	...	91	39	52	1	1	...	...	...	...
10—15 ...	42	24	18	8	8	...	34	16	18	3	3	...	...	...	...
15—20 ...	29	14	15	7	7	...	22	7	15	2	2	...	...	...	...
20 and over ...	179	110	69	57	57	...	122	53	69	3	3	...	...	...	...
Budhist.	452	211	241	6	6	...	446	205	241	...	...	...	...	...	...
0—10 ...	107	49	58	...	...	...	107	49	58	...	...	...	...	...	...
10—15 ...	46	18	28	...	...	...	46	18	28	...	...	...	...	...	...
15—20 ...	31	13	18	...	...	...	31	13	18	...	...	...	...	...	...
20 and over...	268	131	137	6	6	...	262	125	137	...	...	...	...	...	...
Zoroastrian.	5	2	3	4	2	2	1	...	1	...	...	...	...	...	...
0—10 ...	1	...	1	...	...	...	1	...	1	...	...	...	...	...	...
20 and over...	4	2	2	4	2	2	...	...	...	...	...	...	...	...	...
Musalman.	953,293	500,690	452,603	7,368	7,190	178	945,925	493,500	452,425	5,130	5,027	103	803	798	5
0—10 ...	293,561	151,359	142,202	105	96	9	293,456	151,263	142,193	89	84	5	5	5	...
10—15 ...	111,854	61,490	50,364	563	545	18	111,291	60,945	50,346	464	454	10	32	32	...
15—20 ...	80,417	41,553	38,864	756	726	30	79,661	40,827	38,834	568	550	18	64	64	...
20 and over ...	467,461	246,288	221,173	5,944	5,823	121	461,517	240,465	221,052	4,009	3,939	70	702	697	5
Christian.	672	450	222	66	41	25	606	409	197	13	9	4	...	...	...
0—10 ...	211	102	109	3	2	1	208	100	108	1	...	1	...	...	...
10—15 ...	77	52	25	3	1	2	74	51	23	1	1	...	...	...	...
15—20 ...	39	34	5	7	3	4	32	31	1	2	1	1	...	...	...
20 and over...	345	262	83	53	35	18	292	227	65	9	7	2	...	...	...
							(iii) KASHMIR PROVINCE.								
All Religions	1,295,201	691,780	603,421	27,106	26,788	318	1,268,095	664,992	603,103	8,890	8,856	34	9,764	9,730	34
0—10 ...	410,250	210,916	199,334	361	345	16	409,889	210,571	199,318	181	180	1	36	36	...
10—15 ..	148,131	81,764	66,367	2,028	2,000	28	146,103	79,764	66,339	936	930	6	276	272	4
15—20 ...	118,128	63,427	54,701	2,694	2,663	31	115,434	60,764	54,670	927	924	3	542	540	2
20 and over...	618,692	335,673	283,019	22,023	21,780	243	596,669	313,893	282,776	6,846	6,822	24	8,910	8,882	28

TABLE VIII.

Education by Religion and Age.

Jammu and Kashmir State Census 1911.

Part I—Provincial Tables.

LITERATE IN

Arabic.			Dogri.			Hindi.			Bodhi.			Gurmukhi.			Others.			English.		
Persons.	Males.	Females.	Persons.	Males.	Females.	Persons.	Males.	Females.	Persons.	Males.	Females.	Persons.	Males.	Females.	Persons.	Males.	Females.	Persons.	Males.	Females.
17	18	19	20	21	22	23	24	25	26	27	28	29	30	31	32	33	34	35	36	37
						(ii) **JAMMU PROVINCE.**														
794	731	63	7,580	7,488	92	8,312	7,878	434	...	...	...	1,693	1,288	405	327	311	16	2,217	2,159	58
8	5	3	26	25	1	85	55	30	...	...	...	28	10	18	1	1	...	16	13	3
43	36	7	152	150	2	345	295	50	...	...	...	144	66	78	11	9	2	183	174	9
59	47	12	364	354	10	585	528	57	...	...	...	152	80	72	29	28	1	373	363	10
684	643	41	7,038	6,959	79	7,297	7,000	297	...	...	...	1,369	1,132	237	286	273	13	1,645	1,609	36
...	...	...	7,303	7,215	88	7,964	7,550	414	...	...	...	746	517	229	279	267	12	1,637	1,607	30
...	...	...	26	25	1	79	50	29	...	...	...	12	2	10	1	1	...	11	9	2
...	...	...	147	145	2	335	286	49	...	...	...	69	25	44	8	7	1	145	139	6
...	...	...	357	347	10	553	499	54	...	...	...	74	24	50	21	21	...	279	272	7
...	...	...	6,773	6,698	75	6,997	6,715	282	...	...	...	591	466	125	249	238	11	1,202	1187	15
...	...	...	1	1	...	40	28	12	...	...	...	7	5	2	6	6	...	77	75	2
...	...	...	...	...	...	1	1	...	...	...	...	...	...	...	...	...	...	...	...	...
...	...	...	...	...	...	2	2	...	...	...	...	...	...	...	...	...	...	8	8	...
...	...	...	...	...	...	6	5	1	...	...	...	...	...	...	1	1	...	14	14	...
...	...	...	1	1	...	31	20	11	...	...	...	7	5	2	5	5	...	55	53	2
...	...	...	28	27	1	213	206	7	...	...	...	937	763	174	12	8	4	108	108	...
...	...	...	...	...	...	2	1	1	...	...	...	16	8	8	...	...	...	...	...	...
...	...	...	...	...	...	7	6	1	...	...	...	75	41	34	2	1	1	6	6	...
...	...	...	1	1	...	25	23	2	...	...	...	78	56	22	3	2	1	16	16	...
...	...	...	27	26	1	179	176	3	...	...	...	768	658	110	7	5	2	86	86	...
...	...	...	...	...	...	34	34	...	...	...	...	...	...	...	26	26	...	7	7	...
...	...	...	...	...	...	3	3	...	...	...	...	...	...	...	...	...	...	...	...	...
...	...	...	...	...	...	1	1	...	...	...	...	...	...	...	1	1	...	3	3	...
...	...	...	...	...	...	1	1	...	...	...	...	...	...	...	3	3	...	1	1	...
...	...	...	...	...	...	29	29	...	...	...	...	...	...	...	22	22	...	3	3	...
...	...	...	...	...	...	5	5	...	...	...	...	...	...	...	...	...	...	1	1	...
...	...	...	...	...	...	...	...	...	...	...	...	...	...	...	...	...	...	...	...	...
...	...	...	...	...	...	...	...	...	...	...	...	...	...	...	...	...	...	...	...	...
...	...	...	...	...	...	...	...	...	...	...	...	...	...	...	...	...	...	...	...	...
...	...	...	...	...	...	5	5	...	...	...	...	...	...	...	...	...	...	1	1	...
...	...	...	...	...	...	...	...	...	...	...	...	...	...	...	...	...	...	4	2	2
...	...	...	...	...	...	...	...	...	...	...	...	...	...	...	...	...	...	...	...	...
...	...	...	...	...	...	...	...	...	...	...	...	...	...	...	...	...	...	4	2	2
794	731	63	248	245	3	56	55	1	...	...	...	3	3	...	4	4	...	330	327	3
8	5	3	...	...	...	...	...	...	...	...	...	...	...	...	...	...	...	3	2	1
43	36	7	5	5	...	...	...	...	...	...	...	...	...	...	...	...	...	19	18	1
59	47	12	6	6	...	...	...	...	...	...	...	...	...	...	1	1	...	58	58	...
684	643	41	237	234	3	56	55	1	...	...	...	3	3	...	3	3	...	250	249	1
...	...	...	...	...	...	...	...	...	...	...	...	...	...	...	...	...	...	53	32	21
...	...	...	...	...	...	...	...	...	...	...	...	...	...	...	...	...	...	2	2	...
...	...	...	...	...	...	...	...	...	...	...	...	...	...	...	...	...	...	2	...	2
...	...	...	...	...	...	...	...	...	...	...	...	...	...	...	...	...	...	5	2	3
...	...	...	...	...	...	...	...	...	...	...	...	...	...	...	...	...	...	44	28	16
						(iii) **KASHMIR PROVINCE.**														
1,242	1,202	40	116	111	5	2,302	2,267	35	...	...	...	1,080	1,005	75	4	4	...	3,707	3,613	94
14	13	1	...	...	...	26	21	5	...	...	...	23	19	4	...	...	...	81	76	5
66	64	2	6	5	1	136	128	8	...	...	...	58	54	4	...	...	...	550	547	3
97	92	5	6	6	...	181	178	3	...	...	...	107	95	12	...	...	...	833	828	5
1,065	1,033	32	104	100	4	1,959	1,940	19	...	...	...	892	837	55	4	4	...	2,243	2,162	81

VIII
Education.

TABLE VIII.

Education by Religion and Age.

Jammu and Kashmir State Census 1911.

Part I—Provincial Tables.

AGE.	POPULATION.									LITERATE IN					
	Total.			Literate.			Illiterate.			Urdu.			Persian.		
	Persons.	Males.	Females.	Persons.	Males.	Females.	Persons.	Males.	Females.	Persons.	Males.	Females.	Persons.	Males.	Females.
1	2	3	4	5	6	7	8	9	10	11	12	13	14	15	16
Hindu (Brahmanic).	62,368	35,056	27,312	15,989	15,887	102	46,379	19,169	27,210	5,587	5,563	24	4,784	4,770	14
0—10 ...	15,748	8,018	7,730	267	262	5	15,481	7,756	7,725	155	154	1	18	18	...
10—15 ...	6,469	3,736	2,733	1,404	1,387	17	5,065	2,349	2,716	663	658	5	109	108	1
15—20 ...	5,324	3,178	2,146	1,664	1,652	12	3,660	1,526	2,134	541	538	3	194	193	1
20 and over...	34,827	20,124	14,703	12,654	12,586	68	22,173	7,538	14,635	4,228	4,213	15	4,463	4,451	12
Hindu (Arya).	45	27	18	21	15	6	24	12	12	1	1	...	...	...	...
0—10 ...	18	10	8	1	...	1	17	10	7	...	...	...	...	...	...
10—15 ...	6	5	1	4	4	...	2	1	1	...	...	...	...	...	...
15—20 ...	3	2	1	3	2	1	...	...	...	...	...	...	...	...	...
20 and over...	18	10	8	13	9	4	5	1	4	1	1	...	...	...	...
Hindu (Bramho).	1	...	1	1	...	1	...	...	...	...	...	...	...	...	...
20 and over ...	1	...	1	1	...	1	...	...	...	...	...	...	...	...	...
Sikh.	14,772	7,871	6,901	1,187	1,135	52	13,585	6,736	6,849	196	195	1	6	6	...
0—10 ...	4,962	2,557	2,405	28	24	4	4,934	2,533	2,401	5	5	...	...	...	...
10—15 ...	1,648	912	736	88	85	3	1,560	827	733	18	18	...	...	...	...
15—20 ...	1,369	732	637	133	126	7	1,236	606	630	33	33	...	1	1	...
20 and over...	6,793	3,670	3,123	938	900	38	5,855	2,770	3,085	140	139	1	5	5	...
Budhist.	3	3	...	...	...	...	3	3	...	...	...	...	...	...	...
15—20 ...	1	1	...	...	...	...	1	1	...	...	...	...	...	...	...
20 and over ...	2	2	...	...	...	...	2	2	...	...	...	...	...	...	...
Zoroastrian.	26	20	6	18	14	4	8	6	2	...	...	...	...	...	...
0—10 ...	9	8	1	3	3	...	6	5	1	...	...	...	...	...	...
10—15 ...	1	1	...	1	1	...	...	...	...	...	...	...	...	...	...
15—20 ...	2	1	1	2	1	1	...	...	...	...	...	...	...	...	...
20 and over ...	14	10	4	12	9	3	2	1	1	...	...	...	...	...	...
Musalman.	1,217,768	648,685	569,083	9,716	9,647	69	1,208,052	639,038	569,014	3,103	3,094	9	4,974	4,954	20
0—10 ...	389,481	200,304	189,177	56	55	1	389,425	200,249	189,176	21	21	...	18	18	...
10—15 ...	140,001	77,106	62,895	527	521	6	139,474	76,585	62,889	254	253	1	167	164	3
15—20 ...	111,423	59,512	51,911	888	882	6	110,535	58,630	51,905	353	353	...	347	346	1
20 and over ...	576,863	311,763	26,510	8,245	8,189	56	568,628	303,574	265,044	2,475	2,467	8	4,442	4,426	16
Christian.	218	118	100	174	90	84	44	28	16	3	3	...	...	...	...
0—10 ...	32	19	13	6	1	5	26	18	8	...	...	...	...	...	...
10—15 ...	7	5	2	4	2	2	3	3	...	1	1	...	...	...	...
15—20 ...	5	...	5	4	...	4	1	...	1	...	...	...	...	...	...
20 and over...	174	94	80	160	87	73	14	7	7	2	2	...	...	...	...
							***(iv)* KASHMIR VALLEY.**								
All Religions.	1,099,996	587,472	512,524	24,272	24,040	232	1,075,724	563,432	512,292	7,670	7,646	24	9,296	9,265	31
0—10 ...	345,662	177,292	168,370	328	315	13	345,334	176,977	168,357	164	163	1	35	35	...
10—15 ...	125,874	69,211	56,663	1,840	1,819	21	124,034	67,392	56,642	824	820	4	261	257	4
15—20 ...	99,945	54,101	45,844	2,451	2,426	25	97,494	51,675	45,819	812	809	3	527	525	2
20 and over ...	528,515	286,868	241,647	19,653	19,480	173	508,862	267,388	241,474	5,870	5,854	16	8,473	8,448	25
Hindu (Brahmanic).	57,671	32,233	25,438	14,898	14,834	64	42,773	17,399	25,374	5,195	5,178	17	4,673	4,659	14
0—10 ...	14,484	7,348	7,136	254	249	5	14,230	7,099	7,131	143	142	1	18	18	...
10—15 ...	5,958	3,434	2,524	1,343	1,332	11	4,615	2,102	2,513	622	619	3	109	108	1
15—20 ...	4,919	2,961	1,958	1,584	1,574	10	3,335	1,387	1,948	523	520	3	194	193	1
20 and over...	32,310	18,490	13,820	11.717	11,679	38	20,593	6,811	13,782	3,907	3.897	10	4,352	4,340	12

TABLE VIII.

EDUCATION BY RELIGION AND AGE.

Jammu and Kashmir State Census 1911.

Part I—Provincial Tables.

LITERATE IN

ARABIC.			DOGRI.			HINDI.			BODHI.			GURMUKHI.			OTHERS.			ENGLISH.		
Persons.	Males.	Females.	Persons.	Males.	Females.	Persons.	Males.	Females.	Persons.	Males.	Females.	Persons.	Males.	Females.	Persons.	Males.	Females.	Persons.	Males.	Females.
17	18	19	20	21	22	23	24	25	26	27	28	29	30	31	32	33	34	35	36	37
...	...	...	103	101	2	2,273	2,243	30	...	...	...	172	145	27	3	3	...	3,067	3,062	5
...	...	...	...	...	...	25	21	4	...	...	...	...	...	...	...	...	...	69	69	...
...	...	...	4	4	...	136	128	8	...	...	...	4	2	2	...	...	...	488	487	1
...	...	...	6	6	...	181	178	3	...	...	...	13	8	5	...	...	...	729	729	...
...	...	...	93	91	2	1,931	1,916	15	...	...	...	155	135	20	3	3	...	1,781	1,777	4
...	...	...	...	...	...	5	...	5	...	...	...	...	...	...	...	...	...	14	14	...
...	...	...	...	...	...	1	...	1	...	...	...	...	...	...	...	...	...	...	...	...
...	...	...	...	...	...	...	...	...	...	...	...	...	...	...	...	...	...	4	4	...
...	...	...	...	...	...	...	...	...	...	...	...	...	...	...	...	...	...	2	2	...
...	...	...	...	...	...	4	...	4	...	...	...	...	...	...	...	...	...	8	8	...
...	...	...	...	...	...	...	...	...	...	...	...	...	...	...	...	...	...	1	...	1
...	...	...	...	...	...	...	...	...	...	...	...	...	...	...	...	...	...	1	...	1
...	...	...	9	6	3	20	20	...	...	...	...	898	850	48	...	...	...	58	58	...
...	...	...	...	...	...	...	...	...	...	...	...	23	19	4	...	...	...	...	...	...
...	...	...	2	1	1	...	...	...	...	...	...	54	52	2	...	...	...	14	14	...
...	...	...	...	...	...	...	...	...	...	...	...	94	87	7	...	...	...	5	5	...
...	...	...	7	5	2	20	20	...	...	...	...	727	692	35	...	...	...	39	39	...
...	...	...	...	...	...	...	...	...	...	...	...	...	...	...	...	...	...	...	...	...
...	...	...	...	...	...	...	...	...	...	...	...	...	...	...	...	...	...	...	...	...
...	...	...	...	...	...	...	...	...	...	...	...	...	...	...	...	...	...	...	...	...
...	...	...	...	...	...	...	...	...	...	...	...	...	...	...	...	...	...	18	14	4
...	...	...	...	...	...	...	...	...	...	...	...	...	...	...	...	...	...	3	3	...
...	...	...	...	...	...	...	...	...	...	...	...	...	...	...	...	...	...	1	1	...
...	...	...	...	...	...	...	...	...	...	...	...	...	...	...	...	...	...	2	1	1
...	...	...	...	...	...	...	...	...	...	...	...	...	...	...	...	...	...	12	9	3
1,242	1,202	40	4	4	...	4	4	...	...	...	...	10	10	...	1	1	...	378	378	...
14	13	1	...	...	...	...	...	...	...	...	...	...	...	...	...	...	...	3	3	...
66	64	2	...	...	...	...	...	...	...	...	...	...	...	...	...	...	...	40	40	...
97	92	5	...	...	...	...	...	...	...	...	...	...	...	...	...	...	...	91	91	...
1,065	1,033	32	4	4	...	4	4	...	...	...	...	10	10	...	1	1	...	244	244	...
...	...	...	...	...	...	...	...	...	...	...	...	...	...	...	...	...	...	171	87	84
...	...	...	...	...	...	...	...	...	...	...	...	...	...	...	...	...	...	6	1	5
...	...	...	...	...	...	...	...	...	...	...	...	...	...	...	...	...	...	3	1	2
...	...	...	...	...	...	...	...	...	...	...	...	...	...	...	...	...	...	4	...	4
...	...	...	...	...	...	...	...	...	...	...	...	...	...	...	...	...	...	158	85	73
							(iv) KASHMIR VALLEY.													
1,089	1,060	29	108	103	5	1,908	1,884	24	...	...	...	632	603	29	4	4	...	3,565	3,475	90
14	13	1	...	...	...	25	20	5	...	...	...	9	8	1	...	...	...	81	76	5
56	54	2	5	4	1	122	116	6	...	...	...	25	24	1	...	...	...	547	544	3
86	81	5	6	6	...	133	130	[illegible]	...	...	...	63	56	7	...	...	...	824	819	5
933	912	21	97	93	4	1,628	1,618	10	...	...	...	535	515	20	4	4	...	2,113	2,036	77
...	...	...	97	95	2	1,891	1,872	19	...	...	...	71	64	7	3	3	...	2,968	2,963	5
...	...	...	...	...	...	24	20	4	...	...	...	...	...	...	...	...	...	69	69	...
...	...	...	3	3	...	122	116	6	...	...	...	...	...	...	...	...	...	487	486	1
...	...	...	6	6	...	133	130	3	...	...	...	8	5	3	...	...	...	720	720	...
...	...	...	88	86	2	1,612	1,606	6	...	...	...	63	59	4	3	3	...	1,692	1,688	4

VIII
Education.

TABLE VIII.

Education by Religion and Age.

Jammu and Kashmir State Census 1911.

Part I—Provincial Tables.

AGE.	POPULATION.									LITERATE IN					
	Total.			Literate.			Illiterate.			Urdu.			Persian.		
	Persons.	Males.	Females.	Persons.	Males.	Females.	Persons.	Males.	Females.	Persons.	Males.	Females.	Persons.	Males.	Females.
1	2	3	4	5	6	7	8	9	10	11	12	13	14	15	16
Hindu (Arya).	45	27	18	20	15	5	25	12	13	1	1	...	...	...	...
0—10 ...	18	10	8	1	...	1	17	10	7	...	...	...	...	...	...
10—15 ...	6	5	1	4	4	...	2	1	1	...	...	...	...	...	...
15—20 ...	3	2	1	2	2	...	1	...	1	...	...	...	...	...	...
20 and over ...	18	10	8	13	9	4	5	1	4	1	1	...	...	...	...
Hindu (Bramho).	1	...	1	1	...	1	...	...	...	...	...	...	...	...	...
20 and over...	1	...	1	1	...	1	...	...	...	...	...	...	...	...	...
Sikh.	7,161	3,831	3,330	689	663	26	6,472	3,168	3,304	61	60	1	5	5	...
0—10 ...	2,360	1,210	1,150	11	10	1	2,349	1,200	1,149	2	2	...	...	...	...
10—15 ...	783	434	349	45	43	2	738	391	347	5	5	...	...	...	...
15—20 ...	669	359	310	65	61	4	604	298	306	5	5	...	...	...	...
20 and over...	3,349	1,828	1,521	568	549	19	2,781	1,279	1,502	49	48	1	5	5	...
Budhist.	2	2	...	...	...	...	2	2	...	...	...	...	...	...	...
20 and over...	2	2	...	...	...	...	2	2	...	...	...	...	...	...	...
Zoroastrian.	26	20	6	18	14	4	8	6	2	...	...	...	...	...	...
0—10 ...	9	8	1	3	3	...	6	5	1	...	...	...	...	...	...
15—20 ...	3	2	1	3	2	1	...	...	...	...	...	...	...	...	...
20 and over...	14	10	4	12	9	3	2	1	1	...	...	...	...	...	...
Musalman.	1,034,889	551,254	483,635	8,487	8,435	52	1,026,402	542,819	483,583	2,410	2,404	6	4,618	4,601	17
0—10 ...	328,761	168,699	160,062	53	52	1	328,708	168,647	160,061	19	19	...	17	17	...
10—15 ...	119,120	65,333	53,787	444	438	6	118,676	64,895	53,781	196	195	1	152	149	3
15—20 ...	94,346	50,777	43,569	793	787	6	93,553	49,990	43,563	284	284	...	333	332	1
20 and over...	492,662	266,445	226,217	7,197	7,158	39	485,465	259,287	226,178	1,911	1,906	5	4,116	4,103	13
Christian.	201	105	96	159	79	80	42	26	16	3	3	...	...	...	...
0—10 ...	30	17	13	6	1	5	24	16	8	...	...	...	...	...	...
10—15 ...	7	5	2	4	2	2	3	3	...	1	1	...	...	...	...
15—20 ...	5	...	5	4	...	4	1	...	1	...	...	...	...	...	...
20 ond over...	159	83	76	145	76	69	14	7	7	2	2	...	...	...	...
(v) FRONTIER DISTRICTS.															
All Religions.	210,435	106,408	104,027	3,210	3,141	69	207,225	103,267	103,958	810	809	1	529	529	...
0—10 ...	61,072	30,624	30,448	8	7	1	61,064	30,617	30,447	4	4	...	1	1	...
10—15 ...	20,377	10,911	9,466	70	64	6	20,307	10,847	9,460	27	27	...	4	4	...
15—20 ...	18,183	9,748	8,435	235	233	2	17,948	9,515	8,433	86	86	...	36	36	...
20 and over...	110,803	55,125	55,678	2,897	2,837	60	107,906	52,288	55,618	693	692	1	488	488	...
Hindu (Brahmanic).	1,223	1,128	95	615	609	6	608	519	89	250	250	...	18	18	...
0—10 ...	74	39	35	2	2	...	72	37	35	1	1	...	...	...	...
10—15 ...	26	18	8	12	10	2	14	8	6	6	6	...	...	...	...
15—20 ...	60	52	8	17	17	...	43	35	8	9	9	...	...	...	...
20 and over...	1,063	1,019	44	584	580	4	479	439	40	234	234	...	18	18	...
Hindu (Arya).	18	11	7	11	9	2	7	2	5	8	7	1	...	...	...
0—10 ...	3	1	2	...	...	...	3	1	2	...	...	...	...	...	...
20 and over...	15	10	5	11	9	2	4	1	3	8	7	1	...	...	...
Sikh.	98	74	24	58	51	7	40	23	17	18	18	...	...	...	...
0—10 ...	14	6	8	1	...	1	13	6	7	...	...	...	...	...	...
10—15 ...	5	1	4	2	...	2	3	1	2	...	...	...	...	...	...
15—20 ...	13	10	3	9	8	1	4	2	2	6	6	...	...	...	...
20 and over...	66	57	9	46	43	3	20	14	6	12	12	...	...	...	...

TABLE VIII.

Education by Religion and Age.

Jammu and Kashmir State Census 1911.

Part I—Provincial Tables.

LITERATE IN

Arabic.			Dogri.			Hindi.			Bodhi.			Gurmukhi.			Others.			English.		
Persons.	Males.	Females.	Persons.	Males.	Females.	Persons.	Males.	Females.	Persons.	Males.	Females.	Persons.	Males.	Females.	Persons.	Males.	Females.	Persons.	Males.	Females.
17	18	19	20	21	22	23	24	25	26	27	28	29	30	31	32	33	34	35	36	37
...	...	...	...	...	...	5	...	5	...	...	...	...	...	...	...	...	...	14	14	...
...	...	...	...	...	...	1	...	1	...	...	...	...	...	...	...	...	...	...	...	...
...	...	...	...	...	...	...	...	...	...	...	...	...	...	...	...	...	...	4	4	...
...	...	...	...	...	...	...	...	...	...	...	...	...	...	...	...	...	...	2	2	...
...	...	...	...	...	...	4	...	4	...	...	...	...	...	...	...	...	...	8	8	...
...	...	...	...	...	...	...	...	...	...	...	...	...	...	...	...	...	...	1	...	1
...	...	...	...	...	...	...	...	...	...	...	...	...	...	...	...	...	...	1	...	1
...	...	...	8	5	3	11	11	...	...	...	...	555	533	22	...	...	...	49	49	...
...	...	...	...	...	...	...	...	...	...	...	...	9	8	1	...	...	...	...	...	...
...	...	...	2	1	1	...	...	...	...	...	...	25	24	1	...	...	...	13	13	...
...	...	...	...	...	...	...	...	...	...	...	...	55	51	4	...	...	...	5	5	...
...	...	...	6	4	2	11	11	...	...	...	...	466	450	16	...	...	...	31	31	...
...	...	...	...	...	...	...	...	...	...	...	...	...	...	...	...	...	...	...	...	...
...	...	...	...	...	...	...	...	...	...	...	...	...	...	...	...	...	...	...	...	...
...	...	...	...	...	...	...	...	...	...	...	...	...	...	...	...	...	...	18	14	4
...	...	...	...	...	...	...	...	...	...	...	...	...	...	...	...	...	...	3	3	...
...	...	...	...	...	...	...	...	...	...	...	...	...	...	...	...	...	...	3	2	1
...	...	...	...	...	...	...	...	...	...	...	...	...	...	...	...	...	...	12	9	3
1,089	1,060	29	3	3	...	1	1	...	...	...	...	6	6	...	1	1	...	359	359	...
14	13	1	...	...	...	...	...	...	...	...	...	...	...	...	...	...	...	3	3	...
56	54	2	...	...	...	...	...	...	...	...	...	...	...	...	...	...	...	40	40	...
86	81	5	...	...	...	...	...	...	...	...	...	...	...	...	...	...	...	90	90	...
933	912	21	3	3	...	1	1	...	...	...	...	6	6	...	1	1	...	226	226	...
...	...	...	...	...	...	...	...	...	...	...	...	...	...	...	...	...	...	156	76	80
...	...	...	...	...	...	...	...	...	...	...	...	...	...	...	...	...	...	6	1	5
...	...	...	...	...	...	...	...	...	...	...	...	...	...	...	...	...	...	3	1	2
...	...	...	...	...	...	...	...	...	...	...	...	...	...	...	...	...	...	4	...	4
...	...	...	...	...	...	...	...	...	...	...	...	...	...	...	...	...	...	143	74	69
(v) FRONTIER DISTRICTS.																				
30	30	...	45	45	...	183	179	4	1,368	1,323	45	34	24	10	3	2	1	208	200	8
...	...	...	...	...	...	...	...	...	...	...	...	1	...	1	...	...	...	2	2	...
...	...	...	...	...	...	1	...	1	31	29	2	3	...	3	...	...	...	4	4	...
2	2	...	...	...	...	6	6	...	96	95	1	4	3	1	...	...	...	5	5	...
28	28	...	45	45	...	176	173	3	1,241	1,199	42	26	21	5	3	2	1	197	189	8
...	...	...	42	42	...	183	179	4	...	...	...	6	4	2	2	2	...	114	114	...
...	...	...	...	...	...	...	...	...	...	...	...	...	...	...	...	...	...	1	1	...
...	...	...	...	...	...	1	...	1	...	...	...	1	...	1	...	...	...	4	4	...
...	...	...	...	...	...	6	6	...	...	...	...	1	1	...	...	...	...	1	1	...
...	...	...	42	42	...	176	173	3	...	...	...	4	3	1	2	2	...	108	108	...
...	...	...	...	...	...	...	...	...	...	...	...	1	...	1	...	...	...	2	2	...
...	...	...	...	...	...	...	...	...	...	...	...	...	...	...	...	...	...	...	...	...
...	...	...	...	...	...	...	...	...	...	...	...	1	...	1	...	...	...	2	2	...
...	...	...	1	1	...	...	...	...	...	...	...	26	19	7	...	...	...	13	13	...
...	...	...	...	...	...	...	...	...	...	...	...	1	...	1	...	...	...	...	...	...
...	...	...	...	...	...	...	...	...	...	...	...	2	...	2	...	...	...	...	...	...
...	...	...	...	...	...	...	...	...	...	...	...	3	2	1	...	...	...	...	...	...
...	...	...	1	1	...	...	...	...	...	...	...	20	17	3	...	...	...	13	13	...

TABLE VIII.

Education by Religion and Age.

Jammu and Kashmir State Census 1911.

Part I—Provincial Tables.

AGE.	POPULATION.									LITERATE IN					
	Total.			Literate.			Illiterate.			Urdu.			Persian.		
	Persons.	Males.	Females.	Persons.	Males.	Females.	Persons.	Males.	Females.	Persons.	Males.	Females.	Persons.	Males.	Females.
1	2	3	4	5	6	7	8	9	10	11	12	13	14	15	16
Budhist.	35,867	17,956	17,911	1,316	1,277	39	34,551	16,679	17,872	6	6	...	1	1	...
0—10 ...	7,393	3,602	3,791	...	...	...	7,393	3,602	3,791	...	...	...	...	...	...
10—15 ...	3,186	1,615	1,571	28	27	1	3,158	1,588	1,570	...	...	...	...	...	...
15—20 ...	3,090	1,548	1,542	94	93	1	2,996	1,455	1,541	1	1	...	...	...	...
20 and over ...	22,198	11,191	11,007	1,194	1,157	37	21,004	10,034	10,970	5	5	...	1	1	...
Musalman.	173,145	87,190	85,955	1,163	1,163	...	171,982	86,027	85,955	526	526	...	510	510	...
0—10 ...	53,571	26,968	26,603	5	5	...	53,566	26,963	26,603	3	3	...	1	1	...
10—15 ...	17,154	9,272	7,882	25	25	...	17,129	9,247	7,882	21	21	...	4	4	...
15—20 ...	15,011	8,131	6,880	111	111	...	14,900	8,020	6,880	69	69	...	36	36	...
20 and over ...	87,409	42,819	44,590	1,022	1,022	...	86,338	41,797	44,590	433	433	...	469	469	...
Christian.	84	49	35	47	32	15	37	17	20	2	2	...	...	...	...
0—10 ...	17	8	9	...	...	...	17	8	9	...	...	...	...	...	...
10—15 ...	6	5	1	3	2	1	3	3	...	...	...	...	...	...	...
15—20 ...	9	7	2	4	4	...	5	3	2	1	1	...	...	...	...
20 and over ...	52	29	23	40	26	14	12	3	9	1	1	...	...	...	...

TABLE VIII.

Education by Religion and Age.

Jammu and Kashmir State Census 1911.

Part I—Provincial Tables.

LITERATE IN

Arabic.			Dogri.			Hindi.			Bodhi.			Gurmukhi.			Others.			English.		
Persons.	Males.	Females.	Persons.	Males.	Females.	Persons.	Males.	Females.	Persons.	Males.	Females.	Persons.	Males.	Females.	Persons.	Males.	Females.	Persons.	Males.	Females.
17	18	19	20	21	22	23	24	25	26	27	28	29	30	31	32	33	34	35	36	37
...	...	...	...	...	...	...	...	...	1,309	1,270	39	...	...	...	...	...	...	...	...	...
...	...	...	...	...	...	...	...	...	...	...	...	...	...	...	...	...	...	...	...	...
...	...	...	...	...	...	...	...	...	28	27	1	...	...	...	...	...	...	...	...	...
...	...	...	...	...	...	...	...	...	93	92	1	...	...	...	...	...	...	...	...	...
...	...	...	...	...	...	...	...	...	1,188	1,151	37	...	...	...	...	...	...	...	...	...
30	30	...	2	2	...	...	...	...	42	42	...	1	1	...	...	...	...	52	52	...
...	...	...	...	...	...	...	...	...	...	...	...	...	...	...	...	...	...	1	1	...
...	...	...	...	...	...	...	...	...	...	...	...	...	...	...	...	...	...	...	...	...
2	2	...	...	...	...	...	...	...	...	...	...	...	...	...	...	...	...	4	4	...
28	28	...	2	2	...	...	...	...	42	42	...	1	1	...	...	...	...	47	47	...
...	...	...	...	...	...	...	...	...	17	11	6	...	...	...	...	...	...	27	19	8
...	...	...	...	...	...	...	...	...	...	...	...	...	...	...	...	...	...	...	...	...
...	...	...	...	...	...	...	...	...	3	2	1	...	...	...	...	...	...	...	...	...
...	...	...	...	...	...	...	...	...	3	3	...	...	...	...	...	...	...	...	...	...
...	...	...	...	...	...	...	...	...	11	6	5	...	...	...	...	...	...	27	19	8

TABLE VIII.

EDUCATION BY RELIGION AND AGE.

Jammu and Kashmir State Census 1911.

Part II—District Tables.

AGE.	POPULATION.									LITERATE IN					
	TOTAL.			LITERATE.			ILLITERATE.			URDU.			PERSIAN.		
	Persons.	Males.	Females.	Persons.	Males.	Females.	Persons.	Males.	Females.	Persons.	Males.	Females.	Persons.	Males.	Females.
1	2	3	4	5	6	7	8	9	10	11	12	13	14	15	16
(1) JAMMU DISTRICT.															
All Religions.	326,691	180,691	146,000	12,817	12.137	680	313,874	168,554	145,320	4,527	4,410	117	399	389	10
0—10 ...	85,486	44,280	41,206	224	188	36	85,262	44,092	41,170	139	136	3	11	11	...
10—15 ...	36,637	21,868	15,269	1,038	930	108	35,599	20,438	15,161	564	542	22	38	38	...
15—20 ...	27,373	15,332	12,041	1,364	1.245	119	26,009	14,087	11,922	598	575	23	50	49	1
20 and over ...	177,195	99,711	77,484	10,191	9,774	417	67,004	89,937	77,067	3,226	3,157	69	300	291	9
Hindu (Brahmanic).	195,470	108,196	87,274	10,297	9,765	532	185,173	98,431	86,742	3,000	2,943	57	259	252	7
0—10 ...	47,525	24.629	22,896	167	137	30	47,358	24,492	22,866	97	95	2	8	8	...
10—15 ...	21,172	12,640	8,532	821	731	90	20,351	11,909	8,442	409	394	15	32	32	...
15—20 ...	16,569	9,308	7,261	1,057	968	89	15,512	8,340	7,172	429	420	9	28	28	...
20 and over...	110,204	61,619	48,585	8,252	7,929	323	101,952	53,690	48,262	2,065	2,034	31	191	184	7
Hindu (Arya).	604	310	294	95	84	11	509	226	283	36	34	2	...	...	...
0—10 ...	124	73	51	3	3	...	121	70	51	3	3	...	...	...	...
10—15 ...	64	35	29	9	9	...	55	26	29	6	6	...	...	...	...
15—20 ...	64	33	31	15	13	2	49	20	29	2	1	1	...	...	...
20 and over ...	352	169	183	68	59	9	284	110	174	25	24	1	...	...	...
Sikh.	3,156	1,722	1,434	374	321	53	2,782	1,401	1,381	108	101	7	3	2	1
0—10 ...	897	453	344	11	7	4	886	446	440	6	6	...	...	...	...
10—15 ...	364	212	152	34	27	7	330	185	145	16	15	1	...	...	...
15—20 ...	265	153	112	57	46	11	208	107	101	11	9	2	2	1	1
20 and over ...	1,630	904	726	272	241	31	1,358	663	695	75	71	4	1	1	...
Jain.	334	181	153	74	74	...	260	107	153	8	8	...	...	...	...
0—10 ...	93	41	52	3	3	...	90	38	52	...	...	...	...	...	...
10—15 ...	42	24	18	8	8	...	34	16	18	3	3	...	...	...	...
15—20 ...	28	13	15	7	7	...	21	6	15	2	2	...	...	...	...
20 and over ...	171	103	68	56	56	...	115	47	68	3	3	...	...	...	...
Zoroastrian.	5	2	3	4	2	2	1	...	1	...	...	...	...	...	...
0—10 ...	1	...	1	...	...	...	1	...	1	...	...	...	...	...	...
20 and over...	4	2	2	4	2	2	...	...	...	...	...	...	...	...	...
Musalman.	126,659	69,976	56,683	1,943	1,871	72	124,716	68,105	56,611	1,368	1,319	49	137	135	2
0—10 ...	36,681	19,003	17,678	40	38	2	36,641	18,965	17,676	33	32	1	3	3	...
10—15 ...	14,940	8,420	6,520	165	154	11	14,775	8,266	6,509	129	123	6	6	6	...
15—20 ...	10,421	5,803	4,618	223	210	13	10,198	5,593	4,605	153	143	10	20	20	...
20 and over...	64,617	36,750	27,867	1,515	1,469	46	63,102	35,281	27,821	1,053	1,021	32	108	106	2
Christian.	463	304	159	30	20	10	433	284	149	7	5	2	...	...	...
0—10 ...	165	81	84	...	...	...	165	81	84	...	...	...	...	...	...
10—15 ...	55	37	18	5	1	4	50	36	14	2	1	1	...	...	...
15—20 ...	26	22	4	1	1	...	25	21	4	...	...	...	...	...	...
20 and over...	217	164	53	24	18	6	193	146	47	5	4	1	...	...	...
(2) JASROTA DISTRICT.															
All Religions.	151,802	81,375	70,427	3,840	3,764	76	147,962	77,611	70,351	902	894	8	25	25	...
0—10 ...	39,622	20,287	19,335	52	51	1	39,570	20,236	19,334	32	31	1	1	1	...
10—15 ...	16,734	9,334	7,400	261	257	4	16,473	9,077	7,396	139	138	1	2	2	...
15—20 ...	13,563	7,049	6,514	326	318	8	13,237	6,731	6,506	126	124	2	...	...	...
20 and over ...	81,883	44,705	37,178	3,201	3,138	63	78,682	41,567	37,115	605	601	4	22	22	...
Hindu (Brahmanic).	116,267	61,994	54,273	3,503	3,439	64	112,764	58,555	54,209	689	686	3	14	14	...
0—10 ...	28,876	14,786	14,090	44	44	...	28,832	14,742	14,090	24	24	...	1	1	...
10—15 ...	12,351	7,030	5,321	223	220	3	12,128	6,810	5,318	114	114	...	...	...	...
15—20 ...	10,309	5,281	5,028	296	290	6	10,013	4,991	5,022	104	103	1	...	...	...
20 and over...	64,731	34,897	29,834	2,940	2,885	55	61,791	32,012	29,779	447	445	2	13	13	...

TABLE VIII.

Education by Religion and Age.

Jammu and Kashmir State Census 1911.

Part II—District Tables.

LITERATE IN																				
Arabic.			Dogri.			Hindi.			Bodhi.			Gurmukhi.			Others.			English.		
Persons.	Males.	Females.	Persons.	Males.	Females.	Persons.	Males.	Females.	Persons.	Males.	Females.	Persons.	Males.	Females.	Persons.	Males.	Females.	Persons.	Males.	Females.
17	18	19	20	21	22	23	24	25	26	27	28	29	30	31	32	33	34	35	36	37
(1) JAMMU DISTRICT.																				
181	164	17	2,289	2,251	38	3,444	3,161	283	...	...	...	451	285	166	40	33	7	1,486	1,444	42
2	2	...	6	6	...	42	24	18	...	...	...	14	2	12	...	...	...	10	7	3
18	14	4	54	54	...	166	132	34	...	...	...	60	21	39	3	1	2	138	128	10
15	12	3	110	105	5	263	225	38	...	...	...	58	19	39	5	4	1	262	256	6
146	136	10	2,119	2,086	33	2,973	2,780	193	...	...	...	319	243	76	32	28	4	1,076	1,053	23
...	...	...	2,220	2,184	36	3,349	3,076	273	...	...	...	299	171	128	10	7	3	1,160	1,132	28
...	...	...	6	6	...	39	21	18	...	...	...	9	1	8	...	...	...	8	6	2
...	...	...	53	53	...	164	130	34	...	...	...	50	16	34	1	...	1	112	106	6
...	...	...	106	101	5	247	210	37	...	...	...	41	9	32	1	1	...	205	199	6
...	...	...	2,055	2,024	31	2,899	2,715	184	...	...	...	199	145	54	8	6	2	835	821	14
...	...	...	...	...	...	10	2	8	...	...	...	3	3	...	...	...	...	46	45	1
...	...	...	...	...	...	...	...	...	...	...	...	...	...	...	...	...	...	...	...	...
...	...	...	...	...	...	...	...	...	...	...	...	...	...	...	...	...	...	3	3	...
...	...	...	...	...	...	2	1	1	...	...	...	...	...	...	...	...	...	11	11	...
...	...	...	...	...	...	8	1	7	...	...	...	3	3	...	...	...	...	32	31	1
...	...	...	18	17	1	27	25	2	...	...	...	148	110	38	4	...	4	66	66	...
...	...	...	...	...	...	...	...	...	...	...	...	5	1	4	...	...	...	...	...	...
...	...	...	...	...	...	1	1	...	...	...	...	10	5	5	1	...	1	6	6	...
...	...	...	1	1	...	13	13	...	...	...	...	17	10	7	1	...	1	12	12	...
...	...	...	17	16	1	13	11	2	...	...	...	116	94	22	2	...	2	48	48	...
...	...	...	...	...	...	34	34	...	...	...	...	...	...	...	26	26	...	6	6	...
...	...	...	...	...	...	3	3	...	...	...	...	...	...	...	...	...	...	...	...	...
...	...	...	...	...	...	1	1	...	...	...	...	...	...	...	1	1	...	3	3	...
...	...	...	...	...	...	1	1	...	...	...	...	...	...	...	3	3	...	1	1	...
...	...	...	...	...	...	29	29	...	...	...	...	...	...	...	22	22	...	2	2	...
...	...	...	...	...	...	...	...	...	...	...	...	...	...	...	...	...	...	4	2	2
...	...	...	...	...	...	...	...	...	...	...	...	...	...	...	...	...	...	...	...	...
...	...	...	...	...	...	...	...	...	...	...	...	...	...	...	...	...	...	4	2	2
181	164	17	51	50	1	24	24	...	...	...	...	1	1	...	...	...	...	181	178	3
2	2	...	...	...	...	...	...	...	...	...	...	...	...	...	...	...	...	2	1	1
18	14	4	1	1	...	...	...	...	...	...	...	...	...	...	...	...	...	11	10	1
15	12	3	3	3	...	...	...	...	...	...	...	...	...	...	...	...	...	32	32	...
146	136	10	47	46	1	24	24	...	...	...	...	1	1	...	...	...	...	136	135	1
...	...	...	...	...	...	...	...	...	...	...	...	...	...	...	...	...	...	23	15	8
...	...	...	...	...	...	...	...	...	...	...	...	...	...	...	...	...	...	...	...	...
...	...	...	...	...	...	...	...	...	...	...	...	...	...	...	...	...	...	3	...	3
...	...	...	...	...	...	...	...	...	...	...	...	...	...	...	...	...	...	1	1	...
...	...	...	...	...	...	...	...	...	...	...	...	...	...	...	...	...	...	19	14	5
(2) JASROTA DISTRICT.																				
43	41	2	1,046	1,031	15	1,637	1,597	40	...	...	...	82	71	11	...	...	...	101	101	...
...	...	...	7	7	...	11	11	...	...	...	...	1	1	...	...	...	...	...	...	...
6	6	...	26	26	...	74	73	1	...	...	...	4	2	2	...	...	...	10	10	...
2	1	1	70	69	1	115	112	3	...	...	...	3	2	1	...	...	...	10	10	...
35	34	1	943	929	14	1,437	1,401	36	...	...	...	74	66	8	...	...	...	81	81	...
...	...	...	1,032	1,018	14	1,620	1,582	38	...	...	...	70	61	9	4	4	...	74	74	...
...	...	...	7	7	...	11	11	...	...	...	...	1	1	...	...	...	...	...	...	...
...	...	...	26	26	...	73	72	1	...	...	...	4	2	2	...	...	...	6	6	...
...	...	...	70	69	1	115	112	3	...	...	...	3	2	1	...	...	...	4	4	...
...	...	...	929	916	13	1,421	1,387	34	...	...	...	62	56	6	4	4	...	64	64	...

VIII
Education.

TABLE VIII.

Education by Religion and Age.

Jammu and Kashmir State Census 1911.

Part II—District Tables.

AGE.	POPULATION.									LITERATE IN					
	Total.			Literate.			Illiterate.			Urdu.			Persian.		
	Persons.	Males.	Females.	Persons.	Males.	Females.	Persons.	Males.	Females.	Persons.	Males.	Females.	Persons.	Males.	Females.
1	2	3	4	5	6	7	8	9	10	11	12	13	14	15	16
Hindu (Arya).	72	45	27	14	12	2	58	33	25	...	...	...	...	...	...
0—10 ...	11	5	6	...	...	...	11	5	6	...	...	...	...	...	...
10—15 ...	7	5	2	1	1	...	6	4	4	...	...	...	...	...	...
15—20 ...	5	1	4	...	...	...	5	1	2	...	...	...	...	...	...
20 and over ...	49	34	15	13	11	2	36	23	13	...	...	...	...	...	...
Sikh.	108	58	50	15	13	2	93	45	48	5	5	...	...	...	...
0—10 ...	33	15	18	...	...	...	33	15	18	...	...	...	...	...	...
10—15 ...	14	11	3	...	...	...	14	11	3	...	...	...	...	...	...
15—20 ...	6	3	3	...	...	...	6	3	3	...	...	...	...	...	...
20 and over ...	55	29	26	15	13	2	40	16	24	5	5	...	...	...	...
Budhist.	11	4	7	...	...	...	11	4	7	...	...	...	...	...	...
0—10 ...	3	...	3	...	...	...	3	...	3	...	...	...	...	...	...
10—15 ...	2	1	1	...	...	...	2	1	1	...	...	...	...	...	...
15—20 ...	1	...	1	...	...	...	1	...	1	...	...	...	...	...	...
20 and over ...	5	3	2	...	...	...	5	3	2	...	...	...	...	...	...
Musalman.	35,174	19,146	16,028	302	296	6	34,872	18,850	16,022	202	199	3	11	11	...
0—10 ...	10,664	5,463	5,201	7	7	...	10,657	5,456	5,201	7	7	...	...	...	...
10—15 ...	4,340	2,272	2,068	37	36	1	4,303	2,236	2,067	25	24	1	2	2	...
15—20 ...	3,230	1,753	1,477	29	27	2	3,201	1,726	1,475	21	20	1	...	...	...
20 and over ...	16,940	9,658	7,282	229	226	3	16,711	93,42	7,279	149	148	1	9	9	...
Christian.	170	128	42	6	4	2	164	124	40	6	4	2	...	...	...
0—10 ...	35	18	17	1	...	1	34	18	16	1	...	1	...	...	...
10—15 ...	20	15	5	...	...	...	20	15	5	...	...	...	...	...	...
15—20 ...	12	11	1	1	1	...	11	10	1	1	1	...	...	...	...
20 and over ...	103	84	19	4	3	1	99	81	18	4	3	1	...	...	...
(3) UDHAMPUR DISTRICT.															
All Religions.	215,725	113,877	101,848	4,532	4,453	79	211,193	109,424	101,769	1,048	1,038	10	244	241	3
0—10 ...	57,752	29,313	28,439	22	21	1	57,730	29,292	28,438	7	7	...	2	2	...
10—15 ...	21,367	11,642	9,725	218	207	11	21,149	11,435	9,714	118	115	3	8	8	...
15—20 ...	18,089	9,218	8,871	274	262	12	17,815	8,956	8,859	101	99	2	21	21	...
20 and over ...	118,517	63,704	54,813	4,018	3,963	55	114,499	59,741	54,758	822	817	5	213	210	3
Hindu (Brahmanic).	130,748	68,786	61,962	3,844	3,791	53	126,904	64,995	61,909	740	736	4	61	61	...
0—10 ...	30,557	15,432	15,125	18	17	1	30,539	15,415	15,124	3	3	...	2	2	...
10—15 ...	11,718	6,343	5,375	179	174	5	11,539	6,169	5,370	91	90	1	2	2	...
15—20 ...	10,442	5,217	5,225	230	223	7	10,212	4,994	5,218	82	80	2	10	10	...
20 and over ...	78,031	41,794	36,237	3,417	3,377	40	74,614	38,417	36,197	564	563	1	47	47	...
Hindu (Arya).	17	12	5	8	7	1	9	5	4	5	5	...	...	...	...
0—10 ...	5	3	2	...	...	...	5	3	2	...	...	...	...	...	...
20 and over ...	12	9	3	8	7	1	4	2	2	5	5	...	...	...	...
Sikh.	128	61	67	36	25	11	92	36	56	11	11	...	4	2	2
0—10 ...	31	11	20	1	1	...	30	10	20	1	1	...	...	...	...
10—15 ...	16	7	9	2	1	1	14	6	8	1	1	...	...	...	...
15—20 ...	14	6	8	4	2	2	10	4	6	...	...	...	...	...	...
20 and over ...	67	37	30	29	21	8	38	16	22	9	9	...	4	2	2
Jain.	3	2	1	2	2	...	1	...	1	1	1	...	...	...	...
0—10 ...	1	1	...	1	1	...	...	...	...	1	1	...	...	...	...
20 and over ...	2	1	1	1	1	...	1	...	1	...	...	...	...	...	...

TABLE VIII.

Education by Religion and Age.

Jammu and Kashmir State Census 1911.

Part II—District Tables.

LITERATE IN

Arabic.			Dogri.			Hindi.			Bodhi.			Gurmukhi.			Others.			English.		
Persons.	Males.	Females.	Persons.	Males.	Females.	Persons.	Males.	Females.	Persons.	Males.	Females.	Persons.	Males.	Females.	Persons.	Males.	Females.	Persons.	Males.	Females.
17	18	19	20	21	22	23	24	25	26	27	28	29	30	31	32	33	34	35	36	37
...	...	...	...	...	...	11	9	2	...	...	...	1	1	...	...	...	...	2	2	...
...	...	...	...	...	...	...	...	...	...	...	...	...	...	...	...	...	...	...	...	...
...	...	...	...	...	...	1	1	...	...	...	...	...	...	...	...	...	...	...	...	...
...	...	...	...	...	...	...	...	...	...	...	...	...	...	...	...	...	...	...	...	...
...	...	...	...	...	...	10	8	2	...	...	...	1	1	...	...	...	...	2	2	...
...	...	...	...	...	...	...	...	...	...	...	...	9	7	2	...	...	...	1	1	...
...	...	...	...	...	...	...	...	...	...	...	...	...	...	...	...	...	...	...	...	...
...	...	...	...	...	...	...	...	...	...	...	...	...	...	...	...	...	...	...	...	...
...	...	...	...	...	...	...	...	...	...	...	...	...	...	...	...	...	...	...	...	...
...	...	...	...	...	...	...	...	...	...	...	...	9	7	2	...	...	...	1	1	...
...	...	...	...	...	...	...	...	...	...	...	...	...	...	...	...	...	...	...	...	...
...	...	...	...	...	...	...	...	...	...	...	...	...	...	...	...	...	...	...	...	...
...	...	...	...	...	...	...	...	...	...	...	...	...	...	...	...	...	...	...	...	...
...	...	...	...	...	...	...	...	...	...	...	...	...	...	...	...	...	...	...	...	...
...	...	...	...	...	...	...	...	...	...	...	...	...	...	...	...	...	...	...	...	...
43	41	2	14	13	1	6	6	...	...	...	...	2	2	...	...	...	...	24	24	...
...	...	...	...	...	...	...	...	...	...	...	...	...	...	...	...	...	...	...	...	...
6	6	...	...	...	...	...	...	...	...	...	...	...	...	...	...	...	...	4	4	...
2	1	1	...	...	...	...	...	...	...	...	...	...	...	...	...	...	...	6	6	...
35	34	1	14	13	1	6	6	...	...	...	...	2	2	...	...	...	...	14	14	...
...	...	...	...	...	...	...	...	...	...	...	...	...	...	...	...	...	...	...	...	...
...	...	...	...	...	...	...	...	...	...	...	...	...	...	...	...	...	...	...	...	...
...	...	...	...	...	...	...	...	...	...	...	...	...	...	...	...	...	...	...	...	...
...	...	...	...	...	...	...	...	...	...	...	...	...	...	...	...	...	...	...	...	...
...	...	...	...	...	...	...	...	...	...	...	...	...	...	...	...	...	...	...	...	...
(3) UDHAMPUR DISTRICT.																				
65	58	7	2,306	2,289	17	674	660	14	...	...	...	59	31	28	1	1	...	135	135	...
...	...	...	6	6	...	5	5	...	...	...	...	1	...	1	...	...	...	1	1	...
3	...	3	52	51	1	27	25	2	...	...	...	2	...	2	...	...	...	8	8	...
8	5	3	95	93	2	38	37	1	...	...	...	6	2	4	...	...	...	5	5	...
54	53	1	2,153	2,139	14	604	593	11	...	...	...	50	29	21	1	1	...	121	121	...
...	...	...	2,227	2,210	17	667	653	14	...	...	...	41	23	18	1	1	...	107	107	...
...	...	...	6	6	...	5	5	...	...	...	...	1	...	1	...	...	...	1	1	...
...	...	...	52	51	1	27	25	2	...	...	...	1	...	1	...	...	...	6	6	...
...	...	...	93	91	2	38	37	1	...	...	...	2	...	2	...	...	...	5	5	...
...	...	...	2,076	2,062	14	597	586	11	...	...	...	37	23	14	1	1	...	95	95	...
...	...	...	1	1	...	...	...	...	...	...	...	1	...	1	...	...	...	1	1	...
...	...	...	...	...	...	...	...	...	...	...	...	...	...	...	...	...	...	...	...	...
...	...	...	1	1	...	...	...	...	...	...	...	1	...	1	...	...	...	1	1	...
...	...	...	2	2	...	...	...	...	...	...	...	17	8	9	...	...	...	2	2	...
...	...	...	...	...	...	...	...	...	...	...	...	...	...	...	...	...	...	...	...	...
...	...	...	...	...	...	...	...	...	...	...	...	1	...	1	...	...	...	...	...	...
...	...	...	...	...	...	...	...	...	...	...	...	4	2	2	...	...	...	...	...	...
...	...	...	2	2	...	...	...	...	...	...	...	12	6	6	...	...	...	2	2	...
...	...	...	...	...	...	...	...	...	...	...	...	...	...	...	...	...	...	1	1	...
...	...	...	...	...	...	...	...	...	...	...	...	...	...	...	...	...	...	...	...	...
...	...	...	...	...	...	...	...	...	...	...	...	...	...	...	...	...	...	1	1	...

TABLE VIII.

Education by Religion and Age.

Jammu and Kashmir State Census 1911.

Part II—District Tables.

AGE.	POPULATION.									LITERATE IN					
	Total.			Literate.			Illiterate.			Urdu.			Persian.		
	Persons.	Males.	Females.	Persons.	Males.	Females.	Persons.	Males.	Females.	Persons.	Males.	Females.	Persons.	Males.	Females.
1	2	3	4	5	6	7	8	9	10	11	12	13	14	15	16
Budhist.	439	205	234	5	5	...	434	200	234	...	...	...	...	...	...
0—10 ...	104	49	55	...	...	...	104	49	55	...	...	...	...	...	...
10—15 ...	44	17	27	...	...	...	44	17	27	...	...	...	...	...	...
15—20 ...	30	13	17	...	...	...	30	13	17	...	...	...	...	...	...
20 and over ...	261	126	135	5	5	...	256	121	135	...	...	...	...	...	...
Musalman.	84,390	44,811	39,579	637	623	14	83,753	44,188	39,565	291	285	6	179	178	1
0—10 ...	27,054	13,817	13,237	2	2	...	27,052	13,815	13,237	2	2	...	...	...	...
10—15 ...	9,589	5,275	4,314	37	32	5	9,552	5,243	4,309	26	24	2	6	6	...
15—20 ...	7,603	3,982	3,621	40	37	3	7,563	3,945	3,618	19	19	...	11	11	...
20 and over ...	40,144	21,737	18,407	558	552	6	39,586	21,185	18,401	244	240	4	162	161	1
							(4) RIASI DISTRICT.								
All Religions.	206,809	109,026	97,783	2,918	2,880	38	203,891	106,146	97,745	705	698	7	102	100	2
0—10 ...	58,025	28,781	29,244	19	17	2	58,006	28,764	29,242	8	8	...	...	...	...
10—15 ...	22,564	12,052	10,512	98	98	...	22,466	11,954	10,512	63	63	...	4	4	...
15—20 ...	17,678	8,887	8,791	204	194	10	17,774	8,693	8,781	76	74	2	4	4	...
20 and over ...	108,542	59,306	49,236	2,597	2,571	26	105,945	56,735	49,210	558	553	5	94	92	2
Hindu (Brahmanic).	80,886	42,629	38,257	2,337	2,315	22	78,549	40,314	38,235	377	373	4	49	49	...
0—10 ...	17,392	8,087	9,305	13	12	1	17,379	8,075	9,304	5	5	...	...	...	...
10—15 ...	7,913	4,163	3,750	73	73	...	7,840	4,090	3,750	45	45	...	3	3	...
15—20 ...	6,885	3,389	3,496	173	166	7	6,712	3,223	3,489	54	53	1	3	3	...
20 and over ...	48,696	26,990	21,706	2,078	2,064	14	46,618	24,926	21,692	273	270	3	43	43	...
Hindu (Arya).	11	10	1	8	8	...	3	2	1	5	5	...	...	...	...
0—10 ...	1	1	...	...	...	...	1	1	...	...	...	...	...	...	...
10—15 ...	...	...	...	...	...	...	...	...	...	...	...	...	...	...	...
15—20 ...	1	1	...	...	...	...	1	1	...	...	...	...	...	...	...
20 and over ...	9	8	1	8	8	...	1	...	1	5	5	...	...	...	...
Sikh.	487	265	222	95	88	7	392	177	215	28	28	...	1	1	...
0—10 ...	113	57	56	2	1	1	111	56	55	...	...	...	...	...	...
10—15 ...	48	27	21	8	8	...	40	19	21	4	4	...	...	...	...
15—20 ...	43	19	24	7	5	2	36	14	22	1	1	...	...	...	...
20 and over ...	283	162	121	78	74	4	205	88	117	23	23	...	1	1	...
Musalman.	125,424	66,121	59,303	477	468	9	124,947	65,653	59,294	295	292	3	52	50	2
0—10 ...	40,519	20,636	19,883	4	4	...	40,515	20,632	19,883	3	3	...	...	...	...
10—15 ...	14,603	7,862	6,741	17	17	...	14,586	7,845	6,741	14	14	...	1	1	...
15—20 ...	10,749	5,478	5,271	24	23	1	10,725	5,455	5,270	21	20	1	1	1	...
20 and over ...	59,553	32,145	27,408	432	424	8	59,121	31,721	27,400	257	255	2	50	48	2
Christian.	1	1	...	1	1	...	...	...	...	...	...	...	...	...	...
20 and over ...	1	1	...	1	1	...	...	...	...	...	...	...	...	...	...
							(5) MIRPUR DISTRICT.								
All Religions.	324,933	169,276	155,657	6,368	6,063	305	318,565	163,213	155,352	3,039	2,987	52	357	357	...
0—10 ...	92,870	48,527	44,343	80	61	19	92,790	48,466	44,324	48	44	4	...	...	...
10—15 ...	37,287	20,791	16,496	523	477	46	36,764	20,314	16,450	365	359	6	19	19	...
15—20 ...	25,205	12,824	12,381	655	616	39	24,550	12,208	12,342	377	368	9	22	22	...
20 and over ...	169,571	87,134	82,437	5,110	4,909	201	16,446	82,225	82,236	2,249	2,216	33	316	316	...
Hindu (Brahmanic).	57,187	30,956	26,231	3,256	3,120	136	53,931	27,836	26,095	1,179	1,163	16	78	78	...
0—10 ...	15,414	8,112	7,302	44	35	9	15,370	8,077	7,293	24	24	...	...	...	...
10—15 ...	6,337	3,722	2,615	255	237	18	6,082	3,485	2,597	175	171	4	4	4	...
15—20 ...	4,640	2,453	2,187	337	317	20	4,303	2,136	2,167	168	164	4	4	4	...
20 and over ...	30,796	16,669	14,127	2,620	2,531	89	28,176	14,138	14,038	812	804	8	70	70	...

TABLE VIII.

Education by Religion and Age.

Jammu and Kashmir State Census 1911.

Part II—District Tables.

LITERATE IN

Arabic.			Dogri.			Hindi.			Bodhi.			Gurmukhi.			Others.			English.		
Persons.	Males.	Females.	Persons.	Males.	Females.	Persons.	Males.	Females.	Persons.	Males.	Females.	Persons.	Males.	Females.	Persons.	Males.	Females.	Persons.	Males.	Females.
17	18	19	20	21	22	23	24	25	26	27	28	29	30	31	32	33	34	35	36	37
...	...	...	...	...	...	5	5	...	...	...	...	...	...	...	...	...	...	...	...	...
...	...	...	...	...	...	...	...	...	...	...	...	...	...	...	...	...	...	...	...	...
...	...	...	...	...	...	...	...	...	...	...	...	...	...	...	...	...	...	...	...	...
...	...	...	...	...	...	...	...	...	...	...	...	...	...	...	...	...	...	...	...	...
...	...	...	...	...	...	5	5	...	...	...	...	...	...	...	...	...	...	...	...	...
65	58	7	76	76	...	2	2	...	...	...	...	...	...	...	...	...	...	24	24	...
...	...	...	...	...	...	...	...	...	...	...	...	...	...	...	...	...	...	...	...	...
3	...	3	...	...	...	...	...	...	...	...	...	...	...	...	...	...	...	2	2	...
8	5	3	2	2	...	...	...	...	...	...	...	...	...	...	...	...	...	...	...	...
54	53	1	74	74	...	2	2	...	...	...	...	...	...	...	...	...	...	22	22	...
(4) RIASI DISTRICT.																				
81	77	4	1,290	1,284	6	661	653	8	...	...	...	45	34	11	...	...	...	34	34	...
...	...	...	6	5	1	3	3	...	...	...	...	1	...	1	...	...	...	1	1	...
1	1	...	12	12	...	18	18	...	...	...	...	...	...	...	...	...	...	...	...	...
2	2	...	62	62	...	52	47	5	...	...	...	7	4	3	...	...	...	1	1	...
78	74	4	1,210	1,205	5	588	585	3	...	...	...	37	30	7	...	...	...	32	32	...
...	...	...	1,248	1,242	6	621	613	8	...	...	...	22	18	4	...	...	...	20	20	...
...	...	...	6	5	1	2	2	...	...	...	...	...	...	...	...	...	...	...	...	...
...	...	...	11	11	...	14	14	...	...	...	...	...	...	...	...	...	...	...	...	...
...	...	...	62	62	...	49	44	5	...	...	...	4	3	1	...	...	...	1	1	...
...	...	...	1,169	1,164	5	556	553	3	...	...	...	18	15	3	...	...	...	19	19	...
...	...	...	...	...	...	...	...	...	...	...	...	...	...	...	...	...	...	3	3	...
...	...	...	...	...	...	...	...	...	...	...	...	...	...	...	...	...	...	...	...	...
...	...	...	...	...	...	...	...	...	...	...	...	...	...	...	...	...	...	...	...	...
...	...	...	...	...	...	...	...	...	...	...	...	...	...	...	...	...	...	...	...	...
...	...	...	...	...	...	...	...	...	...	...	...	...	...	...	...	...	...	3	3	...
...	...	...	5	5	...	37	37	...	...	...	...	23	16	7	...	...	...	1	1	...
...	...	...	...	...	...	1	1	...	...	...	...	1	...	1	...	...	...	...	...	...
...	...	...	...	...	...	4	4	...	...	...	...	...	...	...	...	...	...	...	...	...
...	...	...	...	...	...	3	3	...	...	...	...	3	1	2	...	...	...	...	...	...
...	...	...	5	5	...	29	29	...	...	...	...	19	15	4	...	...	...	1	1	...
81	77	4	37	37	...	3	3	...	...	...	...	...	...	...	...	...	...	9	9	...
...	...	...	...	...	...	...	...	...	...	...	...	...	...	...	...	...	...	1	1	...
1	1	...	1	1	...	...	...	...	...	...	...	...	...	...	...	...	...	...	...	...
2	2	...	...	...	...	...	...	...	...	...	...	...	...	...	...	...	...	...	...	...
78	74	4	36	36	...	3	3	...	...	...	...	...	...	...	...	...	...	8	8	...
...	...	...	...	...	...	...	...	...	...	...	...	...	...	...	...	...	...	1	1	...
...	...	...	...	...	...	...	...	...	...	...	...	...	...	...	...	...	...	1	1	...
(5) MIRPUR DISTRICT.																				
214	191	23	183	181	2	1,377	1,316	61	...	...	...	619	465	154	282	273	9	297	293	4
3	...	3	...	...	...	19	10	9	...	...	...	8	5	3	1	1	...	1	1	...
7	7	...	5	5	...	42	34	8	...	...	...	59	27	32	8	8	...	18	18	...
16	12	4	6	6	...	96	90	6	...	...	...	55	36	19	24	24	...	59	58	1
188	172	16	172	170	2	1,220	1,182	38	...	...	...	497	397	100	249	240	9	219	216	3
...	...	...	167	166	1	1,224	1,170	54	...	...	...	162	108	54	264	255	9	182	180	2
...	...	...	...	...	...	17	9	8	...	...	...	1	...	1	1	1	...	1	1	...
...	...	...	4	4	...	39	32	7	...	...	...	11	4	7	7	7	...	15	15	...
...	...	...	5	5	1	83	79	4	...	...	...	17	6	11	20	20	...	40	39	1
...	...	...	158	157		1,085	1,050	35	...	...	...	133	98	35	236	227	9	126	125	1

VIII
Education.

TABLE VIII.

Education by Religion and Age.

Jammu and Kashmir State Census 1911.

Part II—District Tables.

AGE.	POPULATION.									LITERATE IN					
	Total.			Literate.			Illiterate.			Urdu.			Persian.		
	Persons.	Males.	Females.	Persons.	Males.	Females.	Persons.	Males.	Females.	Persons.	Males.	Females.	Persons.	Males.	Females.
1	2	3	4	5	6	7	8	9	10	11	12	13	14	15	16
Hindu (Arya).	225	140	85	72	67	5	153	73	80	35	34	1	1	1	...
0—10 ...	52	32	20	4	4	...	48	28	20	3	3	...	...	...	...
10—15 ...	28	18	10	4	3	1	24	15	9	2	1	1	...	...	...
15—20 ...	21	8	13	8	8	...	13	...	13	1	1	...	...	...	...
20 and over ...	124	82	42	56	52	4	68	30	38	29	29	...	1	1	...
Sikh.	3,156	1,779	1,377	792	686	106	2,364	1,093	1,271	167	165	2	7	7	...
0—10 ...	797	432	365	10	7	3	787	425	362	2	2	...	...	...	...
10—15 ...	372	222	150	91	65	26	281	157	124	39	39	...	1	1	...
15—20 ...	249	136	113	76	65	11	173	71	102	23	22	1	...	...	...
20 and over ...	1,738	989	749	615	549	66	1,123	440	683	103	102	1	6	6	...
Jain.	8	8	...	...	...	...	8	8	...	...	...	...	...	...	...
0—10 ...	1	1	...	...	...	...	1	1	...	...	...	...	...	...	...
15—20 ...	1	1	...	...	...	...	1	1	...	...	...	...	...	...	...
20 and over ...	6	6	...	...	...	...	6	6	...	...	...	...	...	...	...
Musalman.	264,347	136,386	127,961	2,241	2,184	57	262,106	134,202	127,904	1,658	1,625	33	271	271	...
0—10 ...	76,603	39,949	36,654	22	15	7	76,581	39,934	36,647	19	15	4	...	...	...
10—15 ...	30,550	16,829	13,721	173	172	1	30,377	16,657	13,720	149	148	1	14	14	...
15—20 ...	20,294	10,226	10,068	234	226	8	20,060	10,000	10,060	185	181	4	18	18	...
20 and over ...	136,900	69,382	67,518	1,812	1,771	41	135,088	67,611	67,477	1,305	1,281	24	239	239	...
Christian.	10	7	3	7	6	1	3	1	2	...	...	...	...	...	...
0—10 ...	3	1	2	...	...	...	3	1	2	...	...	...	...	...	...
20 and over ...	7	6	1	7	6	1	...	...	...	...	...	...	...	...	...
(6) BHADARWAH JAGIR.															
All Religions.	37,512	18,975	18,537	798	775	23	36,714	18,200	18,514	225	222	3	6	6	...
0—10 ...	10,194	5,149	5,045	3	3	...	10,191	5,146	5,045	2	2	...	...	...	...
10—15 ...	3,953	2,180	1,773	36	34	2	3,917	2,146	1,771	28	28	...	...	...	...
15—20 ...	3,179	1,521	1,658	59	56	3	3,120	1,465	1,655	32	32	...	1	1	...
20 and over ...	20,186	10,125	10,061	700	682	18	19,486	9,443	10,043	163	160	3	5	5	...
Hindu (Brahmanic).	22,931	11,375	11,556	665	643	22	22,266	10,732	11,534	183	181	2	4	4	...
0—10 ...	5,815	2,927	2,888	2	2	...	5,813	2,925	2,888	1	1	...	...	...	...
10—15 ...	2,302	1,276	1,026	31	29	2	2,271	1,247	1,024	25	25	...	...	...	...
15—20 ...	1,826	807	1,019	49	46	3	1,777	761	1,016	26	26	...	...	...	...
20 and over ...	12,988	6,365	6,623	583	566	17	12,405	5,799	6,606	131	129	2	4	4	...
Budhist.	1	1	...	...	...	...	1	1	...	...	...	...	...	...	...
20 and over ...	1	1	...	...	...	...	1	1	...	...	...	...	...	...	...
Musalman.	14,580	7,599	6,981	133	132	1	14,447	7,467	6,980	42	41	1	2	2	...
0—10 ...	4,379	2,222	2,157	1	1	...	4,378	2,221	2,157	1	1	...	...	...	...
10—15 ...	1,651	904	747	5	5	...	1,646	899	747	3	3	...	...	...	...
15—20 ...	1,353	714	639	10	10	...	1,343	704	639	6	6	...	1	1	...
20 and over ...	7,197	3,759	3,438	117	116	1	7,080	3,643	3,437	32	31	1	1	1	...
(7) PUNCH ILAQA.															
All Religions.	334,393	173,570	160,823	3,348	3,250	98	331,045	170,320	160,725	1,933	1,915	18	186	185	1
0—10 ...	1,06,822	54,816	52,016	66	59	7	106,766	54,757	52,009	50	47	3	2	2	...
10—15 ...	40,104	22,214	17,890	294	283	11	39,810	21,931	17,879	238	236	2	4	4	...
15—20 ...	29,472	15,109	14,363	377	364	13	29,095	14,745	14,350	269	266	3	20	20	...
20 and over ...	157,985	81,431	76,554	2,611	2,544	67	155,373	78,887	76,487	1,376	1,366	10	160	159	1

TABLE VIII.

Education by Religion and Age.

Jammu and Kashmir State Census 1911.

Part II—District Tables.

LITERATE IN

Arabic.			Dogri.			Hindi.			Bodhi.			Gurmukhi.			Others.			English.		
Persons.	Males.	Females.	Persons.	Males.	Females.	Persons.	Males.	Females.	Persons.	Males.	Females.	Persons.	Males.	Females.	Persons.	Males.	Females.	Persons.	Males.	Females.
17	18	19	20	21	22	23	24	25	26	27	28	29	30	31	32	33	34	35	36	37
...	...	...	...	...	...	16	14	2	...	...	...	2	1	1	6	6	...	12	11	1
...	...	...	...	...	...	1	1	...	...	...	...	...	...	...	...	...	...	...	...	...
...	...	...	...	...	...	1	1	...	...	...	...	...	...	...	...	...	...	1	1	...
...	...	...	...	...	...	4	4	...	...	...	...	...	...	...	1	1	...	2	2	...
...	...	...	...	...	...	10	8	2	...	...	...	2	1	1	5	5	...	9	8	1
...	...	...	2	2	...	119	114	5	...	...	...	455	356	99	8	8	...	34	34	...
...	...	...	...	...	...	1	...	1	...	...	...	7	5	2	...	...	...	...	...	...
...	...	...	...	...	...	2	1	1	...	...	...	48	23	25	1	1	...	...	...	...
...	...	...	...	...	...	9	7	2	...	...	...	38	30	8	2	2	...	4	4	...
...	...	...	2	2	...	107	106	1	...	...	...	362	298	64	5	5	...	30	30	...
...	...	...	...	...	...	...	...	...	...	...	...	...	...	...	...	...	...	...	...	...
...	...	...	...	...	...	...	...	...	...	...	...	...	...	...	...	...	...	...	...	...
...	...	...	...	...	...	...	...	...	...	...	...	...	...	...	...	...	...	...	...	...
...	...	...	...	...	...	...	...	...	...	...	...	...	...	...	...	...	...	...	...	...
214	191	23	14	13	1	18	18	...	...	...	...	...	...	...	4	4	...	62	62	...
3	...	3	...	...	...	...	...	...	...	...	...	...	...	...	...	...	...	...	...	...
7	7	...	1	1	...	...	...	...	...	...	...	...	...	...	...	...	...	2	2	...
16	12	4	1	1	...	...	...	...	...	...	...	...	...	...	1	1	...	13	13	...
188	172	16	12	11	1	18	18	...	...	...	...	...	...	...	3	3	...	47	47	...
...	...	...	...	...	...	...	...	...	...	...	...	...	...	...	...	...	...	...	...	...
...	...	...	...	...	...	...	...	...	...	...	...	...	...	...	...	...	...	7	6	1
...	...	...	...	...	...		...	...	...	...	...	...	...	...	...	...	...	7	6	1
(6) BHADARWAH JAGIR.																				
33	33	...	397	384	13	129	122	7	...	...	...	5	5	...	...	...	...	...	...	...
...	...	...	1	1	...	...	...	...	...	...	...	...	...	...	...	...	...	...	...	...
...	...	...	3	2	1	5	4	1	...	...	...	...	...	...	...	...	...	...	...	...
3	3	...	19	17	2	4	3	1	...	...	...	...	...	...	...	...	...	...	...	...
30	30	...	374	364	10	120	115	5	...	...	...	5	5	...	...	...	...	...	...	...
...	...	...	342	329	13	129	122	7	...	...	...	5	5	...	...	...	...	...	...	...
...	...	...	1	1	...	...	...	...	...	...	...	...	...	...	...	...	...	...	...	...
...	...	...	1	...	1	5	4	1	...	...	...	...	...	...	...	...	...	...	...	...
...	...	...	19	17	2	4	3	1	...	...	...	...	...	...	...	...	...	...	...	...
...	...	...	321	311	10	120	115	5	...	...	...	5	5	...	...	...	...	...	...	...
...	...	...	...	...	...	...	...	...	...	...	...	...	...	...	...	...	...	...	...	...
...	...	...	...	...	...	...	...	...	...	...	...	...	...	...	...	...	...	...	...	...
33	33	...	55	55	...	...	...	...	...	...	...	...	...	...	...	...	...	...	...	...
...	...	...	...	...	...	...	...	...	...	...	...	...	...	...	...	...	...	...	...	...
...	...	...	2	2	...	...	...	...	...	...	...	...	...	...	...	...	...	...	...	...
3	3	...	...	...	...	...	...	...	...	...	...	...	...	...	...	...	...	...	...	...
30	30	...	53	53	...	...	...	...	...	...	...	...	...	...	...	...	...	...	...	...
(7) PUNCH ILAQA.																				
177	167	10	69	68	1	390	369	21	...	...	...	432	397	35	...	...	...	161	149	12
3	3	...	...	...	...	5	2	3	...	...	...	3	2	1	...	...	...	3	3	...
8	8	...	...	...	...	13	9	4	...	...	...	19	16	3	...	...	...	12	10	2
13	12	1	2	2	...	17	14	3	...	...	...	23	17	6	...	...	...	33	33	...
153	144	9	67	66	1	355	344	11	...	...	...	387	362	25	...	...	...	113	103	10

VIII
Education.

TABLE VIII.

Education by Religion and Age.

Jammu and Kashmir State Census 1911.

Part II—District Tables.

AGE.	POPULATION.									LITERATE IN					
	Total.			Literate.			Illiterate.			Urdu.			Persian.		
	Persons.	Males.	Females.	Persons.	Males.	Females.	Persons.	Males.	Females.	Persons.	Males.	Females.	Persons.	Males.	Females.
1	2	3	4	5	6	7	8	9	10	11	12	13	14	15	16
Hindu (Brahmanic).	21,967	11,685	10,282	1,247	1,202	45	20,720	10,483	10,237	559	552	7	28	27	1
0—10 ...	6,061	2,891	3,170	25	20	5	6,036	2,871	3,165	19	17	2	...	...	...
10—15 ...	2,732	1,616	1,116	133	128	5	2,599	1,488	1,111	110	109	1	1	1	...
15—20 ...	1,840	1,031	809	143	136	7	1,697	895	802	87	86	1	6	6	...
20 and over ...	11,334	6,147	5,187	946	918	28	10,388	5,229	5,159	343	340	3	21	20	1
Hindu (Arya).	54	37	17	30	27	3	24	10	14	12	9	3	2	2	...
0—10 ...	12	7	5	3	2	1	9	5	4	3	2	1	...	...	...
10—15 ...	8	5	3	6	5	1	2	...	2	2	1	1	...	...	...
15—20 ...	6	5	1	1	1	...	5	4	1	...	...	...	...	...	...
20 and over ...	28	20	8	20	19	1	8	1	7	7	6	1	2	2	...
Sikh.	9,624	5,186	4,438	413	394	19	9,211	4,792	4,419	88	88	...	5	5	...
0—10 ...	3,090	1,647	1,443	7	6	1	3,083	1,641	1,442	4	4	...	...	...	...
10—15 ...	1,181	605	516	24	21	3	1,157	644	513	8	8	...	...	...	...
15—20 ...	858	475	383	36	33	3	822	442	380	19	19	...	1	1	...
20 and over ...	4,495	2,399	2,096	346	334	12	4,149	2,065	2,084	57	57	...	4	4	...
Jain.	1	1	...	1	1	...	...	...	...	...	...	...	...	...	...
20 and over ...	1	1	...	1	1	...	...	...	...	...	...	...	...	...	...
Musalman.	302,719	156,651	146,068	1,635	1,616	19	301,084	155,035	146,049	1,274	1,266	8	151	151	...
0—10 ...	97,661	50,269	47,392	29	29	...	97,632	50,240	47,392	24	24	...	2	2	...
10—15 ...	36,181	19,928	16,253	129	129	...	36,052	19,799	16,253	118	118	...	3	3	...
15—20 ...	26,767	13,597	13,170	196	193	3	26,571	13,404	13,167	163	161	2	13	13	...
20 and over ...	142,110	72,857	69,253	1,281	1,265	16	140,829	71,592	69,237	969	963	6	133	133	...
Christian.	28	10	18	22	10	12	6	...	6	...	...	...	...	...	...
0—10 ...	8	2	6	2	2	...	6	...	6	...	...	...	...	...	...
10—15 ...	2	...	2	2	...	2	...	...	...	...	...	...	...	...	...
15—20 ...	1	1	...	1	1	...	...	...	...	...	...	...	...	...	...
20 and over ...	17	7	10	17	7	10	...	...	...	...	...	...	...	...	...
(3) KASHMIR NORTH.															
All Religions.	460,786	244,637	216,149	6,082	6,018	64	454,704	238,619	216,085	2,987	2,983	4	1,573	1,563	10
0—10 ...	149,051	76,485	72,566	48	44	4	149,003	76,441	72,562	33	32	1	...	...	...
10—15 ...	52,681	28,782	23,899	307	304	3	52,374	28,478	23,896	195	195	...	20	19	1
15—20 ...	43,157	22,978	20,179	562	549	13	42,595	22,429	20,166	346	344	2	59	58	1
20 and over...	215,897	116,392	99,505	5,165	5,121	44	210,732	111,271	99,461	2,413	2,412	1	1,494	1,486	8
Hindu (Brahmanic).	9,917	5,935	3,982	2,472	2,453	19	7,445	3,482	3,963	1,407	1,403	4	526	523	3
0—10 ...	2,420	1,216	1,204	23	22	1	2,397	1,194	1,203	18	17	1	...	...	...
10—15 ...	1,028	582	446	141	140	1	887	442	445	89	89	...	5	5	...
15—20 ...	777	486	291	217	211	6	560	275	285	145	145	2	10	10	...
20 and over...	5,692	3,651	2,041	2,091	2,080	11	3,601	1,571	2,030	1,155	1,154	1	511	508	3
Hindu (Arya).	5	3	2	3	1	2	2	2	...	...	...	...	...	...	...
0—10 ...	3	2	1	2	1	1	1	1	...	...	...	...	...	...	...
10—15 ...	...	...	...	...	...	...	...	...	...	...	...	...	...	...	...
15—20 ...	...	...	...	...	...	...	...	...	...	...	...	...	...	...	...
20 and over...	2	1	1	1	...	1	1	1	...	...	...	...	...	...	...
Sikh.	4,575	2,383	2,192	509	492	17	4,066	1,891	2,175	23	23	...	1	1	...
0—10 ...	1,521	772	749	9	9	...	1,512	763	749	2	2	...	...	...	...
10—15 ...	518	282	236	32	31	1	486	251	235	5	5	...	...	...	...
15—20 ...	436	217	219	58	54	4	378	163	215	1	1	...	...	...	...
20 and over...	2,100	1,112	988	410	398	12	1,690	714	976	15	15	...	1	1	...

TABLE VIII.

Education by Religion and Age.

Jammu and Kashmir State Census 1911.

Part II—District Tables.

LITERATE IN

Arabic.			Dogri.			Hindi.			Bodhi.			Gurmukhi.			Others.			English.		
Persons.	Males.	Females.	Persons.	Males.	Females.	Persons.	Males.	Females.	Persons.	Males.	Females.	Persons.	Males.	Females.	Persons.	Males.	Females.	Persons.	Males.	Females.
17	18	19	20	21	22	23	24	25	26	27	28	29	30	31	32	33	34	35	36	37
...	...	...	67	66	1	354	334	20	...	...	...	147	131	16	...	...	...	92	92	...
...	...	...	...	...	...	5	2	3	...	...	...	...	...	...	...	...	...	1	1	...
...	...	...	...	...	...	13	9	4	...	...	...	3	3	...	...	...	...	6	6	...
...	...	...	2	2	...	17	14	3	...	...	...	7	4	3	...	...	...	24	24	...
...	...	...	65	64	1	319	309	10	...	...	...	137	124	13	...	...	...	61	61	...
...	...	...	...	...	...	3	3	...	...	...	...	...	...	...	...	...	...	13	13	...
...	...	...	...	...	...	...	...	...	...	...	...	...	...	...	...	...	...	...	...	...
...	...	...	...	...	...	...	...	...	...	...	...	...	...	...	...	...	...	4	4	...
...	...	...	...	...	...	...	...	...	...	...	...	...	...	...	...	...	...	1	1	...
...	...	...	...	...	...	3	3	...	...	...	...	...	...	...	...	...	...	8	8	...
...	...	...	1	1	...	30	30	...	...	...	...	285	266	19	...	...	...	4	4	...
...	...	...	...	...	...	...	...	...	...	...	...	3	2	1	...	...	...	...	...	...
...	...	...	...	...	...	...	...	...	...	...	...	16	13	3	...	...	...	...	...	...
...	...	...	...	...	...	...	...	...	...	...	...	16	13	3	...	...	...	...	...	...
...	...	...	1	1	...	30	30	...	...	...	...	250	238	12	...	...	...	4	4	...
...	...	...	...	...	...	...	...	...	...	...	...	...	...	...	...	...	...	1	1	...
...	...	...	...	...	...	...	...	...	...	...	...	...	...	...	...	...	...	1	1	...
177	167	10	1	1	...	3	2	1	...	...	...	...	...	...	...	...	...	29	29	...
3	3	...	...	...	...	...	...	...	...	...	...	...	...	...	...	...	...	...	...	...
8	8		...	...	...	...	...	...	...	...	...	...	...	...	...	...	...	...	...	...
13	12	1	...	...	...	...	...	...	...	...	...	...	...	...	...	...	...	7	7	...
153	144	9	1	1	...	3	2	1	...	...	...	...	...	...	...	...	...	22	22	...
...	...	...	...	...	...	...	...	...	...	...	...	...	...	...	...	...	...	22	10	12
...	...	...	...	...	...	...	...	...	...	...	...	...	...	...	...	...	...	2	2	...
...	...	...	...	...	...	...	...	...	...	...	...	...	...	...	...	...	...	2	...	2
...	...	...	...	...	...	...	...	...	...	...	...	...	...	...	...	...	...	1	1	...
...	...	...	...	...	...	...	...	...	...	...	...	...	...	...	...	...	...	17	7	10

(8) KASHMIR NORTH.

Arabic.			Dogri.			Hindi.			Bodhi.			Gurmukhi.			Others.			English.		
403	391	12	17	17	...	190	183	7	...	...	...	519	495	24	5	5	...	388	381	7
1	...	1	...	...	...	1	...	1	...	...	...	7	7	...	...	...	...	6	5	1
9	9	...	...	...	...	9	8	1	...	...	...	23	22	1	...	...	...	51	51	...
23	21	2	1	1	...	15	14	1	...	...	...	59	52	7	...	...	...	59	59	...
370	361	9	16	16	...	165	161	4	...	...	...	430	414	16	5	5	...	272	266	6
...	...	...	15	15	...	177	172	5	...	...	...	61	54	7	4	4	...	282	282	...
...	...	...	...	...	...	...	...	...	...	...	...	...	...	...	...	...	...	5	5	...
...	...	...	...	...	...	9	8	1	...	...	...	...	...	...	...	...	...	38	38	...
...	...	...	1	1	...	15	14	1	...	...	...	7	4	3	...	...	...	39	39	...
...	...	...	14	14	...	153	150	3	...	...	...	54	50	4	4	4	...	200	200	...
...	...	...	...	...	...	2	...	2	...	...	...	...	...	...	...	...	...	1	1	...
...	...	...	...	...	...	1	...	1	...	...	...	...	...	...	...	...	...	1	1	...
...	...	...	...	...	...	...	...	...	...	...	...	...	...	...	...	...	...	...	...	...
...	...	...	...	...	...	...	...	...	...	...	...	...	...	...	...	...	...	...	...	...
...	...	...	...	...	...	1	...	1	...	...	...	...	...	...	...	...	...	...	...	...
...	...	...	2	2	...	10	10	...	...	...	...	452	435	17	...	...	...	21	21	...
...	...	...	...	...	...	...	...	...	...	...	...	7	7	...	...	...	...	...	...	...
...	...	...	...	...	...	...	...	...	...	...	...	23	22	1	...	...	...	4	4	...
...	...	...	...	...	...	...	...	...	...	...	...	52	48	4	...	...	...	5	5	...
...	...	...	2	2	...	10	10	...	...	...	...	370	358	12	...	...	...	12	12	...

VIII
Education.

TABLE VIII.

Education by Religion and Age.

Jammu and Kashmir State Census 1911.

Part II—District Tables.

AGE.	POPULATION.									LITERATE IN					
	Total.			Literate.			Illiterate.			Urdu.			Persian.		
	Persons.	Males.	Females.	Persons.	Males.	Females.	Persons.	Males.	Females.	Persons.	Males.	Females.	Persons.	Males.	Females.
1	2	3	4	5	6	7	8	9	10	11	12	13	14	15	16
Budhist.	2	2	...	...	...	...	2	2	...	...	...	...	...	...	...
20 and over...	2	2	...	...	...	...	2	2	...	...	...	...	...	...	...
Musalman.	446,248	236,289	209,959	3,071	3,052	19	443,177	233,237	209,940	1,557	1,557	...	1,046	1,039	7
0—10 ...	145,100	74,491	70,609	14	13	1	145,086	74,478	70,608	13	13	...	...	...	...
10—15 ...	51,135	27,918	23,217	134	133	1	51,001	27,785	23,216	101	101	...	15	14	1
15—20 ...	41,944	22,275	19,660	287	284	3	41,657	21,991	19,666	200	200	...	49	48	1
20 and over...	208,069	111,605	96,464	2,636	2,622	14	205,433	108,983	96,450	1,243	1,243	...	982	977	5
Christian.	39	25	14	27	20	7	12	5	7	...	...	...	...	...	...
0—10 ...	7	4	3	1	...	1	6	4	2	...	...	...	...	...	...
20 and over...	32	21	11	26	20	6	6	1	5	...	...	...	...	...	...
(9) KASHMIR SOUTH.															
All Religions.	639,210	342,835	296,375	18.190	18,022	168	621,020	324,813	296,207	4,683	4.663	20	7,723	7,702	21
0—10 ...	196,611	100,807	95,804	280	271	9	196,331	100,536	95,795	131	131	...	35	35	...
10—15 ...	73,193	40,429	32,764	1,533	1,515	18	71,660	38,914	32,746	629	625	4	241	238	3
15—20 ...	56,788	31,123	25,665	1,889	1,877	12	54,899	29,246	25,653	466	465	1	468	467	1
20 and over...	312,618	170,476	142,142	14,488	14,359	129	298,130	156,117	142,013	3,457	3,442	15	6,979	6,962	17
Hindu (Brahmanic).	47,754	26,298	21,456	12,426	12,381	45	35,328	13,917	21,411	3,788	3,775	13	4,147	4,136	11
0—10 ...	12,064	6,132	5,932	231	227	4	11,833	5,905	5.928	125	125	...	18	18	...
10—15 ...	4,930	2,852	2,078	1,202	1,192	10	3,728	1.660	2,068	533	530	3	104	103	1
15—20 ...	4,142	2,475	1,667	1,367	1,363	4	2,775	1,112	1,663	378	377	1	184	183	1
20 and over...	26,618	14,839	11,779	9.626	9,599	27	16,992	5,240	11,752	2,752	2,743	9	3,841	3,832	9
Hindu (Arya).	40	24	16	17	14	3	23	10	13	1	1	...	...	...	...
0—10 ...	15	8	7	...	...	...	15	8	7	...	...	...	...	...	...
10—15 ...	6	5	1	4	4	...	2	1	1	...	...	...	...	...	...
15—20 ...	3	2	1	2	2	...	1	...	1	...	...	...	...	...	...
20 and over...	16	9	7	11	8	3	5	1	4	1	1	...	...	...	...
Hindu (Bramho).	1	...	1	1	...	1	...	...	...	...	...	...	...	...	...
20 and Over...	1	...	1	1	...	1	...	...	...	...	...	...	...	...	...
Sikh.	2,586	1,448	1,138	180	171	9	2,406	1,277	1,129	38	37	1	4	4	...
0—10 ...	839	438	401	2	1	1	837	437	400	...	...	...	...	...	...
10—15 ...	265	152	113	13	12	1	252	140	112	...	...	...	...	...	...
15—20 ...	233	142	91	7	7	...	226	135	91	4	4	...	...	...	...
20 and over...	1,249	716	533	158	151	7	1,091	565	526	34	33	1	4	4	...
Zoroastrian.	26	20	6	18	14	4	8	6	2	...	...	...	...	...	...
0—10 ...	9	8	1	3	3	...	6	5	1	...	...	...	...	...	...
15—20 ...	3	2	1	3	2	1	...	...	...	...	...	...	...	...	...
20 and over...	14	10	4	12	9	3	2	1	1	...	...	...	...	...	...
Musalman.	588,641	314,965	273,676	5,416	5,383	33	583,225	309.582	273,643	853	847	6	3,572	3,562	10
0—10 ...	183,661	94.208	89,453	39	39	...	183,622	94,169	89,453	6	6	...	17	17	...
10—15 ...	67,985	37,415	30,570	310	305	5	67,675	37,110	30,565	95	94	1	137	135	2
15—20 ...	52,402	28,502	23,900	506	503	3	51,896	27,999	23,897	84	84	...	284	284	...
20 and over...	284,593	154,840	129,753	4,561	4,536	25	280,032	150,304	129,728	668	663	5	3,134	3,126	8
Christian.	162	80	82	132	59	73	30	21	9	3	3	...	...	...	...
0—10 ...	23	13	10	5	1	4	18	12	6	...	...	...	...	...	...
10—15 ...	7	5	2	4	2	2	3	3	...	1	1	...	...	...	...
15—20 ...	5	...	5	4	...	4	1	...	1	...	...	...	...	...	...
20 and over...	127	62	65	119	56	63	8	6	2	2	2	...	...	...	...

TABLE VIII.

VIII
Education.

Education by Religion and Age.

Jammu and Kashmir State Census 1911.

Part II—District Tables.

LITERATE IN

Arabic.			Dogri.			Hindi.			Bodhi.			Gurmukhi.			Others.			English.		
Persons.	Males.	Females.	Persons.	Males.	Females.	Persons.	Males.	Females.	Persons.	Males.	Females.	Persons.	Males.	Females.	Persons.	Males.	Females.	Persons.	Males.	Females.
17	18	19	20	21	22	23	24	25	26	27	28	29	30	31	32	33	34	35	36	37
...	...	...	...	...	...	...	...	...	...	...	...	...	...	...	...	...	...	...	...	...
...	...	...	...	...	...	...	...	...	...	...	...	...	...	...	...	...	...	...	...	...
403	391	12	...	...	...	1	1	...	...	...	...	6	6	...	1	1	...	57	57	...
1	...	1	...	...	...	...	...	...	...	...	...	...	...	...	...	...	...	...	...	...
9	9	...	...	...	...	...	...	...	...	...	...	...	...	...	...	...	...	9	9	...
23	21	2	...	...	...	...	...	...	...	...	...	...	...	...	...	...	...	15	15	...
370	361	9	...	...	...	1	1	...	...	...	...	6	6	...	1	1	...	33	33	...
...	...	...	...	...	...	...	...	...	...	...	...	...	...	...	...	...	...	27	20	7
...	...	...	...	...	...	...	...	...	...	...	...	...	...	...	...	...	...	1	...	1
...	...	...	...	...	...	...	...	...	...	...	...	...	...	...	...	...	...	26	20	6
(9) KASHMIR SOUTH.																				
686	669	17	91	86	5	1,718	1,701	17	...	...	...	112	107	5	...	...	...	3,177	3,094	83
13	13	...	...	...	...	24	20	4	...	...	...	2	1	1	...	...	...	75	71	4
47	45	2	5	4	1	113	108	5	...	...	...	2	2	...	...	...	...	496	493	3
63	60	3	5	5	...	118	116	2	...	...	...	4	4	...	...	...	...	765	760	5
563	551	12	81	77	4	1,463	1,457	6	...	...	...	104	100	4	...	...	...	1,841	1,770	71
...	...	...	82	80	2	1,714	1,700	14	...	...	...	9	9	...	...	...	...	2,686	2,681	5
...	...	...	...	...	...	24	20	4	...	...	...	...	...	...	...	...	...	64	64	...
...	...	...	3	3	...	113	108	5	...	...	...	...	...	...	...	...	...	449	448	1
...	...	...	5	5	...	118	116	2	...	...	...	1	1	...	...	...	...	681	681	...
...	...	...	74	72	2	1,459	1,456	3	...	...	...	8	8	...	...	...	...	1,492	1,488	4
...	...	...	...	...	...	3	...	3	...	...	...	...	...	...	...	...	...	13	13	...
...	...	...	...	...	...	...	...	...	...	...	...	...	...	...	...	...	...	...	...	...
...	...	...	...	...	...	...	...	...	...	...	...	...	...	...	...	...	...	4	4	...
...	...	...	...	...	...	...	...	...	...	...	...	...	...	...	...	...	...	2	2	...
...	...	...	...	...	...	3	...	3	...	...	...	...	...	...	...	...	...	7	7	...
...	...	...	...	...	...	...	...	...	...	...	...	...	...	...	...	...	...	1	...	1
...	...	...	...	...	...	...	...	...	...	...	...	...	...	...	...	...	...	1	...	1
...	...	...	6	3	3	1	1	...	...	...	...	103	98	5	...	...	...	28	28	...
...	...	...	...	...	...	...	...	...	...	...	...	2	1	1	...	...	...	...	...	...
...	...	...	2	1	1	...	...	...	...	...	...	2	2	...	...	...	...	9	9	...
...	...	...	...	...	...	...	...	...	...	...	...	3	3	...	...	...	...	...	...	...
...	...	...	4	2	2	1	1	...	...	...	...	96	92	4	...	...	...	19	19	...
...	...	...	...	...	...	...	...	...	...	...	...	...	...	...	...	...	...	18	14	4
...	...	...	...	...	...	...	...	...	...	...	...	...	...	...	...	...	...	3	3	...
...	...	...	...	...	...	...	...	...	...	...	...	...	...	...	...	...	...	3	2	1
...	...	...	...	...	...	...	...	...	...	...	...	...	...	...	...	...	...	12	9	3
686	669	17	3	3	...	...	...	...	...	...	...	...	...	...	...	...	...	302	302	...
13	13	...	...	...	...	...	...	...	...	...	...	...	...	...	...	...	...	3	3	...
47	45	2	...	...	...	...	...	...	...	...	...	...	...	...	...	...	...	31	31	...
63	60	3	...	...	...	...	...	...	...	...	...	...	...	...	...	...	...	75	75	...
563	551	12	3	3	...	...	...	...	...	...	...	...	...	...	...	...	...	193	193	...
...	...	...	...	...	...	...	...	...	...	...	...	...	...	...	...	...	...	129	56	73
...	...	...	...	...	...	...	...	...	...	...	...	...	...	...	...	...	...	5	1	4
...	...	...	...	...	...	...	...	...	...	...	...	...	...	...	...	...	...	3	1	2
...	...	...	...	...	...	...	...	...	...	...	...	...	...	...	...	...	...	4	...	4
...	...	...	...	...	...	...	...	...	...	...	...	...	...	...	...	...	...	117	54	63

VIII
Education.

TABLE VIII.

Education by Religion and Age.

Jammu and Kashmir State Census 1911.

Part II—District Tables.

Age.	Population.									Literate in					
	Total.			Literate.			Illiterate.			Urdu.			Persian.		
	Persons.	Males.	Females.	Persons.	Males.	Females.	Persons.	Males.	Females.	Persons.	Males.	Females.	Persons.	Males.	Females.
1	2	3	4	5	6	7	8	9	10	11	12	13	14	15	16
(10) MUZAFFARABAD DISTRICT.															
All Religions.	195,205	104,308	90,897	2,833	2,748	85	192,372	101,560	90,812	1,220	1,210	10	468	465	3
0—10 ...	64,588	33,624	30,964	33	30	3	64,555	33,594	30,961	17	17	...	1	1	...
10—15 ...	22,257	12,553	9,704	187	180	7	22,070	12,373	9,697	112	110	2	15	15	...
15—20 ...	18,183	9,326	8,857	243	238	5	17,940	9,088	8,852	115	115	...	15	15	...
20 and over ...	90,177	48,805	41,372	2,370	2,300	70	87,807	46,505	41,302	976	968	8	437	434	3
Hindu (Brahmanic).	4,697	2,823	1,874	1,091	1,053	38	3,606	1,770	1,836	392	385	7	111	111	...
0—10 ...	1,264	670	594	13	13	...	1,251	657	594	12	12	...	...	...	...
10—15 ...	511	302	203	61	55	6	450	247	203	41	39	2	...	...	...
15—20 ...	405	217	188	80	78	2	325	139	186	18	18	...	...	...	...
20 and over ...	2,517	1,634	883	937	907	30	1,580	727	853	321	316	5	111	111	...
Sikh.	7,611	4,040	3,571	498	472	26	7,113	3,568	3,545	135	135	...	1	1	...
0—10 ...	2,602	1,347	1,255	17	14	3	2,585	1,333	1,252	3	3	...	...	...	...
10—15 ...	865	478	387	43	42	1	822	436	386	13	13	...	...	...	...
15—20 ...	700	373	327	68	65	3	632	308	324	28	28	...	1	1	...
20 and over ...	3,444	1,842	1,602	370	351	19	3,074	1,491	1,583	91	91	...	...	...	...
Budhist.	1	1	...	...	...	...	1	1	...	...	...	...	...	...	...
15—20 ...	1	1	...	...	...	...	1	1	...	...	...	...	...	...	...
Musalman.	182,879	97,431	85,448	1,229	1,212	17	181,650	96,219	85,431	693	690	3	356	353	3
0—10 ...	60,720	31,605	29,115	3	3	...	60,717	31,602	29,115	2	2	...	1	1	...
10—15 ...	20,881	11,773	9,108	83	83	...	20,798	11,690	9,108	58	58	...	15	15	...
15—20 ...	17,077	8,735	8,342	95	95	...	16,982	8,640	8,342	69	69	...	14	10	...
20 and over ...	84,201	45,318	38,883	1,048	1,031	17	83,153	44,287	38,866	564	561	3	326	323	3
Christian.	17	13	4	15	11	4	2	2	...	...	...	...	...	...	...
0—10 ...	2	2	...	...	...	...	2	2	...	...	...	...	...	...	...
20 and over ...	15	11	4	15	11	4	...	...	...	...	...	...	...	...	...
(11) LADDAKH DISTRICT.															
All Religions.	186,466	93,109	93,357	2,413	2,357	56	184,053	90,752	93,301	433	432	1	453	453	...
0—10 ...	53,286	26,712	26,574	3	3	...	53,283	26,709	26,574	2	2	...	...	...	...
10—15 ...	18,008	9,584	8,424	51	49	2	17,957	9,535	9,422	15	15	...	2	2	...
15—20 ...	16,197	8,669	7,528	179	177	2	16,018	8,492	7,526	46	46	...	31	31	...
20 and over ...	98,975	48,144	50,831	2,180	2,128	52	96,795	46,016	50,779	370	369	1	420	420	...
Hindu (Brahmanic).	407	358	49	215	213	2	192	145	47	123	123	...	11	11	...
0—10 ...	37	16	25	1	1	...	36	15	21	1	1	...	...	...	...
10—15 ...	10	9	1	5	5	...	5	4	1	2	2	...	...	...	...
15—20 ...	13	11	2	6	6	...	7	5	2	4	4	...	...	...	...
20 and over ...	347	322	25	203	201	2	144	121	23	116	116	...	11	11	...
Hindu (Arya).	18	11	7	11	9	2	7	2	5	8	7	1	...	...	...
0—10 ...	3	1	2	...	...	...	3	1	2	...	...	...	...	...	...
20 and over ...	15	10	5	11	9	2	4	1	3	8	7	1	...	...	...
Sikh.	41	33	8	25	23	2	16	10	6	8	8	...	...	...	...
0—10 ...	5	2	3	...	...	...	5	2	3	...	...	...	...	...	...
15—20 ...	8	6	2	5	4	1	3	2	1	3	3	...	...	...	...
20 and over ...	28	25	3	20	19	1	8	6	2	5	5	...	...	...	...

TABLE VIII.

Education by Religion and Age.

Jammu and Kashmir State Census 1911.

Part II—District Tables.

LITERATE IN

Arabic.			Dogri.			Hindi.			Bodhi.			Gurmukhi.			Others.			English.		
Persons.	Males.	Females.	Persons.	Males.	Females.	Persons.	Males.	Females.	Persons.	Males.	Females.	Persons.	Males.	Females.	Persons.	Males.	Females.	Persons.	Males.	Females.
17	18	19	20	21	22	23	24	25	26	27	28	29	30	31	32	33	34	35	36	37
(10) MUZAFFARABAD DISTRICT.																				
153	142	11	8	8	...	394	383	11	...	...	...	448	402	46	...	...	...	142	138	4
...	...	...	...	...	...	1	1	...	...	...	...	14	11	3	...	...	...	...	...	...
10	10	...	1	1	...	14	12	2	...	...	...	33	30	3	...	...	...	2	2	...
11	11	...	...	...	...	48	48	...	...	...	...	44	39	5	...	...	...	10	10	...
132	121	11	7	7	...	331	322	9	...	...	...	357	322	35	...	...	...	130	126	4
...	...	...	6	6	...	382	371	11	...	...	...	101	81	20	...	...	...	99	99	...
...	...	...	...	...	...	1	1	...	...	...	...	...	...	...	...	...	...	...	...	...
...	...	...	1	1	...	14	12	2	...	...	...	4	2	2	...	...	...	1	1	...
...	...	...	...	...	...	48	48	...	...	...	...	5	3	2	...	...	...	9	9	...
...	...	...	5	5	...	319	310	9	...	...	...	92	76	16	...	...	...	89	89	...
...	...	...	1	1	...	9	9	...	...	...	...	343	317	26	...	...	...	9	9	...
...	...	...	...	...	...	...	...	...	...	...	...	14	11	3	...	...	...	...	...	...
...	...	...	...	...	...	...	...	...	...	...	...	29	28	1	...	...	...	1	1	...
...	...	...	...	...	...	...	...	...	...	...	...	39	36	3	...	...	...	...	...	...
...	...	...	1	1	...	9	9	...	...	...	...	261	242	19	...	...	...	8	8	...
...	...	...	...	...	...	...	...	...	...	...	...	...	...	...	...	...	...	...	...	...
...	...	...	...	...	...	...	...	...	...	...	...	...	...	...	...	...	...	...	...	...
153	142	11	1	1	...	3	3	...	...	...	...	4	4	...	...	...	...	19	19	...
...	...	...	...	...	...	...	...	...	...	...	...	...	...	...	...	...	...	...	...	...
10	10	...	...	...	...	...	...	...	...	...	...	...	...	...	...	...	...	...	...	...
11	11	...	...	...	...	...	...	...	...	...	...	...	...	...	...	...	...	1	1	...
132	121	11	1	1	...	3	3	...	...	...	...	4	4	...	...	...	...	18	18	...
...	...	...	...	...	...	...	...	...	...	...	...	...	...	...	...	...	...	15	11	4
...	...	...	...	...	...	...	...	...	...	...	...	...	...	...	...	...	...	...	...	...
...	...	...	...	...	...	...	...	...	...	...	...	...	...	...	...	...	...	15	11	4
(11) LADDAKH DISTRICT.																				
16	16	...	9	9	...	15	13	2	1,368	1,323	45	13	10	3	3	2	1	103	99	4
...	...	...	...	...	...	...	...	...	...	...	...	...	...	...	...	...	...	1	1	...
...	...	...	...	...	...	...	...	...	31	29	2	...	...	...	...	...	...	3	3	...
...	...	...	...	...	...	1	1	...	96	95	1	2	1	1	...	...	...	3	3	...
16	16	...	9	9	...	14	12	2	1,241	1,199	42	11	9	2	3	2	1	96	92	4
...	...	...	9	9	...	15	13	2	...	...	...	...	...	...	2	2	...	55	55	...
...	...	...	...	...	...	...	...	...	...	...	...	...	...	...	...	...	...	...	...	...
...	...	...	...	...	...	...	...	...	...	...	...	...	...	...	...	...	...	3	3	...
...	...	...	...	...	...	1	1	...	...	...	...	...	...	...	...	...	...	1	1	...
...	...	...	9	9	...	14	12	2	...	...	...	...	...	...	2	2	...	51	51	...
...	...	...	...	...	...	...	...	...	...	...	...	1	...	1	...	...	...	2	2	...
...	...	...	...	...	...	...	...	...	...	...	...	...	...	...	...	...	...	...	...	...
...	...	...	...	...	...	...	...	...	...	...	...	1	...	1	...	...	...	2	2	...
...	...	...	...	...	...	...	...	...	...	...	...	11	9	2	...	...	...	6	6	...
...	...	...	...	...	...	...	...	...	...	...	...	...	...	...	...	...	...	...	...	...
...	...	...	...	...	...	...	...	...	...	...	...	2	1	1	...	...	...	...	...	...
...	...	...	...	...	...	...	...	...	...	...	...	9	8	1	...	...	...	6	6	...

VIII
Education.

TABLE VIII.

Education by Religion and Age.

Jammu and Kashmir State Census 1911.

Part II—District Tables.

AGE.	POPULATION.									LITERATE IN					
	Total.			Literate.			Illiterate.			Urdu.			Persian.		
	Persons.	Males.	Females.	Persons.	Males.	Females.	Persons.	Males.	Females.	Persons.	Males.	Females.	Persons.	Males.	Females.
1	2	3	4	5	6	7	8	9	10	11	12	13	14	15	16
Budhist.	35,867	17,956	17,911	1,316	1,277	39	34,551	16,679	17,872	6	6	...	1	1	...
0—10 ...	7,393	3,602	3,791	...	...	...	7,393	3,602	3,791	...	...	...	...	...	...
10—15 ...	3,186	1,615	1,571	28	27	1	3,158	1,588	1,570	...	...	...	...	...	...
15—20 ...	3,090	1,548	1,542	94	93	1	2,996	1.455	1,541	1	1	...	...	...	...
20 and over...	22,198	11,191	11,007	1,194	1,157	37	21,004	10,034	10,970	5	5	...	1	1	...
Musalman.	150,070	74,719	75,351	818	818	...	149,252	73,901	75,351	287	287	...	441	441	...
0—10 ...	45,833	23,085	22,748	2	2	...	45,831	23,083	22,748	1	1	...	...	...	...
10—15 ...	14,806	7,955	6,851	15	15	...	14,791	7,940	6,851	13	13	...	2	2	...
15—20 ...	13,077	7,097	5,980	70	70	...	13,007	7,027	5,980	37	37	...	31	31	...
20 and over...	76,354	36,582	39,772	731	731	...	75,623	35,851	37,772	236	236	...	408	408	...
Christian.	63	32	31	28	17	11	35	15	20	1	1	...	...	...	...
0—10 ...	15	6	9	...	...	...	15	6	9	...	...	...	...	...	...
10—15 ...	6	5	1	3	2	1	3	3	...	...	...	...	...	...	...
15—20 ...	9	7	2	4	4	...	5	3	2	1	1	...	...	...	...
20 and over...	33	14	19	21	11	10	12	3	9	...	...	...	...	...	...
							(12) GILGIT DISTRICT.								
All Religions.	23,969	13,299	10,670	797	784	13	23,172	12,515	10,657	377	377	...	76	76	...
0—10 ...	7,786	3,912	3,874	5	4	1	7,781	3,908	3,873	2	2	...	1	1	...
10—15 ...	2,369	1,327	1,042	19	15	4	2,350	1,312	1,038	12	12	...	2	2	...
15—20 ...	1,986	1,079	907	56	56	...	1,930	1,023	907	40	40	...	5	5	...
20 and over ...	11,828	6,981	4,847	717	709	8	11,111	6,272	4,839	323	323	...	68	68	...
Hindu (Brahmanic).	816	770	46	400	396	4	416	374	42	127	127	...	7	7	...
0—10 ...	37	23	14	1	1	...	36	22	14	...	...	...	...	...	...
10—15 ...	16	9	7	7	5	2	9	4	5	4	4	...	...	...	...
15—20 ...	47	41	6	11	11	...	36	30	6	5	5	...	...	...	...
20 and over ...	716	697	19	381	379	2	335	318	17	118	118	...	7	7	...
Sikh.	57	41	16	33	28	5	24	13	11	10	10	...	...	...	...
0—10 ...	9	4	5	1	...	1	8	4	4	...	...	...	...	...	...
0—15 ...	5	1	4	2	...	2	3	1	2	...	...	...	...	...	...
15—20 ...	5	4	1	4	4	...	1	...	1	3	3	...	...	...	...
20 and over ...	38	32	6	26	24	2	12	8	4	7	7	...	...	...	...
Musalman.	23,075	12,471	10,604	345	345	...	22,730	12,126	10,604	339	239	...	69	69	...
0—10 ...	7,738	3,883	3,855	3	3	...	7,735	3,880	3,855	2	2	...	1	1	...
10—15 ...	2,348	1,317	1,031	10	10	...	2,338	1,307	1,081	8	8	...	2	2	...
15—20 ...	1,934	1,034	900	41	41	...	1,893	993	900	32	32	...	5	5	...
20 and over...	11,055	6,237	4,818	291	291	...	10,764	5,946	4,818	197	197	...	61	61	...
Christian.	21	17	4	19	15	4	2	2	...	1	1	...	...	...	...
0—10 ...	2	2	...	...	...	...	2	2	...	...	...	...	...	...	...
10—15 ...	...	...	...	...	...	...	...	...	...	...	...	...	...	...	...
15—20 ...	...	...	...	...	...	...	...	...	...	...	...	...	...	...	...
20 and over ...	19	15	4	19	15	4	...	...	...	1	1	...	...	...	...

TABLE VIII.

Education by Religion and Age.

Jammu and Kashmir State Census 1911.

Part II—District Tables.

LITERATE IN

Arabic.			Dogri.			Hindi.			Bodhi.			Gurmukhi.			Others.			English.		
Persons.	Males.	Females.	Persons.	Males.	Females.	Persons.	Males.	Females.	Persons.	Males.	Females.	Persons.	Males.	Females.	Persons.	Males.	Females.	Persons.	Males.	Females.
17	18	19	20	21	22	23	24	25	26	27	28	29	30	31	32	33	34	35	36	37
...	...	...	...	...	...	...	...	...	1,309	1,270	39	...	...	...	...	...	...	...	...	...
...	...	...	...	...	...	...	...	...	...	...	...	...	...	...	...	...	...	...	...	...
...	...	...	...	...	...	...	...	...	28	27	1	...	...	...	...	...	...	...	...	...
...	...	...	...	...	...	...	...	...	93	92	1	...	...	...	...	...	...	...	...	...
...	...	...	...	...	...	...	...	...	1,188	1,151	37	...	...	...	...	...	...	...	...	...
16	16	...	...	...	...	...	...	...	42	42	...	1	1	...	...	...	...	31	31	...
...	...	...	...	...	...	...	...	...	...	...	...	...	...	...	...	...	...	1	1	...
...	...	...	...	...	...	...	...	...	...	...	...	...	...	...	...	...	...	...	...	...
...	...	...	...	...	...	...	...	...	...	...	...	...	...	...	...	...	...	2	2	...
16	16	...	...	...	...	...	...	...	42	42	...	1	1	...	...	...	...	28	28	...
...	...	...	...	...	...	...	...	...	17	11	6	...	...	...	1	...	1	9	5	4
...	...	...	...	...	...	...	...	...	...	...	...	...	...	...	...	...	...	...	...	...
...	...	...	...	...	...	...	...	...	3	2	1	...	...	...	...	...	...	...	...	...
...	...	...	...	...	...	...	...	...	3	3	...	...	...	...	...	...	...	...	...	...
...	...	...	...	...	...	...	...	...	11	6	5	...	...	...	1	...	1	9	5	4
(12) GILGIT DISTRICT.																				
14	14	...	36	36	...	168	166	2	...	...	...	21	14	7	...	...	...	105	101	4
...	...	...	...	...	...	...	...	...	...	...	...	1	...	1	...	...	...	1	1	...
...	...	...	...	...	...	1	...	1	...	...	...	3	...	3	...	...	...	1	1	...
2	2	...	...	...	...	5	5	...	...	...	...	2	2	...	...	...	...	2	2	...
12	12	...	36	36	...	162	161	1	...	...	...	15	12	3	...	...	...	101	97	4
...	...	...	33	33	...	168	166	2	...	...	...	6	4	2	...	...	...	59	59	...
...	...	...	...	...	...	...	...	...	...	...	...	...	...	...	...	...	...	1	1	...
...	...	...	...	...	...	1	...	1	...	...	...	1	...	1	...	...	...	1	1	...
...	...	...	...	...	...	5	5	...	...	...	...	1	1	...	...	...	...	...	...	...
...	...	...	33	33	...	162	161	1	...	...	...	4	3	1	...	...	...	57	57	...
...	...	...	1	1	...	...	...	...	...	...	...	15	10	5	...	...	...	7	7	...
...	...	...	...	...	...	...	...	...	...	...	...	1	...	1	...	...	...	...	...	...
...	...	...	...	...	...	...	...	...	...	...	...	2	...	2	...	...	...	...	...	...
...	...	...	...	...	...	...	...	...	...	...	...	1	1	...	...	...	...	...	...	...
...	...	...	1	1	...	...	...	...	...	...	...	11	9	2	...	...	...	7	7	...
14	14	...	2	2	...	...	...	...	...	...	...	...	...	...	...	...	...	21	21	...
...	...	...	...	...	...	...	...	...	...	...	...	...	...	...	...	...	...	...	...	...
...	...	...	...	...	...	...	...	...	...	...	...	...	...	...	...	...	...	...	...	...
2	2	...	...	...	...	...	...	...	...	...	...	...	...	...	...	...	...	2	2	...
12	12	...	2	2	...	...	...	...	...	...	...	...	...	...	...	...	...	19	19	...
...	...	...	...	...	...	...	...	...	...	...	...	...	...	...	...	...	...	18	14	4
...	...	...	...	...	...	...	...	...	...	...	...	...	...	...	...	...	...	...	...	...
...	...	...	...	...	...	...	...	...	...	...	...	...	...	...	...	...	...	...	...	...
...	...	...	...	...	...	...	...	...	...	...	...	...	...	...	...	...	...	...	...	...
...	...	...	...	...	...	...	...	...	...	...	...	...	...	...	...	...	...	18	14	4

VIII
Education.

TABLE VIII.

EDUCATION BY RELIGION AND AGE.

Jammu and Kashmir State Census 1911.

Part III—City Tables.

AGE.	POPULATION.									LITERATE IN					
	TOTAL.			LITERATE.			ILLITERATE.			URDU.			PERSIAN.		
	Persons.	Males.	Females.	Persons.	Males.	Females.	Persons.	Males.	Females.	Persons.	Males.	Females.	Persons.	Males.	Females.
1	2	3	4	5	6	7	8	9	10	11	12	13	14	15	16
							(a) JAMMU CITY.								
All Religions.	31.726	19,362	12,364	5,563	5.106	457	26,163	14,256	11,907	2,081	1,994	87	90	86	4
0—10 ...	5,610	2,943	2,667	145	116	29	5,465	2,827	2,638	92	89	3	1	1	...
10—15 ...	2,981	1,854	1,127	483	414	69	2,498	1,440	1,058	238	228	10	9	9	...
15—20 ...	2,841	1,800	1,041	616	548	68	2,225	1,252	973	205	191	14	12	11	1
20 and over...	20,294	12,765	7,529	4,319	4,028	291	15,975	8,737	7,234	1,546	1,486	60	68	65	3
Hindu (Brahmanic).	19,778	12,032	7,746	4,304	3,957	347	15.474	8,075	7,399	1,348	1,308	40	62	61	1
0—10 ...	3.259	1,678	1,581	105	82	23	3,154	1,596	1,558	61	59	2	1	1	...
10—15 ...	1,725	1,092	633	368	312	56	1,357	780	577	158	154	4	6	6	...
15—20 ...	1,770	1,132	638	440	395	45	1,330	737	593	127	122	5	3	3	...
20 and over...	13,024	8,130	4,894	3,391	3,168	223	9,633	4,962	4,671	1,002	973	29	52	51	1
Hindu (Arya).	132	87	45	76	68	8	56	19	37	24	23	1	...	...	...
0—10 ...	25	15	10	3	3	...	22	12	10	3	3	...	...	...	...
10—15 ...	9	7	2	7	7	...	2	...	2	4	4	...	...	...	...
15—20 ...	17	15	2	15	13	2	2	2	...	2	1	1	...	...	...
20 and over...	81	50	31	51	45	6	30	5	25	15	15	...	...	...	...
Sikh.	695	414	281	230	187	43	465	227	238	60	56	4	1	...	1
0—10 ...	146	77	69	9	5	4	137	72	65	5	5	...	...	...	...
10—15 ...	80	44	36	19	12	7	61	32	29	7	6	1	...	...	...
15—20 ...	71	46	25	46	37	9	25	9	16	8	7	1	1	...	1
20 and over...	398	247	151	156	133	23	242	114	128	40	38	2	...	...	...
Jain.	334	181	153	74	74	...	260	107	153	8	8	...	...	...	...
0—10 ...	93	41	52	3	3	...	90	38	52	...	...	...	...	...	...
10—15 ...	42	24	18	8	8	...	34	16	18	3	3	...	...	...	...
15—20 ...	28	13	15	7	7	...	21	6	15	2	2	...	...	...	...
20 and over...	171	103	68	56	56	...	115	47	68	3	3	...	...	...	...
Zoroastrian.	5	2	3	4	2	2	1	...	1	...	...	...	...	...	...
0—10 ...	1	...	1	...	...	...	1	...	...	...	...	...	...	...	...
20 and over...	4	2	2	4	2	2	...	...	1	...	...	...	...	...	...
Musalman...	10,618	6,552	4,066	858	808	50	9,760	5,744	4,016	637	596	41	27	25	2
0—10 ...	2,045	1,108	937	25	23	2	2,020	1,085	935	23	22	1	...	...	...
10—15 ...	1,101	671	430	80	74	6	1,021	597	424	65	60	5	3	3	...
15—20 ...	948	589	359	104	96	8	844	493	351	65	59	6	8	8	...
20 and over...	6,524	4,184	2,340	649	615	34	5,875	3,569	2,306	484	455	29	16	14	2
Christian.	164	94	70	17	10	7	147	84	63	4	3	1	...	...	...
0—10 ...	41	24	17	...	...	...	41	24	17	...	...	...	...	...	...
10—15 ...	24	16	8	5	1	4	19	15	4	2	1	1	...	...	...
15—20 ...	7	5	2	...	...	...	7	5	2	...	...	...	...	...	...
20 and over...	92	49	43	12	9	3	80	40	40	2	2	...	...	...	...
							(b) SRINAGAR CITY.								
All Religions.	126,344	63,378	57,966	10,609	10,493	116	115.735	57,885	57,850	3,442	3,528	14	2,695	2,688	7
0—10 ...	33,159	16,546	16,619	237	230	7	32,922	16,316	16,606	114	114	...	21	21	...
10—15 ...	13,825	8,061	5,764	1,169	1,155	14	12,656	6,906	5,750	475	471	4	100	100	...
15—20 ...	11.149	6,421	4,728	1,208	1,199	9	9,941	5,222	4,719	266	265	1	96	96	...
20 and over ...	68,211	37,350	30,861	7,995	7,909	86	60,216	29,441	30,775	2,587	2,578	9	2,478	2,471	7

TABLE VIII.

EDUCATION BY RELIGION AND AGE.

Jammu and Kashmir State Census 1911.

Part III—City Tables.

LITERATE IN

Arabic.			Dogri.			Hindi.			Bodhi.			Gurmukhi.			Others.			English.		
Persons.	Males.	Females.	Persons.	Males.	Females.	Persons.	Males.	Females.	Persons.	Males.	Females.	Persons.	Males.	Females.	Persons.	Males.	Females.	Persons.	Males.	Females.
17	18	19	20	21	22	23	24	25	26	27	28	29	30	31	32	33	34	35	36	37
						(a) JAMMU CITY.														
12	8	4	325	317	8	1,570	1,374	196	...	...	...	222	110	112	36	29	7	1,227	1,188	39
...	...	...	1	1	...	32	18	14	...	...	...	9	...	9	...	...	...	10	7	3
...	...	...	6	6	...	75	51	24	...	...	...	30	4	26	3	1	2	122	115	7
2	...	2	11	11	...	127	106	21	...	...	...	31	11	20	4	3	1	224	215	9
10	8	2	307	299	8	1,336	1,199	137	...	...	...	152	95	57	29	25	4	871	851	20
...	...	...	314	307	7	1.496	1,307	189	...	...	...	128	49	79	6	3	3	950	922	28
...	...	...	1	1	...	29	15	14	...	...	...	5	...	5	...	...	...	8	6	2
...	...	...	5	5	...	73	49	24	...	...	...	24	3	21	1	...	1	101	95	6
...	...	...	11	11	...	111	91	20	...	...	...	17	3	14	...	...	...	171	165	6
...	...	...	297	290	7	1,283	1,152	131	...	...	...	82	43	39	5	3	2	670	656	14
...	...	...	...	...	...	9	2	7	...	...	...	...	...	...	...	...	...	43	43	...
...	...	...	...	...	...	...	...	...	...	...	...	...	...	...	...	...	...	...	...	...
...	...	...	...	...	...	...	...	...	...	...	...	...	...	...	...	...	...	3	3	...
...	...	...	...	...	...	2	1	1	...	...	...	...	...	...	...	...	...	11	11	...
...	...	...	...	...	...	7	1	6	...	...	...	...	...	...	...	...	...	29	29	...
...	...	...	1	...	1	22	22	...	...	...	...	94	61	33	4	...	4	48	48	...
...	...	...	...	...	...	...	...	...	...	...	...	4	...	4	...	...	...	...	...	...
...	...	...	...	...	...	1	1	...	...	...	...	6	1	5	1	...	1	4	4	...
...	...	...	...	...	...	13	13	...	...	...	...	14	8	6	1	...	1	9	9	...
...	...	...	1	...	1	8	8	...	...	...	...	70	52	18	2	...	2	35	35	...
...	...	...	...	...	...	34	34	...	...	...	...	...	...	...	26	26	...	6	6	...
...	...	...	...	...	...	3	3	...	...	...	...	...	...	...	...	...	...	...	...	...
...	...	...	...	...	...	1	1	...	...	...	...	...	...	...	1	1	...	3	3	...
...	...	...	...	...	...	1	1	...	...	...	...	...	...	...	3	3	...	1	1	...
...	...	...	...	...	...	29	29	...	...	...	...	...	...	...	22	22	...	2	2	...
...	...	...	...	...	...	...	...	...	...	...	...	...	...	...	...	...	...	4	2	2
...	...	...	...	...	...	...	...	...	...	...	...	...	...	...	...	...	...	...	...	...
...	...	...	...	...	...	...	...	...	...	...	...	...	...	...	...	...	...	4	2	2
12	8	4	10	10	...	9	9	...	...	...	...	...	...	...	...	...	...	163	160	3
...	...	...	...	...	...	...	...	...	...	...	...	...	...	...	...	...	...	2	1	1
...	...	...	1	1	...	...	...	...	...	...	...	...	...	...	...	...	...	11	10	1
2	...	2	...	...	...	...	...	...	...	...	...	...	...	...	...	...	...	29	29	...
10	8	2	9	9	...	9	9	...	...	...	...	...	...	...	...	...	...	121	120	1
...	...	...	...	...	...	...	...	...	...	...	...	...	...	...	...	...	...	13	7	6
...	...	...	...	...	...	...	...	...	...	...	...	...	...	...	...	...	...	...	...	...
...	...	...	...	...	...	...	...	...	...	...	...	...	...	...	...	...	...	3	...	3
...	...	...	...	...	...	...	...	...	...	...	...	...	...	...	...	...	...	...	...	...
...	...	...	...	...	...	...	...	...	...	...	...	...	...	...	...	...	...	10	7	3
						(b) SRINAGAR CITY.														
174	164	10	22	22	...	1,287	1,271	16	...	...	...	13	10	3	1	...	1	2,975	2,910	56
10	10	...	...	...	...	18	14	4	...	...	...	2	1	1	...	...	...	72	70	2
24	22	2	1	1	...	87	82	5	...	...	...	...	...	...	1	...	1	481	479	2
17	16	1	3	3	...	92	90	2	...	...	...	1	1	...	...	...	...	733	728	5
123	116	7	18	11	...	1,090	1,085	5	...	...	...	10	8	2	...	...	...	1,689	1,633	56

VIII
Education.

TABLE VIII.

EDUCATION BY RELIGION AND AGE.

Jammu and Kashmir State Census 1911.

Part III—City Tables.

AGE.	POPULATION.									LITERATE IN					
	TOTAL.			LITERATE.			ILLITERATE.			URDU.			PERSIAN.		
	Persons.	Males.	Females.	Persons.	Males.	Females.	Persons.	Males.	Females.	Persons.	Males.	Females.	Persons.	Males.	Females.
1	2	3	4	5	6	7	8	9	10	11	12	13	14	15	16
Hindu (Brahmanic).	28,739	15,696	13,043	8,409	8,374	35	20,330	7,322	13,008	2,772	2,760	12	1,778	1,773	5
0—10 ...	7,024	3,511	3,513	203	199	4	6,821	3,312	3,509	109	109	...	12	12	...
10—15 ...	2,834	1,726	1,108	952	943	9	1,882	783	1,099	402	399	3	25	25	...
15—20 ...	2,615	1,587	1,028	1,001	998	3	1,614	589	1,025	215	214	1	32	32	...
20 and over ...	16,266	8,872	7,394	6,253	6,234	19	10,013	2,638	7,375	2,046	2,038	8	1,709	1,704	5
Hindu (Arya).	40	24	16	18	14	4	22	10	12	1	1	...	...	...	...
0—10 ...	15	8	7	...	...	...	15	8	7	...	...	...	...	...	...
10—15 ...	6	5	1	5	4	1	1	1	...	...	...	...	...	...	...
15—20 ...	3	2	1	2	2	...	1	...	1	...	...	...	...	...	...
20 and over ...	16	9	7	11	8	3	5	1	4	1	1	...	...	...	...
Hindu (Bramho).	1	...	1	1	...	1	...	...	...	...	...	...	...	...	...
20 and over ...	1	...	1	1	...	1	...	...	...	...	...	...	...	...	...
Sikh.	486	316	170	60	57	3	426	259	167	25	25	...	...	...	...
0—10 ...	113	45	68	2	1	1	111	44	67	...	...	...	...	...	...
10—15 ...	45	31	14	9	9	...	36	22	14	...	...	...	...	...	...
15—20 ...	47	32	15	...	...	...	47	32	15	...	...	...	...	...	...
20 and over ...	281	208	73	49	47	2	232	161	71	25	25	...	...	...	...
Zoroastrian.	26	20	6	18	14	4	8	6	2	...	...	...	...	...	...
0—10 ...	9	8	1	3	3	...	6	5	1	...	...	...	...	...	...
10—15 ...	...	...	...	...	...	...	...	...	...	...	...	...	...	...	...
15—20 ...	3	2	1	3	2	1	...	...	...	...	...	...	...	...	...
20 and over ...	14	10	4	12	9	3	2	1	1	...	...	...	...	...	...
Musalman.	96,941	52,271	44,670	2,011	1,997	14	94,930	50,274	44,656	643	641	2	917	915	2
0—10 ...	25,982	12,965	13,017	27	27	...	25,955	12,938	13,017	5	5	...	9	9	...
10—15 ...	10,938	6,298	4,640	202	199	3	10,736	6,099	4,637	73	72	1	75	75	...
15—20 ...	8,477	4,798	3,679	198	197	1	8,279	4,601	3,678	51	51	...	64	64	...
20 and over ...	51,544	28,210	23,334	1,584	1,574	10	49,960	26,636	23,324	514	513	1	769	767	2
Christian.	111	51	60	92	37	55	19	14	5	1	1	...	...	...	...
0—10 ...	16	9	7	2	...	2	14	9	5	...	...	...	...	...	...
10—15 ...	2	1	1	1	...	1	1	1	...	...	...	...	...	...	...
15—20 ...	4	...	4	4	...	4	...	...	...	...	...	...	...	...	...
20 and over ...	89	41	48	85	37	48	4	4	...	1	1	...	...	...	...

TABLE VIII.

Education by Religion and Age.

Jammu and Kashmir State Census 1911.

Part III—City Tables.

LITERATE IN

Arabic.			Dogri.			Hindi.			Bodhi.			Gurmukhi.			Others.			English.		
Persons.	Males.	Females.	Persons.	Males.	Females.	Persons.	Males.	Females.	Persons.	Males.	Females.	Persons.	Males.	Females.	Persons.	Males.	Females.	Persons.	Males.	Females.
17	18	19	20	21	22	23	24	25	26	27	28	29	30	31	32	33	34	35	36	37
...	...	...	22	22	...	1,284	1,271	13	...	...	...	5	5	...	...	...	...	2,548	2,543	5
...	...	...	...	...	...	18	14	4	...	...	...	...	...	...	...	...	...	64	64	...
...	...	...	1	1	...	87	82	5	...	...	...	...	...	...	...	...	...	437	436	1
...	...	...	3	3	...	92	90	2	...	...	...	1	1	...	...	...	...	658	658	...
...	...	...	18	18	...	1,087	1,085	2	...	...	...	4	4	...	...	...	...	1,389	1,385	4
...	...	...	...	...	...	3	...	3	...	...	...	...	...	...	1	...	1	13	13	...
...	...	...	...	...	...	...	...	...	...	...	...	...	...	...	...	...	...	...	...	...
...	...	...	...	...	...	...	...	...	...	...	...	...	...	...	1	...	1	4	4	...
...	...	...	...	...	...	...	...	...	...	...	...	...	...	...	...	...	...	2	2	...
...	...	...	...	...	...	3	...	3	...	...	...	...	...	...	...	...	...	7	7	...
...	...	...	...	...	...	...	...	...	...	...	...	...	...	...	...	...	...	1	...	1
...	...	...	...	...	...	...	...	...	...	...	...	...	...	...	...	...	...	1	...	1
...	...	...	...	...	...	...	...	...	...	...	...	8	5	3	...	...	...	27	27	...
...	...	...	...	...	...	...	...	...	...	...	...	2	1	1	...	...	...	...	...	...
...	...	...	...	...	...	...	...	...	...	...	...	...	...	...	...	...	...	9	9	...
...	...	...	...	...	...	...	...	...	...	...	...	...	...	...	...	...	...	...	...	...
...	...	...	...	...	...	...	...	...	...	...	...	6	4	2	...	...	...	18	18	...
...	...	...	...	...	...	...	...	...	...	...	...	...	...	...	...	...	...	18	14	4
...	...	...	...	...	...	...	...	...	...	...	...	...	...	...	...	...	...	3	3	...
...	...	...	...	...	...	...	...	...	...	...	...	...	...	...	...	...	...	...	...	...
...	...	...	...	...	...	...	...	...	...	...	...	...	...	...	...	...	...	3	2	1
...	...	...	...	...	...	...	...	...	...	...	...	...	...	...	...	...	...	12	9	3
174	164	10	...	...	...	...	...	...	...	...	...	...	...	...	...	...	...	277	277	...
10	10	...	...	...	...	...	...	...	...	...	...	...	...	...	...	...	...	3	3	...
24	22	2	...	...	...	...	...	...	...	...	...	...	...	...	...	...	...	30	30	...
17	16	1	...	...	...	...	...	...	...	...	...	...	...	...	...	...	...	66	66	...
123	116	7	...	...	...	...	...	...	...	...	...	...	...	...	...	...	...	178	178	...
...	...	...	...	...	...	...	...	...	...	...	...	...	...	...	...	...	...	91	36	55
...	...	...	...	...	...	...	...	...	...	...	...	...	...	...	...	...	...	2	...	2
...	...	...	...	...	...	...	...	...	...	...	...	...	...	...	...	...	...	1	...	1
...	...	...	...	...	...	...	...	...	...	...	...	...	...	...	...	...	...	4	...	4
...	...	...	...	...	...	...	...	...	...	...	...	...	...	...	...	...	...	84	36	48

TABLE IX.

EDUCATION BY SELECTED CASTES, TRIBES OR RACES.

Jammu and Kashmir State Census 1911.

1. This Table and Tables XIV and XVI deal only with a few typical castes, tribes, etc., selected with reference to their suitability to the subject of the table concerned.

2. Although the caste-totals dealt with here relate to the State as a whole and are the same in these three Tables, they will not be found agreeing with those given in Table XIII. This is because the classification for the latter was made afterwards and on different principles. A large number of persons returned under various designations were, upon enquiry, found to belong to one and the same major head of caste, etc. All these cases were included under such major heads for purposes of Table XIII, whereas they are excluded from Tables IX, XIV and XVI.

3. The figures for Christians, Budhists, Sikhs, etc., have not been shown in this Table and Table XIV as their literacy and civil condition are already seperately indicated by Tables VII and VIII. In Table XVI, however, Christian figures are set out under three main heads, *viz.*, Europeans, Anglo-Indians, and Native Christians.

IX
Education by Selected Castes.

TABLE IX.

Education by Selected Castes, Tribes or Races.

Jammu and Kashmir State Census 1911.

Caste, Tribe or Race.	Population. Total. Persons.	Population. Total. Males.	Population. Total. Females.	Population. Literate. Persons.	Population. Literate. Males.	Population. Literate. Females.	Population. Illiterate. Persons.	Population. Illiterate. Males.	Population. Illiterate. Females.	Literate in English. Persons.	Literate in English. Males.	Literate in English. Females.
1	2	3	4	5	6	7	8	9	10	11	12	13
					HINDU.							
Arora ...	1,879	1,127	752	515	473	42	1,364	654	710	71	71	...
Brahman ...	173,795	93,115	80,680	10,026	9,662	364	163,769	83,453	80,316	480	469	11
Kashmiri Pandit (Brahman).	55,097	30,724	24,373	17,911	17,814	97	37,186	12,910	24,276	3,136	3,122	14
Jat ...	23,388	12,464	10,924	190	184	6	23,198	12,280	10,918	8	8	...
Khatri ...	15,855	9,160	6,695	3,916	3,675	241	11,939	5,485	6,454	664	653	11
Mahajan ...	17,984	9,902	8,082	3,616	3,537	79	14,368	6,365	8,003	97	96	1
Rajput ...	50,264	29,540	20,724	3,562	3,497	65	46,702	26,043	20,659	139	138	1
Thakkar ...	93,596	49,419	44,177	1,598	1,580	18	91,998	47,839	44,159	26	25	1
					MUSALMAN.							
Awan ...	25,831	13,922	11,909	184	181	3	25,647	13,741	11,906	6	6	...
Brukpa ...	4,329	2,189	2,140	5	5	...	4.324	2,184	2,140	1	1	...
Balti ...	11,176	5,522	5,654	20	20	...	11,156	5,502	5,654	...	...	...
Bat ...	152,210	82,012	70,198	609	604	5	151,601	81,408	70,193	26	26	...
Babazada ...	48,843	24,233	24,610	2,529	2.434	95	46,314	21,799	24,515	49	48	1
Dar ...	98,525	53,150	45,375	282	278	4	98,243	52,872	45,371	6	6	...
Malik ...	53,451	27,072	26,379	368	355	13	53,083	26,717	26,366	8	8	...
Moghal ...	33,269	17,696	15,573	471	455	16	32,798	17,241	15,557	26	26	...
Pathan ...	19,902	10,871	9,031	358	307	51	19,544	10,564	8,980	32	32	...
Rishi ...	8,066	4,163	3,903	50	50	...	8,016	4,113	3,903	...	...	...
Shin ...	2,719	1,620	1,099	24	24	...	2,695	1,596	1,099	...	...	...
Sufi ...	14,404	8,261	6,143	60	59	1	14,344	8,202	6,142	1	1	...
Sheikh ...	105,338	58,197	47,141	1,152	1,116	36	104,186	57,081	47,105	121	121	...
Yashkun ...	16,214	7,944	8,270	68	68	...	16,146	7,876	8,270	2	2	...

TABLE X.

LANGUAGES.

Jammu and Kashmir State Census 1911.

The arrangement of the languages, dialects, etc., in this Table is in accordance with the classification scheme of Dr. Grierson. As distinguished from the method of the last census the languages have this time been arranged both territorially and Philologically all in one Table, the parts of the Table being :—

Part I—Languages of the State.
,, II— ,, India.
,, III— ,, Asia.
,, IV— ,, Europe.

Unclassified languages are shown separately at the end of Part IV. The arrangement within each group is alphabetical.

2. Certain names that formed only synonyms of others have been included together and the figures shown under the better known term, *e. g.*, Dardi and Dardistani or Jamwali and Dogri.

3. A greater detail of dialectical distinction having this time been gone into, certain very minute divisions were found to have been returned. Their figures have been thrown into the more important heads to which they belonged. These are discussed individually in the Report Volume.

4. The Sanskrit figures have been thrown into Hindi as it is not a spoken language at all.

5. Gilgit Agency and Mansar figures do not find a place here.

TABLE X.

LANGUAGES.

Jammu and Kashmir State Census 1911.

Part I—Languages of the State.

DISTRICT, JAGIR OR ILAQA.	POPULATION.			*Tibeto-Chinese Family.* Tibeto-Burman Sub-Family. *Tibeto-Himalayan Branch.* TIBETAN GROUP.						*Indo-European Family.* Aryan Sub-Family. *Indian Branch.* Non-Sanskrit Sub-Branch. SHINA-KHOWAR GROUP.															
				Balti.			*Laddakhi.*			*Bambagi.*			*Chitrali. (Chatrari).*			*Dardistani.*			*Dodi.*			*Kaghani (Kohistani).*		
	Persons.	Males.	Females.	Persons.	Males.	Females.	Persons.	Males.	Females.	Persons.	Males.	Females.	Persons.	Males.	Females.	Persons.	Males.	Females.	Persons.	Males.	Females.	Persons.	Males.	Females.
1	2	3	4	5	6	7	8	9	10	11	12	13	14	15	16	17	18	19	20	21	22	23	24	25
Total State ...	3,103,501	1,644,978	1,458,523	132,161	65,537	66,624	54,237	27,346	26,891	1,140	598	542	7	7	...	4,711	2,366	2,345	170	96	74	4,750	2,590	2,160
I—Total Jammu Province (including *Jagirs*).	1,597,865	846,790	751,075	11	11	...	620	322	298	1,140	598	542	2	2	...	22	17	5	4	4	...	4,349	2,403	1,946
1. Jammu District ...	326,691	180,691	146,000	1	1	...	14	11	3	...	...	...	...	...	...	20	17	3	...	...	...	215	147	68
2. Jasrota " ...	151,802	81,375	70,427	...	...	...	16	9	7	...	...	...	...	...	...	...	...	...	...	...	...	231	128	103
3. Udhampur " ...	215,725	113,877	101,848	...	...	...	545	260	285	...	...	...	...	...	...	...	...	...	4	4	...	179	78	101
4. Riasi " ...	206,809	109,026	97,783	...	...	...	2	2	...	1,139	598	541	2	2	...	...	...	...	...	...	...	3,698	2,031	1,667
5. Mirpur " ...	324,933	169,276	155,657	10	10	...	...	...	...	1	...	1	...	...	...	...	...	...	...	...	...	21	15	6
6. Bhadarwah *Jagir* ...	37,512	18,975	18,537	...	...	...	5	2	3	...	...	...	...	...	...	...	...	...	...	...	...	...	...	...
7. Punch *Ilaqa* ...	334,393	173,570	160,823	...	...	...	38	38	...	...	...	...	...	...	...	2	2	...	...	...	...	5	4	1
II—Total Kashmir Province (including *Jagirs*).	1,295,201	691,780	603,421	143	77	66	126	58	68	...	...	...	...	...	...	4,479	2,206	2,273	166	92	74	401	187	214
8. Kashmir North (including Langet *Jagir*).	460,786	244,637	216,149	53	30	23	9	6	3	...	...	...	...	...	...	4,445	2,188	2,257	...	...	...	...	...	...
9. Kashmir South (including city).	639,210	342,835	296,375	90	47	43	117	52	65	...	...	...	...	...	...	34	18	16	166	92	74	398	184	214
Total Kashmir Valley ...	*1,099,996*	*587,472*	*512,524*	*143*	*77*	*66*	*126*	*58*	*68*	...	...	...	...	...	...	*4,479*	*2,206*	*2,273*	*166*	*92*	*74*	*398*	*184*	*214*
10. Muzaffarabad District (*Wizarat Pahar*).	195,205	104,308	90,897	...	...	...	...	...	...	...	...	...	...	...	...	...	...	...	...	...	...	3	3	...
III—Total Frontier Districts.	210,435	106,408	104,027	132,007	65,449	66,558	53,491	26,966	26,525	...	...	...	5	5	...	210	143	67	...	...	...	...	...	...
11. Laddakh District ...	186,466	93,109	93,357	131,774	65,246	66,528	53,491	26,966	26,525	...	...	...	...	...	...	...	...	...	...	...	...	...	...	...
12. Gilgit " ...	23,969	13,299	10,670	233	203	30	...	...	...	...	...	...	5	5	...	210	143	67	...	...	...	...	...	...

TABLE X.

Languages.

Jammu and Kashmir State Census 1911.

Part I—Languages of the State—(Continued).

DISTRICT, JAGIR OR ILAQA.	Indo-European Family. Aryan Sub-Family. Indian Branch. Non-Sanskrit Sub-Branch. Shina-Khowar Group.												Indo-European Family. Aryan Sub-Family. Indian Branch. Sanskrit Sub-Branch. Western Group.					
	Kashmiri.			*Kishtwari.*			*Rambani.*			*Shina.*			*Bhadarwahi.*			*Bhujwali.*		
	Persons.	Males.	Females.	Persons.	Males.	Females.	Persons.	Males.	Females.	Persons.	Males.	Females.	Persons.	Males.	Females.	Persons.	Males.	Females.
	26	27	28	29	30	31	32	33	34	35	36	37	38	39	40	41	42	43
Total State ...	1,155,229	620,505	534,724	7,464	4,029	3,435	2,174	1,088	1,086	21,562	11,236	10,326	24,499	12,332	12,167	432	206	226
I—Total Jammu Province (including *Jagirs*).	114,466	64,784	49,682	7,438	4,009	3,429	2,171	1,085	1,086	28	18	10	24,485	12,322	12,163	432	206	226
1. Jammu District	8,886	8,712	174	27	24	3	6	6	...	3	3	...	141	119	22	...	...	...
2. Jasrota "	1,972	980	992	...	...	...	...	...	...	...	...	...	285	283	2	...	...	...
3. Udhampur "	57,443	30,422	27,021	7,297	3,905	3,392	1,886	932	954	3	1	2	2,906	1,606	1,300	432	206	226
4. Riasi "	20,252	10,536	9,716	32	32	...	279	147	132	3	3	...	133	127	6	...	...	...
5. Mirpur "	136	100	36	...	...	...	...	...	...	3	...	3	...	...	...	...	...	...
6. Bhadarwah *Jagir*	10,461	5,490	4,971	81	48	33	...	...	...	4	3	1	21,012	10,179	10,833	...	...	...
7. Punch *Ilaqa*	15,316	8,544	6,772	1	...	1	...	...	...	12	8	4	8	8	...	...	...	...
II—Total Kashmir Province (including *Jagirs*).	1,039,964	555,083	484,881	19	13	6	3	3	...	33	17	16	3	3	...	...	...	...
8. Kashmir North (including Langet *Jagir*).	413,672	219,266	194,406	2	2	...	3	3	...	2	1	1	3	3	...	...	...	...
9. Kashmir South (including city) ...	608,573	326,158	282,415	17	11	6	...	...	...	26	12	14	...	...	...	...	...	...
Total Kashmir Valley	*1,022,245*	*545,424*	*476,821*	*19*	*13*	*6*	*3*	*3*	...	*28*	*13*	*15*	*3*	*3*	...	...	...	...
10. Muzaffarabad District (*Wizarat Pahar*).	17,719	9,659	8,060	...	...	...	...	...	...	5	4	1	...	...	...	...	...	...
III—Total Frontier Districts	799	638	161	7	7	...	...	...	...	21,501	11,201	10,300	11	7	4	...	...	...
11. Laddakh District	589	450	139	6	6	...	...	...	...	3	3	...	11	7	4	...	...	...
12. Gilgit "	210	188	22	1	1	...	...	...	...	21,498	11,198	10,300	...	...	...	...	...	...

TABLE X.

LANGUAGES.

Jammu and Kashmir State Census 1911.

Part I—Languages of the State—(*Continued*).

Indo-European Family. — Aryan Sub-Family. — *Indian Branch.* — Sanskrit Sub-branch. — WESTERN GROUP.

DISTRICT, JAGIR OR ILAQA.	*Bangri.*			*Budali.*			*Dogri.*			*Gujari.*			*Gaddi (Gadi).*			*Kathiawari.*			*Pahari.*		
	Persons.	Males.	Females.	Persons.	Males.	Females.	Persons.	Males.	Females.	Persons.	Males.	Females.	Persons.	Males.	Females.	Persons.	Males.	Females.	Persons.	Males.	Females.
	44	45	46	47	48	49	50	51	52	53	54	55	56	57	58	59	60	61	62	63	64
Total State ...	125	81	44	849	452	397	516,441	279,562	236,879	252,692	131,712	120,980	6,354	3,108	3,246	5	5	...	488,403	253,770	234,633
I—Total Jammu Province (including *Jagirs.*) ...	125	81	44	849	452	397	514,302	277,759	236,543	192,372	99,213	93,159	6,354	3,108	3,246	5	5	...	321,820	165,531	156,289
1. Jammu District ...	...	...	...	6	6	...	214,646	118,131	96,515	42,656	19,343	23,313	...	...	...	...	...	...	909	704	205
2. Jasrota ,, ...	2	2	...	...	...	...	122,599	65,802	56,797	11,816	6,190	5,626	397	271	126	...	...	...	10,008	4,956	5,052
3. Udhampur ,, ...	...	...	...	...	...	...	87,429	46,099	41,330	17,550	9,160	8,390	5,269	2,515	2,754	1	1	...	2,552	1,668	884
4. Riasi ,, ...	1	...	1	843	446	397	56,447	29,602	26,845	46,698	25,714	20,984	...	...	...	4	4	...	65,389	33,331	32,058
5. Mirpur ,, ...	122	79	43	...	...	...	27,968	15,246	12,722	9,894	5,323	4,571	...	...	...	...	...	...	9,971	5,331	4,640
6. Bhadarwah *Jagir* ...	...	...	...	...	...	...	2,381	1,373	1,008	2,210	1,100	1,110	688	322	366	...	...	...	52	14	38
7. Punch *Ilaqa* ...	...	...	...	...	...	...	2,832	1,506	1,326	61,548	32,383	29,165	...	...	...	...	...	...	232,939	119,527	113,412
II—Total Kashmir Province (including *Jagirs*).	...	...	...	...	...	...	1,239	934	305	60,127	32,453	27,674	...	...	...	...	...	...	166,493	88,165	78,328
8. Kashmir North (including Langet *Jagir*).	...	...	...	...	...	...	257	196	61	12,898	7,251	5,647	...	...	...	...	...	...	17,879	9,360	8,519
9. Kashmir South (including city).	...	...	...	...	...	...	884	666	218	13,781	7,092	6,689	...	...	...	...	...	...	6,460	3,479	2,981
Total Kashmir Valley ...	...	...	...	...	...	...	*1,141*	*862*	*279*	*26,679*	*14,343*	*12,336*	...	...	...	...	...	...	*24,339*	*12,839*	*11,500*
10. Muzaffarabad District (*Wizarat Pahar.*)	...	...	...	...	...	...	98	72	26	33,448	18,110	15,338	...	...	...	...	...	...	142,154	75,326	66,828
III—Total Frontier Districts...	...	...	...	...	...	...	900	869	31	193	46	147	...	...	...	...	...	...	90	74	16
11. Laddakh District ...	...	...	...	...	...	...	135	113	22	1	...	1	...	...	...	...	...	...	15	15	...
12. Gilgit ,, ...	...	...	...	...	...	...	765	756	9	192	46	146	...	...	...	...	...	...	75	59	16

TABLE X.

LANGUAGES.

Jammu and Kashmir State Census 1911.

Part I—Languages of the State—(*Concluded*).

Indo-European Family. — Aryan Sub-Family. — *Indian Branch.* — Sanskrit Sub-Branch. — WESTERN GROUP.

DISTRICT, JAGIR OR ILAQA.	*Pawahdi.*			*Padri.*			*Pangwali.*			*Pogli.*			*Punjabi.*			*Siraji.*			*Sarori.*		
	Persons.	Males.	Females.	Persons.	Males.	Females.	Persons.	Males.	Females.	Persons.	Males.	Females.	Persons.	Males.	Females.	Persons.	Males.	Females.	Persons.	Males.	Females.
	65	66	67	68	69	70	71	72	73	74	75	76	77	78	79	80	81	82	83	84	85
Total State ...	14	13	1	4,813	2,516	2,297	6	6	...	8,158	4,254	3,904	213,339	115,823	97,516	14,562	7,453	7,109	1,599	830	769
I—Total Jammu Province (including *Jagirs*).	14	13	1	4,813	2,516	2,297	6	6	...	8,158	4,254	3,904	193,111	104,359	88,752	14,562	7,453	7,109	1,599	830	769
1. Jammu District ...	3	3	...	...	...	...	...	...	...	...	...	...	54,580	30,326	24,254	16	...	16	...	...	...
2. Jasrota „ ...	...	...	...	1	...	1	...	...	...	...	...	...	3,992	2,440	1,552	6	6	...	...	...	...
3. Udhampur „ ...	9	8	1	4,807	2,511	2,296	6	6	...	8,060	4,192	3,868	1,557	1,086	471	14,344	7,327	7,017	1,599	830	769
4. Riasi „ ...	2	2	...	...	...	...	...	...	...	93	58	35	1,758	1,168	590	171	107	64	...	...	...
5. Mirpur „ ...	...	...	...	...	...	...	...	...	...	...	...	...	109,750	57,910	51,840	...	...	...	...	...	...
6. Bhadarwah *Jagir* ...	...	...	...	5	5	...	...	...	...	5	4	1	133	111	22	25	13	12	...	...	...
7. Punch *Ilaqa* ...	...	...	...	...	...	...	...	...	...	...	...	...	21,341	11,318	10,023	...	...	...	...	...	...
II—Total Kashmir Province (including *Jagirs*).	...	...	...	...	...	...	...	...	...	...	...	...	19,660	11,019	8,641	...	...	...	...	...	...
8. Kashmir North (including Langet *Jagir*).	...	...	...	...	...	...	...	...	...	...	...	...	10,795	5,893	4,902	...	...	...	...	...	...
9. Kashmir South (including city).	...	...	...	...	...	...	...	...	...	...	...	...	7,327	4,142	3,185	...	...	...	...	...	...
Total Kashmir Valley ...	...	...	...	...	...	...	...	...	...	...	...	...	*18,122*	*10,035*	*8.087*	...	...	...	...	...	...
10. Muzaffarabad District (*Wizarat Pahar*).	...	...	...	...	...	...	...	...	...	...	...	...	1,538	984	554	...	...	...	...	...	...
III—Total Frontier Districts.	...	...	...	...	...	...	...	...	...	...	...	...	568	445	123	...	...	...	...	...	...
11. Laddakh District ...	...	...	...	...	...	...	...	...	...	...	...	...	204	144	60	...	...	...	...	...	...
12. Gilgit „ ...	...	...	...	...	...	...	...	...	...	...	...	...	364	301	63	...	...	...	...	...	...

TABLE X.

Languages.

Jammu and Kashmir State Census 1911.

Part II—Languages of India.

DISTRICT, JAGIR OR ILAQA.	*Tibeto-Chinese Family.* Tibito-Burman Sub-Family. *Tibeto Himalayan Branch.* Pronominalized Himalayan Group. Western Sub-Group.			*Indo-European Family.* Aryan Sub-Family. *Indian Branch.* Sanskrit Sub-Branch. North-Western Group.									Southern Group.						Eastern Group.		
	Multani.			*Chibhali (Chhibhali).*			*Puthwari (Pothwari.)*			*Sindhi.*			*Goanese.*			*Marhatti (Marathi).*			*Bengali.*		
	Persons.	Males.	Females.	Persons.	Males.	Females.	Persons.	Males.	Females.	Persons.	Males.	Females.	Persons.	Males.	Females.	Persons.	Males.	Females.	Persons.	Males.	Females.
1	2	3	4	5	6	7	8	9	10	11	12	13	14	15	16	17	18	19	20	21	22
Total State ...	4	4	...	82,206	42,475	39,731	94,125	47,325	46,800	22	20	2	5	5	...	6	4	2	79	48	31
I—Total Jammu Province (including *Jagirs*).	2	2	...	82,048	42,317	39,731	94,100	47,314	46,786	7	5	2	...	...	...	6	4	2	63	36	27
1. Jammu District ...	2	2	...	498	475	23	45	40	5	2	...	2	...	...	...	3	2	1	62	35	27
2. Jasrota " ...	...	...	...	4	4	...	14	12	2	...	...	...	...	...	...	...	...	...	...	...	...
3. Udhampur " ...	...	...	...	842	439	403	12	7	5	2	2	...	...	...	...	...	...	...	...	...	...
4. Riasi " ...	...	...	...	9,152	4,678	4,474	5	3	2	1	1	...	...	...	...	...	...	...	1	1	...
5. Mirpur " ...	...	...	...	71,546	36,716	34,830	93,982	47,223	46,759	2	2	...	...	...	...	1	1	...	...	...	...
6. Bhadarwah *Jagir* ...	...	...	...	...	...	...	1	1	...	...	...	...	...	...	...	...	...	...	...	...	...
7. Punch *Ilaqa* ...	...	...	...	6	5	1	41	28	13	...	...	...	...	...	...	2	1	1	...	...	...
II—Total Kashmir Province (including *Jagirs*).	...	...	...	118	118	...	25	11	14	13	13	...	5	5	...	...	...	...	14	10	4
8. Kashmir North (including Langet *Jagir*).	...	...	...	...	...	...	25	11	14	11	11	...	...	...	...	...	...	...	...	...	...
9. Kashmir South (including city).	...	...	...	118	118	...	...	...	...	2	2	...	5	5	...	...	...	...	13	9	4
Total Kashmir Valley ...	...	...	...	*118*	*118*	...	*25*	*11*	*14*	*13*	*13*	...	*5*	*5*	...	...	...	...	*13*	*9*	*4*
10. Muzaffarabad District (*Wizarat Pahar*).	...	...	...	...	...	...	...	...	...	...	...	...	...	...	...	...	...	...	1	1	...
III—Total Frontier Districts.	2	2	...	40	40	...	...	...	...	2	2	...	...	...	...	...	...	...	2	2	...
11. Laddakh District ...	2	2	...	40	40	...	...	...	...	2	2	...	...	...	...	...	...	...	1	1	...
12. Gilgit " ...	...	...	...	...	...	...	...	...	...	...	...	...	...	...	...	...	...	...	1	1	...

TABLE X.

LANGUAGES.

Jammu and Kashmir State Census 1911.

Part II—Languages of India—(*Continued*).

Indo-European Family. — Aryan Sub-Family. — *Indian Branch.* — Sanskrit Sub-Branch. — WESTERN GROUP.

DISTRICT, JAGIR OR ILAQA.	*Bikaneri.* Persons.	Males.	Females.	*Chambiali.* Persons.	Males.	Females.	*Dakhni.* Persons.	Males.	Females.	*Gujarati.* Persons.	Males.	Females.	*Hindi.* Persons.	Males.	Females.	*Kangri.* Persons.	Males.	Females.	*Kuluwari.* Persons.	Males.	Females.
	23	24	25	26	27	28	29	30	31	32	33	34	35	36	37	38	39	40	41	42	43
Total State ...	4	3	1	923	500	423	13	11	2	44	28	16	556	375	181	276	230	46	24	16	8
I—Total Jammu Province (including *Jagirs*).	4	3	1	923	500	423	13	11	2	16	9	7	380	253	127	270	224	46	24	16	8
1. Jammu District ...	3	2	1	...	...	...	4	4	...	12	6	6	278	184	94	72	67	5	...	...	...
2. Jasrota ,, ...	...	...	...	16	14	2	...	...	...	...	...	...	6	5	1	11	7	4	...	...	...
3. Udhampur ,, ...	...	...	...	698	369	329	...	...	...	1	...	1	2	2	...	88	87	1	...	...	...
4. Riasi ,, ...	...	...	...	...	...	...	4	3	1	...	...	...	2	2	...	...	...	...	...	...	...
5. Mirpur ,, ...	...	...	...	1	1	...	...	...	...	3	3	...	70	51	19	...	...	...	...	...	...
6. Bhadarwah *Jagir* ...	1	1	...	208	116	92	3	3	...	...	...	...	1	1	...	49	33	16	24	16	8
7. Punch *Ilaqa* ...	...	...	...	...	...	...	2	1	1	...	...	...	21	8	13	50	30	20	...	...	...
II—Total Kashmir Province (including *Jagirs*).	...	...	...	...	...	...	...	...	...	27	18	9	171	118	53	6	6	...	...	...	...
8. Kashmir North (including Langet *Jagir*).	...	...	...	...	...	...	...	...	...	...	...	...	15	1	14	3	3	...	...	...	...
9. Kashmir South (including city).	...	...	...	...	...	...	...	...	...	27	18	9	142	111	31	3	3	...	...	...	...
Total Kashmir Valley ...	...	...	...	...	...	...	...	...	...	*27*	*18*	*9*	*157*	*112*	*45*	*6*	*6*	...	...	...	...
10. Muzaffarabad District (*Wizarat Pahar*).	...	...	...	...	...	...	...	...	...	...	...	...	14	6	8	...	...	...	...	...	...
III—Total Frontier Districts.	...	...	...	...	...	...	...	...	...	1	1	...	5	4	1	...	...	...	...	...	...
11. Laddakh District ...	...	...	...	...	...	...	...	...	...	...	...	...	5	4	1	...	...	...	...	...	...
12. Gilgit ,, ...	...	...	...	...	...	...	...	...	...	1	1	...	...	...	...	...	...	...	...	...	...

TABLE X.

LANGUAGES.

Jammu and Kashmir State Census 1911.

Part II—Languages of India—(*Concluded*).

DISTRICT, JAGIR OR ILAQA.	Indo-European Family. Aryan Sub-Family. *Indian Branch.* Sanskrit Sub-Branch.																	
	WESTERN GROUP.															NORTHERN GROUP.		
	Marwari.			*Mewari.*			*Mandiali.*			*Rathi.*			*Urdu.*			*Naipali (Gorkhali).*		
	Persons.	Males.	Females.	Persons.	Males.	Females.	Persons.	Males.	Females.	Persons.	Males.	Females.	Persons.	Males.	Females.	Persons.	Males.	Females.
	44	45	46	47	48	49	50	51	52	53	54	55	56	57	58	59	60	61
Total State ...	127	73	54	4	2	2	97	86	11	4	4	...	1,911	1,388	523	1,844	1,534	310
I—Total Jammu Province (including *Jagirs*).	126	72	54	4	2	2	97	86	11	4	4	...	1,565	1,149	416	1,241	1,059	192
1. Jammu District ...	76	39	37	4	2	2	...	...	...	...	...	...	1,006	734	272	705	573	132
2. Jasrota " ...	...	...	...	...	...	...	...	...	...	...	...	...	71	53	18	101	65	36
3. Udhampur " ...	...	...	...	...	...	...	13	13	...	...	...	...	114	83	31	16	14	2
4. Riasi " ...	...	...	...	...	...	...	...	...	...	...	...	...	53	50	3	47	38	9
5. Mirpur " ...	50	33	17	...	...	...	...	...	...	...	...	...	267	184	83	293	293	...
6. Bhadarwah *Jagir* ...	...	...	...	...	...	...	84	73	11	4	4	...	26	24	2	14	10	4
7. Punch *Ilaqa* ...	...	...	...	...	...	...	...	...	...	...	...	...	28	21	7	65	56	9
II—Total Kashmir Province (including *Jagirs*).	1	1	...	...	...	...	...	...	...	...	...	...	313	212	101	297	181	116
8. Kashmir North (including Langet *Jagirs*).	1	1	...	...	...	...	...	...	...	...	...	...	38	30	8	58	30	28
9. Kashmir South (including city).	...	...	...	...	...	...	...	...	...	...	...	...	245	160	85	239	151	88
Total Kashmir Valley ...	*1*	*1*	...	...	...	...	...	...	...	...	...	...	*283*	*190*	*93*	*297*	*181*	*116*
10. Muzaffarabad District (*Wizarat Pahar*).	...	...	...	...	...	...	...	...	...	...	...	...	30	22	8	...	...	...
III—Total Frontier Districts.	...	...	...	...	...	...	...	...	...	...	...	...	33	27	6	306	304	2
11. Laddakh District ...	...	...	...	...	...	...	...	...	...	...	...	...	5	4	1	32	32	...
12. Gilgit " ...	...	...	...	...	...	...	...	...	...	...	...	...	28	23	5	274	274	...

TABLE X.

LANGUAGES.

Jammu and Kashmir State Census 1911.

Part III—Asiatic Languages.

DISTRICT, JAGIR OR ILAQA.	*Indo-European Family.* Aryan Sub-Family. *Eranian Branch.* EASTERN GROUP.			*Tibeto-Chinese Family.* Tibeto-Burman Sub-Family. *Tibeto-Himalayan Branch.* TIBETAN GROUP.			*Mongolian Family.* URAL ALTAIC GROUP.			*Mongolian Family.* MONOSYLLABIC GROUP.			*Semitic Family.*			*Indo-European Family.* ERANIAN GROUP.		
	Pashto.			*Lhassi.*			*Yarkandi. (Turkistani.)*			*Chinese.*			*Arabic.*			*Persian.*		
	Persons.	Males.	Females.	Persons	Males.	Females.	Persons.	Males.	Females.	Persons.	Males.	Females.	Persons.	Males.	Females.	Persons.	Males.	Females.
1	2	3	4	5	6	7	8	9	10	11	12	13	14	15	16	17	18	19
Total State ...	2,745	1,951	794	115	56	59	29	23	6	2	...	2	7	6	1	58	50	8
I—Total Jammu Province (including *Jagirs*).	1,527	1,221	306	...	...	...	1	1	...	...	...	...	6	5	1	26	24	2
1. Jammu District ...	140	103	37	...	...	...	...	...	...	...	...	...	...	...	...	7	5	2
2. Jasrota " ...	28	22	6	...	...	...	...	...	...	...	...	...	...	...	...	...	...	...
3. Udhampur " ...	54	39	15	...	...	...	...	...	...	...	...	...	...	...	...	5	5	...
4. Riasi " ...	444	265	179	...	...	...	...	...	...	...	...	...	1	1	...	...	...	...
5. Mirpur " ...	717	694	23	...	...	...	...	...	...	...	...	...	5	4	1	9	9	...
6. Bhadarwah *Jagir* ...	35	29	6	...	...	...	...	...	...	...	...	...	...	...	...	...	...	...
7. Punch *Ilaqa* ...	109	69	40	...	...	...	1	1	...	...	...	...	...	...	...	5	5	...
II—Total Kashmir Province (including *Jagirs*).	1,134	653	481	...	...	...	15	13	2	...	...	...	1	1	...	15	10	5
8. Kashmir North (including Langet *Jagir*.)	577	324	253	...	...	...	1	1	...	...	...	...	...	...	...	3	2	1
9. Kashmir South (including city).	389	227	162	...	...	...	14	12	2	...	...	...	1	1	...	3	3	...
Total Kashmir Valley ...	*966*	*551*	*415*	...	...	...	*15*	*13*	*2*	...	...	...	*1*	*1*	...	*6*	*5*	*1*
10. Muzaffarabad District (*Wizarat Pahar.*)	168	102	66	...	...	...	...	...	...	...	...	...	...	...	...	9	5	4
III—Total Frontier Districts.	84	77	7	115	56	59	13	9	4	2	...	2	...	...	...	17	16	1
11. Laddakh District ...	4	4	...	115	56	59	13	9	4	2	...	2	...	...	...	4	4	...
12. Gilgit " ...	80	73	7	...	...	...	...	...	...	...	...	...	...	...	...	13	12	1

TABLE X.

LANGUAGES.

Jammu and Kashmir State Census 1912.

Part IV—European Languages.

DISTRICT, JAGIR OR ILAQA.	Indo-European Family.											
	TUTONIC GROUP.									ROMANIC GROUP.		
	Dutch.			*English.*			*German.*			*French.*		
	Persons.	Males.	Females.	Persons.	Males.	Females.	Persons.	Males.	Females.	Persons.	Males.	Females.
1	2	3	4	5	6	7	8	9	10	11	12	13
Total State ...	2	2	...	257	141	116	14	5	9	1	1	...
I—Total Jammu Province (including *Jagirs*).	...	...	...	54	32	22	...	...	...	...	...	...
1. Jammu District ...	...	...	...	22	15	7	...	...	...	...	...	...
2. Jasrota ,, ...	...	...	...	...	...	...	...	...	...	...	...	...
3. Udhampur ,, ...	...	...	...	...	...	...	...	...	...	...	...	...
4. Riasi ,, ...	...	...	...	1	1	...	...	...	...	...	...	...
5. Mirpur ,, ...	...	...	...	10	7	3	...	...	...	...	...	...
6. Bhadarwah *Jagir* ...	...	...	...	...	...	...	...	...	...	...	...	...
7. Punch *Ilaqa* ...	...	...	...	21	9	12	...	...	...	...	...	...
II—Total Kashmir Province (including *Jagirs*).	2	2	...	183	94	89	3	2	1	1	1	...
8. Kashmir North (including Langet *Jagir*).	2	2	...	31	20	11	3	2	1	...	...	...
9. Kashmir South (including city).	...	...	...	135	61	74	...	...	...	1	1	...
Total Kashmir Valley ...	*2*	*2*	...	*166*	*81*	*85*	*3*	*2*	*1*	*1*	*1*	...
10. Muzaffarabad District (*Wizarat Pahar*).	...	...	...	17	13	4	...	...	...	...	...	...
III—Total Frontier Districts.	...	...	...	20	15	5	11	3	8	...	...	...
11. Laddakh District ...	...	...	...	1	...	1	11	3	8	...	...	...
12. Gilgit ,, ...	...	...	...	19	15	4	...	...	...	...	...	...

Unclassified Languages.

DISTRICT, JAGIR OR ILAQA.	*Bazgari.*			*Karnathi.*			*Labani.*		
	Persons.	Males.	Females.	Persons.	Males.	Females.	Persons.	Males.	Females.
1	2	3	4	5	6	7	8	9	10
Total State ...	38	21	17	2	1	1	2,061	1,069	992
I—Total Jammu Province (including *Jagirs*).	38	21	17	1	...	1	2,061	1,069	992
1. Jammu District ...	...	...	...	1	...	1	1,620	850	770
2. Jasrota ,, ...	38	21	17	...	...	...	188	105	83
3. Udhampur ,, ...	...	...	...	...	...	...	...	...	...
4. Riasi ,, ...	...	...	...	...	...	...	152	73	79
5. Mirpur ,, ...	...	...	...	...	...	...	101	41	60
6. Bhadarwah *Jagir* ...	...	...	...	...	...	...	...	...	...
7. Punch *Ilaqa* ...	...	...	...	...	...	...	...	...	...
II—Total Kashmir Province (including *Jagirs*).	...	...	...	1	1	...	...	...	...
8. Kashmir North (including Langet *Jagir*).	...	...	...	...	...	...	...	...	...
9. Kashmir South (including city)	...	...	...	...	...	...	...	...	...
Total Kashmir Valley	...	...	...	1	1	...	...	...	...
10. Muzaffarabad District (*Wizarat Pahar*).	...	...	...	...	...	...	...	...	...
III—Total Frontier Districts	...	...	...	...	...	...	...	...	...
11. Laddakh District ...	...	...	...	...	...	...	...	...	...
12. Gilgit ,,	...	...	...	...	...	...	...	...	...

TABLE XI.

BIRTH-PLACE.

Jammu and Kashmir State Census 1911.

---

1. The units which were to be returned as birth-place were districts in case of the internal territorial divisions of the State, districts with the name of Province in case of British Indian Provinces and countries in case of places beyond India. The divisions of Kashmir Valley having come on rather late in the first year of our operations, the accuracy of figures for Kashmir North and South as Revenue districts cannot be fully vouched for, as the general public had not come to realise the distinction well by the time the Preliminary Record was prepared.

2. The arrangement of the birth-places in column 1 (except in case of our own internal divisions) is alphabetical within each major head. In arranging the birth-places the districts and countries adjoining the boundaries of the State have been shown first under separate heading as "Conterminous" and the rest under "Remote." The internal territorial divisions of the State are ranged on four consecutive pages for each unit of birth-place shown in the first column. The two cities have been shown separately at the end, but the figures of the Revenue districts to which they belong also include the city figures.

3. The districts within the State have all been shown in this table, but in the case of other Provinces the district is given only when emigrants from it exceed 300. The district figures in all such cases, therefore, do not work up to the Provincial total below which they appear.

4. As pointed out in § 3 of the title-page remarks to Table I, this table does not deal with the population of the Frontier *Ilaqas* (54,435 persons), the special schedule used there having had no column for registration of birth-places. Mansar figures (190 persons) have, however, been included as its inhabitants were all born where they live.

TABLE XI.

Birth-Place.

Jammu and Kashmir State Census 1911.

District, State, Province or Country where born.	District, Jagir, Ilaqa or City where enumerated.								
	Population of the State.			*Jammu District (including city).*			*Jasrota District.*		
	Persons.	Males.	Females.	Persons.	Males.	Females.	Persons.	Males.	Females.
1	2	3	4	5	6	7	8	9	10
Entire State ...	**3,103,691**	**1,645,089**	**1,458,602**	**326,691**	**180,691**	**146,000**	**151,802**	**81,375**	**70,427**
A.—Born in District, Ilaqa or Jagir within the State Territories.	**3,026,716**	**1,606,430**	**1,420,286**	**298,115**	**168,074**	**130,041**	**139,323**	**75,747**	**63,576**
Jammu Province ...	1,533,751	815,694	718,057	296,777	167,078	129,699	138,931	75,514	63,417
Jammu District ...	299,173	167,835	131,338	285,192	161,173	124,019	3,745	1,636	2,109
Jasrota ,, ...	136,738	73,998	62,740	2,701	1,095	1,606	132,195	72,047	60,148
Udhampur ,, ...	215,753	113,521	102,232	3,161	1,685	1,476	1,699	950	749
Riasi ,, ...	200,578	105,408	95,170	3,403	1,710	1,693	242	139	103
Mirpur ,, ...	311,070	163,628	147,442	1,849	1,069	780	140	79	61
Bhadarwah *Jagir* ...	37,195	18,250	18,945	240	195	45	797	591	206
Punch *Ilaqa* ...	333,244	173,054	160,190	231	151	80	113	72	41
Kashmir Province ...	1,284,767	686,368	598,399	1,251	919	332	253	162	91
Kashmir (North) ...	456,189	242,994	213,195	746	530	216	19	9	10
Kashmir (South) ...	634,500	340,174	294,326	457	355	102	194	126	68
Kashmir Valley ...	*1,090,689*	*583,168*	*507,521*	*1,203*	*885*	*318*	*213*	*135*	*78*
Muzaffarabad District ...	194,078	103,200	90,878	48	34	14	40	27	13
Frontier Districts ...	207,446	103,866	103,580	27	17	10	13	8	5
Laddakh District ...	186,221	92,881	93,340	7	4	3	13	8	5
Gilgit ,, ...	21,225	10,985	10,240	20	13	7	...	...	...
Frontier *Ilaqas* ...	752	502	250	60	60	...	126	63	63
Chilas ...	*97*	*53*	*44*	...	...	...	...	...	...
Hunza ...	*189*	*120*	*69*	...	...	...	...	...	...
Punial ...	*464*	*329*	*135*	*60*	*60*	...	*120*	*63*	*63*
Yasin ...	*2*	...	*2*	...	...	...	...	...	...
B.—Born in Provinces, Districts or States in India beyond the State	**74,397**	**36.550**	**37,847**	**27,878**	**12,056**	**15.822**	**12,455**	**5,625**	**6,830**
N.-W. F. Province ...	12,904	7,193	5,711	416	278	138	154	105	49
Conterminous ...	*12,257*	*6,755*	*5,502*	*282*	*195*	*87*	*134*	*87*	*47*
Districts ...	10,516	5,782	4,734	252	183	69	130	87	43
Hazara	10,516	5,782	4,734	252	183	69	130	87	43
Agencies and Tribal Areas ...	1,741	973	768	30	12	18	4	...	4
Swat	322	113	209	2	1	1	4		4
Yaghistan	1,416	858	558	28	11	17			...
Remote	*647*	*438*	*209*	*134*	*83*	*51*	*20*	*18*	*2*
Peshawar	575	389	186	114	70	44	8	8	...
Punjab Province ...	59,707	28.020	31,687	26,832	11,291	15,541	12,204	5,458	6.746
Districts	58,500	27,191	31,309	26,724	11,223	15,501	11,784	5,245	6,539
Conterminous	*51,236*	*22,277*	*28,959*	*23,602*	*9,423*	*14,179*	*11,218*	*4,913*	*6,305*
Gujrat	8,493	3,337	5,156	1,728	853	875	48	33	15
Gardaspur	14,124	6,202	7,922	3,983	1,638	2,345	9,524	4,205	5,319
Jhelum	2,592	1,483	1,109	136	58	78	25	19	6
Kangra	2,795	1,342	1,453	858	251	607	929	273	656
Rawalpindi	2,995	1,930	1,065	395	259	136	33	26	7
Sialkot ...	20,237	7,983	12,254	16,502	6,364	10,138	659	357	302
Remote	*7,264*	*4,914*	*2,350*	*3,122*	*1,800*	*1,322*	*566*	*332*	*234*
Amritsar	914	531	383	497	249	248	98	62	36
Gujranwala	1,650	1,030	620	995	555	440	40	26	14
Hoshiarpur	769	516	253	248	182	66	213	93	120
Jallundar	788	597	191	308	189	119	76	60	16
Lahore	1,278	876	402	465	260	205	45	25	20
Shahpur	733	552	181	199	103	96	19	14	5
States	1,207	829	378	108	68	40	420	213	207
Conterminous	*679*	*370*	*309*	*13*	*8*	*5*	*394*	*199*	*195*
Chamba	679	370	309	13	8	5	394	199	195
Remote	*528*	*459*	*69*	*95*	*60*	*35*	*26*	*14*	*12*
Patiala ...	343	323	20	39	27	12	8	5	3

TABLE XI.

BIRTH-PLACE.

Jammu and Kashmir State Census 1911.

District, Jagir, Ilaqa or City where enumerated.											
Udhampur District.			*Riasi District.*			*Mirpur District.*			*Bhadarwah Jagir.*		
Persons.	Males.	Females.	Persons.	Males.	Females.	Persons.	Males.	Females.	Persons.	Males.	Females.
11	12	13	14	15	16	17	18	19	20	21	22
215,725	**113,877**	**101,848**	**206,809**	**109,026**	**97,783**	**324,933**	**169,276**	**155,657**	**37,512**	**18,975**	**18,537**
213,994	112,732	101,262	204,016	107,197	96,819	311,089	162,673	148,416	36,833	18,435	18,398
212,052	111,348	100,704	201,774	105,907	95,867	310,320	162,137	148,183	36,611	18,289	18,322
2,359	1,205	1,154	3,221	1,399	1,822	1,854	611	1,243	101	83	18
1,398	546	852	56	27	29	76	65	11	172	121	51
206,054	108,438	97,616	2,184	907	1,277	38	25	13	1,666	948	718
1,538	678	860	192,188	101,226	90,962	1,737	678	1,059	131	77	54
85	61	24	1,901	1,103	798	304,679	159,906	144,773	2	2	...
438	323	115	34	29	5	1,123	39	1,084	34,535	17,055	17,480
180	97	83	2,190	1,216	974	813	813	...	4	3	1
1,873	1,341	532	2,241	1,289	952	755	525	230	201	131	70
640	551	89	700	461	239	413	269	144	34	26	8
1,199	766	433	635	320	315	175	116	59	161	101	60
1,839	*1,317*	*522*	*1,335*	*781*	*554*	*588*	*385*	*203*	*195*	*127*	*68*
34	24	10	906	508	398	167	140	27	6	4	2
62	42	20	1	1	...	14	11	3	2	1	1
41	25	16	1	1	...	9	9	...	2	1	1
21	17	4	...	...	...	5	2	3	...	...	...
7	1	6	...	...	...	...	...	...	19	14	5
7	*1*	*6*	...	...	...	...	...	...	...	...	...
...	...	...	...	...	...	...	...	...	...	...	...
...	...	...	...	...	...	...	...	...	*19*	*14*	*5*
...	...	...	...	...	...	...	...	...	...	...	...
1,633	1,048	585	2,677	1,747	930	12,983	5,765	7,218	659	520	139
141	73	68	1,320	751	569	471	272	199	4	4	...
116	*56*	*60*	*1,211*	*672*	*539*	*379*	*205*	*174*	*1*	*1*	...
105	55	50	889	506	383	185	100	85	1	1	...
105	55	50	889	506	383	185	100	85	1	1	...
11	1	10	322	166	156	194	105	89	...	...	...
8	...	8	209	105	104	25		25			...
3	1	2	113	61	52	169	105	64			...
25	*17*	*8*	*109*	*79*	*30*	*92*	*67*	*25*	*3*	*3*	...
22	16	6	108	78	30	76	57	19	2	2	...
1,412	906	506	1,260	917	343	12,112	5,213	6,899	626	487	139
1,314	839	475	1,237	901	336	12,095	5,202	6,893	393	328	65
955	*578*	*377*	*613*	*321*	*292*	*11,386*	*4,715*	*66,71*	*293*	*245*	*48*
79	57	22	130	53	77	6,260	2,159	4,101	7	5	2
222	128	94	26	16	10	219	106	113	22	18	4
51	31	20	46	18	28	1,773	964	809	1	1	
277	210	67	129	117	12	158	133	25	224	187	37
85	58	27	123	82	41	1,026	542	484	14	12	2
241	94	147	159	35	124	1,950	811	1,139	25	22	3
359	*261*	*98*	*624*	*580*	*44*	*709*	*487*	*222*	*100*	*83*	*17*
37	30	7	14	11	3	65	42	23	9	6	3
111	71	40	157	141	16	196	125	71	4	4	
49	37	12	13	8	5	93	79	14	4	4	
32	23	9	200	198	2	62	49	13	...		
42	33	9	6		6	37	16	21	14	13	1
32	22	10	195	186	9	36		30	2	2	
98	67	31	23	16	7	17	11	6	233	159	74
63	*33*	*30*	*10*	*6*	*4*	...	...	...	*192*	*119*	*73*
63	33	30	10	6	4	...	...	...	192	119	73
35	*34*	*1*	*13*	*10*	*3*	*17*	*11*	*6*	*41*	*40*	*1*
7	7	...	1	1	...	7	6	1	3	3	...

XI
Birth-Place.

TABLE XI.

BIRTH-PLACE.

Jammu and Kashmir State Census 1911.

District, State, Province or Country where born.	Punch *Ilaqa*. Persons.	Males.	Females.	Kashmir (North). Persons.	Males.	Females.	Kashmir (South) (including Srinagar City). Persons.	Males.	Females.
	23	24	25	26	27	28	29	30	31
Entire State ...	**334,393**	**173,570**	**160,823**	**460,786**	**244,637**	**216,149**	**639,210**	**342,835**	**296,375**
A.—Born in District, Ilaqa or Jagir within the State Territories	**332,163**	**172,035**	**160,069**	**455,026**	**241,597**	**213,429**	**634,831**	**340,237**	**294,594**
Jammu Province ...	330,715	171,109	159,608	1,545	905	640	3,030	1,863	1,187
Jammu District ...	1,290	697	593	128	108	20	791	529	262
Jasrota ,, ...	66	31	35	8	7	1	44	37	7
Udhampur ,, ...	217	87	130	50	42	8	562	343	219
Riasi ,, ...	431	235	196	70	51	19	614	405	209
Mirpur ,, ...	1,865	988	877	83	49	34	159	83	76
Bhadarwah *Jagir* ...	17	10	7	...	...	...	...	...	...
Punch *Ilaqa* ...	326,829	169,061	157,770	1,206	648	558	860	466	394
Kashmir Province ...	1,215	765	450	453,238	240,569	212,669	631,411	338,148	293,263
Kashmir (North) ...	315	188	127	452,087	239,938	212,149	37	18	19
Kashmir (South) ...	292	186	106	27	21	6	631,092	337,963	293,129
Kashmir Valley ...	*607*	*374*	*233*	*452,114*	*239,959*	*212.155*	*631,129*	*337,981*	*293,148*
Muzaffarabad District ...	608	391	217	1,124	610	514	282	167	115
Frontier Districts ...	107	104	3	176	85	91	181	86	95
Laddakh District ...	107	104	3	41	21	20	118	48	70
Gilgit ,, ...	...	...	...	135	64	71	63	38	25
Frontier *Ilaqas* ...	65	57	8	67	38	29	209	140	69
Chilas ...	...	...	...	*66*	*37*	*29*	*15*	*7*	*8*
Hunza ...	...	...	...	...	...	...	...	...	...
Punial ...	*65*	*57*	*8*	*1*	*1*	...	*192*	*133*	*59*
Yasin ...	...	...	...	...	...	...	*2*	...	*2*
B.—Born in Provinces, Districts or States in India beyond the State	**2,267**	**1,519**	**748**	**5,628**	**2,949**	**2,679**	**4,225**	**2,507**	**1,718**
N.-W. F. Province ...	589	362	227	4,555	2,305	2,250	2,978	1,591	1,387
Conterminous ...	*548*	*329*	*219*	*4,458*	*2,251*	*2,207*	*2,911*	*1,547*	*1,364*
Districts ...	476	296	180	4,284	2,164	2,120	2,586	1,383	1,203
Hazara	476	296	180	4,284	2,164	2,120	2,586	1,383	1,203
Agencies and Tribal Areas ...	72	33	39	174	87	87	325	164	161
Swat	8		8	19	5	14	26	..	26
Yaghistan	64	33	31	153	81	72	298	163	135
Remote ...	*41*	*33*	*8*	*97*	*54*	*43*	*67*	*44*	*23*
Peshawar ...	41	33	8	93	51	42	60	38	22
Punjab Province ...	1,615	1,115	500	1,021	609	412	1,017	741	276
Districts ...	1,599	1,104	495	1,014	603	411	1,000	729	271
Conterminous ...	*1,391*	*956*	*435*	*543*	*195*	*348*	*322*	*231*	*91*
Gujrat	90	65	25	16	14	2	77	48	29
Gurdaspur	37	24	13	2	1	1	20	19	1
Jhelum ...	397	274	123	54	35	19	25	21	4
Kangra	71	49	22	13	8	5	26	23	3
Rawalpindi	622	443	179	180	116	64	77	59	18
Sialkot	174	101	73	278	21	257	97	61	36
Remote ...	*208*	*148*	*60*	*471*	*408*	*63*	*673*	*498*	*180*
Amritsar	23	16	7	27	19	8	87	56	31
Gujranwala	55	38	17	19	16	3	23	16	7
Hoshiarpur	8	4	4	11	9	2	49	39	10
Jallundur	26	20	6	13	8	5	38	28	10
Lahore	24	16	8	347	319	28	233	138	95
Shahpur	24	16	8	18	12	6	170	170	..
States ...	16	11	5	7	6	1	17	12	5
Conterminous ...	*5*	*4*	*1*	...	...	...	...	...	...
Chamba	5	4	1				..	...	..
Remote ...	*11*	*7*	*4*	*7*	*6*	*1*	*17*	*12*	*5*
Patiala	1	1	.	7	6	1	9	6	3

TABLE XI.

Birth-Place.

Jammu and Kashmir State Census 1911.

District, Jagir, Ilaqa or City where enumerated.														
Muzaffarabad District.			*Laddakh District.*			*Gilgit District.*			*Jammu City.*			*Srinagar City.*		
Persons.	Males.	Females.	Persons.	Males.	Females.	Persons.	Males.	Females.	Persons.	Males.	Females.	Persons.	Males.	Females.
32	33	34	35	36	37	38	39	40	41	42	43	44	45	46
195,205	**104,308**	**90,897**	**186,656**	**93,220**	**93,436**	**23,969**	**13,299**	**10,670**	**31,726**	**19,362**	**12,364**	**126,344**	**68,378**	**57.966**
192,404	**102,455**	**89,949**	**186,210**	**92,916**	**93,294**	**22,773**	**12,332**	**10,441**	**25,298**	**15,534**	**9,764**	**125,127**	**67,540**	**57,597**
981	637	344	289	198	91	726	709	17	24,174	14,616	9,558	890	729	161
116	88	28	135	78	57	241	228	13	20,926	12,175	8,751	419	308	111
...	...	...	4	4	...	18	18	...	500	392	108	31	30	1
15	13	2	59	35	24	48	48	...	1,149	817	332	124	110	14
38	31	7	35	28	7	151	150	1	882	645	237	195	177	18
65	47	18	36	36	...	206	205	1	493	422	71	73	66	7
...	...	...	11	8	3	...	...	...	106	82	24	1	1	...
747	458	289	9	9	...	62	60	2	118	83	35	47	37	10
191,406	101,802	89,604	611	455	156	312	262	50	1,042	845	197	123,963	66,637	57,326
535	498	37	517	376	141	146	130	16	666	530	136	18	18	...
30	29	1	87	74	13	151	117	34	356	300	56	123,894	66,576	57,318
565	*527*	*38*	*604*	*450*	*154*	*297*	*247*	*50*	*1,022*	*830*	*192*	*123,912*	*66,594*	*57,318*
190,841	101,275	89,566	7	5	2	15	15	...	20	15	5	51	43	8
8	8	...	185,310	92,263	93,047	21,545	11,240	10,305	22	13	9	79	40	39
8	8	...	185,294	92,247	93,047	580	405	175	7	4	3	31	10	21
...	...	...	16	16	...	20,965	10,835	10,130	15	9	6	48	30	18
9	8	1	...	...	...	190	121	69	60	60	...	193	134	59
9	*8*	*1*	...	...	...	...	...	...	...	...	...	*1*	*1*	...
...	...	...	...	...	...	*189*	*120*	*69*	...	...	...	...	...	...
...	...	...	...	...	...	*1*	*1*	...	*60*	*60*	...	*192*	*133*	*59*
...	...	...	...	...	...	...	...	...	...	...	...	...	...	...
2,623	**1,723**	**900**	**245**	**188**	**57**	**1,124**	**903**	**221**	**6,375**	**3,801**	**2,574**	**1,110**	**773**	**337**
1,675	1,033	642	13	9	4	588	410	178	140	89	51	294	201	93
1,640	*1,012*	*628*	*7*	*5*	*2*	*570*	*395*	*175*	*44*	*29*	*15*	*262*	*177*	*85*
1,583	983	600	4	4	...	21	20	1	34	19	15	243	166	77
1,583	983	600	4	4	...	21	20	1	34	19	15	243	166	77
57	29	28	3	1	2	549	375	174	10	10	...	19	11	8
15	1	14	2		2	4	1	3				8		8
42	28	14	1	1		545	374	171	10	10	...	10	10	
35	*21*	*14*	*6*	*4*	*2*	*18*	*15*	*3*	*96*	*60*	*36*	*32*	*24*	*8*
32	20	12	1	1	...	18	15	3	85	51	34	28	20	8
900	667	233	212	160	52	496	456	40	5,768	3,347	2,421	632	441	191
895	663	232	212	160	52	233	194	39	5,700	3,304	2,396	616	430	186
654	*488*	*166*	*131*	*106*	*25*	*128*	*106*	*22*	*3,569*	*2,060*	*1,509*	*272*	*202*	*70*
42	35	7				16	15	1	429	224	205	60	39	21
54	38	16	7	6	1	8	3	5	349	209	140	19	19	
60	43	17	12	10	2	12	9	3	112	58	54	19	16	3
34	30	4	66	51	15	10	10		175	134	41	19	19	
392	297	95	10	8	2	38	28	10	266	161	105	68	50	18
72	45	27	36	31	5	44	41	3	2,238	1,274	964	87	59	28
241	*175*	*66*	*81*	*54*	*27*	*105*	*88*	*17*	*2,131*	*1,244*	*887*	*344*	*228*	*116*
26	20	6	18	10	8	13	10	3	359	181	178	70	45	25
30	22	8	8	6	2	12	10	2	684	373	311	21	14	7
43	37	6	24	11	13	14	13	1	140	123	17	45	36	9
25	17	8	2	1	1	6	4	2	231	140	91	30	22	8
18	15	3	3	1	2	44	40	4	347	202	145	112	66	46
14	6	8	20	19	1	4	2	2	147	69	78	8	8	
5	4	1	...	...	...	263	262	1	68	43	25	16	11	5
2	*1*	*1*	...	...	...	...	...	...	*3*	*3*	...	...	...	...
2	1	1	...	...	...	...	...	...	3	3	...	...	...	...
3	*3*	...	...	...	...	*263*	*262*	*1*	*65*	*40*	*25*	*16*	*11*	*5*
2	2	...	...	...	...	259	259	...	19	10	9	8	5	3

XI
Birth-Place.

TABLE XI.

Birth-Place.

Jammu and Kashmir State Census 1911.

District, State, Province or Country where born.	District, Jagir, Ilaqa or City where enumerated.								
	Population of the State.			*Jammu District.*			*Jasrota District.*		
	Persons.	Males.	Females.	Persons.	Males.	Females.	Persons.	Males.	Females.
1	2	3	4	5	6	7	8	9	10
U. P. of Agra and Oudh ...	982	778	204	403	314	89	50	37	13
Districts	974	770	204	395	306	89	50	37	13
States	8	8	...	8	8	...	...	...	...
Bengal	131	83	48	44	28	16	14	6	8
Behar and Orissa ...	79	58	21	17	17	...	...	...	...
Ajmere (Merwara) ...	27	23	4	11	11	...	...	...	...
Bombay Presidency ...	184	139	45	68	56	12	17	8	9
Districts	166	121	45	65	53	12	17	8	9
States	18	18	...	3	3	...	...	...	...
Madras Presidency ...	27	23	4	11	8	3	...	...	...
Central Provinces ...	11	8	3	4	4	...	...	...	...
Baluchistan	20	17	3	8	7	1	1	...	1
Andamans	7	2	5	3	1	2	...	...	...
Haiderabad (Deccan) ...	11	8	3	4	3	1	2	...	2
Central India Agency ...	35	28	7	8	5	3	9	8	1
Mysore	10	3	7	...	...	...	...	...	...
Baroda	4	3	1	...	...	...	...	...	...
Rajputana	250	156	94	48	32	16	4	3	1
Portuguese Settlements (Goa)	8	8	...	1	1	...	...	...	...
C.—Born in Countries in Asia beyond India	**2,233**	**1,860**	**373**	**688**	**554**	**134**	**20**	**1**	**19**
Conterminous	*177*	*96*	*81*	*2*	*1*	*1*	...	...	...
Chinese Tartary	28	22	6	...	...	...	...	...	...
Tibet	149	74	75	2	1	1	...	...	...
Remote	*2,056*	*1,764*	*292*	*686*	*553*	*133*	*20*	*1*	*19*
Afghanistan	943	806	137	63	38	25	2	1	1
Arabia	1	1	...	...	...	...	...	...	...
Bhutan	2	2	...	2	2	...	...	...	...
China	2	1	1	1	1	...	...	...	...
Nepal	1,077	926	151	620	512	108	18	...	18
Persia	29	26	3	...	...	...	...	...	...
Russia (Asiatic)	1	1	...	...	...	...	...	...	...
Turkey	1	1	...	...	...	...	...	...	...
D.—Born in Countries in Europe ...	**126**	**76**	**50**	**9**	**7**	**2**		...	...
United Kingdom ...	109	69	40	9	7	2	...	...	...
England and Wales	90	58	32	4	4		...	.	...
Ireland ...	9	5	4	1	1	...	...	.	...
Scotland ...	10	6	4	4	2	2	...	.	...
Denmark	1	...	1	...	...	...	...	...	...
France	3	3	...	...	...	...	...	...	...
Germany	6	1	5	...	...	...	...	...	...
Holland	2	2	...	...	...	...	...	...	...
Sweden	1	1	...	...	...	...	...	...	...
Switzerland	4	...	4	...	...	...	...	...	...
E.—Countries in Africa ...	**6**	**2**	**4**		.	.	**4**	**2**	**2**
Africa	6	2	4	...	...	...	4	2	2
F.—Born in Countries in America ...	**10**	**6**	**4**			...		...	...
North America	9	5	4	...	...	...	...	...	...
South America	1	1	...	...	...	...	...	...	...
G.—Born in Australia	**1**	**1**	...	.		...		...	
Australia	1	1	...	...	...	...	...	...	...
Birth-Place not returned ...	**202**	**166**	**36**	**1**	...	**1**			

TABLE XI.

Birth-Place.

Jammu and Kashmir State Census 1911.

District, Jagir, Ilaqa or City where enumerated.											
Udhampur District.			*Riasi District.*			*Mirpur District.*			*Bhadarwah Jagir.*		
Persons.	Males.	Females.	Persons.	Males.	Females.	Persons.	Males.	Females.	Persons.	Males.	Females.
11	12	13	14	15	16	17	18	19	20	21	22
39	**32**	**7**	**33**	**31**	**2**	**165**	**136**	**29**	**11**	**11**	...
39	32	7	33	31	2	165	136	29	11	11	...
...	...	...	...	...	...	...	...	...	...	...	...
21	21	...	1	1	...	17	10	7	3	3	...
1	1	...	...	...	...	1	...	1	3	3	...
1	...	1	...	...	...	11	8	3	2	2	...
4	3	1	53	39	14	12	9	3	1	1	...
3	2	1	48	34	14	6	3	3	1	1	...
1	1	...	5	5	...	6	6	...	...	...	...
...	...	...	...	...	...	1	1	...	...	...	...
2	1	1	3	3	...	...	...	...	...	...	...
...	...	...	1	...	1	6	6	...	...	...	...
...	...	...		...	...	4	1	3	...	...	...
...	...	...	1	1	...	...	...	...	2	2	...
7	6	1	1	...	1	4	4	...	2	2	...
...	...	...	...	...	...	...	...	...	...	...	...
1	1	...	1	1	...	1	1	...	...	...	...
4	4	...	3	3	...	178	104	74	5	5	...
...	...	...	...	...	...	...	...	...	...	...	...
48	**46**	**2**	**115**	**82**	**33**	**856**	**834**	**22**	**4**	**4**	...
1	*1*	...	*1*	*1*	...	...	...	...	...	...	...
1	1	...	1	1	...	...	...	...	...	...	...
...	...	...	...	...	...	...	...	...	...	...	...
47	*45*	*2*	*114*	*81*	*33*	*856*	*834*	*22*	*4*	*4*	...
17	17	...	71	45	26	531	513	18	4	4	...
...	...	...	...	...	...	...	...	...	...	...	...
...	...	...	...	...	...	...	...	...	...	...	...
...	...	...	1	...	1	...	...	...	...	...	...
30	28	2	42	36	6	296	295	1	...	...	...
...	...	...	...	...	...	29	26	3	...	...	...
...	...	...	...	...	...	...	...	...	...	...	...
...	...	...	...	...	...	...	...	...	...	...	...
...	...	...	1	1	...	4	4	...	...	...	...
...	...	...	1	1	...	4	4	...	...	...	...
...	...	...	1	1	...	4	4	...	...	...	...
...	...	...	...	...	...	...	...	...	...	...	...
...	...	...	...	...	...	...	...	...	...	...	...
...	...	...	...	...	...	...	...	...	...	...	...
...	...	...	...	...	...	...	...	...	...	...	...
...	...	...	...	...	...	...	...	...	...	...	...
...	...	...	...	...	...	...	...	...	...	...	...
...	...	...	...	...	...	...	...	...	...	...	...
...	...	...	...	...	...	...	...	...	...	...	...
...	...	...	...	...	...	1	...	1	...	...	...
...	...	...	...	...	...	1	...	1	...	...	...
...	...	...	...	...	...	...	...	...	...	...	...
...	...	...	...	...	...	...	...	...	...	...	...
...	...	...	...	...	...	...	...	...	...	...	...
...	...	...	...	...	...	...	...	...	...	...	...
...	...	...	...	...	...	...	...	...	...	...	...
50	**50**	...	...	...	...	...	...	...	**16**	**16**	...

XI
Birth-Place.

TABLE XI.

Birth-Place.

Jammu and Kashmir State Census 1911.

District, State, Province or Country where born.	District, Jagir, Ilaqa or City where enumerated.								
	Punch Ilaqa.			*Kashmir (North).*			*Kashmir (South).*		
	Persons.	Males.	Females.	Persons.	Males.	Females.	Persons.	Males.	Females.
	23	24	25	26	27	28	29	30	31
U. P. of Agra and Oudh ...	36	24	12	40	30	10	147	115	32
Districts ...	36	24	12	40	30	10	147	115	32
States ...	...	...	...	...	...	...	...	...	...
Bengal ...	4	1	3	7	...	7	12	5	7
Behar and Orissa ...	13	9	4	...	...	...	19	16	3
Ajmere (Merwara) ...	...	...	...	2	2	...	...	...	...
Bombay Presidency ...	2	2	...	1	1	...	21	15	6
Districts ...	2	2	...	...	...	...	21	15	6
States ...	...	...	...	1	1	...	...	...	...
Madras Presidency ...	...	...	...	...	...	...	14	13	1
Central Provinces ...	2	...	2	...	...	...	...	...	...
Baluchistan ...	3	3	...	...	...	...	...	...	...
Andamans ...	...	...	...	...	...	...	...	...	...
Haiderabad (Deccan) ...	1	1	...	...	...	...	1	1	...
Central India Agency ...	...	...	...	...	1	...	2	2	...
Mysore ...	...	...	...	...	...	...	6	1	5
Baroda ...	...	...	...	...	...	...	1	...	1
Rajputana ...	2	2	...	1	1	...	2	2	...
Portuguese Settlements (Goa)	...	...	...	...	...	...	5	5	...
C.—Born in Countries in Asia beyond India	**16**	**13**	**3**	**113**	**76**	**37**	**42**	**26**	**16**
Conterminous ...	*2*	*2*	...	...	...	...	*14*	*10*	*4*
Chinese Tartary ...	1	1	...	...	...	...	12	10	2
Tibet ...	1	1	...	...	...	...	2	...	2
Remote ...	*14*	*11*	*3*	*113*	*76*	*37*	*28*	*16*	*12*
Afghanistan ...	14	11	3	78	52	26	21	12	9
Arabia ...	...	...	...	...	...	...	1	1	...
Bhutan ...	...	...	...	...	...	...	...	...	...
China ...	...	...	...	...	...	...	...	...	...
Nepal ...	...	...	...	35	24	11	6	3	3
Persia ...	...	...	...	...	...	...	...	...	...
Russia (Asiatic) ...	...	...	...	...	...	...	...	...	...
Turkey ...	...	...	...	...	...	...	...	...	...
D.—Born in Countries in Europe ...	**8**	**5**	**3**	**15**	**13**	**2**	**59**	**28**	**31**
United Kingdom ...	6	4	2	12	10	2	54	26	28
England and Wales	4	3	1	11	9	2	48	24	24
Ireland	1	1	...	..	...		3	...	3
Scotland	1	...	1	1	1		3	2	1
Denmark ...	1	...	1	...	...	...	...	...	...
France ...	...	...	...	1	1	...	2	2	...
Germany ...	...	...	...	...	...	...	2	...	2
Holland ...	...	...	...	2	2	...	...	...	...
Sweden ...	1	1	...	...	...	...	...	...	...
Switzerland ...	...	...	...	...	...	...	1	...	1
E.—Born in Countries in Africa	...	.	.		..		**1**		**1**
Africa ...	...	...	...	...	...	...	1	...	1
F.—Born in Countries in America.	.	.	..	**4**	**2**	**2**	**6**	**4**	**2**
North America ...	...	...	...	4	2	2	5	3	2
South America ...	...	...	...	...	...	...	1	1	...
G.—Born in Australia	..	...				...	**1**	**1**	...
Australia ...	...	...	...	...	...	...	1	1	...
Birth-Place not returned ..		...	...	...	...	...	**45**	**32**	**13**

TABLE XI.

Birth-Place.

Jammu and Kashmir State Census 1911.

District, Jagir, Ilaqa or City where enumerated.														
Muzaffarabad District.			*Laddakh District.*			*Gilgit District.*			*Jammu City.*			*Srinagar City.*		
Persons.	Males.	Females.	Persons.	Males.	Females.	Persons.	Males.	Females.	Persons.	Males.	Females.	Persons.	Males.	Females.
32	33	34	35	36	37	38	39	40	41	42	43	44	45	46
26	**20**	**6**	**13**	**12**	**1**	**19**	**16**	**3**	**289**	**228**	**61**	**119**	**88**	**31**
26	20	6	13	12	1	19	16	3	281	220	61	119	88	31
...	...	...	...	...	...	...	...	...	8	8	...	...	...	...
...	...	...	2	2	...	6	6	...	40	24	16	11	4	7
14	1	13	4	4	...	7	7	...	15	15	...	14	11	3
...	...	...	...	...	...	...	...	...	11	11	...	...	...	...
...	...	...	1	1	...	4	4	...	48	40	8	21	15	6
...	...	...	1	1	...	2	2	...	48	40	8	21	15	6
...	...	...	...	...	...	2	2	...	...	...	...	...	...	...
...	...	...	...	...	...	1	1	...	11	8	3	13	12	1
...	...	...	...	...	...	...	...	...	2	2	...	...	...	...
1	1	...	...	...	...	...	...	...	5	4	1	...	...	...
...	...	...	...	...	...	...	...	...	2	1	1	...	...	...
...	...	...	...	...	...	...	...	...	4	3	1	...	...	...
1	...	1	...	...	...	...	...	...	6	4	2	1	1	...
3	1	2	...	...	...	1	1	...	...	...	...	5	...	5
...	...	...	...	...	...	...	...	...	...	...	...	...	...	...
3	...	3	...	...	...	...	...	...	34	25	9	...	...	...
...	...	...	...	...	...	2	2	...	...	...	...	...	...	...
75	**52**	**23**	**191**	**113**	**78**	**65**	**59**	**6**	**51**	**25**	**26**	**21**	**16**	**5**
...	...	...	*156*	*80*	*76*	*1*	*1*	...	...	...	...	*12*	*10*	*2*
...	...	...	12	8	4	1	1	...	...	...	...	12	10	2
...	...	...	144	72	72	...	...	...	...	...	...	...	...	...
75	*52*	*23*	*35*	*33*	*2*	*64*	*58*	*6*	*51*	*25*	*26*	*9*	*6*	*3*
73	50	23	6	6	...	63	57	6	32	24	8	5	5	...
...	...	...	...	...	...	...	...	...	...	...	...	...	...	...
...	...	...	...	...	...	...	...	...	...	...	...	...	...	...
...	...	...	...	...	...	...	...	...	1	1	...	...	...	...
1	1	...	28	26	2	1	1	...	18	...	18	4	1	3
...	...	...	...	...	...	...	...	...	...	...	...	...	...	...
...	...	...	1	1	...	...	...	...	...	...	...	...	...	...
1	1	...	...	...	...	...	...	...	...	...	...	...	...	...
15	**11**	**4**	**9**	**2**	**7**	**6**	**5**	**1**	**2**	**2**	...	**40**	**13**	**27**
15	11	4	2	1	1	6	5	1	2	2	...	37	16	21
13	10	3	1		1	4	3	1	2	2		35	15	20
1	..	1	1	1		2	2					1		1
1	1											1	1	
...	...	...	...	...	...	...	...	...	...	...	...	...	...	...
...	...	...	...	...	...	...	...	...	...	...	...	1	1	...
...	...	...	4	1	3	...	...	...	...	...	...	2	...	2
...	...	...	...	...	...	...	...	...	...	...	...	...	...	...
...	...	...	...	...	...	...	...	...	...	...	...	...	...	...
...	...	...	3	...	3	...	...	...	...	...	...	...	...	...
..	..													
...	...	...	...	...	...	...	...	...	...	...	...	...	...	...
..	..											**5**	**4**	**1**
...	...	...	...	...	...	...	...	...	...	...	...	4	3	1
...	...	...	...	...	...	...	...	...	...	...	...	1	1	...
...	..													
...	...	...	...	...	...	...	...	...	...	...	...	...	...	...
88	**67**	**21**	**1**	**1**		**1**		**1**				**41**	**28**	**13**

TABLE XII.

INFIRMITIES.

Jammu and Kashmir State Census 1911.

1. The infirmities recorded at the Census were insanity, deaf-mutism, blindness and leprosy.

2. The table is divided into two parts :—Part I shows the distribution by age of the entire afflicted population and Part II deals with distribution of the infirmities by territorial divisions of the State.

3. In addition to the above there is Table XII-A in which such castes, tribes, etc., as have a total number of infirms in excess of 10 have been shown seperately, and the rest put together under a general head "others." The detail of the latter is :—

Caste.	*Persons.*	*Caste.*	*Persons.*
Banjara ...	... 1	Mussalli ...	... 5
Brukpa ...	... 3	Mazhabi ...	... 3
Bazigar ...	... 2	Naddaf ...	... 1
Beldar ...	... 2	Qassab ...	... 4
Bhirai ...	... 1	Rangrez ...	... 5
Churigar ...	... 7	Ratal ...	... 5
Darzi ...	... 5	Sapiada ...	... 1
Dosali ...	... 1	Saryara ...	... 6
Gadri ...	... 3	Sikh ...	... 7
Khokhar ...	... 1	Thiar ...	... 2
Kamangar ...	... 1	Watal ..	... 7
Kanjar ...	... 2	TOTAL ...	86
Koli ...	... 7		
Machhi ...	... 3	Castes not specified ...	356
Memar ...	... 1	GRAND TOTAL ...	442

4. The special tracts (*vide* title-page of Table I) do not, ofcourse, come within the purview of this table as the special schedule used there provided no column for record of infirmities.

5. For the purposes of this table persons suffering from more than one infirmity have been counted twice or three times over, according to the number of infirmities they were suffering from. The total number of such cases is, however, very insignificant. The same appears to have been done here at the previous Census.

TABLE XII—INFIRMITIES.

Part I—Distribution by age.

Jammu and Kashmir State Census 1911.

Entire State.

AGE.	*Population afflicted.*			*Insane.*			*Deaf-mute.*			*Blind.*			*Leper.*		
	Persons.	Males.	Females.	Persons.	Males.	Females.	Persons.	Males.	Females.	Persons.	Males.	Females.	Persons.	Males.	Females.
1	2	3	4	5	6	7	8	9	10	11	12	13	14	15	16
All Ages...	10.370	6,064	4,306	1,228	786	442	3,043	1,767	1,276	4,747	2,534	2,213	1,352	977	375
0—1	13	8	5	...	...	...	1	1	...	12	7	5	...	...	...
1—2	9	7	2	...	...	...	1	1	...	8	6	2	...	...	...
2—3	54	33	21	5	5	...	20	10	10	23	15	8	6	3	3
3—4	108	63	45	15	9	6	58	32	26	31	19	12	4	3	1
4—5	140	79	61	15	9	6	100	55	45	25	15	10	...	...	...
Total 0—5	324	190	134	35	23	12	180	99	81	99	62	37	10	6	4
5—10	860	462	398	107	72	35	510	268	242	214	112	102	29	10	19
10—15	954	550	404	146	87	59	497	275	222	253	157	96	58	31	27
15—20	970	564	406	139	96	43	459	256	203	291	156	135	81	56	25
20—25	993	554	439	151	95	56	385	228	157	346	171	175	111	60	51
25—30	746	440	306	101	63	38	263	147	116	270	149	121	112	81	31
30—35	805	515	290	140	93	47	236	165	71	289	168	121	140	89	51
35—40	582	371	211	81	51	30	152	97	55	224	123	101	125	100	25
40—45	807	497	310	112	41	71	164	109	55	345	176	169	186	141	45
45—50	450	259	191	52	32	20	46	29	17	250	119	131	102	79	23
50—55	655	413	242	66	42	24	59	37	22	376	210	166	154	124	30
55—60	169	103	66	17	11	6	22	15	7	107	58	49	23	19	4
60—65	781	444	337	38	25	13	38	21	17	572	288	284	133	110	23
65—70	169	107	62	10	8	2	11	10	1	131	75	56	17	14	3
70 & over	1,105	595	510	33	17	16	21	11	10	980	510	470	71	57	14

Part II.—Distribution by Districts.

DISTRICT, JAGIR OR ILAQA.	*Population afflicted.*			*Insane.*			*Deaf-mute.*			*Blind.*			*Leper.*		
	Persons.	Males.	Females.	Persons.	Males.	Females.	Persons.	Males.	Females.	Persons.	Males.	Females.	Persons.	Males.	Females.
1	2	3	4	5	6	7	8	9	10	11	12	13	14	15	16
Total State ...	10,370	6,064	4,306	1,228	786	442	3,043	1,767	1,276	4,747	2,534	2,213	1,352	977	375
I.—Total Jammu Province.	5,303	3,228	2,075	521	302	219	1,654	972	682	2,243	1,275	968	885	679	206
1. Jammu District ...	1,005	601	404	121	66	55	214	144	70	629	357	272	41	34	7
2. Jasrota ,, ...	717	436	281	78	50	28	197	120	77	363	201	162	79	65	14
3. Udhampur ,, ...	1,030	621	409	66	36	30	503	279	224	284	171	113	177	135	42
4. Riasi ,, ...	302	199	103	20	13	7	79	50	29	129	80	49	74	56	18
5. Mirpur ,, ...	1,216	706	510	118	64	54	438	251	187	532	296	236	128	95	33
6. Bhadarwah *Jagir*.	221	117	104	13	8	5	70	44	26	81	35	46	57	30	27
7. Punch *Ilaqa* ...	812	548	264	105	65	40	153	84	69	225	135	90	329	264	65
II.—Total Kashmir Province.	3,895	2,321	1,574	652	448	204	938	557	381	1,865	1,035	830	440	281	159
8. Kashmir North ...	1,409	842	567	197	135	62	261	156	105	747	411	336	204	140	64
9. Kashmir South ...	2,096	1,246	850	390	274	116	564	337	227	989	555	434	153	80	73
Total Kashmir Valley...	*3,505*	*2,038*	*1,417*	*587*	*409*	*178*	*825*	*493*	*332*	*1,736*	*966*	*770*	*357*	*220*	*137*
10. Muzaffarabad District.	390	233	157	65	39	26	113	64	49	129	69	60	83	61	22
III.—Total Frontier Districts.	1,172	515	657	55	36	19	451	238	213	639	224	415	27	17	10
11. Laddakh District ...	1,008	428	580	48	31	17	326	172	154	609	210	399	25	15	10
12. Gilgit ,, ...	164	87	77	7	5	2	125	66	59	30	14	16	2	2	...

TABLE XII-A.

Infirmities by selected castes, tribes or races.

Jammu and Kashmir State Census 1911.

Caste, Tribe or Race.	*Population dealt with.*			*Insane.*			*Deaf-Mute.*			*Blind.*			*Leper.*		
	Persons.	Males.	Females.	Persons.	Males.	Females.	Persons.	Males.	Females.	Persons.	Males.	Females.	Persons.	Males.	Females.
1	2	3	4	5	6	7	8	9	10	11	12	13	14	15	16
Total ...	2,942,852	1,558,250	1,384,602	1,228	786	442	3,043	1,767	1,276	4,747	2,534	2,213	1,352	977	375
1. Arain ...	20,654	11,508	9,146	12	7	5	35	25	10	41	24	17	3	2	1
2. Arora ...	3,472	2,028	1,444	3	3	...	4	4	...	4	3	1	...	...	...
3. Bafinda ...	26,830	14,795	12,035	22	16	6	38	30	8	47	26	21	21	13	8
4. Balti ...	72,439	40,597	31,842	35	24	11	318	168	150	559	191	368	21	13	8
5. Barwala ...	11,355	6,142	5,213	9	2	7	13	8	5	27	19	8	2	2	...
6. Basith ...	7,659	3,735	3,924	1	...	1	7	3	4	7	6	1	1	...	1
7. Bhatti ...	4,468	2,416	2,052	2	1	1	5	4	1	4	2	2	4	1	3
8. Brahman ...	236,662	130,169	106,493	103	66	37	179	115	64	342	211	131	71	55	16
9. Budhan ...	6,586	3,022	3,564	...	...	...	6	4	2	5	4	1	9	9	...
10. Chamiar ...	38,219	20,017	18,202	17	11	6	52	33	19	69	35	34	11	10	1
11. Chuhra ...	6,829	3,540	3,289	2	1	1	6	...	6	11	7	4	4	4	...
12. Darwesh ...	1,168	527	641	5	4	1	7	4	3	21	9	12	2	1	1
13. Dhobi ...	5,981	3,362	2,619	1	...	1	9	9	...	23	18	5	1	...	1
14. Dhund ...	15,858	7,867	7,991	4	4	...	7	4	3	11	5	6	8	6	2
15. Dum ...	51,447	26,677	24,770	14	8	6	76	44	32	90	48	42	41	37	4
16. Domal ...	7,610	3,921	3,689	4	3	1	6	4	2	7	5	2	7	5	2
17. Gaddi ...	10,563	5,172	5,391	3	2	1	10	6	4	17	10	7	11	8	3
18. Gujjar ...	328,003	183,798	144,205	77	49	28	127	78	49	277	150	127	173	141	32
19. Hajjam ...	34,456	18,697	15,759	12	9	3	23	9	14	51	36	15	15	11	4
20. Hanji ...	18,275	10,244	8,031	10	10	...	16	6	10	56	36	20	6	3	3
21. Jat ...	141,409	72,895	68,514	52	27	25	186	115	71	238	131	107	46	34	12
22. Jhiwar ...	13,500	7,285	6,215	5	2	3	13	8	5	31	17	14	3	3	...
23. Jogi ...	5,553	3,125	2,428	4	1	3	7	4	3	10	7	3	2	2	...
24. Kumhiar ...	18,958	10,154	8,804	9	8	1	23	19	4	39	22	17	8	6	2
25. Kashmiri (Musalmans.)	758,044	387,821	370,223	395	252	143	860	492	368	1,268	672	596	333	216	117
26. Khatik ...	668	360	308	1	...	1	4	1	3	6	6	...	...	...	...
27. Khatri ...	18,509	10,697	7,812	16	10	6	15	10	5	30	16	14	7	3	4
28. Labana ...	5,309	2,899	2,410	...	...	...	5	3	2	8	4	4	...	...	...
29. Lohar ...	28,876	15,098	13,778	9	3	6	38	20	18	33	22	11	15	10	5
30. Mahajan ...	20,462	11,585	8,877	10	7	3	5	4	1	37	23	14	4	2	2
31. Mangriks ...	62,892	30,867	32,025	6	5	1	10	6	4	36	14	22	3	2	1
32. Megh ...	75,128	39,236	35,892	20	11	9	83	32	51	163	80	83	40	43	17
33. Mirasi ...	7,693	4,097	3,596	3	2	1	6	2	4	15	7	8	3	3	...
34. Mochi ...	14,694	7,644	7,050	6	5	1	22	18	4	24	13	11	6	3	3
35. Mughal ...	49,887	28,037	21,850	10	7	3	27	14	13	45	32	13	14	9	5
36. Pathan ...	20,822	11,159	9,663	21	12	9	41	21	20	67	40	27	17	10	7
37. Rajput ...	157,639	85,175	72,464	46	24	22	139	92	47	231	121	110	92	79	13
38. Sadhu ...	3,068	1,882	1,186	...	...	...	2	...	2	17	12	5	9	1	8
39. Sheikh ...	101,239	57,313	43,926	56	38	18	126	69	57	155	95	60	43	28	15
40. Shin ...	11,080	5,930	5,150	...	...	...	11	5	6	1	1	...	...	...	...
41. Sudhan ...	56,754	28,160	28,594	14	8	6	25	15	10	41	22	19	76	58	18
42. Sayed ...	75,445	40,083	35,362	55	45	10	61	33	28	119	65	54	30	21	9
43. Tarkhan ...	27,871	15,080	12,791	17	6	11	39	20	19	43	25	18	20	15	5
44. Teli ...	19,309	10,206	9,103	4	2	2	13	7	6	15	8	7	1	...	1
45. Thakkar ...	104,622	54,597	50,025	39	28	11	117	68	49	188	116	72	91	64	27
46. Yashkun ...	35,011	17,965	17,046	5	4	1	92	50	42	22	13	9	---	...	...
47. Zargar ...	6,379	3,366	3,013	6	6	...	9	4	5	14	7	7	1	1	...
48. Others ...	193,497	97,300	96,197	83	53	30	120	77	43	182	98	84	57	43	14

TABLE XIII.

CASTE, TRIBE, RACE OR NATIONALITY.

Jammu and Kashmir State Census 1911.

1. This table is divided into three parts :—Part I— Hindus, Part II—Musalmans and Part III—Other Religions.

2. It deals with the entire population (except that of Europeans and Anglo-Indians) classified by caste, tribe, etc., the figures of each class being ranged under the various religions returned. All this detail is given in respect of the State as a whole as well as its internal territorial divisions. The total population returned under each head, irrespective of religion and locality, is also given as an Index to the table.

3. In making the classification, only such names have been shown separately as constitute real ethnic units either as castes and sub-castes, or tribes and races, or even true functional groups. Certain geographical names such as Baltis, Kashmiri Musalmans, Kashmiri Brahmans, etc., have also been retained, as the communities indicated by such terms are commonly recognised as distinct races. Differentiations, however, based *purely* on territorial, linguistic, occupational, titular and other similar distinctions such as *gotras*, nicknames, family-titles, etc., and whose number in this country is legion, have been carefully discarded.

4. Some of the divisions under the main castes, tribes, etc., were either of doubtful identity or were not of sufficient numbers and importance to be shown as separate 'sub-caste.' They have been grouped together under the general head "others" as a sub-division of the principal caste or tribe concerned. Similarly, the untraced and minor items under the three chief religions of the State have been classed together as 'Unclassified Hindus,' 'Musalmans' and 'Sikh' as the case was.

5. In case of Indian Christians, the original caste, tribe, etc., even when returned, have been disregarded and they have all been put together under the head 'Indian Christians.' Europeans and Anglo-Indians have been excluded from the table as they are dealt with by Table XVIII *infra* (*vide* the note to § 14, Chapter IV, p. 51, Imperial Census Code, Part II). Their detail by races and nationality is as follows :—

RACE OR NATIONALITY.	BRAMHO.			MUSALMAN.			CHRISTIAN.			TOTAL.		
	Persons.	Males.	Females.	Persons.	Males.	Females.	Persons.	Males.	Females.	Persons.	Males.	Females.
1	2	3	4	5	6	7	8	9	10	11	12	13
American (unspecified).	1	...	1	...	...	...	2	1	1	3	1	2
Anglo-Indian ...	...	...	...	1	1	...	16	9	7	17	10	7
Canadian ...	...	...	...	...	...	...	1	...	1	1	...	1
Dutch ...	...	...	...	...	...	...	2	2	...	2	2	...
English ...	...	...	...	...	...	...	199	103	96	199	103	96
French ...	...	...	...	...	...	...	3	3	...	3	3	...
German ...	...	...	...	...	...	...	10	4	6	10	4	6
Irish ...	...	...	...	...	...	...	12	7	5	12	7	5
Scotch ...	...	...	...	...	...	...	21	14	7	21	14	7
TOTAL ...	1	...	1	1	1	...	266	143	123	268	144	124

6. As to the detail of certain lower classes who, though returned as Hindus, are regarded as of doubtful religious *status vide* § 7 of the remarks on the title-page of Table VI *Supra*.

INDEX.

Serial No.	Name of caste and sub-caste.	Population.
1	Arain ...	20,621
2	Arghun ...	1,517
3	Arora ...	3,527
4	Bafinda ...	26,830
5	Bakarwal ...	583
6	Balti ...	72,439
7	Banjara ...	136
8	Barwala ...	11,355
9	Basith ...	7,647
10	Bawaria ...	34
11	Bazigar ...	1,276
12	Beda ...	224
13	Beldar ...	2,418
14	Bhatti ...	4,451
15	Bhirai ...	542
16	Brahman ...	241,362
,,	*Acharji* ...	*660*
,,	*Gujrati* ...	*516*
,,	*Kashmiri Pandit*	*55,279*
,,	*Mohyal* ...	*6,119*
,,	*Others* ...	*173,788*
17	Brukpa ...	8,890
18	Budhan ...	6,586
19	Chamiar ...	3,999
20	Changar ...	455
21	Chhimba ...	364
22	Chuhra ...	8,699
23	Churigar ...	446
24	Darugar ...	41
25	Darwesh ...	9,175
26	Darzi ...	3,958
27	Dhobi ...	5,991
28	Dhund ...	15,858
29	Domal ...	6,953
30	Dosali ...	181
31	Dum ...	52,099
32	Gaddi ...	10,563
33	Gadri ...	354
34	Ghrit ...	131
35	Gujjar ...	328,003
36	Gorkha ...	1,330
37	Hajjam ...	34,456
38	Hanji ...	18.275
39	Harni ...	654
40	Indian Christian ...	709
41	Jat ...	141,439
42	Jhiwar ...	13,500
43	Jogi ...	5,553
44	Kamangar ...	491
45	Kanjar ...	312
46	Kashmiri Musalman	765,442
,,	*Aito* ...	*7,472*
,,	*Bat* ...	*149,315*
,,	*Dar* ...	*98,321*
,,	*Ganai* ...	*46,424*
,,	*Khwaja* ...	*1,462*
,,	*Lon* ...	*56,931*
,,	*Malik* ...	*8,397*
,,	*Mir* ...	*77,532*
,,	*Parai* ...	*15,629*
,,	*Pandit* ...	*3,326*

Serial No.	Name of caste and sub-caste.	Population.
,,	*Raina* ...	*3,264*
,,	*Rathar* ...	*33,951*
,,	*Rishi* ...	*7,685*
,,	*Tantre* ...	*8,056*
,,	*Wain* ...	*59,487*
,,	*Others* ...	*187,689*
47	Kayasth ...	6
48	Khatri ...	18,517
49	Khatik ...	1,230
50	Khoja ...	5,816
51	Khusra ...	9
52	Koli ...	1,784
53	Kumhiar ...	18,958
54	Labana ...	5,321
55	Lama ...	28
56	Lohar ...	28,884
57	Machhi ...	196
58	Mahajan ...	20,462
59	Malik ...	46,162
60	Mangriks ...	98,508
61	Megh ...	75,409
62	Memar ...	325
63	Mirasi ...	7,699
64	Mochi ...	14.694
65	Mughal ...	49,875
,,	*Beg* ...	*6,831*
,,	*Choghatta* ...	*3,397*
,,	*Mir* ...	*17,556*
,,	*Mirza* ...	*1,336*
,,	*Qazilbash* ...	*48*
,,	*Others* ...	*20,707*
66	Naddaf ...	184
67	Parsi ...	31
68	Pathan ...	52,263
,,	*Afridi* ...	*119*
,,	*Baloch* ...	*144*
,,	*Barakzai* ...	*133*
,,	*Durrani* ...	*65*
,,	*Hasanzai* ...	*64*
,,	*Hazara* ...	*89*
,,	*Kabuli* ...	*49*
,,	*Kakezai* ...	*471*
,,	*Khan* ...	*30.338*
,,	*Khaibari* ...	*370*
,,	*Yusufzai* ...	*1,844*
,,	*Zakakhel* ...	*10*
,,	*Others* ...	*18,567*
69	Patoi ...	26
70	Qalandar ...	100
71	Rajput ...	204,742
,,	*Awan* ...	*27,588*
,,	*Bains* ...	*6,193*
,,	*Bamba* ...	*1,462*
,,	*Bhau* ...	*3,093*
,,	*Chauhan* ...	*3,933*
,,	*Chibh* ...	*13,562*
,,	*Duli* ...	*3,099*
,,	*Gakkhar* ...	*13,825*

Serial No.	Name of caste and sub-caste.	Population.
,,	*Janhal* ...	*1,180*
,,	*Janjua* ...	*8,132*
,,	*Jaral* ...	*8,887*
,,	*Khakha* ...	*1,391*
,,	*Khokhar* ...	*7,736*
,,	*Maldial* ...	*11,643*
,,	*Mangral* ...	*7,027*
,,	*Manihas* ...	*12,250*
,,	*Narma* ...	*6,651*
,,	*Sau* ...	*3,047*
,,	*Others* ...	*64,043*
72	Rangrez ...	1,331
73	Ratal ...	970
74	Rigzang ...	4,888
75	Sadhu ...	3,068
76	Sansi ...	97
77	Sapiada ...	145
78	Saryara ...	2,626
79	Sayed ...	102,195
,,	*Akhun* ...	*17,436*
,,	*Baba and Babazada*	*11,267*
,,	*Bukhari* ...	*9,237*
,,	*Gilani* ...	*2,579*
,,	*Hamdani* ...	*282*
,,	*Husaini and Hasani*	*235*
,,	*Jafari* ...	*48*
,,	*Jalali* ...	*59*
,,	*Mashhadi* ...	*6,472*
,,	*Naqshbandi* ...	*35*
,,	*Pirzada* ...	*6,165*
,,	*Qadri* ...	*262*
,,	*Shirazi* ...	*834*
,,	*Sufi* ...	*14,655*
,,	*Others* ...	*32,629*
80	Sheikh ...	10,585
,,	*Makhdumi* ...	*67*
,,	*Qadri* ...	*915*
,,	*Qazi* ...	*637*
,,	*Qureshi* ...	*6,947*
,,	*Ulma* ...	*1,380*
,,	*Others* ...	*95,339*
81	Shin ...	11,080
82	Sudhan ...	56,800
83	Tarkhan ...	27,871
84	Teli ...	19,309
85	Thakkar ...	104,613
86	Tharhiar ...	63
87	Thiar ...	2,755
88	Turk ...	2,407
89	Watal ...	6,467
90	Yashkun ...	35,011
91	Zargar ...	6,379
92	Unclassified Hindu ...	6,420
93	,, Arya ...	144
94	,, Sikh ...	12,494
95	,, Musalman ...	119,243
	GRAND TOTAL ...	3,157,858

TABLE XIII.

Caste, Tribe, Race or Nationality.

Jammu and Kashmir State Census 1911.

Part I—Hindus.

DISTRICT, JAGIR OR ILAQA.	HINDU (*Brahmanic*).																													
	Arora.			Barwala (and Batwal).			Basith.			Bawaria.			Bazigar.			Beldar.			Brahman.											
																			Acharji.			*Gujrati.*			*Kashmiri Pandit.*			*Mohyal.*		
	Persons.	Males.	Females.	Persons.	Males.	Females.	Persons.	Males.	Females.	Persons.	Males.	Females.	Persons.	Males.	Females.	Persons.	Males.	Females.	Persons.	Males.	Females.	Persons.	Males.	Females.	Persons.	Males.	Females.	Persons.	Males.	Females.
1	2	3	4	5	6	7	8	9	10	11	12	13	14	15	16	17	18	19	20	21	22	23	24	25	26	27	28	29	30	31
Total State ...	1,950	1,182	768	11,175	6,040	5,135	7,372	3,604	3,768	33	20	13	121	73	48	9	6	3	654	340	314	516	282	234	55,276	30,768	24,508	4,960	2,506	2,454
I—Total Jammu Province (including *Jagirs*).	1,811	1,079	732	11,175	6,040	5,135	7,369	3,603	3,766	33	20	13	121	73	48	9	6	3	654	340	314	516	282	234	2,330	1,469	861	4,712	2,358	2,354
1. Jammu District (including city).	1,084	650	434	9,715	5,307	4,408	238	114	124	33	20	13	85	58	27	9	6	3	180	86	94	210	120	90	818	615	203	1,001	502	499
2. Jasrota ,, ...	32	17	15	215	108	107	1	1	...	...	...	...	36	15	21	...	...	...	255	138	117	182	88	94	233	107	126	14	6	8
3. Udhampur ,, ...	68	47	21	238	118	120	1	1	...	...	...	...	...	...	...	...	...	...	115	60	55	60	33	27	707	397	310	577	357	220
4. Riasi ,, ...	265	151	114	121	39	82	3,770	1,820	1,950	...	...	...	...	...	...	...	...	...	47	26	21	30	18	12	145	95	50	676	317	359
5. Mirpur ,, ...	310	192	118	631	340	291	3,359	1,667	1,692	...	...	...	...	...	...	...	...	...	44	21	23	33	22	11	41	33	8	1,595	754	841
6. Bhadarwah *Jagir* ...	...	...	...	187	89	98	...	...	...	...	...	...	...	...	...	...	...	...	2	1	1	...	...	...	253	140	113	52	...	52
7. Punch *Ilaqa*	52	22	30	68	39	29	...	...	...	...	...	...	...	...	...	...	...	...	11	8	3	1	1	...	133	82	51	797	422	375
II—Total Kashmir Province (including *Jagirs*).	102	74	28	...	...	...	1	1	...	...	...	...	...	...	...	...	...	...	...	...	...	...	...	...	52,678	29,064	23,614	247	147	100
8. Kashmir North (including Langet *Jagir*).	52	43	9	...	...	...	1	1	...	...	...	...	...	...	...	...	...	...	...	...	...	...	...	...	8,061	4,750	3,311	8	2	6
9. Kashmir South (including city).	28	16	12	...	...	...	...	...	...	...	...	...	...	...	...	...	...	...	...	...	...	...	...	...	44,306	24,031	20,275	11	7	4
Total Kashmir Valley ...	*80*	*59*	*21*	...	...	...	*1*	*1*	...	...	...	...	...	...	...	...	...	...	...	...	...	...	...	...	*52,367*	*28,781*	*23,586*	*19*	*9*	*10*
10. Muzaffarabad District (*Wizarat Pahar*).	22	15	7	...	...	...	...	...	...	...	...	...	...	...	...	...	...	...	...	...	...	...	...	...	311	283	28	228	138	90
III—Total Frontier Districts.	37	29	8	...	...	...	...	...	...	...	...	...	...	...	...	...	...	...	...	...	...	...	...	...	268	235	33	1	1	...
11. Laddakh District (including Mansar).	6	6	...	...	...	...	...	...	...	...	...	...	...	...	...	...	...	...	...	...	...	...	...	...	165	143	22	1	1	...
12. Gilgit ,, ...	11	8	3	...	...	...	...	...	...	...	...	...	...	...	...	...	...	...	...	...	...	...	...	...	43	32	11	...	...	...
13. Frontier *Ilaqas*	20	15	5	...	...	...	...	...	...	...	...	...	...	...	...	...	...	...	...	...	...	...	...	...	60	60	...	...	...	...

TABLE XIII.

Caste, Tribe, Race or Nationality.

Jammu and Kashmir State Census 1911.

Part I—Hindus.

DISTRICT, JAGIR OR ILAQA.	HINDU (*Brahmanic*).																							
	Brahman.						Chamiar.			Chhimba.			Chuhra.			Darzi (Sochi).			Dosali.			Dum.		
	Others.			*Total Brahman.*																				
	Persons.	Males.	Females.	Persons.	Males.	Females.	Persons.	Males.	Females.	Persons.	Males.	Females.	Persons.	Males.	Females.	Persons.	Males.	Females.	Persons.	Males.	Females.	Persons.	Males.	Females.
	32	33	34	35	36	37	38	39	40	41	42	43	44	45	46	47	48	49	50	51	52	53	54	55
Total State ...	168,120	90,082	78,038	229,526	123,978	105,548	39,094	20,459	18,635	339	173	166	231	125	106	558	295	263	181	98	83	36,785	19,391	17,394
I—Total Jammu Province (includng *Jagirs*).	166,622	89,017	77,605	174,834	93,466	81,368	38,927	20,401	18,526	339	173	166	125	20	105	554	291	263	181	98	83	36,782	19,388	17,394
1. Jammu District (including city).	50,217	27,591	22,626	52,426	28.914	23,512	12,915	6,917	5,998	77	28	49	104	10	94	78	32	46	137	75	62	11,283	5,995	5,288
2. Jasrota „	31,656	16,589	15,067	32,340	16,928	15,412	7,684	4,126	3,558	7	3	4	...	...	...	190	97	93	15	11	4	11,892	6,345	5,547
3. Udhampur „	29,660	15,754	13,906	31,119	16,601	14,518	5,093	2,663	2,430	21	8	13	...	...	...	232	114	118	...	...	...	9,489	4,938	4,551
4. Riasi „	25,082	13,289	11,793	25,980	13,745	12,235	5,795	2,934	2,861	23	12	11	21	10	11	38	35	3	...	...	...	2,796	1,402	1,394
5. Mirpur „	11,516	6,127	5,389	13,229	6,957	6,272	6,558	3,363	3,195	211	122	89	...	...	...	13	13	...	4	2	2	296	187	109
6. Bhadarwah *Jagir* ...	1,908	1,025	883	2,215	1.166	1,049	628	269	359	...	...	...	...	...	...	...	...	...	...	...	...	845	436	409
7. Punch *Ilaqa*	16,583	8,642	7,941	17,525	9,155	8,370	254	129	125	...	...	...	...	...	...	3	...	3	25	10	15	181	85	96
II-Total Kashmir Province (including *Jagirs*).	1.297	886	411	54,222	30,097	24,125	130	25	105	...	...	...	106	105	1	4	4	...	...	...	...	3	3	...
8. Kashmir North (including Langet *Jagir*).	617	431	186	8,686	5,183	3,503	39	22	17	...	...	...	...	...	...	...	...	...	...	...	...	...	...	...
9. Kashmir South (including city).	321	237	84	44,638	24,275	20,363	64	...	64	...	...	...	106	105	1	4	4	...	...	...	...	3	3	...
Total Kashmir Valley ...	*938*	*668*	*270*	*53,324*	*29,458*	*23,866*	*103*	*22*	*81*	...	...	...	*106*	*105*	*1*	*4*	*4*	...	...	...	...	*3*	*3*	...
10. Muzaffarabad District (*Wizarat Pahar*).	359	218	141	898	639	259	27	3	24	...	...	...	...	...	...	...	...	...	...	...	...	...	...	...
III—Total Frontier Districts.	201	179	22	470	415	55	37	33	4	...	...	...	...	...	...	...	...	...	...	...	...	...	...	...
11. Laddakh District (including Mansar).	79	63	16	245	207	38	...	...	...	...	...	...	...	...	...	...	...	...	...	...	...	...	...	...
12. Gilgit „	113	111	2	156	143	13	37	33	4	...	...	...	...	...	...	...	...	...	...	...	...	...	...	...
13. Frontier *Ilaqas* ...	9	5	4	69	65	4	...	...	...	...	...	...	...	...	...	...	...	...	...	...	...	...	...	...

TABLE XIII.

Caste, Tribe, Race or Nationality.

Jammu and Kashmir State Census 1911.

Part I—Hindus.

DISTRICT, JAGIR OR ILAQA.	HINDU (*Brahmanic*).																				
	Gaddi.			Gadri.			Ghrit.			Gorkha.			Hajjam.			Jat.			Jhiwar.		
	Persons.	Males.	Females.	Persons.	Males.	Females.	Persons.	Males.	Females.	Persons.	Males.	Females.	Persons.	Males.	Females.	Persons.	Males.	Females.	Persons.	Males.	Females.
	56	57	58	59	60	61	62	63	64	65	66	67	68	69	70	71	72	73	74	77	76
Total State ...	10,550	5,164	5,386	354	246	108	131	71	60	1,304	1,160	144	3,893	2,142	1,751	25,191	13,595	11,596	11,272	5,987	5,285
I—Total Jammu Province (including *Jagirs*).	10,549	5,163	5,386	354	246	108	131	71	60	799	657	142	3,875	2,129	1,746	25,163	13,572	11,591	11,171	5,906	5,265
1. Jammu District (including city).	47	35	12	231	172	59	...	...	...	706	578	128	1,884	1,063	821	7,827	4,352	3,475	7,162	3,862	3,300
2. Jasrota "	4,028	1,940	2,088	...	...	...	131	71	60	44	42	2	1,179	630	549	2,256	1,280	976	2,237	1,112	1,125
3. Udhampur "	5,908	2,932	2,976	...	...	...	...	...	...	11	6	5	616	324	292	285	173	112	378	174	204
4. Riasi "	3	...	3	36	21	15	...	...	...	5	5	...	...	...	...	76	55	21	252	152	100
5. Mirpur "	...	...	...	87	53	34	...	...	...	...	...	...	138	79	59	14,654	7,671	6,983	975	520	455
6. Bhadarwah *Jagir* ...	562	255	307	...	...	...	...	...	...	...	...	...	...	...	...	2	...	2	9	6	3
7. Punch *Ilaqa*	1	1	...	...	...	...	...	...	...	33	26	7	58	33	25	63	41	22	158	80	78
II—Total Kashmir Province (including *Jagirs*).	...	...	...	...	...	...	...	...	...	27	27	...	10	5	5	9	4	5	60	40	20
8. Kashmir North (including Langet *Jagir*).	...	...	...	...	...	...	...	...	...	...	...	...	...	...	...	...	...	...	4	2	2
9. Kashmir South (including city).	...	...	...	...	...	...	...	...	...	27	27	...	10	5	5	...	...	...	51	38	13
Total Kashmir Valley ...	...	...	...	...	...	...	...	...	...	*27*	*27*	...	*10*	*5*	*5*	...	...	...	*55*	*40*	*15*
10. Muzaffarabad District (*Wizarat Pahar*).	...	...	...	...	...	...	...	...	...	...	...	...	...	...	...	9	4	5	5	...	5
III—Total Frontier Districts.	1	1	...	...	...	...	...	...	...	478	476	2	8	8	...	19	19	...	41	41	...
11. Laddakh District (including Mansar).	...	...	...	...	...	...	...	...	...	29	29	...	2	2	...	3	3	...	3	3	...
12. Gilgit "	1	1	...	...	...	...	...	...	...	267	267	...	6	6	...	15	15	...	34	34	...
13. Frontier *Ilaqas*	...	...	...	...	...	...	...	...	...	182	180	2	...	...	...	1	1	...	4	4	...

TABLE XIII.

Caste, Tribe, Race or Nationality.

Jammu and Kashmir State Census 1911.

Part I—Hindus.

DISTRICT, JAGIR OR ILAQA.	HINDU (*Brahmanic*).																							
	Jogi.			Kayasth.			Khatri.			Koli.			Kumhiar.			Labana.			Lohar.			Mahajan.		
	Persons.	Males.	Females.	Persons.	Males.	Females.	Persons.	Males.	Females.	Persons.	Males.	Females.	Persons.	Males.	Females.	Persons.	Males.	Females.	Persons.	Males.	Females.	Persons.	Males.	Females.
	77	78	79	80	81	82	83	84	85	86	87	88	89	90	91	92	93	94	95	96	97	98	99	100
Total State ...	3,081	1,734	1,347	6	3	3	15,948	9,228	6,720	1,784	888	896	4,729	2,527	2,202	3,642	1,977	1,665	10,937	5,715	5,222	20,206	11,428	8,778
I—Total Jammu Province (including *Jagirs*).	3,074	1,727	1,347	...	...	...	12,464	7,170	5,294	1,784	888	896	4,712	2,517	2,195	2,965	1,586	1,379	10,900	5,682	5,218	20,079	11,348	8,731
1. Jammu District (including city).	1,295	740	555	...	...	...	4,355	2,503	1,852	...	...	...	2,118	1,139	979	1,749	928	821	2,941	1,593	1,348	9,002	5,404	3,598
2. Jasrota ,, ...	969	523	446	...	...	...	748	455	293	578	312	266	1,561	822	739	323	185	138	1,923	1,055	868	3,186	1,691	1,495
3. Udhampur ,, ...	437	240	197	...	...	...	836	511	325	1,206	576	630	269	147	122	...	...	...	2,114	1,026	1,088	3,341	1,828	1,513
4. Riasi ,, ...	252	147	105	...	...	...	1,804	1,000	804	...	...	...	461	240	221	552	290	262	2,715	1,417	1,298	1,094	580	514
5. Mirpur ,, ...	118	77	41	...	...	...	3,357	1,909	1,448	...	...	...	279	153	126	111	50	61	298	161	137	2,979	1,557	1,422
6. Bhadarwah *Jagir* ...	...	...	...	...	...	...	143	90	53	...	...	...	...	...	...	...	...	...	768	365	403	188	105	83
7. Punch *Ilaqa*	3	...	3	...	...	...	1,221	702	519	...	...	...	24	16	8	230	133	97	141	65	76	289	183	106
II—Total Kashmir Province (including *Jagirs*).	6	6	...	6	3	3	3,394	1,995	1,399	...	...	...	17	10	7	677	391	286	30	26	4	119	75	44
8. Kashmir North (including Langet *Jagir*).	1	1	...	...	...	...	584	320	264	...	...	...	2	...	2	16	2	14	3	3	...	5	1	4
9. Kashmir South (including city).	3	3	...	6	3	3	1,206	704	502	...	...	...	15	10	5	...	...	...	27	23	4	36	25	11
Total Kashmir Valley ...	*4*	*4*	...	*6*	*3*	*3*	*1,790*	*1,024*	*766*	...	...	...	*17*	*10*	*7*	*16*	*2*	*14*	*30*	*26*	*4*	*41*	*26*	*15*
10. Muzaffarabad District (*Wizarat Pahar*).	2	2	...	...	...	...	1,604	971	633	...	...	...	...	...	...	661	389	272	...	...	...	78	49	29
III—Total Frontier Districts.	1	1	...	...	...	...	90	63	27	...	...	...	...	...	...	...	...	...	7	7	...	8	5	3
11. Laddak Disrrict (including Mansar).	...	...	...	...	...	...	34	24	10	...	...	...	...	...	...	...	...	...	...	...	...	1	1	...
12. Gilgit ,, ...	1	1	...	...	...	...	50	33	17	...	...	...	...	...	...	...	...	...	6	6	...	7	4	3
13. Frontier *Ilaqas*	...	...	...	...	...	...	6	6	...	...	...	...	...	...	...	...	...	...	1	1	...	...	...	...

TABLE XIII.

Caste, Tribe, Race or Nationality.

Jammu and Kashmir State Census 1911.

Part I—Hindus.

DISTRICT, JAGIR OR ILAQA.	HINDU (*Brahmanic*).																										
	Megh.			Rajput.																							
				Bhau.			*Chauhan.*			*Chibh.*			*Janjua.*			*Jaral.*			*Manihas.*			*Narma.*			*Sau.*		
	Persons.	Males.	Females.	Persons.	Males.	Females.	Persons.	Males.	Females.	Persons.	Males.	Females.	Persons.	Males.	Females.	Persons.	Males.	Females.	Persons.	Males.	Females.	Persons.	Males.	Females.	Persons.	Males.	Females.
	101	102	103	104	105	106	107	108	109	110	111	112	113	114	115	116	117	118	119	120	121	122	123	124	125	126	127
Total State ...	74,762	39,000	35,762	2,501	1,325	1,176	216	156	60	3,897	2,426	1,471	70	39	31	381	233	148	5,453	2,845	2,608	34	16	18	86	49	37
I—Total Jammu Province (including *Jagirs*.)	74,743	38,997	35,746	2,501	1,325	1,176	216	156	60	3,894	2,423	1,471	70	39	31	381	233	148	5,448	2,843	2,605	34	16	18	86	49	37
1. Jammu District (including city).	30,560	16,028	14,532	2,184	1,185	999	68	45	23	527	336	191	11	7	4	71	33	38	3,799	2,037	1,762	3	3	...	86	49	37
2. Jasrota ,, ...	7,131	3,768	3,363	...	...	...	34	25	9	11	5	6	...	...	...	36	35	1	128	94	34	...	...	...	...	...	...
3. Udhampur ,, ...	20,995	10,918	10,077	100	29	71	27	20	7	244	151	93	28	14	14	150	92	58	904	396	508	...	...	...	...	...	...
4. Riasi ,, ...	7,209	3,712	3,497	139	65	74	2	2	...	205	95	110	30	17	13	119	68	51	223	104	119	31	13	18	...	...	...
5. Mirpur ,, ...	1,582	877	705	69	40	29	72	52	20	2,895	1,826	1,069	...	...	...	...	...	...	372	196	176	...	...	...	...	...	...
6. Bhadarwah *Jagir* ...	7,074	3,503	3,571	2	2	...	11	11	...	...	...	...	...	...	...	...	...	...	5	5	...	...	...	...	...	...	...
7. Punch *Ilaqa*	192	191	1	7	4	3	2	1	1	12	10	2	1	1	...	5	5	...	17	11	6	...	...	...	...	...	...
II—Total Kashmir Province (including *Jagirs*).	19	3	16	...	...	...	...	...	...	3	3	...	...	...	...	...	...	...	5	2	3	...	...	...	...	...	...
8. Kashmir North (including Langet *Jagir*).	...	...	...	...	...	...	...	...	...	3	3	...	...	...	...	...	...	...	...	...	...	...	...	...	...	...	...
9. Kashmir South (including city).	6	3	3	...	...	...	...	...	...	...	...	...	...	...	...	...	...	...	5	2	3	...	...	...	...	...	...
Total Kashmir Valley ...	*6*	*3*	*3*	...	...	...	...	...	...	*3*	*3*	...	...	...	...	...	...	...	*5*	*2*	*3*	...	...	...	...	...	...
10. Muzaffarabad District (*Wizarat Pahar*).	13	...	13	...	...	...	...	...	...	...	...	...	...	...	...	...	...	...	...	...	...	...	...	...	...	...	...
III—Total Frontier Districts.	...	...	...	...	...	...	...	...	...	...	...	...	...	...	...	...	...	...	...	...	...	...	...	...	...	...	...
11. Laddakh District (including Mansar).	...	...	...	...	...	...	...	...	...	...	...	...	...	...	...	...	...	...	...	...	...	...	...	...	...	...	...
12. Gilgit ,, ...	...	...	...	...	...	...	...	...	...	...	...	...	...	...	...	...	...	...	...	...	...	...	...	...	...	...	...
13. Frontier *Ilaqas*	...	...	...	...	...	...	...	...	...	...	...	...	...	...	...	...	...	...	...	...	...	...	...	...	...	...	...

TABLE XIII.

Caste, Tribe, Race or Nationality.

Jammu and Kashmir State Census 1911.

Part I—Hindus.

DISTRICT, JAGIR OR ILAQA.	HINDU (*Brahmanic*).																				
	RAJPUT.						RATAL.			SADHU.			SANSI.			SARYARA.			TARKHAN.		
	Others.			*Total Rajput.*																	
	Persons.	Males.	Females.	Persons.	Males.	Females.	Persons.	Males.	Females.	Persons.	Males.	Females.	Persons.	Males.	Females.	Persons.	Males.	Females.	Persons.	Males.	Females.
	128	129	130	131	132	133	134	135	136	137	138	139	140	141	142	143	144	145	146	147	148
Total State ...	38,061	22,658	15,403	50,699	29,747	20,952	970	531	439	3,068	1,862	1.186	59	41	18	2,626	1,330	1,296	9,149	5,019	4,130
I—Total Jammu Province (including *Jagirs*).	36,964	21,846	15,138	49,614	28,930	20,684	970	531	439	2,992	1,819	1,173	57	40	17	2,626	1,330	1,296	9,145	5,015	4,130
1. Jammu District (including city).	16,220	10,049	6,171	22,969	13,744	9,225	...	...	...	938	621	317	56	39	17	925	451	474	4,439	2,499	1,940
2. Jasrota ,, ...	8,074	4.524	3,550	8,283	4,683	3.600	496	263	233	355	201	154	...	...	...	801	403	398	2,890	1,561	1,329
3. Udhampur ,, ...	6,605	3,716	2,889	8,058	4,418	3,640	226	114	112	662	344	318	...	...	...	448	226	222	818	426	392
4. Riasi ,, ...	2,401	1,265	1,136	3,150	1,629	1.521	248	154	94	390	223	167	...	...	...	452	250	202	543	286	257
5. Mirpur ,, ...	2,573	1,650	923	5,981	3,764	2,217	...	...	...	244	184	60	1	1	...	...	...	...	402	207	195
6. Bhadarwah *Jagir* ...	637	342	295	655	360	295	...	...	...	365	214	151	...	...	...	...	...	...	2	2	...
7. Punch *Ilaqa*	474	300	174	518	332	186	...	...	...	38	32	6	...	...	...	...	...	...	51	34	17
II—Total Kashmir Province (including *Jagirs*).	862	604	258	870	609	261	...	...	...	76	63	13	2	1	1	...	...	...	...	...	...
8. Kashmir North (including Langet *Jagir*).	104	80	24	107	83	24	...	...	...	...	...	...	...	...	...	...	...	...	...	...	...
9. Kashmir South (including city).	695	478	217	700	480	220	...	...	...	76	63	13	2	1	1	...	...	...	...	...	...
Total Kashmir Valley ...	*799*	*558*	*241*	*807*	*563*	*244*	...	...	...	*76*	*63*	*13*	*2*	*1*	*1*	...	...	...	...	...	...
10. Muzaffarabad District (*Wizarat Pahar*).	63	46	17	63	46	17	...	...	...	...	...	...	...	...	...	...	...	...	...	...	...
III—Total Frontier Districts.	215	208	7	215	208	7	...	...	...	...	...	...	...	...	...	...	...	...	4	4	...
11. Laddakh District (including Mansar).	60	59	1	60	59	1	...	...	...	...	...	...	...	...	...	...	...	...	...	...	...
12. Gilgit ,, ...	155	149	6	155	149	6	...	...	...	...	...	...	...	...	...	...	...	...	4	4	...
13. Frontier *Ilaqas*	...	...	...	...	...	...	...	...	...	...	...	...	...	...	...	...	...	...	...	...	...

TABLE XIII.

Caste, Tribe, Race or Nationality.

Jammu and Kashmir State Census 1911.

Part I—Hindus.

DISTRICT, JAGIR OR ILAQA.	HINDU (*Brahmanic*).																				
	Teli.			Thakkar.			Thathiar.			Thiar.			Zargar.			Hindu Brahmanic unclassified.			Total Hindu (Brahmanic).		
	Persons.	Males.	Females.	Persons.	Males.	Females.	Persons.	Males.	Females.	Persons.	Males.	Females.	Persons.	Males.	Females.	Persons.	Males.	Females.	Persons.	Males.	Females.
	149	150	151	152	153	154	155	156	157	158	159	160	161	162	163	164	165	166	167	168	169
Total State ...	53	26	27	94,150	49,678	44,472	47	28	19	2,755	1,345	1,410	4,182	2,188	1,994	6,420	3,965	2,455	689,342	372,089	317,253
I—Total Jammu Province (including *Jagirs*).	53	26	27	94.033	49,568	44,465	47	28	19	2,755	1,345	1,410	4,170	2,179	1,991	3,969	2,493	1,476	625,456	335,621	289,835
1. Jammu District (including city).	36	16	20	5,419	2,915	2,504	...	...	...	53	53	...	1,402	660	742	1,170	675	495	195,470	108,196	87,274
2. Jasrota „	...	...	...	23,893	12,890	11,003	38	21	17	...	...	...	636	357	279	169	78	91	116,267	61,994	54,273
3. Udhampur „	8	6	2	37,032	19,461	17,571	7	7	...	...	...	...	613	331	282	219	108	111	130,748	68,786	61,962
4. Riasi „	2	2	...	18,158	9,640	8,518	2	...	2	2,576	1,221	1,355	486	259	227	1,611	1,198	413	80,886	42,629	38,257
5. Mirpur „	7	2	5	93	66	27	...	...	...	118	71	47	863	465	398	289	246	43	57,187	30,956	26,231
6. Bhadarwah *Jagir* ...	...	...	...	9,025	4,376	4,649	...	...	...	...	...	...	...	...	...	263	139	124	22,931	11,375	11,556
7. Punch *Ilaqa*	...	...	...	413	220	193	...	...	...	8	...	8	170	107	63	248	49	199	21,967	11,685	10,282
II—Total Kashmir Province (including *Jagirs*).	...	...	...	65	58	7	...	...	...	...	...	...	12	9	3	2,401	1,422	979	62,368	35,056	27,312
8. Kashmir North (including Langet *Jagir*).	...	...	...	22	22	...	...	...	...	...	...	...	...	...	...	395	252	143	9,917	5,935	3,982
9. Kashmir South (including city).	...	...	...	22	18	4	...	...	...	...	...	...	12	9	3	712	483	229	47,754	26,298	21,456
Total Kashmir Valley ...	...	...	...	*44*	*40*	*4*	...	...	...	...	...	...	*12*	*9*	*3*	*1,107*	*735*	*372*	*57,671*	*32,233*	*25,438*
10. Muzaffarabad District (*Wizarat Pahar*).	...	...	...	21	18	3	...	...	...	...	...	...	...	...	...	1,294	687	607	4,697	2,823	1,874
III—Total Frontier Districts.	...	...	...	52	52	...	...	...	...	...	...	...	...	...	...	50	50	...	1,518	1,412	106
11. Laddakh District (including Mansar).	...	...	...	16	16	...	...	...	...	...	...	...	...	...	...	8	8	...	407	358	49
12. Gilgit „	...	...	...	36	36	...	...	...	...	...	...	...	...	...	...	30	30	...	816	770	46
13. Frontier *Ilaqas*	...	...	...	...	...	...	...	...	...	...	...	...	...	...	...	12	12	...	295	284	11

TABLE XIII.

Caste, Tribe, Race or Nationality.

Jammu and Kashmir State Census 1911.

Part I—Hindus.

DISTRICT, JAGIR OR ILAQA.	HINDU (*Arya*). Arora. Persons.	Arora. Males.	Arora. Females.	Brahman. Kashmiri Pandit. Persons.	Kashmiri Pandit. Males.	Kashmiri Pandit. Females.	Mohyal. Persons.	Mohyal. Males.	Mohyal. Females.	Others. Persons.	Others. Males.	Others. Females.	Total Brahman. Persons.	Total Brahman. Males.	Total Brahman. Females.	Chuhra. Persons.	Chuhra. Males.	Chuhra. Females.	Dum. Persons.	Dum. Males.	Dum. Females.	Jat. Persons.	Jat. Males.	Jat. Females.	Khatri. Persons.	Khatri. Males.	Khatri. Females.
	170	171	172	173	174	175	176	177	178	179	180	181	182	183	184	185	186	187	188	189	190	191	192	193	194	195	196
Total State ...	8	5	3	3	1	2	25	14	11	80	67	13	108	82	26	16	6	10	9	9	...	3	3	...	170	112	58
I—Total Jammu Province (including *Jagirs*).	8	5	3	3	1	2	23	12	11	78	66	12	104	79	25	16	6	10	9	9	...	3	3	...	165	110	55
1. Jammu District (including city)	6	4	2	3	1	2	10	6	4	3	2	1	16	9	7	16	6	10	...	...	...	...	...	...	92	60	32
2. Jasrota ,, ...	...	...	...	...	...	...	...	...	...	34	34	...	34	34	...	...	...	...	9	9	...	...	...	...	...	...	...
3. Udhampur ,, ...	...	...	...	...	...	...	...	...	...	2	2	...	2	2	...	...	...	...	...	...	...	...	...	...	14	9	5
4. Riasi ,, ...	1	...	1	...	...	...	1	1	...	1	1	...	2	2	...	...	...	...	...	...	...	1	1	...	5	5	...
5. Mirpur ,, ...	1	1	...	...	...	...	8	1	7	18	12	6	26	13	13	...	...	...	...	...	...	2	2	...	36	24	12
6. Bhadarwah *Jagir* ...	...	...	...	...	...	...	...	...	...	...	...	...	...	...	...	...	...	...	...	...	...	...	...	...	...	...	...
7. Punch *Ilaqa*	...	...	...	...	...	...	4	4	...	20	15	5	24	19	5	...	...	...	...	...	...	...	...	...	18	12	6
II—Total Kashmir Province (including *Jagirs*).	...	...	...	...	...	...	...	...	...	...	...	...	...	...	...	...	...	...	...	...	...	...	...	...	...	...	...
8. Kashmir North (including Langet *Jagir*).	...	...	...	...	...	...	...	...	...	...	...	...	...	...	...	...	...	...	...	...	...	...	...	...	...	...	...
9. Kashmir South (including city).	...	...	...	...	...	...	...	...	...	...	...	...	...	...	...	...	...	...	...	...	...	...	...	...	...	...	...
Total Kashmir Valley ...	...	...	...	...	...	...	...	...	...	...	...	...	...	...	...	...	...	...	...	...	...	...	...	...	...	...	...
10. Muzffarabad District (*Wizarat Pahar*).	...	...	...	...	...	...	...	...	...	...	...	...	...	...	...	...	...	...	...	...	...	...	...	...	...	...	...
III—Total Frontier Districts.	...	...	...	...	...	...	2	2	...	2	1	1	4	3	1	...	...	...	...	...	...	...	...	...	5	2	3
11. Laddakh District (including Mansar).	...	...	...	...	...	...	2	2	...	2	1	1	4	3	1	...	...	...	...	...	...	...	...	...	5	2	3
12. Gilgit ,, ...	...	...	...	...	...	...	...	...	...	...	...	...	...	...	...	...	...	...	...	...	...	...	...	...	...	...	...
13. Frontier *Ilaqas*	...	...	...	...	...	...	...	...	...	...	...	...	...	...	...	...	...	...	...	...	...	...	...	...	...	...	...

TABLE XIII.

Caste, Tribe, Race or Nationality.

Jammu and Kashmir State Census 1911.

Part I—Hindus.

District, Jagir or Ilaqa.	Hindu (Arya). Mahajan. Persons.	Mahajan. Males.	Mahajan. Females.	Megh. Persons.	Megh. Males.	Megh. Females.	Rajput. Persons.	Rajput. Males.	Rajput. Females.	Thakkar. Persons.	Thakkar. Males.	Thakkar. Females.	Hindu Arya Unclassified. Persons.	Hindu Arya Unclassified. Males.	Hindu Arya Unclassified. Females.	Total Hindu Arya. Persons.	Total Hindu Arya. Males.	Total Hindu Arya. Females.	Total Hindu. Persons.	Total Hindu. Males.	Total Hindu. Females.
	197	198	199	200	201	202	203	204	205	206	207	208	209	210	211	212	213	214	215	216	217
Total State ...	136	81	55	429	225	204	12	9	3	12	11	1	144	50	94	1,047	593	454	690,389	372,682	317,707
I—Total Jammu Province (including *Jagirs*).	132	79	53	429	225	204	8	6	2	12	11	1	97	21	76	983	554	429	626,439	336,175	290,264
1. Jammu District (including city).	24	12	12	380	193	187	4	2	2	12	11	1	54	13	41	604	310	294	196,074	108,506	87,568
2. Jasrota ,, ...	2	2	...	...	...	...	...	...	...	...	...	...	27	...	27	72	45	27	116,339	62,039	54,300
3. Udhampur ,, ...	1	1	...	...	...	...	...	...	...	...	...	...	...	...	...	17	12	5	130,765	68,798	61,967
4. Riasi ,, ...	...	...	...	...	...	...	...	...	...	...	...	...	2	2	...	11	10	1	80,897	42,639	38,258
5. Mirpur ,, ...	105	64	41	49	32	17	4	4	...	...	...	...	2	...	2	225	140	85	57,412	31,096	26,316
6. Bhadarwah *Jagir* ...	...	...	...	...	...	...	...	...	...	...	...	...	...	...	...	...	...	...	22,931	11,375	11,556
7. Punch *Ilaqa*	...	...	...	...	...	...	...	...	...	...	...	...	12	6	6	54	37	17	22,021	11,722	10,299
II—Total Kashmir Province (including *Jagirs*).	...	...	...	...	...	...	...	...	...	...	...	...	45	27	18	45	27	18	62,413	35,083	27,330
8. Kashmir North (including Langet *Jagir*).	...	...	...	...	...	...	...	...	...	...	...	...	5	3	2	5	3	2	9,922	5,938	3,984
9. Kashmir South (including city).	...	...	...	...	...	...	...	...	...	...	...	...	40	24	16	40	24	16	47,794	26,322	21,472
Total Kashmir Valley...	...	...	...	...	...	..	...	...	...	...	...	...	*45*	*27*	*18*	*45*	*27*	*18*	*57,716*	*32,260*	*25,456*
10. Muzaffarabad District (*Wizarat Pahar*).	...	...	...	...	...	...	...	...	...	...	...	...	...	...	...	...	...	...	4,697	2,823	1,874
III—Total Frontier Districts.	4	2	2	...	...	...	4	3	1	...	...	...	2	2	...	19	12	7	1,537	1,424	113
11. Laddakh District (including Mansar).	4	2	2	...	...	...	4	3	1	...	...	...	1	1	...	18	11	7	425	369	56
12. Gilgit ,, ...	...	...	...	...	...	...	...	...	...	...	...	...	...	...	...	...	...	...	816	770	46
13. Frontier *Ilaqas*	...	...	...	...	...	...	...	...	...	...	...	...	1	1	...	1	1	...	296	285	11

TABLE XIII

Caste, Tribe, Race or Nationality.

Jammu and Kashmir State Census 1911.

Part II—Musalmans.

District, Jagir or Ilaqa.	Arain.			Arghun.			Arora.			Bafinda (Julaha).			Bakarwal.			Balti.			Banjara.			Barwala (and Batwal).		
	Persons.	Males.	Females.	Persons.	Males.	Females.	Persons.	Males.	Females.	Persons.	Males.	Females.	Persons.	Males.	Females.	Persons.	Males.	Females.	Persons.	Males.	Females.	Persons.	Males.	Females.
1	2	3	4	5	6	7	8	9	10	11	12	13	14	15	16	17	18	19	20	21	22	23	24	25
Total State ...	20,621	11,497	9,124	1,517	1,001	516	71	43	28	26,830	14,795	12,035	583	290	293	72,439	40,597	31,842	136	.72	64	180	102	78
I—Total Jammu Province (including *Jagirs*).	20,121	11,239	8,882	...	...	...	...	...	...	25,971	14,402	11,569	486	264	222	122	111	11	98	34	64	48	18	30
1. Jammu District (including city).	11,748	6,693	5,055	...	...	...	...	...	...	784	409	375	...	...	...	8	6	2	44	3	41	41	13	28
2. Jasrota ,, ...	1,711	1,020	691	...	...	...	...	...	...	5,434	2,933	2,501	158	97	61	...	...	...	36	21	15	5	3	2
3. Udhampur ,, ...	255	148	107	...	...	...	...	...	...	347	184	163	127	80	47	4	3	1	12	7	5	1	1	...
4. Riasi ,, ...	314	212	102	...	...	...	...	...	...	1,063	512	551	200	86	114	...	...	...	6	3	3	...	...	...
5. Mirpur ,, ...	5,890	3,019	2,871	...	...	...	...	...	...	10,420	5,531	4,889	...	...	...	3	3	...	...	...	...	...	...	...
6. Bhadarwah *Jagir* ...	...	...	...	...	...	...	...	...	...	...	...	...	...	...	...	...	...	...	...	...	...	...	...	...
7. Punch *Ilaqa*	203	147	56	...	...	...	...	...	...	7,923	4,833	3,090	1	1	...	107	99	8	...	...	...	1	1	...
II—Total Kashmir Province (including *Jagirs*).	500	258	242	89	48	41	71	43	28	859	393	466	97	26	71	7,150	6,831	319	...	...	...	132	84	48
8. Kashmir North (including Langet *Jagir*).	164	80	84	...	...	...	...	...	...	28	17	11	...	...	...	6,876	6,603	273	...	...	...	61	22	39
9. Kashmir South (including city).	317	178	139	89	48	41	...	...	...	73	32	41	47	26	21	274	228	46	...	...	...	37	35	2
Total Kashmir Valley ...	*481*	*258*	*223*	*89*	*48*	*41*	...	...	...	*101*	*49*	*52*	*47*	*26*	*21*	*7,150*	*6,831*	*319*	...	...	...	*98*	*57*	*41*
10. Muzaffarabad District (*Wizarat Pahar*).	19	...	19	...	...	...	71	43	28	758	344	414	50	...	50	...	...	...	...	...	...	34	27	7
III—Total Frontier Districts.	...	...	...	1,428	953	475	...	...	...	...	...	...	...	...	...	65,167	33,655	31,512	38	38	...	...	...	...
11. Laddakh District (including Mansar).	...	...	...	1,428	953	475	...	...	...	...	...	...	...	...	...	64,744	33,412	31,332	...	...	...	...	...	...
12. Gilgit ,, ...	...	...	...	...	...	...	...	...	...	...	...	...	...	...	...	418	238	180	38	38	...	...	...	...
13. Frontier *Ilaqas*	...	...	...	...	...	...	...	...	...	...	...	...	...	...	...	5	5	...	...	...	...	...	...	...

TABLE XIII.

Caste, Tribe, Race or Nationality.

Jammu and Kashmir State Census 1911.

Part II—Musalmans.

District, Jagir or Ilaqa.	Basith.			Bawaria.			Bazigar.			Beda.			Beldar.			Bhatti.			Bhirai.			Brukpa.			Budhan.		
	Persons.	Males.	Females.	Persons.	Males.	Females.	Persons.	Males.	Females.	Persons.	Males.	Femaless.	Persons.	Males.	Females.	Persons.	Males.	Females.	Persons.	Males.	Females.	Persons.	Males.	Females.	Persons.	Males.	Females.
	26	27	28	29	30	31	32	33	34	35	36	37	38	39	40	41	42	43	44	45	46	47	48	49	50	51	52
Total State ...	55	22	33	1	1	...	1.155	643	512	219	69	150	2,409	1,220	1.189	4,451	2,399	2,052	542	300	242	8,890	3,983	4.907	6,586	3,022	3,564
I—Total Jammu Province (including *Jagirs*).	49	22	27	...	...	...	1,155	643	512	...	...	...	2,407	1,220	1,187	3,292	1,791	1,501	542	300	242	...	...	...	6,079	2,835	3,244
1. Jammu District (including city).	...	...	...	...	...	...	176	98	78	...	...	...	1,472	705	767	502	385	117	243	146	97	...	...	...	...	...	...
2. Jasrota „	...	...	...	...	...	...	467	267	200	...	...	...	911	500	411	...	...	...	232	123	109	...	...	...	...	...	...
3. Udhampur „	...	...	...	...	...	...	151	74	77	...	...	...	12	3	9	...	...	...	4	1	3	...	...	...	...	...	...
4. Riasi „	49	22	27	...	...	...	8	6	2	...	...	...	...	...	...	1,900	870	1,030	...	...	...	...	...	...	79	19	60
5. Mirpur „	...	...	...	...	...	...	352	198	154	...	...	...	12	12	...	347	199	148	63	30	33	...	...	...	1,393	684	709
6. Bhadarwah *Jagir* ...	...	...	...	...	...	...	...	...	...	...	...	...	...	...	...	...	...	...	...	...	...	...	...	...	...	...	...
7. Punch *Ilaqa*	...	...	...	...	...	...	1	...	1	...	...	...	...	...	...	543	337	206	...	...	...	...	...	...	4,607	2,132	2,475
II—Total Kashmir Province (including *Jagirs*).	6	...	6	1	1	...	...	...	...	...	...	...	2	...	2	1,140	594	546	...	...	...	5	4	1	505	185	320
8. Kashmir North (including Langet *Jagir*).	...	...	...	...	...	...	...	...	...	...	...	...	...	...	...	27	12	15	...	...	...	...	...	...	...	...	...
9. Kashmir South (including city).	...	...	...	...	...	...	...	...	...	...	...	...	2	...	2	2	2	...	...	...	...	5	4	1	...	...	...
Total Kashmir Valley ...	...	...	...	...	...	...	...	...	...	...	...	...	*2*	...	*2*	*29*	*14*	*15*	...	...	...	*5*	*4*	*1*	...	...	...
10. Muzaffarabad District (*Wizarat Pahar*).	6	...	6	1	1	...	...	...	...	...	...	...	...	...	...	1,111	580	531	...	...	...	...	...	...	505	185	320
III—Total Frontier Districts.	...	...	...	...	...	...	...	...	...	219	69	150	...	...	...	19	14	5	...	...	...	8,885	3,979	4,906	2	2	...
11.—Laddakh District (including Mansar).	...	...	...	...	...	...	...	...	...	216	67	149	...	...	...	3	2	1	...	...	...	8,173	3,618	4,555	...	...	...
12. Gilgit „	...	...	...	...	...	...	...	...	...	3	2	1	...	...	...	...	...	...	...	...	...	1	1	...	2	2	...
13. Frontier *Ilaqas*	...	...	...	...	...	...	...	...	...	...	...	...	...	...	...	16	12	4	...	...	...	711	360	351	...	...	...

TABLE XIII.

Caste, Tribe Race or Nationality.

Jammu and Kashmir State Census 1911.

Part II—Musalmans.

DISTRICT, JAGIR OR ILAQA.	Changar.			Chuhra (including Musallis).			Churigar (Manihar).			Darugar.			Darwesh (and Fakir).			Darzi.			Dhobi.			Dhund.			Domal.		
	Persons.	Males.	Females.	Persons.	Males.	Females.	Persons.	Males.	Females.	Persons.	Males.	Females.	Persons.	Males.	Females.	Persons.	Males.	Females.	Persons.	Males.	Females.	Persons.	Males.	Females.	Persons.	Males.	Females.
	53	54	55	56	57	58	59	60	61	62	63	64	65	66	67	68	69	70	71	72	73	74	75	76	77	78	79
Total State ...	455	238	217	8,364	4,285	4,079	446	228	218	41	21	20	9,175	4,850	4,325	3,400	1,701	1,699	5,991	3,362	2,629	15,858	7,867	7,991	6,953	3,264	3,689
I—Total Jammu Province (including *Jagirs*).	455	238	217	7,756	3,987	3,769	437	224	213	41	21	20	7,536	4,048	3,488	3,005	1,529	1,476	5,017	2,840	2,177	9,611	4,984	4,627	6,635	2,946	3,689
1. Jammu District (including city).	...	...	...	1,305	715	590	165	82	83	29	15	14	2,750	1,427	1,323	168	86	82	2,553	1,372	1,181	...	...	...	...	...	...
2. Jasrota ,, ...	256	137	119	129	68	61	40	21	19	...	...	...	1,257	683	574	29	13	16	850	484	366	...	...	...	...	...	...
3. Udhampur ,, ...	...	...	...	180	86	94	...	...	...	...	...	...	411	301	110	21	8	13	214	118	96	...	...	...	9	9	...
4. Riasi ,, ...	...	...	...	1,191	652	539	...	...	...	...	...	...	461	264	197	57	24	33	667	495	172	...	...	...	2,599	1,210	1,389
5. Mirpur ,, ...	199	101	98	2,857	1,450	1,407	232	121	111	12	6	6	2,363	1,229	1,134	2,437	1,216	1,221	550	295	255	...	...	...	1,035	511	524
6. Bhadarwah *Jagir* ...	...	...	...	...	...	...	...	...	...	...	...	...	51	26	25	...	...	...	...	...	...	...	...	...	...	...	...
7. Punch *Ilaqa*	...	...	...	2,094	1,016	1,078	...	...	...	...	...	...	243	118	125	293	182	111	183	76	107	9,611	4,984	4,627	2,992	1,216	1,776
II—Total Kashmir Province (including *Jagirs*).	...	...	...	556	263	293	9	4	5	...	...	...	1,488	722	766	392	172	220	961	511	450	6,280	2,872	3,358	308	308	...
8. Kashmir North (including Langet *Jagir*).	...	...	...	366	178	188	...	...	...	...	...	...	674	300	374	71	36	35	335	176	159	...	...	...	302	302	...
9. Kashmir South (including city).	...	...	...	65	33	32	9	4	5	...	...	...	811	420	391	244	125	119	550	317	233	5	5	...	...	...	...
Total Kashmir Valley ...	...	...	...	*431*	*211*	*220*	*9*	*4*	*5*	...	...	...	*1,485*	*720*	*765*	*315*	*161*	*154*	*885*	*493*	*392*	*5*	*5*	...	*302*	*302*	...
10. Muzaffarabad District (*Wizarat Pahar*).	...	...	...	125	52	73	...	...	...	...	...	...	3	2	1	77	11	66	76	18	58	6,225	2,867	3,358	6	6	...
III—Total Frontier Districts.	...	...	...	52	35	17	...	...	...	...	...	...	151	80	71	3	...	3	13	11	2	17	11	6	10	10	...
11. Laddakh District (including Mansar).	...	...	...	...	...	...	...	...	...	...	...	...	21	8	13	...	...	...	1	1	...	...	...	...	...	...	...
12. Gilgit ,, ...	...	...	...	40	27	13	...	...	...	...	...	...	26	17	9	3	...	3	10	8	2	2	1	1	9	9	...
13. Frontier *Ilaqas*	...	...	...	12	8	4	...	...	...	...	...	...	104	55	49	...	...	...	2	2	...	15	10	5	1	1	...

TABLE XIII.

Caste, Tribe, Race or Nationality.

Jammu and Kashmir State Census 1911.

Part II—Musalmans.

DISTRICT, JAGIR OR ILAQA.	Dum.			Gaddi.			Gujjar.			Gorkha.			Hajjam.			Hanji.			Harni.			Jat.		
	Persons.	Males.	Females.	Persons.	Males.	Females.	Persons.	Males.	Females.	Persons.	Males.	Females.	Persons.	Males.	Females.	Persons.	Males.	Females.	Persons.	Males.	Females.	Persons.	Males.	Females.
	80	81	82	83	84	85	86	87	88	89	90	91	92	93	94	95	96	97	98	99	100	101	102	103
Total State ...	15,284	7,921	7,363	13	8	5	328,003	183,798	144,205	25	5	20	30,557	16,549	14,008	18,275	10,244	8,031	654	347	307	115,530	58,905	56,625
I—Total Jammu Province (including *Jagirs*).	97	58	39	13	8	5	237,702	127,211	110,491	1	1	...	10,828	5,676	5,152	1,036	639	397	631	347	284	114,746	58,585	56,161
1. Jammu District (including city)	...	...	...	...	...	...	54,140	29,368	24,772	1	1	...	2,106	1,130	976	161	90	71	631	347	284	8,378	4,967	3,411
2. Jasrota „	3	3	...	13	8	5	15,762	8,381	7,381	...	...	...	267	159	108	8	8	...	...	...	...	442	251	191
3. Udhampur „	89	50	39	...	...	...	18,762	9,873	8,889	...	...	...	901	463	438	711	479	232	...	...	...	110	72	38
4. Riasi „	...	...	...	...	...	...	58,843	31,384	27,459	...	...	...	1,311	646	665	81	37	44	...	...	...	2,877	1,477	1,400
5. Mirpur „	...	...	...	...	...	...	26,199	14,306	11,893	...	...	...	4,116	2,152	1,964	1	1	...	...	...	...	91,169	46,053	45,116
6. Bhadarwah *Jagir* ...	...	...	...	...	...	...	2,486	1,254	1,232	...	...	...	17	11	6	74	24	50	...	...	...	14	...	14
7. Punch *Ilaqa*	5	5	...	...	...	...	61,510	32,645	28,865	...	...	...	2,110	1,115	995	...	...	...	...	...	...	11,756	5,765	5,991
II—Total Kashmir Province (including *Jagirs*).	11,975	6,139	5,836	...	...	...	87,198	54,892	32,306	23	3	20	19,550	10,774	8,776	17,238	9,604	7,634	23	...	23	744	286	458
8. Kashmir North (including Langet *Jagir*).	7,304	3,660	3,644	...	...	...	28,265	19,648	8,617	...	...	...	4,064	2,140	1,924	4,361	2,731	1,630	23	...	23	46	18	28
9. Kashmir South (including) city).	4,665	2,473	2,192	...	...	...	22,845	12,419	10,426	23	3	20	14,881	8,385	6,496	12,874	6,873	6,001	...	...	...	236	186	50
Total Kashmir Valley ...	*11,969*	*6,133*	*5,836*	...	...	...	*51,110*	*32,067*	*19,043*	*23*	*3*	*20*	*18,945*	*10,525*	*8,420*	*17,235*	*9,604*	*7,631*	*23*	...	*23*	*282*	*204*	*78*
10. Muzaffarabad District (*Wizarat Pahar*).	6	6	...	...	...	...	36,088	22,825	13,263	...	...	...	605	249	356	3	...	3	...	...	...	462	82	380
III—Total Frontier Districts.	3,212	1,724	1,488	...	...	...	3,103	1,695	1,408	1	1	...	179	99	80	1	1	...	...	...	...	40	34	6
11. Laddakh District (including Mansar).	3	...	3	...	...	...	85	85	...	...	...	...	119	63	56	1	1	...	...	...	...	9	3	6
12. Gilgit	785	407	378	...	...	...	299	137	162	1	1	...	59	35	24	...	...	...	...	...	...	23	23	...
13. Frontier *Ilaqas*	2,424	1,317	1,107	...	...	...	2,719	1,473	1,246	...	...	...	1	1	...	...	...	...	...	...	...	8	8	...

TABLE XIII.

Caste, Tribe, Race or Nationality.

Jammu and Kashmir State Census 1911.

Part II—Musalmans.

DISTRICT, JAGIR OR ILAQA.	Jhiwar (Mashki).			Jogi.			Kamangar			Kanjar (and Gan).			Kashmiri Musalman. Aito.			Kashmiri Musalman. Bat.			Kashmiri Musalman. Dar.			Kashmiri Musalman. Ganai.		
	Persons.	Males.	Females.	Persons.	Males.	Females.	Persons.	Males.	Females.	Persons.	Males.	Females.	Persons.	Males.	Females.	Persons.	Males.	Females.	Persons.	Males.	Females.	Persons.	Males.	Females.
	104	105	106	107	108	109	110	111	112	113	114	115	116	117	118	119	120	121	122	123	124	125	126	127
Total State ...	2,203	1,285	918	2,472	1,391	1,081	491	230	261	312	134	178	7,472	3,821	3,651	149,315	79,764	69,551	98,321	52,085	46,236	46,424	21,795	24,629
I—Total Jammu Province (including *Jagirs*).	2,081	1,173	908	2,433	1,371	1,062	404	200	204	82	33	49	267	181	86	14,415	8,234	6,181	5,239	2,718	2,521	2,897	1,453	1,444
1. Jammu District (including city).	90	37	53	634	314	320	45	26	19	77	33	44	11	7	4	1,053	643	410	386	245	141	47	43	4
2. Jasrota ,, ...	3	2	1	67	45	22	...	...	...	...	...	...	...	...	...	284	148	136	95	39	56	91	41	50
3. Udhampur ,, ...	...	...	...	103	49	54	13	2	11	...	...	...	212	155	57	5,814	3,558	2,256	909	486	423	1,440	755	685
4. Riasi ,, ...	32	14	18	110	55	55	...	...	...	...	...	...	10	4	6	1,708	915	793	809	438	371	201	96	105
5. Mirpur ,, ...	1,570	902	668	1,167	720	447	117	48	69	5	...	5	23	12	11	1,640	912	728	1,068	650	415	263	149	114
6. Bhadarwah *Jagir* ...	...	...	...	...	...	...	...	...	...	...	...	...	...	...	...	2,236	1,253	983	387	182	205	299	154	145
7. Punch *Ilaqa*	386	218	168	352	188	164	229	124	105	...	...	...	11	3	8	1,680	805	875	1,588	678	910	556	215	341
II—Total Kashmir Province (including *Jagirs*).	122	112	10	39	20	19	87	30	57	230	101	129	7,205	3,640	3,565	134,545	71,363	63,182	92,946	49,289	43,657	43,504	20,329	23,175
8. Kashmir North (including Langet *Jagir*.)	3	1	2	...	...	...	...	...	...	...	...	...	2,079	729	1,350	47,876	24,671	23,205	47,616	24,890	22,726	16,611	5,373	11,238
9. Kashmir South (including city).	118	111	7	39	20	19	...	...	...	196	101	95	5,068	2,911	2,157	84,164	45,323	38,841	44,348	24,122	20,226	26,245	14,578	11,667
Total Kashmir Valley ...	*121*	*112*	*9*	*39*	*20*	*19*	...	...	...	*196*	*101*	*95*	*7,147*	*3,640*	*3,507*	*132,040*	*69,994*	*62,046*	*91,964*	*49,012*	*42,952*	*42,856*	*19,951*	*22,905*
10. Muzaffarabad District (*Wizarat Pahar*).	1	...	1	...	...	...	87	30	57	34	...	34	58	...	58	2,505	1,369	1,136	982	277	705	648	378	270
III—Total Frontier Districts.	...	...	...	...	...	...	...	...	...	...	...	...	...	...	...	355	167	188	136	78	58	23	13	10
11. Laddakh District (including Mansar).	...	...	...	...	...	...	...	...	...	...	...	...	...	...	...	239	101	138	105	56	49	23	13	10
12. Gilgit ,, ...	...	...	...	...	...	...	...	...	...	...	...	...	...	...	...	116	66	50	31	22	9	...	...	...
13. Frontier *Ilaqas*	...	...	...	...	...	...	...	...	...	...	...	...	...	...	...	...	...	...	...	...	...	...	...	...

TABLE XIII.

CASTE, TRIBE, RACE OR NATIONALITY.

Jammu and Kashmir State Census 1911.

Part II—Musalmans.

DISTRICT, JAGIR OR ILAQA.	KASHMIRI MUSALMAN.																				
	Khwaja.			*Lon.*			*Malik.*			*Mir.*			*Parai.*			*Pandit.*			*Raina.*		
	Persons.	Males.	Females.	Persons.	Males.	Females.	Persons.	Males.	Females.	Persons.	Males.	Females.	Persons.	Males.	Females.	Persons.	Males.	Females.	Persons.	Males.	Females.
	128	129	130	131	132	133	134	135	136	137	138	139	140	141	142	143	144	145	146	147	148
Total State ...	1,462	672	790	56,931	29,718	27,213	8,897	4,622	4,275	77,532	42,204	35,328	15,629	8,448	7,181	3,326	1,696	1,630	3,264	1,434	1,830
I—Total Jammu Province (including *Jagirs*).	411	172	239	8,126	4,131	3,995	4,979	2,654	2,325	7,719	4,070	3,649	893	442	451	127	19	108	136	70	66
1. Jammu District (including city).	...	...	...	202	130	72	317	241	76	428	270	158	2	2	...	...	...	...	1	1	...
2. Jasrota ,, ...	36	31	5	25	10	15	8	8	...	63	41	22	...	...	...	...	...	...	...	...	...
3. Udhampur ,, ...	23	2	21	4,293	2,246	2,047	296	187	109	653	489	164	394	200	194	5	5	...	130	69	61
4. Riasi ,, ...	...	...	...	944	503	441	1,964	995	969	1,334	685	649	...	...	...	...	...	...	3	...	3
5. Mirpur ,, ...	...	...	...	863	420	443	430	242	188	1,740	922	818	126	63	63	30	14	16	...	...	...
6. Bhadarwah *Jagir* ...	1	1	...	243	160	83	773	398	375	699	368	331	290	151	139	...	...	...	2	...	2
7. Punch *Ilaqa*	351	138	213	1,556	662	894	1,191	583	608	2,802	1,295	1,507	81	26	55	92	...	92	...	...	...
II—Total Kashmir Province (including *Jagirs*).	1,051	500	551	48,451	25,367	23,084	3,655	1,901	1,754	68,731	37,554	31,177	14,736	8,006	6,730	3,199	1,677	1,522	3,124	1,364	1,760
8. Kashmir North (including Langet *Jagir*).	887	407	480	28,709	14,829	13,880	754	406	348	31,917	18,284	13,633	8,812	4,740	4,072	1,430	744	686	612	329	283
9. Kashmir South (including city).	164	93	71	17,344	9,377	7,967	2,244	1,380	864	36,333	18,832	17,501	5,777	3,205	2,572	1,710	895	815	1,927	1,035	892
Total Kashmir Valley ...	*1,051*	*500*	*551*	*46,053*	*24,206*	*21,847*	*2,998*	*1,786*	*1,212*	*68,250*	*37,116*	*31,134*	*14,589*	*7,945*	*6,644*	*3,140*	*1,639*	*1,501*	*2,539*	*1,364*	*1,175*
10. Muzaffarabad District (*Wizarat Pahar*).	...	...	...	2,398	1,161	1,237	657	115	542	481	438	43	147	61	86	59	38	21	585	...	585
III—Total Frontier Districts.	...	...	...	354	220	134	263	67	196	1,082	580	502	...	...	...	...	...	...	4	...	4
11. Laddakh District (including Mansar).	...	...	...	96	91	5	89	...	89	461	261	200	...	...	...	...	...	...	4	...	4
12. Gilgit ,, ...	...	...	...	258	129	129	174	67	107	621	319	302	...	...	...	...	...	...	...	...	...
13. Frontier *Ilaqas*	...	...	...	...	...	...	...	...	...	...	...	...	...	...	...	...	...	...	...	...	...

TABLE XIII.

Caste, Tribe, Race or Nationality.

Jammu and Kashmir State Census 1911.

Part II—Musalmans.

DISTRICT, JAGIR OR ILAQA.	Kashmiri Musalman. Rathar. Persons.	Rathar. Males.	Rathar. Females.	Rishi. Persons.	Rishi. Males.	Rishi. Females.	Tantre. Persons.	Tantre. Males.	Tantre. Females.	Wani. Persons.	Wani. Males.	Wani. Females.	Others. Persons.	Others. Males.	Others. Females.	Total Kashmiri. Persons.	Total Kashmiri. Males.	Total Kashmiri. Females.	Khatik. Persons.	Khatik. Males.	Khatik. Females.
	149	150	151	152	153	154	155	156	157	158	159	160	161	162	163	164	165	166	167	168	169
Total State ...	33,951	18,151	15,800	7,685	3,964	3,721	8,056	4,431	3,625	59,487	32,113	27,374	187,689	86,565	101,124	765,442	391,484	373,958	1,230	726	504
I—Total Jammu Province (including *Jagirs*).	2,545	1,256	1,289	459	277	182	1,050	791	259	7,237	3,701	3,536	21,971	11,016	10,955	78,471	41,185	37,286	1,204	711	493
1. Jammu District (including city).	25	18	7	1	1	...	4	...	4	407	255	152	1,552	773	779	4,436	2,629	1,807	547	319	228
2. Jasrota "	89	50	39	28	17	11	7	...	7	23	13	10	367	239	128	1,116	637	479	270	164	106
3. Udhampur "	1,272	644	628	234	175	59	459	251	208	4,538	2,381	2,157	3,140	1,249	1,891	23,813	12,852	10,960	42	23	19
4. Riasi "	286	169	117	21	4	17	12	12	...	995	392	603	5,212	2,859	2,353	13,499	7,072	6,427	46	34	12
5. Mirpur "	220	118	102	4	4	...	6	1	5	256	126	130	3,417	1,778	1,639	10,083	5,411	4,672	277	149	128
6. Bhadarwah *Jagir* ...	295	139	156	79	37	42	25	...	25	822	430	392	4,337	2,221	2,116	10,488	5,494	4,994	...	...	...
7. Punch *Ilaqa*	258	118	240	92	39	53	537	527	10	196	104	92	3,946	1,897	2,049	15,037	7,090	7,947	22	22	...
II—Total Kashmir Province (including *Jagirs*).	31,280	16,883	14,397	7,204	3,672	3,532	6,990	3,632	3,358	52,137	28,349	23,788	163,790	74,592	89,198	682,548	348,118	334,430	26	15	11
8. Kashmir North (including Langet *Jagir*).	13,977	7,491	6,486	2,776	1,396	1,380	3,427	1,751	1,676	20,373	11,152	9,221	34,139	10,279	23,860	261,995	127,471	134,524	...	...	...
9. Kashmir South (including city).	17,236	9,392	7,844	4,428	2,276	2,152	3,456	1,881	1,575	31,663	17,121	14,542	68,872	33,621	35,251	350,979	186,042	164,937	26	15	11
Total Kashmir Valley ...	*31,213*	*16,883*	*14,330*	*7,204*	*3,672*	*3,532*	*6,883*	*3,632*	*3,251*	*52,036*	*28,273*	*23,763*	*103,011*	*43,900*	*59,111*	*612,974*	*313,513*	*299,461*	*26*	*15*	*11*
10. Muzaffarabad District (*Wizarat Pahar*).	67	...	67	...	...	...	107	...	107	101	76	25	60,779	30,692	30,087	69,574	34,605	34,969	...	...	...
III—Total Frontier Districts.	126	12	114	22	15	7	16	8	8	113	63	50	1,928	957	971	4,422	2,180	2,242	...	...	...
11. Laddakh District (including Mansar).	112	11	101	12	7	5	7	7	...	73	35	38	1,249	565	684	2,470	1,147	1,323	...	...	...
12. Gilgit "	14	1	13	10	8	2	9	1	8	40	28	12	155	104	51	1,428	745	683	...	...	...
13. Frontier *Ilaqas*	...	...	...	...	...	...	...	...	...	...	...	...	524	288	236	524	288	236	...	...	...

TABLE XIII.
Caste, Tribe, Race or Nationality.
Jammu and Kashmir State Census 1911.
Part II—Musalmans.

District, Jagir or Ilaqa.	Khoja.			Khusra.			Kumhar.			Labana.			Lohar.			Machhi.			Malik.			Mangriks.			Megh.		
	Persons.	Males.	Females.	Persons.	Males.	Females.	Persons.	Males.	Females.	Persons.	Males.	Females.	Persons.	Males.	Females.	Persons.	Males.	Females.	Persons.	Males.	Females.	Persons.	Males.	Females.	Persons.	Males.	Females.
	170	171	172	173	174	175	176	177	178	179	180	181	182	183	184	185	186	187	188	189	190	191	192	193	194	195	196
Total State ...	5,816	3,162	2,654	9	9	...	14,189	7,608	6,581	52	31	21	17,332	9,375	8,557	196	102	94	46,162	23,764	22,398	62,892	30,867	32,025	184	95	89
I—Total Jammu Province (including *Jagirs*).	3,750	2,432	1,318	9	9	...	10,113	5,384	4,729	52	31	21	12,075	6,398	5,677	94	41	53	18,065	9,082	8,983	...	...	...	23	20	3
1. Jammu District (including city).	38	31	7	9	9	...	954	531	423	...	...	...	1,228	650	578	52	17	35	41	21	20	...	...	...	14	14	...
2. Jasrota ,, ...	106	41	65	...	...	...	140	68	72	...	...	...	40	17	23	1	1	...	210	91	119	...	...	...	3	3	...
3. Udhampur ,, ...	577	365	212	...	...	...	1,211	608	603	...	...	...	541	232	309	...	...	...	4,079	2,180	1,899	...	...	...	...	...	...
4. Riasi ,, ...	295	180	115	...	...	...	598	333	265	15	9	6	1,521	815	706	2	1	1	628	186	442	...	...	...	...	...	...
5. Mirpur ,, ...	287	141	146	...	...	...	3,970	2,191	1,779	37	22	15	4,612	2,406	2,206	39	22	17	7,503	3,766	3,737	...	...	...	...	...	...
6. Bhadarwah *Jagir* ...	10	5	5	...	...	...	43	20	23	...	...	...	22	1	21	...	...	...	...	...	...	...	...	...	...	...	...
7. Punch *Ilaqa*	2,437	1,669	768	...	...	...	3,197	1,633	1,564	...	...	...	4,111	2,277	1,834	...	...	...	5,604	2,838	2,766	...	...	...	6	3	3
II—Total Kashmir Province (including *Jagirs*).	2,063	728	1,335	...	...	...	3,982	2,178	1,804	...	...	...	5,482	2,777	2,705	102	61	41	28,051	14,666	13,385	...	...	...	161	75	86
8. Kashmir North (including Langet *Jagir*).	11	8	3	...	...	...	1,564	832	732	...	...	...	1,101	512	589	2	1	1	11,993	6,427	5,566	...	...	...	...	...	...
9. Kashmir South (including city).	296	101	195	...	...	...	2,281	1,287	994	...	...	...	2,612	1,259	1,353	100	60	40	13,736	6,913	6,823	...	...	...	...	...	...
Total Kashmir Valley ...	*307*	*109*	*198*	...	...	...	*3,845*	*2,119*	*1,726*	...	...	...	*3,713*	*1,771*	*1,942*	*102*	*61*	*41*	*25,729*	*13,340*	*12,389*	...	...	...	...	...	...
10. Muzaffarabad District (*Wizarat Pahar*).	1,756	619	1,137	...	...	...	137	59	78	...	...	...	1,769	1,006	763	...	...	...	2,322	1,326	996	...	...	...	161	75	86
III—Total Frontier Districts.	3	2	1	...	...	...	94	46	48	...	...	...	375	200	175	...	...	...	46	16	30	62,892	30,867	32,025	...	...	...
11. Laddakh District (including Mansar).	3	2	1	...	...	...	9	4	5	...	...	...	80	32	48	...	...	...	44	14	30	62,892	30,867	32,025	...	...	...
12. Gilgit	...	...	...	...	...	...	85	42	43	...	...	...	118	62	56	...	...	...	...	...	...	...	...	...	...	...	...
13. Frontier *Ilaqas*	...	...	...	...	...	...	...	...	...	...	...	...	177	106	71	...	...	...	2	2	...	...	...	...	...	...	...

TABLE XIII.

Caste, Tribe, Race or Nationality.

Jammu and Kashmir State Census 1911.

Part II—Musalmans.

District, Jagir or Ilaqa.	Memar.			Mirasi.			Mochi.			Mughal.																	
										Beg.			*Choghatta.*			*Mir.*			*Mirza.*			*Qazilbash.*			*Others.*		
	Persons.	Males.	Females.	Persons.	Males.	Females.	Persons.	Males.	Females.	Persons.	Males.	Females.	Persons.	Males.	Females.	Persons.	Males.	Females.	Persons.	Males.	Females.	Persons.	Males.	Females.	Persons.	Males.	Females.
	197	198	199	200	201	202	203	204	205	206	207	208	209	210	211	212	213	214	215	216	217	218	219	220	221	222	223
Total State ...	325	177	148	7,690	4,097	3,602	14,694	7,644	7,050	6,831	3,466	3,365	3,397	2,106	1,291	17,556	9,159	8,397	1,336	868	468	48	25	23	20,707	12,413	8,294
I—Total Jammu Province (including *Jagirs*).	324	177	147	7,192	3,849	3,343	9,838	5,257	4,581	208	95	113	2,362	1,325	1,037	1,220	750	770	51	40	11	1	1	...	12,078	6,825	5,253
1. Jammu District (including city).	233	128	105	1,635	927	708	654	335	319	...	...	...	45	34	11	...	...	...	...	...	...	...	...	...	566	347	219
2. Jasrota „	87	45	42	335	176	159	32	13	19	5	3	2	...	...	...	...	...	...	...	...	...	1	1	...	57	28	29
3. Udhampur „	...	...	...	85	46	39	1,055	538	517	114	81	33	20	12	8	1,487	750	737	10	4	6	...	...	...	390	227	163
4. Riasi „	...	...	...	772	406	366	408	274	134	81	7	74	509	241	268	1	...	1	25	25	...	...	...	...	5,116	2,821	2,295
5. Mirpur „	4	4	...	1,368	664	704	4,558	2,324	2,234	4	4	...	298	161	137	4	...	4	16	11	5	...	...	...	3,773	2,024	1,749
6. Bhadarwah *Jagir* ...	...	...	...	9	5	4	4	...	4	...	...	...	5	3	2	...	...	...	...	...	...	...	...	...	66	39	27
7. Punch *Ilaqa*	...	...	...	2,988	1,625	1,363	3,127	1,773	1,354	4	...	4	1,485	874	611	28	...	28	...	...	...	...	...	...	2,110	1,339	771
II—Total Kashmir Province (including *Jagirs*).	...	...	...	498	239	259	4,783	2,340	2,443	6,593	3,345	3,248	1,035	781	254	16,008	8,386	7,622	1,217	782	435	26	3	23	8,330	5,410	2,920
8. Kashmir North (including Langet *Jagir*).	...	...	...	10	4	6	1,872	996	876	2,188	1,064	1,124	1	...	1	9,456	3,715	5,741	152	32	120	4	3	1	1,180	582	598
9. Kashmir South (including city).	...	...	...	97	59	38	2,435	1,171	1,264	4,228	2,281	1,947	1	...	1	1,721	1,715	6	884	750	134	...	...	...	1,237	586	651
Total Kashmir Valley ...	...	...	...	*107*	*63*	*44*	*4,307*	*2,167*	*2,140*	*6,416*	*3,345*	*3,071*	*2*	...	*2*	*11,177*	*5,430*	*5,747*	*1,036*	*782*	*254*	*4*	*3*	*1*	*2,417*	*1,168*	*1,249*
10. Muzaffarabad District (*Wizarat Pahar*).	...	...	...	391	176	215	476	173	303	177	...	177	1,033	781	252	4,831	2,956	1,875	181	...	181	22	...	22	5,913	4,242	1,671
III—Total Frontier Districts.	1	...	1	9	9	...	73	47	26	30	26	4	...	...	...	28	23	5	68	46	22	21	21	...	299	178	121
11. Laddakh District (including Mansar).	...	...	...	5	5	...	67	42	25	8	4	4	...	...	...	28	23	5	68	46	22	...	...	...	97	61	36
12. Gilgit „	1	...	1	4	4	...	6	5	1	22	22	...	...	...	...	...	...	...	...	...	...	21	21	...	181	106	75
13. Frontier *Ilaqas*	...	...	...	...	...	...	...	...	...	...	...	...	...	...	...	...	...	...	...	...	...	...	...	...	21	11	10

TABLE XIII.

Caste, Tribe, Race or Nationality.

Jammu and Kashmir State Census 1911.

Part II—Musalmans.

DISTRICT, JAGIR OR ILAQA.	Mughal. Total Mughal. Persons.	Males.	Females.	Naddaf. Persons.	Males.	Females.	Pathan. Afridi. Persons.	Males.	Females.	Baloch. Persons.	Males.	Females.	Barakzai. Persons.	Males.	Females.	Durrani. Persons.	Males.	Females.	Hasanzai. Persons.	Males.	Females.	Hazara. Persons.	Males.	Females.	Kabuli. Persons.	Males.	Females.	Kakezai. Persons.	Males.	Females.
	224	225	226	227	228	229	230	231	232	233	234	235	236	237	238	239	240	241	242	243	244	245	246	247	248	249	250	251	252	253
Total State ...	49,875	28,037	21,838	184	91	93	119	63	56	144	59	85	133	71	62	65	36	29	64	31	33	89	62	27	49	29	20	471	180	291
I—Total Jammu Province (including *Jagirs*).	16,220	9,036	7,184	...	...	...	18	8	10	84	49	35	115	60	55	41	24	17	28	9	19	...	...	...	...	...	...	451	176	275
1. Jammu District (including city).	611	381	230	...	...	...	2	2	...	3	3	...	12	7	5	14	8	6	...	...	...	...	...	...	...	...	...	1	1	...
2. Jasrota „	63	32	31	...	...	...	...	...	...	11	10	1	2	2	...	...	...	...	...	...	...	...	...	...	...	...	...	...	...	...
3. Udhampur „	2,021	1,074	947	...	...	...	...	...	...	1	...	1	50	28	22	5	5	...	...	...	...	...	...	...	...	...	...	36	35	1
4. Riasi „	5,732	3,094	2,638	...	...	...	12	2	10	1	1	...	...	...	...	5	5	...	25	9	16	...	...	...	...	...	...	70	9	61
5. Mirpur „	4,095	2,200	1,895	...	...	...	4	4	...	...	...	...	...	...	...	...	...	...	1	...	1	...	...	...	...	...	...	236	127	159
6. Bhadarwah *Jagir*. ...	71	42	29	...	...	...	...	...	...	...	...	...	...	...	...	3	1	2	...	...	...	...	...	...	...	...	...	5	4	1
7. Punch *Ilaqa*	3,627	2,213	1,414	...	...	...	...	...	...	68	35	33	51	23	28	14	5	9	2	...	2	...	...	...	...	...	...	53	...	53
II—Total Kashmir Province (including *Jagirs*).	33,209	18,707	14,502	184	91	93	99	53	46	60	10	50	18	11	7	24	12	12	36	22	14	89	62	27	49	29	20	18	2	16
8. Kashmir North (including Langet *Jagir*).	12,981	5,396	7,585	45	6	39	96	53	43	...	...	...	...	...	...	...	...	...	...	...	...	...	...	...	29	21	8	...	...	...
9. Kashmir South (including city).	8,071	5,332	2,739	123	73	50	...	...	...	...	...	...	18	11	7	24	12	12	...	...	...	51	48	3	20	8	12	...	...	...
Total Kashmir Valley ...	*21,052*	*10,728*	*10,324*	*168*	*79*	*89*	*96*	*53*	*43*	...	...	...	*18*	*11*	*7*	*24*	*12*	*12*	...	...	...	*51*	*48*	*3*	*49*	*29*	*20*	...	...	...
10. Muzaffarabad District (*Wizarat Pahar*).	12,157	7,979	4,178	16	12	4	3	...	3	60	10	50	...	...	...	...	...	...	36	22	14	38	14	24	...	...	...	18	2	16
III—Total Frontier Districts.	446	294	152	...	...	...	2	2	...	...	...	...	...	...	...	...	...	...	...	...	...	...	...	...	...	...	...	2	2	...
11. Laddakh District (including Mansar).	201	134	67	...	...	...	...	...	...	...	...	...	...	...	...	...	...	...	...	...	...	...	...	...	...	...	...	1	1	...
12. Gilgit „	224	149	75	...	...	...	2	2	...	...	...	...	...	...	...	...	...	...	...	...	...	...	...	...	...	...	...	1	1	...
13. Frontier *Ilaqas*	21	11	10	...	...	...	...	...	...	...	...	...	...	...	...	...	...	...	...	...	...	...	...	...	...	...	...	...	...	...

TABLE XIII.

Caste, tribe, Race or Nationality.

Jammu and Kashmir State Census 1911.

Part II—Musalmans.

DISTRICT, JAGIR OR ILAQA.	Pathan.																		Patoi.			Qalandar.			Rajput.		
	Khan.			*Khaibari.*			*Yusufzai.*			*Zakakhel.*			*Others.*			*Total Pathan.*									*Awan.*		
	Persons.	Males.	Females.	Persons.	Males.	Females.	Persons.	Males.	Females.	Persons.	Males.	Females.	Persons.	Males.	Females.	Persons.	Males.	Females.	Persons.	Males.	Females.	Persons.	Males.	Females.	Persons.	Males.	Females.
	254	255	256	257	258	259	260	261	262	263	264	265	266	267	268	269	270	271	272	273	274	275	276	277	278	279	280
Total State ...	30,338	16,273	14,065	370	197	173	1,844	965	879	10	4	6	18,567	9,961	8,606	52,263	27,931	24,332	26	12	14	100	56	44	27,588	13,782	13,806
I—Total Jammu Province (including *Jagirs*).	574	266	308	...	...	...	1,367	720	647	7	4	3	8,496	4,919	3,577	11,131	6,235	4,946	26	12	14	70	39	31	14,988	8,096	6,892
1. Jammu District (including city).	...	...	...	...	...	...	171	98	73	...	...	...	1,425	883	542	1,628	1,002	626	21	12	9	9	5	4	1,978	1,154	824
2. Jasrota ,, ...	13	...	13	...	...	...	11	5	6	...	...	...	147	89	58	184	106	78	...	...	...	27	15	12	127	74	53
3. Udhampur ,, ...	515	249	266	...	...	...	104	62	42	...	...	...	699	379	320	1,410	758	652	5	...	5	...	...	...	108	98	10
4. Riasi ,, ...	15	7	8	...	...	...	218	106	112	...	...	...	914	510	404	1,260	649	611	...	...	...	...	...	...	324	196	128
5. Mirpur ,, ...	...	...	...	...	...	...	389	212	177	...	...	...	979	761	218	1,659	1,104	555	...	...	...	34	19	15	6,280	3,330	2,950
6. Bhadarwah *Jagir* ...	...	...	...	...	...	...	78	38	40	...	...	...	348	173	175	434	216	218	...	...	...	...	...	...	...	...	...
7. Punch *Ilaqa*	31	10	21	...	...	...	396	199	197	7	4	3	3,984	2,124	1,860	4,606	2,400	2,206	...	...	...	...	...	...	6,171	3,244	2,927
II—Total Kashmir Province (including *Jagirs*).	29,687	15,979	13,708	370	197	173	475	243	232	3	...	3	8,522	4,036	4,426	39,450	20,716	18,734	...	...	...	29	17	12	12,455	5,609	6,846
8. Kashmir North (including Langet *Jagir*).	13,878	7,407	6,471	318	171	147	149	76	73	...	...	...	2,429	1,059	1,370	16,899	8,787	8,112	...	...	...	...	...	...	580	321	259
9. Kashmir South (including city)	15,795	8,561	7,234	50	26	24	7	6	1	...	...	...	1,637	962	675	17,602	9,634	7,968	...	...	...	29	17	12	233	117	116
Total Kashmir Valley ...	*29,673*	*15,968*	*13,705*	*368*	*197*	*171*	*156*	*82*	*74*	...	...	...	*4,066*	*2,021*	*2,045*	*34,501*	*18,421*	*16,080*	...	...	...	*29*	*17*	*12*	*813*	*438*	*375*
10. Muzaffarabad District (*Wizarat Pahar*).	14	11	3	2	...	2	319	161	158	3	...	3	4,456	2,075	2,381	4,949	2,295	2,654	...	...	...	...	...	...	11,642	5,171	6,471
III—Total Frontier Districts.	77	28	49	...	...	...	2	2	...	...	...	...	1,549	946	603	1,632	980	652	...	...	...	1	...	1	145	77	68
11. Laddakh District (including Mansar).	52	14	38	...	...	...	1	1	...	...	...	...	75	41	34	129	57	72	...	...	...	1	...	1	6	4	2
12. Gilgit ,, ...	25	14	11	...	...	...	1	1	...	...	...	...	309	267	132	428	285	143	...	...	...	...	...	...	139	73	66
13. Frontier *Ilaqas*	...	...	...	...	...	...	...	...	...	...	...	...	1,075	638	437	1,075	638	437	...	...	...	...	...	...	...	...	...

TABLE XIII.

Caste, Tribe, Race or Nationality.

Jammu and Kashmir State Census 1911.

Part II—Musalmans.

DISTRICT, JAGIR OR ILAQA.	RAJPUT.																										
	Bains.			*Bamba.*			*Bhau.*			*Chauhan.*			*Chibh.*			*Duli.*			*Gakkhar.*			*Janhal.*			*Janjua.*		
	Persons.	Males.	Females.	Persons.	Males.	Females.	Persons.	Males.	Females.	Persons.	Males.	Females.	Persons.	Males.	Females.	Persons.	Males.	Females.	Persons.	Males.	Females.	Persons.	Males.	Females.	Persons.	Males.	Females.
	281	282	283	284	285	286	287	288	289	290	291	992	293	294	295	296	297	298	299	300	301	302	303	304	305	306	307
Total State ...	6,193	3,070	3,123	1,462	823	639	592	302	290	3,646	1,771	1,875	9,665	4.673	4,992	3,099	1,202	1,897	13,825	6,815	7,010	1,180	598	582	8,062	4,545	3,517
I—Total Jammu Province (including *Jagirs*).	6,089	3,063	3,026	4	4	...	592	302	290	263	150	113	9,501	4,567	4,934	3,068	1,178	1,890	12,934	6,566	6,368	1,180	598	582	6,490	3,490	3,000
1. Jammu District (including city)	1	1	...	...	...	...	66	45	21	147	88	59	198	159	39	...	...	...	121	87	34	...	...	...	186	109	77
2. Jasrota ,, ...	...	...	...	...	...	...	...	...	...	23	...	23	2	2	...	...	...	...	5	...	5	...	...	...	2	1	1
3. Udhampur ,, ...	...	...	...	...	...	...	2	2	...	4	4	...	13	12	1	...	...	...	170	88	82	...	...	...	11	5	6
4. Riasi ,, ...	167	81	86	...	...	...	51	22	29	6	5	1	336	172	164	...	...	...	357	89	268	...	...	...	1,404	751	653
5. Mirpur ,, ...	5,862	2,922	2,940	4	4	...	457	223	234	46	36	10	8,659	4,092	4,567	248	132	116	4,095	2,072	2,023	236	95	141	427	257	170
6. Bhadarwah *Jagir* ...	...	...	...	...	...	...	...	...	...	5	...	5	23	14	9	...	...	...	...	...	...	...	...	...	...	...	...
7. Punch *Ilaqa*	59	59	...	...	...	...	16	10	6	32	17	15	270	116	154	2,820	1,046	1,774	8,186	4,230	3,956	944	503	441	4,460	2,367	2,093
II—Total Kashmir Province (including *Jagirs*).	98	1	97	1,388	781	607	...	...	...	3,379	1,619	1,760	110	52	58	31	24	7	877	236	641	...	...	...	1,566	1,050	516
8. Kashmir North (including Langet *Jagir*).	1	...	1	165	73	92	...	...	...	2,219	1,064	1,155	8	6	2	...	...	...	95	58	37	...	...	...	248	143	105
9. Kashmir South (including city).	...	...	...	33	...	33	...	...	...	792	425	367	2	2	...	8	7	1	23	3	20	...	...	...	5	5	...
Total Kashmir Valley ...	*1*	...	*1*	*198*	*73*	*125*	...	...	...	*3,011*	*1,489*	*1,522*	*10*	*8*	*2*	*8*	*7*	*1*	*118*	*61*	*57*	...	...	...	*253*	*148*	*105*
10. Muzaffarabad District (*Wizarat Pahar*).	97	1	96	1,190	708	482	...	...	...	368	130	238	100	44	56	23	17	6	759	175	584	...	...	...	1,313	902	411
III—Total Frontier Districts.	6	6	...	70	38	32	...	...	...	4	2	2	54	54	...	...	...	...	14	13	1	...	...	...	6	5	1
11. Laddakh District (including Mansar).	...	...	...	...	...	...	...	...	...	...	...	...	10	10	...	...	...	...	...	...	...	...	...	...	...	...	...
12. Gilgit ,, ...	6	6	...	70	38	32	...	...	...	4	2	2	44	44	...	...	...	...	14	13	1	...	...	...	6	5	1
13. Frontier *Ilaqas*	...	...	...	...	...	...	...	...	...	...	...	...	...	...	...	...	...	...	...	...	...	...	...	...	...	...	...

TABLE XIII.

Caste, Tribe, Race or Nationality.

Jammu and Kashmir State Census 1911.

Part II—Musalmans.

DISTRICT, JAGIR OR ILAQA.	Rajput.																								
	Jatal.			*Khakha.*			*Khokhar.*			*Maldial.*			*Mangral.*			*Manhas.*			*Narma.*			*Sau.*			
	Persons.	Males.	Females.	Persons.	Males.	Females.	Persons.	Males.	Females.	Persons.	Males.	Females.	Persons.	Males.	Females.	Persons.	Males.	Females.	Persons.	Males.	Females.	Persons.	Males.	Females.	
	308	309	310	311	312	313	314	315	316	317	318	319	320	321	322	323	324	325	326	327	328	329	330	331	
Total State ...	8,506	4,068	4,438	1,391	827	564	7,736	3,980	3,756	11,643	5,787	5,856	7,027	3,505	3,522	6,797	3,522	3,275	6,617	3,346	3,271	2,961	1,639	1,322	
I—Total Jammu Province (including *Jagirs*).	8,184	3,862	4,322	1,211	662	549	5,182	2,579	2,603	11,500	5,701	5,799	6,924	3,419	3,505	5,675	3,018	2,657	6,594	3,323	3,271	2,960	1,638	1,322	
1. Jammu District (including city).	214	195	19	...	...	...	486	331	155	...	...	...	17	17	...	1,000	590	410	2	2	...	26	17	9	
2. Jasrota ,, ...	20	13	7	...	...	...	72	44	28	...	...	...	2	2	...	42	24	18	...	...	...	...	...	...	
3. Udhampur ,, ...	52	35	17	1	...	1	23	...	23	...	...	...	...	...	...	110	59	51	...	...	...	...	...	...	
4. Riasi ,, ...	3,893	1,485	2,408	...	...	...	1,115	598	517	...	...	...	429	257	172	403	153	250	127	92	35	...	...	...	
5. Mirpur ,, ...	3,434	1,674	1,760	4	1	3	949	340	609	8	2	6	5,937	2,817	3,120	490	306	184	1,970	895	1,075	2,934	1,621	1,313	
6. Bhadarwah *Jagir* ...	2	...	2	...	...	...	...	...	...	...	...	...	...	...	...	...	...	...	...	...	...	...	...	...	
7. Punch *Ilaqa*	569	460	109	1,206	661	545	2,537	1,266	1,271	11,492	5,699	5,793	539	326	213	3,630	1,886	1,744	4,495	2,334	2,161	...	...	...	
II—Total Kashmir Province (including *Jagirs*).	222	109	113	180	165	15	2,549	1,399	1,150	143	86	57	103	86	17	1,115	497	618	14	14	...	...	...	...	
8. Kashmir North (including Langet *Jagir*).	...	...	...	...	...	...	169	111	58	...	...	...	...	...	...	39	19	20	...	...	...	...	...	...	
9. Kashmir South (including city).	50	24	26	1	1	...	75	32	43	20	12	8	27	13	14	52	16	36	...	...	...	...	...	...	
Total Kashmir Valley ...	*50*	*24*	*26*	*1*	*1*	...	*244*	*143*	*101*	*20*	*12*	*8*	*27*	*13*	*14*	*91*	*35*	*56*	...	...	...	...	...	...	
10. Muzaffarabad District (*Wizarat Pahar*).	172	85	87	179	164	15	2,305	1,256	1,049	123	74	49	76	73	3	1,024	462	562	14	14	...	...	...	...	
III—Total Frontier Districts.	100	97	3	...	...	...	5	2	3	...	...	...	...	...	...	7	7	...	9	9	...	1	1	...	
11. Laddakh District (including Mansar).	...	...	...	...	...	...	4	2	2	...	...	...	...	...	...	...	...	...	...	...	...	1	1	...	
12. Gilgit ,, ...	100	97	3	...	...	...	1	...	1	...	...	...	...	...	...	7	7	...	9	9	...	...	...	...	
13. Frontier *Ilaqas*	...	...	...	...	...	...	...	...	...	...	...	...	...	...	...	...	...	...	...	...	...	...	...	...	

TABLE XIII.

Caste, Tribe, Race or Nationality.

Jammu and Kashmir State Census 1911.

Part II—Musalmans.

District, Jagir or Ilaqa.	Rajput.						Rangrez or (Lilari).			Rigzang (Tarakchos).			Sapiada.			Sayed.					
	Others.			*Total Rajput.*												*Akhun.*			*Baba (and Babazada).*		
	Persons.	Males.	Females.	Persons.	Males.	Females.	Persons.	Males.	Females.	Persons.	Males.	Females.	Persons.	Males.	Females.	Persons.	Males.	Females.	Persons.	Males.	Females.
	332	333	334	335	336	337	338	339	340	341	342	343	344	345	346	347	348	349	350	351	352
Total State ...	25,687	14,183	11,504	153,677	78,438	75,239	1,331	616	715	4,026	1,994	2,032	145	74	71	17,436	7,259	10,177	11,267	5,810	5,457
I—Total Jammu Province (including *Jagirs*).	24,497	13,420	11,077	127,836	65,636	62,200	1,196	540	656	1	...	1	145	74	71	213	180	33	63	36	27
1. Jammu District (including city).	8,150	4,604	3,546	12,592	7,399	5,193	158	84	74	...	...	...	122	65	57	...	...	...	...	...	...
2. Jasrota "	372	260	112	667	420	247	8	2	6	...	...	...	...	...	...	...	...	...	...	...	...
3. Udhampur "	949	371	578	1,443	674	769	8	5	3	...	...	...	...	...	...	78	45	33	58	36	22
4. Riasi "	2,833	1,370	1,463	11,445	5,271	6,174	53	38	15	...	...	...	...	...	...	24	24	...	...	...	...
5. Mirpur "	8,081	4,117	3,964	50,121	24,936	25,185	870	349	521	...	...	...	15	9	6	...	...	...	...	...	...
6. Bhadarwah *Jagir* ...	6	1	5	36	15	21	...	...	...	...	...	...	...	...	...	...	...	...	...	...	...
7. Punch *Ilaqa*	4,106	2,697	1,409	51,532	26,921	24,611	99	62	37	1	...	1	8	...	8	111	111	...	5	...	5
II—Total Kashmir Province (including *Jagirs*).	905	565	340	25,135	12,293	12,842	135	76	59	...	...	...	...	...	...	16,276	6,545	9,731	11,198	5,771	5,427
8. Kashmir North (including Langet *Jagir*).	49	21	28	3,573	1,816	1,757	14	8	6	...	...	...	...	...	...	4,985	1,150	3,835	4,055	2,012	2,043
9. Kashmir South (including city).	260	183	77	1,581	840	741	121	68	53	...	...	...	...	...	...	11,144	5,395	5,749	6,934	3,759	3,175
Total Kashmir Valley ...	*309*	*204*	*105*	*5,154*	*2,656*	*2,498*	*135*	*76*	*59*	...	...	...	...	...	...	*16,129*	*6,545*	*9,584*	*10,989*	*5,771*	*5,218*
10. Muzaffarabad District (*Wizarat Pahar*).	596	361	235	19,981	9,637	10,344	...	...	...	...	...	...	...	...	...	147	...	147	209	...	209
III—Total Frontier Districts.	285	198	87	706	509	197	...	...	...	4,025	1,994	2,031	...	...	...	947	534	413	6	3	3
11. Laddakh District (including Mansar).	56	47	9	77	64	13	...	...	...	4,025	1,994	2,031	...	...	...	890	504	386	...	...	...
12. Gilgit "	38	20	18	438	314	124	...	...	...	...	...	...	...	...	...	57	30	27	6	3	3
13. Frontier *Ilaqas*	191	131	60	191	131	60	...	...	...	...	...	...	...	...	...	...	...	...	...	...	...

TABLE XIII.

Caste, Tribe, Race or Nationality,

Jammu and Kashmir State Census 1911.

Part II—Musalmans.

DISTRICT, JAGIR OR ILAQA.	SAYED.																													
	Bokhari.			*Gilani.*			*Hamdani.*			*Hasani (and Husaini).*			*Jafari.*			*Jalali.*			*Mashhadi.*			*Naqshbandi.*			*Pirzada.*			*Qadri.*		
	Persons.	Males.	Females.	Persons.	Males.	Females.	Persons.	Males.	Females.	Persons.	Males.	Females.	Persons.	Males.	Females.	Persons.	Males.	Females.	Persons.	Males.	Females.	Persons.	Males.	Females.	Persons.	Males.	Females.	Persons.	Males.	Females.
	353	354	355	356	357	358	359	360	361	362	363	364	365	366	367	368	369	370	371	372	373	374	375	376	377	378	379	380	381	382
Total State ...	9,237	4,821	4,416	2,579	1,519	1,060	282	154	128	235	178	57	48	21	27	59	30	29	6,472	3,201	3,271	35	15	20	6,165	3,277	2,888	262	184	78
I—Total Jammu Province (including *Jagirs*).	6,973	3,520	3,453	2,287	1,264	1,023	107	79	28	155	119	36	48	21	27	59	30	29	3,842	2,026	1,816	16	2	14	33	17	16	110	64	46
1. Jammu District (including city).	644	349	295	186	134	52	4	3	1	100	97	3	...	...	...	24	13	11	221	75	146	...	...	...	...	...	...	3	3	...
2. Jasrota ,, ...	27	21	6	8	6	2	...	...	...	2	2	...	...	...	...	5	5	...	2	2	...	12	...	12	1	1	...	...	...	...
3. Udhampur ,, ...	161	86	75	144	78	66	...	...	...	...	...	...	...	...	...	24	11	13	28	14	14	...	...	...	2	...	2	105	61	44
4. Riasi ,, ...	804	457	347	442	231	211	...	...	...	7	7	...	...	...	...	1	1	...	415	199	216	...	...	...	...	...	...	...	...	...
5. Mirpur ,, ...	2,687	1,360	1,327	585	317	268	12	3	9	...	...	...	...	...	...	...	...	...	720	383	337	...	...	...	...	...	...	...	...	...
6. Bhadarwah *Jagir* ...	8	3	5	5	3	2	...	...	...	...	...	...	...	...	...	...	...	...	9	4	5	...	...	...	...	...	...	...	...	...
7. Punch *Ilaqa*	2,642	1,244	1,398	917	495	422	91	73	18	46	13	33	48	21	27	5	...	5	2,447	1,349	1,098	4	2	2	30	16	14	2	...	2
II—Total Kashmir Province (including *Jagirs*).	2,263	1,301	962	292	255	37	175	75	100	58	58	...	...	...	...	...	...	...	2,630	1,175	1,455	19	13	6	6,046	3,216	2,830	152	120	32
8. Kashmir North (including Langet *Jagir*).	187	187	...	...	...	...	...	...	...	...	...	...	...	...	...	...	...	...	...	...	...	4	...	4	4,039	2,169	1,870	95	92	3
9. Kashmir South (including city).	53	26	27	...	...	...	...	...	...	43	43	...	...	...	...	...	...	...	...	...	...	15	13	2	1,941	1,047	894	7	7	...
Total Kashmir Valley ...	*240*	*213*	*27*	...	...	...	...	...	...	*43*	*43*	...	...	...	...	...	...	...	...	...	...	*19*	*13*	*6*	*5,980*	*3,216*	*2,764*	*102*	*99*	*3*
10. Muzaffarabad District (*Wizarat Pahar*).	2,023	1,088	935	292	255	37	175	75	100	15	15	...	...	...	...	...	...	...	2,630	1,175	1,455	...	...	...	66	...	66	50	21	29
III—Total Frontier Districts.	1	...	1	...	...	...	...	...	...	22	1	21	...	...	...	...	...	...	...	...	...	...	...	...	86	44	42	...	...	...
11. Laddakh District (including Mausar).	...	...	...	...	...	...	...	...	...	10	1	9	...	...	...	...	...	...	...	...	...	...	...	...	1	1	...	...	...	...
12. Gilgit ,, ...	1	...	1	...	...	...	...	...	...	12	...	12	...	...	...	...	...	...	...	...	...	...	...	...	85	43	42	...	...	...
13. Frontier *Ilaqas*	...	...	...	...	...	...	...	...	...	...	...	...	...	...	...	...	...	...	...	...	...	...	...	...	...	...	...	...	...	...

TABLE XIII.

Caste, Tribe, Race or Nationality.

Jammu and Kashmir State Census 1911.

Part II—Musalmans.

DISTRICT, JAGIR OR ILAQA.	Sayed.												Sheikh.														
	Shirazi.			*Sufi.*			*Others.*			*Total Sayed.*			*Makhdumi.*			*Qadri.*			*Qazi.*			*Qureshi.*			*Ulma.*		
	Persons.	Males.	Females.	Persons.	Males.	Females.	Persons.	Males.	Females.	Persons.	Males.	Females.	Persons.	Males.	Females.	Persons.	Males.	Females.	Persons.	Males.	Females.	Persons.	Males.	Females.	Persons.	Males.	Females.
	383	384	385	386	387	388	389	390	391	392	393	394	395	396	397	398	399	400	401	402	403	404	405	406	407	408	409
Total State ...	834	458	376	14,655	7,712	6,943	32,629	19,427	13,202	102,195	54,066	48,129	67	9	58	915	391	524	637	355	282	6,947	3,510	3,437	1,380	619	761
I—Total Jammu Province (including *Jagirs*).	803	427	376	26	14	12	7,919	4,707	3,212	22,654	12,506	10,148	...	...	...	20	7	13	37	17	20	5,476	2,934	2,542	1,380	619	761
1. Jammu District (including city).	155	96	59	...	...	...	1,124	588	536	2,461	1,358	1,103	...	...	...	...	...	...	15	10	5	327	176	151	287	114	173
2. Jasrota ,, ...	1	1	...	...	...	...	58	39	19	116	77	39	...	...	...	...	...	...	12	...	12	9	8	1	1	1	...
3. Udhampur ,, ...	...	...	...	26	14	12	369	217	152	995	562	433	...	...	...	...	...	...	10	7	3	38	28	10	...	...	...
4. Riasi ,, ...	38	19	19	...	...	...	499	265	234	2,230	1,203	1,027	...	...	...	...	...	...	...	...	...	330	161	169	15	13	2
5. Mirpur ,, ...	54	38	16	...	...	...	994	489	505	5,052	2,590	2,462	...	...	...	...	...	...	...	...	...	1,912	1,078	834	1,077	491	586
6. Bhadarwah *Jagir* ...	1	1	...	...	...	...	47	37	10	68	46	22	...	...	...	...	...	...	...	...	...	1	...	1	...	...	...
7. Punch *Ilaqa*	554	272	282	...	...	...	4,828	3,072	1,756	11,732	6,670	5,062	...	...	...	20	7	13	...	...	...	2,859	1,483	1,376	...	...	...
II—Total Kashmir Province (including *Jagirs*).	1	1	...	14,586	7,698	6,888	19,908	12,609	7,299	73,604	38,837	34,767	67	9	58	884	384	500	594	334	260	1,449	555	894	...	...	...
8. Kashmir North (including Langet *Jagir*).	...	...	...	7,550	4,055	3,495	8,005	5,749	2,256	28,920	15,414	13,506	5	2	3	43	43	...	55	55	...	577	246	331	...	...	...
9. Kashmir South (including city).	...	...	...	6,983	3,604	3,379	7,077	4,259	2,818	34,197	18,153	16,044	62	7	55	237	11	226	532	279	253	277	126	151	...	...	...
Total Kashmir Valley ...	...	...	...	*14,533*	*7,659*	*6,874*	*15,082*	*10,008*	*5,074*	*63,117*	*33,567*	*29,550*	*67*	*9*	*58*	*280*	*54*	*226*	*587*	*334*	*253*	*854*	*372*	*482*	...	...	...
10. Muzaffarabad District (*Wizarat Pahar*).	1	1	...	53	39	14	4,826	2,601	2,225	10,487	5,270	5,217	...	...	...	604	330	274	7	...	7	595	183	412	...	...	...
III—Total Frontier Districts.	30	30	...	43	...	43	4,802	2,111	2,691	5,937	2,723	3,214	...	...	...	11	...	11	6	4	2	22	21	1	...	...	...
11. Laddakh District (including Mansar).	30	30	...	43	...	43	3,201	1,242	1,959	4,175	1,778	2,397	...	...	...	...	...	...	6	4	2	10	9	1	...	...	...
12. Gilgit ,, ...	...	...	...	...	...	...	295	170	125	456	246	210	...	...	...	11	...	11	...	...	...	12	12	...	...	...	...
13. Frontier *Ilaqas*	...	...	...	...	...		1,306	699	607	1,306	699	607	...	...	...	...	...	...	...	...	...	...	...	...	...	...	...

TABLE XIII.

Caste, Tribe, Race or Nationality.

Jammu and Kashmir State Census 1911.

Part II—Musalmans.

District, Jagir or Ilaqa.	Sheikh. Others.			Sheikh. Total Sheikh.			Shin.			Sudhan.			Tarkhan.			Teli.			Thakkar.		
	Persons.	Males.	Females.	Persons.	Males.	Females.	Persons.	Males.	Females.	Persons.	Males.	Females.	Persons.	Males.	Females.	Persons.	Males.	Females.	Persons.	Males.	Females.
	410	411	412	413	414	415	416	417	418	419	420	421	422	423	424	425	426	427	428	429	430
Total State ...	95,339	54,778	40,561	105,285	59,662	45,623	11,080	5,930	5,150	56,800	28,206	28,594	18,568	9,968	8,600	19,256	10,180	9,076	10,451	4,899	5,552
I—Total Jammu Province (including *Jagirs*).	25,425	13,527	11,898	32,338	17,104	15,234	4	2	2	56,631	28,100	28,531	12,640	6,753	5,887	14,321	7,582	6,739	3,873	1,909	1,964
1. Jammu District (including city).	1,880	1,086	794	2,509	1,386	1,123	...	...	...	...	...	...	1,664	959	705	5,587	2,842	2,745	5	1	4
2. Jasrota "	566	285	281	588	294	294	...	...	...	...	...	...	22	18	4	2,563	1,431	1,132	9	7	2
3. Udhampur "	8,125	4,205	3,920	8,173	4,240	3,933	3	1	2	...	...	...	73	43	30	435	230	205	66	52	14
4. Riasi "	3,129	1,650	1,479	3,474	1,824	1,650	...	...	...	73	54	19	1,415	707	708	920	487	433	3,038	1,486	1,552
5. Mirpur "	1,619	934	685	4,608	2,503	2,105	...	...	...	1,482	748	734	6,612	3,531	3,081	3,892	2,093	1,799	16	12	4
6. Bhadarwah *Jagir* ...	422	233	189	423	233	190	...	...	...	...	...	...	3	...	3	1	...	1	11	7	4
7. Punch *Ilaqa*	9,684	5,134	4,550	12,563	6,624	5,939	1	1	...	55,076	27,298	27,778	2,851	1,495	1,356	923	499	424	728	344	384
II—Total Kashmir Province (including *Jagirs*).	69,295	40,910	28,385	72,289	42,192	30.097	4	...	4	159	96	63	5,659	3,084	2,575	4,925	2,598	2,327	6,462	2,919	3,543
8. Kashmir North (including Langet *Jagir*).	23,581	15,351	8,230	24,261	15,697	8,564	...	...	...	...	...	...	1,393	1,289	1,104	1,880	1,004	876	2,542	1,273	1,269
9. Kashmir South (including city).	37,992	21,214	16,778	39,100	21,637	17,463	4	...	4	11	11	...	2,753	1,530	1,223	2,860	1,559	1,301	3,561	1,450	2,111
Total Kashmir Valley ...	*61,573*	*36,565*	*25,008*	*63,361*	*37,334*	*26,027*	*4*	...	*4*	*11*	*11*	...	*5,146*	*2,819*	*2,327*	*4,740*	*2,563*	*2,177*	*6,103*	*2,723*	*3,380*
10 Muzaffarabad District (*Wizarat Pahar*).	7,722	4,345	3,377	8,928	4,858	4,070	...	...	...	148	85	63	513	265	248	185	35	150	359	196	163
III—Total Frontier Districts.	619	341	278	658	366	292	11,072	5,928	5,144	10	10	...	269	131	138	10	...	10	116	71	45
11. Laddakh District (including Mansar).	419	221	198	435	234	201	367	...	367	...	...	...	31	13	18	10	...	10	116	71	45
12. Gilgit "	87	62	25	110	74	36	2,065	1,342	723	10	10	...	130	60	70	...	...	...	...	...	...
13. Frontier *Ilaqas*	113	58	55	113	58	55	8,640	4,586	4,054	...	...	...	108	58	50	...	...	...	...	...	...

TABLE XIII.

Caste, Tribe, Race or Nationality.

Jammu and Kashmir State Census 1911.

Part II—Musalmans.

DISTRICT, JAGIR OR ILAQA.	Thathiar.			Turk.			Watal.			Yashkun.			Zargar.			Unclassified Musalman.			TOTAL MUSALMAN.*		
	Persons.	Males.	Females.	Persons.	Males.	Females.	Persons.	Males.	Females.	Persons.	Males.	Females.	Persons.	Males.	Females.	Persons.	Males.	Females.	Persons.	Males.	Females.
	431	432	433	434	435	436	437	438	439	440	441	442	443	444	445	446	447	448	449	450	451
Total State ...	16	8	8	2,407	1,200	1,207	6,467	3,685	2,782	35,011	17,965	17,046	1,905	1,018	887	119,243	65,669	53,574	2,398,319	1,265,534	1,132,785
I—Total Jammu Province (including *Jagirs*).	16	8	8	216	72	144	1,232	593	639	...	...	...	516	299	217	40,050	20,616	19,434	953,293	500,690	452,603
1. Jammu District (including city).	5	3	2	...	...	...	46	23	23	...	...	...	171	99	72	978	278	700	126,659	69,976	56,683
2. Jasrota ,, ...	8	4	4	...	...	...	41	37	4	...	...	...	62	38	24	396	182	214	35,174	19,146	16,028
3. Udhampur ,, ...	3	1	2	...	...	...	476	146	330	...	...	...	115	63	52	15,325	8,107	7,218	84,390	44,811	39,579
4. Riasi ,, ...	...	...	...	...	...	...	201	90	111	...	...	...	40	25	15	5,911	3,895	2,016	125,424	66,121	59,303
5. Mirpur ,, ...	...	...	...	...	...	...	...	...	...	...	...	...	104	60	44	540	345	195	264,347	136,386	127,961
6. Bhadarwah *Jagir* ...	...	...	...	...	...	...	310	195	115	...	...	...	2	2	...	3	3	...	14,580	7,599	6,981
7. Punch *Ilaqa*	...	...	...	216	72	144	158	102	56	...	...	...	22	12	10	16,897	7,806	9,091	302,719	156,651	146,068
II—Total Kashmir Province (including *Jagirs*).	...	...	...	2,176	1,123	1,053	5,235	3,092	2,143	16	13	3	1,055	541	514	62,627	35,813	26,814	1,217,767	648,684	569,083
8. Kashmir North (including Langet *Jagir*).	...	...	...	553	311	242	423	160	263	16	13	3	221	105	116	20,009	12,835	7,174	446,248	236,289	209
9. Kashmir South (including city).	...	...	...	162	85	77	4,196	2,334	1,862	...	...	...	828	431	397	42,472	22,875	19,597	588,640	314,964	273,676
Total Kashmir Valley ...	...	...	...	*715*	*396*	*319*	*4,619*	*2,494*	*2,125*	*16*	*13*	*3*	*1,049*	*536*	*513*	*62,481*	*35,710*	*26,771*	*1,034,888*	*551,253*	*483,635*
10. Muzaffarabad District (*Wizarat Pahar*).	...	...	...	1,461	727	734	616	598	18	...	...	...	6	5	1	146	103	43	182,879	97,431	85,448
III—Total Frontier Districts.	...	...	...	15	5	10	...	...	...	34,995	17,952	17,043	334	178	156	16,566	9,240	7,326	227,259	116,160	111,099
11. Laddakh District (including Mansar).	...	...	...	...	...	...	...	...	...	105	37	68	25	11	14	4	4	...	150,070	74,719	75,351
11. Gilgit ,, ...	...	...	...	...	...	...	...	...	...	14,087	6,832	7,255	215	112	103	1,579	1,267	312	23,075	12,471	10,604
13. Frontier *Ilaqas*	...	...	...	15	5	10	...	...	...	20,803	11,083	9,720	94	55	39	14,983	7,969	7,014	54,114	28,970	25,144

* This total differs from that of Musalman males given in Table VI by 1 because one male is Anglo-Indian, and European and Anglo-Indian figures are excluded from this Table.

TABLE XIII.

Caste, Tribe, Race or Nationality.

Jammu and Kashmir State Census 1911.

Part III—Other Religions.

DISTRICT, JAGIR OR ILAQA.	SIKH.																										
	Arora.			Basith.			Brahman.												Chamiar.			Chhimba.			Dum.		
							Acharji.			*Mohyal.*			*Others.*			*Total Brahman.*											
	Persons.	Males.	Females.	Persons.	Males.	Females.	Persons.	Males.	Females.	Persons.	Males.	Females.	Persons.	Males.	Females.	Persons.	Males.	Females.	Persons.	Males.	Females.	Persons.	Males.	Females.	Persons.	Males.	Females.
1	2	3	4	5	6	7	8	9	10	11	12	13	14	15	16	17	18	19	20	21	22	23	24	25	26	27	28
Total State ...	1,498	852	646	220	109	111	6	2	4	1,134	493	641	10,588	5,699	4,889	11,728	6,194	5,534	5	3	2	25	12	13	21	9	12
I—Total Jammu Province (including *Jagirs*).	1,484	842	642	220	109	111	6	2	4	665	320	345	8,562	4,594	3,968	9,233	4,916	4,317	5	3	2	25	12	13	21	9	12
1. Jammu District (including city).	319	195	124	6	...	6	...	...	...	25	16	9	27	21	6	52	37	15	...	...	...	15	9	6	1	1	...
2. Jasrota „	1	1	...	...	...	...	...	...	...	...	...	...	6	5	1	6	5	1	5	3	2	...	...	...	19	7	12
3. Udhampur „	9	5	4	...	...	...	...	...	...	2	1	1	32	20	12	34	21	13	...	...	...	...	...	...	...	...	...
4. Riasi „	188	107	81	111	58	53	...	...	...	11	9	2	49	26	23	60	35	25	...	...	...	...	...	...	...	...	...
5. Mirpur „	925	505	420	103	51	52	...	...	...	55	23	32	92	53	39	147	76	71	...	...	...	10	3	7	...	...	...
6. Bhadarwah *Jagir* ...	...	...	...	...	...	...	...	...	...	...	...	...	...	...	...	...	...	...	...	...	...	...	...	...	...	...	...
7. Punch *Ilaqa*	42	29	13	...	...	...	6	2	4	572	271	301	8,356	4,469	3,887	8,934	4,742	4,192	...	...	...	...	...	...	1	1	...
II—Total Kashmir Province (including *Jagirs*).	14	10	4	...	...	...	...	...	...	469	173	296	2,019	1,098	921	2,488	1,271	1,217	...	...	...	...	...	...	...	...	...
8. Kashmir North (including Langet *Jagir*).	5	5	...	...	...	...	...	...	...	457	168	289	142	88	54	599	256	343	...	...	...	...	...	...	...	...	...
9. Kashmir South (including city).	7	4	3	...	...	...	...	...	...	12	5	7	345	164	181	357	169	188	...	...	...	...	...	...	...	...	...
Total Kashmir Valley ...	*12*	*9*	*3*	...	...	...	...	...	...	*469*	*173*	*296*	*487*	*252*	*235*	*956*	*425*	*531*	...	...	...	...	...	...	...	...	...
10. Muzaffarabad District (*Wizarat Pahar*).	2	1	1	...	...	...	...	...	...	...	...	...	1,532	846	686	1,532	846	686	...	...	...	...	...	...	...	...	...
III—Total Frontier Districts.	...	...	...	...	...	...	...	...	...	...	...	...	7	7	...	7	7	...	...	...	...	...	...	...	...	...	...
11. Laddakh District (including Mansar).	...	...	...	...	...	...	...	...	...	...	...	...	...	...	...	...	...	...	...	...	...	...	...	...	...	...	...
12. Gilgit „	...	...	...	...	...	...	...	...	...	...	...	...	7	7	...	7	7	...	...	...	...	...	...	...	...	...	...
13. Frontier *Ilaqas*	...	...	...	...	...	...	...	...	...	...	...	...	...	...	...	...	...	...	...	...	...	...	...	...	...	...	...

TABLE XIII.

CASTE, TRIBE, RACE OR NATIONALITY.

Jammu and Kashmir State Census 1911.

Part III—Other Religions.

DISTRICT, JAGIR OR ILAQA.	SIKH.																										
	HAJJAM.			JAT.			JHIWAR.			KHATRI.			KUMHIAR.			LABANA.			LOHAR.			MAHAJAN.			MAZHABI (CHUHRA).		
	Persons.	Males.	Females.	Persons.	Males.	Females.	Persons.	Males.	Females.	Persons.	Males.	Females.	Persons.	Males.	Females.	Persons.	Males.	Females.	Persons.	Males.	Females.	Persons.	Males.	Females.	Persons.	Males.	Females.
	29	30	31	32	33	34	35	36	37	38	39	40	41	42	43	44	45	46	47	48	49	50	51	52	53	54	55
Total State ...	6	6	...	715	392	323	25	13	12	2,054	1,174	880	40	19	21	1,627	891	736	15	11	4	120	76	44	88	37	51
I—Total Jammu Province (including *Jagirs*). ...	6	6	...	658	386	272	16	10	6	1,955	1.113	842	40	19	21	1,627	891	736	15	11	4	120	76	44	...	...	...
1. Jammu District (including city).	6	6	...	292	159	133	16	10	6	229	111	118	5	3	2	1,426	755	671	...	...	...	46	29	17	...	...	...
2. Jasrota „	...	...	...	7	3	4	...	...	...	13	7	6	...	...	...	36	19	17	9	5	4	2	1	1	...	...	...
3. Udhampur „ ...	...	...	...	...	...	...	...	...	...	28	10	18	...	...	...	...	...	...	...	...	...	9	4	5	...	...	...
4. Riasi „ ...	...	...	...	...	...	...	...	...	...	72	34	38	...	...	...	9	4	5	4	4	...	13	9	4	...	...	...
5. Mirpur „ ...	...	...	...	358	223	135	...	...	...	1,331	757	574	35	16	19	10	10	...	2	2	...	32	20	12	...	...	...
6. Bhadarwah *Jagir* ...	...	...	...	...	...	...	...	...	...	...	...	...	...	...	...	...	...	...	...	...	...	...	...	...	...	...	...
7. Punch *Ilaqa* ...	...	...	...	1	1	...	...	...	...	282	194	88	...	...	...	146	103	43	...	...	...	18	13	5	...	...	...
II—Total Kashmir Province (including *Jagirs*).	...	...	...	54	3	51	9	3	6	57	38	19	...	...	...	...	...	...	...	...	...	...	...	...	88	37	51
8. Kashmir North (including Langet *Jagir*).	...	...	...	...	...	...	...	...	...	15	8	7	...	...	...	...	...	...	...	...	...	...	...	...	...	...	...
9. Kashmir South (including city).	...	...	...	1	1	...	9	3	6	28	21	7	...	...	...	...	...	...	...	...	...	...	...	...	88	37	51
Total Kashmir Valley ...	...	...	...	*1*	*1*	...	*9*	*3*	*6*	*43*	*29*	*14*	...	...	...	...	...	...	...	...	...	...	...	...	*88*	*37*	*61*
10. Muzaffarabad District (*Wizarat Pahar*).	...	...	...	53	2	51	...	...	...	14	9	5	...	...	...	...	...	...	...	...	...	...	...	...	...	...	...
III—Total Frontier Districts.	...	...	...	3	3	...	...	...	...	42	23	19	...	...	...	...	...	...	...	...	...	...	...	...	...	...	...
11. Laddakh District (including Mausar).	...	...	...	...	...	...	...	...	...	6	2	4	...	...	...	...	...	...	...	...	...	...	...	...	...	...	...
12. Gilgit „ ...	...	...	...	1	1	...	...	...	...	22	9	13	...	...	...	...	...	...	...	...	...	...	...	...	...	...	...
13. Frontier *Ilaqas* ...	...	...	...	2	2	...	...	...	...	14	12	2	...	...	...	...	...	...	...	...	...	...	...	...	...	...	...

TABLE XIII.

Caste, Tribe, Race or Nationality.

Jammu and Kashmir State Census 1911.

Part III—Other Religions.

District, Jagir or Ilaqa.	SIKH. Megh. Persons.	Megh. Males.	Megh. Females.	Rajput. Chauhan. Persons.	Chauhan. Males.	Chauhan. Females.	Rajput. Others. Persons.	Others. Males.	Others. Females.	Total Rajput. Persons.	Total Rajput. Males.	Total Rajput. Females.	Sansi. Persons.	Sansi. Males.	Sansi. Females.	Tarkhan. Persons.	Tarkhan. Males.	Tarkhan. Females.	Zargar. Persons.	Zargar. Males.	Zargar. Females.	Sikh Unclassified. Persons.	Sikh Unclassified. Males.	Sikh Unclassified. Females.	TOTAL SIKH. Persons.	TOTAL SIKH. Males.	TOTAL SIKH. Females.
	56	57	58	59	60	61	62	63	64	65	66	67	68	69	70	71	72	73	74	75	76	77	78	79	80	81	82
Total State ...	34	11	23	71	32	39	283	148	135	354	180	174	38	17	21	154	93	61	292	160	132	12,494	6,770	5,724	31,553	17,038	14,515
I—Total Jammu Province (including *Jagirs*).	34	11	23	71	32	39	239	123	116	310	155	155	...	...	...	152	91	61	286	155	131	452	256	196	16,659	9,071	7,588
1. Jammu District (including city).	16	3	13	65	32	33	203	99	104	268	131	137	...	...	...	97	54	43	6	3	3	356	216	140	3,156	1,722	1,434
2. Jasrota ,, ...	4	2	2	...	...	...	...	...	...	...	...	...	...	...	...	...	...	...	2	1	1	4	4	...	108	58	50
3. Udhampur ,, ...	12	4	8	...	...	...	16	5	11	16	5	11	...	...	...	...	...	...	...	...	...	20	12	8	128	61	67
4. Riasi ,, ...	...	...	...	...	...	...	2	2	...	2	2	...	...	...	...	1	1	...	1	...	1	26	11	15	487	265	222
5. Mirpur ,, ...	...	...	...	...	...	...	12	12	...	12	12	...	...	...	...	54	36	18	108	55	53	29	13	16	3,156	1,779	1,377
6. Bhadarwah *Jagir* ...	...	...	...	...	...	...	...	...	...	...	...	...	...	...	...	...	...	...	...	...	...	...	...	...	...	...	...
7. Punch *Ilaqa* ...	2	2	...	6	...	6	6	5	1	12	5	7	...	...	...	...	...	...	169	96	73	17	...	17	9,624	5,186	4,438
II—Total Kashmir Province (including *Jagirs*).	...	...	...	...	...	...	38	20	18	38	20	18	38	17	21	...	...	...	6	5	1	11,930	6,458	5,522	14,772	7,871	6,901
8. Kashmir North (including Langet *Jagir*).	...	...	...	...	...	...	14	9	5	14	9	5	...	...	...	...	...	...	...	...	...	3,942	2,105	1,837	4,575	2,383	2,192
9. Kashmir South (including city).	...	...	...	...	...	...	7	6	1	7	6	1	38	17	21	...	...	...	...	...	...	2,051	1,190	861	2,586	1,448	1,138
Total Kashmir Valley ...	...	...	...	...	...	...	*21*	*15*	*6*	*21*	*15*	*6*	*38*	*17*	*21*	...	...	...	...	...	...	*5,993*	*3,295*	*2,698*	*7,161*	*3,831*	*3,330*
10. Muzaffarabad District (*Wizarat Pahar*).	...	...	...	...	...	...	17	5	12	17	5	12	...	...	...	...	...	...	6	5	1	5,987	3,163	2,824	7,611	4,040	3,571
III—Total Frontier Districts.	...	...	...	...	...	...	6	5	1	6	5	1	...	...	...	2	2	...	...	...	...	62	56	6	122	96	26
11. Laddakh District (including Mansar).	...	...	...	...	...	...	...	...	...	...	...	...	...	...	...	...	...	...	...	...	...	35	31	4	41	33	8
12. Gilgit ,, ...	...	...	...	...	...	...	4	3	1	4	3	1	...	...	...	2	2	...	...	...	...	21	19	2	57	41	16
13. Frontier *Ilaqas* ...	...	...	...	...	...	...	2	2	...	2	2	...	...	...	...	...	...	...	...	...	...	6	6	...	24	22	2

TABLE XIII.

Caste, Tribe, Race or Nationality.

Jammu and Kashmir State Census 1911.

Part III Other Religions.

DISTRICT, JAGIR OR ILAQA.	JAIN.			BUDHIST.																		TOTAL BUDHIST.			PARSI.			INDIAN CHRISTIAN.*		
	Khatri.			Beda.			Gorkha.			Lama.			Mangriks.			Rigzang.													
	Persons.	Males.	Females.	Persons.	Males.	Females.	Persons.	Males.	Females.	Persons.	Males.	Females.	Persons.	Males.	Females.	Persons.	Males.	Females.	Persons.	Males.	Females.	Persons.	Males.	Females.	Persons.	Males.	Females.
	83	84	85	86	87	88	89	90	91	92	93	94	95	96	97	98	99	100	101	102	103	104	105	106	107	108	109
Total State ...	345	191	154	5	1	4	1	1	...	28	27	1	35,616	17,691	17,925	862	561	301	36,512	18,281	18,231	31	22	9	709	475	234
I—Total Jammu Province (including *Jagirs*).	345	191	154	...	...	...	1	1	...	...	...	...	451	210	241	...	...	...	452	211	241	5	2	3	623	420	203
1. Jammu District (including city).	334	181	153	...	...	...	...	...	...	...	...	...	...	...	...	...	...	...	...	...	...	5	2	3	445	291	154
2. Jasrota " ...	...	...	...	...	...	...	...	...	...	...	...	...	11	4	7	...	...	...	11	4	7	...	...	...	170	128	42
3. Udhampur " ...	3	2	1	...	...	...	...	...	...	...	...	...	439	205	234	...	...	...	439	205	234	...	...	...	...	...	...
4. Riasi " ...	...	...	...	...	...	...	...	...	...	...	...	...	...	...	...	...	...	...	...	...	...	...	...	...	...	...	...
5. Mirpur " ...	8	8	...	...	...	...	...	...	...	...	...	...	...	...	...	...	...	...	...	...	...	...	...	...	...	...	...
6. Bhadarwah *Jagir* ...	...	...	...	...	...	...	...	...	...	...	...	...	1	1	...	...	...	...	1	1	...	...	...	...	...	...	...
7. Punch *Ilaqa* ...	...	...	...	...	...	...	1	1	...	...	...	...	...	...	...	...	...	...	1	1	...	...	...	...	8	1	7
II—Total Kashmir Province (including *Jagirs*).	...	...	...	...	...	...	...	...	...	...	...	...	3	3	...	...	...	...	3	3	...	26	20	6	33	24	9
8. Kashmir North (including Langet *Jagir*).	...	...	...	...	...	...	...	...	...	...	...	...	2	2	...	...	...	...	2	2	...	...	...	...	...	...	...
9. Kashmir South (including city).	...	...	...	...	...	...	...	...	...	...	...	...	...	...	...	...	...	...	...	...	...	26	20	6	31	22	9
Total Kashmir Valley ...	...	...	...	...	...	...	...	...	...	...	...	...	*2*	*2*	...	...	...	...	*2*	*2*	...	*23*	*20*	*6*	*31*	*22*	*9*
10. Muzaffarabad District (*Wizarat Pahar*).	...	...	...	...	...	...	...	...	...	...	...	...	1	1	...	...	...	...	1	1	...	...	...	...	2	2	...
III—Total Frontier Districts.	...	...	...	5	1	4	...	...	...	28	27	1	35,162	17,478	17.684	862	561	301	36,057	18,067	17,990	...	...	...	53	31	22
11. Laddakh District (including Mansar).	...	...	...	5	1	4	...	...	...	28	27	1	35,162	17,478	17,684	862	561	301	36,057	18,067	17,990	...	...	...	51	29	22
12. Gilgit " ...	...	...	...	...	...	...	...	...	...	...	...	...	...	...	...	...	...	...	...	...	...	...	...	...	2	2	...
13. Frontier *Ilaqas* ...	...	...	...	...	...	...	...	...	...	...	...	...	...	...	...	...	...	...	...	...	...	...	...	...	...	...	...

* Europeans and Anglo-Indians have been excluded under Section 14, Note Chapter IV, page 51 Imperial Census Code, Part II.

TABLE XIV.

CIVIL CONDITION BY AGE FOR SELECTED CASTES.

Jammu and Kashmir State Census 1911.

Vide Title Page remarks to Table IX above.

Civil condition by age for selected castes.

TABLE XIV.

Civil condition by age for selected castes.

	Caste, Tribe or Race.	Total.	Sexes.	Population dealt with.	Unmarried. Total.	0–5	5–12	12–15	15–20	20–40	40 & over.	Married. Total.	0–5	5–12	12–15	15–20	20–40	40 & over.	Widowed. Total.	0–5	5–12	12–15	15–20	20–40	40 & over.
	1	2	3	4	5	6	7	8	9	10	11	12	13	14	15	16	17	18	19	20	21	22	23	24	25
Hindu.	1. Arora ...	1,879	Males ...	1,127	556	92	156	69	77	119	43	458	...	1	...	17	260	180	113	...	...	...	1	36	76
			Females ...	752	230	87	115	20	4	3	1	348	...	11	25	56	200	56	174	...	1	3	4	51	115
	2. Brahman ...	173,795	Males ...	93,115	48,568	10,102	13,905	6,015	6,297	9,554	2,695	35,973	8	232	772	2,398	16,988	15,575	8,574	1	9	118	361	2,175	5,910
			Females ...	80,680	24,523	9,775	12,101	1,501	447	477	222	36,934	67	2,562	2,843	5,975	18,899	6,588	19,223	3	82	188	477	5,620	12,853
	3. Chamiar ...	37,860	Males ...	19,971	9,621	2,534	3,495	1,293	961	1,102	236	8,995	7	120	392	614	4,385	3,477	1,355	...	2	9	67	422	855
			Females ...	17,889	5,873	2,539	2,843	326	94	53	18	9,435	6	589	736	1,476	5,014	1,614	2,581	1	10	18	86	672	1,794
	4. Kashmiri Pandit	55,097	Males ...	30,724	17,283	3,345	4,847	1,827	2,276	3,722	1,266	11,312	...	35	178	523	6,084	4,492	2,129	...	2	6	11	484	1,626
			Females ...	24,373	8,668	3,222	4,590	731	98	25	2	10,954	2	152	522	1,712	6,547	2,019	4,751	...	9	13	64	1,214	3,451
	5. Megh ...	73,440	Males ...	37,570	17,613	4,208	5,998	2,073	2,020	2,652	662	16,356	16	205	330	1,138	8,022	6,645	3,601	...	24	24	76	898	2,579
			Females ...	35,870	10,577	4,666	4,965	573	187	126	60	18,714	13	1,139	1,370	2,848	9,934	3,410	6,579	...	20	37	143	1,566	4,813
	6. Rajput ...	50,264	Males ...	29,540	16,490	3,102	4,658	2,073	2,264	3,562	831	10,822	3	44	159	625	5,274	4,717	2,228	...	1	26	12	606	1,583
			Females ...	20,724	4,802	1,806	2,466	361	106	43	20	10,597	8	435	618	1,744	6,030	1,762	5,325	...	19	24	73	1,450	3,759
	7. Thakkar ...	93,596	Males ...	49,419	25,307	5,134	7,189	2,708	3,089	5,400	1,787	19,941	11	320	902	1,674	8,842	8,192	4,171	1	7	138	275	1,118	2,632
			Females ...	44,177	13,943	5,480	6,196	1,068	459	455	285	20,704	37	1,330	1,585	3,390	10,785	3,577	9,530	1	54	120	183	2,181	6,991
Musalman.	1. Awan ...	25,831	Males ...	13,922	7,723	2,139	2,869	966	816	825	108	5,525	3	38	87	269	2,853	2,275	674	...	2	2	4	184	482
			Females ...	11,909	5,122	2,074	2,328	432	198	84	6	5,644	1	150	292	786	3,234	1,181	1,143	...	6	5	30	182	920
	2. Brukpa ...	4,329	Males ...	2,189	1,118	392	432	126	102	63	3	998	...	13	33	66	508	378	73	...	...	...	1	22	50
			Females ...	2,140	915	388	379	84	37	24	3	1,004	...	6	54	128	590	226	221	...	...	1	5	28	187
	3. Balti ...	11,176	Males ...	5,522	2,712	839	1,061	322	295	186	9	2,617	...	20	56	191	1,403	947	193	1	1	...	2	58	131
			Females ...	5,654	2,280	1,001	964	219	74	19	3	2,772	...	9	114	316	1,664	669	602	...	...	2	17	84	499
	4. Bat ...	152,210	Males ...	82,012	42,601	12,405	16,000	5,096	4,936	3,790	374	35,226	10	156	657	2,691	18,676	13,036	4,185	...	2	16	55	1,147	2,965
			Females ...	70,198	28,726	11,966	13,266	2,445	627	300	122	35,237	6	550	2,235	5,636	19,312	7,498	6,235	4	5	28	245	1,097	4,856
	5. Bains ...	6,069	Males ...	3,015	1,653	479	623	231	153	152	15	1,205	...	7	24	54	549	571	157	...	1	1	2	33	120
			Females ...	3,054	1,127	445	504	103	40	26	9	1,524	5	35	78	179	898	329	403	...	1	1	5	107	289
	6. Chibh ...	9,164	Males ...	4,605	2,622	624	937	342	278	375	66	1,772	...	3	13	74	807	875	211	...	...	...	6	58	147
			Females ...	4,559	1,653	595	708	169	110	56	15	2,168	1	40	97	261	1,301	468	738	...	1	2	13	145	577
	7. Dar ...	98,525	Males ...	53,150	27,467	8,517	10,332	3,216	2,953	2,284	165	23,146	1	135	409	1,739	12,494	8,368	2,537	...	6	16	88	621	1,806
			Females ...	45,375	18,600	7,945	8,592	1,532	373	122	36	22,952	1	434	1,361	3,538	12,728	4,890	3,823	...	4	37	95	627	3,060
	8. Ganai ...	55,554	Males ...	29,777	15,552	4,622	5,812	1,831	1,885	1,290	112	12,806	...	53	207	869	7,057	4,620	1,419	...	1	10	51	384	973
			Females ...	25,777	10,709	4,412	5,068	857	200	74	98	12,880	...	196	716	2,072	7,228	2,668	2,188	...	2	8	43	353	1,782
	9. Gujjar ...	304,117	Males ...	164,675	87,108	25,770	31,889	10,968	9,419	8,022	1,040	68,804	178	1,311	1,784	4,692	33,846	26,993	8,763	86	66	271	314	2,398	5,628
			Females ...	139,442	57,069	24,483	25,248	4,431	1,684	847	376	70,130	88	3,822	5,087	11,482	35,057	14,594	12,243	1	41	76	333	2,307	9,485
	10. Gakkhar ...	15,175	Males ...	7,733	4,315	1,131	1,571	536	518	498	61	3,118	...	17	53	195	1,593	1,260	300	...	1	...	10	91	198
			Females ...	7,442	3,089	1,138	1,338	359	176	69	9	3,562	1	94	202	527	1,986	752	791	...	...	4	8	149	630
	11. Hanji ...	18,090	Males ...	9,826	4,991	1,476	2,026	588	478	397	26	4,253	4	32	82	350	2,504	1,281	582	7	...	3	19	132	421
			Females ...	8,264	3,443	1,359	1,634	298	81	54	17	4,045	1	76	212	608	2,300	848	776	...	...	3	6	204	563
	12. Jat ...	113,563	Males ...	58,002	31,686	8,362	11,259	3,852	3,337	4,200	676	22,617	17	156	384	1,057	11,102	9,901	3,699	3	4	10	22	956	2,704
			Females ...	55,561	20,694	7,331	9,101	2,416	1,256	473	117	28,722	24	696	1,273	3,067	17,527	6,135	6,145	...	18	15	91	1,227	4,794
	13. Malik ...	53,451	Males ...	27,072	14,436	4,111	5,462	1,717	1,685	1,291	170	11,444	5	86	187	770	6,058	4,338	1,192	...	1	6	24	290	871
			Females ...	26,379	11,405	4,339	5,195	1,014	507	129	221	12,454	10	238	739	1,921	7,062	2,484	2,520	...	5	13	63	434	2,005
	14. Megh ...	184	Males ...	95	46	19	14	5	5	2	1	49	...	...	1	2	27	19	...	...	...	...	...	...	...
			Females ...	89	32	6	18	3	4	1	...	50	...	...	2	9	30	9	7	...	...	...	...	1	6
	15. Mughal ...	33,269	Males ...	17,696	9,575	2,639	3,501	1,214	1,129	998	94	7,304	2	28	86	421	3,725	3,042	817	2	6	18	28	213	550
			Females ...	15,573	6,525	2,520	2,964	623	226	182	10	7,442	...	157	405	1,169	4,109	1,602	1,606	...	1	21	36	335	1,213
	16. Pathan ...	19,902	Males ...	10,871	5,946	1,519	1,969	690	765	881	122	4,414	3	31	60	283	2,208	1,829	511	...	...	3	7	136	365
			Females ...	9,031	3,973	1,540	1,810	383	166	60	14	4,231	2	95	218	693	2,389	834	827	...	3	2	38	165	619
	17. Sayed ...	56,493	Males ...	29,809	16,052	4,288	5,885	2,097	1,939	1,655	188	12,496	5	87	153	747	6,500	5,004	1,261	...	4	6	21	376	854
			Females ...	26,684	11,273	4,146	5,200	1,122	543	215	47	12,680	...	243	615	1,872	7,371	2,579	2,731	...	2	11	59	565	2,094
	18. Shin ...	2,719	Males ...	1,620	848	244	307	80	99	113	5	705	1	8	11	40	361	284	67	...	1	...	...	15	51
			Females ...	1,099	492	210	199	50	22	10	1	532	...	7	29	52	318	120	75	...	...	1	...	11	63
	19. Yashkun ...	16,214	Males ...	7,944	4,385	1,411	1,690	469	435	353	27	3,293	...	17	67	192	1,842	1,175	266	...	1	1	1	84	179
			Females ...	8,270	3,757	1,662	1,596	277	176	39	7	3,902	...	82	178	474	2,486	682	611	...	2	4	12	101	492

TABLE XV.

OCCUPATION OR MEANS OF LIVELIHOOD.

Jammu and Kashmir State Census 1911.

1. This table is divided into the following parts:—

PART A.—General Table. It deals with the entire population of the State and the figures are given by territorial divisions. The city totals are shown separately as well as along with those of the district, province, etc. to which they belong.

PART B.—Subsidiary occupations of agriculturists (actual workers only). This is sub-divided into:—

(1) In respect of Rent-Receivers.
(2) ,, ,, Rent-Payers.
(3) ,, ,, Agricultural labourers.

This part does not include the Agency *Ilaqas* as their special schedule of enumeration did not provide for details of this sort.

PART C.—Not prepared in this State as its utility would not have been commensurate with its cost.

PART D.—Distribution of occupation by religion. This also includes all the population but the figures are arranged only in respect of the following units:—

(1) Entire State (including the cities.)
(2) City totals : (*a*) Jammu, (*b*) Srinagar.

PART E.—Statistics of Industries, sub-divided into :—

(1) Provincial summary.
(2) Distribution by districts.
(3) Particulars as to ownership of factories, etc.
(4) Caste or race of the Managers of factories.

This part records the results of the special Industrial Census taken this time in accordance with the Government of India Resolutions Home Department Nos. 233-249, dated 28th July 1910.

2. The present classification of occupations differs considerably from that of the previous Census to secure uniformity for purposes of international statistics. It is based on Monsieur Bertillon's scheme as adapted to the local conditions of India.

3. To make a comparison of the present figures with those of the last Census possible the figures of the latter have been recast according to the new scheme and these are published in the form of a separate statement along with the text volume of the Census Report.

4. In the case of Military and Civil services, the persons under direct employment of the British Government have alone been shown in groups 139 and 144 and the rest under groups 140 and 145 as servants of this State. In group 146 are shown the servants of the Municipalities and of the internal Jagir Managements.

5. The heads (major or minor) under which no figures were returned here have been omitted. The occupations peculiar to this part of the country have been duly classified under the proper heads of the new scheme.

TABLE XV-A.

Occupation or Means of Livelihood.

Jammu and Kashmir State Census 1911.

DISTRICT, JAGIR, ILAQA OR CITY.	ENTIRE STATE.						CLASS A.—PRODUCTION OF RAW MATERIALS.						Sub-Class I.—Exploitation of the surface of the earth.					
	Total workers and dependents.	Actual Workers. Total.		Actual Workers. Partially Agriculturists.		Dependents.	Total workers and dependents.	Actual Workers. Total.		Actual Workers. Partially Agriculturists.		Dependents.	Total workers and dependents.	Actual Workers. Total.		Actual Workers. Partially Agriculturists.		Dependents.
		Males.	Females.	Males.	Females.			Males.	Females.	Males.	Females.			Males.	Females.	Males.	Females.	
1	2	3	4	5	6	7	8	9	10	11	12	13	14	15	16	17	18	19
Total State ...	**3,158,126**	**1,024,661**	**461,628**	**20,940**	**1,030**	**1,671,837**	**2,519,742**	**796,769**	**397,631**	**1,338**	**25**	**1,325,342**	**2,519,709**	**796,760**	**397,630**	**1,338**	**25**	**1,325,319**
I—Total Jammu Province (including *Jagirs*).	1,597,865	533,131	170,026	12,914	744	894,708	1,298,263	421,624	143,028	522	15	733,611	1,298,238	421,616	143,027	522	15	733,595
1. Jammu District (including city).	326,691	116,311	27,339	4,668	252	193,041	205,968	71,346	17,355	94	...	117,267	205,968	71,346	17,355	94	...	117,647
2. Jasrota ,, ...	151,802	53,305	21,831	2,282	213	76,666	104,867	37,758	17,230	119	7	49,879	104,867	37,758	17,230	119	7	49,879
3. Udhampur ,, ...	215,725	74,413	31,813	1,540	139	109,499	189,199	63,896	28,890	126	3	96,413	189,189	63,896	28,890	126	3	96,413
4. Riasi ,, ...	206,809	69,698	18,419	1,014	42	118,692	182,448	60,082	16,788	106	3	105,578	182,448	60,082	16,788	106	3	105,578
5. Mirpur ,, ...	324,933	109,208	30,841	2,631	77	184,884	267,673	87,680	25,964	43	...	154,029	267,648	87,672	25,963	43	...	154,013
6. Bhadarwah *Jagir* ...	37,512	12,900	9,253	423	13	15,359	33,610	11,126	8,722	32	2	13,762	33,610	11,126	8,722	32	2	13,762
7. Punch *Ilaqa*	334,393	97,296	30,530	356	8	206,567	314,498	89,736	28,079	2	...	196,683	314,498	89,736	28,079	2	...	196,683
II—Total Kashmir Province (including *Jagirs*).	1,295,201	398,498	237,060	7,289	274	659,643	972,917	191,694	201,810	791	10	479,413	972,917	291,694	201,810	791	10	479,413
8. Kashmir North (including Langet *Jagir*).	460,786	140,906	96,155	1,893	180	223,825	390,260	117,431	87,883	295	8	184,946	390,260	117,431	87,883	295	8	184,946
9. Kashmir South (including city).	639,210	199,814	102,457	4,975	47	336,939	401,310	122,470	76,160	478	2	202,680	401,310	122,470	76,160	478	2	202,680
Total Kashmir Valley...	*1,099,996*	*340,720*	*198,512*	*6,868*	*227*	*560,764*	*791,570*	*239,901*	*164,043*	*773*	*10*	*387,626*	*791,570*	*239,901*	*164,043*	*773*	*10*	*387,626*
10. Muzaffarabad District ...	195,205	57,778	38,548	421	47	98,879	181,347	51,793	37,767	18	...	91,787	181,347	51,793	37,767	18	...	91,787
III—Total Frontier Districts.	265,060	93,032	54,542	737	12	117,486	248,562	83,451	52,793	25	...	112,318	248,554	83,450	52,793	25	...	112,311
11. Laddakh District (including Mansar).	186,656	55,804	49,321	200	12	81,531	176,808	50,710	47,619	21	...	78,479	176,800	50,709	47,619	21	...	78,472
12. Gilgit ,, ...	23,969	7,950	5,221	537	...	10,798	21,179	5,885	5,174	4	...	10,120	21,179	5,885	5,174	4	...	10,120
13. Frontier *Ilaqas*	54,435	29,278	...	...	...	25,157	50,575	26,856	...	...	...	23,719	50,575	26,856	...	...	...	23,719
Cities.																		
Jammu	31,726	13,111	2,132	106	543	16,483	2,122	870	145	5	...	1,107	2,122	870	145	5	...	1,107
Srinagar	126,344	43,634	8,048	506	163	74,662	7,386	2,233	1,048	4	...	4,095	7,386	2,233	1,048	4	...	4,095

TABLE XV-A.

Occupation or Means of Livelihood.

Jammu and Kashmir State Census 1911.

District, Jagir, Ilaqa or City.	Order 1.—Pasture and Agriculture.						Order 1 (a).—Ordinary Cultivation.						*Group (1).—Income from rent of agricultural land.*					
	Total workers and dependents.	Actual Workers. Total.		Actual Workers. Partially Agriculturists.		Dependents.	Total workers and dependents.	Actual Workers. Total.		Actual Workers. Partially Agriculturists.		Dependents.	Total workers and dependents.	Actual Workers. Total.		Actual Workers. Partially Agriculturists.		Dependents.
		Males.	Females.	Males.	Females.			Males.	Females.	Males.	Females.			Males.	Females.	Males.	Females.	
	20	21	22	23	24	25	26	27	28	29	30	31	32	33	34	35	36	37
Total State ...	**2,515,519**	**795,289**	**397,307**	**1,234**	**25**	**1,322,923**	**2,474,991**	**777,010**	**392,917**	**16**	..	**1,305,064**	**32,470**	**8,385**	**3,983**	...	...	**20,102**
I—Total Jammu Province (including *Jagirs*).	1,298,154	421,573	143,025	522	15	733,556	1,281,266	411,767	141,559	13	...	727,940	19,402	4,724	3,147	...	...	11,531
1. Jammu District (including city).	205,930	71,328	117,354	94	...	117,628	203,246	69,694	17,263	...	...	116,289	6,320	1,625	892	...	...	3,803
2. Jasrota ,, ...	104,866	37,757	17,230	119	7	48,879	102,529	36,517	16,994	4	...	49,018	3,955	1,006	605	...	...	2,344
3. Udhampur ,, ...	189,189	63,896	28,890	126	3	96,413	186,482	62,579	28,469	7	...	95,434	1,913	488	417	...	...	1,008
4. Riasi ,, ...	182,445	60,080	16,788	106	3	105,577	173,918	58,244	16,559	2	...	104,115	856	174	220	...	...	462
5. Mirpur ,, ...	267,625	87,667	25,963	43	...	153,995	264,666	85,640	25,764	...	...	153,262	4,226	971	717	...	...	2,548
6. Bhadarwah *Jagir* ...	33,610	11,126	8,722	32	2	13,762	32,862	10,736	8,521	...	...	13,605	231	64	38	...	...	129
7. Punch *Ilaqa*	314,479	89,719	28,078	2	...	196,682	312,563	88,357	27,989	...	...	196,217	1,901	406	258	...	...	1,237
II—Total Kashmir Province (including *Jagirs*).	969,216	290,492	201,489	691	10	477,235	946,625	282,583	198,738	2	...	465,304	11,111	2,667	745	...	...	7,699
8. Kashmir North (including Langet *Jagir*).	388,555	116,882	87,698	272	8	183,975	378,397	113,312	86,161	2	...	178,924	2,202	570	263	...	...	1,369
9. Kashmir South (including city).	399,326	121,822	76,024	402	2	201,480	387,409	117,828	74,832	...	...	194,749	7,948	1,865	409	...	...	5,674
Total Kashmir Valley ...	*787,881*	*238,704*	*163,722*	*674*	*10*	*385,455*	*765,806*	*231,140*	*160,993*	*2*	...	*373,673*	*10,150*	*2,435*	*672*	...	...	*7,043*
10. Muzaffarabad District ...	181,335	51,788	37,767	17	...	91,780	180,819	51,443	37,745	...	...	91,631	961	232	73	...	...	656
III—Total Frontier Districts.	248,149	83,224	52,793	21	...	112,132	247,100	82,660	52,620	1	...	111,820	1,957	994	91	...	...	872
11. Laddakh District (including Mansar).	176,800	50,709	47,619	21	...	78,472	175,886	50,209	47,448	1	...	78,229	1,843	959	86	...	...	798
12. Gilgit ,, ...	21,166	5,873	5,174	...	...	10,119	21,122	5,851	5,172	...	...	10,099	114	35	5	...	...	74
13. Frontier *Ilaqas*	50,183	26,642	...	...	...	23,541	50,092	26,600	...	...	...	23,492	...	...	...	...	...	...
Cities.																		
Jammu	2,088	856	144	5	...	1,088	2,018	822	143	...	...	1,053	292	74	33	...	...	185
Srinagar	7,069	2,137	1,014	4	...	3,908	5,627	1,732	1,013	...	...	2,882	897	210	16	...	...	671

TABLE XV-A.

Occupation or Means of Livelihood.

Jammu and Kashmir State Census 1911.

District, Jagir, Ilaqa or City.	Group (2).—Ordinary Cultivators.						Group (3).—Agents, managers of landed estates (not planters), clerks, rent collectors, etc.						Group (4).—Farm servants and field labourers.						Order 1 (b).—Growers of special products and market gardening.					
	Total workers and dependents.	Actual Workers. Total.		Actual Workers. Partially Agriculturists.		Dependents.	Total workers and dependents.	Actual Workers. Total.		Actual Workers. Partially Agriculturists.		Dependents.	Total workers and dependents.	Actual Workers. Total.		Actual Workers. Partially Agriculturists.		Dependents.	Total workers and dependents.	Actual Workers. Total.		Actual Workers. Partially Agriculturists.		Dependents.
		Males.	Females.	Males.	Females.			Males.	Females.	Males.	Females.			Males.	Females.	Males.	Females.			Males.	Females.	Males.	Females.	
	38	39	40	41	42	43	44	45	46	47	48	49	50	51	52	53	54	55	56	57	58	59	60	61
Total State ...	**2,400,806**	**752,509**	**381,837**	...		**1,266,460**	**1,434**	**648**	...	**16**	...	**786**	**40,281**	**15,468**	**7,097**	...	...	**17,716**	**4,407**	**1,600**	**606**	**48**	...	**2,201**
I—Total Jammu Province (including *Jagirs*).	1,239,460	397,398	135,316	...	...	706,766	900	514	...	13	...	386	21,484	9,131	3,096	...	...	9,257	319	138	52	6	...	129
1. Jammu District (including city).	187,391	64,559	15,126	...	...	102,992	523	258	...	...	...	265	9,012	3,252	1,245	...	...	4,515	160	74	3	5	...	83
2. Jasrota ,, ...	94,500	33,938	15,513	...	...	45,049	88	58	...	4	...	30	3,986	1,515	876	...	...	1,595	29	19	1	...	...	9
3. Udhampur ,, ...	182,765	61,072	27,799	...	...	93,894	181	141	...	7	...	40	1,623	878	253	...	...	492	14	6	...	1	...	8
4. Riasi ,, ...	176,155	57,004	16,159	...	...	103,012	88	48	...	2	...	40	1,819	1,018	180	...	...	621	3	2	...	...	...	1
5. Mirpur ,, ...	258,239	83,560	24,826	...	...	149,853	16	7	...	...	...	9	2,185	1,112	221	...	...	852	59	1	48	...	...	10
6. Bhadarwah *Jagir*. ...	32,328	10,454	8,416	...	...	13,458	1	...	...	...	...	1	302	218	67	...	...	17	7	2	...	...	...	5
7. Punch *Ilaqa*	308,102	86,811	27,477	...	...	193,814	3	2	...	...	...	1	2,557	1,138	254	...	...	1,165	47	34	...	...	...	13
II—Total Kashmir Province (including *Jagirs*).	918,645	274,428	194,732	...	...	446,805	418	55	...	2	...	363	16,451	5,433	3,261	...	...	7,757	4,024	1,426	549	31	...	2,049
8. Kashmir North (including Langet *Jagir*).	366,292	109,557	83,923	...	...	172,812	4	2	...	2	...	2	9,899	3,183	1,975	...	...	4,741	3,129	1,031	540	12	...	1,558
9. Kashmir South (including city).	374,918	114,471	73,612	...	...	186,835	106	45	...	...	...	361	4,137	1,447	811	...	...	1,879	886	391	9	18	...	486
Total Kashmir Valley ...	*741,210*	*224,028*	*157,535*	...	...	*359,647*	*410*	*47*	...	*2*	...	*363*	*14,036*	*4,630*	*2,786*	...	...	*6,620*	*4,015*	*1,422*	*549*	*30*	...	*2,044*
10. Muzaffarabad District ...	177,435	50,400	37,197	...	...	89,838	8	8	...	...	...	...	2,415	803	475	...	...	1,137	9	4	...	1	...	5
III—Total Frontier Districts.	242,681	80,683	51,789	...	...	110,209	116	79	...	1	...	37	2,346	904	740	...	...	702	64	36	5	11	...	23
11. Laddakh District (including Mansar).	172,146	48,449	46,759	...	...	76,938	116	79	...	1	...	37	1,781	722	603	...	...	456	56	29	5	11	...	22
12. Gilgit ,, ...	20,490	5,662	5,030	...	...	9,798	...	...	...	...	...	...	518	154	137	...	...	227	8	7	...	...	...	1
13. Frontier *Ilaqas*	50,045	26,572	...	...	...	23,473	...	...	...	...	...	...	47	28	...	...	...	19	...	...	...	...	...	...
Cities.																								
Jammu	1,685	733	107	...	...	845	11	...	...	...	...	11	30	15	3	...	...	12	7	7	...	...	...	...
Srinagar	3,521	1,238	791	...	...	1,492	348	28	...	...	...	320	861	256	206	...	...	399	593	207	1	2	...	385

TABLE XV-A.

Occupation or Means of Livelihood.

Jammu and Kashmir State Census 1911.

DISTRICT, JAGIR, ILAQA OR CITY.	Group (6).—Fruit, flower, vegetable, betel, vine, areca nut, etc. growers. Total workers and dependents.	Actual Workers. Total. Males.	Actual Workers. Total. Females.	Actual Workers. Partially Agriculturists. Males.	Actual Workers. Partially Agriculturists. Females.	Dependents.
	62	63	64	65	66	67
Total State ...	4,407	1,600	606	48	...	2,201
I—Total Jammu Province (including *Jagirs*).	319	138	52	6	...	129
1. Jammu District (including city).	160	74	3	5	...	83
2. Jasrota "	29	19	1	...	...	9
3. Udhampur "	14	6	...	1	...	8
4. Riasi "	3	2	...	...	...	1
5. Mirpur "	59	1	48	...	...	10
6. Bhadarwah *Jagir* ...	7	2	...	...	...	5
7. Punch *Ilaqa*	47	34	...	...	...	13
II—Total Kashmir Province (including *Jagirs*).	4,024	1,426	549	31	...	2,049
8. Kashmir North (including Langet *Jagir*).	3,129	1,031	540	12	...	1,558
9. Kashmir South (including city).	886	391	9	18	...	486
Total Kashmir Valley ...	*4,015*	*1,422*	*549*	*30*	...	*2,044*
10. Muzaffarabad District ...	9	4	...	1	...	5
III—Total Frontier Districts.	64	36	5	11	...	23
11. Laddakh District (including Mansar).	56	29	5	11	...	22
12. Gilgit "	8	7	...	...	...	1
13. Frontier *Ilaqas*	...	...	...	...	...	...
Cities.						
Jammu	7	7	...	...	...	...
Srinagar	593	207	1	2	...	385

DISTRICT, JAGIR, ILAQA OR CITY.	Order 1 (c).—Forestry. Total workers and dependents.	Actual Workers. Total. Males.	Actual Workers. Total. Females.	Actual Workers. Partially Agriculturists. Males.	Actual Workers. Partially Agriculturists. Females.	Dependents.
	68	69	70	71	72	73
Total State ...	3,085	1,328	172	69	...	1,585
I—Total Jammu Province (including *Jagirs*).	1,282	669	3	55	...	610
1. Jammu District (including city).	309	122	...	7	...	187
2. Jasrota	134	50	...	7	...	84
3. Udhampur	359	220	...	13	...	139
4. Riasi	95	53	...	1	...	42
5. Mirpur	214	124	3	15	...	87
6. Bhadarwah *Jagir*	72	41	...	12	...	31
7. Punch *Ilaqa*	99	59	...	...	...	40
II—Total Kashmir Province (including *Jagirs*).	1,743	635	159	12	...	949
8. Kashmir North (including Langet *Jagir*).	369	168	21	1	...	180
9. Kashmir South (including city).	1,242	366	138	9	...	738
Total Kashmir Valley ...	*1,611*	*534*	*159*	*10*	...	*918*
10. Muzaffarabad District	132	101	...	2	...	31
III—Total Frontier Districts.	60	24	10	2	...	26
11. Laddakh District (including Mansar).	57	23	10	2	...	24
12. Gilgit	3	1	...	...	...	2
13. Frontier *Ilaqas*	...	...	...	...	...	...
Cities.						
Jammu	52	20	...	...	...	32
Srinagar	717	183	...	2	...	538

DISTRICT, JAGIR, ILAQA OR CITY.	Group (7).—Forest Officers, Rangers, Guards, etc. Total workers and dependents.	Actual Workers. Total. Males.	Actual Workers. Total. Females.	Actual Workers. Partially Agriculturists. Males.	Actual Workers. Partially Agriculturists. Females.	Dependents.
	74	75	76	77	78	79
Total State ...	2,140	913	...	64	...	1,227
I—Total Jammu Province (including *Jagirs*).	1,153	570	...	51	...	583
1. Jammu District (including city).	281	102	...	5	...	179
2. Jasrota	132	48	...	6	...	84
3. Udhampur	319	190	...	13	...	129
4. Riasi	95	53	...	1	...	42
5. Mirpur	157	79	...	14	...	78
6. Bhadarwah *Jagir*	72	41	...	12	...	31
7. Punch *Ilaqa*	97	57	...	...	...	40
II—Total Kashmir Province (including *Jagirs*).	979	338	...	12	...	641
8. Kashmir North (including Langet *Jagir*).	238	115	...	1	...	123
9. Kashmir South (including city).	697	190	...	9	...	507
Total Kashmir Valley ...	*935*	*305*	...	*10*	...	*630*
10. Muzaffarabad District	44	33	...	2	...	11
III—Total Frontier Districts.	8	5	...	1	...	3
11. Laddakh District (including Mansar).	5	4	...	1	...	1
12. Gilgit	3	1	...	...	...	2
13. Frontier *Ilaqas*	...	...	...	...	...	...
Cities.						
Jammu	52	20	...	...	...	32
Srinagar	473	86	...	2	...	387

DISTRICT, JAGIR, ILAQA OR CITY.	Group (8).—Wood-cutters, fire-wood, lac, catechu, rubber, etc. collectors and charcoal burners. Total workers and dependents.	Actual Workers. Total. Males.	Actual Workers. Total. Females.	Actual Workers. Partially Agriculturists. Males.	Actual Workers. Partially Agriculturists. Females.	Dependents.
	80	81	82	83	84	85
Total State ...	945	415	172	5	...	358
I—Total Jammu Province (including *Jagirs*).	129	99	3	4	...	27
1. Jammu District (including city).	28	20	...	2	...	8
2. Jasrota	2	2	...	1	...	...
3. Udhampur	40	30	...	...	...	10
4. Riasi	...	...	...	...	...	...
5. Mirpur	57	45	3	1	...	9
6. Bhadarwah *Jagir*	...	...	...	...	...	...
7. Punch *Ilaqa*	2	2	...	...	...	...
II—Total Kashmir Province (including *Jagirs*).	764	297	159	...	...	308
8. Kashmir North (including Langet *Jagir*).	131	53	21	...	...	57
9. Kashmir South (including city).	545	176	38	...	...	231
Total Kashmir Valley ...	*676*	*229*	*159*	...	...	*288*
10. Muzaffarabad District	88	68	...	...	...	20
III—Total Frontier Districts.	52	19	10	1	...	23
11. Laddakh District (including Mansar).	52	19	10	1	...	23
12. Gilgit	...	...	...	...	...	...
13. Frontier *Ilaqas*	...	...	...	...	...	...
Cities.						
Jammu	...	...	...	...	...	...
Srinagar	244	97	...	...	...	147

TABLE XV-A.

Occupation or Means of Livelihood.

Jammu and Kashmir State Census 1911.

District, Jagir, Ilaqa or City.	Order 1 (a).—Raising of Farm Stock. Total workers and dependents.	Actual Workers. Total. Males.	Actual Workers. Total. Females.	Actual Workers. Partially Agriculturists. Males.	Actual Workers. Partially Agriculturists. Females.	Dependents.	Group (9).—Cattle and buffalo breeders and keepers. Total workers and dependents.	Actual Workers. Total. Males.	Actual Workers. Total. Females.	Actual Workers. Partially Agriculturists. Males.	Actual Workers. Partially Agriculturists. Females.	Dependents.	Group (10).—Sheep, goat and pig breeders. Total workers and dependents.	Actual Workers. Total. Males.	Actual Workers. Total. Females.	Actual Workers. Partially Agriculturists. Males.	Actual Workers. Partially Agriculturists. Females.	Dependents.	Group (12).—Herdsmen, Shepherds, goat-herds, etc. Total workers and dependents.	Actual Workers. Total. Males.	Actual Workers. Total. Females.	Actual Workers. Partially Agriculturists. Males.	Actual Workers. Partially Agriculturists. Females.	Dependents.
	86	87	88	89	90	91	92	93	94	95	96	97	98	99	100	101	102	103	104	105	106	107	108	109
Total State ...	**32,284**	**14 944**	**3,607**	**1,050**	**24**	**13,733**	**23,785**	**11.014**	**2,900**	**674**	**20**	**9,871**	**736**	**363**	**32**	**25**	...	**341**	**7,763**	**3,567**	**675**	**351**	**4**	**3,521**
I—Total Jammu Province (including *Jagirs*).	15,283	8,995	1,411	447	15	4,877	10,292	6,572	1,050	216	13	2,670	671	359	19	23	...	293	4,320	2,064	342	208	2	1,914
1. Jammu District (including city).	2,215	1,438	88	82	...	689	1,418	1,030	49	26	...	339	...	...	...	...	...	...	797	408	39	56	...	350
2. Jasrota ,, ...	2,174	1,171	235	108	7	768	1,035	579	143	27	6	313	...	...	...	...	...	...	1,139	592	92	81	1	455
3. Udhampur ,, ...	2,340	1,087	421	104	3	832	2,088	940	418	84	3	730	6	2	...	...	...	4	246	145	3	20	...	98
4. Riasi ,, ...	3,429	1,781	229	103	3	1,419	2,135	1,239	163	63	2	733	648	342	18	23	...	288	646	200	48	17	1	398
5. Mirpur ,, ...	2,686	1,902	148	28	...	636	1,698	1,512	17	12	...	169	6	5	...	...	...	1	982	385	131	16	...	466
6. Bhadarwah *Jagir* ...	669	347	201	20	2	121	353	81	201	2	2	71	4	4	...	...	...	...	312	262	...	18	...	50
7. Punch *Ilaqa*	1,770	1,269	89	2	...	412	1,565	1,191	59	2	...	315	7	6	1	...	...	...	198	72	29	...	...	97
II—Total Kashmir Province (including *Jagirs*).	16,076	5,445	2,038	596	9	8,593	12,624	3,973	1,695	451	7	6,956	65	4	13	2	...	48	3,387	1,468	330	143	2	1,589
8. Kashmir North (including Langet *Jagir*).	6,409	2,225	974	245	7	3,210	4,983	1,559	888	173	7	2,536	25	...	8	...	...	17	1,401	666	78	72	...	657
9. Kashmir South (including city).	9,292	2,980	1,042	337	2	5,270	7,570	2,374	802	277	...	4,394	40	4	5	2	...	31	1,682	602	235	58	2	845
Total Kashmir Valley ...	*15,701*	*5,205*	*2,016*	*582*	*9*	*8,480*	*12,553*	*3,933*	*1,690*	*450*	*7*	*6,930*	...	...	...	...	...	...	*3,083*	*1,268*	*313*	*130*	*2*	*1,502*
10. Muzaffarabad District ...	375	240	22	14	...	113	71	40	5	1	...	26	...	...	...	...	...	...	304	200	17	13	...	87
III—Total Frontier Districts.	925	504	158	7	...	263	869	469	155	7	...	245	...	...	...	...	...	...	56	35	3	...	...	18
11. Laddakh District (including Mansar).	801	448	156	7	...	197	778	427	155	7	...	196	...	...	...	...	...	...	23	21	1	...	...	1
12. Gilgit ,, ...	33	14	2	...	...	17	...	...	...	...	...	...	...	...	...	...	...	...	33	14	2	...	...	17
13. Frontier *Ilaqas*	91	42	...	...	...	49	91	42	...	...	...	49	...	...	...	...	...	...	...	...	...	...	...	...
Cities.																								
Jammu	11	7	1	5	...	3	...	...	...	...	...	...	...	...	...	...	...	...	11	7	1	5	...	3
Srinagar	105	2	...	...	...	103	105	2	...	...	...	103	...	...	...	...	...	...	...	...	...	...	...	...

TABLE XV-A.

Occupation or Means of Livelihood.

Jammu and Kashmir State Census 1911.

District, Jagir, Ilaqa or City.	Order 1 (e).—Raising of small Animals.						Group (13).—Birds, bees, silk-worms, etc.						Order 2.—Fishing and hunting.						Group (14).—Fishing.						Group (15).—Hunting.					
	Total workers and dependents.	Actual Workers. Total. Males.	Actual Workers. Total. Females.	Partially Agriculturists. Males.	Partially Agriculturists. Females.	Dependents.	Total workers and dependents.	Actual Workers. Total. Males.	Actual Workers. Total. Females.	Partially Agriculturists. Males.	Partially Agriculturists. Females.	Dependents.	Total workers and dependents.	Actual Workers. Total. Males.	Actual Workers. Total. Females.	Partially Agriculturists. Males.	Partially Agriculturists. Females.	Dependents.	Total workers and dependents.	Actual Workers. Total. Males.	Actual Workers. Total. Females.	Partially Agriculturists. Males.	Partially Agriculturists. Females.	Dependents.	Total workers and dependents.	Actual Workers. Total. Males.	Actual Workers. Total. Females.	Partially Agriculturists. Males.	Partially Agriculturists. Females.	Dependents.
	110	111	112	113	114	115	116	117	118	119	120	121	122	123	124	125	126	127	128	129	130	131	132	133	134	135	136	137	138	139
Total State ...	752	407	5	51	1	340	752	407	5	51	1	340	4,190	1,471	323	104	...	2,396	3,326	1,071	323	98	...	1,932	864	400	...	6	...	464
I—Total Jammu Province (including *Jagirs*).	4	4	...	1	...	...	4	4	...	1	...	...	84	43	2	...	...	39	67	26	2	...	...	39	17	17	...	...	...	...
1. Jammu District (including city).	...	...	...	...	...	...	...	...	...	...	...	...	38	18	1	...	...	19	35	15	1	...	...	19	3	3	...	...	...	...
2. Jasrota "	...	...	...	...	...	...	...	...	...	...	...	...	1	1	...	...	...	...	1	1	...	...	...	...	...	...	...	...	...	...
3. Udhampur "	4	4	...	1	...	...	4	4	...	1	...	...	...	...	...	...	...	...	...	...	...	...	...	...	...	...	...	...	...	...
4. Riasi "	...	...	...	...	...	...	...	...	...	...	...	...	3	2	...	...	...	1	3	2	...	...	...	1	...	...	...	...	...	...
5. Mirpur "	...	...	...	...	...	...	...	...	...	...	...	...	23	5	...	...	...	18	23	5	...	...	...	18	...	...	...	...	...	...
6. Bhadarwah *Jagir*. ...	...	...	...	...	...	...	...	...	...	...	...	...	...	...	...	...	...	...	...	...	...	...	...	...	...	...	...	...	...	...
7. Punch *Ilaqa*	...	...	...	...	...	...	...	...	...	...	...	...	19	17	1	...	...	1	5	3	1	...	...	1	14	14	...	...	...	...
II—Total Kashmir Province (including *Jagirs*).	748	403	5	50	1	340	748	403	5	50	1	340	3,701	1,202	321	100	...	2,178	3,255	1,041	321	95	...	1,893	446	161	...	5	...	285
8. Kashmir North (including Langet *Jagir*).	251	146	2	12	1	103	251	146	2	12	1	103	1,705	549	185	23	...	971	1,660	532	185	23	...	943	45	17	...	...	...	28
9. Kashmir South (including city).	497	257	3	38	...	237	497	257	3	38	...	237	1,984	648	136	76	...	1,200	1,583	504	136	71	...	943	401	144	...	5	...	257
Total Kashmir Valley ...	*748*	*403*	*5*	*50*	*1*	*340*	*748*	*403*	*5*	*50*	*1*	*340*	*3,089*	*1,107*	*321*	*99*	...	*2,171*	*3,243*	*1,036*	*321*	*94*	...	*1,886*	*446*	*161*	...	*5*	...	*285*
10. Muzaffarabad District ...	...	...	...	...	...	...	...	...	...	...	...	...	12	5	...	1	...	7	12	5	...	1	...	7	...	...	...	...	...	...
III—Total Frontier Districts.	...	...	...	...	...	...	...	...	...	...	...	...	405	226	...	4	...	179	4	4	...	3	...	...	401	222	...	1	...	179
11. Laddakh District (including Mansar).	...	...	...	...	...	...	...	...	...	...	...	...	...	...	...	...	...	...	...	...	...	...	...	...	...	...	...	...	...	...
12. Gilgit "	...	...	...	...	...	...	...	...	...	...	...	...	13	12	...	4	...	1	4	4	...	3	...	...	9	8	...	1	...	1
13. Frontier *Ilaqas*	...	...	...	...	...	...	...	...	...	...	...	...	392	214	...	...	...	178	...	...	...	...	...	...	392	214	...	...	...	178
Cities.																														
Jammu	...	...	...	...	...	...	...	...	...	...	...	...	34	14	1	...	...	19	34	14	1	...	...	19	...	...	...	...	...	...
Srinagar	27	13	...	...	...	14	27	13	...	...	...	14	317	96	34	...	...	187	254	72	34	...	...	148	63	24	...	...	...	39

TABLE XV-A.

Occupation or Means of Livelihood.

Jammu and Kashmir State Census 1911.

DISTRICT, JAGIR, ILAQA OR CITY.	Sub-class II.—Extraction of minerals.						Order 3.—Mines.						Group (17).—Mines, metallic minerals, (gold, iron, manganese, etc.).						CLASS B.—PREPARATION AND SUPPLY OF MATERIAL SUBSTANCES.					
	Total workers and dependents.	Actual Workers. Total.		Actual Workers. Partially Agriculturists.		Dependents.	Total workers and dependents.	Actual Workers. Total.		Actual Workers. Partially Agriculturists.		Dependents.	Total workers and dependents.	Actual Workers. Total.		Actual Workers. Partially Agriculturists.		Dependents.	Total workers and dependents.	Actual Workers. Total.		Actual Workers. Partially Agriculturists.		Dependents.
		Males.	Females.	Males.	Females.			Males.	Females.	Males.	Females.			Males.	Females.	Males.	Females.			Males.	Females.	Males.	Females.	
	140	141	142	143	144	145	146	147	148	149	150	151	152	153	154	155	156	157	158	159	160	161	162	163
Total State ...	**33**	**9**	**1**	...	...	**23**	**33**	**9**	**1**	...	...	**23**	**33**	**9**	**1**	...	...	**23**	**433,421**	**147,018**	**51,173**	**13,663**	**823**	**235,230**
I—Total Jammu Province (including *Jagirs*).	25	8	1	...	...	16	25	8	1	...	...	16	25	8	1	...	...	16	192,933	67,830	17,475	8,994	565	107,628
1. Jammu District (including city).	...	...	...	...	...	...	...	...	...	...	...	...	...	...	...	...	...	...	70,460	24,984	6,187	3,229	215	39,289
2. Jasrota ,, ...	...	...	...	...	...	...	...	...	...	...	...	...	...	...	...	...	...	...	33,473	11,048	3,367	1,634	168	19,058
3. Udhampur ,, ...	...	...	...	...	...	...	...	...	...	...	...	...	...	...	...	...	...	...	18,142	6,772	2.185	1,093	99	9,185
4. Riasi ,, ...	...	...	...	...	...	...	...	...	...	...	...	...	...	...	...	...	...	...	17,124	6,100	987	636	28	10,037
5. Mirpur ,, ...	25	8	1	...	...	16	25	8	1	...	...	16	25	8	1	...	...	16	40,042	14,372	3,109	1,927	41	22,561
6. Bhadarwah *Jagir* ...	...	...	...	...	...	...	...	...	...	...	...	...	...	...	...	...	...	...	2,444	993	354	256	8	1,097
7. Punch *Ilaqa*	...	...	...	...	...	...	...	...	...	...	...	...	...	...	...	...	...	...	11,248	3,561	1,286	219	6	6,401
II-Total Kashmir Province (including *Jagirs*).	...	...	...	...	...	...	...	...	...	...	...	...	...	...	...	...	...	...	235,283	76,445	32,962	4,532	255	125,871
8. Kashmir North (including Langet *Jagir*).	...	...	...	...	...	...	...	...	...	...	...	...	...	...	...	...	...	...	52,150	16,470	7,666	1,146	171	28,114
9. Kashmir South (including city).	...	...	...	...	...	...	...	...	...	...	...	...	...	...	...	...	...	...	176,521	57,473	25,151	3,136	38	93,897
Total Kashmir Valley ...	...	...	...	...	...	...	...	...	...	...	...	...	...	...	...	...	...	...	*228,671*	*73,943*	*32,717*	*4,282*	*209*	*122,011*
10. Muzaffarabad District ...	...	...	...	...	...	...	...	...	...	...	...	...	...	...	...	...	...	...	6,612	2,502	245	250	46	3,865
III—Total Frontier Districts.	8	1	...	...	...	7	8	1	...	...	...	7	8	1	...	...	...	7	5,205	2,743	736	137	3	1,726
11. Laddakh District (including Mansar).	8	1	...	...	...	7	8	1	...	...	...	7	8	1	...	...	...	7	3,965	1,950	725	101	3	1,290
12. Gilgit ,, ...	...	...	...	...	..	...	...	...	...	...	...	...	...	...	...	...	...	...	602	398	11	36	...	193
13. Frontier *Ilaqas* ...	...	...	...	...	...	...	...	...	...	...	...	...	...	...	...	...	...	...	638	395	...	...	...	243
Cities.																								
Jammu	...	...	...	...	...	...	...	...	...	...	...	...	...	...	...	...	...	...	12,725	5,139	645	42	470	6,941
Srinagar	...	...	...	...	...	...	...	...	...	...	...	...	...	...	...	...	...	...	84,579	30,688	6,398	226	163	47,493

TABLE XV-A.

Occupation or Means of Livelihood.

Jammu and Kashmir State Census 1911.

DISTRICT, JAGIR, ILAQA OR CITY.	Sub-class III.—Industry.						Order 6.—Textiles.						Group (21).—Cotton ginning, clearing and pressing.						Group (22).—Cotton spinning, sizing and weaving.					
	Total workers and dependents.	Actual Workers. Total. Males.	Actual Workers. Total. Females.	Actual Workers. Partially Agriculturists. Males.	Actual Workers. Partially Agriculturists. Females.	Dependents.	Total workers and dependents.	Actual Workers. Total. Males.	Actual Workers. Total. Females.	Actual Workers. Partially Agriculturists. Males.	Actual Workers. Partially Agriculturists. Females.	Dependents.	Total workers and dependents.	Actual Workers. Total. Males.	Actual Workers. Total. Females.	Actual Workers. Partially Agriculturists. Males.	Actual Workers. Partially Agriculturists. Females.	Dependents.	Total workers and dependents.	Actual Workers. Total. Males.	Actual Workers. Total. Females.	Actual Workers. Partially Agriculturists. Males.	Actual Workers. Partially Agriculturists. Females.	Dependents.
	164	165	166	167	168	169	170	171	172	173	174	175	176	177	178	179	180	181	182	183	184	185	186	187
Total State ...	**280,397**	**92,262**	**40,771**	**9,519**	**621**	**147,364**	**95,619**	**26,306**	**29,444**	**1,988**	**366**	**39,869**	**180**	**71**	**8**	**8**	**3**	**101**	**61,184**	**11,347**	**28,309**	**1,602**	**359**	**21,528**
I—Total Jammu Province (including *Jagirs*).	115,939	39,743	13,567	6,175	373	62,629	31,375	8,480	7,422	1,466	150	15,473	158	70	8	7	3	80	28,660	7,693	6,790	1,395	144	14,177
1. Jammu District (including city).	48,646	17,216	5,101	2,591	132	26,329	12,206	3,329	2,702	731	38	6,175	39	15	1	...	1	23	11,244	3,074	2,462	722	37	5,708
2. Jasrota "	17,519	5,725	2,178	1,025	111	9,616	4,893	1,318	1,082	283	53	2,493	5	5	...	4	...	...	4,634	1,252	968	273	53	2,414
3. Udhampur "	8,342	3,035	1,433	548	62	3,874	1,691	369	741	50	27	581	...	...	...	...	...	...	1,426	262	698	34	24	466
4. Riasi "	5,451	1,990	594	383	20	2,867	1,198	315	320	44	8	563	5	5	...	...	...	...	1,109	289	319	44	8	501
5. Mirpur "	28,250	9,257	2,823	1,334	37	16,170	9,301	2,768	1,526	317	22	5,007	96	39	3	...	...	54	8,477	2,534	1,328	293	22	4,615
6. Bhadarwah *Jagir* ...	1,501	627	245	163	7	629	198	56	88	11	...	54	1	1	...	...	...	...	174	39	87	8	...	48
7. Punch *Ilaqa*	6,230	1,893	1,193	131	4	3,144	1,888	325	963	30	2	600	12	5	4	3	2	3	1,596	243	928	21	...	425
II—Total Kashmir Province (including *Jagirs*).	161,971	51,494	26,509	3,271	246	83,968	63,019	17,490	21,352	497	216	24,177	22	1	...	1	...	21	31,845	3,420	21,169	202	215	7,256
8. Kashmir North (including Langet *Jagir*).	33,588	9,742	6,132	820	166	17,714	10,439	2,251	4,664	51	149	3,524	6	...	...	...	...	6	6,912	811	4,567	25	148	1,534
9. Kashmir South (including city).	124,550	40,458	20,171	2,296	35	63,921	51,669	14,959	16,590	420	26	20,120	...	...	...	...	...	...	24,065	2,339	16,504	152	26	5,222
Total Kashmir Valley ...	*158,138*	*50,200*	*26,303*	*3,116*	*201*	*81,635*	*62,108*	*17,210*	*21,254*	*471*	*175*	*23,644*	*6*	...	...	...	...	*6*	*30,977*	*3,150*	*21'071*	*177*	*174*	*6,756*
10. Muzaffarabad District ...	3,833	1,294	206	155	45	2,333	911	280	98	26	41	533	16	1	...	1	...	15	868	270	98	25	41	500
III—Total Frontier Districts	2,487	1,025	695	73	2	767	1,225	336	670	25	...	219	...	...	...	...	...	...	679	234	350	5	...	95
11. Laddakh District (including Mansar).	1,648	523	684	51	2	441	1,156	295	667	21	...	194	...	...	...	...	...	...	653	221	350	2	...	82
12. Gilgit "	285	174	11	22	...	100	54	32	3	4	...	19	...	...	...	...	...	...	12	5	...	3	...	7
13. Frontier *Ilaqas*	554	328	...	...	...	226	15	9	...	...	...	6	...	...	...	...	...	...	14	8	...	...	...	6
Cities.																								
Jammu	7,656	3,236	559	20	469	3,861	650	158	243	...	...	249	...	...	...	...	...	...	87	34	17	...	...	36
Srinagar	60,572	22,954	3,976	173	163	33,642	26,085	10,042	2,927	139	1	13,116	...	...	...	...	...	...	5,354	589	2,907	4	1	1,858

TABLE XV-A.

Occupation or Means of Livelihood.

Jammu and Kashmir State Census 1911.

DISTRICT, JAGIR, ILAQA OR CITY.	Group (24).—Rope, twine and string.						Group (25).—Other fibres (Cocoanut, aloes, flax, hemp, straw, etc.).						Group (26).—Wool carders and spinners, weavers of woollen blankets, carpets, etc.					
	Total workers and dependents.	Actual Workers. Total.		Actual Workers. Partially Agriculturists.		Dependents.	Total workers and dependents.	Actual Workers. Total.		Actual Workers. Partially Agriculturists.		Dependents.	Total workers and dependents.	Actual Workers. Total.		Actual Workers. Partially Agriculturists.		Dependents.
		Males.	Females.	Males.	Females.			Males.	Females.	Males.	Females.			Males.	Females.	Males.	Females.	
	188	189	190	191	192	193	194	195	196	197	198	199	200	201	202	203	204	205
Total State ...	**194**	**85**	**8**	**1**	...	**101**	**22**	**3**	...	...	...	**19**	**23,677**	**10,795**	**237**	**302**	**4**	**12,645**
1—Total Jammu Province (including *Jagirs*).	99	31	8	1	...	60	6	1	...	...	...	5	599	198	156	30	3	245
1. Jammu District (including city).	22	5	3	...	...	14	1	1	...	...	...	...	56	24	1	...	...	31
2. Jasrota "	65	20	4	...	...	41	...	...	...	...	...	...	164	31	109	5	...	24
3. Udhampur "	3	...	1	...	...	2	...	...	...	...	...	...	195	75	41	15	3	79
4. Riasi "	2	1	...	...	...	1	...	...	...	...	...	...	26	10	...	...	...	16
5. Mirpur "	7	5	...	1	...	2	5	...	...	...	...	5	68	22	2	1	...	44
6. Bhadarwah *Jagir* ...	...	...	...	...	...	...	...	...	...	...	...	...	23	16	1	3	...	6
7. Punch *Ilaqa*	...	...	...	...	...	...	...	...	...	...	...	...	67	20	2	6	...	45
II—Total Kashmir Province (including *Jagirs*).	95	54	...	...	...	41	15	1	...	...	...	14	22,850	10,531	25	253	1	12,294
8. Kashmir North (including Langet *Jagir*).	...	...	...	...	...	...	2	...	...	...	...	2	1,249	574	1	24	1	674
9. Kashmir South (including city).	95	54	...	...	...	41	13	1	...	...	...	12	21,590	9,953	24	229	...	11,613
Total Kashmir Valley ...	*95*	*54*	...	...	...	*41*	*15*	*1*	...	...	...	*14*	*22,839*	*10,527*	*25*	*253*	*1*	*12,287*
10. Muzaffarabad District ...	...	...	...	...	...	...	...	...	...	...	...	...	11	4	...	...	...	7
III—Total Frontier Districts.	...	...	...	...	...	...	1	1	...	...	...	...	228	66	56	19	...	106
11. Laddakh District (including Mansar).	...	...	...	...	...	...	...	...	...	...	...	...	228	66	56	19	...	106
12. Gilgit "	...	...	...	...	...	...	...	...	...	...	...	...	...	...	...	...	...	...
13. Frontier *Ilaqas*	...	...	...	...	...	...	1	1	...	...	...	...	...	...	...	...	...	...
Cities.																		
Jammu	...	...	...	...	...	...	...	...	...	...	...	...	34	13	...	...	...	21
Srinagar	90	53	...	...	...	37	4	1	...	...	...	3	16,154	7,341	6	126	...	8,807

DISTRICT, JAGIR, ILAQA OR CITY.	Group (27).—Silk spinners and weavers.						Group (30).—Dyeing, bleaching, printing, preparation and sponging of textiles.					
	Total workers and dependents.	Actual Workers. Total.		Actual Workers. Partially Agriculturists.		Dependents.	Total workers and dependents.	Actual Workers. Total.		Actual Workers. Partially Agriculturists.		Dependents.
		Males.	Females.	Males.	Females.			Males.	Females.	Males.	Females.	
	206	207	208	209	210	211	212	213	214	215	216	217
Total State ...	**5,724**	**2,248**	**631**	**8**	...	**2,845**	**2,375**	**821**	**41**	**49**	...	**1,513**
1—Total Jammu Province (including *Jagirs*).	475	64	217	1	...	194	1,063	366	38	32	...	659
1. Jammu District (including city).	332	38	211	...	...	83	435	153	11	9	...	271
2. Jasrota "	1	1	...	...	...	...	24	9	1	1	...	14
3. Udhampur "	31	14	...	1	...	17	36	18	1	...	...	17
4. Riasi "	26	4	...	...	...	22	30	6	1	...	...	23
5. Mirpur "	12	2	...	...	...	10	435	143	21	22	...	271
6. Bhadarwah *Jagir* ...	...	...	...	...	...	...	...	...	...	...	...	...
7. Punch *Ilaqa*	73	5	6	...	...	62	103	37	3	...	...	63
II—Total Kashmir Province (including *Jagirs*).	4,981	2,183	153	7	...	2,615	1,310	453	3	17	...	854
8. Kashmir North (including Langet *Jagir*).	1,917	725	95	...	...	1,097	351	139	1	2	...	211
9. Kashmir South (including city).	3,063	1,457	58	7	...	1,548	944	310	2	15	...	632
Total Kashmir Valley ...	*4,980*	*2,182*	*153*	*7*	...	*2,645*	*1,295*	*440*	*3*	*17*	...	*843*
10. Muzaffarabad District ...	1	1	...	...	...	...	15	4	...	...	...	11
III—Total Frontier Districts.	268	1	261	...	...	6	2	2	...	...	...	...
11. Laddakh District (including Mansar).	268	1	261	...	...	6	1	1	...	...	...	...
12. Gilgit "	...	...	...	...	...	...	1	1	...	...	...	...
13. Frontier *Ilaqas*	...	...	...	...	...	...	...	...	...	...	...	...
Cities.												
Jammu	331	38	211	...	...	82	121	54	2	...	...	65
Srinagar	2,595	1,209	10	4	...	1,286	616	210	2	...	...	404

TABLE XV-A.

Occupation or Means of Livelihood.

Jammu and Kashmir State Census 1911.

DISTRICT, JAGIR, ILAQA OR CITY.	Group (31).—Other (lace, crape, embroideries, fringes, etc.) and insufficiently described textile industries.						Order 7.—Hides, skins and hard materials from the animal kingdom.						Group (32).—Tanners, curriers, leather dressers and dyers, etc.						Order 8.—Wood.					
	Total workers and dependents.	Actual Workers.				Dependents.	Total workers and dependents.	Actual Workers.				Dependents.	Total workers and dependents.	Actual Workers.				Dependents.	Total workers and dependents.	Actual Workers.				Dependents.
		Total.		Partially Agriculturists.				Total.		Partially Agriculturists.				Total.		Partially Agriculturists.				Total.		Partially Agriculturists.		
		Males.	Females.	Males.	Females.			Males.	Females.	Males.	Females.			Males.	Females.	Males.	Females.			Males.	Females.	Males.	Females.	
	218	219	220	221	222	223	224	225	226	227	228	229	230	231	232	233	234	235	236	237	238	239	240	241
Total State ...	**2,263**	**936**	**210**	**18**	...	**1,117**	**620**	**238**	**22**	**24**	...	**360**	**620**	**238**	**22**	**24**	...	**360**	**31,045**	**10,154**	**2,400**	**1,389**	**34**	**18,491**
I—Total Jammu Province (including *Jagirs*).	315	57	205	...	...	53	400	163	17	18	...	220	400	163	17	18	...	220	13,105	4,697	649	770	33	7,759
1. Jammu District (including city).	77	19	13	...	...	45	186	83	6	13	...	97	186	83	6	13	...	97	5,535	1,830	261	312	16	3,444
2. Jasrota "	...	...	...	...	...	...	34	10	...	...	...	24	34	10	...	...	...	24	2,558	898	145	159	14	1,515
3. Udhampur "	...	...	...	...	...	...	...	...	...	...	...	...	...	...	...	...	...	...	839	353	68	38	1	418
4. Riasi "	...	...	...	...	...	...	63	25	5	5	...	33	63	25	5	5	...	33	668	220	22	56	...	426
5. Mirpur "	201	23	172	...	...	6	82	39	...	...	...	43	82	39	...	...	...	43	2,384	921	50	177	1	1,413
6. Bhadarwah *Jagir* ...	...	...	...	...	...	...	...	...	...	...	...	...	...	...	...	...	...	...	351	204	61	21	...	86
7. Punch *Ilaqa*	37	15	20	...	...	2	35	6	6	...	...	23	35	6	6	...	...	23	770	271	42	7	1	457
II—Total Kashmir Province (including *Jagirs*).	1.901	847	2	17	...	1,052	220	75	5	6	...	140	220	75	5	6	...	140	17,838	5,396	1,748	616	1	10,694
8. Kashmir North (including Langet *Jagir*).	2	2	...	...	...	...	184	55	3	4	...	126	184	55	3	4	...	126	5,378	1,638	335	189	...	3,405
9. Kashmir South (including city).	1.899	845	2	17	...	1,052	36	20	2	2	...	14	36	20	2	2	...	14	12,006	3,594	1,403	420	1	7,009
Total Kashmir Valley ...	*1,901*	*847*	*2*	*17*	...	*1,052*	*220*	*75*	*5*	*6*	...	*140*	*220*	*75*	*5*	*6*	...	*140*	*17,384*	*5,232*	*1,738*	*609*	*1*	*10,414*
10. Muzffarabad District ...	...	...	...	...	...	...	...	...	...	...	...	...	...	...	...	...	...	...	454	164	10	7	...	280
III—Total Frontier Districts.	47	32	3	1	...	12	...	...	...	...	...	...	...	...	...	...	...	...	102	61	3	3	...	38
11. Laddakh District (including Mansar).	6	6	...	...	...	...	...	...	...	...	...	...	...	...	...	...	...	...	66	36	3	1	...	27
12. Gilgit "	41	26	3	1	...	12	...	...	...	...	...	...	...	...	...	...	...	...	36	25	...	2	...	11
13. Frontier *Ilaqas*	...	...	...	...	...	...	...	...	...	...	...	...	...	...	...	...	...	...	...	...	...	...	...	...
Cities.																								
Jammu	77	19	13	...	...	45	17	1	3	...	...	13	17	1	3	...	...	13	553	245	3	7	...	305
Srinagar	1,272	549	2	5	...	721	12	8	...	...	...	4	12	8	...	...	...	4	4,315	1,407	223	15	...	2,685

TABLE XV-A.

Occupation or Means of Livelihood.

Jammu and Kashmir State Census 1911.

DISTRICT, JAGIR, ILAQA OR CITY.	Group (36).—Sawyers, carpenters, turners, joiners, etc.						Group (37).—Basket-makers and other industries of woody material including leaves.					
	Total workers and dependents.	Actual Workers. Total.		Partially Agriculturists.		Dependents.	Total workers and dependents.	Actual Workers. Total.		Partially Agriculturists.		Dependents.
		Males.	Females.	Males.	Females.			Males.	Females.	Males.	Females.	
	242	243	244	245	246	247	248	249	250	251	252	253
Total State	**19,999**	**6.964**	**213**	**1,047**	**6**	**12,822**	**11,046**	**3,190**	**2,187**	**342**	**28**	**5,669**
I—Total Jammu Province (including *Jagirs*).	8.118	3,115	195	558	6	4,808	4,987	1,582	454	212	27	2,951
1. Jammu District (including city).	3,362	1,137	77	176	3	2,148	2,173	693	184	136	13	1,296
2. Jasrota "	1,346	514	12	121	1	820	1,212	384	133	38	13	695
3. Udhampur "	440	225	14	27	...	201	399	128	54	11	1	217
4. Riasi "	437	152	2	42	...	283	231	68	20	14	...	143
5. Mirpur "	1,897	737	22	165	1	1,138	487	184	28	12	...	275
6. Bhadarwah *Jagir* ...	340	200	61	21	...	79	11	4	...	...	...	7
7. Punch *Ilaqa*	296	150	7	6	1	139	474	121	35	1	...	318
II—Total Kashmir Province (including *Jagirs*).	11,779	3,788	15	486	...	7,976	6,059	1,608	1,733	130	1	2,718
8. Kashmir North (including Langet *Jagir*).	3,625	1,101	6	172	...	2,518	1,753	537	329	17	...	887
9. Kashmir South (including city).	7,830	2,562	3	308	...	5,265	4,176	1,032	1,400	112	1	1,744
Total Kashmir Valley ...	*11,455*	*3,663*	*9*	*480*	...	*7,783*	*5,929*	*1,569*	*1,729*	*129*	*1*	*2,631*
10. Muzaffarabad District ...	324	125	6	6	...	193	130	39	4	1	...	87
III—Total Frontier Districts.	102	61	3	3	...	38	...	...	...	...	...	...
11. Laddakh District (including Mansar).	66	36	3	1	...	27	...	...	...	...	...	...
12. Gilgit "	36	25	...	2	...	11	...	...	...	...	...	...
13. Frontier *Ilaqas*	...	...	...	...	...	...	...	...	...	...	...	...
Cities.												
Jammu	500	238	...	7	...	262	53	7	3	...	...	43
Srinagar	3,825	1,299	...	15	...	2,526	494	109	223	...	...	162

DISTRICT, JAGIR, ILAQA OR CITY.	Order 9.—Metals.						Group (40).—Makers of arms, guns, etc.					
	Total workers and dependents.	Actual Workers. Total.		Partially Agriculturists.		Dependents.	Total workers and dependents.	Actual Workers. Total.		Partially Agriculturists.		Dependents.
		Males.	Females.	Males.	Females.			Males.	Females.	Males.	Females.	
	254	255	256	257	258	259	260	261	262	263	264	265
Total State	**13,104**	**4,675**	**163**	**819**	**6**	**8,266**	**20**	**11**	...	**1**	...	**9**
I—Total Jammu Province (including *Jagirs*).	6,192	2,247	109	574	1	3,836	7	3	...	1	...	4
1. Jammu District (including city).	2,640	940	31	200	...	1,669	...	...	...	...	...	...
2. Jasrota "	829	300	9	85	...	520	7	3	...	1	...	4
3. Udhampur "	555	196	8	64	1	351	...	...	...	...	...	...
4. Riasi "	444	194	5	70	...	245	...	...	...	...	...	...
5. Mirpur "	1,377	469	40	130	...	868	...	...	...	...	...	...
6. Bhadarwah *Jagir* ...	56	30	1	14	...	25	...	...	...	...	...	...
7. Punch *Ilaqa*	291	118	15	11	...	158	...	...	...	...	...	...
II—Total Kashmir Province (including *Jagirs*).	6,526	2,217	52	233	3	4,257	13	8	...	...	...	5
8. Kashmir North (including Langet *Jagir*).	1,350	427	4	60	...	919	...	...	...	...	...	...
9. Kashmir South (including city).	4,862	1,708	10	154	...	3,144	13	8	...	...	...	5
Total Kashmir Valley ...	*6,212*	*2,135*	*14*	*214*	...	*4,063*	*13*	*8*	...	...	...	*5*
10. Muzaffarabad District ...	314	82	38	19	3	194	...	...	...	...	...	...
III—Total Frontier Districts.	386	211	2	12	2	173	...	...	...	...	...	...
11. Laddakh District (including Mansar).	109	54	2	10	2	53	...	...	...	...	...	...
12. Gilgit "	29	12	...	2	...	17	...	...	...	...	...	...
13. Frontier *Ilaqas*	248	145	...	...	...	103	...	...	...	...	...	...
Cities.												
Jammu	410	184	...	9	...	226	...	...	...	...	...	...
Srinagar	2,546	964	4	1	...	1,584	13	8	...	...	...	5

TABLE XV-A.

Occupation or Means of Livelihood.

Jammu and Kashmir State Census 1911.

DISTRICT, JAGIR, ILAQA OR CITY.	*Group (41).—Other workers in iron and makers of implements and tools principally or exclusively of iron.*						*Group (42).—Workers in brass, copper and bell metal.*						*Group (43).—Workers in other metals (tin, zinc, lead, quicksilver, etc).*						*Group (44).—Workers in mints, die-sinkers, etc.*						Order 10—Ceramics.					
	Total workers and dependents.	Actual Workers. Total. Males.	Actual Workers. Total. Females.	Actual Workers. Partially Agriculturists. Males.	Actual Workers. Partially Agriculturists. Females.	Dependents.	Total workers and dependents.	Actual Workers. Total. Males.	Actual Workers. Total. Females.	Actual Workers. Partially Agriculturists. Males.	Actual Workers. Partially Agriculturists. Females.	Dependants.	Total workers and dependents.	Actual Workers. Total. Males.	Actual Workers. Total. Females.	Actual Workers. Partially Agriculturists. Males.	Actual Workers. Partially Agriculturists. Females.	Dependents.	Total workers and dependents.	Actual Workers. Total. Males.	Actual Workers. Total. Females.	Actual Workers. Partially Agriculturists. Males.	Actual Workers. Partially Agriculturists. Females.	Dependents.	Total workers and dependents.	Actual Workers. Total. Males.	Actual Workers. Total. Females.	Actual Workers. Partially Agriculturists. Males.	Actual Workers. Partially Agriculturists. Females.	Dependents.
	266	267	268	269	270	271	272	273	274	275	276	277	278	279	280	281	282	283	284	285	286	287	288	289	290	291	292	293	294	295
Total State ..	**12,041**	**4,262**	**116**	**815**	**3**	**7.663**	**312**	**103**	**7**	...	...	**202**	**188**	**80**	**2**	**2**	...	**106**	**543**	**219**	**38**	**1**	**3**	**286**	**14,201**	**4,825**	**1,620**	**725**	**24**	**7,756**
I—Total Jammu Province (including *Jagirs*).	5,970	2,164	102	572	1	3,704	164	57	7	...	...	100	43	16	...	1	...	27	8	7	...	...	...	1	6,345	2,279	439	300	12	3,627
1. Jammu District (including city).	2,481	878	31	199	...	1,572	114	40	...	...	...	74	37	15	...	1	...	22	8	7	...	...	...	1	1,982	703	115	56	...	1,164
2. Jasrota „	809	292	8	84	...	509	13	5	1	...	...	7	...	...	...	...	...	...	...	...	...	...	...	...	1,001	329	66	38	3	606
3. Udhampur „	549	195	8	64	1	346	...	...	...	...	...	...	...	...	...	...	...	...	...	...	...	...	...	...	680	266	89	65	8	325
4. Riasi „	444	194	5	70	...	245	...	...	...	...	...	...	...	...	...	...	...	...	...	...	...	...	...	...	281	103	23	25	...	155
5. Mirpur „	1,374	469	40	130	...	865	3	...	...	...	...	3	6	1	...	...	...	5	...	...	...	...	...	...	1,970	724	110	79	1	1,136
6. Bhadarwah *Jagir* ...	50	29	1	14	...	20	6	1	...	...	...	5	...	...	...	...	...	...	...	...	...	...	...	...	58	23	18	14	...	17
7. Punch *Ilaqa*	263	107	9	11	...	147	28	11	6	...	...	11	...	...	...	...	...	...	...	...	...	...	...	...	373	131	18	23	...	224
II—Total Kashmir Province (including *Jagirs*).	5,688	1,889	12	231	...	3,787	148	46	...	...	...	102	143	62	2	1	...	79	534	212	38	1	3	284	7,826	2,531	1,180	418	12	4,115
8. Kashmir North (including Langet *Jagir*).	1,266	405	2	59	...	859	27	9	...	...	...	18	36	13	...	1	...	23	21	...	2	...	...	19	2,532	800	430	114	9	1,302
9. Kashmir South (including city).	4,217	1,413	9	153	...	2,795	111	33	...	...	...	78	91	42	1	...	...	48	430	212	...	1	...	218	5,176	1,657	750	290	3	2,769
Total Kashmir Valley ...	*5,483*	*1,818*	*11*	*212*	...	*3,654*	*138*	*42*	...	...	...	*96*	*127*	*55*	*1*	*1*	...	*71*	*451*	*212*	*2*	*1*	...	*237*	*7,708*	*2,457*	*1,180*	*404*	*12*	*4,071*
10. Muzaffarabad District ...	205	71	1	19	...	133	10	4	...	...	...	6	16	7	1	...	...	8	83	...	36	...	3	47	118	74	...	14	...	44
III—Total Frontier Districts.	383	209	2	12	2	172	...	...	...	...	...	...	2	2	...	...	...	...	1	...	...	...	...	1	30	15	1	7	...	14
11. Laddakh District (including Mansar).	108	54	2	10	2	52	...	...	...	...	...	...	...	...	...	...	...	...	1	...	...	...	...	1	28	13	1	7	...	14
12. Gilgit „	27	10	...	2	...	17	...	...	...	...	...	...	2	2	...	...	...	...	...	...	...	...	...	...	2	2	...	...	...	...
13. Frontier *Ilaqas*	248	145	...	...	...	103	...	...	...	...	...	...	...	...	...	...	...	...	...	...	...	...	...	...	...	...	...	...	...	...
Cities.																														
Jammu	280	136	...	8	...	144	85	26	...	...	...	59	37	15	...	1	...	22	8	7	...	...	...	1	180	69	10	...	...	101
Srinagar	1,963	688	1	...	...	1,274	107	30	...	...	...	77	68	38	1	...	...	29	398	199	...	1	...	199	777	298	73	...	...	406

TABLE XV-A.

Occupation or Means of Livelihood.

Jammu and Kashmir State Census 1911.

District, Jagir, Ilaqa or City.	Group (47)—Potters and earthen pipe and bowl makers.						Group (48)—Brick and tile makers.					
	Total workers and dependents.	Actual Workers. Total. Males.	Actual Workers. Total. Females.	Actual Workers. Partially Agriculturists. Males.	Actual Workers. Partially Agriculturists. Females.	Dependents.	Total workers and dependents.	Actual Workers. Total. Males.	Actual Workers. Total. Females.	Actual Workers. Partially Agriculturists. Males.	Actual Workers. Partially Agriculturists. Females.	Dependents.
	296	297	298	299	300	301	302	303	304	305	306	307
Total State	**13,377**	**4,446**	**1,604**	**723**	**24**	**7,327**	**824**	**379**	**16**	**2**	...	**429**
I—Total Jammu Province (including *Jagirs*).	6,076	2,134	423	299	12	3,519	269	145	16	1	...	108
1. Jammu District (including city)	1,921	669	115	56	...	1,137	61	34	...	...	...	27
2. Jasrota ,, ...	941	307	64	38	3	570	60	22	2	...	...	36
3. Udhampur ,, ...	678	266	89	65	8	323	2	...	...	...	...	2
4. Riasi ,, ...	280	103	23	25	...	154	1	...	...	...	...	1
5. Mirpur ,, ...	1,828	638	96	78	1	1,094	142	26	14	1	...	42
6. Bhadarwah *Jagir* ...	58	23	18	14	...	17	...	...	...	...	...	...
7. Punch *Ilaqa*	370	128	18	23	...	224	3	3	...	...	...	...
II—Total Kashmir Province (including *Jagirs*).	7,273	2,299	1.180	417	12	3,794	553	232	...	1	...	321
8. Kashmir North (including Languet *Jagir*).	2,520	797	430	114	9	1,293	12	3	...	...	...	9
9. Kashmir South (including city).	4,651	1,440	750	289	3	2,461	525	217	...	1	...	308
Total Kashmir Valley ...	*7,171*	*2,237*	*1,180*	*403*	*12*	*3,754*	*537*	*220*	...	*1*	...	*317*
10. Muzaffarabad District ...	102	62	...	14	...	40	16	12	...	...	...	4
III—Total Frontier Districts.	28	13	1	7	...	14	2	2	...	...	...	...
11. Laddakh District (including Mansar).	28	13	1	7	...	14	...	...	...	...	...	...
12. Gilgit	...	...	...	...	...	...	2	2	...	...	...	...
13. Frontier *Ilaqas*	...	...	...	...	...	...	...	...	...	...	...	...
Cities.												
Jammu	149	53	10	...	...	86	31	16	...	...	...	15
Srinagar	411	156	73	...	...	182	422	167	...	...	...	255

District, Jagir, Ilaqa or City.	Order 11—Chemical products, properly so called and analogous.						Group (50)—Manufacture of matches and explosive materials.						Group (51)—Manufacture of ærated and mineral waters.					
	Total workers and dependents.	Actual Workers. Total. Males.	Actual Workers. Total. Females.	Actual Workers. Partially Agriculturists. Males.	Actual Workers. Partially Agriculturists. Females.	Dependents.	Total workers and dependents.	Actual Workers. Total. Males.	Actual Workers. Total. Females.	Actual Workers. Partially Agriculturists. Males.	Actual Workers. Partially Agriculturists. Females.	Dependents.	Total workers and dependents.	Actual Workers. Total. Males.	Actual Workers. Total. Females.	Actual Workers. Partially Agriculturists. Males.	Actual Workers. Partially Agriculturists. Females.	Dependents.
	308	309	310	311	312	313	314	315	316	317	318	319	320	321	322	323	324	325
Total State	**13,044**	**4,303**	**572**	**656**	**20**	**8,169**	**274**	**91**	**2**	**3**	...	**181**	**64**	**19**	...	...	...	**45**
I—Total Jammu Province (including *Jagirs*).	4,725	1,545	415	234	14	2,765	244	84	1	3	...	159	35	6	...	...	...	29
1. Jammu District (including city)	2,117	650	190	90	9	1,277	113	40	...	...	...	73	13	2	...	...	...	11
2. Jasrota ,, ...	593	193	42	30	2	358	11	5	...	...	...	6	5	...	...	...	...	5
3. Udhampur ,, ...	486	183	67	32	1	186	...	...	...	...	...	...	...	...	...	...	...	...
4. Riasi ,, ...	258	109	21	35	2	128	2	2	...	...	...	...	...	...	...	...	...	...
5. Mirpur ,, ...	1,138	359	70	45	...	709	118	37	1	3	...	80	17	4	...	...	...	13
6. Bhadarwah *Jagir* ...	4	3	...	...	...	1	...	...	...	...	...	...	...	...	...	...	...	...
7. Punch *Ilaqa*	179	48	25	2	...	106	...	...	...	...	...	...	...	...	...	...	...	...
II—Total Kashmir Province (including *Jagirs*).	8,319	2,758	157	422	6	5,404	30	7	1	...	...	22	29	13	...	...	...	16
8. Kashmir North (including Languet *Jagir*).	2,274	759	34	110	1	1,481	5	1	1	...	...	3	29	13	...	...	...	16
9. Kashmir South (including city).	5,854	1,942	119	301	4	3,793	25	6	...	...	...	19	...	...	...	...	...	...
Total Kashmir Valley ...	*8,128*	*2,701*	*153*	*411*	*5*	*5,274*	*30*	*7*	*1*	...	...	*22*	*29*	*13*	...	...	...	*16*
10. Muzaffarabad District ...	191	57	4	11	1	130	...	...	...	...	...	...	...	...	...	...	...	...
III—Total Frontier Districts.	...	...	...	...	...	...	...	...	...	...	...	...	...	...	...	...	...	...
11. Laddakh District (including Mansar).	...	...	...	...	...	...	...	...	...	...	...	...	...	...	...	...	...	...
12. Gilgit	...	...	...	...	...	...	...	...	...	...	...	...	...	...	...	...	...	...
13. Frontier *Ilaqas*	...	...	...	...	...	...	...	...	...	...	...	...	...	...	...	...	...	...
Cities.																		
Jammu	249	113	...	...	...	136	90	33	...	...	...	57	13	2	...	...	...	11
Srinagar	1,203	462	29	...	...	712	5	1	...	...	...	4	...	...	...	...	...	...

TABLE XV-A.

Occupation or Means of Livelihood.

Jammu and Kashmir State Census 1911.

District, Jhgir, Ilaqa or City.	Group (52).—Manufacture of dyes, paint and ink.						Group (53).—Manufacture and refining of vegetable and mineral oil.					
	Total workers and dependents.	Actual Workers. Total.		Partially Agriculturists.		Dependents.	Total workers and dependents.	Actual Workers. Total.		Partially Agriculturists.		Dependents.
		Males.	Females.	Males.	Females.			Males.	Females.	Males.	Females.	
	326	327	328	329	330	331	332	333	334	335	336	337
Total State ...	**136**	**65**	...	**3**	...	**71**	**11,309**	**3,651**	**567**	**643**	**20**	**7,091**
I—Total Jammu Province (including *Jagirs*).	20	15	...	...	...	5	4,239	1,358	414	231	14	2,467
1. Jammu District (including city).	17	15	...	...	...	2	1,837	523	190	90	9	1,124
2. Jasrota "	...	...	...	...	...	...	575	186	42	30	2	347
3. Udhampur "	...	...	...	...	...	...	436	183	67	32	1	186
4. Riasi "	...	...	...	...	...	...	256	107	21	35	2	128
5. Mirpur "	3	...	...	...	...	3	975	311	69	42	...	595
6. Bhadarwah *Jagir* ...	...	...	...	...	...	...	4	3	...	...	...	1
7. Punch *Ilaqa*	...	...	...	...	...	...	156	45	25	2	...	86
II—Total Kashmir Province (including *Jagirs*).	116	50	...	3	...	66	7,070	2,293	153	412	6	4,624
8. Kashmir North (including Langet *Jagir*).	19	10	...	3	...	9	2,151	709	30	106	1	1,412
9. Kashmir South (including city).	97	40	...	...	...	57	4,728	1,527	119	295	4	3,082
Total Kashmir Valley ...	*116*	*50*	...	*3*	...	*66*	*6,879*	*2,236*	*149*	*401*	*5*	*4,494*
10. Muzaffarabad District ...	...	...	...	...	...	...	191	57	4	11	1	130
III—Total Frontier Districts.	...	...	...	...	...	...	...	...	...	...	...	...
11. Laddakh District (including Mansar).	...	...	...	...	...	...	...	...	...	...	...	...
12. Gilgit "	...	...	...	...	...	...	...	...	...	...	...	...
13. Frontier *Ilaqas*	...	...	...	...	...	...	...	...	...	...	...	...
Cities.												
Jammu	17	15	...	...	...	2	15	1	...	...	...	14
Srinagar	85	36	...	...	...	49	461	169	29	...	...	263

District, Jhgir, Ilaqa or City.	Group (54).—Manufacture of paper, card-board and papier mache.						Group (55).—Others (Soap, candles, lac, cutch, perfumes and miscellaneous drugs).					
	Total workers and dependents.	Actual Workers. Total.		Partially Agriculturists.		Dependents.	Total workers and dependents.	Actual Workers. Total.		Partially Agriculturists.		Dependents.
		Males.	Females.	Males.	Females.			Males.	Females.	Males.	Females.	
	338	339	340	341	342	343	344	345	346	347	348	349
Total State ...	**279**	**92**	...	...	...	**187**	**982**	**385**	**3**	**7**	...	**594**
I—Total Jammu Province (including *Jagirs*).	...	...	...	...	...	...	187	82	...	...	...	105
1. Jammu District (including city).	...	...	...	...	...	...	137	70	...	...	...	67
2. Jasrota "	...	...	...	...	...	...	2	2	...	...	...	...
3. Udhampur "	...	...	...	...	...	...	...	...	...	...	...	...
4. Riasi "	...	...	...	...	...	...	...	...	...	...	...	...
5. Mirpur "	...	...	...	...	...	...	25	7	...	...	...	18
6. Bhadarwah *Jagir* ...	...	...	...	...	...	...	...	...	...	...	...	...
7. Punch *Ilaqa*	...	...	...	...	...	...	23	3	...	...	...	20
II—Total Kashmir Province (including *Jagirs*).	279	92	...	...	...	187	795	303	3	7	...	489
8. Kashmir North (including Langet *Jagir*).	...	...	...	...	...	...	70	26	3	1	...	41
9. Kashmir South (including city).	279	92	...	...	...	187	725	277	...	6	...	448
Total Kashmir Valley ...	*279*	*92*	...	...	...	*187*	*795*	*303*	*3*	*7*	...	*489*
10. Muzaffarabad District ...	...	...	...	...	...	...	...	...	...	...	...	...
III—Total Frontier Districts.	...	...	...	...	...	...	...	...	...	...	...	...
11. Laddakh District (including Mansar).	...	...	...	...	...	...	...	...	...	...	...	...
12. Gilgit "	...	...	...	...	...	...	...	...	...	...	...	...
13. Frontier *Ilaqas*	...	...	...	...	...	...	...	...	...	...	...	...
Cities.												
Jammu	...	...	...	...	...	...	116	62	...	...	...	54
Srinagar	35	14	...	...	...	21	621	244	...	...	...	377

District, Jhgir, Ilaqa or City.	Order 12.—Food Industries.					
	Total workers and dependents.	Actual Workers. Total		Partially Agriculturists.		Dependents.
		Males.	Females.	Males.	Females.	
	350	351	352	353	354	355
Total State ...	**20,858**	**7,412**	**2,352**	**322**	**34**	**11,094**
I—Total Jammu Province (including *Jagirs*).	10,476	3,880	1,430	207	34	5,166
1. Jammu District (including city).	4,473	1,721	509	45	12	2,243
2. Jasrota "	1,866	594	396	18	10	876
3. Udhampur "	883	472	67	40	2	344
4. Riasi "	744	333	80	24	5	331
5. Mirpur "	1,779	486	311	55	4	982
6. Bhadarwah *Jagir* ...	133	64	13	20	1	54
7. Punch *Ilaqa*	598	210	54	5	...	334
II—Total Kashmir Province (including *Jagirs*).	10,263	3,471	919	108	...	5,242
8. Kashmir North (including Langet *Jagir*).	2,090	682	216	17	...	1,192
9. Kashmir South (including city).	7,708	2,617	684	79	...	4,407
Total Kashmir Valley ...	*9,798*	*3,299*	*900*	*96*	...	*5,599*
10. Muzaffarabad District ...	463	172	19	12	...	272
III—Total Frontier Districts.	121	61	3	7	...	57
11. Laddakh District (including Mansar).	89	37	2	4	...	50
12. Gilgit "	15	12	1	3	...	2
13. Frontier *Ilaqas*	17	12	...	...	...	5
Cities.						
Jammu	1,906	819	66	2	469	1,021
Srinagar	4,099	1,415	322	1	162	2,362

TABLE XV-A.

Occupation or Means of Livelihood.

Jammu and Kashmir State Census 1911.

DISTRICT, JAGIR, ILAQA OR CITY.	Group (56).—*Rice pounders and huskers and flour grinders.* Total workers and dependents.	Actual Workers. Total. Males.	Actual Workers. Total. Females.	Actual Workers. Partially Agriculturists. Males.	Actual Workers. Partially Agriculturists. Females.	Dependents.	Group (57)—*Bakers and biscuit makers.* Total workers and dependents.	Total Workers. Total. Males.	Total Workers. Total. Females.	Total Workers. Partially Agriculturists. Males.	Total Workers. Partially Agriculturists. Females.	Dependents.
	356	357	358	359	360	361	362	363	364	365	366	367
Total State	**8,736**	**3,238**	**1,475**	**203**	**33**	**4,023**	**5,638**	**1,977**	**808**	**36**	...	**2,853**
I—Total Jammu Province (including *Jagirs*).	7,618	2,817	1,351	165	33	3,450	620	276	27	8	...	317
1. Jammu District (including city).	3,095	1,216	478	38	12	1,401	380	183	6	1	...	191
2. Jasrota "	1,557	470	393	14	10	694	11	5	...	...	...	6
3. Udhampur "	669	384	59	38	2	226	24	7	3	...	...	14
4. Riasi "	593	265	78	21	4	250	23	8	1	...	...	14
5. Mirpur "	1,289	329	280	47	4	680	57	17	14	...	...	26
6. Bhadarwah *Jagir* ...	63	36	10	4	1	17	25	9	3	5	...	13
7. Punch *Ilaqa*	352	117	53	3	...	182	100	47	...	2	...	53
II—Total Kashmir Province (including *Jagirs*).	1,100	411	122	36	...	567	4,981	1,683	780	27	...	2,518
8. Kashmir North (including Langet *Jagir*).	158	67	13	2	...	78	1,240	407	196	7	...	637
9. Kashmir South (including city).	900	326	108	32	...	466	3,553	1,205	567	17	...	1,781
Total Kashmir Valley ...	*1,058*	*393*	*121*	*34*	...	*544*	*4,793*	*1,612*	*763*	*24*	...	*2,418*
10. Muzaffarabad District ...	42	18	1	2	...	23	188	71	17	3	...	100
III—Total Frontier Districts.	18	10	2	2	...	6	37	18	1	1	...	18
11. Laddakh District (including Mansar).	13	7	1	2	...	5	21	8	1	1	...	12
12. Gilgit "	5	3	1	...	...	1	2	1	...	...	...	1
13. Frontier *Ilaqas*	...	...	...	...	...	...	14	9	...	...	...	5
Cities.												
Jammu	965	447	49	1	469	469	332	160	4	...	...	168
Srinagar	337	120	55	...	162	162	1,561	557	261	...	...	743

DISTRICT, JAGIR, ILAQA OR CITY.	Group (58).—*Grain parchers, etc.* Total workers and dependents.	Actual Workers. Total. Males.	Actual Workers. Total. Females.	Actual Workers. Partially Agriculturists. Males.	Actual Workers. Partially Agriculturists. Females.	Dependents.	Group (59).—*Butchers.* Total workers and dependents.	Actual Workers. Total. Males.	Actual Workers. Total. Females.	Actual Workers. Partially Agriculturists. Males.	Actual Workers. Partially Agriculturists. Females.	Dependents.
	368	369	370	371	372	373	374	375	376	377	378	379
Total State	**123**	**39**	**26**	**2**	...	**58**	**4,081**	**1,322**	**24**	**58**	...	**2,735**
I—Total Jammu Province (including *Jagirs*).	77	17	26	2	...	34	893	291	20	18	...	582
1. Jammu District (including city).	21	7	11	...	...	3	352	113	10	2	...	229
2. Jasrota "	21	3	3	...	...	15	118	39	...	2	...	79
3. Udhampur "	4	1	...	...	...	3	69	26	5	1	...	38
4. Riasi "	11	5	...	1	...	6	30	11	...	...	...	19
5. Mirpur "	20	1	12	1	...	7	165	49	4	3	...	112
6. Bhadarwah *Jagir* ...	...	...	...	...	...	...	39	16	...	10	...	23
7. Punch *Ilaqa*	...	...	...	...	...	...	120	37	1	...	...	82
II—Total Kashmir Province (including *Jagirs*).	45	21	...	...	...	24	3,133	1,009	4	39	...	2,120
8. Kashmir North (including Langet *Jagir*).	...	...	...	...	...	...	594	192	1	7	...	401
9. Kashmir South (including city).	32	18	...	...	...	14	2,397	771	3	29	...	1,623
Total Kashmir Valley ...	*32*	*18*	...	...	...	*14*	*2,991*	*963*	*4*	*36*	...	*2,024*
10. Muzaffarabad District ...	13	3	...	...	...	10	142	46	...	3	...	96
III—Total Frontier Districts.	1	1	...	...	...	...	55	22	...	1	...	33
11. Laddakh District (including Mansar).	...	...	...	...	...	...	55	22	...	1	...	33
12. Gilgit "	1	1	...	...	...	...	...	...	...	...	...	...
13. Frontier *Ilaqas*	...	...	...	...	...	...	...	...	...	...	...	...
Cities.												
Jammu	9	2	4	...	...	3	241	76	9	...	...	156
Srinagar	32	18	...	...	...	14	1,494	477	...	...	...	1,017

DISTRICT, JAGIR, ILAQA OR CITY.	Group (62).—*Makers of sugar, molasses and gur.* Total workers and dependents.	Actual Workers. Total. Males.	Actual Workers. Total. Females.	Actual Workers. Partially Agriculturists. Males.	Actual Workers. Partially Agriculturists. Females.	Dependents.
	380	381	382	383	384	385
Total State	**19**	**2**	...	..	...	**17**
I—Total Jammu Province (including *Jagirs*).	19	2	...	...	...	17
1. Jammu District (including city).	...	...	...	...	...	...
2. Jasrota "	19	2	...	...	...	17
3. Udhampur "	...	...	...	...	...	...
4. Riasi "	...	...	...	...	...	...
5. Mirpur "	...	...	...	...	...	...
6. Bhadarwah *Jagir* ...	...	...	...	...	...	...
7. Punch *Ilaqa*	...	...	...	...	...	...
II—Total Kashmir Province (including *Jagirs*).	...	...	...	...	...	...
8. Kashmir North (including Langet *Jagir*).	...	...	...	...	...	...
9. Kashmir South (including city).	...	...	...	...	...	...
Total Kashmir Valley ...	...	...	...	...	...	...
10. Muzaffarabad District ...	...	...	...	...	...	...
III—Total Frontier Districts.	...	...	...	...	...	...
11. Laddakh District (including Mansar).	...	...	...	...	...	...
12. Gilgit "	...	...	...	...	...	...
13. Frontier *Ilaqas*	...	...	...	...	...	...
Cities.						
Jammu	...	...	...	...	...	...
Srinagar	...	...	...	...	...	...

TABLE XV-A.

Occupation or Means of Livelihood.

Jammu and Kashmir State Census 1911.

DISTRICT, JAGIR, ILAQA OR CITY.	Group (63).—Sweetmeat makers, preparers of jam and condiments, etc.						Group (64).—Brewers and distillers.					
	Total workers and dependents.	Actual Workers. Total. Males.	Actual Workers. Total. Females.	Actual Workers. Partially Agriculturists. Males.	Actual Workers. Partially Agriculturists. Females.	Dependents.	Total workers and dependents.	Actual Workers. Total. Males.	Actual Workers. Total. Females.	Actual Workers. Partially Agriculturists. Males.	Actual Workers. Partially Agriculturists. Females.	Dependents.
	386	387	388	389	390	391	392	393	394	395	396	397
Total State ...	**2,246**	**826**	**19**	**22**	**1**	**1,401**	**15**	**8**	...	**1**	...	**7**
I—Total Jammu Province (including *Jagirs*).	1,246	475	6	13	1	765	3	2	...	1	...	1
1. Jammu District (including city).	625	202	4	4	...	419	...	...	...	...	...	...
2. Jasrota "	140	75	...	2	...	65	...	...	...	...	...	...
3. Udhampur "	117	54	...	1	...	63	...	...	...	...	...	...
4. Riasi "	87	44	1	2	1	42	...	...	...	...	...	...
5. Mirpur "	248	90	1	4	...	157	...	...	...	...	...	...
6. Bhadarwah *Jagir* ...	3	1	...	...	...	2	3	2	...	1	...	1
7. Punch *Ilaqa*	26	9	...	...	...	17	...	...	...	...	...	...
II—Total Kashmir Province (including *Jagirs*).	943	344	13	6	...	636	9	3	...	...	...	6
8. Kashmir North (including Langet *Jagir*).	98	16	6	1	...	76	...	...	...	...	...	...
9. Kashmir South (including city).	817	294	6	1	...	517	9	3	...	...	...	6
Total Kashmir Valley ...	*915*	*310*	*12*	*2*	...	*593*	*9*	*3*	...	...	...	*6*
10. Muzaffarabad District ...	78	34	1	4	...	43	...	...	...	...	...	...
III—Total Frontier Districts.	7	7	...	3	...	...	3	3	...	...	...	...
11. Laddakh District (including Mansar).	...	...	...	...	...	...	...	...	...	...	...	...
12. Gilgit "	7	7	...	3	...	...	...	...	...	...	...	...
13. Frontier *Ilaqas*	...	...	...	...	...	...	3	3	...	...	...	...
Cities.												
Jammu	359	134	...	1	...	225	...	...	...	...	...	...
Srinagar	666	240	6	1	...	420	9	3	...	...	...	6

DISTRICT, JAGIR, ILAQA OR CITY.	Order 13.—Industries of dress and the toilet.						Group (67).—Hat, cap and turban makers.						Group (68).—Tailors, milliners, dress-makers and darners, embroiderers on linen.					
	Total workers and dependents.	Actual Workers. Total. Males.	Actual Workers. Total. Females.	Actual Workers. Partially Agriculturists. Males.	Actual Workers. Partially Agriculturists. Females.	Dependents.	Total workers and dependents.	Actual Workers. Total. Males.	Actual Workers. Total. Females.	Actual Workers. Partially Agriculturists. Males.	Actual Workers. Partially Agriculturists. Females.	Dependents.	Total workers and dependents.	Actual Workers. Total. Males.	Actual Workers. Total. Females.	Actual Workers. Partially Agriculturists. Males.	Actual Workers. Partially Agriculturists. Females.	Dependents.
	398	399	400	401	402	403	404	405	406	407	408	409	410	411	412	413	414	415
Total State ...	**66,985**	**25,138**	**3,116**	**3,056**	**83**	**38,731**	**11**	**8**	**1**	**4**	...	**2**	**21,580**	**8.663**	**626**	**477**	**12**	**12.291**
I—Total Jammu Province (including *Jagirs*).	32,086	11,982	2,386	2,194	75	17,718	6	3	1	...	...	2	5,272	2,102	595	302	11	2,575
1. Jammu District (including city).	13,536	5,386	928	978	23	7,222	2	...	1	...	...	1	2,403	1,102	194	164	2	1,107
2. Jasrota "	4,218	1,584	264	356	10	2,370	...	...	...	...	...	...	327	93	53	6	...	181
3. Udhampur "	2,441	870	361	213	22	1,210	3	2	...	...	...	1	441	153	69	22	4	219
4. Riasi "	1,301	502	99	98	5	700	...	...	...	...	...	...	249	88	16	6	...	145
5. Mirpur "	8,459	2,831	615	450	9	5,013	...	...	...	...	...	...	1,348	439	242	75	3	667
6. Bhadarwah *Jagir* ...	498	183	60	53	6	255	...	...	...	...	...	...	126	58	8	19	2	60
7. Punch *Ilaqa*	1,633	626	59	46	...	948	1	1	...	...	...	...	378	169	13	10	...	196
II—Total Kashmir Province (including *Jagirs*).	34,689	13,043	721	857	8	20,925	5	5	...	4	...	...	16,221	6,512	29	173	1	9,680
8. Kashmir North (including Langet *Jagir*).	7,057	2,393	279	242	7	4,385	...	...	...	...	...	...	2,189	872	8	29	1	1,309
9. Kashmir South (including city).	26,587	10,280	415	553	1	15,892	5	5	...	4	...	...	13,674	5,500	9	132	...	8,165
Total Kashmir Valley ...	*33,644*	*12,673*	*694*	*795*	*8*	*20,277*	*5*	*5*	...	*4*	...	...	*15,863*	*6,372*	*17*	*161*	*1*	*9,474*
10. Muzaffarabad District ...	1,045	370	27	62	...	648	...	...	...	...	...	...	358	140	12	12	...	206
III—Total Frontier Districts.	210	113	9	5	...	88	...	...	...	...	...	...	87	49	2	2	...	36
11. Laddakh District (including Mansar).	126	56	8	2	...	62	...	...	...	...	...	...	62	30	2	1	...	30
12. Gilgit "	64	44	1	3	...	19	...	...	...	...	...	...	16	13	...	1	...	3
13. Frontier *Ilaqas*	20	13	...	...	...	7	...	...	...	...	...	...	9	6	...	...	...	3
Cities.																		
Jammu	2,104	938	155	2	...	1,011	...	...	...	...	...	...	877	410	57	2	...	410
Srinagar	13,129	5,466	213	10	...	7,450	...	...	...	...	...	...	9,831	4,275	1	10	...	5,555

TABLE XV-A.

Occupation or Means of Livelihood.

Jammu and Kashmir State Census 1911.

DISTRICT, JAGIR, ILAQA OR CITY.	Group (69).—Shoe, boot and sandal makers.						Group (70).—Other industries pertaining to dress, gloves, socks, gaiters, belts, buttons, umbrellas, canes, etc.					
	Total workers and dependents.	Actual Workers. Total.		Actual Workers. Partially Agriculturists.		Dependents.	Total workers and dependents.	Actual Workers. Total.		Actual Workers. Partially Agriculturists.		Dependents.
		Males.	Females.	Males.	Females.			Males.	Females.	Males.	Females.	
	416	417	418	419	420	421	422	423	424	425	426	427
Total State	**27,318**	**9,875**	**1,540**	**1,580**	**55**	**15,903**	**151**	**78**	**6**	**2**	...	**67**
I—Total Jammu Province (including *Jagirs*).	17,943	6,417	1,377	1,330	54	10,149	50	29	...	1	...	21
1. Jammu District (including city).	7,479	2,704	485	596	20	4,290	12	7	...	1	...	5
2. Jasrota ,, ...	2,125	847	162	260	5	1,116	...	...	...	...	...	...
3. Udhampur ,, ...	1,589	526	277	149	16	786	6	2	...	...	...	4
4. Riasi ,, ...	697	272	79	66	4	346	1	1	...	...	...	...
5. Mirpur ,, ...	4,935	1,687	288	222	5	2,960	30	18	...	...	...	12
6. Bhadarwah *Jagir* ...	328	98	51	18	4	179	...	...	...	...	...	...
7. Punch *Ilaqa*	790	283	35	19	...	472	1	1	...	...	...	...
II—Total Kashmir Province (including *Jagirs*).	9,351	3,444	163	249	1	5,744	93	43	6	...	...	44
8. Kashmir North (including Langet *Jagir*).	2,212	640	130	59	1	1,442	...	...	...	...	...	...
9. Kashmir South (including city).	6,733	2,671	22	165	...	4,040	93	43	6	...	...	64
Total Kashmir Valley ...	*8,945*	*3,311*	*152*	*224*	*1*	*5,482*	*93*	*43*	*6*	...	...	*44*
10. Muzaffarabad District ...	406	133	11	25	...	262	...	...	...	...	...	...
III—Total Frontier Districts.	24	14	...	1	...	10	8	6	...	1	...	2
11. Laddakh District (including Mansar).	...	...	...	...	...	...	8	6	...	1	...	2
12. Gilgit ,, ...	13	7	...	1	...	6	...	...	...	...	...	...
13. Frontier *Ilaqas*	11	7	...	...	...	4	...	...	...	...	...	...
Cities.												
Jammu ...	699	349	68	...	...	282	7	4	...	...	...	3
Srinagar ...	1,222	392	7	...	...	823	93	43	6	...	...	44

DISTRICT, JAGIR, ILAQA OR CITY.	Group (71).—Washing, cleaning and dyeing.						Group (72).—Barbers, hair-dressers and wig makers.					
	Total workers and dependents.	Actual Workers. Total.		Actual Workers. Partially Agriculturists.		Dependents.	Total workers and dependents.	Actual Workers. Total.		Actual Workers. Partially Agriculturists.		Dependents.
		Males.	Females.	Males.	Females.			Males.	Females.	Males.	Females.	
	428	429	430	431	432	433	434	435	436	437	438	439
Total State	**5,198**	**1,816**	**735**	**136**	**9**	**2,647**	**12,727**	**4,698**	**208**	**857**	**7**	**7,821**
I—Total Jammu Province (including *Jagirs*).	2,982	1,048	216	93	3	1,718	5,833	2,383	197	468	7	3,253
1. Jammu District (including city).	1,593	536	134	55	...	923	2,047	1,037	114	162	1	896
2. Jasrota ,, ...	664	241	30	7	3	393	1,102	403	19	83	2	680
3. Udhampur ,, ...	81	40	8	5	...	33	321	147	7	37	2	167
4. Riasi ,, ...	84	39	2	6	...	43	270	102	2	20	1	166
5. Mirpur ,, ...	457	158	35	13	...	264	1,689	529	50	140	1	1,110
6. Bhadarwah *Jagir* ...	18	10	1	7	...	7	26	17	...	9	...	9
7. Punch *Ilaqa*	85	24	6	...	...	55	378	148	5	17	...	225
II—Total Kashmir Province (including *Jagirs*).	2,166	740	513	43	6	913	6,853	2,299	10	388	...	4,544
8. Kashmir North (including Langet *Jagir*).	614	195	134	18	5	285	2,042	686	7	136	...	1,349
9. Kashmir South (including city).	1,523	534	376	22	1	613	4,559	1,527	2	230	...	3,030
Total Kashmir Valley ...	*2,137*	*729*	*510*	*40*	*6*	*898*	*6,601*	*2,213*	*9*	*366*	...	*4,379*
10. Muzaffarabad District ...	29	11	3	3	...	15	252	86	1	22	...	165
III—Total Frontier Districts.	50	28	6	...	...	16	41	16	1	1	...	24
11. Laddakh District (including Mansar).	33	14	5	...	...	14	23	6	1	1	...	16
12. Gilgit ,, ...	17	14	1	...	...	2	18	10	...	...	...	8
13. Frontier *Ilaqas*	...	...	...	...	...	...	...	...	...	...	...	...
Cities.												
Jammu ...	228	71	26	...	...	131	320	118	4	...	...	198
Srinagar ...	831	309	202	...	...	320	1,155	447	...	...	...	708

TABLE XV-A.

Occupation or Means of Livelihood.

Jammu and Kashmir State Census, 1911.

DISTRICT, JAGIR, ILAQA OR CITY.	Order 15.—Building industries.						*Group (76).—Lime burners, cement workers.*					
	Total workers and dependents.	Actual Workers. Total. Males.	Actual Workers. Total. Females.	Actual Workers. Partially Agriculturists. Males.	Actual Workers. Partially Agriculturists. Females.	Dependents.	Total workers and dependents.	Actual Workers. Total. Males.	Actual Workers. Total. Females.	Actual Workers. Partially Agriculturists. Males.	Actual Workers. Partially Agriculturists. Females.	Dependents.
	440	441	442	443	444	445	446	447	448	449	450	451
Total State ...	**7,953**	**2,878**	**227**	**146**	**17**	**4,848**	**114**	**26**	**2**	**2**	...	**86**
I—Total Jammu Province (including *Jagirs*).	2,232	882	118	122	17	1,232	5	3	...	...	...	2
1. Jammu District (including city).	1,554	657	59	75	17	838	3	2	...	...	...	1
2. Jasrota "	467	145	41	37	...	281	...	...	...	...	...	...
3. Udhampur "	80	37	6	6	...	37	...	...	...	...	...	...
4. Riasi "	1	1	...	...	...	...	...	...	...	...	...	...
5. Mirpur "	70	21	3	3	...	46	2	1	...	...	...	1
6. Bhadarwah *Jagir* ...	3	...	...	...	...	3	...	...	...	...	...	...
7. Punch *Ilaqa*	57	21	9	1	...	27	...	...	...	...	...	...
II—Total Kashmir Province (including *Jagirs*).	5,704	1,985	109	24	...	3,610	109	23	2	2	...	84
8. Kashmir North (including Langet *Jagir*).	396	123	7	5	...	266	...	...	...	...	...	...
9. Kashmir South (including city).	5,298	1,855	102	19	...	3,341	109	23	2	2	...	84
Total Kashmir Valley ...	*5,694*	*1,978*	*109*	*24*	...	*2,607*	*109*	*23*	*2*	*2*	...	*84*
10. Muzaffarabad District ...	10	7	...	...	...	3	...	...	...	...	...	...
III—Total Frontier Districts.	17	11	...	...	...	6	...	...	...	...	...	...
11. Laddakh District (including Mansar).	...	...	...	...	...	...	...	...	...	...	...	...
12. Gilgit "	7	5	...	...	...	2	...	...	...	...	...	...
13. Frontier *Ilaqas* ...	10	6	...	...	...	4	...	...	...	...	...	...
Cities.												
Jammu	60	31	...	...	...	29	...	...	...	...	...	...
Srinagar	4,469	1,548	92	6	...	2,829	...	...	...	...	...	...

DISTRICT, JAGIR, ILAQA OR CITY.	*Group (77).—Excavators, plinth builders and well sinkers.*						*Group (79).—Others (thatchers, building contractors, house painters, tilers, plumbers, locksmiths, etc.).*						Order 16.—Construction of means of transport.					
	Total workers and dependents.	Actual Workers. Total. Males.	Actual Workers. Total. Females.	Actual Workers. Partially Agriculturists. Males.	Actual Workers. Partially Agriculturists. Females.	Dependents.	Total workers and dependents.	Actual Workers. Total. Males.	Actual Workers. Total. Females.	Actual Workers. Partially Agriculturists. Males.	Actual Workers. Partially Agriculturists. Females.	Dependants.	Total workers and dependents.	Actual Workers. Total. Males.	Actual Workers. Total. Females.	Actual Workers. Partially Agriculturists. Males.	Actual Workers. Partially Agriculturists. Females.	Dependents.
	452	453	454	455	456	457	458	459	460	461	462	463	464	465	466	467	468	469
Total State ...	**5,079**	**1,969**	**210**	**132**	**17**	**2,900**	**2,760**	**883**	**15**	**12**	...	**1,862**	**256**	**119**	**9**	...	...	**128**
I—Total Jammu Province (including *Jagirs*).	2,045	810	108	119	17	1,127	182	69	10	3	...	103	114	31	9	...	...	74
1. Jammu District (including city).	1,477	615	59	75	17	803	74	40	...	...	...	34	60	24	...	...	...	36
2. Jasrota "	435	136	34	37	...	265	32	9	7	...	...	16	...	...	...	...	...	...
3. Udhampur "	66	34	4	6	...	28	14	3	2	...	...	9	27	...	5	...	...	22
4. Riasi "	...	...	...	...	...	...	1	1	...	...	...	...	1	1	...	...	...	...
5. Mirpur "	23	8	2	...	...	13	45	12	1	3	...	32	26	6	4	...	...	16
6. Bhadarwah *Jagir* ...	3	...	...	...	...	3	...	...	...	...	...	...	...	...	...	...	...	...
7. Punch *Ilaqa*	41	17	9	1	...	15	16	4	...	...	...	12	...	...	...	...	...	...
II—Total Kashmir Province (including *Jagirs*).	3,033	1,158	102	13	...	1,773	2,562	804	5	9	...	1,753	141	87	...	...	...	54
8. Kashmir North (including Langet *Jagir*).	286	79	7	...	...	200	110	44	...	5	...	66	3	...	...	...	...	3
9. Kashmir South (including city).	2,747	1,079	95	13	...	1,573	2,442	753	5	4	...	1,684	137	86	...	...	...	51
Total Kashmir Valley ...	*3,033*	*1,158*	*102*	*13*	...	*1,773*	*2,552*	*797*	*5*	*9*	...	*1,750*	*140*	*86*	...	...	...	*54*
10. Muzaffarabad District ...	...	...	...	...	...	...	10	7	...	...	...	3	1	1	...	...	...	...
III—Total Frontier Districts.	1	1	...	...	...	...	16	10	...	...	...	6	1	1	...	...	...	...
11. Laddakh District (including Mansar).	...	...	...	...	...	...	...	...	...	...	...	...	...	...	...	...	...	...
12. Gilgit "	1	1	...	...	...	...	6	4	...	...	...	2	1	1	...	...	...	...
13. Frontier *Ilaqas* ...	...	...	...	...	...	...	10	6	...	...	...	4	...	...	...	...	...	...
Cities.																		
Jammu	...	...	...	...	...	...	60	31	...	...	...	29	60	24	...	...	...	36
Srinagar	2,258	870	90	4	...	1,298	2,211	678	2	2	...	1,531	131	84	...	...	...	47

TABLE XV-A.

Occupation or Means of Livelihood.

Jammu and Kashmir State Census, 1911.

DISTRICT, JAGIR, ILAQA OR CITY.	Group (81).—Saddlers, harness makers, whip and lash makers.						Order 17.—Production and transmission of physical forces (heat, light, electricity, motive power, etc.).						Group (83).—Gas workers, electric light and ice factories.						Order 18.—Industries of luxury and those pertaining to literature and the arts and sciences.						Group (86).—Book-binders and stitchers, envelope makers, etc.					
	Total workers and dependents.	Actual Workers. Total. Males.	Actual Workers. Total. Females.	Actual Workers. Partially Agriculturists. Males.	Actual Workers. Partially Agriculturists. Females.	Dependents.	Total workers and dependents.	Actual Workers. Total. Males.	Actual Workers. Total. Females.	Actual Workers. Partially Agriculturists. Males.	Actual Workers. Partially Agriculturists. Females.	Dependents.	Total workers and dependents.	Actual Workers. Total. Males.	Actual Workers. Total. Females.	Actual Workers. Partially Agriculturists. Males.	Actual Workers. Partially Agriculturists. Females.	Dependents.	Total workers and dependents.	Actual Workers. Total. Males.	Actual Workers. Total. Females.	Actual Workers. Partially Agriculturists. Males.	Actual Workers. Partially Agriculturists. Females.	Dependents.	Total workers and dependents.	Actual Workers. Total. Males.	Actual Workers. Total. Females.	Actual Workers. Partially Agriculturists. Males.	Actual Workers. Partially Agriculturists. Females.	Dependents.
	470	471	472	473	474	475	476	477	478	479	480	481	482	483	484	485	486	487	488	489	490	491	492	493	494	495	496	497	498	499
Total State ...	**256**	**119**	**9**	...	...	**128**	**208**	**58**	...	...	...	**150**	**208**	**58**	...	...	...	**150**	**12,254**	**4,804**	**72**	**293**	**3**	**7,378**	**147**	**44**	**1**	**1**	...	**102**
I—Total Jammu Province (including *Jagirs*).	144	31	9	...	...	74	7	6	...	...	...	1	7	6	...	...	...	1	6,652	2,889	65	195	3	3,698	49	12	...	...	...	37
1. Jammu District (including city).	60	24	...	...	...	36	7	6	...	...	...	1	7	6	...	...	...	1	3,111	1,553	22	49	2	1,536	27	6	...	...	...	21
2. Jasrota ,, ...	...	...	...	...	...	...	...	...	...	...	...	...	...	...	...	...	...	...	825	303	13	19	...	509	1	1	...	...	...	...
3. Udhampur ,, ...	27	...	5	...	...	22	...	...	...	...	...	...	...	...	...	...	...	...	675	279	10	31	...	386	...	...	...	...	...	...
4. Riasi ,, ...	1	1	...	...	...	...	...	...	...	...	...	...	...	...	...	...	...	...	395	156	2	26	...	237	...	...	...	...	...	...
5. Mirpur ,, ...	26	6	4	...	...	16	...	...	...	...	...	...	...	...	...	...	...	...	1,080	425	12	36	...	643	13	5	...	...	...	8
6. Bhadarwah *Jagir* ...	...	...	...	...	...	...	...	...	...	...	...	...	...	...	...	...	...	...	199	64	4	30	...	131	...	...	...	...	...	...
7. Punch *Ilaqa*	...	...	...	...	...	...	...	...	...	...	...	...	...	...	...	...	...	...	367	109	2	5	1	256	8	...	...	...	...	8
II—Total Kashmir Province (including *Jagirs*).	141	87	...	...	...	54	201	52	...	...	...	149	201	52	...	...	...	149	5,355	1,778	6	90	...	357	92	30	1	1	...	61
8. Kashmir North (including Langet *Jagir*).	3	...	...	...	...	3	12	6	...	...	...	6	12	6	...	...	...	6	1,135	402	5	28	...	728	1	1	...	...	...	...
9. Kashmir South (including city).	137	86	...	...	...	51	182	39	...	...	...	143	182	39	...	...	...	143	3,990	1,315	1	58	...	2,674	91	29	1	1	...	61
Total Kashmir Valley ...	*140*	*86*	...	...	...	*54*	*194*	*45*	...	...	...	*149*	*194*	*45*	...	...	...	*149*	*5,125*	*1,717*	*6*	*86*	...	*3,402*	*92*	*30*	*1*	*1*	...	*61*
10. Muzaffarabad District ...	1	1	...	...	...	...	7	7	...	...	...	...	7	7	...	...	...	...	230	61	...	4	...	169	...	...	...	...	...	...
III—Total Frontier Districts.	1	1	...	...	...	...	...	...	...	...	...	...	...	...	...	...	...	...	247	137	1	8	...	109	6	2	...	...	...	4
11. Laddakh District (including Mansar).	...	...	...	...	...	...	...	...	...	...	...	...	...	...	...	...	...	...	57	21	1	6	...	35	6	2	...	...	...	4
12. Gilgit ,, ...	1	1	...	...	...	...	...	...	...	...	...	...	...	...	...	...	...	...	6	5	...	2	...	1	...	...	...	...	...	...
13. Frontier *Ilaqas*	...	...	...	...	...	...	...	...	...	...	...	...	...	...	...	...	...	...	184	111	...	...	...	73	...	...	...	...	...	...
Cities.																														
Jammu ...	60	24	...	...	...	36	7	6	...	...	...	1	7	6	...	...	...	1	1,145	567	1	...	...	577	27	6	...	...	...	21
Srinagar ...	180	38	...	...	...	142	180	38	...	...	...	142	180	38	...	...	...	142	2,637	873	1	1	...	1,763	90	29	1	1	...	60

TABLE XV-A.

Occupation or Means of Livelihood.

Jammu and Kashmir State Census, 1911.

District, Jagir, Ilaqa or City.	Group (87).—Makers of musical instruments. Total workers and dependents.	Actual Workers. Total. Males.	Actual Workers. Total. Females.	Actual Workers. Partially Agriculturists. Males.	Actual Workers. Partially Agriculturists. Females.	Dependents.
	500	501	502	503	504	505
Total State ...	**18**	**4**	...	...	...	**14**
I—Total Jammu Province (including *Jagirs*).	4	1	...	...	...	3
1. Jammu District (including city).	4	1	...	...	...	3
2. Jasrota "	...	...	...	...	...	...
3. Udhampur "	...	...	...	...	...	...
4. Riasi "	...	...	...	...	...	...
5. Mirpur "	...	...	...	...	...	...
6. Bhadarwah *Jagir* ...	...	...	...	...	...	...
7. Punch *Ilaqa*	...	...	...	...	...	...
II—Total Kashmir Province (including *Jagirs*).	14	3	...	...	...	11
8. Kashmir North (including Langet *Jagir*).	...	...	...	...	...	...
9. Kashmir South (including city).	14	3	...	...	...	11
Total Kashmir Valley ...	*14*	*3*	...	...	...	*11*
10. Muzaffarabad District ...	...	...	...	...	...	...
III—Total Frontier Districts.	...	...	...	...	...	...
11. Laddakh District (including Mansar).	...	...	...	...	...	...
12. Gilgit	...	...	...	...	...	...
13. Frontier *Ilaqas*	...	...	...	...	...	...
Cities.						
Jammu	4	1	...	...	...	3
Srinagar	14	3	...	...	...	11

District, Jagir, Ilaqa or City.	Group (88).—Makers of watches and clocks and optical, photographic and surgical instruments. Total workers and dependents.	Actual Workers. Total. Males.	Actual Workers. Total. Females.	Actual Workers. Partially Agriculturists. Males.	Actual Workers. Partially Agriculturists. Females.	Dependents.
	506	507	508	509	510	511
Total State ...	**178**	**69**	...	...	...	**109**
I—Total Jammu Province (including *Jagirs*).	78	28	...	...	...	50
1. Jammu District (including city).	74	24	...	...	...	50
2. Jasrota "	1	1	...	...	...	...
3. Udhampur "	...	...	...	...	...	...
4. Riasi "	1	1	...	...	...	...
5. Mirpur "	2	2	...	...	...	...
6. Bhadarwah *Jagir* ...	...	...	...	...	...	...
7. Punch *Ilaqa*	...	...	...	...	...	...
II—Total Kashmir Province (including *Jagirs*).	99	40	...	...	...	59
8. Kashmir North (including Langet *Jagir*).	6	6	...	...	...	...
9. Kashmir South (including city).	92	33	...	...	...	59
Total Kashmir Valley ...	*98*	*39*	...	...	...	*59*
10. Muzaffarabad District ...	1	1	...	...	...	...
III—Total Frontier Districts.	1	1	...	...	...	...
11. Laddakh District (including Mansar).	1	1	...	...	...	...
12. Gilgit	...	...	...	...	...	...
13. Frontier *Ilaqas*	...	...	...	...	...	...
Cities.						
Jammu	69	24	...	...	...	45
Srinagar	89	33	...	...	...	56

District, Jagir, Ilaqa or City.	Group (89).—Workers in precious stones and metals, enamellers, imitation jewellery makers, gilders, etc. Total workers and dependents.	Actual Workers. Total. Males.	Actual Workers. Total. Females.	Actual Workers. Partially Agriculturists. Males.	Actual Workers. Partially Agriculturists. Females.	Dependents.
	512	513	514	515	516	517
Total State ...	**10,947**	**4,230**	**65**	**273**	**3**	**6,652**
I—Total Jammu Province (including *Jagirs*).	5,921	2,504	60	178	3	3,357
1. Jammu District (including city).	2,485	1,215	19	34	2	1,251
2. Jasrota "	780	280	12	17	...	488
3. Udhampur "	675	279	10	31	...	386
4. Riasi "	390	155	2	26	...	233
5. Mirpur "	1,055	411	12	35	...	632
6. Bhadarwah *Jagir* ...	199	64	4	30	...	131
7. Punch *Ilaqa*	337	100	1	5	1	236
II—Total Kashmir Province (including *Jagirs*).	4,791	1,596	4	87	...	3,191
8. Kashmir North (including Langet *Jagir*).	1,107	389	4	28	...	714
9. Kashmir South (including city).	3,463	1,147	...	55	...	2,316
Total Kashmir Valley ...	*4,570*	*1,536*	*4*	*83*	...	*3,030*
10. Muzaffarabad District ...	221	60	...	4	...	161
III—Total Frontier Districts.	235	130	1	8	...	104
11. Laddakh District (including Mansar).	45	14	1	6	...	30
12. Gilgit	6	5	...	2	...	1
13. Frontier *Ilaqas*	184	111	...	...	...	73
Cities.						
Jammu	639	299	...	...	...	340
Srinagar	2,196	728	...	...	...	1,468

District, Jagir, Ilaqa or City.	Group (90).—Makers of bangles, rosaries, bead and other necklaces, spangles, lingams and sacred thread. Total workers and dependents.	Actual Workers. Total. Males.	Actual Workers. Total. Females.	Actual Workers. Partially Agriculturists. Males.	Actual Workers. Partially Agriculturists. Females.	Dependents.
	518	519	520	521	522	523
Total State ...	**765**	**396**	**4**	**17**	...	**365**
I—Total Jammu Province (including *Jagirs*).	523	322	3	17	...	198
1. Jammu District (including city).	485	302	2	15	...	181
2. Jasrota "	19	12	...	2	...	7
3. Udhampur "	...	...	...	...	...	...
4. Riasi "	4	...	...	...	...	4
5. Mirpur "	...	...	...	...	...	...
6. Bhadarwah *Jagir* ...	...	...	...	...	...	...
7. Punch *Ilaqa*	15	8	1	...	...	6
II—Total Kashmir Province (including *Jagirs*).	242	74	1	...	...	167
8. Kashmir North (including Langet *Jagir*).	20	5	1	...	...	14
9. Kashmir South (including city).	214	69	...	...	...	145
Total Kashmir Valley ...	*234*	*74*	*1*	...	...	*159*
10. Muzaffarabad District ...	8	...	...	...	...	8
III—Total Frontier Districts.	...	...	...	...	...	...
11. Laddakh District (including Mansar).	...	...	...	...	...	...
12. Gilgit	...	...	...	...	...	...
13. Frontier *Ilaqas*	...	...	...	...	...	...
Cities.						
Jammu	394	237	...	...	...	157
Srinagar	176	56	...	...	...	120

District, Jagir, Ilaqa or City.	Group (91).—Toy, kite, cage, fishing, etc., makers, taxidermists, etc. Total workers and dependents.	Actual Workers. Total. Males.	Actual Workers. Total. Females.	Actual Workers. Partially Agriculturists. Males.	Actual Workers. Partially Agriculturists. Females.	Dependents.
	524	525	526	527	528	529
Total State ...	**137**	**42**	**2**	...	...	**93**
I—Total Jammu Province (including *Jagirs*).	63	16	2	...	...	45
1. Jammu District (including city).	30	4	1	...	...	25
2. Jasrota "	24	9	1	...	...	14
3. Udhampur "	...	...	...	...	...	...
4. Riasi "	...	...	...	...	...	...
5. Mirpur "	5	3	...	...	...	2
6. Bhadarwah *Jagir* ...	...	...	...	...	...	...
7. Punch *Ilaqa*	4	...	...	...	...	4
II—Total Kashmir Province (including *Jagirs*).	74	26	...	...	...	48
8. Kashmir North (including Langet *Jagir*).	1	1	...	...	...	...
9. Kashmir South (including city).	73	25	...	...	...	48
Total Kashmir Valley ...	*74*	*26*	...	...	...	*48*
10. Muzaffarabad District ...	...	...	...	...	...	...
III—Total Frontier Districts.	...	...	...	...	...	...
11. Laddakh District (including Mansar).	...	...	...	...	...	...
12. Gilgit	...	...	...	...	...	...
13. Frontier *Ilaqas*	...	...	...	...	...	...
Cities.						
Jammu	10	...	1	...	...	9
Srinagar	73	25	...	...	...	48

TABLE XV-A.

Occupation or Means of Livelihood.

Jammu and Kashmir State Census, 1911.

DISTRICT, JAGIR, ILAQA OR CITY.	Group (92).—Others (including managers, persons other than performers employed in theatres and other places of public entertainment, employes of public societies, race-course service, huntsmen, etc.)						Order 19.—Industries concerned with refuse matter.						Group (93).—Sweepers, scavangers, dust and sweeping contractors.						Sub-class IV.—Transport.					
	Total workers and dependents.	Actual Workers. Total		Actual Workers. Partially Agriculturists.		Dependents.	Total workers and dependents.	Actual Workers. Total.		Actual Workers. Partially Agriculturists.		Dependents.	Total workers and dependents.	Actual Workers. Total.		Actual Workers. Partially Agriculturists.		Dependents.	Total workers and dependents.	Actual Workers. Total.		Actual Workers. Partially Agriculturists.		Dependents.
		Males.	Females.	Males.	Females.			Males.	Females.	Males.	Females.			Males.	Females.	Males.	Females.			Males.	Females.	Males.	Females.	
	530	531	532	533	534	535	536	537	538	539	540	541	542	543	544	545	546	547	548	549	550	551	552	553
Total State ...	**62**	**19**	...	**2**	...	**43**	**4 250**	**1,352**	**774**	**101**	**34**	**2,124**	**4 250**	**1,352**	**774**	**101**	**34**	**2,124**	**33,667**	**14,022**	**3,037**	**784**	**22**	**16,608**
I—Total Jammu Province (including *Jagirs*).	14	6	...	...	...	8	2,230	662	508	95	34	1,010	2,230	662	508	95	34	1,010	11,554	5,544	102	480	18	5,908
1. Jammu District (including city).	6	1	...	...	...	5	1,239	334	278	42	15	627	1,239	334	278	42	15	627	3,905	1,653	26	144	14	2,226
2. Jasrota ,, ...	...	...	...	...	...	...	235	51	120	...	19	64	235	51	120	...	19	64	2,631	993	13	65	3	1,625
3. Udhampur ,, ...	...	...	...	...	...	...	35	10	11	9	...	14	35	10	11	9	...	14	468	222	3	16	...	243
4. Riasi ,, ...	...	...	...	...	...	...	97	31	17	...	...	49	97	31	17	...	...	49	1,054	354	...	14	...	700
5. Mirpur ,, ...	5	4	...	...	...	1	584	208	82	43	...	294	584	208	82	43	...	294	3,135	2,138	57	214	1	940
6. Bhadarwah *Jagir* ...	...	...	...	...	...	...	1	...	...	...	...	1	1	...	...	...	...	1	70	48	...	21	...	22
7. Punch *Ilaqa*	3	1	...	...	...	2	39	28	...	1	...	11	39	28	...	1	...	11	291	136	3	6	...	152
II—Total Kashmir Province (including *Jagirs*).	43	9	...	2	...	34	1,872	611	260	...	...	1,001	1,872	111	260	...	...	1,001	20,841	7,415	2,935	276	3	10,491
8. Kashmir North (including Langet *Jagir*).	...	...	...	...	...	...	738	206	155	...	...	377	738	206	155	...	...	377	5,099	1,826	540	78	...	2,733
9. Kashmir South (including city).	43	9	...	2	...	34	1,045	386	95	...	...	564	1,045	386	95	...	...	564	15,165	5,247	2,381	175	2	7,537
Total Kashmir Valley ...	*43*	*9*	...	*2*	...	*34*	*1,783*	*592*	*250*	...	...	*941*	*1,783*	*592*	*250*	...	...	*941*	*20,264*	*7,073*	*2,921*	*253*	*2*	*10,270*
10. Muzaffarabad District ...	...	...	...	...	...	...	89	19	10	...	...	60	89	19	10	...	...	60	577	342	14	23	1	221
III—Total Frontier Districts.	5	4	...	...	...	1	148	79	6	6	...	63	148	79	6	6	...	63	1,372	1,063	...	28	1	209
11. Laddakh District (including Mansar).	5	4	...	...	...	1	17	11	...	...	...	6	17	11	...	...	...	6	1,110	933	...	26	1	177
12. Gilgit ,, ...	...	...	...	...	...	...	71	36	6	6	...	29	71	36	6	6	...	29	89	74	...	2	...	15
13. Frontier *Ilaqas*	...	...	...	...	...	...	60	32	...	...	...	28	60	32	...	...	...	28	73	56	...	...	...	17
Cities.																								
Jammu ...	2	...	...	...	...	2	286	67	78	...	...	141	286	67	78	...	...	141	819	426	1	22	...	392
Srinagar ...	2	1	...	...	...	1	916	320	91	...	...	505	916	320	91	...	...	505	7,478	2,630	1,317	3	...	3,531

TABLE XV-A.

Occupation or Means of Livelihood.

Jammu and Kashmir State Census 1911.

DISTRICT, JAGIR, ILAQA OR CITY.	Order 20.—Transport by water.						*Group (95).—Ship owners and their employes, ship brokers, ships' officers, engineers, mariners & firemen.*						*Group (96).—Persons employed on the maintenance of streams, rivers and canals (including construction).*						*Group (97).—Boat owners, boat men and tow men.*					
	Total workers and dependents.	Actual Workers. Total.		Actual Workers. Partially Agriculturists.		Dependents.	Total workers and dependents.	Actual Workers. Total.		Actual Workers. Partially Agriculturists.		Dependents.	Total workers and dependents.	Actual Workers. Total.		Actual Workers. Partially Agriculturists.		Dependents.	Total workers and dependents.	Actual Workers. Total.		Actual Workers. Partially Agriculturists.		Dependents.
		Males.	Females.	Males.	Females.			Males.	Females.	Males.	Females.			Males.	Females.	Males.	Females.			Males.	Females.	Males.	Females.	
	554	555	556	557	558	559	560	561	562	563	564	565	566	567	568	569	570	571	572	573	574	575	576	577
Total State ...	**15,968**	**6,402**	**2,985**	**221**	**3**	**6,581**	**67**	**13**	**18**	...	**1**	**36**	**2,524**	**1,910**	**52**	**188**	**1**	**562**	**13,377**	**4,479**	**2,915**	**33**	**1**	**5,983**
I—Total Jammu Province (including *Jagirs*).	2,970	2,063	70	191	2	837	67	13	18	...	1	36	2,454	1,875	52	187	1	527	449	175	...	4	...	274
1. Jammu District (including city).	666	299	7	10	...	360	...	...	...	...	...	...	283	164	7	6	...	112	383	135	...	4	...	248
2. Jasrota ,, ...	117	45	6	2	1	66	...	...	...	...	...	...	114	42	6	2	1	66	3	3	...	...	...	...
3. Udhampur ,, ...	9	7	...	...	...	2	...	...	...	...	...	...	7	7	...	...	...	...	2	...	...	...	...	2
4. Riasi ,, ...	34	26	...	...	...	8	...	...	...	...	...	...	1	1	...	...	...	...	33	25	...	...	...	8
5. Mirpur ,, ...	2,126	1,679	57	178	1	390	67	13	18	...	1	36	2,038	1,658	39	178	...	341	21	8	...	...	...	13
6. Bhadarwah *Jagir* ...	...	...	...	...	...	...	...	...	...	...	...	...	...	...	...	...	...	...	...	...	...	...	...	...
7. Punch *Ilaqa*	18	7	...	1	...	11	...	...	...	...	...	...	11	3	...	1	...	8	7	4	...	...	...	3
II—Total Kashmir Province (including *Jagirs*).	12,946	4,302	2,915	30	1	5,729	...	...	...	...	...	...	37	8	...	1	...	29	12,909	4,294	2,915	29	1	5,700
8. Kashmir North (including Langet *Jagir*).	3,043	947	539	11	...	1,557	...	...	...	...	...	...	10	3	...	1	...	7	3,033	994	539	10	...	1,550
9. Kashmir South (including city).	9,902	3,354	2,376	19	1	4,172	...	...	...	...	...	...	26	4	...	...	...	22	9,876	3,350	2,376	19	1	4,150
Total Kashmir Valley ...	*12,945*	*4,301*	*2,915*	*30*	*1*	*5,729*	...	...	...	...	...	...	*36*	*7*	...	*1*	...	*29*	*12,909*	*4,294*	*2,915*	*29*	*1*	*5,700*
10 Muzaffarabad District ...	1	1	...	...	...	...	...	...	...	...	...	...	1	1	...	...	...	...	...	...	...	...	...	...
III—Total Frontier Districts.	52	37	...	...	...	15	...	...	...	...	...	...	33	27	...	...	...	6	19	10	...	...	...	9
11. Laddakh District (including Mansar).	23	23	...	...	...	...	...	...	...	...	...	...	23	23	...	...	...	...	...	...	...	...	...	...
12. Gilgit ,, ...	...	...	...	...	...	...	...	...	...	...	...	...	...	...	...	...	...	...	...	...	...	...	...	...
13. Frontier *Ilaqas*	29	14	...	...	...	15	...	...	...	...	...	...	10	4	...	...	...	6	19	10	...	...	...	9
Cities.																								
Jammu ...	9	6	...	...	...	3	...	...	...	...	...	...	4	2	...	...	...	2	5	4	...	...	...	1
Srinagar ...	5,735	2,082	1,314	1	...	2,339	...	...	...	...	...	...	...	...	...	...	...	...	5,735	2,082	1,314	1	...	2,339

TABLE XV-A.

Occupation or Means of Livelihood.

Jammu and Kashmir State Census 1911.

DISTRICT, JAGIR, ILAQA OR CITY.	Order 21.—Transport by road.						Group (98).—Persons employed on the construction and maintenance of roads and bridges.					
	Total workers and dependents.	Actual Workers. Total. Males.	Actual Workers. Total. Females.	Actual Workers. Partially Agriculturists. Males.	Actual Workers. Partially Agriculturists. Females.	Dependents.	Total workers and dependents.	Actual Workers. Total. Males.	Actual Workers. Total. Females.	Actual Workers. Partially Agriculturists. Males.	Actual Workers. Partially Agriculturists. Females.	Dependents.
	578	579	580	581	582	583	584	585	586	587	588	589
Total State	**15.504**	**6,610**	**52**	**472**	**19**	**8.842**	**1.549**	**682**	**17**	**67**	**2**	**850**
I—Total Jammu Province (including *Jagirs*).	7,665	3,030	32	245	16	4,603	233	115	4	2	...	114
1. Jammu District (including city).	2,826	1,144	19	106	14	1,663	26	23	1	...	...	2
2. Jasrota "	2,437	915	7	59	2	1.525	...	...	...	...	...	...
3. Udhampur "	352	151	3	6	...	198	124	25	...	...	...	99
4. Riasi "	971	297	...	12	...	674	21	13	...	1	...	8
5. Mirpur "	829	384	...	36	...	445	4	3	...	...	...	1
6. Bhadarwah *Jagir* ...	62	43	...	21	...	19	1	1	...	1	...	...
7. Punch *Ilaqa*	188	96	3	5	...	89	57	50	3	...	...	4
II—Total Kashmir Province (including *Jagirs*).	6,853	2,708	20	226	2	4,125	1,263	516	13	64	2	734
8. Kashmir North (including Langet *Jagir*).	1,781	728	1	62	...	1,052	321	167	1	3	...	153
9. Kashmir South (including city).	4,534	1,669	5	145	1	2,860	635	200	1	59	1	434
Total Kashmir Valley ...	*6,315*	*2,397*	*6*	*207*	*1*	*3,912*	*956*	*367*	*2*	*62*	*1*	*587*
10. Muzaffarabad District ...	538	311	14	19	1	213	307	149	11	2	1	147
III—Total Frontier Districts.	986	872	...	1	1	114	53	51	...	1	...	2
11. Laddakh District (including Mansar).	918	806	...	...	1	112	...	...	...	...	...	...
12. Gilgit "	25	25	...	1	...	...	16	16	...	1	...	...
13. Frontier *Ilaqas*	43	41	...	...	...	2	37	35	...	...	...	2
Cities.												
Jammu ...	688	375	1	22	...	312	...	...	...	...	...	...
Srinagar ...	1,262	428	...	1	...	834	135	43	...	...	...	92

DISTRICT, JAGIR, ILAQA OR CITY.	Group (99).—Cart owners and drivers, coachmen, stable boys, tramway mail carriage, etc., managers and employes (excluding private servants).						Group (100).—Palki, etc. bearers and owners.						Group (101).—Pack elephant, camel, mule, ass and bullock owners and drivers.					
	Total workers and dependents.	Actual Workers. Total. Males.	Actual Workers. Total. Females.	Actual Workers. Partially Agriculturists. Males.	Actual Workers. Partially Agriculturists. Females.	Dependents.	Total workers and dependents.	Actual Workers. Total. Males.	Actual Workers. Total. Females.	Actual Workers. Partially Agriculturists. Males.	Actual Workers. Partially Agriculturists. Females.	Dependents.	Total workers and dependents.	Actual Workers. Total. Males.	Actual Workers. Total. Females.	Actual Workers. Partially Agriculturists. Males.	Actual Workers. Partially Agriculturists. Females.	Dependents.
	590	591	592	593	594	595	596	597	598	599	600	601	602	603	604	605	606	607
Total State	**698**	**406**	**3**	**15**		**289**	**29**	**8**	...	...	...	**21**	**10,902**	**4,768**	...	**315**	**5**	**6,134**
I—Total Jammu Province (including *Jagirs*).	228	132	...	...	...	96	19	3	...	...	...	16	5,933	2,362	...	170	4	3,571
1. Jammu District (including city).	202	119	...	...	...	83	15	2	...	...	...	13	2,004	843	...	70	2	1,161
2. Jasrota "	1	...	...	...	...	1	4	1	...	...	...	3	2,061	801	...	34	2	1,260
3. Udhampur "	1	1	...	...	...	...	...	...	...	...	...	...	79	50	...	3	...	29
4. Riasi "	...	...	...	...	...	...	...	...	...	...	...	...	946	284	...	11	...	662
5. Mirpur "	12	3	...	...	...	9	...	...	...	...	...	...	701	319	...	27	...	382
6. Bhadarwah *Jagir* ...	...	...	...	...	...	...	...	...	...	...	...	...	61	42	...	20	...	19
7. Punch *Ilaqa*	12	9	...	...	...	3	...	...	...	...	...	...	81	23	...	5	...	58
II—Total Kashmir Province (including *Jagirs*).	464	268	3	15	...	193	6	1	...	...	...	5	4,048	1,597	...	145	...	2,451
8. Kashmir North (including Langet *Jagir*).	132	85	...	8	...	47	...	...	...	...	...	...	1,151	432	...	51	...	719
9. Kashmir South (including city).	150	60	...	1	...	90	4	1	...	...	...	3	2,850	1,126	...	83	...	1,724
Total Kashmir Valley ...	*282*	*145*	...	*9*	...	*137*	*4*	*1*	...	...	...	*3*	*4,001*	*1,558*	...	*134*	...	*2,443*
10. Muzaffarabad District ...	182	123	3	6	...	56	2	...	...	...	...	2	47	39	...	11	...	8
III—Total Frontier Districts.	6	6	...	...	...	...	4	4	...	...	...	...	921	809	...	...	1	112
11. Laddakh District (including Mansar).	1	1	...	...	...	...	...	...	...	...	...	...	917	805	...	...	1	112
12. Gilgit "	5	5	...	...	...	...	...	...	...	...	...	...	4	4	...	...	...	...
13. Frontier *Ilaqas*	...	...	...	...	...	...	4	4	...	...	...	...	...	...	...	...	...	...
Cities.																		
Jammu ...	199	117	...	...	...	82	...	...	...	...	...	...	485	258	...	22	...	227
Srinagar ...	112	46	...	1	...	66	4	1	...	...	...	3	678	220	...	...	...	458

TABLE XV-A.

Occupation or Means of Livelihood.

Jammu and Kashmir State Census 1911.

District, Jagir, Ilaqa or City.	Group (102).—Porters and messengers.						Order 22.-Transport by rail.						Group (103).—Railway employes of all kinds other than construction coolies.						Group (104).—Labourers employed on railway construction.						Order 23.—Post office, telegraph and telephone services.					
	Total workers and dependents.	Actual Workers. Total.		Actual Workers. Partially Agriculturists.		Dependents.	Total workers and dependents.	Actual Workers. Total.		Actual Workers. Partially Agriculturists.		Dependents	Total workers and dependents.	Actual Workers. Total.		Actual Workers. Partially Agriculturists.		Dependents.	Total workers and dependents.	Actual Workers. Total.		Actual Workers. Partially Agriculturists.		Dependents.	Total workers and dependents.	Actual Workers. Total.		Actual Workers. Partially Agriculturists.		Dependents.
		Males.	Females.	Males.	Females.			Males.	Females.	Males.	Females.			Males.	Females.	Males.	Females.			Males.	Females.	Males.	Females.			Males.	Females.	Males.	Females.	
	608	609	610	611	612	613	614	615	616	617	618	619	620	621	622	623	624	625	626	627	628	629	630	631	632	633	634	635	636	637
Total State ...	**2,326**	**746**	**32**	**75**	**12**	**1,548**	**426**	**217**	...	**25**	...	**209**	**399**	**201**	...	**25**	...	**198**	**27**	**16**	...	...	...	**11**	**1,769**	**793**	...	**66**	...	**976**
I—Total Jammu Province (including *Jagirs*).	1,252	418	28	73	12	806	400	199	...	25	...	201	389	194	...	25	...	195	11	5	...	...	...	6	519	252	...	19	...	267
1. Jammu District (including city).	579	157	18	36	12	404	234	135	...	21	...	99	234	135	...	21	...	99	...	...	...	...	...	...	179	75	...	7	...	104
2. Jasrota „	371	113	7	25	...	251	21	11	...	4	...	10	21	11	...	4	...	10	...	...	...	...	...	...	56	22	...	...	...	34
3. Udhampur „	148	75	3	3	...	70	4	2	...	...	...	2	4	2	...	...	...	2	...	...	...	...	...	...	103	62	...	10	...	41
4. Riasi „	4	...	...	...	...	4	5	1	...	...	...	4	5	1	...	...	...	4	...	...	...	...	...	...	44	30	...	2	...	14
5. Mirpur „	112	59	...	9	...	53	92	33	...	...	...	59	82	29	...	...	...	53	10	4	...	...	...	6	88	42	...	...	...	46
6. Bhadarwah *Jagir*	...	...	...	...	...	...	...	...	...	...	...	...	...	...	...	...	...	...	...	...	...	...	...	...	8	5	...	...	...	3
7. Punch *Ilaqa*	38	14	...	...	...	24	44	17	...	...	...	27	43	16	...	...	...	27	1	1	...	...	...	...	41	16	...	...	...	25
II—Total Kashmir Province (including *Jagirs*).	1,072	326	4	2	...	742	25	17	...	...	...	8	9	6	...	...	...	3	16	11	...	...	...	5	1,017	388	...	20	...	629
8. Kashmir North (including Langet *Jagir*).	177	44	...	...	...	133	20	15	...	...	...	5	4	4	...	...	...	...	16	11	...	...	...	5	255	136	...	5	...	119
9. Kashmir South (including city).	895	285	4	2	...	609	4	2	...	...	...	2	4	2	...	...	...	2	...	...	...	...	...	...	725	222	...	11	...	503
Total Kashmir Valley ...	*1,072*	*326*	*4*	*2*	...	*742*	*24*	*17*	...	...	...	*7*	*8*	*6*	...	...	...	*2*	*16*	*11*	...	...	...	*5*	*980*	*358*	...	*16*	...	*622*
10. Muzaffarabad District ...	...	...	...	...	...	...	1	...	...	...	...	1	1	...	...	...	...	1	...	...	...	...	...	...	37	30	...	4	...	7
III—Total Frontier Districts.	2	2	...	...	...	...	1	1	...	...	...	...	1	1	...	...	...	...	...	...	...	...	...	...	233	153	...	27	...	80
11. Laddakh District (including Mansar).	...	...	...	...	...	...	...	...	...	...	...	...	...	...	...	...	...	...	...	...	...	...	...	...	169	104	...	26	...	65
12. Gilgit „	...	...	...	...	...	...	1	1	...	...	...	...	1	1	...	...	...	...	...	...	...	...	...	...	63	48	...	1	...	15
13. Frontier *Ilaqas*	2	2	...	...	...	...	...	...	...	...	...	...	...	...	...	...	...	...	...	...	...	...	...	...	1	1	...	...	...	...
Cities.																														
Jammu ...	4	...	1	...	...	3	10	3	...	...	...	7	10	3	...	...	...	7	...	...	...	...	...	...	112	42	...	...	...	70
Srinagar ...	333	118	...	...	...	215	4	2	...	...	...	2	4	2	...	...	...	2	...	...	...	...	...	...	477	118	...	1	...	359

TABLE XV-A.

Occupation or Means of Livelihood.

Jammu and Kashmir State Census 1911.

DISTRICT, JAGIR, ILAQA OR CITY.	Group (105).—*Post Office, telegraph and telephone services.*						Sub-class V.—Trade.						Order 24.—Banks, establishments of credit, exchange and insurance.						Group (106).—*Bank managers, money-lenders, exchange and insurance agents, money changers and brokers and their employes.*					
	Total workers and dependents.	Actual Workers.				Dependents.	Total workers and dependents.	Actual Workers.				Dependents.	Total workers and dependents.	Actual Workers.				Dependents.	Total workers and dependents.	Actual Workers.				Dependents.
		Total.		*Partially Agriculturists.*				*Total.*		*Partially Agriculturists.*				*Total.*		*Partially Agriculturists.*				*Total.*		*Partially Agriculturists.*		
		Males.	Females.	Males.	Females.			Males.	Females.	Males.	Females.			Mal s.	Females.	Males.	Females.			Males.	Females.	Males.	Females.	
	638	639	640	541	642	643	644	645	646	647	648	649	650	651	652	653	654	655	656	657	658	659	660	661
Total State ...	**1,769**	**793**		**66**		**976**	**119,357**	**40,734**	**7.365**	**3,360**	**180**	**71,258**	**10.239**	**2,986**	**266**	**528**	**12**	**6,987**	**10,239**	**2,986**	**266**	**528**	**12**	**6,987**
I—Total Jammu Province (including *Jagirs*).	519	252	...	19	...	267	65,440	22,543	3,806	2,339	174	39,091	9,548	2,784	254	223	12	6,510	9,548	2,784	254	223	12	6,510
1. Jammu District (including city).	179	75	...	7	...	104	17,909	61,115	1,060	494	69	10,734	1,986	521	60	76	3	1,405	1,986	521	60	76	3	1,405
2. Jasrota ,, ...	56	22	...	...	...	34	13,323	4,330	1,176	544	54	7,817	1,787	494	84	100	2	1,209	1,787	494	84	100	2	1,209
3. Udhampur ,, ...	103	62	...	10	...	41	9,332	3,515	749	529	37	5,068	1,395	446	43	38	2	906	1,395	446	43	38	2	906
4. Riasi ,, ...	44	30	...	2	...	14	10,619	3,756	393	239	8	6,470	962	349	20	56	2	593	962	349	20	56	2	593
5. Mirpur ,, ...	88	42	...	...	...	46	8,657	2,977	229	379	3	5,451	3,167	921	40	241	3	2,206	3,167	921	40	241	3	2,206
6. Bhadarwah *Jagir* ...	8	5	...	...	...	3	873	318	109	72	1	446	28	13	1	3	...	14	28	13	1	3	...	14
7. Punch *Ilaqa* ...	41	16	...	...	...	25	4,727	1,532	90	82	2	3,105	223	40	6	9	...	177	223	40	6	9	...	177
II—Total Kashmir Province (including *Jagirs*).	1,017	388	...	20	...	629	52,471	17,536	3,518	985	6	31,417	682	200	12	5	...	470	682	200	12	5	...	470
8. Kashmir North (including Langet *Jagir*).	255	136	...	5	...	119	13,463	4,902	894	248	5	7,667	39	10	...	...	...	29	39	10	...	...	...	29
9. Kashmir South (including city).	725	222	...	11	...	503	36,806	11,768	2,599	665	1	22,439	641	190	11	5	...	440	641	190	11	5	...	440
Total Kashmir Valley ...	*980*	*358*	...	*16*	...	*622*	*50,269*	*16,670*	*3,493*	*913*	*6*	*30,106*	*680*	*200*	*11*	*5*	...	*469*	*680*	*200*	*11*	*5*	...	*469*
10 Muzaffarabad District ...	37	30	...	4	...	7	2,202	866	25	72	...	1,311	2	...	1	...	...	1	2	...	1	...	...	1
III—Total Frontier Districts.	233	153	...	27	...	80	1,446	655	41	36	...	750	9	2	...	...	...	7	9	2	...	...	...	7
11. Laddakh District (including Mansar).	169	104	...	26	...	65	1,207	494	41	24	...	672	2	1	...	...	...	1	2	1	...	...	...	1
12. Gilgit ,, ...	63	48	...	1	...	15	228	150	...	12	...	78	7	1	...	...	...	6	7	1	...	...	...	6
13. Frontier *Ilaqas* ...	1	1	...	...	...	...	11	11	...	...	...	...	...	...	...	...	...	...	...	...	...	...	...	...
Cities.																								
Jammu ...	112	42	...	...	...	70	4,250	1,477	85	...	1	2,688	324	119	3	...	...	202	324	119	3	...	...	202
Srinagar ...	477	118	...	1	...	359	16,529	5,104	1,105	50	...	10,320	513	149	9	1	...	355	513	149	9	1	...	355

TABLE XV-A.

Occupation or Means of Livelihood.

Jammu and Kashmir State Census 1911.

DISTRICT, JAGIR, ILAQA OR CITY.	Order 26.—Trade in textiles.						*Group (108).—Trade in piece goods, wool, cotton, silk, hair and other textiles.*					
	Total workers and dependents.	Actual Workers. Total. Males.	Actual Workers. Total. Females.	Actual Workers. Partially Agriculturists. Males.	Actual Workers. Partially Agriculturists. Females.	Dependents.	Total workers and dependents.	Actual Workers. Total. Males.	Actual Workers. Total. Females.	Actual Workers. Partially Agriculturists. Males.	Actual Workers. Partially Agriculturists. Females.	Dependents.
	662	663	664	665	666	667	668	669	670	671	672	673
Total State	**6,032**	**2,105**	**23**	**103**	...	**3,904**	**6,032**	**2,105**	**23**	**103**	...	**3,904**
I—Total Jammu Province (including *Jagirs*).	2,097	866	14	62	...	1,217	2,097	866	14	62	...	1,217
1. Jammu District (including city).	474	182	1	3	...	291	474	182	1	3	...	291
2. Jasrota „	204	87	2	4	...	115	204	87	2	4	...	115
3. Udhampur „ ...	505	225	1	32	...	279	505	225	1	32	...	279
4. Riasi „ ...	283	127	2	5	...	154	283	127	2	5	...	154
5. Mirpur „ ...	280	101	6	4	...	173	280	101	6	4	...	173
6. Bhadarwah *Jagir* ...	126	47	1	7	...	78	126	47	1	7	...	78
7. Punch *Ilaqa* ...	225	97	1	7	...	127	225	97	1	7	...	127
II—Total Kashmir Province (including *Jagirs*).	3,742	1,146	5	36	...	2,591	3,742	1,146	5	36	...	2,591
8. Kashmir North (including Langet *Jagir*).	514	185	...	5	...	329	514	185	...	5	...	329
9. Kashmir South (including city).	3,157	955	5	30	...	2,197	3,157	955	5	30	...	2,197
Total Kashmir Valley ...	*3,671*	*1,140*	*5*	*35*	...	*2,526*	*3,671*	*1,140*	*5*	*35*	...	*2,526*
10. Muzaffarabad District	71	6	...	1	...	65	71	6	...	1	...	65
III—Total Frontier Districts.	193	93	4	5	...	96	193	93	4	5	...	96
11. Laddakh District (including Mansar).	169	83	4	5	...	82	169	83	4	5	...	82
12. Gilgit „ ...	24	10	...	...	...	14	24	10	...	...	...	14
13. Frontier *Ilaqas* ...	...	...	...	...	...	...	...	...	...	...	...	...
Cities.												
Jammu	170	79	...	...	...	91	170	79	...	...	...	91
Srinagar	2,584	789	3	17	...	1,792	2,584	789	3	17	...	1,792

DISTRICT, JAGIR, ILAQA OR CITY.	Order 27.—Trade in skins, leather and furs.						*Group (109).—Trade in skins, leather, furs, feathers, horn, etc.*					
	Total workers and dependents.	Actual Workers. Total. Males.	Actual Workers. Total. Females.	Actual Workers. Partially Agriculturists. Males.	Actual Workers. Partially Agriculturists. Females.	Dependents.	Total workers and dependents.	Actual Workers. Total. Males.	Actual Workers. Total. Females.	Actual Workers. Partially Agriculturists. Males.	Actual Workers. Partially Agriculturists. Females.	Dependents.
	674	675	676	677	678	679	680	681	682	683	684	685
Total State	**1,140**	**398**	**17**	**32**	...	**725**	**1,140**	**398**	**17**	**32**	...	**725**
I—Total Jammu Province (including *Jagirs*).	713	267	11	28	...	435	713	267	11	28	...	435
1. Jammu District (including city).	293	78	...	13	...	215	293	78	...	13	...	215
2. Jasrota „	105	81	2	...	...	22	105	81	2	...	...	22
3. Udhampur „ ...	145	53	2	11	...	90	145	53	2	11	...	90
4. Riasi „ ...	71	13	7	...	...	51	71	13	7	...	...	51
5. Mirpur „ ...	76	22	...	4	...	54	76	22	...	4	...	54
6. Bhadarwah *Jagir* ...	1	...	...	...	...	1	1	...	...	...	...	1
7. Punch *Ilaqa* ...	22	20	...	...	...	2	22	20	...	...	...	2
II—Total Kashmir Province (including *Jagirs*).	427	131	6	4	...	290	427	131	6	4	...	290
8. Kashmir North (including Langet *Jagir*).	213	45	5	4	...	163	213	45	5	4	...	163
9. Kashmir South (including city).	182	68	...	...	...	114	182	68	...	...	...	114
Total Kashmir Valley ...	*395*	*113*	*5*	*4*	...	*277*	*395*	*113*	*5*	*4*	...	*277*
10. Muzaffarabad District	32	18	1	...	...	13	32	18	1	...	...	13
III—Total Frontier Districts.	...	...	...	...	...	...	...	...	...	...	...	...
11. Laddakh District (including Mansar).	...	...	...	...	...	...	...	...	...	...	...	...
12. Gilgit „ ...	...	...	...	...	...	...	...	...	...	...	...	...
13. Frontier *Ilaqas* ...	...	...	...	...	...	...	...	...	...	...	...	...
Cities.												
Jammu	63	21	...	...	...	42	63	21	...	...	...	42
Srinagar	104	26	...	...	...	78	104	26	...	...	...	78

TABLE XV-A.

Occupation or Means of Livelihood.

Jammu and Kashmir State Census 1911.

DISTRICT, JAGIR, ILAQA OR CITY.	Order 28.—Trade in Wood.						Group (110).—Trade in wood (not firewood) cork, bark, etc.						Order 32.—Hotels, cafes, restaurants, etc.						Group (114).—Vendors of wine, liquors, ærated waters, etc.						Group (115).—Owners and managers of hotels, cookshops, sarais, etc. and their employes.					
	Total workers and dependents.	Actual Workers. Total.		Actual Workers. Partially Agriculturists.		Dependents.	Total workers and dependents.	Actual Workers. Total.		Actual Workers. Partially Agriculturists.		Dependents.	Total workers and dependents.	Actual Workers. Total.		Actual Workers. Partially Agriculturists.		Dependents.	Total workers and dependents.	Actual Workers. Total.		Actual Workers. Partially Agriculturists.		Dependents.	Total workers and dependents.	Actual Workers. Total.		Actual Workers. Partially Agriculturists.		Dependents.
		Males.	Females.	Males.	Females.			Males.	Females.	Males.	Females.			Males.	Females.	Males.	Females.			Males.	Females.	Males.	Females.			Males.	Females.	Males.	Females.	
	686	687	688	689	690	691	692	693	694	695	696	697	698	699	700	701	702	703	704	705	706	707	708	709	710	711	712	713	714	715
Total State ...	**895**	**370**	**64**	**10**	..	**461**	**895**	**370**	**64**	**10**	...	**461**	**196**	**84**	**4**	**9**	...	**108**	**109**	**43**	...	**3**	...	**66**	**87**	**41**	**4**	**6**	...	**42**
I—Total Jammu Province (including *Jagirs*).	113	31	5	...	...	77	113	31	5	...	...	77	72	29	...	2	...	43	69	26	...	2	...	43	3	3	...	...	...	...
1. Jammu District (including city).	40	11	...	...	...	29	40	11	...	...	...	29	39	15	...	...	...	24	39	15	...	...	...	24	...	...	...	...	...	...
2. Jasrota ,, ...	1	...	...	...	...	1	1	...	...	...	...	1	6	2	...	1	...	4	6	2	...	1	...	4	...	...	...	...	...	...
3. Udhampur ,, ...	11	...	1	...	...	10	11	...	1	...	...	10	4	4	...	...	...	...	2	2	...	...	...	...	2	2	...	...	...	...
4. Riasi ,, ...	35	8	2	...	...	25	35	8	2	...	...	25	3	2	...	...	...	1	3	2	...	...	...	1	...	...	...	...	...	...
5. Mirpur ,, ...	24	11	2	...	...	11	24	11	2	...	...	11	17	4	...	1	...	13	17	4	...	1	...	13	...	...	...	...	...	...
6. Bhadarwah *Jagir* ...	2	1	...	...	...	1	2	1	...	...	...	1	1	...	...	...	...	1	1	...	...	...	...	1	...	...	...	...	...	...
7. Punch *Ilaqa*	...	...	...	...	...	...	...	...	...	...	...	...	2	2	...	...	...	...	1	1	...	...	...	...	1	1	...	...	...	...
II—Total Kashmir Province (including *Jagirs*).	770	329	59	8	...	382	770	329	59	8	...	382	121	54	4	7	...	63	40	17	...	1	...	23	81	37	4	6	...	40
8. Kashmir North (including Langet *Jagir*).	147	44	57	1	...	46	147	44	57	1	...	46	37	19	...	6	...	18	5	2	...	...	...	3	32	17	...	6	...	15
9. Kashmir South (including city).	605	274	2	7	...	329	605	274	2	7	...	329	64	27	1	1	...	36	35	15	...	1	...	20	29	12	1	...	...	16
Total Kashmir Valley ...	*752*	*318*	*59*	*8*	...	*375*	*752*	*318*	*59*	*8*	...	*375*	*101*	*46*	*1*	*7*	...	*54*	*40*	*17*	...	*1*	...	*23*	*61*	*29*	*1*	*6*	...	*31*
10. Muzaffarabad District ...	18	11	...	...	...	7	18	11	...	...	...	7	20	8	3	...	...	9	...	...	...	...	...	...	20	8	3	...	...	9
III—Total Frontier Districts.	12	10	...	2	...	2	12	10	...	2	...	2	3	1	...	...	...	2	...	...	...	...	...	...	3	1	...	...	...	2
11. Laddakh District (including Mansar).	2	...	...	...	...	2	2	...	...	...	...	2	3	1	...	...	...	2	...	...	...	...	...	...	3	1	...	...	...	2
12. Gilgit ,, ...	10	10	...	2	...	...	10	10	...	2	...	...	...	...	...	...	...	...	...	...	...	...	...	...	...	...	...	...	...	...
13. Frontier *Ilaqas*	...	...	...	...	...	...	...	...	...	...	...	...	...	...	...	...	...	...	...	...	...	...	...	...	...	...	...	...	...	...
Cities.																														
Jammu	5	2	...	...	...	3	5	2	...	...	...	3	37	13	...	...	...	24	37	13	...	...	...	24	...	...	...	...	...	...
Srinagar	237	109	...	...	...	128	237	109	...	...	...	128	37	16	1	...	...	20	26	8	...	...	...	18	11	8	1	...	...	2

TABLE XV-A.

Occupation or Means of Livelihood.

Jammu and Kashmir State Census 1911.

DISTRICT, JAGIR, ILAQA OR CITY.	Order 33.—Other trade in food stuffs.						*Group (118).—Sellers of milk, butter, ghee, poultry, eggs, etc.*						*Group (120).—Cardamum, betel leaf, vegetables, fruit and areca-nut sellers.*						*Group (121).—Grain and pulse dealers.*					
	Total workers and dependents.	Actual Workers.				Dependents.	Total workers and dependents.	Actual Workers.				Dependents.	Total workers and dependents.	Actual Workers.				Dependents.	Total workers and dependents.	Actual Workers.				Dependents.
		Total.		*Partially Agriculturists.*				*Total.*		*Partially Agriculturists.*				*Total.*		*Partially Agriculturists.*				*Total.*		*Partially Agriculturists.*		
		Males.	Females.	Males.	Females.			Males.	Females.	Males.	Females.			Males.	Females.	Males.	Females.			Males.	Females.	Males.	Females.	
	716	717	718	719	720	721	722	723	724	725	726	727	728	729	730	731	732	733	734	735	736	737	738	739
Total State ...	**82,174**	**28,743**	**5,986**	**2,304**	**68**	**47,445**	**23,343**	**6,880**	**3,784**	**991**	**46**	**12,679**	**5,384**	**1,876**	**878**	**70**	**4**	**2,630**	**41,657**	**15,379**	**612**	**995**	**1**	**25,666**
I—Total Jammu Province (including *Jagirs*).	41,539	14,692	2,686	1,424	62	24,161	11,446	3,315	1,303	577	40	6,828	1,017	269	305	46	4	443	19,509	7,782	433	573	1	11,294
1. Jammu District (including city).	9,322	3,357	581	264	13	5,384	763	221	130	32	2	412	590	169	180	34	...	241	6,860	2,654	99	168	...	4,107
2. Jasrota ,, ...	9,190	3,199	934	375	18	5,057	4,507	1,253	635	166	14	2,619	289	45	115	8	3	129	3,234	1,413	77	123	...	1,744
3. Udhampur ,, ...	5,923	2,235	537	409	24	3,160	3,346	1,129	394	339	23	1,823	14	5	3	2	...	6	2,141	937	78	52	1	1,126
4. Riasi ,, ...	8,769	3,067	348	162	6	5,354	1,737	484	83	17	1	1,170	...	...	...	...	...	...	2,263	958	19	78	...	1,286
5. Mirpur ,, ...	3,826	1,424	103	97	...	2,299	232	62	21	3	...	149	85	42	1	2	...	42	3,433	1,269	78	89	...	2,086
6. Bhadarwah *Jagir* ...	660	216	105	59	...	339	178	69	35	10	...	74	...	...	...	...	...	...	480	146	70	49	...	264
7. Punch *Ilaqa*	3,840	1,194	78	58	1	2,568	683	97	5	10	...	581	39	8	6	...	1	25	1,098	405	12	14	...	681
II—Total Kashmir Province (including *Jagirs*).	39,476	13,539	3,265	851	6	22,672	11,893	3,564	2,481	414	6	5,848	4,338	1,596	572	24	...	2,170	21,049	7,108	155	393	...	13,786
8. Kashmir North (including Langet *Jagir*).	11,317	4,220	758	217	5	6,339	2,488	782	498	123	5	1,208	1,120	243	143	...	...	734	6,877	2,465	99	93	...	4,313
9. Kashmir South (including city).	26,359	8,613	2,488	567	1	15,258	9,362	2,768	1,979	291	1	4,615	3,211	1,352	429	24	...	1,430	12,445	3,963	41	233	...	8,441
Total Kashmir Valley...	*37,676*	*12,833*	*3,246*	*784*	*6*	*21,597*	*11,850*	*3,550*	*2,477*	*414*	*6*	*5,823*	*4,331*	*1,595*	*572*	*24*	...	*2,164*	*19,322*	*6,423*	*140*	*326*	...	*12,754*
10. Muzaffarabad District ...	1,800	706	19	67	...	1,075	43	14	4	...	...	25	7	1	...	...	...	6	1,727	680	15	67	...	1,032
III—Total Frontier Districts.	1,159	512	35	29	...	612	4	1	...	...	...	3	29	11	1	...	...	17	1,099	489	24	29	...	586
11. Laddakh District (including Mansar).	976	386	35	19	...	555	4	1	...	...	...	3	28	10	1	...	...	17	917	364	24	19	...	529
12. Gilgit ,, ...	183	126	...	10	...	57	...	...	...	...	...	...	1	1	...	...	...	...	182	125	...	10	...	57
13. Frontier *Ilaqas* ...	...	...	...	...	...	...	...	...	...	...	...	...	...	...	...	...	...	...	...	...	...	...	...	...
Cities.																								
Jammu	2,658	1,097	15	1	...	1,546	110	45	1	...	...	64	141	60	7	...	...	74	1,796	743	2	...	...	1,051
Srinagar	10,486	3,346	1,024	19	...	6,116	2,939	1,006	627	4	...	1,306	1,694	562	360	...	...	772	4,518	1,306	15	12	...	3,197

TABLE XV-A.

Occupation or Means of Livelihood.

Jammu and Kashmir State Census 1911.

DISTRICT, JAGIR, ILAQA OR CITY.	Group (122).—Tobacco, opium, ganja, etc. sellers.						Group (123).—Dealers in sheep, goats and pigs.					
	Total workers and dependents.	Actual Workers. Total. Males.	Actual Workers. Total. Females.	Actual Workers. Partially Agriculturists. Males.	Actual Workers. Partially Agriculturists. Females.	Dependents.	Total workers and dependents.	Actual Workers. Total. Males.	Actual Workers. Total. Females.	Actual Workers. Partially Agriculturists. Males.	Actual Workers. Partially Agriculturists. Females.	Dependents.
	740	741	742	743	744	745	746	747	748	749	750	751
Total State ...	**876**	**358**	**16**	**10**	...	**502**	**8,248**	**3,005**	**269**	**190**	**1**	**4,974**
I—Total Jammu Province (including *Jagirs*).	409	206	4	8	...	199	7,849	2,786	269	180	1	4,794
1. Jammu District (including city).	294	132	4	...	...	158	265	78	1	13	...	186
2. Jasrota "	52	35	...	3	...	17	785	355	33	62	1	397
3. Udhampur "	38	24	...	5	...	14	278	103	24	11	...	151
4. Riasi "	10	8	...	...	...	2	4,514	1,575	156	58	...	2,783
5. Mirpur "	11	6	...	...	...	5	14	7	...	2	...	7
6. Bhadarwah *Jagir* ...	...	...	...	...	...	...	...	...	...	...	...	...
7. Punch *Ilaqa*	4	1	...	...	...	3	1,993	668	55	34	...	1,270
II—Total Kashmir Province (including *Jagirs*).	465	151	12	2	...	302	393	213	...	10	...	180
8. Kashmir North (including Langet *Jagir*).	40	11	7	...	...	22	60	23	...	1	...	37
9. Kashmir South (including city).	424	139	5	2	...	280	332	189	...	9	...	143
Total Kashmir Valley ...	*464*	*150*	*12*	*2*	...	*302*	*392*	*212*	...	*10*	...	*180*
10. Muzaffarabad District ...	1	1	...	...	...	...	1	1	...	...	...	...
III—Total Frontier Districts.	2	1	...	...	...	1	6	6	...	...	...	...
11. Laddakh District (including Mansar).	2	1	...	...	...	1	6	6	...	...	...	...
12. Gilgit "	...	...	...	...	...	...	...	...	...	...	...	...
13. Frontier *Ilaqas*	...	...	...	...	...	...	...	...	...	...	...	...
Cities.												
Jammu	247	114	2	...	...	131	...	...	...	...	...	...
Srinagar	347	118	5	2	...	224	103	36	...	...	...	67

DISTRICT, JAGIR, ILAQA OR CITY.	Group (124).—Dealers in hay, grass and fodder.						Order 34.—Trade in clothing and toilet articles.						Group (125).—Trade in ready made clothing and other articles of dress and the toilet (hats, umbrellas, socks, ready-made shoes, perfumes, etc.)					
	Total workers and dependents.	Actual Workers. Total. Males.	Actual Workers. Total. Females.	Actual Workers. Partially Agriculturists. Males.	Actual Workers. Partially Agriculturists. Females.	Dependents.	Total workers and dependents.	Actual Workers. Total. Males.	Actual Workers. Total. Females.	Actual Workers. Partially Agriculturists. Males.	Actual Workers. Partially Agriculturists. Females.	Dependents.	Total workers and dependents.	Actual Workers. Total. Males.	Actual Workers. Total. Females.	Actual Workers. Partially Agriculturists. Males.	Actual Workers. Partially Agriculturists. Females.	Dependents.
	752	753	754	755	756	757	758	759	760	761	762	763	764	765	766	767	768	769
Total State ...	**2,666**	**1,245**	**427**	**48**	**16**	**994**	**1,315**	**188**	**115**	**49**	**33**	**1,012**	**1,315**	**188**	**115**	**49**	**33**	**1,012**
I—Total Jammu Province (including *Jagirs*).	1,309	334	372	40	16	603	1,077	124	77	47	33	876	1,077	124	77	47	33	876
1. Jammu District (including city).	550	103	167	17	11	280	176	20	...	...	...	156	176	20	...	...	...	156
2. Jasrota "	323	98	78	13	...	151	840	78	67	38	33	695	840	78	67	38	33	695
3. Udhampur "	115	37	38	...	...	40	6	1	...	...	...	5	6	1	...	...	...	5
4. Riasi "	245	42	90	9	5	113	21	14	1	3	...	6	21	14	1	3	...	6
5. Mirpur "	51	38	3	1	...	10	34	11	9	6	...	14	34	11	9	6	...	14
6. Bhadarwah *Jagir* ...	2	1	...	...	...	1	...	...	...	...	...	...	...	...	...	...	...	...
7. Punch *Ilaqa*	23	15	...	...	...	8	...	...	...	...	...	...	...	...	...	...	...	...
II—Total Kashmir Province (including *Jagirs*).	1,338	907	45	8	...	386	238	64	38	...	...	136	238	64	38	...	...	136
8. Kashmir North (including Langet *Jagir*).	732	696	11	...	...	25	47	10	...	...	...	37	47	10	...	...	...	37
9. Kashmir South (including city).	585	202	34	8	...	349	190	54	38	2	...	98	190	54	38	2	...	98
Total Kashmir Valley ...	*1,317*	*898*	*45*	*8*	...	*374*	*237*	*64*	*38*	*2*	...	*135*	*237*	*64*	*38*	*2*	...	*135*
10. Muzaffarabad District ...	21	9	...	...	...	12	1	...	...	...	...	1	1	...	...	...	...	1
III—Total Frontier Districts.	19	4	10	...	...	5	...	...	...	...	...	...	...	...	...	...	...	...
11. Laddakh District (including Mansar).	19	4	10	...	...	5	...	...	...	...	...	...	...	...	...	...	...	...
12. Gilgit "	...	...	...	...	...	...	...	...	...	...	...	...	...	...	...	...	...	...
13. Frontier *Ilaqas*	...	...	...	...	...	...	...	...	...	...	...	...	...	...	...	...	...	...
Cities.																		
Jammu	5	1	3	...	...	1	96	18	...	...	...	58	96	18	...	...	...	58
Srinagar	216	78	11	...	...	127	143	40	35	...	...	68	143	40	35	...	...	68

TABLE XV-A.

OCCUPATION OR MEANS OF LIVELIHOOD.

Jammu and Kashmir State Census, 1911.

DISTRICT, JAGIR, ILAQA OR CITY.	Order 35—Trade in furniture.						*Group (126).—Trade in furniture, carpets, curtains and bedding.*					
	Total worker and dependents.	ACTUAL WORKERS. *Total.* Males.	ACTUAL WORKERS. *Total.* Females.	ACTUAL WORKERS. *Partially Agriculturists.* Males.	ACTUAL WORKERS. *Partially Agriculturists.* Females.	Dependents.	Total workers and dependents.	ACTUAL WORKERS. *Total.* Males.	ACTUAL WORKERS. *Total.* Females.	ACTUAL WORKERS. *Partially Agriculturists.* Males.	ACTUAL WORKERS. *Partially Agriculturists.* Females.	Dependents.
	770	771	772	773	774	775	776	777	778	779	780	781
Total State ...	**147**	**55**	**7**	**9**	...	**85**	**13**	**5**	...	...	...	**8**
I—Total Jammu Province (including *Jagirs*).	63	38	...	9	...	25	3	...	...	...	...	3
1. Jammu District (including city).	3	...	...	...	...	3	3	...	...	...	...	3
2. Jasrota ,, ...	56	37	...	9	...	19	...	...	...	...	...	...
3. Udhampur ,, ...	4	1	...	...	...	3	...	...	...	...	...	...
4. Riasi ,, ...	...	...	...	...	...	...	...	...	...	...	...	...
5. Mirpur ,, ...	...	...	...	...	...	...	...	...	...	...	...	...
6. Bhadarwah *Jagir* ...	...	...	...	...	...	...	...	...	...	...	...	...
7. Punch *Ilaqa*	...	...	...	...	...	...	...	...	...	...	...	...
II—Total Kashmir Province (including *Jagirs*).	83	16	7	...	...	60	9	4	...	...	...	5
8. Kashmir North (including Langet *Jagir*).	14	3	4	...	...	7	...	...	...	...	...	...
9. Kashmir South (including city).	69	13	3	...	...	53	9	4	...	...	...	5
Total Kashmir Valley ...	*83*	*16*	*7*	...	...	*60*	*9*	*4*	...	...	...	*5*
10. Muzaffarabad District ...	...	...	...	...	...	...	...	...	...	...	...	...
III—Total Frontier Districts.	1	1	...	...	...	...	1	1	...	...	...	...
11.—Laddakh District (including Mansar).	1	1	...	...	...	...	1	1	...	...	...	...
12. Gilgit ,, ...	...	...	...	...	...	...	...	...	...	...	...	...
13. Frontier *Ilaqas*	...	...	...	...	...	...	...	...	...	...	...	...
Cities.												
Jammu	3	...	...	...	...	3	3	...	...	...	...	3
Srinagar	38	4	...	...	...	34	6	3	...	...	...	3

DISTRICT, JAGIR, ILAQA OR CITY.	*Group (127).—Hardware, cooking utensils, porcelain, crockery, glassware, bottles, articles for gardening, the cellar, etc.*					
	Total workers and dependents.	ACTUAL WORKERS. *Total.* Males.	ACTUAL WORKERS. *Total.* Females.	ACTUAL WORKERS. *Partially Agriculturists.* Males.	ACTUAL WORKERS. *Partially Agriculturists.* Females.	Dependents.
	782	783	784	785	786	787
Total State ...	**134**	**50**	**7**	**9**	...	**77**
I—Total Jammu Province (including *Jagirs*).	60	38	...	9	...	22
1. Jammu District (including city).	...	...	...	...	...	...
2. Jasrota ,, ...	56	37	...	9	...	19
3. Udhampur ,, ...	4	1	...	...	...	3
4. Riasi ,, ...	...	...	...	...	...	...
5. Mirpur ,, ...	...	...	...	...	...	...
6. Bhadarwah *Jagir* ...	...	...	...	...	...	...
7. Punch *Ilaqa*	...	...	...	...	...	...
II—Total Kashmir Province (including *Jagirs*).	74	12	7	...	...	55
8. Kashmir North (including Langet *Jagir*).	14	3	4	...	...	7
9. Kashmir South (including city).	60	9	3	...	...	48
Total Kashmir Valley ...	*74*	*12*	*7*	...	...	*55*
10. Muzaffarabad District ...	...	...	...	...	...	...
III—Total Frontier Districts.	...	...	...	...	...	...
11.—Laddakh District (including Mansar).	...	...	...	...	...	...
12. Gilgit ,, ...	...	...	...	...	...	...
13. Frontier *Ilaqas*	...	...	...	...	...	...
Cities.						
Jammu	...	...	...	...	...	...
Srinagar	32	1	...	...	...	31

DISTRICT, JAGIR, ILAQA OR CITY.	Order 36.—Trade in building materials.						*Group (128).—Trade in building materials, stones, bricks, plaster, cement, sand, tiles, thatch, etc.*					
	Total workers and dependents.	ACTUAL WORKERS. *Total.* Males.	ACTUAL WORKERS. *Total.* Females.	ACTUAL WORKERS. *Partially Agriculturists.* Males.	ACTUAL WORKERS. *Partially Agriculturists.* Females.	Dependents.	Total workers and dependents.	ACTUAL WORKERS. *Total.* Males.	ACTUAL WORKERS. *Total.* Females.	ACTUAL WORKERS. *Partially Agriculturists.* Males.	ACTUAL WORKERS. *Partially Agriculturists.* Females.	Dependents.
	788	789	790	791	792	793	794	795	796	797	798	799
Total State ...	**45**	**24**	**1**	**2**	...	**20**	**45**	**24**	**1**	**2**	...	**20**
I—Total Jammu Province (including *Jagirs*).	7	6	...	2	...	1	7	6	...	2	...	1
1. Jammu District (including city).	3	2	...	...	...	1	3	2	...	...	...	1
2. Jasrota ,, ...	...	...	...	...	...	...	...	...	...	...	...	...
3. Udhampur ,, ...	4	4	...	2	...	...	4	4	...	2	...	...
4. Riasi ,, ...	...	...	...	...	...	...	...	...	...	...	...	...
5. Mirpur ,, ...	...	...	...	...	...	...	...	...	...	...	...	...
6. Bhadarwah *Jagir* ...	...	...	...	...	...	...	...	...	...	...	...	...
7. Punch *Ilaqa*	...	...	...	...	...	...	...	...	...	...	...	...
II—Total Kashmir Province (including *Jagirs*).	38	18	1	...	...	19	38	18	1	...	...	19
8. Kashmir North (including Langet *Jagir*).	7	...	...	...	...	7	7	...	...	...	...	7
9. Kashmir South (including city).	31	18	1	...	...	12	31	18	1	...	...	12
Total Kashmir Valley ...	*38*	*18*	*1*	...	...	*19*	*38*	*18*	*1*	...	...	*19*
10. Muzaffarabad District ...	...	...	...	...	...	...	...	...	...	...	...	...
III—Total Frontier Districts.	...	...	...	...	...	...	...	...	...	...	...	...
11.—Laddakh District (including Mansar).	...	...	...	...	...	...	...	...	...	...	...	...
12. Gilgit ,, ...	...	...	...	...	...	...	...	...	...	...	...	...
13. Frontier *Ilaqas*	...	...	...	...	...	...	...	...	...	...	...	...
Cities.												
Jammu	3	2	...	...	...	1	3	2	...	...	...	1
Srinagar	9	4	...	...	...	5	9	4	...	...	...	5

TABLE XV-A.

Occupation or Means of Livelihood.

Jammu and Kashmir State Census, 1911.

DISTRICT, JAGIR, ILAQA OR CITY.	Order 37.—Trade in means of transport.						*Group (129).—Dealers & hirers of elephants, camel, horses, cattle, asses, mules, etc., sellers (not makers) of carriages, saddlery, etc.*						Order 38.—Trade in fuel.						*Group (130).—Dealers in firewood, charcoal, coal, cowdung, etc.*					
	Total workers and dependents.	Actual Workers. Total. Males.	Actual Workers. Total. Females.	Actual Workers. Partially Agriculturists. Males.	Actual Workers. Partially Agriculturists. Females.	Dependents.	Total workers and dependents.	Actual Workers. Total. Males.	Actual Workers. Total. Females.	Actual Workers. Partially Agriculturists. Males.	Actual Workers. Partially Agriculturists. Females.	Dependents.	Total workers and dependents.	Actual Workers. Total. Males.	Actual Workers. Total. Females.	Actual Workers. Partially Agriculturists. Males.	Actual Workers. Partially Agriculturists. Females.	Dependents.	Total workers and dependents.	Actual Workers. Total. Males.	Actual Workers. Total. Females.	Actual Workers. Partially Agriculturists. Males.	Actual Workers. Partially Agriculturists. Females.	Dependents.
	800	801	802	803	804	805	806	807	808	809	810	811	812	813	814	815	816	817	818	819	820	821	822	823
Total State	**703**	**286**	**25**	**3**	**1**	**392**	**703**	**286**	**25**	**3**	**1**	**392**	**3,883**	**1,458**	**613**	**106**	**62**	**1,812**	**3,883**	**1,458**	**613**	**106**	**62**	**1,812**
I—Total Jammu Province (including *Jagirs*).	654	260	23	3	1	371	654	260	23	3	1	371	2,472	1,020	512	102	62	940	2,472	1,020	512	102	62	940
1. Jammu District (including city).	144	42	4	2	...	98	144	42	4	2	...	98	1,618	690	297	66	50	631	1,618	690	297	66	50	631
2. Jasrota ,, ...	49	25	15	...	1	9	49	25	15	...	1	9	357	153	60	9	...	144	357	153	60	9	...	144
3. Udhampur ,, ...	107	54	...	1	...	53	107	54	...	1	...	53	317	87	143	25	11	87	317	87	143	25	11	87
4. Riasi ,, ...	4	1	...	...	...	3	4	1	...	...	...	3	63	35	8	2	...	20	63	35	8	2	...	20
5. Mirpur ,, ...	339	138	4	...	...	197	339	138	4	...	...	197	53	18	...	...	...	35	53	18	...	...	...	35
6. Bhadarwah *Jagir* ...	...	...	...	...	...	...	...	...	...	...	...	...	5	...	2	...	1	3	5	...	2	...	1	3
7. Punch *Ilaqa*	11	...	...	...	...	11	11	...	...	...	...	11	59	37	2	...	...	20	59	37	2	...	...	20
II—Total Kashmir Province (including *Jagirs*).	41	23	2	...	...	16	41	23	2	...	...	16	1,390	429	100	4	...	861	1,390	429	100	4	...	861
8. Kashmir North (including Langet *Jagir*).	8	2	2	...	...	4	8	2	2	...	...	4	452	135	68	2	...	249	452	135	68	2	...	249
9. Kashmir South (including city).	12	4	...	...	...	8	12	4	...	...	...	8	921	283	32	2	...	606	921	283	32	2	...	606
Total Kashmir Valley ...	*20*	*6*	*2*	...	...	*12*	*20*	*6*	*2*	...	...	*12*	*1,373*	*418*	*100*	*4*	...	*355*	*1,373*	*418*	*100*	*4*	...	*855*
10. Muzaffarabad District ...	21	17	...	...	...	4	21	17	...	...	...	4	17	11	...	...	...	6	17	11	...	...	...	6
III—Total Frontier Districts.	8	3	...	...	...	5	8	3	...	...	...	5	21	9	1	...	...	11	21	9	1	...	...	11
11. Laddakh District (including Mansar).	8	3	...	...	...	5	8	3	...	...	...	5	18	7	1	...	...	10	18	7	1	...	...	10
12. Gilgit ,, ...	...	...	...	...	...	...	...	...	...	...	...	...	3	2	...	...	...	1	3	2	...	...	...	1
13. Frontier *Ilaqas*	...	...	...	...	...	...	...	...	...	...	...	...	...	...	...	...	...	...	...	...	...	...	...	...
Cities.																								
Jammu	3	3	...	...	...	...	3	3	...	...	...	...	197	80	51	...	1	66	197	80	51	...	1	66
Srinagar	10	4	...	...	...	6	10	4	...	...	...	6	541	163	24	...	...	354	541	163	24	...	...	354

TABLE XV-A.

Occupation or Means of Livelihood.

Jammu and Kashmir State Census, 1911.

Order 39.—Trade in articles of luxury and those pertaining to letters and the arts and sciences (824–829). Group (131).—Dealers in precious stones, jewellery (real and imitation), clocks, optical instruments, etc. (830–835). Group (132).—Dealers in common bangles, bead, necklaces, fans, small articles, toys, hunting and fishing tackle, flowers, etc. (836–841). Group (133).—Publishers, book-sellers, stationers, dealers in music, pictures, musical instruments and curiosities (842–847). Order 40.—Trade in refuse matter (848–853).

District, Jagir, Ilaqa or City.	Order 39. Total workers and dependents.	Actual Workers. Total. Males.	Actual Workers. Total. Females.	Actual Workers. Partially Agriculturists. Males.	Actual Workers. Partially Agriculturists. Females.	Dependents.	Group (131). Total workers and dependents.	Actual Workers. Total. Males.	Actual Workers. Total. Females.	Actual Workers. Partially Agriculturists. Males.	Actual Workers. Partially Agriculturists. Females.	Dependents.	Group (132). Total workers and dependents.	Actual Workers. Total. Males.	Actual Workers. Total. Females.	Actual Workers. Partially Agriculturists. Males.	Actual Workers. Partially Agriculturists. Females.	Dependents.	Group (133). Total workers and dependents	Actual Workers. Total. Males.	Actual Workers. Total. Females.	Actual Workers. Partially Agriculturists. Males.	Actual Workers. Partially Agriculturists. Females.	Dependents.	Order 40. Total workers and dependents.	Actual Workers. Total. Males.	Actual Workers. Total. Females.	Actual Workers. Partially Agriculturists. Males.	Actual Workers. Partially Agriculturists. Females.	Dependents.
	824	825	826	827	828	829	830	831	832	833	834	835	836	837	838	839	840	841	842	843	844	845	846	847	848	849	850	851	852	853
Total State ...	3,115	841	126	35	1	2,148	1,524	410	3	7	...	1,111	1,432	373	123	27	1	936	159	58	...	1	...	101	180	55	...	1	...	125
I—Total Jammu Province (including *Jagirs*).	742	176	121	16	1	445	95	29	...	...	...	66	620	137	121	16	1	362	27	10	...	...	...	17	1	1	...	...	...	...
1. Jammu District (including city).	314	55	60	...	1	199	76	23	...	...	...	53	218	29	60	...	1	129	20	3	...	...	...	17	...	...	...	...	...	...
2. Jasrota	130	38	2	2	...	90	...	...	...	...	...	...	130	38	2	2	...	90	...	...	...	...	...	...	...	...	...	...	...	...
3. Udhampur	40	23	3	1	...	14	3	3	...	...	...	...	33	16	3	1	...	14	4	4	...	...	...	...	...	...	...	...	...	...
4. Riasi	20	16	...	...	...	4	...	...	...	...	...	...	20	16	...	...	...	4	...	...	...	...	...	...	...	...	...	...	...	...
5. Mirpur	211	40	55	13	...	116	16	3	...	...	...	13	192	34	55	13	...	103	3	3	...	...	...	...	...	...	...	...	...	...
6. Bhadarwah *Jagir* ...	2	...	...	...	...	2	...	...	...	...	...	...	2	...	...	...	...	2	...	...	...	...	...	...	...	...	...	...	...	...
7. Punch *Ilaqa*	25	4	1	...	...	20	...	...	...	...	...	...	25	4	1	...	...	20	...	...	...	...	...	...	1	1	...	...	...	...
II—Total Kashmir Province (including *Jagirs*).	2,359	661	4	19	...	1,694	1,418	382	2	7	...	1,036	812	236	2	11	...	574	129	45	...	1	...	84	179	54	...	1	...	125
8. Kashmir North (including Langet *Jagir*).	92	32	...	...	...	60	36	6	...	...	...	30	45	19	...	...	...	26	11	7	...	...	...	4	...	...	...	...	...	...
9. Kashmir South (including city).	2,240	620	4	19	...	1,616	1,382	374	2	7	...	1,006	740	208	2	11	...	530	118	38	...	1	...	80	179	54	...	1	...	125
Total Kashmir Valley ...	*2,332*	*652*	*4*	*19*	...	*1,676*	*1,418*	*380*	*2*	*7*	...	*1,036*	*785*	*227*	*2*	*11*	...	*556*	*129*	*45*	...	*1*	...	*84*	*179*	*54*	...	*1*	...	*125*
10. Muzaffarabad District ...	27	9	...	...	...	18	...	...	...	...	...	...	27	9	...	...	...	18	...	...	...	...	...	...	...	...	...	...	...	...
III—Total Frontier Districts.	14	4	1	...	...	9	11	1	1	...	...	9	...	...	...	...	...	...	3	3	...	...	...	...	...	...	...	...	...	...
11. Laddakh District (including Mansar).	10	...	1	...	...	9	10	...	1	...	...	9	...	...	...	...	...	...	...	...	...	...	...	...	...	...	...	...	...	...
12. Gilgit	1	1	...	...	...	...	1	1	...	...	...	...	...	...	...	...	...	...	...	...	...	...	...	...	...	...	...	...	...	...
13. Frontier *Ilaqas*	3	3	...	...	...	...	...	...	...	...	...	...	...	...	...	...	...	...	3	3	...	...	...	...	...	...	...	...	...	...
Cities.																														
Jammu	145	36	12	...	...	97	76	23	...	...	...	53	49	10	12	...	...	27	20	3	...	...	...	17	...	...	...	...	...	...
Srinagar	1,747	462	2	13	...	1,283	1,273	341	...	7	...	932	368	87	2	4	...	279	106	34	...	1	...	72	176	52	...	1	...	124

TABLE XV-A.

Occupation or Means of Livelihood.

Jammu and Kashmir State Census, 1911.

District, Jagir, Ilaqa or City.	Group (134).—Dealers in rags, stable refuse, etc.						Order 41.—Trade of other sorts.						Group (135).—Shopkeepers otherwise unspecified.						Group (136).—Itinerant traders, pedlars, hawkers etc.						Group ([illegible]).—Conjurers, acrobats, fortune tellers, reciters, exhibitors of curiosities and wild animals.					
	Total workers and dependents.	Actual Workers. Total. Males.	Actual Workers. Total. Females.	Actual Workers. Partially Agriculturists. Males.	Actual Workers. Partially Agriculturists. Females.	Dependents.	Total workers and dependents.	Actual Workers. Total. Males.	Actual Workers. Total. Females.	Actual Workers. Partially Agriculturists. Males.	Actual Workers. Partially Agriculturists. Females.	Dependents.	Total workers and dependents.	Actual Workers. Total. Males.	Actual Workers. Total. Females.	Actual Workers. Partially Agriculturists. Males.	Actual Workers. Partially Agriculturists. Females.	Dependents.	Total workers and dependents.	Actual Workers. Total. Males.	Actual Workers. Total. Females.	Actual Workers. Partially Agriculturists. Males.	Actual Workers. Partially Agriculturists. Females.	Dependents.	Total workers and dependents.	Actual Workers. Total. Males.	Actual Workers. Total. Females.	Actual Workers. Partially Agriculturists. Males.	Actual Workers. Partially Agriculturists. Females.	Dependents.
	854	855	856	857	858	859	860	861	862	863	864	865	866	867	868	869	870	871	872	873	874	875	876	877	878	879	880	881	882	883
Total State	**180**	**55**	...	**1**	...	**125**	**9,293**	**3,141**	**118**	**169**	**3**	**6,034**	**7,400**	**2,441**	**54**	**128**	**3**	**4,905**	**1,112**	**412**	**19**	**16**	...	**681**	**779**	**287**	**45**	**24**	...	**447**
I—Total Jammu Province (including *Jagirs*).	1	1	...	...	...	...	6,342	2,249	103	121	3	3,990	5,341	1,847	52	101	3	3,442	510	211	6	13	...	293	489	190	45	6	...	254
1. Jammu District (including city)	...	...	...	...	...	...	3,477	1,122	57	70	2	2,298	3,155	986	24	70	2	2,145	156	79	...	...	...	77	166	57	33	...	...	76
2. Jasrota ,, ...	...	...	...	...	...	...	598	136	10	6	...	452	418	59	2	3	...	357	36	17	...	2	...	19	142	59	8	...	...	75
3. Udhampur	...	...	...	...	...	...	862	382	19	10	...	461	521	253	11	1	...	257	261	92	5	9	...	164	80	37	3	...	...	40
4. Riasi ,, ...	...	...	...	...	...	...	408	144	5	11	...	259	367	123	5	6	...	239	36	16	...	2	...	20	5	5	...	3	...	...
5. Mirpur ,, ...	...	...	...	...	...	...	630	287	10	13	...	333	552	264	8	10	...	280	20	7	1	...	...	12	58	16	1	3	...	41
6. Bhadarwah *Jagir* ...	...	...	...	...	...	...	48	41	...	3	...	7	48	41	...	3	...	7	...	...	...	...	...	...	...	...	...	...	...	...
7. Punch *Ilaqa*	1	1	...	...	...	...	319	137	2	8	1	180	280	121	2	8	1	157	1	...	...	...	...	1	38	16	...	...	...	22
II—Total Kashmir Province (including *Jagirs*).	179	54	...	1	...	125	2,925	872	15	98	...	2,038	2,047	586	2	27	...	1,459	602	201	13	3	...	388	276	85	...	18	...	191
8. Kashmir North (including Langet *Jagir*).	...	...	...	...	...	...	576	197	...	13	...	379	375	140	...	10	...	235	30	10	...	3	...	20	171	47	...	...	...	124
9. Kashmir South (including city).	179	54	...	1	...	125	2,156	595	14	31	...	1,547	1,521	386	1	13	...	1,134	569	188	13	...	...	368	66	21	...	18	...	45
Total Kashmir Valley...	*179*	*54*	...	*1*	...	*125*	*2,732*	*792*	*14*	*44*	...	*1,926*	*1,896*	*526*	*1*	*23*	...	*1,360*	*599*	*198*	*13*	*3*	...	*388*	*237*	*68*	...	*18*	...	*160*
10. Muzaffarabad District ...	...	...	...	...	...	...	193	80	1	4	...	112	151	60	1	4	...	90	3	3	...	...	...	...	39	17	...	...	...	22
III—Total Frontier Districts.	...	...	...	...	...	...	26	20	...	...	...	6	12	8	...	...	...	4	...	...	...	...	...	...	14	12	...	...	...	2
11. Laddakh District (including Mansar).	...	...	...	...	...	...	18	12	...	...	...	6	4	...	...	...	...	4	...	...	...	...	...	...	14	12	...	...	...	2
12. Gilgit ,, ...	...	...	...	...	...	...	...	...	...	...	...	...	...	...	...	...	...	...	...	...	...	...	...	...	...	...	...	...	...	...
13. Frontier *Ilaqas* ...	...	...	...	...	...	...	8	8	...	...	...	...	8	8	...	...	...	...	...	...	...	...	...	...	...	...	...	...	...	...
Cities.																														
Jammu	...	...	...	...	...	...	925	141	4	...	...	780	781	69	4	...	...	708	140	69	...	...	...	71	4	3	...	...	...	1
Srinagar	176	52	...	1	...	124	573	180	13	...	...	380	160	41	1	...	...	118	397	136	12	...	...	249	16	3	...	...	...	13

TABLE XV-A.

Occupation or Means of Livelihood.

Jammu and Kashmir State Census, 1911.

DISTRICT, JAGIR, ILAQA OR CITY.	Group (138).—Other trades (including farmers of pounds, tolls and markets). Total workers and dependents.	Actual Workers. Total. Males.	Total. Females.	Partially Agriculturists. Males.	Partially Agriculturists. Females.	Dependents.	CLASS C.—PUBLIC ADMINISTRATION AND LIBERAL ARTS. Total workers and dependents.	Actual Workers. Total. Males.	Total. Females.	Partially Agriculturists. Males.	Partially Agriculturists. Females.	Dependents.
	884	885	886	887	888	889	890	891	892	893	894	895
Total State ...	**2**	**1**	...	**1**	...	**1**	**104,541**	**40,915**	**1,957**	**3,959**	**90**	**61,669**
I—Total Jammu Province (including *Jagirs*).	2	1	...	1	...	1	52,969	22,153	1,610	2,030	78	29,206
1. Jammu District (including city).	...	...	...	...	...	...	27,172	11,796	793	732	24	14 583
2. Jasrota ,, ...	2	1	...	1	...	1	7,133	2,390	300	315	11	4,443
3. Udhampur ,, ...	...	...	...	...	...	...	4,437	1,854	148	209	12	2,435
4. Riasi ,, ...	...	...	...	...	...	...	2,768	1,228	58	165	6	1.482
5. Mirpur ,, ...	...	...	...	...	...	...	7,618	2,881	239	428	22	4,498
6. Bhadarwah *Jagir*. ...	...	...	...	...	...	...	554	269	3	77	1	282
7. Punch *Ilaqa*	...	...	...	...	...	...	3,287	1,735	69	104	2	1,483
II—Total Kashmir Province (including *Jagirs*).	...	...	...	...	...	...	45,960	14,711	218	1,407	6	31,031
8. Kashmir North (including Langet *Jagir*).	...	...	...	...	...	...	8,902	3,379	55	339	...	5,468
9. Kashmir South (including city).	...	...	...	...	...	...	35,123	10,334	150	965	6	24,639
Total Kashmir Valley ...	...	...	...	...	...	...	*44,025*	*13,713*	*205*	*1,304*	*6*	*30,107*
10. Muzaffarabad District ...	...	...	...	...	...	...	1,935	998	13	103	...	924
III—Total Frontier Districts.	...	...	...	...	...	...	5,612	4,051	129	522	6	1,432
11. Laddakh District (including Mansar).	...	...	...	...	...	...	2,639	1,866	127	48	6	646
12. Gilgit ,, ...	...	...	...	...	...	...	1,437	1,231	2	474	...	204
13. Frontier *Ilaqas*	...	...	...	...	...	...	1,536	954	...	...	...	582
Cities.												
Jammu	...	...	...	...	...	...	10,208	4,675	304	49	72	5,229
Srinagar	...	...	...	...	...	...	21,699	6,349	83	239	...	15,277

DISTRICT, JAGIR, ILAQA OR CITY.	Sub-class VI.—Public force. Total workers and dependents.	Actual Workers. Total. Males.	Total. Females.	Partially Agriculturists. Males.	Partially Agriculturists. Females.	Dependents.
	896	897	898	899	900	901
Total State ...	**20.513**	**10,573**	**18**	**1.203**	**4**	**9.922**
I—Total Jammu Province (including *Jagirs*).	13,148	6,786	18	349	4	6,344
1. Jammu District (including city).	8,683	5,036	17	135	2	3,630
2. Jasrota ,, ...	1.314	350	...	46	...	964
3. Udhampur ,, ...	704	327	...	33	...	377
4. Riasi ,, ...	461	237	...	31	...	224
5. Mirpur ,, ...	1,122	379	...	63	1	743
6. Bhadarwah *Jagir*. ...	49	30	...	10	...	19
7. Punch *Ilaqa*	815	427	1	31	1	387
II—Total Kashmir Province (including *Jagirs*).	5,893	2,480	...	398	...	3,413
8. Kashmir North (including Langet *Jagir*).	906	473	...	141	...	433
9. Kashmir South (including city).	4,781	1,880	...	240	...	2,901
Total Kashmir Valley ...	*5,687*	*2,353*	...	*381*	...	*3,334*
10. Muzaffarabad District ...	206	127	...	17	...	79
III—Total Frontier Districts.	1,472	1,307	...	456	...	165
11. Laddakh District (including Mansar).	390	275	...	3	...	115
12. Gilgit ,, ...	1,013	978	...	453	...	35
13. Frontier *Ilaqas*	69	54	...	...	...	15
Cities.						
Jammu	2,889	1,918	...	12	...	971
Srinagar	3,015	1,324	...	155	...	1,691

DISTRICT, JAGIR, ILAQA OR CITY.	Order 42.—Army. Total workers and dependents.	Actual Workers. Total. Males.	Total. Females.	Partially Agriculturists. Males.	Partially Agriculturists. Females.	Dependents.	Group (139).—Army (Imperial). Total workers and dependents.	Actual Workers. Total. Males.	Total. Females.	Partially Agriculturists. Males.	Partially Agriculturists. Females.	Dependents.
	902	903	904	905	906	907	908	909	910	911	912	913
Total State ...	**10,706**	**6,970**	**18**	**781**	...	**3,718**	**9**	**9**	...	...	...	...
I—Total Jammu Province (including *Jagirs*).	8,255	4,965	18	122	...	3,272	7	7	...	...	...	...
1. Jammu District (including city).	6,070	4,174	17	32	...	1,879	7	7	...	...	...	...
2. Jasrota ,, ...	593	96	...	17	...	497	...	...	...	...	...	...
3. Udhampur ,, ...	327	123	...	12	...	204	...	...	...	...	...	...
4. Riasi ,, ...	191	108	...	4	...	83	...	...	...	...	...	...
5. Mirpur ,, ...	573	183	...	31	...	390	...	...	...	...	...	...
6. Bhadarwah *Jagir*. ...	1	1	...	...	...	...	...	...	...	...	...	...
7. Punch *Ilaqa*	500	280	1	26	...	219	...	...	...	...	...	...
II—Total Kashmir Province (including *Jagirs*).	1,238	851	...	210	...	387	...	...	...	...	...	...
8. Kashmir North (including Langet *Jagir*).	188	137	...	58	...	51	...	...	...	...	...	...
9. Kashmir South (including city).	1,037	706	...	152	...	331	...	...	...	...	...	...
Total Kashmir Valley ...	*1,225*	*843*	...	*210*	...	*382*	...	...	...	...	...	...
10. Muzaffarabad District ...	13	8	...	...	...	5	...	...	...	...	...	...
III—Total Frontier Districts.	1,213	1,154	...	449	...	59	2	2	...	...	...	...
11. Laddakh District (including Mansar).	210	194	...	...	...	16	...	...	...	...	...	...
12. Gilgit ,, ...	973	945	...	449	...	28	2	2	...	...	...	...
13. Frontier *Ilaqas*	30	15	...	...	...	15	...	...	...	...	...	...
Cities.												
Jammu	2,099	1,559	...	1	...	540	...	...	...	...	...	...
Srinagar	991	683	...	146	...	308	...	...	...	...	...	...

TABLE XV-A.

Occupation or Means of Livelihood.

Jammu and Kashmir State Census, 1911.

DISTRICT, JAGIR, ILAQA OR CITY.	Group (140).—Army (Native States). Total workers and dependents.	Actual Workers. Total. Males.	Total. Females.	Partially Agriculturists. Males.	Partially Agriculturists. Females.	Dependents.	Order 44.—Police. Total workers and dependents.	Actual Workers. Total. Males.	Total. Females.	Partially Agriculturists. Males.	Partially Agriculturists. Females.	Dependents.
	914	915	916	917	918	919	920	921	922	923	924	925
Total State ...	**10,697**	**6.961**	**18**	**781**	...	**3.718**	**9,807**	**3.603**	...	**422**	**4**	**6,204**
I—Total Jammu Province (including *Jagirs*).	8,248	4,958	18	122	...	3,272	4,893	1,821	...	227	4	3,072
1. Jammu District (including city).	6,063	4,167	17	32	...	1,879	2,613	862	...	103	2	1,751
2. Jasrota ,, ...	593	96	...	17	...	497	721	254	...	29	...	467
3. Udhampur ,, ...	327	123	...	12	...	204	377	204	...	21	...	173
4. Riasi ,, ...	191	108	...	4	...	83	270	129	...	27	...	141
5. Mirpur ,, ...	573	183	...	31	...	390	549	196	...	32	1	353
6. Bhadarwah *Jagir* ...	1	1	...	...	...	...	48	29	...	10	...	19
7. Punch *Ilaqa*	500	280	1	26	...	219	315	147	...	5	1	168
II—Total Kashmir Province (including *Jagirs*).	1,238	851	...	210	...	387	4,655	1,629	...	188	...	3,026
8. Kashmir North (including Langet *Jagir*).	188	137	...	58	...	51	718	336	...	83	...	382
9. Kashmir South (including city).	1,037	706	...	152	...	331	3,744	1,174	...	88	...	2,570
Total Kashmir Valley ...	*1,225*	*843*	...	*210*	...	*382*	*4,462*	*1,510*	...	*171*	...	*2,952*
10. Muzaffarabad District ...	13	8	...	...	...	5	193	119	...	17	...	74
III—Total Frontier Districts.	1,211	1,152	...	449	...	59	259	153	...	7	...	106
11. Laddakh District (including Mansar).	210	194	...	...	...	16	180	81	...	3	...	99
12. Gilgit ,, ...	971	943	...	449	...	28	40	33	...	4	...	7
13. Frontier *Ilaqas*	30	15	...	...	...	15	39	39	...	...	...	...
Cities.												
Jammu	2,099	1,559	...	1	...	540	790	359	...	11	...	431
Srinagar	991	683	...	146	...	308	2,024	641	...	9	...	1,383

DISTRICT, JAGIR, ILAQA OR CITY.	Group (142).—Police. Total workers and dependents.	Actual Workers. Total. Males.	Total. Females.	Partially Agriculturists. Males.	Partially Agriculturists. Females.	Dependents.	Group (143).—Village watchmen. Total workers and dependents.	Actual Workers. Total. Males.	Total. Females.	Partially Agriculturists. Males.	Partially Agriculturists. Females.	Dependents.
	926	927	928	929	930	931	932	933	934	935	936	937
Total State ...	**4,672**	**1,866**	...	**113**	...	**2,806**	**5,135**	**1,737**	...	**309**	**4**	**3.398**
I—Total Jammu Province (including *Jagirs*).	2,159	951	...	72	...	1,208	2,734	870	...	155	4	1,864
1. Jammu District (including city).	1,082	448	...	40	...	634	1,531	414	...	63	2	1,117
2. Jasrota ,, ...	175	65	...	4	...	110	546	189	...	25	...	357
3. Udhampur ,, ...	193	113	...	4	...	80	184	91	...	17	...	93
4. Riasi ,, ...	106	62	...	4	...	44	164	67	...	23	...	97
5. Mirpur ,, ...	285	112	...	9	...	173	264	84	...	23	1	180
6. Bhadarwah *Jagir* ...	41	24	...	9	...	17	7	5	...	1	...	2
7. Punch *Ilaqa*	277	127	...	2	...	150	38	20	...	3	...	18
II—Total Kashmir Province (including *Jagirs*).	2,468	887	...	35	...	1,581	2,187	742	...	153	...	1,445
8. Kashmir North (including Langet *Jagir*).	158	114	...	4	...	44	560	222	...	79	...	338
9. Kashmir South (including city).	2,178	682	...	19	...	1,496	1,566	492	...	69	...	1,074
Total Kashmir Valley ...	*2,336*	*796*	...	*23*	...	*1,540*	*2,126*	*714*	...	*148*	...	*1,412*
10. Muzaffarabad District ...	132	91	...	12	...	41	61	28	...	5	...	33
III—Total Frontier Districts.	45	28	...	6	...	17	214	125	...	1	...	89
11. Laddakh District (including Mansar).	22	12	...	2	...	10	158	69	...	1	...	89
12. Gilgit ,, ...	23	16	...	4	...	7	17	17	...	...	...	...
13. Frontier *Ilaqas*	...	...	...	...	...	...	39	39	...	...	...	...
Cities.												
Jammu	715	308	...	11	...	407	75	51	...	...	...	24
Srinagar	1,846	525	...	6	...	1,321	178	116	...	3	...	62

DISTRICT, JAGIR, ILAQA OR CITY.	Sub-class VII.—Public administration. Total workers and dependents.	Actual Workers. Total. Males.	Total. Females.	Partially Agriculturists. Males.	Partially Agriculturists. Females.	Dependents.
	938	939	940	941	942	943
Total State ...	**28,707**	**11,157**	**241**	**709**	**17**	**17,309**
I—Total Jammu Province (including *Jagirs*).	13,998	6,180	212	445	17	7,606
1. Jammu District (including city).	8,147	3,382	111	204	4	4,654
2. Jasrota ,, ...	1,024	376	31	42	1	617
3. Udhampur ,, ...	1,167	521	35	45	...	611
4. Riasi ,, ...	530	265	...	19	...	265
5. Mirpur ,, ...	1,770	808	17	78	12	945
6. Bhadarwah *Jagir* ...	194	110	...	24	...	84
7. Punch *Ilaqa*	1,166	918	18	33	...	430
II—Total Kashmir Province (including *Jagirs*).	13,349	4,131	27	242	...	9,191
8. Kashmir North (including Langet *Jagir*).	1,699	936	...	72	...	763
9. Kashmir South (including city).	10,938	2,714	26	141	...	8,198
Total Kashmir Valley ...	*12,637*	*3,650*	*26*	*213*	...	*8,961*
10. Muzaffarabad District ...	712	481	1	29	...	230
III—Total Frontier Districts.	1,360	846	2	22	...	512
11. Laddakh District (including Mansar).	388	212	1	15	...	175
12. Gilgit ,, ...	202	137	1	7	...	64
13. Frontier *Ilaqas*	770	497	...	...	...	273
Cities.						
Jammu	4,493	1,892	81	36	71	2,520
Srinagar	8,969	1,987	20	50	...	6,962

TABLE XV-A.

Occupation or Means of Livelihood.

Jammu and Kashmir State Census, 1911.

DISTRICT, JAGIR, ILAQA OR CITY.	Order 45.—Public administration.						Group 144.—Service of the State.						*Group (145).—Service of Native and Foreign States.*						*Group (146).—Municipal and other local (not village) service.*						*Group (147).—Village officials and servants other than watchmen.*					
	Total workers and dependents.	Actual Workers. Total. Males.	Actual Workers. Total. Females.	Actual Workers. Partially Agriculturists. Males.	Actual Workers. Partially Agriculturists. Females.	Dependents.	Total workers and dependents.	Actual Workers. Total. Males.	Actual Workers. Total. Females.	Actual Workers. Partially Agriculturists. Males.	Actual Workers. Partially Agriculturists. Females.	Dependents.	Total workers and dependents.	Actual Workers. Total. Males.	Actual Workers. Total. Females.	Actual Workers. Partially Agriculturists. Males.	Actual Workers. Partially Agriculturists. Females.	Dependents.	Total workers and dependents.	Actual Workers. Total. Males.	Actual Workers. Total. Females.	Actual Workers. Partially Agriculturists. Males.	Actual Workers. Partially Agriculturists. Females.	Dependents.	Total workers and dependents.	Actual Workers. Total. Males.	Actual Workers. Total. Females.	Actual Workers. Partially Agriculturists. Males.	Actual Workers. Partially Agriculturists. Females.	Dependents.
	944	945	946	947	948	949	950	951	952	953	954	955	956	957	958	959	960	961	962	963	964	965	966	967	968	969	970	971	972	973
Total State ...	**28,707**	**11,157**	**241**	**709**	**17**	**17,309**	**34**	**34**	...	...	...	...	**23,617**	**8,755**	**192**	**461**	**17**	**14,670**	**1,765**	**946**	**49**	**57**	...	**770**	**3,291**	**1,422**	...	**191**	...	**1,869**
I—Total Jammu Province (including *Jagirs*).	13,998	6,180	212	445	17	7,606	2	2	...	...	...	...	11,412	4,868	173	317	17	6,371	1,325	757	39	55	...	529	1,259	553	...	73	...	706
1. Jammu District (including city).	8,147	3,382	111	204	4	4,654	...	...	...	...	...	...	7,735	3,227	101	145	4	4,407	30	6	10	2	...	14	382	149	...	37	...	233
2. Jasrota ,, ...	1,024	376	31	42	1	617	...	...	...	...	...	...	813	294	29	30	1	490	15	7	2	4	...	6	196	75	...	8	...	121
3. Udhampur ,, ...	1,167	521	35	45	...	611	...	...	...	...	...	...	1,069	476	27	42	...	566	31	3	8	...	...	20	67	72	...	3	...	25
4. Riasi ,, ...	530	265	...	19	...	265	...	...	...	...	...	...	370	175	...	11	...	195	7	6	...	...	...	1	153	54	...	8	...	59
5. Mirpur ,, ...	1,770	808	17	78	12	945	2	2	...	...	...	...	1,425	696	16	69	12	713	44	7	1	...	...	36	229	103	...	9	...	196
6. Bhadarwah *Jagir* ...	194	110	...	24	...	84	...	...	...	...	...	...	...	...	...	...	...	...	185	102	...	21	...	83	9	8	...	3	...	1
7. Punch *Ilaqa*	1,166	918	18	33	...	430	...	...	...	...	...	...	...	...	...	...	...	...	1,013	626	18	28	...	369	153	92	...	5	...	61
II—Total Kashmir Province (including *Jagirs*).	13,349	4,131	27	242	...	9,191	32	32	...	...	...	...	10,967	3,128	17	130	...	7,822	438	187	10	2	...	241	1,912	784	...	110	...	1,128
8. Kashmir North (including Langet *Jagir*).	1,699	936	...	72	...	763	12	12	...	...	...	...	1,106	590	...	34	...	543	10	3	...	...	...	7	571	331	...	38	...	240
9. Kashmir South (including city).	10,938	2,714	26	141	...	8,198	20	20	...	...	...	...	9,232	2,115	16	71	...	7,001	422	178	10	2	...	234	1,264	401	...	68	...	863
Total Kashmir Valley ...	*12,637*	*3,650*	*26*	*213*	...	*8,961*	*32*	*32*	...	...	...	...	*10,328*	*2,705*	*16*	*105*	...	*7,617*	*432*	*181*	*10*	*2*	...	*241*	*1,835*	*732*	...	*106*	...	*1,103*
10. Muzaffarabad District ...	712	481	1	29	...	230	...	...	...	...	...	...	629	423	1	25	...	205	6	6	...	...	...	...	77	52	...	4	...	25
III—Total Frontier Districts	1,360	846	2	22	...	512	...	...	...	...	...	...	1,228	759	2	14	...	497	2	2	...	...	...	...	120	85	...	8	...	35
11. Laddakh District (including Mansar).	388	212	1	15	...	175	...	...	...	...	...	...	283	133	1	8	...	148	...	...	...	...	...	...	106	79	...	7	...	27
12. Gilgit ,, ...	202	137	1	7	...	64	...	...	...	...	...	...	186	129	1	6	...	56	2	2	...	...	...	...	14	6	...	1	...	8
13. Frontier *Ilaqas*	770	497	...	...	...	273	...	...	...	...	...	...	770	497	...	...	...	273	...	...	...	...	...	...	...	...	...	...	...	...
Cities.																														
Jammu	4,493	1,892	81	36	71	2,520	...	...	...	...	...	...	4,468	1,890	71	36	...	2,507	24	1	10	...	...	13	1	1	...	...	...	...
Srinagar	8,969	1,987	20	50	...	6,962	20	20	...	...	...	...	8,208	1,747	16	6	...	6,445	358	164	4	2	...	190	383	50	...	2	...	327

TABLE XV-A.

Occupation or Means of Livelihood.

Jammu and Kashmir State Census, 1911.

DISTRICT, JAGIR, ILAQA OR CITY.	Sub-Class VIII.—Professions and Liberal Arts.						Order 46.—Religion.						*Group (148).—Priests, Ministers, etc.*						*Group (149).—Religious mendicants, inmates of monastries, etc.*					
	Total workers and dependents.	Actual Workers.				Dependents.	Total workers and dependents.	Actual Workers.				Dependents.	Total workers and dependents.	Actual Workers.				Dependents.	Total workers and dependents.	Actual Workers.				Dependents.
		Total.		*Partially Agriculturists.*				*Total.*		*Partially Agriculturists.*				*Total.*		*Partially Agriculturists.*				*Total.*		*Partially Agriculturists.*		
		Males.	Females.	Males.	Females.			Males.	Females.	Males.	Females.			Males.	Females.	Males.	Females.			Males.	Females.	Males.	Females.	
	974	975	976	977	978	979	980	981	982	983	984	985	986	987	988	989	990	991	992	993	994	995	996	997
Total State ...	**52,889**	**18,434**	**1,528**	**1,899**	**60**	**32,927**	**38,592**	**13,026**	**1,173**	**1,577**	**52**	**24,393**	**6,737**	**2,842**	**281**	**232**	**10**	**3,614**	**31,614**	**10,109**	**890**	**1,343**	**41**	**20,615**
I—Total Jammu Province (including *Jagirs*).	24,292	8,724	1,245	1,113	51	14,323	17,641	6,012	962	937	43	10,667	2,093	1,317	153	180	8	2,423	13,734	4,692	809	757	35	8,233
1. Jammu District (including city).	9,558	3,111	593	322	18	5,854	6,840	2,125	467	283	17	4,248	1,946	659	56	55	3	1,231	4,880	1,463	411	228	14	3,006
2. Jasrota "	4,617	1,611	259	216	9	2,747	3,926	1,349	215	189	5	2,362	130	58	3	4	...	69	3,796	1,291	212	185	5	2,293
3. Udhampur "	2,392	982	106	123	12	1,304	1,852	742	76	103	9	1,034	251	109	13	20	...	129	1,601	633	63	83	9	905
4. Riasi "	1,698	695	45	106	4	958	1,381	518	45	97	4	818	445	183	15	35	1	247	936	335	30	62	3	571
5. Mirpur "	4,424	1,611	191	264	6	2,622	2,949	1,009	131	209	6	1,809	1,010	273	45	60	4	692	1,939	736	86	149	2	1,117
6. Bhadarwah *Jagir* ...	310	128	3	43	1	179	211	86	3	24	1	122	28	20	...	2	...	8	183	66	3	22	1	114
7. Punch *Ilaqa*	1,293	586	48	39	1	659	482	183	25	32	1	274	83	15	21	4	...	47	399	168	4	28	1	227
II—Total Kashmir Province (including *Jagirs*).	25,945	7,881	160	444	6	17,904	18,831	5,524	95	628	6	13,212	1,517	429	22	47	...	1,066	17,087	5,023	71	579	5	11,993
8. Kashmir North (including Langet *Jagir*).	6,199	1,943	53	125	...	4,203	5,054	1,516	40	115	...	3,498	440	72	8	7	...	360	4,598	1,444	32	108	...	3,119
9. Kashmir South (including city).	18,788	5,563	96	568	6	13,129	13,060	3,765	48	466	6	9,247	986	321	11	28	...	654	11,866	3,372	35	436	5	8,459
Total Kashmir Valley ...	*24,987*	*7,506*	*149*	*693*	*6*	*17,322*	*18,114*	*5,281*	*88*	*581*	*6*	*12,745*	*1,426*	*393*	*19*	*35*	...	*1,014*	*16,461*	*4,816*	*67*	*544*	*5*	*11,578*
10. Muzaffarabad District ...	958	375	11	51	...	572	717	243	7	47	...	467	91	36	3	12	...	44	626	207	4	35	...	415
III—Total Frontier Districts.	2,652	1,829	123	42	3	700	2,120	1,490	116	12	3	514	1,327	1,096	106	5	2	125	793	394	10	7	1	389
11. Laddakh District (including Mansar).	1,845	1,375	122	28	3	348	1,554	1,203	116	5	3	235	1,326	1,095	106	4	2	125	228	108	10	1	1	110
12. Gilgit "	200	107	1	14	...	92	117	50	...	7	...	67	1	1	...	1	...	...	116	49	...	6	...	67
13. Frontier *Ilaqas*	607	347	...	...	...	260	449	237	...	...	...	212	...	...	...	...	...	...	449	237	...	...	...	212
Cities.																								
Jammu	2,240	729	169	1	1	1,542	695	148	119	1	1	428	227	65	9	...	1	153	464	82	110	1	...	272
Srinagar	9,199	2,888	41	24	...	6,270	5,180	1,622	10	9	...	3,548	693	197	...	...	...	496	4,459	1,409	10	9	...	3,040

TABLE XV-A.

Occupation or Means of Livelihood.

Jammu and Kashmir State Census, 1911.

DISTRICT, JAGIR, ILAQA OR CITY.	Group (151).—Temple, burial or burning ground service, pilgrim conductors, circumcisers.					
	Total workers and dependents.	Actual Workers. Total. Males.	Actual Workers. Total. Females.	Actual Workers. Partially Agriculturists. Males.	Actual Workers. Partially Agriculturists. Females.	Dependents.
	998	999	1000	1001	1002	1003
Total State ...	**241**	**75**	**2**	**2**	**1**	**164**
I—Total Jammu Province (including *Jagirs*).	14	3	...	...	...	11
1. Jammu District (including city).	14	3	...	...	...	11
2. Jasrota "	...	...	...	...	...	...
3. Udhampur "	...	...	...	...	...	...
4. Riasi "	...	...	...	...	...	...
5. Mirpur "	...	...	...	...	...	...
6. Bhadarwah *Jagir* ...	...	...	...	...	...	...
7. Punch *Ilaqa*	...	...	...	...	...	...
II—Total Kashmir Province (including *Jagirs*).	227	72	2	2	1	153
8. Kashmir North (including Langet *Jagir*).	19	...	...	...	...	19
9. Kashmir South (including city).	208	72	2	2	1	134
Total Kashmir Valley ...	*227*	*72*	*2*	*2*	*1*	*153*
10. Muzaffarabad District ...	...	...	...	...	...	...
III—Total Frontier Districts.	...	...	...	...	...	...
11. Laddakh District (including Mansar).	...	...	...	...	...	...
12. Gilgit	...	...	...	...	...	...
13. Frontier *Ilaqas* ...	...	...	...	...	...	...
Cities.						
Jammu	4	1	...	...	...	3
Srinagar	28	16	...	...	...	12

DISTRICT, JAGIR, ILAQA OR CITY.	Order 47.—Law.					
	Total workers and dependents.	Actual Workers. Total. Males.	Actual Workers. Total. Females.	Actual Workers. Partially Agriculturists. Males.	Actual Workers. Partially Agriculturists. Females.	Dependents.
	1004	1005	1006	1007	1008	1009
Total State ...	**1,523**	**402**	...	**29**	..	**1,121**
I—Total Jammu Province (including *Jagirs*).	735	213	...	17	...	522
1. Jammu District (including city).	372	97	...	3	...	275
2. Jasrota "	49	14	...	1	...	35
3. Udhampur "	66	21	...	...	...	45
4. Riasi "	31	11	...	1	...	20
5. Mirpur "	164	54	...	8	...	110
6. Bhadarwah *Jagir* ...	20	6	...	4	...	14
7. Punch *Ilaqa*	33	10	...	...	...	23
II—Total Kashmir Province (including *Jagirs*).	742	172	...	12	...	570
8. Kashmir North (including Langet *Jagir*).	97	35	...	1	...	62
9. Kashmir South (including city).	604	121	...	11	...	483
Total Kashmir Valley ...	*701*	*156*	...	*12*	...	*542*
10. Muzaffarabad District ...	41	16	...	...	...	25
III—Total Frontier Districts.	46	17	...	...	...	29
11. Laddakh District (including Mansar).	29	5	...	...	...	24
12. Gilgit	6	3	...	...	...	3
13. Frontier *Ilaqas* ...	11	9	...	...	...	2
Cities.						
Jammu	271	66	...	...	...	205
Srinagar	492	82	...	7	...	410

DISTRICT, JAGIR, ILAQA OR CITY.	Group (152).—Lawyers of all kinds including Kazis, Law Agents and Mukhtiars.					
	Total workers and dependents.	Actual Workers. Total. Males.	Actual Workers. Total. Females.	Actual Workers. Partially Agriculturists. Males.	Actual Workers. Partially Agriculturists. Females.	Dependents.
	1010	1011	1012	1013	1014	1015
Total State ...	**481**	**98**	...	**12**	...	**383**
I—Total Jammu Province (including *Jagirs*).	168	42	...	6	...	126
1. Jammu District (including city).	65	14	...	1	...	51
2. Jasrota "	14	4	...	...	...	10
3. Udhampur "	18	4	...	...	...	14
4. Riasi "	3	1	...	...	...	2
5. Mirpur "	67	18	...	4	...	49
6. Bhadarwah *Jagir* ...	1	1	...	1	...	...
7. Punch *Ilaqa*	...	...	...	...	...	...
II—Total Kashmir Province (including *Jagirs*).	313	56	...	6	...	257
8. Kashmir North (including Langet *Jagir*).	12	6	...	...	...	6
9. Kashmir South (including city).	301	50	...	6	...	251
Total Kashmir Valley ...	*313*	*56*	...	*6*	...	*257*
10. Muzaffarabad District ...	...	...	...	...	...	...
III—Total Frontier Districts.	...	...	...	...	...	...
11. Laddakh District (including Mansar).	...	...	...	...	...	...
12. Gilgit	...	...	...	...	...	...
13. Frontier *Ilaqas* ...	...	...	...	...	...	...
Cities.						
Jammu	30	2	...	...	...	28
Srinagar	283	39	...	6	...	244

DISTRICT, JAGIR, ILAQA OR CITY.	Group (153).—Lawyer's clerks, petition-writers, etc.					
	Total workers and dependents.	Actual Workers. Total. Males.	Actual Workers. Total. Females.	Actual Workers. Partially Agriculturists. Males.	Actual Workers. Partially Agriculturists. Females.	Dependents.
	1016	1017	1018	1019	1020	1021
Total State ...	**1,042**	**304**	...	**17**	...	**738**
I—Total Jammu Province (including *Jagirs*).	567	171	...	11	...	396
1. Jammu District (including city).	307	83	...	2	...	224
2. Jasrota "	35	10	...	1	...	25
3. Udhampur "	48	17	...	...	...	31
4. Riasi "	28	10	...	1	...	18
5. Mirpur "	97	36	...	4	...	61
6. Bhadarwah *Jagir* ...	19	5	...	3	...	14
7. Punch *Ilaqa*	33	10	...	...	...	23
II—Total Kashmir Province (including *Jagirs*).	429	116	...	6	...	313
8. Kashmir North (including Langet *Jagir*).	85	29	...	1	...	56
9. Kashmir South (including city).	303	71	...	5	...	232
Total Kashmir Valley ...	*388*	*100*	...	*6*	...	*288*
10. Muzaffarabad District ...	41	16	...	...	...	25
III—Total Frontier Districts.	46	17	...	...	...	29
11. Laddakh District (including Mansar).	29	5	...	...	...	24
12. Gilgit	6	3	...	...	...	3
13. Frontier *Ilaqas* ...	11	9	...	...	...	2
Cities.						
Jammu	241	64	...	...	...	177
Srinagar	209	43	...	1	...	166

DISTRICT, JAGIR, ILAQA OR CITY.	Order 48.—Medicine.					
	Total workers and dependents.	Actual Workers. Total. Males.	Actual Workers. Total. Females.	Actual Workers. Partially Agriculturists. Males.	Actual Workers. Partially Agriculturists. Females.	Dependents.
	1022	1023	1024	1025	1026	1027
Total State ...	**2,769**	**928**	**168**	**58**	**5**	**1,673**
I—Total Jammu Province (including *Jagirs*).	930	349	118	28	5	463
1. Jammu District (including city).	237	77	41	4	1	119
2. Jasrota "	260	82	37	8	4	141
3. Udhampur "	95	40	15	3	...	40
4. Riasi "	27	16	...	1	...	11
5. Mirpur "	151	52	22	4	...	77
6. Bhadarwah *Jagir* ...	30	9	...	6	...	21
7. Punch *Ilaqa*	130	73	3	2	...	54
II—Total Kashmir Province (including *Jagirs*).	1,742	511	47	26	...	1,184
8. Kashmir North (including Langet *Jagir*).	408	114	10	5	...	284
9. Kashmir South (including city).	1,288	364	37	21	...	887
Total Kashmir Valley ...	*1,696*	*478*	*47*	*26*	...	*1,171*
10. Muzaffarabad District ...	46	33	...	...	...	13
III—Total Frontier Districts.	97	68	3	4	...	26
11. Laddakh District (including Mansar).	37	23	2	2	...	12
12. Gilgit	46	38	1	2	...	7
13. Frontier *Ilaqas* ...	14	7	...	...	...	7
Cities.						
Jammu	95	27	9	...	...	59
Srinagar	735	207	22	3	...	506

TABLE XV-A.

Occupation or Means of Livelihood.

Jammu and Kashmir State Census, 1911.

DISTRICT, JAGIR, ILAQA OR CITY.	Group (154).—Medical practitioners of all kinds including dentists, oculists and veterinary surgeons.						Group (155).—Midwives, vaccinators, compounders, nurses, masseurs, etc.						Order 49.—Instruction.						Group (156).—Professors and teachers of all kinds and clerks and servants connected with education.						Order 50.—Letters and arts and sciences.					
	Total workers and dependents.	Actual Workers. Total.		Actual Workers. Partially Agriculturists.		Dependents.	Total workers and dependents.	Actual Workers. Total.		Actual Workers. Partially Agriculturists.		Dependents.	Total workers and dependents.	Actual Workers. Total.		Actual Workers. Partially Agriculturists.		Dependents.	Total workers and dependents.	Actual Workers. Total.		Actual Workers. Partially Agriculturists.		Dependents.	Total workers and dependents.	Actual Workers. Total.		Actual Workers. Partially Agriculturists.		Dependents.
		Males.	Females.	Males.	Females.			Males.	Females.	Males.	Females.			Males.	Females.	Males.	Females.			Males.	Females.	Males.	Females.			Males.	Females.	Males.	Females.	
	1028	1029	1030	1031	1032	1033	1034	1035	1036	1037	1038	1039	1040	1041	1042	1043	1044	1045	1046	1047	1048	1049	1050	1051	1052	1053	1054	1055	1056	1057
Total State ...	**2,093**	**767**	**31**	**50**	...	**1,295**	**676**	**161**	**137**	**8**	**5**	**378**	**3,053**	**1,174**	**18**	**79**	...	**1,861**	**3,053**	**1,174**	**18**	**79**	...	**1,861**	**6,952**	**2,904**	**169**	**156**	**3**	**3,879**
I—Total Jammu Province (including *Jagirs*).	774	323	23	26	...	428	156	26	95	2	5	35	1,066	523	10	17	...	533	1,066	523	10	17	...	533	3,920	1,627	155	114	3	2,138
1. Jammu District (including city).	192	69	12	4	...	111	45	8	29	...	1	8	434	178	8	1	...	248	434	178	8	1	...	248	1,675	634	77	31	...	964
2. Jasrota ,, ...	217	76	7	8	...	134	43	6	30	...	4	7	88	40	...	5	...	48	88	40	...	5	...	48	294	126	7	13	...	161
3. Udhampur ,, ...	73	37	...	3	...	36	22	3	15	...	...	4	77	40	...	1	...	37	77	40	...	1	...	37	302	139	15	16	3	148
4. Riasi ,, ...	25	15	...	1	...	10	2	1	...	...	...	1	76	43	...	...	...	33	76	43	...	...	...	33	183	107	...	7	...	76
5. Mirpur ,, ...	114	47	3	4	...	64	37	5	19	...	...	13	160	71	2	6	...	87	160	71	2	6	...	87	1,000	425	36	37	...	539
6. Bhadarwah *Jagir* ...	25	6	...	4	...	19	5	3	...	2	...	2	17	9	...	...	...	8	17	9	...	...	...	8	32	18	...	9	...	14
7. Punch *Ilaqa*	128	73	1	2	...	54	2	...	2	...	...	...	214	142	...	4	...	72	214	142	...	4	...	72	434	178	20	1	...	286
II—Total Kashmir Province (including *Jagirs*).	1,269	414	8	22	...	847	473	97	39	4	...	337	1,900	581	8	58	...	1,311	1,900	581	8	58	...	1,311	2,730	1,093	10	20	...	1,627
8. Kashmir North (including Langet *Jagir*).	294	103	...	2	...	191	114	11	10	3	...	93	213	103	1	1	...	109	213	103	1	1	...	109	427	175	2	3	...	250
9. Kashmir South (including city).	929	278	8	20	...	643	359	86	29	1	...	244	1,670	461	7	56	...	1,202	1,670	461	7	56	...	1,202	2,166	852	4	14	...	1,310
Total Kashmir Valley ...	*1,223*	*381*	*8*	*22*	...	*834*	*473*	*97*	*39*	*4*	...	*337*	*1,883*	*564*	*8*	*57*	...	*1,311*	*1,883*	*564*	*8*	*57*	...	*1,311*	*2,593*	*1,027*	*6*	*17*	...	*1,560*
10. Muzaffarabad District ...	46	33	...	...	...	13	...	...	...	...	...	...	17	17	...	1	...	...	17	17	...	1	...	...	137	66	4	3	...	67
III—Total Frontier Districts.	50	30	...	2	...	20	47	38	3	2	...	6	87	70	...	4	...	17	87	70	...	4	...	17	302	184	4	22	...	114
11. Laddakh District (including Mansar).	30	20	...	2	...	10	7	3	2	...	...	2	38	21	...	4	...	17	38	21	...	4	...	17	187	123	4	17	...	60
12. Gilgit ,, ...	9	5	...	...	...	4	37	33	1	2	...	3	2	2	...	...	...	...	2	2	...	...	...	...	29	14	...	5	...	15
13. Frontier *Ilaqas*	11	5	...	...	...	6	3	2	...	...	...	1	47	47	...	...	...	...	47	47	...	...	...	...	86	47	...	...	...	39
Cities.																														
Jammu	78	24	1	...	...	53	17	3	8	...	...	6	260	94	8	...	...	158	260	94	8	...	...	158	1,119	394	33	...	...	692
Srinagar	471	149	8	3	...	314	264	58	14	...	...	192	1,063	324	6	2	...	733	1,063	324	6	2	...	733	1,729	653	3	3	...	1,073

TABLE XV-A.

Occupation or Means of Livelihood.

Jammu and Kashmir State Census, 1911.

District, Jagir, Ilaqa or City.	Group (158).—Architects, surveyors, engineers and their employes.						Group (159).—Others (authors, photographers, artists, sculptors, astronomers, meteorologists, botanists, astrologers, etc.).					
	Total workers and dependents.	Actual Workers. Total. Males.	Actual Workers. Total. Females.	Actual Workers. Partially Agriculturists. Males.	Actual Workers. Partially Agriculturists. Females.	Dependents.	Total workers and dependents.	Actual Workers. Total. Males.	Actual Workers. Total. Females.	Actual Workers. Partially Agriculturists. Males.	Actual Workers. Partially Agriculturists. Females.	Dependents.
	1058	1059	1060	1061	1062	1063	1064	1065	1066	1067	1068	1069
Total State ...	**3,797**	**1,517**	**61**	**68**	..	**2,219**	**1,352**	**579**	**25**	**19**	**3**	**748**
I—Total Jammu Province (including *Jagirs*).	2,114	855	60	42	...	1,199	694	300	23	18	3	371
1. Jammu District (including city).	1,056	377	36	...	...	643	238	77	8	...	...	153
2. Jasrota ,, ...	160	66	2	4	...	92	45	15	1	2	...	29
3. Udhampur ,, ...	116	86	1	11	...	29	170	49	14	5	3	107
4. Riasi ,, ...	63	55	...	2	...	8	41	18	...	3	...	23
5. Mirpur ,, ...	471	177	13	18	...	281	149	117	...	6	...	32
6. Bhadarwah *Jagir*. ...	17	12	...	6	...	5	11	5	...	2	...	6
7. Punch *Ilaqa*	231	82	8	1	...	141	40	19	...	...	...	21
II—Total Kashmir Province (including *Jagirs*).	1,526	541	1	5	...	984	648	275	2	1	...	371
8. Kashmir North (including Langet *Jagir*).	56	30	...	...	...	26	155	48	...	...	...	107
9. Kashmir South (including city).	1,447	504	1	5	...	942	486	225	2	1	...	259
Total Kashmir Valley ...	*1,503*	*534*	*1*	*5*	...	*968*	*641*	*273*	*2*	*1*	...	*366*
10. Muzaffarabad District ...	23	7	...	...	...	16	7	2	...	...	...	5
III—Total Frontier Districts.	157	121	...	21	...	36	10	4	...	...	...	6
11. Laddakh District (including Mansar).	121	100	...	16	...	21	9	3	...	...	...	6
12. Gilgit ,, ...	28	13	...	5	...	15	1	1	...	...	...	...
13. Frontier *Ilaqas*	8	8	...	...	...	...	...	...	...	...	...	...
Cities.												
Jammu	779	281	6	...	...	492	188	46	8	...	...	134
Srinagar	1,220	411	...	3	...	809	367	176	2	...	...	189

District, Jagir, Ilaqa or City.	Group (160).—Music composers and masters, players on all kinds of musical instruments (not military,) singers, actors and dancers.						Sub-class IX.—Persons living on their income.						Order 51.—Persons living principally on their income.					
	Total workers and dependents.	Actual Workers. Total. Males.	Actual Workers. Total. Females.	Actual Workers. Partially Agriculturists. Males.	Actual Workers. Partially Agriculturists. Females.	Dependents.	Total workers and dependents.	Actual Workers. Total. Males.	Actual Workers. Total. Females.	Actual Workers. Partially Agriculturists. Males.	Actual Workers. Partially Agriculturists. Females.	Dependents.	Total workers and dependents.	Actual Workers. Total. Males.	Actual Workers. Total. Females.	Actual Workers. Partially Agriculturists. Males.	Actual Workers. Partially Agriculturists. Females.	Dependents.
	1070	1071	1072	1073	1074	1075	1076	1077	1078	1079	1080	1081	1082	1083	1084	1085	1086	1087
Total State ...	**1,803**	**808**	**83**	**69**	...	**912**	**2,432**	**751**	**170**	**148**	**9**	**1,511**	**2,432**	**751**	**170**	**148**	**9**	**1,511**
I—Total Jammu Province (including *Jagirs*).	1,112	472	72	54	...	568	1,531	463	135	123	6	933	1,531	463	135	123	6	933
1. Jammu District (including city).	381	180	33	31	...	168	784	267	72	71	...	445	784	267	72	71	...	445
2. Jasrota ,, ...	89	45	4	7	...	40	178	53	10	11	1	115	178	53	10	11	1	115
3. Udhampur ,, ...	16	4	...	...	...	12	174	24	7	8	...	143	175	24	7	8	...	143
4. Riasi ,, ...	79	34	...	2	...	45	79	31	13	9	2	35	79	31	13	9	2	35
5. Mirpur ,, ...	380	131	23	13	...	226	302	83	31	23	3	188	302	83	31	23	3	188
6. Bhadarwah *Jagir*. ...	4	1	...	1	...	3	1	1	...	...	...	...	1	1	...	...	...	...
7. Punch *Ilaqa*	163	77	12	...	...	74	13	4	2	1	...	7	13	4	2	1	...	7
II—Total Kashmir Province (including *Jagirs*).	556	277	7	14	...	272	773	219	31	23	...	523	773	219	31	23	...	523
8. Kashmir North (including Langet *Jagir*).	216	97	2	3	...	117	98	27	2	1	...	69	98	27	2	1	...	69
9. Kashmir South (including city).	233	123	1	8	...	109	616	177	28	16	...	411	616	177	28	16	...	411
Total Kashmir Valley ...	*449*	*220*	*3*	*11*	...	*226*	*710*	*204*	*30*	*17*	...	*480*	*714*	*204*	*30*	*17*	...	*480*
10. Muzaffarabad District ...	107	57	4	3	...	46	59	15	1	6	...	43	59	15	1	6	...	43
III—Total Frontier Districts.	135	59	4	1	...	72	128	69	4	2	3	55	128	69	4	2	3	55
11. Laddakh District (including Mansar).	57	20	4	1	...	33	16	4	4	2	3	8	16	4	4	2	3	8
12. Gilgit ,, ...	...	...	...	...	...	...	22	9	...	...	...	13	22	9	...	...	...	13
13. Frontier *Ilaqas*	78	39	...	...	...	39	90	56	...	...	...	34	90	56	...	...	...	34
Cities.																		
Jammu	152	67	19	6	...	66	386	136	54	...	...	196	386	136	54	...	...	196
Srinagar	142	66	1	...	...	75	516	140	22	10	...	354	516	140	22	10	...	354

TABLE XV-A.

Occupation or Means of Livelihood.

Jammu and Kashmir State Census, 1911.

DISTRICT, JAGIR, ILAQA OR CITY.	Group (161).—*Proprietors (other than of agricultural land), fund and scholarship holders and pensioners.*						Class D.—Miscellaneous.					
	Total workers and dependents.	Actual Workers. Total.		Actual Workers. *Partially Agriculturists.*		Dependents.	Total workers and dependents.	Actual Workers. Total.		Actual Workers. *Partially Agriculturists.*		Dependents.
		Males.	Females.	Males.	Females.			Males.	Females.	Males.	Females.	
	1088	1089	1090	1091	1092	1093	1094	1095	1096	1097	1098	1099
Total State ...	**2,432**	**751**	**170**	**148**	**9**	**1,511**	**100,422**	**39,959**	**10,867**	**1,980**	**92**	**49,596**
I—Total Jammu Province (including *Jagirs*).	1,531	463	135	123	6	933	53,700	21,524	7,913	1,367	86	24,263
1. Jammu District (including city).	784	267	72	71	...	445	23,091	8,185	3,004	612	13	11,902
2. Jasrota ,, ...	178	53	10	11	1	115	6,329	2,109	934	214	27	3,286
3. Udhampur ,, ...	175	24	7	8	...	143	3,947	1,891	590	112	25	1,466
4. Riasi ,, ...	79	31	13	9	2	35	4,469	2,288	586	107	5	1,595
5. Mirpur ,, ...	302	83	31	23	3	188	9,600	4,275	1,529	233	14	3,796
6. Bhadarwah *Jagir* ...	1	1	...	...	...	...	904	512	174	58	2	218
7. Punch *Ilaqa*	13	4	2	1	...	7	5,360	2,264	1,096	31	...	2,000
II—Total Kashmir Province (including *Jagirs*).	773	219	31	23	...	523	41,041	15,648	2,070	560	3	23,323
8. Kashmir North (including Langet *Jagir*).	98	27	2	1	...	69	9,474	3,626	551	113	1	5,297
9. Kashmir South (including city).	616	177	28	16	...	411	26,252	9,537	996	397	1	15,723
Total Kashmir Valley ...	*714*	*204*	*30*	*17*	...	*480*	*35,730*	*13,163*	*1,547*	*510*	*2*	*21,020*
10. Muzffarabad District ...	59	15	1	6	...	43	5,311	2,485	523	50	1	2,303
III—Total Frontier Districts.	128	69	4	2	3	55	5,681	2,787	884	53	3	2,010
11. Laddakh District (including Mansar).	16	4	4	2	3	8	3,244	1,278	850	30	3	1,116
12. Gilgit ,, ...	22	9	...	...	...	13	751	436	34	23	...	281
13. Frontier *Ilaqas*	90	56	...	...	...	34	1,686	1,075	...	...	...	613
Cities.												
Jammu	386	136	54	...	...	196	6,671	2,427	1,038	10	1	3,206
Srinagar	516	140	22	10	...	354	12,680	4,364	519	37	...	7,797

DISTRICT, JAGIR, ILAQA OR CITY.	Sub-class X.—Domestic Service.						Order 52.—Domestic Service.					
	Total workers and dependents.	Actual Workers. Total.		Actual Workers. *Partially Agriculturists.*		Dependents.	Total workers and dependents.	Actual Workers. Total.		Actual Workers. *Partially Agriculturists.*		Dependents.
		Males.	Females.	Males.	Females.			Males.	Females.	Males.	Females.	
	1100	1101	1102	1103	1104	1105	1106	1107	1108	1109	1110	1111
Total State ...	**37,766**	**16,788**	**3,415**	**480**	**16**	**17,563**	**37,766**	**16,788**	**3,415**	**480**	**16**	**17,563**
I—Total Jammu Province (including *Jagirs*).	17,167	7,802	2,413	288	16	6,952	17,167	7,802	2,413	288	16	6,952
1. Jammu District (including city).	8,088	2,767	1,185	95	7	4,136	8,088	2,767	1,185	95	7	4,136
2. Jasrota ,, ...	9,297	960	421	70	2	916	9,297	960	421	70	2	916
3. Udhampur ,, ...	1,171	729	144	23	2	298	1,171	729	144	23	2	298
4. Riasi ,, ...	1,398	981	150	14	1	267	1,398	981	150	14	1	267
5. Mirpur ,, ...	2,963	1,647	335	62	4	981	2,963	1,647	335	62	4	581
6. Bhadarwah *Jagir* ...	148	120	...	11	...	28	148	120	...	11	...	28
7. Punch *Ilaqa*	1,102	598	178	13	...	326	1,102	598	178	13	...	326
II—Total Kashmir Province (including *Jagirs*).	18,946	7,992	735	172	...	10,219	18,946	7,992	735	172	...	10,219
8. Kashmir North (including Langet *Jagir*).	2,620	1,408	77	40	...	1,135	2,620	1,408	77	40	...	1,135
9. Kashmir South (including city).	14,084	5,245	476	113	...	8,363	14,084	5,245	476	113	...	8,363
Total Kashmir Valley ...	*16,704*	*6,653*	*553*	*153*	...	*9,498*	*16,704*	*6,053*	*553*	*153*	...	*9,498*
10. Muzffarabad District ...	2,242	1,339	182	19	...	721	2,242	1,339	182	19	...	721
III—Total Frontier Districts.	1,653	994	267	20	...	392	1,653	994	267	20	...	392
11. Laddakh District (including Mansar).	983	479	267	8	...	237	983	479	267	8	...	237
12. Gilgit ,, ...	290	205	...	12	...	85	290	205	...	12	...	85
13. Frontier *Ilaqas*	380	310	...	...	...	70	380	310	...	...	...	70
Cities.												
Jammu	3,082	901	426	6	...	1,755	3,082	901	426	6	...	1,755
Srinagar	8,944	3,135	356	32	...	5,453	8,944	3,135	356	32	...	5,453

TABLE XV-A.

Occupation or Means of Livelihood.

Jammu and Kashmir State Census, 1911.

District, Jagir, Ilaqa or City.	Group (162).—Cooks, water carriers, door-keepers, watchmen and other indoor servants.						Group (163).—Private grooms, coachmen, dog boys, etc.					
	Total workers and dependents.	Actual Workers. Total.		Actual Workers. Partially Agriculturists.		Dependents.	Total workers and dependents.	Actual Workers. Total.		Actual Workers. Partially Agriculturists.		Dependents.
		Males.	Females.	Males.	Females.			Males.	Females.	Males.	Females.	
	1112	1113	1114	1115	1116	1117	1118	1119	1120	1121	1122	1123
Total State ...	**36,911**	**16,296**	**3,413**	**470**	**16**	**17,202**	**855**	**492**	**2**	**10**	**...**	**361**
I—Total Jammu Province (including *Jagirs*).	16,990	7,671	2,411	282	16	6,908	177	131	2	6	...	44
1. Jammu District (including city).	8,061	2,747	1,185	95	7	4,129	27	20	...	...	...	7
2. Jasrota ,, ...	2,267	944	420	70	2	903	30	16	1	...	...	13
3. Udhampur ,, ...	1,158	718	144	22	2	296	13	11	...	1	...	2
4. Riasi ,, ...	1,398	981	150	14	1	267	...	...	...	...	...	...
5. Mirpur ,, ...	2,938	1,630	335	62	4	973	25	17	...	...	...	8
6. Bhadarwah *Jagir* ...	148	120	...	11	...	28	...	...	...	...	...	...
7. Punch *Ilaqa*	1,020	531	177	8	...	312	82	67	1	5	...	14
II—Total Kashmir Province (including *Jagirs*).	18,326	7,677	735	168	...	9,914	620	315	...	4	...	305
8. Kashmir North (including Langet *Jagir*).	2,486	1,338	77	39	...	1,071	134	70	...	1	...	64
9. Kashmir South (including city).	13,605	5,007	476	110	...	8,122	479	238	...	3	...	241
Total Kashmir Valley ...	*16,091*	*6,345*	*553*	*149*	...	*9,193*	*613*	*308*	...	*4*	...	*305*
10. Muzaffarabad District ...	2,235	1,332	182	19	...	721	7	7	...	...	...	...
III—Total Frontier Districts.	1,595	548	267	20	...	380	58	46	...	...	...	12
11. Laddakh District (including Mansar).	946	453	267	8	...	226	37	26	...	...	...	11
12. Gilgit ,, ...	272	187	...	12	...	85	18	18	...	...	...	...
13. Frontier *Ilaqas*	377	308	...	...	...	69	3	2	...	...	...	1
Cities.												
Jammu	3,082	901	426	6	...	1,755	...	...	...	...	...	...
Srinagar	8,760	3,023	356	32	...	5,381	184	112	...	...	...	72

District, Jagir, Ilaqa or City.	Sub-class XI.—Insufficiently described occupations.						Order 53.—General terms which do not indicate a definite occupation.					
	Total workers and dependents.	Actual Workers. Total.		Actual Workers. Partially Agriculturists.		Dependents.	Total workers and dependents.	Actual Workers. Total.		Actual Workers. Partially Agriculturists.		Dependents.
		Males.	Females.	Males.	Females.			Males.	Females.	Males.	Females.	
	1124	1125	1126	1127	1128	1129	1130	1131	1132	1133	1134	1135
Total State ...	**23,004**	**8,364**	**2,111**	**478**	**33**	**12,529**	**23,004**	**8,364**	**2,111**	**478**	**33**	**12,529**
I—Total Jammu Province (including *Jagirs*).	14,088	5,309	1,964	403	32	6,815	14,088	5,309	1,964	403	32	6,815
1. Jammu District (including city).	7,415	2,645	1,058	200	2	3,712	7,415	2,645	1,058	200	2	3,712
2. Jasrota ,, ...	1,036	355	133	38	10	548	1,036	355	133	38	10	548
3. Udhampur ,, ...	1,343	458	226	25	15	659	1,343	458	226	25	15	659
4. Riasi ,, ...	878	367	68	31	2	443	878	367	68	31	2	443
5. Mirpur ,, ...	2,018	745	232	81	1	971	2,018	745	232	81	1	971
6. Bhadarwah *Jagir* ...	450	220	142	24	2	88	450	220	142	24	2	88
7. Punch *Ilaqa*	948	449	105	4	...	394	948	449	105	4	...	394
II—Total Kashmir Province (including *Jagirs*).	7,035	2,155	106	56	1	4,774	7,035	2,155	106	56	1	4,774
8. Kashmir North (including Langet *Jagir*).	1,712	540	35	13	...	1,137	1,712	540	35	13	...	1,137
9. Kashmir South (including city).	3,813	1,069	21	26	...	2,713	3,813	1,069	21	26	...	2,713
Total Kashmir Valley ...	*5,525*	*1,609*	*56*	*39*	...	*3,860*	*5,525*	*1,609*	*56*	*39*	...	*3,860*
10. Muzaffarabad District ...	1,510	546	50	17	1	914	1,510	546	50	17	1	914
III—Total Frontier Districts.	1,881	900	41	19	...	940	1,881	900	41	19	...	940
11. Laddakh District (including Mansar).	508	124	32	8	...	352	508	124	32	8	...	352
12. Gilgit ,, ...	238	119	9	11	...	110	238	119	9	11	...	110
13. Frontier *Ilaqas*	1,135	657	...	...	...	478	1,135	657	...	...	...	478
Cities.												
Jammu	2,686	933	483	...	...	1,270	2,686	933	483	...	...	1,270
Srinagar	2,332	554	15	5	...	1,763	2,332	554	15	5	...	1,763

TABLE XV-A.

Occupation or Means of Livelihood.

Jammu and Kashmir State Census, 1911.

District, Jagir, Ilaqa or City.	Group (164).—Manufacturers, business-men and contractors, otherwise unspecified.						Group (165).—Cashiers, accountants, book-keepers, clerks and other employes in unspecified offices, ware-houses and shops.					
	Total workers and dependents.	Actual Workers. Total. Males.	Actual Workers. Total. Females.	Actual Workers. Partially Agriculturists. Males.	Actual Workers. Partially Agriculturists. Females.	Dependents.	Total workers and dependents.	Actual Workers. Total. Males.	Actual Workers. Total. Females.	Actual Workers. Partially Agriculturists. Males.	Actual Workers. Partially Agriculturists. Females.	Dependents.
	1136	1137	1138	1139	1140	1141	1142	1143	1144	1145	1146	1147
Total State ...	**6,543**	**2,038**	**71**	**180**	**4**	**4,434**	**66**	**36**	...	**2**	...	**30**
I—Total Jammu Province (including *Jagirs*).	2,722	966	40	141	3	1,716	32	14	...	1	...	18
1. Jammu District (including city).	1,186	444	7	81	1	735	11	4	...	...	...	7
2. Jasrota "	239	46	1	7	...	192	7	4	...	...	...	3
3. Udhampur "	636	194	16	12	1	426	...	...	...	...	...	...
4. Riasi "	326	124	3	7	1	199	9	2	...	...	...	7
5. Mirpur "	250	113	12	29	...	125	...	...	...	...	...	...
6. Bhadarwah *Jagir* ...	12	11	...	5	...	1	...	...	...	...	...	...
7. Punch *Ilaqa*	73	34	1	...	...	38	5	4	...	1	...	1
II—Total Kashmir Province (including *Jagirs*).	3,062	796	23	32	1	2,243	33	21	...	1	...	12
8. Kashmir North (including Langet *Jagir*).	618	198	2	6	...	418	8	3	...	1	...	5
9. Kashmir South (including city).	1,508	341	1	12	...	1,166	23	16	...	...	...	7
Total Kashmir Valley ...	*2,126*	*539*	*3*	*18*	...	*1,584*	*31*	*19*	...	*1*	...	*12*
10. Muzaffarabad District ...	936	257	20	14	1	659	2	2	...	...	...	...
III—Total Frontier Districts.	759	276	8	7	...	475	1	1	...	...	...	...
11. Ladakh District (including Mansar).	420	96	8	7	...	316	...	...	...	...	...	...
12. Gilgit "	30	5	...	...	...	25	1	1	...	...	...	...
13. Frontier *Ilaqas*	309	175	...	...	...	134	...	...	...	...	...	...
Cities.												
Jammu	430	102	...	...	...	328	7	2	...	...	...	5
Srinagar	1,139	237	...	3	...	902	22	15	...	...	...	7

District, Jagir, Ilaqa or City.	Group (166).—Mechanics, otherwise unspecified.						Group (167).—Labourers and workmen, otherwise unspecified.						Sub-Class XII—Unproductive.					
	Total workers and dependents.	Actual Workers. Total. Males.	Actual Workers. Total. Females.	Actual Workers. Partially Agriculturists. Males.	Actual Workers. Partially Agriculturists. Females.	Dependents.	Total workers and dependents.	Actual Workers. Total. Males.	Actual Workers. Total. Females.	Actual Workers. Partially Agriculturists. Males.	Actual Workers. Partially Agriculturists. Females.	Dependents.	Total workers and dependents.	Actual Workers. Total. Males.	Actual Workers. Total. Females.	Actual Workers. Partially Agriculturists. Males.	Actual Workers. Partially Agriculturists. Females.	Dependents.
	1148	1149	1150	1151	1152	1153	1154	1155	1156	1157	1158	1159	1160	1161	1162	1163	1164	1165
Total State ...	**167**	**71**	**6**	...	...	**50**	**16,228**	**6,219**	**2,034**	**296**	**29**	**7,975**	**39,652**	**14,807**	**5,341**	**1,822**	**43**	**19,504**
I—Total Jammu Province (including *Jagirs*).	60	35	...	...	...	25	11,274	4,294	1,924	261	29	5,056	22,445	8,413	3,536	676	38	10,496
1. Jammu District (including city).	51	28	...	...	...	23	6,167	2,169	1,051	109	1	2,947	7,588	2,773	761	317	4	4,054
2. Jasrota "	...	...	...	...	...	...	780	305	132	31	10	353	2,996	793	380	106	15	1,822
3. Udhampur "	3	3	...	...	...	...	704	261	210	13	14	233	1,433	704	220	64	8	509
4. Riasi "	...	...	...	...	...	...	543	241	65	24	1	237	2,193	940	368	62	2	885
5. Mirpur "	6	4	...	...	...	2	1,762	698	220	52	1	844	4,619	1,813	962	90	9	1,844
6. Bhadarwah *Jagir* ...	...	...	...	...	...	...	438	209	142	19	2	87	306	172	32	23	...	102
7. Punch *Ilaqa*	...	...	...	...	...	...	870	411	104	3	...	355	7,310	1,217	813	14	...	1,280
II—Total Kashmir Province (including *Jagirs*).	96	27	6	...	...	63	3,844	1,311	77	23	...	2,456	15,060	5,501	1,229	332	2	5,330
8. Kashmir North (including Langet *Jagir*).	3	...	...	...	...	3	1,083	339	33	6	...	711	5,142	1,678	439	60	1	3,025
9. Kashmir South (including city).	91	25	6	...	...	60	2,191	687	11	14	...	1,490	8,359	3,223	499	258	1	4,637
Total Kashmir Valley ...	*94*	*25*	*6*	...	...	*63*	*3,274*	*1,026*	*47*	*20*	...	*2,201*	*13,501*	*4,901*	*938*	*318*	*2*	*7,662*
10. Muzaffarabad District ...	2	2	...	...	...	...	570	385	30	3	...	255	1,559	600	291	14	...	668
III—Total Frontier Districts.	11	9	...	...	...	2	1,110	614	33	12	...	463	2,147	893	576	14	3	678
11. Ladakh District (including Mansar).	11	9	...	...	...	2	77	19	24	1	...	34	1,753	675	551	14	3	527
12. Gilgit "	...	...	...	...	...	...	207	113	9	11	...	85	223	112	25	...	...	86
13. Frontier *Ilaqas*	...	...	...	...	...	...	826	492	...	...	...	344	171	106	...	...	...	65
Cities.																		
Jammu	35	23	...	...	...	12	2,214	806	483	...	...	925	1,127	807	139	4	1	181
Srinagar	63	25	6	...	...	32	1,108	277	9	2	...	822	1,404	675	148	...	...	581

TABLE XV-A.

Occupation or Means of Livelihood.

Jammu and Kashmir State Census, 1911.

DISTRICT, JAGIR, ILAQA OR CITY.	Order 54.—Inmates of Jails, asylums and hospitals.						*Group (168).—Inmates of Jails, asylums and hospitals.*					
	Total workers and dependents.	Actual Workers.				Dependents.	Total workers and dependents.	Actual Workers.				Dependents.
		Total.		*Partially Agriculturists.*				*Total.*		*Partially Agriculturists.*		
		Males.	Females.	Males.	Females.			Males.	Females.	Males.	Females.	
	1166	1167	1168	1169	1170	1171	1172	1173	1174	1175	1176	1177
Total State	**658**	**621**	**18**	...	...	**19**	**658**	**621**	**18**	...	...	**19**
I—Total Jammu Province (including *Jagirs*).	391	358	14	...	...	19	391	358	14	...	...	19
1. Jammu District (including city)	224	214	10	...	...	...	224	214	10	...	...	...
2. Jasrota ,, ...	3	3	...	...	...	...	3	3	...	...	...	...
3. Udhampur ,, ...	2	1	...	...	...	1	2	1	...	...	...	1
4. Riasi ,, ...	...	...	...	...	...	...	...	...	...	...	...	...
5. Mirpur ,, ...	79	61	...	...	...	18	79	61	...	...	...	18
6. Bhadarwah *Jagir* ...	...	...	...	...	...	...	...	...	...	...	...	...
7. Punch *Ilaqa*	83	79	4	...	...	...	83	79	4	...	...	...
II—Total Kashmir Province (including *Jagirs*).	247	243	4	...	...	...	247	243	4	...	...	...
8. Kashmir North (including Langet *Jagir*).	...	...	...	...	...	...	...	...	...	...	...	...
9. Kashmir South (including city).	247	243	4	...	...	...	247	243	4	...	...	...
Total Kashmir Valley ...	*247*	*243*	*4*	...	...	...	*247*	*243*	*4*	...	...	...
10. Muzaffarabad District ...	...	...	...	...	...	...	...	...	...	...	...	...
III—Total Frontier Districts.	20	20	...	...	...	...	20	20	...	...	...	...
11. Laddakh District (including Mansar).	3	3	...	...	...	...	3	3	...	...	...	...
12. Gilgit ,, ...	17	17	...	...	...	...	17	17	...	...	...	...
13. Frontier *Ilaqas*	...	...	...	...	...	...	...	...	...	...	...	...
Cities.												
Jammu	224	214	10	...	...	...	224	214	10	...	...	...
Srinagar	247	243	4	...	...	...	247	243	4	...	...	...

DISTRICT, JAGIR, ILAQA OR CITY.	Order 55.—Beggars, vagrants, prostitutes.						*Group (169).—Beggars, vagrants, procurers, prostitutes, receivers of stolen goods, cattle poisoners.*					
	Total workers and dependents.	Actual Workers.				Dependents.	Total workers and dependents.	Actual Workers.				Dependents.
		Total.		*Partially Agriculturists.*				*Total.*		*Partially Agriculturists.*		
		Males.	Females.	Males.	Females.			Males.	Females.	Males.	Females.	
	1178	1179	1180	1181	1182	1183	1184	1185	1186	1187	1188	1189
Total State	**38,994**	**14,186**	**5,323**	**1,022**	**43**	**19,485**	**38,994**	**14,186**	**5,323**	**1,022**	**43**	**19,485**
I—Total Jammu Province (including *Jagirs*).	22,054	8,055	3,522	676	38	10,477	22,054	8,055	3,522	676	38	10,477
1. Jammu District (including city)	7,364	2,559	751	317	4	4,054	7,364	2,559	751	317	4	4,054
2. Jasrota ,, ...	2,993	791	380	106	15	1,822	2,993	791	380	106	15	1,822
3. Udhampur ,, ...	1,431	703	220	64	8	508	1,431	703	220	64	8	508
4. Riasi ,, ...	2,193	940	368	62	2	885	2,193	940	368	62	2	885
5. Mirpur ,, ...	4,540	1,752	962	90	9	1,826	4,540	1,752	962	70	9	1,826
6. Bhadarwah *Jagir* ...	306	172	32	23	...	102	306	172	32	23	...	102
7. Punch *Ilaqa*	3,227	1,138	809	14	...	1,280	3,227	1,138	809	14	...	1,280
II—Total Kashmir Province (including *Jagirs*).	14,813	5,258	1,225	332	2	8,330	14,813	5,258	1,225	332	2	8,330
8. Kashmir North (including Langet *Jagir*).	5,142	1,678	439	60	1	3,025	5,142	1,678	439	60	1	3,025
9. Kashmir South (including city).	8,112	2,980	495	258	1	4,637	8,112	2,980	495	258	1	4,637
Total Kashmir Valley ...	*13,254*	*4,658*	*934*	*318*	*2*	*7,662*	*13,254*	*4,658*	*934*	*318*	*2*	*7,662*
10. Muzaffarabad District ...	1,559	600	291	14	...	668	1,559	600	291	14	...	668
III—Total Frontier Districts.	2,127	873	576	14	3	678	2,127	873	576	14	3	678
11. Laddakh District (including Mansar).	1,750	672	551	14	3	527	1,750	672	551	14	3	527
12. Gilgit ,, ...	206	95	25	...	...	86	206	95	25	...	...	86
13. Frontier *Ilaqas*	171	106	...	...	...	65	171	106	...	...	...	65
Cities.												
Jammu	679	379	119	4	1	181	679	379	119	4	1	181
Srinagar	1,157	432	144	...	...	581	1,157	432	144	...	...	581

TABLE XV-B.

Subsidiary Occupations of Agriculturists—Actual Workers only.

(1) Rent-receivers.

Jammu and Kashmir State Census, 1911.

DISTRICT, JAGIR, ILAQA OR CITY.	Total number of Rent-receivers (actual workers).		Number of actual workers who returned Subsidiary occupations.				Detail of subsidiary occupations returned.																											
			Agriculturist.		*Non-Agriculturist.*		*Rent-payers.*		*Agricultural labourers.*		*Government servants of all kinds.*		*Money lenders and grain dealers.*		*Other trades of all kinds.*		*Priests.*		*Clerks of all kinds.*		*School Masters.*		*Lawyers.*		*Estate Managers*		*Medical Practitioners.*		*Artisans.*		*Others.*		*Cocoon rearers.*	
	Males.	Females.	Males.	Females.	Males.	Females.	Males.	Females.	Males.	Females.	Males.	Females.	Males.	Females.	Males.	Females.	Males.	Females.	Males.	Females.	Males.	Females.	Males.	Females.	Males.	Females.	Males.	Females.	Males.	Females.	Males.	Females.	Males.	Females.
1	2	3	4	5	6	7	8	9	10	11	12	13	14	15	16	17	18	19	20	21	22	23	24	25	26	27	28	29	30	31	32	33	34	35
Total State ...	**5.385**	**3,983**	**843**	**118**	**1,373**	**168**	**810**	**115**	**33**	**3**	**342**	**18**	**100**	**2**	**181**	**6**	**210**	**18**	**19**	**5**	**4**	...	...	...	**1**	...	**12**	**1**	**40**	**6**	**385**	**111**	**79**	**1**
I—Total Jammu Province ...	4,724	3,147	656	99	723	140	627	96	29	3	157	16	83	2	89	6	84	17	5	5	2	...	...	...	...	...	6	1	17	4	280	89	...	...
1. Jammu District ...	1,625	892	93	19	171	32	86	16	7	3	45	4	23	...	12	1	8	5	3	3	1	...	...	...	...	...	2	...	4	1	73	18	...	...
2. Jasrota ,, ...	1,006	605	242	27	177	52	227	27	15	...	8	3	29	1	31	2	25	9	...	...	...	...	...	...	...	...	2	1	...	...	82	36	...	...
3. Udhampur ,, ...	488	417	97	11	33	7	97	11	...	...	6	...	3	1	2	3	5	...	1	...	...	...	...	...	...	...	...	...	1	...	15	3	...	...
4. Riasi ,, ...	174	220	19	9	10	4	19	19	...	...	4	1	2	...	...	...	...	...	...	...	...	...	...	...	...	...	...	...	...	...	4	3	...	...
5. Mirpur ,, ...	961	717	179	19	252	41	174	19	5	...	83	7	15	...	24	...	37	3	1	2	1	...	...	...	...	...	1	...	11	3	79	26	...	...
6. Bahadarwah *Jagir* ...	64	38	8	4	18	1	8	4	...	...	5	...	...	...	1	...	4	...	...	...	...	...	...	...	...	...	1	...	...	...	7	1	...	...
7. Punch *Ilaqa* ...	406	258	18	...	62	3	16	...	2	...	6	1	11	...	19	...	5	...	...	...	...	...	...	...	...	...	...	...	1	...	20	2	...	...
II—Total Kashmir Province...	2,667	745	168	18	634	27	164	18	4	...	183	2	17	...	91	...	125	1	14	...	2	...	...	...	1	...	6	...	20	2	96	21	79	1
8. Kashmir North ...	570	263	19	...	146	7	18	...	1	...	45	1	3	...	19	...	23	...	2	...	...	...	...	...	1	...	...	...	5	2	30	3	18	1
9. Kashmir South ...	1,865	409	139	17	455	20	136	17	3	...	132	1	10	...	68	...	101	1	11	...	2	...	...	...	...	...	6	...	15	...	49	18	61	...
Total Kashmir valley ...	*2,435*	*672*	*158*	*17*	*601*	*27*	*154*	*17*	*4*	...	*177*	*2*	*13*	...	*87*	...	*124*	*1*	*13*	...	*2*	...	...	...	*1*	...	*6*	...	*20*	*2*	*79*	*21*	*79*	*1*
10. Muzaffarabad District ...	232	73	10	1	33	...	10	1	...	...	6	...	4	...	4	...	1	...	1	...	...	...	...	...	...	...	...	...	...	...	17	...	...	...
III—Total Frontier Districts.	994	91	19	1	16	1	19	1	...	...	2	...	...	...	1	...	1	...	...	...	...	...	...	...	...	...	...	...	3	...	9	1	...	...
11. Laddakh District ...	959	86	19	1	15	1	19	1	...	...	1	...	...	...	1	...	1	...	...	...	...	...	...	...	...	...	...	...	3	...	9	1	...	...
12. Gilgit ,, ...	35	5	...	...	1	...	...	...	...	...	1	...	...	...	...	...	...	...	...	...	...	...	...	...	...	...	...	...	...	...	...	...	...	...
Cities.																																		
Jammu ...	74	33	...	...	6	...	...	...	...	...	3	...	...	...	...	...	...	...	...	...	...	...	...	...	...	...	...	...	1	...	2	...	...	...
Srinagar ...	210	16	2	...	21	1	2	...	...	...	3	...	...	...	2	...	4	...	6	...	...	...	...	...	...	...	...	...	...	...	4	1	...	...

TABLE XV-B.

SUBSIDIARY OCCUPATIONS OF AGRICULTURISTS—ACTUAL WORKERS ONLY.

(2) Rent-payers.

Jammu and Kashmir State Census, 1911.

DISTRICT, JAGIR, ILAQA OR CITY.	TOTAL NUMBER OF RENT-PAYERS, (ACTUAL WORKERS).		NUMBER OF ACTUAL WORKERS WHO RETURNED SUBSIDIARY OCCUPATIONS.				DETAIL OF SUBSIDIARY OCCUPATIONS RETURNED.													
			Agriculturist.		*Non-Agriculturist.*		*Rent-receivers.*		*Agricultural labourers.*		*General labourers.*		*Government servants of all kinds.*		*Money lenders and grain dealers.*		*Other traders of all kinds.*		*Fishermen and boatmen.*	
	Males.	Females.	Males.	Females.	Males.	Females.	Males.	Females.	Males.	Females.	Males.	Females.	Males.	Females.	Males.	Females.	Males.	Females.	Males.	Females.
1	2	3	4	5	6	7	8	9	10	11	12	13	14	15	16	17	18	19	20	21
Total State ...	**725,937**	**381,837**	**12,406**	**826**	**105,021**	**7,391**	**10,385**	**678**	**2,021**	**148**	**12,008**	**179**	**6,375**	**120**	**868**	**61**	**5,904**	**247**	**338**	...
I—Total Jammu Province...	397,398	135,316	9,569	700	51,005	2,257	8,450	621	1,119	79	8,601	150	2,848	113	594	26	2,816	227	31	...
1. Jammu District	64,559	15,126	2,462	178	7,296	707	1,943	125	519	53	1,178	56	488	27	123	13	337	58	1	...
2. Jasrota ,, ...	33,938	15,513	1,503	113	4,487	266	1,346	108	157	5	320	2	76	5	84	2	222	15	1	...
3. Udhampur ,, ...	61,072	27,799	1,933	113	8,737	470	1,828	108	105	5	1,489	10	438	30	145	7	838	105	...	...
4. Riasi ,, ...	57,004	16,159	1,229	112	5,831	200	1,167	107	62	5	136	8	328	25	97	2	621	34	5	...
5. Mirpur ,, ...	83,560	24,826	1,438	131	14,853	327	1,364	126	74	5	4,830	59	581	25	83	2	488	10	19	...
6. Bhadarwah *Jagir* ...	10,454	8,416	134	24	2,645	208	110	18	24	6	221	4	78	1	17	...	16	...	...	...
7. Punch *Ilaqa*	86,811	87,477	870	29	3,413	35	692	29	178	...	427	11	859	...	45	...	294	5	5	...
II—Total Kashmir Province.	274,428	194,732	2,375	96	49,211	4,663	1,497	32	878	64	3,280	29	2,999	6	274	34	2,684	16	305	...
8. Kashmir North	109,557	83,923	1,001	80	20,026	4,486	305	16	696	64	1,449	13	1,108	3	176	34	867	2	69	...
9. Kashmir South	114,471	73,612	777	5	24,940	121	645	5	132	...	1,328	5	1,231	1	86	...	1,580	13	231	...
Total Kashmir Valley ...	*224,028*	*157,535*	*1,778*	*85*	*44,966*	*4,607*	*950*	*21*	*828*	*64*	*2,777*	*18*	*2,339*	*4*	*262*	*34*	*2,447*	*15*	*300*	...
10. Muzaffarabad District ...	50,400	37,197	597	11	4,245	56	547	11	50	...	503	11	660	2	12	...	237	1	5	...
III—Total Frontier Districts.	54,111	51,789	462	30	4,805	471	438	25	24	5	127	...	528	1	...	1	404	4	2	...
11. Laddakh District ...	48,449	46,759	452	28	4,032	81	428	23	24	5	117	...	399	1	...	1	399	3	2	...
12. Gilgit ,, ...	5,662	5,030	10	2	773	390	10	2	...	...	10	...	129	...	...	...	5	1	...	...
Cities.																				
Jammu	733	107	2	...	41	...	1	...	1	...	16	...	13	...	...	...	...	...	...	...
Srinagar	1,238	791	20	...	147	15	8	...	12	...	19	...	5	...	...	...	20	7	...	...

TABLE XV-B.

Subsidiary Occupations of Agriculturists—Actual Workers only.

(2) Rent-payers.

Jammu and Kashmir State Census, 1911.

District, Jagir, Ilaqa or City.	Detail of subsidiary occupations returned.																			
	Cattle breeders and milkmen.		*Village watchmen.*		*Weavers.*		*Barbers.*		*Oil pressers.*		*Washermen.*		*Potters.*		*Black-smiths and carpenters.*		*Others.*		*Cocoon rearers.*	
	Males.	Females.	Males.	Females.	Males.	Females.	Males.	Females.	Males.	Females.	Males.	Females.	Males.	Females.	Males.	Females.	Males.	Females.	Males.	Females.
	22	23	24	25	26	27	28	29	30	31	32	33	34	35	36	37	38	39	40	41
Total State ...	**6.125**	**298**	**1,345**	**13**	**10,529**	**237**	**3,528**	**46**	**2,033**	**47**	**326**	**15**	**1,562**	**69**	**7,224**	**91**	**30,937**	**5.923**	**15,909**	**45**
I—Total Jammu Province ...	4,230	196	895	13	5,146	228	1,697	35	773	40	221	10	1,050	46	4,591	77	17,512	1,096	...	...
1. Jammu District.... ...	526	72	89	1	783	24	142	20	84	12	43	5	47	2	388	29	3,067	328	...	...
2. Jasrota ,, ...	568	32	75	1	516	29	112	2	60	3	21	1	47	11	325	4	2,060	159	...	...
3. Udhampur ,, ...	1,355	32	192	7	528	33	227	3	73	...	15	1	182	6	708	16	2,547	220	...	...
4. Riasi	548	9	120	...	529	14	367	3	118	9	70	2	139	6	620	8	2,133	80	...	...
5. Mirpur	147	1	199	2	1,699	57	408	5	283	11	48	1	272	9	1,222	11	4.574	134	...	...
6. Bhadarwah *Jagir* ...	1,033	48	48	2	109	...	20	1	18	1	6	...	52	4	535	4	492	143	...	...
7. Punch *Ilaqa*	53	2	172	...	982	11	421	1	137	4	18	...	311	8	793	5	2,639	32	...	...
II—Total Kashmir Province.	1,761	102	413	...	4,921	8	1,779	11	1,260	7	104	5	490	23	2,309	13	10,713	4,364	15,919	45
8. Kashmir North	1,121	99	166	...	1,423	3	691	8	666	6	48	5	233	18	1,207	10	5,129	4,253	5,673	32
9. Kashmir South	556	2	153	...	3,157	4	850	3	581	1	40	...	147	3	661	...	4,093	76	10,246	13
Total Kashmir Valley ...	*1,677*	*101*	*319*	...	*4,580*	7	*1,541*	*11*	*1,247*	*7*	*88*	*5*	*380*	*21*	*1,868*	*10*	*9,222*	*4,329*	*15,919*	*45*
10. Muzaffarabad District ...	84	1	94	...	341	1	238	...	13	...	16	...	110	2	441	3	1,491	35	...	...
III—Total Frontier Districts.	134	...	37	...	462	1	52	...	...	...	1	...	22	...	324	1	2,712	463	...	...
11. Laddakh District ...	9	...	3	...	439	1	43	...	...	...	1	...	20	...	298	1	2,302	74	...	...
12. Gilgit ,, ...	125	...	34	...	23	...	9	...	...	...	...	...	2	...	26	...	410	389	...	...
Cities.																				
Jammu	...	...	...	...	...	...	...	...	...	...	...	...	...	...	...	...	12	...	...	...
Srinagar	2	...	...	...	3	...	2	...	...	...	...	...	...	...	4	...	81	8	11	...

TABLE XV-B.

Subsidiary Occupations of Agriculturists—Actual Workers only.

(3) Agricultural Labourers.

Jammu and Kashmir State Census, 1911.

District, Jagir, Ilaqa or City.	Total Number of Agricultural Labourers (actual workers).		No. of actual workers who returned subsidiary occupations. Agriculturist.		Non-Agriculturist.		Detail of subsidiary occupations returned. Rent-receivers.		Rent-payers.		General labourers.		Village watchmen.		Cattle breeders and Milkmen.		Mill hands.		Fishermen & boatmen.		Rice pounders.		Traders of all kinds.		Oil-pressers.		Weavers.		Potters.		Leather workers.		Washermen.		Blacksmith and carpenters.		Others.		Cocoon rearers.	
	Males.	Females.	Males.	Females.	Males.	Females.	Males.	Females.	Males.	Females.	Males.	Females.	Males.	Females.	Males.	Females.	Males.	Females.	Males.	Females.	Males.	Females.	Males.	Females.	Males.	Females.	Males.	Females.	Males.	Females.	Males.	Females.	Males.	Females.	Males.	Females.	Males.	Females.	Males.	Females.
1	2	3	4	5	6	7	8	9	10	11	12	13	14	15	16	17	18	19	20	21	22	23	24	25	26	27	28	29	30	31	32	33	34	35	36	37	38	39	40	41
Total State ...	**15,440**	**7,097**	**352**	**7**	**1,209**	**74**	**37**	**3**	**315**	**4**	**179**	**6**	**18**	**1**	**102**	**2**	...	...	**5**	**1**	**2**	...	**15**	...	**12**	...	**97**	**4**	**14**	...	**25**	...	**5**	...	**58**		**1569**	**59**	**108**	...
I—Total Jammu Province...	9,131	3,096	210	5	468	44	35	2	175	3	60	6	11	1	39	1	...	...	...	...	2	...	5	...	2	...	25	3	2	...	15	...	4	...	22	...	281	33	...	...
1. Jammu District ...	3,252	1,245	133	4	194	16	19	1	114	3	41	4	7	1	3	...	...	...	...	...	...	...	...	...	...	...	17	2	2	...	14	...	4	...	17	...	89	9	...	...
2. Jasrota „	1,515	876	39	1	88	15	5	1	34	...	7	1	...	...	...	...	...	...	...	...	1	...	2	...	...	...	...	...	...	...	...	...	...	...	1	...	77	14	...	...
3. Udhampur „	878	253	4	...	25	9	1	...	3	...	2	...	2	...	4	1	...	...	...	...	...	...	...	...	2	...	1	...	...	...	...	...	...	...	...	...	14	8	...	...
4. Riasi „	1,018	180	6	...	42	1	...	...	6	...	6	...	...	...	26	...	...	...	...	...	...	...	...	...	...	...	2	...	...	...	...	...	...	...	...	...	8	1	...	...
5. Mirpur „	1,112	221	27	...	83	3	9	...	18	...	2	1	2	...	...	...	...	...	...	...	...	...	...	...	...	...	...	1	...	...	...	...	...	...	3	...	76	1	...	...
6. Bhadarwah *Jagir* ...	218	67	1	...	...	...	1	...	...	...	...	...	...	...	...	...	...	...	...	...	...	...	...	...	...	...	...	...	...	...	...	...	...	...	...	...	...	...	...	...
7. Punch *Ilaqa*	1,138	254	...	...	36	...	...	...	...	...	2	...	...	...	6	...	...	...	...	...	1	...	3	...	...	...	5	...	...	...	1	...	...	...	1	...	17	...	...	...
II—Total Kashmir Province...	5,434	3,261	140	1	712	29	2	...	138	1	119	...	4	...	63	1	...	...	5	1	...	...	9	...	10	...	68	...	12	...	10	...	1	...	35		1268	26	108	...
8. Kashmir North	3,183	1,975	124	1	456	10	...	...	124	1	90	...	3	...	58	1	...	...	3	...	...	...	1	...	6	...	32	...	10	...	6	...	1	...	21		1155	8	70	...
9. Kashmir South	1,447	811	6	...	196	19	...	...	6	...	23	...	...	...	5	...	...	...	2	1	...	...	8	...	4	...	30	...	1	...	2	...	...	...	4	...	79	18	38	...
Total Kashmir Valley ...	*4,630*	*2,786*	*130*	*1*	*652*	*29*	...	...	*130*	*1*	*113*	...	*3*	...	*63*	*1*	...	...	*5*	*1*	...	...	*9*	...	*10*	...	*62*	...	*11*	...	*8*	...	*1*	...	*25*		*1234*	*26*	*108*	...
10. Muzaffarabad District ...	749	...	10	...	60	...	2	...	8	...	6	...	1	...	...	...	...	...	...	...	...	...	...	...	...	...	6	...	1	...	2	...	...	...	10	...	34	...	...	...
III.—Total Frontier Districts	876	740	2	1	29	1	...	1	2	...	...	...	3	...	...	...	...	...	...	...	...	...	...	...	...	...	4	1	...	...	...	...	...	...	1	...	20	...	...	...
11. Laddakh District ...	722	603	1	1	20	1	...	1	1	...	...	...	...	...	...	...	...	...	...	...	...	...	1	...	...	...	3	1	...	...	...	...	...	...	1	...	15	...	...	...
12. Gilgit „	154	137	1	...	9	...	...	...	1	...	...	...	3	...	...	...	...	...	...	...	...	...	...	...	...	...	1	...	...	...	...	...	...	...	...	...	5	...	...	...
Cities.																																								
Jammu	15	3	...	...	...	...	...	...	...	...	...	...	...	...	...	...	...	...	...	...	...	...	...	...	...	...	...	...	...	...	...	...	...	...	...	...	...	...	...	...
Srinagar	256	206	...	...	60	18	...	...	...	...	19	...	...	...	...	...	...	...	...	...	...	...	4	...	...	...	1	...	...	...	...	...	...	...	...	...	36	18	...	...

XV-D
Occupation by Religion.

TABLE XV-D.

Occupations by Religion.

Jammu and Kashmir State Census, 1911.

Entire State.

OCCUPATION.	Total number of workers and dependents.	Distribution by Religion.								
		Hindu.	Arya.	Bramho.	Sikh.	Jain.	Budh.	Parsi.	Musalman.	Christian.
1	2	3	4	5	6	7	8	9	10	11
All Occupations ...	3,158,126	689,342	1,047	1	31,553	345	36,512	31	2,398,320	975
Class A.—Production of raw materials ...	2,519,742	480,750	199	...	25,064	25	32,732	...	1,980,762	210
Sub-class I.—Exploitation of the surface of the earth	2,519,709	480,727	199	...	25,064	25	32,730	...	1,980,754	210
Order 1.—Pasture and Agriculture	2,515,519	480,700	197	...	25,052	25	32,730	...	1,976,203	210
Sub-order 1 (a).—Ordinary cultivation ...	2,474,991	470,080	186	...	25,022	25	31,940	...	1,947,538	200
Group 1. Income from rent of agricultural land ...	32,470	16,951	2	...	1,036	...	29	...	14,452	...
,, 2. Ordinary cultivators ...	2,400,806	438,343	144	...	23,824	25	31,129	...	1,907,257	84
,, 3. Agents, managers of landed estates (not planters), clerks, rent collectors, etc.	1,434	1,117	12	...	51	...	3	...	206	45
,, 4. Farm servants and field labourers ...	40,281	13,669	28	...	111	...	779	...	25,623	71
Sub-order 1 (b).—Growers of special products and market gardening	4,407	158	4	...	7	...	30	...	4,205	3
Group 6. Fruit, flower, vegetable, betel, vine, areca nut, etc. growers	4,407	158	4	...	7	...	30	...	4,205	3
Sub-order 1 (c).—Forestry ...	3,085	1,594	9	...	2	...	52	...	1,421	7
Group 7. Forest officers, rangers, guards, etc. ...	2,140	1,548	9	...	...	...	2	...	574	7
,, 8. Wood-cutters, fire wood, lac, catechu, rubber, etc. collectors and charcoal burners	945	46	...	...	2	...	50	...	847	...
Sub-order 1 (d).—Raising of farm stock ...	32,284	8,857	...	...	20	...	708	...	22,699	...
Group 9. Cattle and buffalo breeders and keepers ...	23,785	3,132	...	...	12	...	708	...	19,933	...
,, 10. Sheep, goat, and pig breeders ...	736	129	...	...	...	...	...	...	607	...
,, 12. Herdsmen, shepherds, goat-herds, etc. ...	7,763	5,596	...	...	8	...	...	...	2,159	...
Sub-order 1 (e).—Raising of small animals ...	752	11	...	...	1	...	...	...	740	...
Group 13. Birds, bees, silkworms, etc. ...	752	11	...	...	1	...	...	...	740	...
Order 2.—Fishing and hunting	4,190	27	...	...	12	...	...	...	4,151	...
Group 14. Fishing ...	3,326	27	...	...	...	...	...	...	3,299	...
,, 15. Hunting ...	864	...	...	...	12	...	...	...	852	...
Sub-class II.—Extraction of minerals ...	33	23	...	...	...	...	2	...	8	...
Order 3.—Mines	33	23	...	...	...	...	2	...	8	...
Group 17. Mines and metallic minerals (gold, iron, manganese, etc.)	33	23	...	...	...	...	2	...	8	...
Class B.—Preparation and supply of material substances.	433,421	114,783	504	...	3,857	281	900	14	312,632	450
Sub-class III.—Industry ...	280.397	62,749	338	...	1,076	7	251	...	215,655	321
Order 6.—Textiles	95,619	17,104	230	...	218	...	106	...	77,944	15
Group 21. Cotton ginning, clearing and pressing ...	180	10	...	...	...	...	...	...	170	...
,, 22. Cotton spinning, sizing and weaving ...	61,184	15.530	227	...	175	...	72	...	45,178	2
,, 24. Rope, twine, and string ...	194	31	...	...	...	...	...	...	163	...
,, 25. Other fibres, cocoanut, aloes, flax, hemp, straw, etc.	22	6	...	...	...	...	...	...	16	...
,, 26. Wood carders and spinners, weavers of woollen blankets, carpets, etc.	23,677	201	...	...	17	...	34	...	23,424	1
,, 27. Silk spinners and weavers ...	5,724	933	3	...	18	...	...	...	4,758	12
,, 30. Dyeing, bleaching, printing, preparation and sponging of textiles	2,375	181	...	...	8	...	...	...	2,186	...
,, 31. Other (lace, crape, embroideries, fringes, etc.) and insufficiently described textile industries	2,263	212	...	...	...	...	...	...	2,051	...
Order 7.—Hides, skins and hard materials from the animal kingdom	620	109	...	...	...	...	...	...	511	...
Group 32. Tanners, curriers, leather dressers and dyers, etc.	620	109	...	...	...	...	...	...	511	...
Order 8.—Wood	31,045	8,209	...	...	100	...	30	...	22,696	10
Group 36. Sawyers, carpenters, turners and joiners, etc.	19,999	4,608	...	...	99	...	30	...	15,253	9
,, 37. Basket makers and other industries of woody material, including leaves.	11,046	3,601	...	...	1	...	...	...	7,443	1
Order 9.—Metals	13,104	3,249	2	...	125	2	59	...	9,667	...
Group 40. Makers of arms, guns, etc. ...	20	2	...	...	...	...	...	...	18	...
,, 41. Other workers in iron and makers of implements and tools principally or exclusively of iron	12,041	3,216	2	...	125	1	59	...	8,638	...
,, 42. Workers in brass, copper and bell metal ...	312	30	...	...	...	1	...	...	281	...
,, 43. Workers in other metals (tin, zinc, lead, quicksilver, etc.)	188	...	...	...	...	...	...	...	188	...
,, 44. Workers in mints, die-sinkers, etc. ...	543	1	...	...	...	...	...	...	542	...
Order 10.—Ceramics	14,201	1,368	6	...	4	5	...	...	12,758	60
Group 47. Potters and earthen pipe and bowl makers ...	13,377	1,314	...	...	...	5	...	...	12,058	...
,, 48. Brick and tile makers ...	824	54	6	...	4	...	...	...	700	60
Order 11.—Chemical products properly so called, and analogous.	13,044	729	...	...	5	...	...	...	12.309	1
Group 50. Manufacture of matches and explosive materials	274	3	...	...	...	...	...	...	271	...
,, 51. Manufacture of ærated and mineral waters	64	20	...	...	...	...	...	...	44	...
,, 52. Manufacture of dyes, paint and ink ...	136	1	...	...	...	...	..	...	134	1

TABLE XV-D.

Occupations by Religion.

Jammu and Kashmir State Census, 1911.

Entire State.

OCCUPATION.	Total number of workers and dependents.	Distribution by Religion. Hindu.	Arya.	Bramho.	Sikh.	Jain.	Budh.	Parsi.	Musalman.	Christian.
1	2	3	4	5	6	7	8	9	10	11
Group 53. Manufacture and refining of vegetable and mineral oil	11,309	92	...	...	...	...	...	...	11,217	...
,, 54. Manufacture of paper cardboard and *papier mache*	279	5	...	...	...	...	...	...	274	...
,, 55. Others (Soap, candles, lac, cutch, perfumes and miscellaneous drugs)	982	608	...	...	5	...	...	...	369	...
Order 12.—Food Industries	20,858	7,454	3	...	122	...	3	...	13,276	...
Group 56. Rice pounders and husker and flour grinders,	8,736	5,345	1	...	17	...	3	...	3,370	...
,, 57. Bakers and biscuit makers	5,638	564	...	...	6	...	...	...	5,068	...
,, 58. Grain parchers, etc.	123	76	...	...	...	...	...	...	47	...
,, 59. Butchers	4,081	8	...	...	12	...	...	...	4,061	...
,, 62. Makers of sugar, molasses and *gur*	19	19	...	...	...	...	...	...	...	...
,, 63. Sweetmeat makers, preparers of jam and condiments, etc.	2,246	1,442	2	...	87	...	...	...	715	...
,, 64. Brewers and distillers	15	...	...	...	...	...	...	...	15	...
Order 13.—Industries of dress and the toilet	66,985	17,339	1	...	35	...	28	...	49,582	...
Group 67. Hat, cap and turban makers	11	...	...	...	...	...	...	...	11	...
,, 68. Tailors, milliners, dress-makers and darners, embroiderers on linen	21,580	1,315	1	...	16	...	21	...	20,227	...
,, 69. Shoe, boot and sandal makers	27,318	13,414	...	...	8	...	1	...	13,895	...
,, 70. Other industries pertaining to dress, gloves, socks, gaiters, belts, buttons, umbrellas, canes, etc.	151	25	...	...	...	...	...	...	126	...
,, 71. Washing, cleaning and dyeing	5,198	175	...	...	9	...	6	...	5,008	...
,, 72. Barbers, hairdressers and wig-makers	12,727	2,410	...	...	2	...	...	...	10,315	...
Order 15.—Building Industries	7,953	1,208	1	...	29	...	...	...	6,715	...
Group 76. Lime burners, cement workers	114	...	...	...	2	...	...	...	112	...
,, 77. Excavators, plinth builders and well sinkers	5,079	1,088	1	...	14	...	...	...	3,976	...
,, 79. Others (thatchers, building contractors, house painters, tilers, plumbers, locksmiths, etc.)	2,760	120	...	...	13	...	...	...	2,627	...
Order 16.—Construction of means of transport	256	27	...	...	...	...	...	...	229	...
Group 81. Saddlers, hornessmakers, whip and lash makers	256	27	...	...	...	...	...	...	229	...
Order 17.—Production and transmission of physical orces (heat, light, electricity, motive power, etc.)	208	162	...	...	4	...	...	...	28	14
Group 83. Gas workers, electric light and ice factories	208	162	...	...	4	...	...	...	28	14
Order 18.—Industries of luxury and those pertaining to literature and the arts and sciences	12,254	4,688	5	...	424	...	13	...	7,116	8
Group 86. Book binders and stichers, envelope makers, etc.	147	17	...	...	...	...	...	...	130	...
,, 87. Makers of musical instruments	18	...	...	...	...	...	...	...	18	...
,, 88. Makers of watches and clocks and optical, photographic and surgical instruments	178	99	...	...	3	...	1	...	74	1
,, 89. Workers in precious stones and metals, enamellers, imitation jewellery makers, gilders, etc.	10,947	4,166	5	...	421	...	10	...	6,338	7
,, 90. Makers of bangles, rosaries, bead and other necklaces, spangles, *lingams* and sacred thread	765	403	...	...	...	...	...	...	362	...
,, 91. Toy, kite, cage, fishing tackle, etc, makers, taxi-dermists, etc.	137	3	...	...	...	...	...	...	134	...
,, 92. Others including managers, persons other than performers employed in theatres and other places of public entertainment, employes of public societies, race-course service, huntsmen, etc.	62	...	...	...	...	...	2	...	60	...
Order 19.—Industries concerned with refuse matter	4,250	1,103	90	...	10	...	12	...	2,822	213
Group 93. Sweepers, scavengers, dust and sweeping contractors	4,250	1,103	90	...	10	...	12	...	2,822	213
Sub-Class IV.—Transport	33,667	4,355	21	...	307	...	170	1	28,728	85
Order 20.—Transport by water	15,968	644	11	...	122	...	2	1	15,188	...
Group 95. Ship owners, and their employes, ship brokers, ships' officers, engineers, mariners and firemen	67	...	...	...	...	...	...	...	67	...
,, 96. Persons employed on the maintenance of streams, rivers and canals (including construction)	2,524	603	11	...	122	...	2	...	1,786	...
,, 97. Boat-owners, boat-men and tow-men.	13,377	41	...	...	...	...	...	1	13,335	...
Order 21.—Transport by road	15,504	2,787	2	...	144	...	135	...	12,430	6
Group 98. Persons employed on the construction and maintenance of roads and bridges	1,549	140	...	...	18	...	...	...	1,389	2
,, 99. Cart owners and drivers, coach men, stable-boys tramway mail carriage, etc., managers and employes (excluding private servants)	698	43	...	...	12	...	...	...	643	...

XV-D
Occupation by Religion.

TABLE XV-D.

Occupations by Religion.

Jammu and Kashmir State Census, 1911.

Entire State.

OCCUPATION.	Total number of workers and dependents.	Distribution by Religion.								
		Hindu.	Arya.	Bramho.	Sikh.	Jain.	Budh.	Parsi.	Musalman.	Christian.
1	2	3	4	5	6	7	8	9	10	11
Group 100. *Palki*, etc., bearers and owners ...	29	23	...	...	...	...	...	...	6	...
,, 101. Pack elephant, camel, mule, ass and bullock owners and drivers	10,902	1,633	2	...	107	...	135	...	9,021	4
,, 102. Porters and messengers	2,326	948	...	...	7	...	...	...	1,371	...
Order 22.—Transport by rail ...	426	117	...	...	14	...	...	...	295	...
Group 103. Railway employes of all kinds other than construction coolies	399	116	...	...	14	...	...	...	269	...
,, 104. Labourers employed on railway construction	27	1	...	...	...	...	...	...	26	...
Order 23.—Post Office, Telegraph and Telephone services	1,769	807	8	...	27	...	33	...	815	79
Group 105. Post Office, Telegraph and Telephone services	1,769	807	8	...	27	...	33	...	815	79
Sub-Class V.—Trade	119,357	47,679	145	...	2,474	274	479	13	68,249	44
Order 24.—Banks, establishments of credit, exchange and insurance	10,239	8,848	46	...	724	...	...	13	603	5
Group 106. Bank managers, money lenders, exchange and insurance agents, money changers and brokers and their employes	10,239	3,848	46	...	724	...	...	13	603	5
Order 26.—Trade in Textiles	6,032	2,794	9	...	210	22	71	...	2,926	...
Group 108. Trade in piece-goods, wool, cotton, silk, hair and other textiles	6,032	2,794	9	...	210	22	71	...	2,926	...
Order 27.—Trade in skins, leather and furs ...	1,140	72	1	...	1	...	...	...	1,034	32
Group 109. Trade in skins, leather, furs, feathers, horns, etc.	1,140	72	1	...	1	...	...	...	1,034	32
Order 28.—Trade in wood	895	88	...	...	8	...	2	...	797	...
Group 110. Trade in wood (not firewood) cork, bark, etc.	895	88	...	...	8	...	2	...	797	...
Order 32.—Hotels, cafes, restaurants, etc. ...	196	80	...	...	31	...	...	...	79	6
Group 114. Vendors of wine, liquors, aerated waters, etc.	109	69	...	...	20	...	...	...	20	...
,, 115. Owners and managers of hotels, cookshops, and *sarais*, etc., and their employes	87	11	...	...	11	...	...	...	59	6
Order 33. Other trade in food stuffs	82,174	25,648	37	...	1,165	12	374	...	54,938	...
Group 118. Sellers of milk, butter, *ghee*, poultry, eggs, etc.	23,343	1,060	...	...	37	2	3	...	22,241	...
,, 120. Cardamum, betel leaf, . vegetables, fruit arecanuts sellers	5,384	225	1	...	13	...	2	...	5,143	...
,, 121. Grain and pulse dealers	41,657	22,198	34	...	1,114	10	349	...	17,952	...
,, 122. Tobacco, opium, *ganja*, etc., sellers ...	876	466	...	...	1	...	...	...	409	...
,, 123. Dealers in sheep, goats and pigs ...	8,248	553	...	...	...	...	6	...	7,689	...
,, 124. Dealers in hay, grass and fodder ...	2,666	1,146	2	...	...	...	14	...	1,504	...
Order 34.—Trade in clothing and toilet articles	1,315	924	...	...	5	...	...	...	386	...
Group 125. Trade in ready-made clothing and other articles of dress and the toilet (hats, umbrellas, socks, ready-made shoes, perfumes, etc.)	1,315	924	...	...	5	...	...	...	386	...
Order 35.—Trade in furniture	147	94	...	...	...	...	...	...	53	...
Group 126. Trade in furniture, carpets, curtains and bedding	13	3	...	...	...	...	...	...	10	...
,, 127. Hardware, cooking utensils, porcelain crockery, glass-ware, bottles, articles for gardening, the cellar, etc.	134	91	...	...	...	...	...	...	43	...
Order 36.—Trade in building materials	45	6	...	...	...	...	...	...	39	...
Group 128. Trade in building materials (stones, brick, plaster, cement, and, tiles thatch, etc.)	45	6	...	...	...	...	...	...	39	...
Order 37.—Trade in means of transport	703	146	...	...	3	...	6	...	548	...
Group 129. Dealers and hirers of elephants, camels horses, cattle, asses, mules, etc., sellers (not makers) of carriages, saddlery, etc.	703	146	...	...	3	...	6	...	548	...
Order 38.—Trade in fuel ...	3,883	2,238	...	...	1	...	12	...	1,632	...
Group 130. Dealers in firewood, charcoal, coal, cowdung, etc.	3,883	2,238	...	...	1	...	12	...	1,632	...
Order 39.—Trade in articles of luxury and those pertaining to letters and the arts and sciences	3,115	1,600	3	...	21	30	...	...	1,461	...
Group 131. Dealers in precious stones, jewellery (real and imitation) clocks, optical instruments, etc.	1,524	1,427	3	...	3	21	...	...	70	...
,, 132. Dealers in common bangles, bead, necklaces, fans, small articles, toys, hunting and fishing tackle, flowers, etc.	1,432	137	...	...	18	9	...	...	1,268	...
,, 133. Publishers, booksellers, stationers, dealers in music, pictures, musical instruments and curiosities	159	36	...	...	...	...	...	...	123	...
Order 40.—Trade in refuse matter ...	180	1	...	...	...	...	...	...	179	...
Group 134. Dealers in rags, stable refuse, etc. ...	180	1	...	...	...	...	...	...	179	...
Order 41.—Trade of other sorts	9,293	5,140	49	...	305	210	14	...	3,574	1
Group 137. Shopkeepers, otherwise unspecified ...	7,400	4,556	49	...	281	210	...	...	2,303	1
,, 136. Itinerant traders, pedlars, hawkers, etc. ...	1,112	466	...	...	24	...	...	...	622	...
,, 137. Conjurers, acrobats, fortune-tellers, reciters, exhibitors of curiosities and wild animals	779	118	...	...	...	...	14	...	647	...
,, 138. Other trades (including farmers of pounds, tolls and markets)	2	...	...	...	...	...	...	...	2	...

TABLE XV-D.
Occupations by Religion.
Jammu and Kashmir State Census, 1911.
Entire State.

OCCUPATION.	Total number of workers and dependents.	Hindu.	Arya.	Bramho.	Sikh.	Jain.	Budh.	Parsi.	Musalman.	Christian.
		DISTRIBUTION BY RELIGION.								
1	2	3	4	5	6	7	8	9	10	11
Class C.—Public administration and liberal arts	104,541	60,153	275	1	1,535	21	1,580	17	40,681	278
SUB-CLASS VI.—PUBLIC FORCE ...	20,513	12,952	14	...	238	4	137	1	7,124	43
Order 42.—Army ...	10,706	7,998	...	...	102	4	...	...	2,560	42
Group 139. Army (Imperial) ...	9	2	...	...	...	...	...	...	...	7
,, 140. Army (Native States) ...	10,697	7,996	...	...	102	4	...	...	2,560	35
Order 44.—Police ...	9,807	4,954	14	...	136	...	37	1	4,564	1
Group 142. Police ...	4,672	2,801	7	...	83	...	...	1	1,779	1
,, 143. Village watchmen ...	5,135	2,153	7	...	53	...	37	...	2,785	...
SUB-CLASS VII.—PUBLIC ADMINISTERATION ...	28,707	18,139	139	...	881	4	26	8	9,412	98
Order 45.—Public Administration ...	28,707	18,139	139	...	881	4	26	8	9,412	98
Group 144. Service of the State (British Government)...	34	20	...	...	2	...	...	2	8	2
,, 145. Service of Native State (J. and K. State)...	23,617	15,044	65	...	575	4	19	6	7,829	75
,, 146. Municipal and other local (not village) service	1,765	1,055	65	...	239	...	...	...	385	21
,, 147. Village officials and servants other than watchmen	3,291	2,020	9	...	65	...	7	...	1,190	...
SUB-CLASS VIII.—PROFESSIONS AND LIBERAL ARTS ...	52,889	27,402	118	...	385	3	1,416	8	23,455	102
Order 46.—Religion ...	38,592	21,216	25	...	149	...	1,344	...	15,823	35
Group 148. Priests, ministers, etc. ...	6,737	4,487	1	...	8	...	1,307	...	929	5
,, 149. Religious mendicants, inmates of monastries, etc.	31,614	16,729	24	...	141	...	34	...	14,656	30
,, 151. Temple, burial or burning ground service, pilgrim conductors, circumcisers	241	...	...	...	...	...	3	...	238	...
Order 47.—Law	1,523	1,051	24	...	30	1	...	3	412	2
Group 152. Lawyers of all kinds including *Kazis*, Law agents and *mukhtiars*.	481	345	15	...	3	1	...	3	114	...
,, 153. Lawyers' clerks, petition-writers, etc. ...	1,042	706	9	...	27	...	...	...	298	2
Order 48.—Medicine	2,769	1,052	7	...	36	1	14	...	1,631	28
Group 154. Medical practitioners of all kinds including dentists, occulists and veterinary surgeons	2,093	816	7	...	29	...	...	...	1,222	19
,, 155. Midwives, vaccinators, compounders, nurses, masseurs, etc.	676	236	...	...	7	1	14	...	409	9
Order 49.—Instruction ...	3,053	1,473	32	...	25	...	1	5	1,495	22
Group 156. Professors and teachers of all kinds or clerks and servants connected with education	3,053	1,473	32	...	25	...	1	5	1,495	22
Order 50.—Letters and arts and sciences	6,952	2,610	30	...	145	1	57	...	4,094	15
Group 158. Architects, surveyors, engineers and their employes	3,797	1,596	22	...	140	...	...	...	2,027	12
,, 159. Others (authors, photographers, artists, sculptors, astronomers, meteorologists, botanists, astrologers, etc.)	1,352	721	...	...	2	1	5	...	620	3
,, 160. Music composers and masters, players on all kinds of musical instruments (not military), singers, actors and dancers	1,803	293	8	...	3	...	52	...	1,447	...
SUB-CLASS IX.—PERSONS LIVING ON THEIR INCOME ...	2,432	1,660	4	1	31	10	1	...	690	35
Order 51.—Persons living principally on their income	2,432	1,660	4	1	31	10	1	...	690	35
Group 161. Proprietors (other than of agricultural land) fund and scholarship holders and pensioners	2,432	1,660	4	1	31	10	1	...	690	35
Class D.—Miscellaneous ...	100,422	33,656	69	...	1,097	18	1,300	...	64,245	37
SUB-CLASS X.—DOMESTIC SERVICE ...	37,766	17,817	18	...	560	7	382	...	18,966	16
Order 52.—Domestic service	37,766	17,817	18	...	560	7	382	...	18,966	16
Group 162. Cooks, water-carriers, door-keepers, watchmen and other indoor servants	36,911	17,757	17	...	558	7	369	...	18,190	13
,, 163. Private grooms, coachmen, dog-boys, etc...	855	60	1	...	2	...	13	...	776	3
SUB-CLASS XI.—INSUFFICIENTLY DESCRIBED OCCUPATIONS	23,004	10,117	12	...	248	7	269	...	12,338	13
Order 53.—General terms which do not indicate a definite occupation	23,004	10,117	12	...	248	7	269	...	12,338	13
Group 164. Manufacturers, business men and contractors otherwise unspecified	6,543	2,739	10	...	174	...	254	...	3,361	5
,, 165. Cashiers, accountants, book-keepers, clerks and other employes in unspecified offices, ware-houses and shops	66	44	...	...	6	...	...	...	16	...
,, 166. Mechanics otherwise unspecified ...	167	6	...	...	...	...	6	...	155	...
,, 167. Labourers and workmen otherwise unspecified	16,228	7,328	2	...	68	7	9	...	8,806	8
SUB-CLASS XII.—UNPRODUCTIVE ...	39,652	5,722	39	...	289	4	649	...	32,941	8
Order 54.—Inmates of jails, asylums and hospitals ...	658	9	...	...	4	...	1	...	644	...
Group 168. Inmates of jails, asylums and hospitals ...	658	9	...	...	4	...	1	...	644	...
Order 55.—Beggars, vagrants, prostitutes ...	38,994	5,713	39	...	285	4	648	...	32,297	8
Group 169. Beggars, vagrants, procurers, prostitutes, receivers of stolen goods, cattle poisoners	38,994	5,713	39	...	285	4	648	...	32,297	8

XV-D
Occupation by Religion.

TABLE XV-D.
Occupations by Religion.
Jammu and Kashmir State Census, 1911.
Jammu City.

OCCUPATION	Total number of workers and dependents.	Distribution by Religion.								
		Hindu.	Arya.	Bramho.	Sikh.	Jain.	Budh.	Parsi.	Musalman.	Christian.
1	2	3	4	5	6	7	8	9	10	11
All Occupations ...	31,726	19,778	132	...	695	334	...	5	10,618	164
Class A—Production of raw materials ...	2,122	1,165	9	...	41	23	...	...	884	...
Sub-class I—Exploitation of the surface of the earth	2,122	1,165	9	...	41	23	...	...	884	...
Order 1—Pasture and Agriculture	2,088	1,136	9	...	41	23	...	...	879	...
Sub-order 1 (a) Ordinary cultivation	2,018	1,086	8	...	32	23	...	...	869	...
Group 1. Income from rent of agricultural land ...	292	239	...	...	1	...	...	...	52	...
,, 2. Ordinary cultivators ...	1,685	823	8	...	31	23	...	...	800	...
,, 3. Agents, managers of landed estates (not planters), clerks, rent collectors, etc.	11	6	...	...	...	...	...	...	5	...
,, 4. Farm servants and field labourers ...	30	18	...	...	...	...	...	...	12	...
Sub-order 1 (b) Growers of special products and market gardening.	7	...	...	...	4	...	...	...	3	...
Group 6. Fruit, flower, vegetable, betel, vine, areca-nut, etc., growers	7	...	...	...	4	...	...	...	3	...
Sub-order 1 (c) Forestry	52	39	1	...	5	...	...	...	7	...
Group 7. Forest officers, rangers, guards, etc. ...	52	39	1	...	5	...	...	...	7	...
Sub-order 1 (d) Raising of farm stock	11	11	...	...	...	...	...	...	...	...
Group 12. Herdsmen, shepherds, goat-herds, etc. ...	11	11	...	...	...	...	...	...	...	...
Order 2—Fishing and hunting	34	29	...	...	...	...	...	...	5	...
Group 14. Fishing ...	34	29	...	...	...	...	...	...	5	...
Class B—Preparation and supply of material substances	12,725	7,357	41	...	280	281	...	...	4,673	93
Sub-class III.—Industry ...	7,656	3,449	4	...	176	7	...	...	3,928	92
Order 6—Textiles	650	77	...	...	...	...	...	...	573	...
Group 22. Cotton spinning, sizing and weaving ...	87	45	...	...	...	...	...	...	42	...
,, 26. Wool carders and spinners, weavers of woollen blankets, carpets, etc.	34	12	...	...	...	...	...	...	22	...
,, 27. Silk spinners and weavers ...	331	...	...	...	...	...	...	...	331	...
,, 30. Dyeing, bleaching, printing, preparation and sponging of textiles	121	...	...	...	...	...	...	...	121	...
,, 31. Other (lace, crape, embroideries, fringes, etc. and insufficiently described textile industries	77	20	...	...	...	...	...	...	57	...
Order 7—Hides, skins and hard materials from the animal kingdom	17	...	...	...	...	...	...	...	17	...
Group 32. Tanners, curriers, leather dressers and dyers, etc.	17	...	...	...	...	...	...	...	17	...
Order 8—Wood	553	226	...	...	50	...	...	...	277	...
Group 36. Sawyers, carpenters, turners and joiners, etc.	500	173	...	...	50	...	...	...	277	...
,, 37. Basket makers and other industries of woody material including leaves	53	53	...	...	...	...	...	...	...	...
Order 9—Metals	410	171	...	...	4	2	...	...	233	...
Group 41. Other workers in iron and makers of implements and tools principally or exclusively of iron	280	87	...	...	4	1	...	...	188	...
,, 42. Workers in brass, copper and bell metal ...	85	84	...	...	...	1	...	...	...	...
,, 43. Workers in other metals (tin, zinc, lead, quick-silver, etc.)	37	...	...	...	...	...	...	...	37	...
,, 44. Workers in mints, die-sinkers, etc. ...	8	...	...	...	...	...	...	...	8	...
Order 10—Ceramics	180	4	...	...	...	5	...	...	142	29
Group 47. Potters and earthen pipe and bowl makers ...	149	4	...	...	...	5	...	...	140	...
,, 48. Brick and tile makers ...	31	...	...	...	...	...	...	...	2	29
Order 11—Chemical products properly so called and analogous	251	80	...	...	...	...	...	...	171	...
Group 50. Manufacture of matches and explosive materials	90	...	...	...	...	...	...	...	90	...
,, 51. Manufacture of aerated and mineral waters ...	13	13	...	...	...	...	...	...	...	...
,, 52. Manufacture of dyes, paint and ink ...	17	...	...	...	...	...	...	...	17	...
,, 53. Manufacture and refining of vegetable and mineral oils	15	...	...	...	...	...	...	...	15	...
,, 55. Others (soap, candles, lac, cutch, perfumes and miscellaneous drugs)	116	67	...	...	...	...	...	...	49	...

TABLE XV-D.

OCCUPATIONS BY RELIGION.

Jammu and Kashmir State Census, 1911.

Jammu City.

OCCUPATION.	Total number of workers and dependents.	Distribution by Religion.								
		Hindu.	Arya.	Bramho.	Sikh.	Jain.	Budh.	Parsi.	Musalman.	Christian.
1	2	3	4	5	6	7	8	9	10	11
Order 12.—Food industries	1,906	1,180	...	...	54	...	...	...	672	...
Group 56. Rice pounders and huskers and flour grinders	965	710	...	...	1	...	...	...	254	...
,, 57. Bakers and biscuit makers	332	151	...	...	...	...	...	...	181	...
,, 58. Grain parchers, etc.	9	9	...	...	...	...	...	...	...	...
,, 59. Butchers	241	4	...	...	...	...	...	...	237	...
,, 63. Sweetmeat makers, preparers of jam and condiments, etc.	359	306	...	...	53	...	...	...	...	...
Order 13.—Industries of dress and the toilet.	2,131	651	...	...	9	...	...	...	1,471	...
Group 68. Tailors, milliners, dress makers and darners, embroiderers on linen	877	69	...	...	8	...	...	...	800	...
,, 69. Shoe, boot and sandal makers	699	434	...	...	...	...	...	...	265	...
Group 70. Other industries pertaining to dress, gloves, socks, gaiters, belts, buttons, umbrellas, canes, etc.	7	7	...	...	...	...	...	...	...	...
,, 71. Washing, cleaning and dyeing	228	...	...	...	...	...	...	...	228	...
,, 72. Barbers, hairdressers and wig-makers	320	141	...	...	1	...	...	...	178	...
Order 15.—Building industries	60	39	...	...	12	...	...	...	9	...
Group 79. Others (thatchers, building contractors, house painters, tilers, plumbers, lock-smith, etc.)	60	39	...	...	12	...	...	...	9	...
Order 16.—Construction of means of transport	60	...	...	...	...	...	...	...	60	...
Group 81. Saddlers, harness-makers whip and lash makers	60	...	...	...	...	...	...	...	60	...
Order 17.—Production and transmission of physical forces (heat, light, electricity, motive power, etc.)	7	7	...	...	...	...	...	...	...	...
Group 83. Gas works, electric light and ice factories...	7	7	...	...	...	...	...	...	...	...
Order 18.—Industries of luxury and those pertaining to literature and the arts and sciences	1,145	874	...	...	47	...	...	...	224	...
Group 86. Book binders and stichers, envelope makers...	27	11	...	...	...	...	...	...	16	...
,, 87. Makers of musical instruments	4	...	...	...	...	...	...	...	4	...
,, 88. Makers of watches and clocks and optical, photographic and surgical instruments	69	42	...	...	3	...	...	...	24	...
,, 89. Workers in precious stones and metals, enamellars, imitation jewellery makers, gilders, etc.	639	426	...	...	44	...	...	...	169	...
,, 90. Makers of bangles, rosaries, bead and other necklaces, spangles, *lingams* and sacred threads	394	392	...	...	...	...	...	...	2	...
,, 91. Toy, kite, cage, fishing tackle, etc., makers, taxidermists, etc.	10	3	...	...	...	...	...	...	7	...
,, 92. Others including managers, persons other than performers employed in theatres and other places of public entertainment, employes of public societies, race course service, huntsmen, etc.	2	...	...	...	...	...	...	...	2	...
Order 19.—Industries concerned with refuse matter	286	140	4	...	...	...	...	...	79	63
Group 93. Sweepers, scavangers, dust and sweeping contractors	286	140	4	...	...	...	...	...	79	63
SUB-CLASS IV.—TRANSPORT	819	501	11	...	6	...	...	...	300	1
Order 20.—Transport by Water	9	...	4	...	...	...	...	...	5	...
Group 96. Persons employed on the maintenance of streams, rivers and canals including construction	4	...	4	...	...	...	...	...	...	...
,, 97. Boat owners, boat men and tow men	5	...	...	...	...	...	...	...	5	...
Order 21.—Transport by road	688	406	...	...	5	...	...	...	276	1
Group 99. Cart owners and drivers, coachmen, stable boys, tramway, mail carriage, etc., managers and employes (excluding private servants	199	3	...	...	1	...	...	...	195	...
,, 101. Pack elephant, camel, mule, ass and bullock owners and drivers	485	403	...	...	...	...	...	...	81	1
,, 102. Porters and messengers	4	...	...	...	4	...	...	...	...	...
Order 22.—Transport by rail	10	8	...	...	...	...	...	...	2	...
Group 103. Railway employes of all kinds other than construction coolies	10	8	...	...	...	...	...	...	2	...
Order 23.—Post office, Telegraph and Telephone services.	112	87	7	...	1	...	...	...	17	...
Group 105. Post office, telegraph and telephone services...	112	87	7	...	1	...	...	...	17	...

XV-D
Occupation by Religion.

TABLE XV-D.

Occupations by Religion.

Jammu and Kashmir State Census, 1911.

Jammu City.

OCCUPATION.	Total number of workers and dependents.	Distribution by Religion. Hindu.	Arya.	Bramho.	Sikh.	Jain.	Budh	Parsi.	Musalman.	Christian.
1	2	3	4	5	6	7	8	9	10	11
Sub-class V.—Trade ...	4,250	3,407	26	...	98	274	...	...	445	...
Order 24.—Banks, establishments of credit, exchange and insurance	324	310	1	...	5	...	...	...	8	...
Group 106. Bank managers, money lenders, exchange and insurance agents, money changers and brokers and their employes	324	310	1	...	5	...	...	...	8	...
Order 26—Trade in textiles	170	137	...	...	...	22	...	...	11	...
Group 108. Trade in piece-goods, wool, cotton, silk, hair and other textiles	170	137	...	...	...	22	...	...	11	...
Order 27—Trade in skins, leather and furs	63	...	...	...	...	...	...	...	63	...
Group 109. Trade in skins, leather, furs, feathers, horn, etc.	63	...	...	...	...	...	...	...	63	...
Order 28—Trade in wood	5	...	...	...	...	...	...	...	5	...
Group 110. Trade in wood (not firewood), cork, bark, etc.	5	...	...	...	...	...	...	...	5	...
Order 32.—Hotels, cafes, restaurants, etc. ...	37	34	...	...	3	...	...	...	...	...
Group 114. Vendors of wine, liquors, aerated water, etc.	37	34	...	...	3	...	...	...	...	...
Order 33.—Other trade in food stuffs	2,299	2,042	1	...	63	12	...	...	181	...
Group 118. Sellers of milk, butter, ghee, poultry, eggs, etc.	110	75	...	...	...	2	...	...	33	...
,, 120. Cardamom, betel leaf, vegetables, fruit and areca nut sellers	141	87	...	...	2	...	...	...	52	...
,, 121. Grain and pulse dealers ...	1,796	1,637	1	...	61	10	...	...	87	...
,, 122. Tobacco, opuim, *ganja*, etc., sellers ...	247	239	...	...	...	...	...	...	8	...
,, 124. Dealers in hay, grass and fodder ...	5	4	...	...	...	...	...	...	1	...
Order 34—Trade in clothing and toilet articles	76	33	...	...	...	...	...	...	43	...
Group 125. Trade in ready-made clothing and other articles of dress and the toilet (hats, umbrellas, socks, ready-made shoes, perfumes, etc.)	76	33	...	...	...	...	...	...	43	...
Order 35—Trade in furniture	3	3	...	...	...	...	...	...	...	...
Group 126. Trade in furniture, carpets, curtains and bedding	3	3	...	...	...	...	...	...	...	...
Order 36—Trade in building materials	3	...	...	...	...	...	...	...	3	...
Group 128. Trade in building materials (stones, bricks, plaster, cement, sand, tiles, thatch, etc.	3	...	...	...	...	...	...	...	3	...
Order 37—Trade in means of transport	3	...	...	...	...	...	...	...	3	...
Group 129. Dealers and hirers of elephants, camels horses, cattle, asses, mules, etc. sellers (not makers) of carriages, saddlery, etc.	3	...	...	...	...	...	...	...	3	...
Order 38—Trade in fuel	197	165	...	...	...	...	...	...	32	...
Group 130. Dealers in firewood, charcoal, coal, cowdung, etc.	197	165	...	...	...	...	...	...	32	...
Order 39—Trade in articles of luxury and those pertaining to letters and the arts and sciences	145	92	...	...	6	30	...	...	17	...
Group 131. Dealers in precious stones, jewellery (real and imitation), clocks, optical instruments, etc.	76	55	...	...	...	21	...	...	...	...
,, 132. Dealers in common bangles, bead, necklaces, fans, small articles, toys, hunting and fishing tackle, flowers, etc.	49	27	...	...	6	9	...	...	7	...
,, 133. Publishers, booksellers, stationers, dealers in music pictures, musical instruments and curiosities	20	10	...	...	...	...	...	...	10	...
Order 41—Trade of other sorts ...	925	591	24	...	21	210	...	...	79	...
Group 135. Shopkeepers otherwise unspecified ...	781	455	24	...	14	210	...	...	78	...
,, 136. Itinerant traders, pedlars, hawkers, etc. ...	140	133	...	...	7	...	...	...	...	...
,, 137. Conjurers, acrobats, fortune-tellers, reciters exhibitors of curiosities and wild animals	4	3	...	...	...	...	...	...	1	...
Class C.—Public administration and liberal arts	10,208	6,533	76	...	233	19	...	5	3,280	62
Sub-class VI.—Public force ...	2,889	2,033	3	...	26	4	...	...	822	1
Order 42—Army	2,099	1,529	...	...	19	4	...	...	546	1
Group 140. Army (Native states) ...	2,099	1,529	...	...	19	4	...	...	546	1
Order 44—Police ...	790	504	3	...	7	...	...	...	276	...
Group 142. Police ...	715	435	3	...	7	...	...	...	270	...
,, 143. Village watchmen ...	75	69	...	...	...	...	...	...	6	...
Sub-class VII.—Public Administration ...	4,493	2,771	59	...	179	4	...	...	1,433	47

TABLE XV-D.

Occupations by Religion.

Jammu and Kashmir State Census, 1911.

Jammu City.

OCCUPATION.	Total number of workers and dependents.	Hindu.	Arya.	Bramho.	Sikh.	Jain.	Budh.	Parsi.	Musalman.	Christian.
1	2	3	4	5	6	7	8	9	10	11
Order 45—Public Administration ...	4,493	2,771	59	...	179	4	...	...	1,433	47
Group 145. Service of native and foreign States ...	4,468	2,771	59	...	179	4	...	...	1,429	26
,, 146. Municipal and other local (not village) service	24	...	...	...	...	...	...	...	3	21
,, 147. Village officials and servants other than watchmen	1	...	...	...	...	...	...	...	1	...
Sub-class VIII—Professions and liberal arts ...	2,440	1,394	10	...	24	1	...	5	992	14
Order 46—Religion ...	695	476	1	...	11	...	...	...	207	...
Group 148. Priests, ministers, etc. ...	227	126	...	...	9	...	...	...	92	...
,, 149. Religious mendicants, inmates of monasteries, etc.	464	350	1	...	2	...	...	...	111	...
,, 151. Temple, burial or burning ground service, pilgrim conductors, circumcisers	4	...	...	...	...	...	...	...	4	...
Order 47—Law ...	271	238	...	...	3	1	...	...	29	...
Group 152. Lawyers of all kinds including *Kazis*, Law agents and *mukhtiars*	30	17	...	...	1	1	...	...	11	...
,, 153. Lawyers' clerks, petition-writers, etc. ...	241	221	...	...	2	...	...	...	18	...
Order 48—Medicine ...	95	51	4	...	2	...	...	...	36	2
Group 154. Medical practitioners of all kinds including dentists, occulists and veterinary surgeons	78	51	4	...	2	...	...	...	19	2
,, 155. Midwives, vaccinators, compounders, nurses, masseurs, etc.	17	...	...	...	...	...	...	...	17	...
Order 49—Instruction ...	260	182	2	...	8	...	...	5	51	12
Group 156. Professors and teachers of all kinds and clerks and servants connected with education	260	182	2	...	8	...	...	5	51	12
Order 50—Letters and arts and sciences	1,119	447	3	...	...	...	...	...	669	...
Group 158. Architects, surveyors, engineers and their employes	779	258	3	...	...	...	...	...	518	...
,, 159. Others (authors, photographers, artists, sculptors, astronomers, meteorologists, botanists, astrologers, etc.)	188	187	...	...	...	...	...	...	1	...
,, 160. Music composers and masters, players on all kinds of musical instruments (not military), singers, actors and dancers	152	2	...	...	...	...	...	...	150	...
Sub class IX—Persons living on their income ...	386	335	4	...	4	10	...	...	33	...
Order 51—Persons living principally on their income	386	335	4	...	4	10	...	...	33	...
Group 161. Proprietors (other than of agricultural land) funds and scholarship holders and pensioners	386	335	4	...	4	10	...	...	33	...
Class D.—Miscellaneous ...	6,671	4,723	6	...	141	11	...	...	1,781	9
Sub-class X.—Domestic Service ...	3,082	2,359	4	...	32	7	...	...	679	1
Order 52—Domestic Service	3,082	2,359	4	...	32	7	...	...	679	1
Group 162. Cooks, water-carriers, door-keepers, watchmen and other indoor servants	3,082	2,359	4	...	32	7	...	...	679	1
Sub-class XI.—Insufficiently described occupations	2,686	1,834	2	...	44	...	...	...	798	8
Order 53—General terms which do not indicate a definite occupation	2,686	1,834	2	...	44	...	...	...	798	8
Group 164. Manufacturers, business men and contractors otherwise unspecified	430	347	2	...	34	...	...	...	47	...
,, **165. Cashiers, accountants, book-keepers, clerks and other employes in unspecified offices, warehouses and shops**	7	...	...	...	...	...	...	...	7	...
,, 166. Mechanics otherwise unspecified. ...	35	...	...	...	...	...	...	...	35	...
,, 167. Labourers and workmen otherwise unspecified	2,214	1,487	...	...	10	...	...	...	709	8
Sub-class XII.—Unproductive ...	903	530	...	...	65	4	...	...	304	...
Order 54—Inmates of jails, asylums and hospitals ...	224	80	...	...	7	...	...	...	137	...
Group 168. Inmates of jails, asylums and hospitals ...	224	80	...	...	7	...	...	...	137	...
Order 55—Beggars, Vagrants, Prostitutes ...	679	450	...	...	58	4	...	...	167	...
Group 169. Beggars, vagrants, procurers, prostitutes, receivers of stolen goods, cattle poisoners	679	450	...	...	58	4	...	...	167	...

XV-D
Occupation by Religion.

TABLE XV-D.
Occupations by Religion.
Jammu and Kashmir State Census, 1911.
Srinagar City.

OCCUPATION.	Total number of workers and dependents.	Distribution by Religion.								
		Hindu.	Arya.	Bramho.	Sikh.	Jain.	Budh.	Parsi.	Musalman.	Christian.
1	2	3	4	5	6	7	8	9	10	11
All Occupations ...	126,344	28,739	40	1	486	...	...	26	96,941	111
Class A—Production of raw materials. ...	7,386	1,533	...	...	17	...	...	...	5,836	..
Sub-class I—Exploitation of the surface of the earth	7,386	1,533	...	...	17	...	...	...	5,836	...
Order 1—Pasture and Agriculture	7,069	1,533	...	...	17	...	...	...	5,519	...
Sub-Order 1—(a) Ordinary cultivation	5,627	1,077	...	...	15	...	...	...	4,535	...
Group 1. Income from rent of agricultural land ...	897	628	...	...	5	...	...	...	264	...
,, 2. Ordinary cultivators ...	3,521	102	...	...	10	...	...	...	3,409	...
,, 3. Agents, managers of landed estates (not planters), clerks, rent collectors, etc.	348	345	...	...	...	...	...	...	3	...
,, 4. Farm servants and field labourers	861	2	...	...	...	...	...	...	859	...
Sub-Order 1—(b) Growers of special products and market gardening	593	25	...	...	...	...	...	...	568	...
Group 6. Fruit, flower, vegetable, betel, vine, areca-nut, etc. growers	593	25	...	...	...	...	...	...	568	...
Sub-Order 1—(c) Forestry	717	430	...	...	2	...	...	...	285	...
Group 7. Forest officers, rangers, guards, etc. ...	473	428	...	...	2	...	...	...	43	...
,, 8. Wood cutters, fire-wood, lac, catechu, rubber, etc. collectors and charcoal burners	244	2	...	...	...	...	...	...	242	...
Sub-Order 1—(d) Raising of farm stock	105	1	...	...	...	...	...	...	104	...
Group 9. Cattle and buffalo breeders and keepers ...	105	1	...	...	...	...	...	...	104	...
Sub-Order 1—(e) Raising of small animals	27	...	...	...	...	...	...	...	27	...
Group 13. Birds, bees, silkworms, etc.	27	...	...	...	...	...	...	...	27	...
Order 2—Fishing and hunting	317	...	...	...	...	...	...	...	317	...
,, 14. Fishing	254	...	...	...	...	...	...	...	254	...
,, 15. Hunting	63	...	...	...	...	...	...	...	63	...
Class B—Preparation and supply of material substances	84,579	8,514	5	...	140	...	...	14	75,875	31
Sub-class III—Industry	60,572	3,364	...	...	68	...	...	...	57,128	12
Order 6—Textiles	26,085	1,525	...	...	24	...	...	...	24,530	6
Group 22. Cotton spining, sizing and weaving ...	5,354	544	...	...	7	...	...	...	4,803	...
,, 24. Rope, twine and string	90	5	...	...	...	...	...	...	85	...
,, 25. Other fibres (cocoanut, aloes, flax, hemp, straw, etc.)	4	...	...	...	...	...	...	...	4	...
,, 26. Wool carders and spinners, weavers of woolen blankets, carpets, etc.	16,154	77	...	...	7	...	...	...	16,070	...
,, 27. Silk spinners and weavers ...	2,595	806	...	...	10	...	...	...	1,773	6
,, 30. Dyeing, bleaching, printing, preparation and sponging of textiles	616	2	...	...	...	...	...	...	614	...
,, 31. Other (lace, crape, embroideries, fringes, etc.) and insufficiently described textile industries	1,272	91	...	...	...	...	...	...	1,181	...
Order 7—Hides, skins and hard materials from the animal kingdom	12	...	...	...	...	...	...	...	12	...
Group 32. Tanners, curriers, leather dressers and dyers, etc.	12	...	...	...	...	...	...	...	12	...
Order 8—Wood	4,319	25	...	...	21	...	...	...	4,273	...
Group 36. Sawyers, carpenters, turners, joiners, etc.	3,825	22	...	...	21	...	...	...	3,782	...
,, 37. Basket makers and other industries of woody material including leaves	494	3	...	...	...	...	...	...	491	...
Order 9—Metals	2,549	9	...	...	...	...	...	...	2,540	...
Group 40. Makers of arms, guns, etc.	13	...	...	...	...	...	...	...	13	...
,, 41. Other workers in iron and makers of implements and tools, principally or exclusively of iron	1,963	9	...	...	...	...	...	...	1,954	...
,, 42. Workers in brass, copper and bell metal ...	107	...	...	...	...	...	...	...	107	...
,, 43. Workers in other metals (tin, zinc, lead, quick silver, etc.)	68	...	...	...	...	...	...	...	68	...
,, 44. Workers in mints, die-sinkers, etc. ...	398	...	...	...	...	...	...	...	398	...
Order 10—Ceramics	833	61	...	...	...	...	...	...	772	...
Group 47. Potters and earthen pipe and bowl makers...	411	55	...	...	...	...	...	...	356	...
,, 48. Brick and tile makers	422	6	...	...	...	...	...	...	416	...
Order 11—Chemical products properly so called and analogous	1,207	486	...	...	...	...	...	...	721	...
Group 50. Manufacture of matches and explosive materials	5	...	...	...	...	...	...	...	5	...
,, 52. Manufacture of dyes, paint and ink ...	85	...	...	...	...	...	...	...	85	...
,, 53. Manufacture and refining of vegetable and mineral oils	461	...	...	...	...	...	...	...	461	...
,, 54. Manufacture of paper, card-board and papier macho	35	...	...	...	...	...	...	...	35	...
,, 55. Others. (soap, candles, lac, cutch, perfumes and miscellaneous drugs)	621	486	...	...	...	...	...	...	135	...
Order 12 Food Industries	4,099	371	...	...	12	...	...	...	3,716	...

TABLE XV-D.

Occupations by Religion.

Jammu and Kashmir State Census, 1911.

Srinagar City.

OCCUPATION.	Total number of workers and dependents.	Distribution by Religion. Hindu.	Arya.	Bramho.	Sikh.	Jain.	Budh.	Parsi.	Musalman.	Christian.
1	2	3	4	5	6	7	8	9	10	11
Group 56. Rice pounders and huskers and flour grinders	337	...	...	...	...	...	...	...	337	...
,, 57. Bakers and biscuit makers	1,561	174	...	...	...	...	...	...	1,387	...
,, 58. Grain parchers, etc.	32	21	...	...	...	...	...	...	11	...
,, 59. Butchers	1,494	...	...	...	12	...	...	...	1,482	...
,, 63. Sweetmeat makers, preparers of jam and condiments, etc.	666	176	...	...	...	...	...	...	490	...
,, 64. Brewers and distillers	9	...	...	...	...	...	...	...	9	...
Order 13—Industries of dress and the toilet	13,129	526	...	...	...	...	...	...	12,606	...
Group 68. Tailors, milliners, dress-makers and darners, embroiderers on linen	9,831	490	...	...	...	...	...	...	9,341	...
,, 69. Shoe, boot and sandal makers	1,222	18	...	...	...	...	...	...	1,204	...
,, 70. Other industries pertaining to dress, gloves, socks, gaiters, belts, buttons, umbrellas, canes, etc.	93	18	...	...	...	...	...	...	75	...
,, 71. Washing, cleaning and dyeing	831	...	...	...	...	...	...	...	831	...
,, 72. Barbers, hair-dressers and wig-makers	1,155	...	...	...	...	...	...	...	1,155	...
Order 15—Building industries	4,469	20	...	...	2	...	...	...	4,446	1
Group 77. Excavators, plinth builders and well sinkers	2,258	...	...	...	2	...	...	...	2,256	...
,, 79. Others (thatchers, building contractors, house painters, tilers, plumbers, locksmiths. etc.)	2,211	20	...	...	...	...	...	...	2,190	...
Order 16—Construction of means of transport	131	...	...	...	...	...	...	...	131	...
Group 81. Saddlers, harness makers, whip and lash makers.	180	...	...	...	...	...	...	...	131	...
Order 17—Production and transmission of physical forces (heat, light, electricity, motive power, etc.)	180	151	...	...	3	...	...	...	22	4
Group 83. Gas works, electric light and ice factories	180	151	...	...	3	...	...	...	22	4
Order 18—Industries of luxury and those pertaining to literature and the arts and sciences.	2,640	71	...	...	...	...	...	...	2,568	1
Group 86. Book binders and stichers, envelope makers, etc.	90	2	...	...	...	...	...	...	88	...
,, 87. Makers of musical instruments	14	...	...	...	...	...	...	...	14	...
,, 88. Makers of watches and clocks and optical, photographic and surgical instruments	89	53	...	...	...	...	...	...	36	...
,, 89. Workers in precious stones and metals, enamellers, imitation jewellery makers, gilders, etc.	2,196	16	...	...	...	...	...	...	2,179	1
,, 90. Makers of bangles, rosaries, bead and other necklaces, spangles, *lingams* and sacred threads.	176	...	...	...	...	...	...	...	176	...
,, 91. Toy, kite, cage, fishing tackle, etc., makers, taxidermists, etc.	73	...	...	...	...	...	...	...	73	...
,, 92. Others (including managers, persons other than performers, employed in theatres and other places of public entertainment, employes of public societies, race course service, huntsmen, etc.)	2	...	...	...	...	...	...	...	2	...
Order 19—Industries concerned with refuse matter	916	119	...	...	6	...	...	...	791	...
Group 93. Sweepers, scavangers, dust and sweeping contractors.	916	119	...	...	6	...	...	...	791	...
Sub-class IV—Transport	7,478	459	...	...	15	...	...	1	6,996	7
Order 20—Transport by water	5,735	1	...	...	...	...	...	1	5,733	...
Group 97. Boat owners, boatmen and towmen	5,735	1	...	...	...	...	...	1	5,733	...
Order 21—Transport by road	1,262	54	...	...	11	...	...	...	1,197	...
Group 98. Persons employed on the construction and maintenance of roads and bridges	135	33	...	...	...	...	...	...	102	...
,, 99. Cart owners and drivers, coachmen, stable boys, tramway, mail carriage, etc., managers and employes (excluding private servants)	112	21	...	...	4	...	...	...	87	...
,, 100. *Palki*, etc., bearers and owners	4	...	...	...	...	...	...	...	4	...
,, 101. Pack elephant, camel, mule, ass and bullock owners and drivers	678	...	...	...	7	...	...	...	671	...
,, 102. Porters and messengers	333	...	...	...	...	...	...	...	333	...
Order 22—Transport by rail	4	4	...	...	...	...	...	...	...	...
Group 103. Railway employes of all kinds other than construction coolies	4	4	...	...	...	...	...	...	...	...
Order 23—Post Office, telegraph and telephone services	477	400	...	...	4	...	...	...	66	7
Group 105. Post Office, telegraph and telephone services	477	400	...	...	4	...	...	...	66	7
Sub-class V—Trade	16,529	4,691	5	...	57	...	...	13	11,751	12
Order 24—Banks, establishments of credit, exchange and insurance	513	268	1	...	14	...	...	13	212	5
Group 106. Bank managers, money lenders, exchange and insurance agents, money changers and brokers and their employes	513	268	1	...	14	...	...	13	212	5

XV-D
Occupation by Religion.

TABLE XV-D.
Occupations by Religion.
Jammu and Kashmir State Census, 1911.
Srinagar City.

OCCUPATION.	Total number of workers and dependents.	Distribution by Religion.								
		Hindu.	Arya.	Bramho.	Sikh.	Jain.	Budh.	Parsi.	Musalman.	Christian.
1	2	3	4	5	6	7	8	9	10	11
Order 26—Trade in textiles ...	2,584	1,089	...	...	4	...	...	...	1,491	...
Group 108. Trade in piece-goods, wool, cotton, silk, hair and other textiles	2,584	1,089	...	...	4	...	...	...	1,491	...
Order 27—Trade in skins, leather and furs ..	104	...	...	...	...	...	...	...	104	...
Group 109. Trade in skins, leather, furs, feathers, horn, etc.	104	...	...	...	...	...	...	...	104	...
Order 28—Trade in wood	237	5	...	...	6	...	...	...	226	...
Group 110. Trade in wood (not firewood), cork, bark, etc.	237	5	...	...	6	...	...	...	226	...
Order 32—Hotels, cafes, restaurants, etc.	37	11	...	...	8	...	...	...	12	6
Group 114. Vendors of wine, liquors, ærated waters, etc.	26	10	...	...	7	...	...	...	9	...
,, 115. Owners and managers of hotels, cook-shops, *sarais*, etc., and their employes.	11	1	...	...	1	...	...	...	3	6
Order 33—Other trade in food stuffs	9,817	1,909	...	...	18	...	...	...	7,890	...
Group 118. Sellers of milk, butter, ghee, poultry, eggs, etc.	2,939	4	...	...	...	...	...	...	2,935	...
,, 120. Cardamom, betel leaf, vegetables, fruit and areca nut	1,694	9	...	...	...	...	...	...	1,685	...
,, 121. Grain and pulse dealers ...	4,518	1,877	...	...	18	...	...	...	2,623	...
,, 122. Tobacco, opium, *ganja*, etc., sellers ...	347	19	...	...	...	...	...	...	328	...
,, 123. Dealers in sheep, goats and pigs ...	103	...	...	...	...	...	...	...	103	...
,, 124. Dealers in hay, grass and fodder ...	216	...	...	...	...	...	...	...	216	...
Order 34—Trade in clothing and toilet articles	143	21	...	...	...	...	...	...	122	...
Group 125. Trade in ready-made clothing and other articles of dress and the toilet (hats, umbrellas, socks, ready-made shoes, perfumes, etc.)	143	21	...	...	...	...	...	...	122	...
Order 35—Trade in furniture	38	29	...	...	...	...	...	...	9	...
Group 126. Trade in furniture, carpets, curtains and bedding	6	...	...	...	...	...	...	...	6	...
,, 127. Hardware, cooking utensils, porcelain, crockery, glassware, bottles, articles for gardening, the cellar, etc.	32	29	...	...	...	...	...	...	3	...
Order 36—Trade in building materials	9	...	...	...	...	...	...	...	9	...
Group 128. Trade in building materials (stones, bricks, plaster, cement, sand, tiles, thatch, etc.	9	...	...	...	...	...	...	...	9	...
Order 37—Trade in means of Transport	10	...	...	...	...	...	...	...	10	...
Group 129. Dealers and hirers of elephants, camels, horses, cattle, asses, mules, etc., sellers (not makers) of carriages, saddlery, etc.	10	...	...	...	...	...	...	...	10	...
Order 38—Trade in fuel	541	1	...	...	1	...	...	...	539	...
Group 130. Dealers in firewood, charcoal, coal, cow-dung, etc.	541	1	...	...	1	...	...	...	539	...
Order 39—Trade in articles of luxury and those pertaining to letters and the arts and sciences	1,747	1,298	...	...	...	...	...	...	449	...
Group 131. Dealers in precious stones, jewellery (real and imitation), clocks, optical instruments, etc.	1,273	1,245	...	...	...	...	...	...	28	...
Group 132. Dealers in common bangles, bead, necklaces, fans, small articles, toys, hunting and fishing tackle, flowers, etc.	368	32	...	...	...	...	...	...	336	...
,, 133. Publishers, books-sellers, stationers, dealers in music pictures, musical instruments and curiosities	106	21	...	...	...	...	...	...	85	...
Order 40—Trade in refuse matter	176	...	...	...	...	...	...	...	176	...
Group 134. Dealers in rags, stable refuse, etc. ...	176	...	...	...	...	...	...	...	176	...
Order 41—Trade of other sorts	573	60	4	...	6	...	...	...	502	1
Group 135. Shopkeepers otherwise unspecified ...	160	13	4	...	...	...	...	...	142	1
,, 136. Itinerant, traders, paddlers, hawkers, etc....	397	47	...	...	6	...	...	...	344	...
,, 137. Conjurers, acrobats, fortune-tellers, reciters, exhibitors of curiosities and wild animals	16	...	...	...	...	...	...	...	16	...
Class C. Public administration and liberal arts	21,699	13,816	28	1	229	...	...	12	7,538	75
Sub-class VI—Public force ...	3,015	1,910	...	...	43	...	...	1	1,055	6
Order 42—Army ...	991	620	...	...	4	...	...	...	361	6
Group 140. Army (Native States) ...	991	620	...	...	4	...	...	...	361	6
Order 44—Police ...	2,024	1,290	...	...	39	...	...	1	694	...
Group 142. Police ...	1,846	1,261	...	...	24	...	...	1	560	...
,, 143. Village watchmen ...	178	29	...	...	15	...	...	...	134	...

TABLE XV-D.

Occupations by Religion.

Jammu and Kashmir State Census, 1911.

Srinagar City.

XV-D
Occupation by Religion.

OCCUPATION.	Total number of workers and dependents.	Distribution by Religion.								
		Hindu.	Arya.	Btambo.	Sikh.	Jain.	Budh.	Parsi.	Musalman.	Christian.
1	2	3	4	5	6	7	8	9	10	11
SUB-CLASS VII—PUBLIC ADMINISTRATION ...	8,969	6,555	17	...	116	...	...	8	2,257	16
Order 45.—Public administration ...	8,969	6,555	17	...	116	...	...	8	2,257	16
Group 144. Service of the State ...	20	12	...	...	1	...	...	1	5	1
,, 145. Service of Native and Foreign States ...	8,208	6,119	17	...	110	...	...	7	1,940	15
,, 146. Municipal and other local (not village) service	358	102	...	...	5	...	...	...	251	...
,, 147. Village officials and servants other than watchmen	383	322	...	...	...	...	...	...	61	...
SUB-CLASS VIII—PROFESSIONS AND LIBERAL ARTS ...	9,199	5,023	11	...	64	...	...	3	4,064	34
Order 46—Religion ...	5,180	2,873	...	...	17	...	...	...	2,281	9
Group 148. Priests, ministers, etc. ...	693	599	...	...	13	...	...	...	81	...
,, 149. Religious mendicants, inmates of monasteries, etc.	4,459	2,274	...	...	4	...	...	...	2,172	9
,, 151. Temple, burial or burning ground service, pilgrim conductors, circumcisors	28	...	...	...	...	...	...	...	28	...
Order 47—Law ...	492	334	...	...	...	...	...	3	153	2
Group 152. Lawyers of all kinds including *Kazis*, Law agents and *mukhtiars*	283	190	...	...	...	...	...	3	90	...
,, 153. Lawyers' clerks, petition-writers, etc. ...	209	144	...	...	...	...	...	...	63	2
Order 48—Medicine	735	336	...	...	...	...	...	..	388	11
Group 154. Medical practitioners of all kinds including dentists, oculists & veterinary surgeons	471	218	...	...	...	...	...	...	244	9
,, 155. Midwives, vaccinators, compounders, nurses, masseurs, etc.	264	118	...	...	...	...	...	...	144	2
Order 49—Instriction	1,063	733	6	...	1	...	...	...	315	8
Group 156. Professors and teachers of all kinds and clerk and servants connected with education	1,063	733	6	...	1	...	...	...	315	8
Order 50—Letters and arts and sciences	1,729	747	5	...	46	...	...	...	927	4
Group 158. Architects, surveyors, engineers and their employes	1,220	630	5	...	46	...	...	...	538	1
,, 159. Others (authors, photographers, artists, sculptors, astronomers, meteorologists, botanists, astrologers, etc.	367	106	...	...	...	...	...	...	258	3
,, 160. Music composers and masters, players on all kinds of musical instruments (not military), singers, actors and dancers	142	11	...	...	...	...	...	...	131	...
SUB-CLASS IX.—PERSONS LIVING ON THEIR INCOME ...	516	328	...	1	6	...	...	...	162	19
Order 51—Persons living principally on their income ...	516	328	...	1	6	...	...	...	162	19
Group 161. Proprietors (other than of agricultural land), fund and scholarship holders and pensioners	516	328	...	1	6	...	...	...	162	19
Class D. Miscellaneous ...	12,680	4,876	7	...	100	...	...	...	7,692	5
SUB-CLASS X.—DOMESTIC SERVICE ...	8,944	3,860	...	...	76	...	...	...	5,006	2
Order 52—Domestic service ...	8,944	3,860	...	...	76	...	...	...	5,006	2
Group 162. Cooks, water-carriers, door-keepers, watchmen and other indoor servants	8,760	3,860	...	...	76	...	...	...	4,822	2
,, 163 Private grooms, coachmen, dog boys, etc. ...	184	...	...	...	...	...	...	...	184	...
SUB-CLASS XI—INSUFFICIENTLY DESCRIBED OCCUPATIONS...	2,332	793	7	...	5	...	...	...	1,524	3
Order 53—General terms which do not indicate a definite occupation.	2,332	793	7	...	5	...	...	...	1,524	3
Group 164. Manufacturers, business-men and contractors otherwise unspecified	1,139	647	7	...	5	...	...	...	477	3
,, 165. Cashiers, accountants, book-keepers, clerks and other employes in unspecified offices, warehouses and shops.	22	14	...	...	...	...	...	...	8	...
,, 166. Mechanics otherwise unspecified ...	63	1	...	...	...	...	...	...	62	...
,, 167. Labourers and workmen otherwise unspecified	1,108	131	...	...	...	...	...	...	977	...
SUB-CLASS XII—UNPRODUCTIVE ...	1,404	223	...	...	19	...	...	...	1,162	...
Order 54—Inmates of jails, asylums and hospitals	247	4	...	...	2	...	...	...	241	...
Group 168. Inmates of jails, asylums and hospitals ...	247	4	...	...	2	...	...	...	241	...
Order 55—Beggars, vagrants, prostitutes ...	1,157	219	...	...	17	...	...	...	921	...
Group 169. Beggars, vagrants, procurers, prostitutes, receivers of stolen goods, cattle poisoners	1,157	219	...	...	17	...	...	...	921	...

TABLE XV-E.

Statistics of Industries.

Part I—Provincial Summary.

Description of factory, mine, etc.	Classification of factory, etc., according to number of persons employed (including management).	Number of factories.	Total Number of persons employed. Males.	Total Number of persons employed. Females.	Classification of persons employed. Direction, supervision and clerical work. Europeans and Anglo-Indians. Males.	Direction, etc. Europeans and Anglo-Indians. Females.	Direction, etc. Indians. Males.	Direction, etc. Indians. Females.	Skilled workmen. Europeans and Anglo-Indians. Males.	Skilled workmen. Europeans and Anglo-Indians. Females.	Skilled workmen. Indians. Males.	Skilled workmen. Indians. Females.	Unskilled workmen. Age 14 and over. Males.	Unskilled workmen. Age 14 and over. Females.	Unskilled workmen. Under 14. Males.	Unskilled workmen. Under 14. Females.	Remarks. Power.	Remarks. State of business.
1	2	3	4	5	6	7	8	9	10	11	12	13	14	15	16	17	18	
Entire State	Total	57	12,128	266	20	..	641	..	1	..	5,703	26	5,518	230	245	10		
I—Growing of special products	Total	1	18	8	..	..	..	..	..	..	..	..	18	8	..	..		
1. Extraction of *Rasaunt* (juice of *berberis lycium*)	20—50	1	18	8	..	..	..	..	..	..	..	..	18	8	..	..	..	(3)—1
II—Textile Industries	Total	14	4,901	29	9	..	289	..	..	..	4,247	5	281	16	75	8		
2. Weaving factories (Jail) *Khaddi khana* (cotton weaving and carpet making)	20—50	2	57	..	..	..	..	..	..	..	24	..	33	..	..	..	..	(4)—2
3. Carpet factories	Total	4	2,203	..	3	..	79	..	..	..	2,050	..	51	..	20	..		
Using mechanical power	400 & over	1	601	..	1	..	53	..	..	..	532	..	15	..	..	..	Steam	(2)—1
Using no mechanical power	Total	3	1,602	..	2	..	26	..	..	..	1,518	..	36	..	20	..		
	20—50	1	24	..	..	..	..	..	..	..	18	..	6	..	..	..	..	(2)—2; (4)—1; 3
	50—100	1	59	..	1	..	8	..	..	..	50	..	..	..	..	..		
	400 & over	1	1,519	..	1	..	18	..	..	..	1,450	..	30	..	20	..		
4. Shawl weaving factories	20—50	5	142	6	..	..	6	..	..	..	107	5	6	..	23	1	..	(4)—4; (7)—1; 5
5. *Hashiabafi* (weaving of shawl fringes)	20—50	1	23	..	..	..	..	..	..	..	23	..	..	..	..	..	..	(4)—1
6. Silk factories (*Using mechanical power,*)	Total	2	2,476	23	6	..	204	..	..	..	2,043	..	191	16	32	7		
	100—200	1	135	23	..	..	14	..	..	..	51	..	38	16	32	7	Steam	(4)—1
	400 & over	1	2,341	..	6	..	190	..	..	..	1,992	..	153	..	..	..	Steam	(7)—1; 2
III—Wood, etc. Industries	Total	9	1,398	47	4	..	65	..	..	..	397	..	917	45	15	2		
7. Timber cutting and floating	Total	9	1,398	47	4	..	65	..	..	..	397	..	917	45	15	2		
Using mechanical power	Total	3	606	5	3	..	37	..	..	..	394	..	171	5	1	..		
	50—100	2	153	5	..	..	5	..	..	..	54	..	93	5	1	..	Hydraulic power	(1)—1; (2)—1
	400 & over	1	453	..	3	..	32	..	..	..	340	..	78	..	..	..	"	(6)—1
Using no mechanical power	Total	6	792	42	1	..	28	..	..	..	3	..	746	40	14	2		
	20—50	2	58	..	..	..	..	..	..	..	..	..	56	..	2	..	..	(5)—1; (6)—1
	50—100	1	67	9	..	..	3	..	..	..	..	..	60	8	4	1	..	(6)—1
	100—200	2	260	33	..	..	20	..	..	..	2	..	230	32	8	1	..	(6)—1; (7)—1
	400 & over	1	407	..	1	..	5	..	..	..	1	..	400	..	..	..	..	(4)—1; 9
IV—Metal Industries	Total	2	126	..	..	..	11	..	..	..	76	..	39	..	..	..		
8. Iron and wood work	50—100	1	73	..	..	..	9	..	..	..	39	..	25	..	..	..	..	(4)—1
9. P. W. Workshop	50—100	1	53	..	..	..	2	..	..	..	37	..	14	..	..	..	Steam	(4)—1
V—Industries of Dress	Total	8	213	11	..	..	2	..	..	..	135	11	44	..	32	..		
10. *Yarmadozi* and *jalakdozi* (embroidery) factories	20—50	5	131	3	..	..	2	..	..	..	73	3	39	..	17	..	..	(1)—1; (2)—1; (3)—1; (4)—2; 5
11. *Rafugari* (darning) factory	20—50	3	82	8	..	..	..	..	..	..	62	8	5	..	15	..	..	(3)—1; (4)—1; (7)—1; 3
VI—Furniture Industries	Total	1	26	..	..	..	2	..	..	..	20	..	4	..	..	..		
12. Table and chair manufacturing factory	20—50	1	26	..	..	..	2	..	..	..	20	..	4	..	..	..	..	(4)—1
VII—Industries connected with building	Total	7	556	32	..	..	15	..	..	..	165	10	346	22	30	..		
13. Brick kilns	Total	6	532	32	..	..	14	..	..	..	163	10	325	22	30	..		
Using mechanical power	Total	2	271	9	..	..	3	..	..	..	53	..	205	9	10	..		
	50—100	1	88	1	..	..	2	..	..	..	20	..	66	1	..	..	Steam	(2)—2
	100—200	1	183	8	..	..	1	..	..	..	33	..	139	8	10	..		
Using no mechanical power	Total	4	261	23	..	..	11	..	..	..	110	10	120	13	20	..		
	20—50	1	40	10	..	..	..	..	..	..	15	10	15	..	10	..	..	(2)—1
	50—100	3	221	13	..	..	11	..	..	..	95	..	105	13	10	..	..	(1)—1; (5)—1; (6)—1; 3
14. *Surkhi* grinding mill	20—50	1	21	..	..	..	1	..	..	..	2	..	21	..	..	..	Steam	(2)—1
VIII—Construction of means of transport	Total	5	4,389	139	5	..	184	..	..	..	486	..	3,621	139	94	..		
15. Dredging work	400 & over	1	425	..	2	..	10	..	..	..	88	..	325	..	..	..	Electricity	(2)—1
16. Upper Jhelum canal construction	400 & over	4	3,964	139	3	..	174	..	..	..	398	..	3,296	139	94	..	Steam	(2)—3; (6)—1; 4
IX—Production and transmission of physical forces	Total	6	214	..	2	..	21	..	1	..	68	..	122	..	..	..		
17. Electric power and generating station	20—50	3	115	..	2	..	10	..	1	..	48	..	54	..	..	..	Hydraulic and electricity.	(4)—2; (2)—1; 3
18. Hydro-electric Installation*	20—50	1	35	..	..	..	11	..	..	..	15	..	9	..	..	..	Steam and electricity	(4)—1
19. Electric transmission line	20—50	1	26	..	..	..	..	..	..	..	1	..	25	..	..	..	Electricity	(4)—1
20. Flume channel and head work	20—50	1	38	..	..	..	..	..	..	..	4	..	34	..	..	..	Hydraulic	(4)—1
X—Industries of Luxury	Total	4	287	..	..	..	52	..	..	..	109	..	126	..	..	..		
21. Printing Press	Total	3	259	..	..	..	43	..	..	..	95	..	121	..	..	..		
Using mechanical power	100—200	1	121	..	..	..	13	..	..	..	69	..	39	..	..	..	Oil Engine	(2)—1
Using no mechanical power	Total	2	138	..	..	..	30	..	..	..	26	..	82	..	..	..		
	20—50	1	23	..	..	..	3	..	..	..	8	..	12	..	..	..	..	(2)—1
	100—200	1	115	..	..	..	27	..	..	..	18	..	70	..	..	..	....	(4)—1
22. Photography, rubber stamp manufacturing and printing press	20—50	1	28	..	..	..	9	..	..	..	14	..	5	..	..	..	....	(2)—1

Remarks (column 18): The state of business is shown in this column by the following notation:— (1). Much brisker than usual. (2). Brisker than usual. (3). Somewhat brisker than usual. (4). Normal. (5). Somewhat slacker than usual. (6). Slacker than usual. (7). Much slacker than usual.

* This includes the Water Works at Jammu.

TABLE XV-E.

STATISTICS OF INDUSTRIES.

Part II—Distribution by Districts.

DESCRIPTION OF FACTORIES, MINES, ETC.	DISTRICT.	Number of factories.	TOTAL NUMBER OF PERSONS EMPLOYED.		CLASSIFICATION OF PERSONS EMPLOYED.											
					DIRECTION, SUPERVISION AND CLERICAL WORK.				SKILLED WORKMEN.				UNSKILLED LABOURERS.			
					Europeans and Anglo-Indians.		*Indians.*		*Europeans and Anglo-Indians.*		*Indians.*		*Age 14 and over.*		*Under 14.*	
			Males.	Females.	Males.	Females.	Males.	Females.	Males.	Females.	Males.	Females.	Males.	Females.	Males.	Females.
1	2	3	4	5	6	7	8	9	10	11	12	13	14	15	16	17
Entire State	**Total ...**	57	12,128	266	20	...	641	...	1	...	5,703	26	5,518	230	245	10
	Jammu District	8	644	32	...	...	42	...	...	...	224	...	336	25	42	7
Weaving factory (Jail) ...	,,	1	34	...	...	...	...	...	...	...	16	...	18	...	...	...
Carpet factory ...	,,	1	24	...	...	...	...	...	...	...	18	...	6	...	...	...
Silk factory ...	,,	1	135	23	...	...	14	...	...	...	51	...	38	16	32	7
Brick kiln ...	,,	2	271	9	...	...	3	...	...	...	53	...	205	9	10	...
Surkhi grinding mill ...	,,	1	24	...	...	...	1	...	...	...	2	...	21	...	...	...
Hydro-electric Installation ...	,,	1	35	...	...	...	11	...	...	...	15	...	9	...	...	...
Printing Press	,,	1	121	...	...	...	13	...	...	...	69	...	39	...	...	...
	Udhampur District	4	269	25	...	...	8	...	...	...	...	...	247	23	14	2
Extraction of *Rasaunt* (juice of *berberis lycium*)	,,	1	18	8	...	...	...	...	...	...	...	...	18	8	...	...
Timber cutting and floating factory	,,	3	251	17	...	...	8	...	...	...	...	...	229	15	14	2
	Riasi District ...	1	20	...	...	...	...	...	...	...	...	...	20	...	...	...
Timber cutting and floating factory.	,,	1	20	...	...	...	...	...	...	...	...	...	20	...	...	...
	Mirpur District ...	9	4,348	152	3	...	194	...	...	...	586	...	3,461	152	104	...
Timber floating factory ...	,,	1	90	...	...	...	...	...	...	...	54	...	35	...	1	...
Iron and wood work ...	,,	1	73	...	...	...	9	...	...	...	39	...	25	...	...	...
Brick kiln	,,	3	221	13	...	...	11	...	...	...	95	...	105	13	10	...
Upper Jhelum canal construction	,,	4	3,964	139	3	...	174	...	...	...	398	...	3,296	139	93	...
	Bhadarwah *Jagir*,	3	584	30	1	...	25	...	...	...	3	...	555	30	...	...
Timber floating factory ...	,,	1	63	5	...	...	5	...	...	...	...	...	58	5	...	...
Timber cutting and floating factory,	,,	2	521	25	1	...	20	...	...	...	3	...	497	25	...	...
	Punch *Ilaqa* ...	1	23	...	...	...	3	...	...	...	8	...	12	...	...	...
Printing Press	,,	1	23	...	...	...	3	...	...	...	8	...	12	...	...	...
	Kashmir North ...	3	472	...	2	...	11	...	...	...	89	...	361	...	9	...
Yarmadozi factory	,,	1	21	...	...	...	1	...	...	...	...	...	11	...	9	...
Dredging work	,,	1	425	...	2	...	10	...	...	...	88	...	325	...	...	...
Electric transmission line ...	,,	1	26	...	...	...	...	...	...	...	1	...	25	...	...	...
	Kashmir South ...	25	5,255	27	9	...	326	...	...	...	4,440	26	404	...	76	1
Weaving factory	..	1	23	...	...	...	...	...	...	...	8	...	15	...	...	...
Carpet factories	..	3	2,179	...	3	...	79	...	...	...	2,032	...	45	...	20	...
Shawl weaving factories ...	..	5	142	6	...	...	6	...	...	...	107	5	6	...	23	1
Hashiabafi (making of shawl fringes)	,,	1	23	...	...	...	...	...	...	...	23	...	...	...	...	...
Silk factory	,,	1	2,341	...	6	...	190	...	...	...	1,992	...	153	...	...	...
P. W. Workshop	,,	1	53	...	...	...	2	...	...	...	37	...	14	...	...	...
Brick kiln	,,	1	40	10	...	...	...	...	...	...	15	10	15	...	10	...
Yarmadozi and *Jalakdozi* factories.	,,	4	110	3	...	...	1	...	...	...	73	3	28	...	8	...
Rafugari (darning) factories ...	,,	3	82	8	...	...	...	...	...	...	62	8	5	...	15	...
Furniture manufacturing factory	,,	1	26	...	...	...	2	...	...	...	20	...	4	...	...	...
Electric power and generating stations	,,	2	93	...	...	...	10	...	...	...	39	...	44	...	...	...
Printing Press	,,	1	115	...	...	...	27	...	...	...	18	...	70	...	...	...
Photography, rubber stamp manufacturing and printing press	,,	1	28	...	...	...	9	...	...	...	14	...	5	...	...	...
	Muzaffarabad District	3	513	...	5	...	32	...	1	...	353	...	122	...	...	...
Wood works	,,	1	453	...	3	...	32	...	...	...	340	...	78	...	...	...
Flume channel and head works...	..	1	38	...	...	...	...	...	...	...	4	...	34	...	...	...
Electric power and generating station	,,	1	22	...	2	...	...	...	1	...	9	...	10	...	...	...

XV-E
Industries.

TABLE XV-E.

Statistics of Industries.

Part III—Particulars as to ownership of factories, etc.

Description of factories, mines, etc.	Number of factories.	Number owned by Companies of which the directors are: Europeans and Anglo-Indians.	Number owned by Companies of which the directors are: Indians.	Number owned by Companies of which the directors are: Of both races.	Number privately owned by: European and Anglo-Indians.	Indians: Total.	Hindu: Arora.	Hindu: Brahman.	Hindu: Arora and Brahman.	Hindu: Kayasth.	Hindu: Kashmiri pandit.	Hindu: Khatri.	Sikh: Arora.	Sikh: Others.	Musalman: Kashmiri Musalman: Bat.	Kashmiri Musalman: Dar.	Kashmiri Musalman: Mir.	Kashmiri Musalman: Pandit.	Kashmiri Musalman: Rishi.	Kashmiri Musalman: Sufi.	Kashmiri Musalman: Others.	Musalman: Kumhiar.	Musalman: Sheikh.	Musalman: Others.	Remarks.
1	2	3	4	5	6	7	8	9	10	11	12	13	14	15	16	17	18	19	20	21	22	23	24	25	26
Entire State ...	57	11	18	...	...	28	1	1	1	2	1	2	1	3	2	1	1	1	1	1	4	1	1	3	
I.—Growing of special products	1	...	...	...	...	1	...	...	...	...	...	1	...	...	...	...	...	...	...	...	...	...	...	...	
1. Extraction of *Rasaunt* (juice of *berberis lycium*)	1	...	...	...	...	1	...	...	...	...	...	1	...	...	...	...	...	...	...	...	...	...	...	...	
II.—Textile Industries ...	14	3	5	...	...	6	...	...	...	...	...	...	...	...	...	1	...	...	...	...	1	...	1	3	
2. Weaving factories ...	2	...	2	...	...	...	...	...	...	...	...	...	...	...	...	...	...	...	...	...	...	...	...	...	State.
3. Carpet factories ...	4	3	1	...	...	...	...	...	...	...	...	...	...	...	...	...	...	...	...	...	...	...	...	...	,,
4. Shawl weaving factories ...	5	...	...	...	...	5	...	...	...	...	...	...	...	...	...	...	...	...	...	...	1	...	1	3	
5. *Hashiabafi* (weaving of shawl fringes)	1	...	...	...	...	1	...	...	...	...	...	...	...	...	...	1	...	...	...	...	...	...	...	...	
6. Silk factories ...	2	...	2	...	...	...	...	...	...	...	...	...	...	...	...	...	...	...	...	...	...	...	...	...	State.
III.—Wood, etc., Industries	9	3	2	...	...	4	1	1	1	...	...	...	1	...	...	...	...	...	...	...	...	...	...	...	
7. Timber cutting and floating factories	9	3	2	...	...	4	1	1	1	...	...	...	1	...	...	...	...	...	...	...	...	...	...	...	
IV.—Metal Industries ...	2	1	1	...	...	...	...	...	...	...	...	...	...	...	...	...	...	...	...	...	...	...	...	...	
8. Iron and wood workshop ...	1	1	...	...	...	...	...	...	...	...	...	...	...	...	...	...	...	...	...	...	...	...	...	...	
9. P. W. Workshop ...	1	...	1	...	...	...	...	...	...	...	...	...	...	...	...	...	...	...	...	...	...	...	...	...	State.
V.—Industries of Dress ...	8	...	...	...	...	8	...	...	...	...	...	...	...	...	2	...	1	1	...	1	3	...	...	...	
10. *Yarmadozi* and *jalakdozi* (embroidery) factories	5	...	...	...	...	5	...	...	...	...	...	...	...	...	2	...	1	...	...	1	1	...	...	...	
11. *Rafugari* (darning) ...	3	...	...	...	...	3	...	...	...	...	...	...	...	...	...	...	...	1	...	...	2	...	...	...	
VI.—Furniture Industries ...	1	...	...	...	...	1	...	...	...	...	...	...	...	...	...	...	...	...	1	...	...	...	...	...	
12. Table and chair manufacturing factory	1	...	...	...	...	1	...	...	...	...	...	...	...	...	...	...	...	...	1	...	...	...	...	...	
VII.—Industries connected with building	7	...	...	...	...	7	...	...	...	2	...	1	...	3	...	...	...	...	...	...	...	1	...	...	
13. Brick kiln ...	6	...	...	...	...	6	...	...	...	1	...	1	...	3	...	...	...	...	...	...	...	1	...	...	
14. *Surkhi* grinding mill ...	1	...	...	...	...	1	...	...	...	1	...	...	...	...	...	...	...	...	...	...	...	...	...	...	
VIII.—Construction of means of transport	5	4	1	...	...	...	...	...	...	...	...	...	...	...	...	...	...	...	...	...	...	...	...	...	
15. Dredging work ...	1	...	1	...	...	...	...	...	...	...	...	...	...	...	...	...	...	...	...	...	...	...	...	...	State.
16. Upper Jhelum canal construction.	4	4	...	...	...	...	...	...	...	...	...	...	...	...	...	...	...	...	...	...	...	...	...	...	British Government.
IX.—Production and transmission of physical forces	6	...	6	...	...	...	...	...	...	...	...	...	...	...	...	...	...	...	...	...	...	...	...	...	
17. Electric power and generating station	3	...	3	...	...	...	...	...	...	...	...	...	...	...	...	...	...	...	...	...	...	...	...	...	State.
18. Hydro-electric Installation ...	1	...	1	...	...	...	...	...	...	...	...	...	...	...	...	...	...	...	...	...	...	...	...	...	
19. Electric Transmission ...	1	...	1	...	...	...	...	...	...	...	...	...	...	...	...	...	...	...	...	...	...	...	...	...	
20. Flume channel and head work	1	...	1	...	...	...	...	...	...	...	...	...	...	...	...	...	...	...	...	...	...	...	...	...	
X.—Industries of Luxury ...	4	...	3	...	...	1	...	...	...	...	1	...	...	...	...	...	...	...	...	...	...	...	...	...	
21. Printing Press ...	3	...	3	...	...	...	...	...	...	...	...	...	...	...	...	...	...	...	...	...	...	...	...	...	
22. Photography & rubber stamp manufacturing and printing press	1	...	...	...	...	1	...	...	...	...	1	...	...	...	...	...	...	...	...	...	...	...	...	...	

TABLE XV-E.

Statistics of Industries.

Part IV—Caste or race of the managers of factories.

DESCRIPTION OF FACTORIES.	Number of factories.	EUROPEANS AND ANGLO-INDIANS.	NUMBER MANAGED BY — INDIANS.																				
				Hindu.										*Musalman.*									
														Kashmiri Musalman.									
			Total.	Arora.	Brahman.	Gaddi.	Kayasth.	Kashmiri Pandit.	Khatri.	Rajput.	Thakkar.	Others.	*Sikh.*	Bat.	Dar.	Mir.	Pandit.	Rishi.	Sufi.	Others.	Kumhar.	Sheikh.	Others.
1	2	3	4	5	6	7	8	9	10	11	12	13	14	15	16	17	18	19	20	21	22	23	24
Entire State	57	17	40	2	1	1	2	1	9	1	1	3	3	2	1	1	1	1	1	4	1	1	3
I—Growing of special products	1	...	1	...	...	...	...	...	1	...	...	...	...	...	...	...	...	...	...	...	...	...	...
1. Extraction of *Rasaunt*, (juice of *berberis lycium*)	1	...	1	...	...	...	...	...	1	...	...	...	...	...	...	...	...	...	...	...	...	...	...
II—Textile Industries ...	14	4	10	...	...	...	...	...	4	...	...	...	...	...	1	...	...	...	...	1	...	1	3
2. Weaving factories ...	2	...	2	...	...	...	...	...	2	...	...	...	...	...	...	...	...	...	...	...	...	...	...
3. Carpet factories	4	3	1	...	...	...	...	...	1	...	...	...	...	...	...	...	...	...	...	...	...	...	...
4. Shawl weaving factories ...	5	...	5	...	...	...	...	...	...	...	...	...	...	...	...	...	...	...	...	1	...	1	3
5. *Hashiabafi* (weaving of shawl fringes)	1	...	1	...	...	...	...	...	...	...	...	...	...	...	1	...	...	...	...	...	...	...	...
6. Silk factories	2	1	1	...	...	...	...	...	1	...	...	...	...	...	...	...	...	...	...	...	...	...	...
III—Wood, etc., Industries...	9	3	6	1	1	1	...	...	...	1	1	1	...	...	...	...	...	...	...	...	...	...	...
7. Timber cutting and floating factories	9	3	6	1	1	1	...	...	...	1	1	1	...	...	...	...	...	...	...	...	...	...	...
IV—Metal Industries ...	2	...	2	1	...	...	...	...	...	...	...	1	...	...	...	...	...	...	...	...	...	...	...
8. Iron and wood workshop ...	1	...	1	1	...	...	...	...	...	...	...	...	...	...	...	...	...	...	...	...	...	...	...
9. P. W. Workshop... ...	1	...	1	...	...	...	...	...	...	...	...	1	...	...	...	...	...	...	...	...	...	...	...
V—Industries of Dress ...	8	...	8	...	...	...	...	...	...	...	...	...	...	2	...	1	1	...	1	3	...	...	...
10. *Yarmadozi* and *Jalakdozi* (embroidery) factories	5	...	5	...	...	...	...	...	...	...	...	...	...	2	...	1	...	...	1	1	...	...	...
11. *Rafugari* (darning) ...	3	...	3	...	...	...	...	...	...	...	...	...	...	...	...	...	1	...	...	2	...	...	...
VI—Furniture Industries ...	1	...	1	...	...	...	...	...	...	...	...	...	...	...	...	...	...	1	...	...	...	...	...
12. Table and chair manufacturing factory	1	...	1	...	...	...	...	...	...	...	...	...	...	...	...	...	...	1	...	...	...	...	...
VII—Industries connected with building	7	...	7	...	...	...	2	...	1	...	...	...	3	...	...	...	...	...	...	...	1	...	...
13. Brick kiln	6	...	6	...	...	...	1	...	1	...	...	...	3	...	...	...	...	...	...	...	1	...	...
14. *Surkhi* grinding mill ...	1	...	1	...	...	...	1	...	...	...	...	...	...	...	...	...	...	...	...	...	...	...	...
VIII—Construction of means of transport	5	5	...	...	...	...	...	...	...	...	...	...	...	...	...	...	...	...	...	...	...	...	...
15. Dredging work	1	1	...	...	...	...	...	...	...	...	...	...	...	...	...	...	...	...	...	...	...	...	...
16. Upper Jhelum canal construction	4	4	...	...	...	...	...	...	...	...	...	...	...	...	...	...	...	...	...	...	...	...	...
IX—Production and transmission of physical forces	6	5	1	...	...	...	...	...	...	...	...	1	...	...	...	...	...	...	...	...	...	...	...
17. Electric power and generating station	3	2	1	...	...	...	...	...	...	...	...	1	...	...	...	...	...	...	...	...	...	...	...
18. Hydro-electric Installation ...	1	1	...	...	...	...	...	...	...	...	...	...	...	...	...	...	...	...	...	...	...	...	...
19. Electric Transmission line ...	1	1	...	...	...	...	...	...	...	...	...	...	...	...	...	...	...	...	...	...	...	...	...
20. Flume channel and head works	1	1	...	...	...	...	...	...	...	...	...	...	...	...	...	...	...	...	...	...	...	...	...
X.—Industries of Luxury ...	4	...	4	...	...	...	...	1	3	...	...	...	...	...	...	...	...	...	...	...	...	...	...
21. Printing Press	3	...	3	...	...	...	...	...	3	...	...	...	...	...	...	...	...	...	...	...	...	...	...
22. Photography and rubber stamp manufacturing and printing press	1	...	1	...	...	...	...	1	...	...	...	...	...	...	...	...	...	...	...	...	...	...	...

TABLE XVI.

OCCUPATION BY SELECTED CASTES, TRIBES OR RACES.

Jammu and Kashmir State Census, 1911.

---

1. For the principle and method of selection of castes, etc., and the numbers dealt with see the title-page remarks of Table IX.

2. The detail of actual workers given in column 12 and onwards is exclusive of the figures entered in columns 6, 7, 10 and 11.

3. The Christian figures do not, of course, include the Anglo-Indian *Musalman* male and the American *Bramho* female.

TABLE XVI.

Occupation by selected Castes, Tribes or Races.

Jammu and Kashmir State Census, 1911.

Column headings:

- Population dealt with: 3 Actual workers, Males; 4 Actual workers, Females; 5 Dependents, Both sexes.
- Number of actual workers whose traditional caste-occupation was returned as their: 6 Principal means of livelihood, Males; 7 Principal means of livelihood, Females; 8 Subsidiary means of livelihood, Males; 9 Subsidiary means of livelihood, Females.
- Number of actual workers returning their traditional occupation as their principal means of livelihood who had some subsidiary occupation: 10 Males; 11 Females.
- Recorded principal occupation of actual workers.
  - I. Exploitation of the surface of the soil: 12–13 Income from rent of land (Males, Females); 14–15 Cultivation of all kinds (Males, Females); 16–17 Agents and managers of landed estates, forest officers, and their clerks, rent-collectors, etc. (Males, Females); 18–19 Field labourers, wood-cutters, etc. (Males, Females); 20–21 Raisers of live-stock, milkmen and herdsmen (Males, Females); 22–23 Fishing and hunting (Males, Females).
  - II. Extraction of minerals: 24–25 Owners, managers, clerks, etc. (Males, Females); 26–27 Labourers (Males, Females).

	Caste, tribe or race.	Traditional occupation.	3	4	5	6	7	8	9	10	11	12	13	14	15	16	17	18	19	20	21	22	23	24	25	26	27
	1	2	3	4	5	6	7	8	9	10	11	12	13	14	15	16	17	18	19	20	21	22	23	24	25	26	27
Hindu.	Chamiar ...	Cobbler and coolie ...	12,745	4,820	20,295	3,308	1,325	2,591	224	1,288	130	11	15	7,106	2,757	...	...	348	257	117	27	...	...	...	...	2	4
	Jat ...	Agriculture ...	7,914	3,382	12,092	6,558	3,122	34	...	456	10	64	48	80	108	2	...	85	8	120	11	2	...	...	...	...	...
	Jhiwar ...	Water bearing and menial service	4,081	1,594	5,528	1,142	1,073	354	24	226	44	13	6	500	140	1	...	78	26	10	...	7	2	...	...	...	...
	Kashmiri Pandit (Brahman)	State service ...	17,507	1,187	36,403	5,240	32	243	2	344	3	886	106	5,095	284	11	...	28	...	14	...	...	...	...	...	3	...
	Khatri ...	Money-lending and trade ...	5,854	399	9,602	2,441	81	130	18	391	11	94	25	856	162	15	...	33	1	3	...	...	...	...	...	2	...
	Nai (Hajjam) ...	Barber ...	1,705	400	2,268	775	120	281	13	214	4	22	6	550	204	...	...	32	7	2	1	...	...	...	...	...	...
	Thakkar ...	Agriculture ...	35,081	16,201	42,314	27,803	11,932	204	7	4,344	67	137	155	136	3,609	12	...	264	49	606	54	...	...	1	...	4	...
	Tarkhan ...	Carpenter ...	3,380	735	5,010	1,395	51	478	24	414	6	69	10	1,222	570	...	3	138	17	4	3	...	...	...	...	1	...
	Lohar ...	Blacksmith ...	3,709	944	5,633	802	88	504	15	462	1	9	18	2,062	739	...	...	90	17	73	6	...	...	...	...	1	...
	Soniar (Zargar) ...	Gold and silver smith ...	1,565	139	2,933	1,145	47	60	10	169	2	1	4	129	42	1	...	9	...	...	...	...	...	...	...	...	...
	Sochi (Darzi) ...	Tailoring ...	210	75	262	73	22	28	5	20	...	1	2	86	43	1	...	...	1	...	...	...	...	...	...	...	...
Musalman.	Bafinda (Julaha) ...	Weaver ...	8,802	2,485	16,336	1,941	677	2,269	67	674	19	95	65	5,394	1,421	3	...	124	28	77	3	...	...	...	...	1	5
	Chibh ...	Agriculture ...	2,853	516	5,795	1,987	353	112	3	351	14	104	21	19	21	1	1	22	...	50	3	...	...	...	...	...	...
	Darzi ...	Tailoring ...	1,089	365	1,857	342	176	159	12	65	15	...	4	598	143	...	...	3	...	3	...	...	...	...	...	...	...
	Dum, Chuhra and Watal	Scavenging ...	6,206	2,969	9,929	360	280	64	90	65	12	18	12	3,711	2,006	32	...	195	65	414	153	2	...	...	...	7	...
	Mochi ...	Cobbler class ...	5,800	1,638	9,831	2,210	294	880	16	292	3	8	7	2,423	934	5	...	53	11	234	38	1	...	...	...	2	4
	Gaddi and Gujjar ...	Cattle breading ...	94,996	37,358	174,563	7,500	2,129	3,537	157	4,158	120	256	167	74,648	32,565	22	13	1,710	453	785	104	19	11	...	...	47	14
	Hanji ...	Boatmen ...	5,616	3,343	8,631	1,295	1,376	34	2	52	45	4	2	1,824	1,659	1	...	72	21	24	7	...	...	...	...	12	...
	Jat ...	Agriculture ...	37,705	13,382	62,476	24,950	11,404	119	305	4,127	72	121	106	5,141	1,153	15	...	382	14	670	46	1	...	...	...	40	...
	Kumhiar ...	Potter ...	4,568	1,810	9,025	1,414	713	530	21	303	6	5	19	2,430	943	...	4	21	4	62	10	1	...	3	...	2	...
	Lohar ...	Blacksmith ...	5,286	1,401	9,769	1,200	83	950	13	312	...	53	6	3,372	1,197	1	...	76	17	29	6	...	...	...	...	11	2
	Mirasi and Bhand ...	Singing ...	2,572	716	4,266	323	86	54	1	51	2	57	6	1,158	345	1	...	67	4	23	...	...	...	...	...	4	...
	Shin ...	Agriculture ...	914	528	1,276	724	373	3	...	70	21	...	...	3	125	1	...	14	4	2	...	1	...	...	...	3	...
	Tantre ...	Do. ...	2,606	1,699	4,358	1,919	1,035	6	...	391	11	8	2	55	342	...	...	13	13	21	1	2	...	...	...	3	...
	Yashkun ...	Do. ...	4,226	4,074	7,914	3,400	3,554	...	...	440	358	10	5	32	...	...	...	102	126	8	1	2	...	...	...	3	...
	Wani ...	Shopkeeper ...	17,795	10,764	28,542	1,193	77	213	4	300	31	68	27	12,335	9,065	20	1	252	84	123	24	1	...	...	1	16	...
	Teli ...	Oil pressing ...	6,191	1,996	10,146	1,818	555	704	80	632	76	16	11	2,335	1,058	2	40	45	12	61	6	2	...	...	...	20	1
Christian.	European ...	... ...	117	34	99	...	...	...	...	...	...	...	...	...	...	5	...	...	...	...	...	...	...	...	...	...	...
	Anglo-Indian ...	... ...	8	4	4	...	...	...	...	...	...	...	...	...	...	...	...	...	...	...	...	...	...	...	...	...	...
	Indian Christian ...	... ...	285	134	290	...	...	...	...	...	...	4	...	58	20	...	...	17	21	...	...	...	...	...	...	...	...

TABLE XVI.

Occupation by selected castes, Tribes or Races.

Jammu and Kashmir State Census, 1911.

RECORDED PRINCIPAL OCCUPATION OF ACTUAL WORKERS.

Religion	Caste, Tribe or Race.	Traditional Occupation.	III. Industry. Owners, managers, clerks, etc. Males.	III. Industry. Owners, managers, clerks, etc. Females.	III. Industry. Artisans and other workmen. Males.	III. Industry. Artisans and other workmen. Females.	IV. Transport. Owner, managers and ships' officers. Males.	IV. Transport. Owner, managers and ships' officers. Females.	IV. Transport. Labourers, boatmen, Palki bearers. Males.	IV. Transport. Labourers, boatmen, Palki bearers. Females.	V. Trade. Males.	V. Trade. Females.	VI. Public Force. Commissioned and gazetted officers. Males.	VI. Public Force. Commissioned and gazetted officers. Females.	VI. Public Force. Others. Males.	VI. Public Force. Others. Females.	VII. Public Administration. Gazetted officers. Males.	VII. Public Administration. Gazetted officers. Females.	VII. Public Administration. Others. Males.	VII. Public Administration. Others. Females.	VIII. Arts and Professions. Religious. Males.	VIII. Arts and Professions. Religious. Females.	VIII. Arts and Professions. Lawyers, doctors and teachers. Males.	VIII. Arts and Professions. Lawyers, doctors and teachers. Females.	VIII. Arts and Professions. Others. Males.	VIII. Arts and Professions. Others. Females.	IX. Persons living on their income. Males.	IX. Persons living on their income. Females.	X. Domestic service. Males.	X. Domestic service. Females.	XI. Contractors, clerks, cashiers, etc. Males.	XI. Contractors, clerks, cashiers, etc. Females.	XII. Labourers unspecified. Males.	XII. Labourers unspecified. Females.	XIII. Beggars, criminals and inmates of jails. Males.	XIII. Beggars, criminals and inmates of jails. Females.
			28	29	30	31	32	33	34	35	36	37	38	39	40	41	42	43	44	45	46	47	48	49	50	51	52	53	54	55	56	57	58	59	60	61
Hindu.	Chamiar ...	Cobbler and coolie ...	8	1	45	113	...	...	13	...	80	1	11	...	19	...	21	...	29	16	2	...	...	...	6	2	110	4	55	38	3	...	133	81	30	49
	Jat ...	Agriculture ...	...	...	17	22	5	...	37	...	36	5	25	...	78	2	1	...	75	3	...	...	3	...	1	1	4	1	189	9	21	...	36	29	19	3
	Jhiwar ...	Water bearing and menial service	...	...	729	102	..	...	17	...	89	7	...	...	64	...	42	...	327	2	54	3	3	...	16	...	354	22	146	93	4	...	238	63	21	11
	Kashmiri Pandit (Brahman)	State service ...	125	...	810	698	7	...	38	...	2,581	15	...	...	2	...	13	...	82	...	69	1	136	2	17	7	142	17	1,650	16	14	...	122	...	78	6
	Khatri ...	Money-lending and trade ...	5	...	116	53	46	...	23	3	256	6	57	...	73	...	35	3	952	1	9	...	69	...	25	2	40	12	198	23	43	1	34	11	38	4
	Nai (Hajjam) ...	Barber ...	...	1	2	11	...	...	1	1	3	...	5	...	32	...	...	...	32	...	...	3	2	1	2	...	...	3	9	12	...	...	6	13	16	13
	Thakkar ...	Agriculture ...	...	...	107	120	1	...	7	1	132	9	97	...	520	1	2	...	469	2	7	...	6	...	22	12	21	8	266	59	12	...	77	21	28	12
	Tarkhan ...	Carpenter ...	...	...	63	40	...	...	3	1	4	...	5	...	6	...	...	...	7	2	...	...	...	...	7	3	3	1	15	1	3	...	14	22	7	5
	Lohar ...	Blacksmith ...	...	...	64	36	...	...	1	1	7	...	4	...	47	...	3	...	23	...	...	...	...	...	1	2	18	...	19	2	2	...	15	28	6	6
	Soniar (Zargar) ...	Gold and silver smith ...	...	...	50	17	1	...	10	1	20	...	...	...	9	...	1	...	10	...	...	...	1	...	...	...	1	4	5	8	...	...	3	11	...	3
	Sochi (Darzi) ...	Tailoring ...	...	...	...	6	...	...	...	...	3	...	...	...	7	...	...	...	8	...	...	...	...	...	...	...	...	...	8	1	...	...	1	...	2	...
Musalman.	Bafinda (Julaha) ...	Weaver ...	3	4	50	77	2	...	28	1	37	3	...	...	6	...	...	...	36	...	22	1	6	...	14	36	1	13	112	28	6	...	76	13	94	91
	Chibh ...	Agriculture ...	...	...	6	26	2	...	32	...	11	...	64	...	77	50	...	...	45	...	1	...	...	...	...	1	14	2	33	8	...	...	19	12	15	4
	Darzi ...	Tailoring ...	...	...	24	15	...	...	7	1	9	...	3	1	3	...	...	...	3	...	1	...	...	...	1	...	1	...	12	5	...	...	6	2	8	3
	Dum, Chuhra and Watal,	Scavenging ...	28	...	421	248	1	...	73	4	84	7	...	...	35	...	2	...	205	46	5	...	1	...	28	29	27	19	308	4	14	...	61	45	109	39
	Mochi ...	Cobbler class ...	2	...	252	158	...	...	23	...	39	3	...	...	4	...	...	...	77	37	5	...	...	...	1	76	4	1	54	10	...	...	17	15	94	47
	Gaddi and Gujjar ...	Cattle breading ...	2	...	268	777	4	168	272	7	2,181	80	24	...	86	1	2	...	283	6	76	3	36	...	68	44	47	11	1,529	169	3	...	189	77	781	459
	Hanji ...	Boatmen ...	...	...	1,241	105	...	...	345	3	550	48	...	...	8	...	...	1	37	6	1	...	...	...	2	44	1	...	39	3	11	...	79	8	18	15
	Jat ...	Agriculture ...	1	...	117	239	11	...	398	3	149	7	45	...	115	1	...	...	166	...	41	2	23	2	35	20	16	5	532	38	10	...	231	68	368	202
	Kumhiar ...	Potter ...	...	...	36	50	...	...	137	7	32	6	...	...	...	...	...	...	6	...	...	...	...	...	7	2	6	...	31	4	1	...	31	13	40	29
	Lohar ...	Blacksmith ...	...	...	58	55	3	1	11	...	12	2	...	...	3	...	...	...	19	...	12	...	4	...	2	4	4	5	25	5	2	...	40	7	37	11
	Mirasi and Bhand ...	Singing ...	...	2	63	11	...	...	11	2	10	...	7	...	15	1	...	...	55	6	3	...	2	...	9	4	7	...	52	4	...	...	38	11	616	232
	Shin ...	Agriculture ...	4	...	5	1	1	...	1	...	16	...	...	...	5	...	...	...	19	...	4	...	...	...	...	...	1	...	8	2	2	...	8	...	22	2
	Tantre ...	Do. ...	...	...	80	265	...	...	20	11	28	1	...	...	2	...	...	...	3	...	2	...	1	...	1	...	...	1	16	10	...	...	12	2	29	5
	Yashkun ...	Do. ...	...	...	13	...	...	...	12	...	10	1	...	...	...	...	...	...	72	...	9	...	1	...	1	...	5	...	45	6	...	...	27	6	34	17
	Wani ...	Shopkeeper ...	2	1,008	2,432	293	1	16	108	9	177	20	...	...	29	...	...	...	69	...	22	1	16	...	31	3	18	3	186	31	12	...	181	18	203	52
	Teli ...	Oil pressing ...	...	...	74	91	...	...	831	36	173	24	...	...	8	...	...	...	22	3	3	...	1	1	4	4	14	5	33	3	1	...	31	27	65	43
Christian.	European ...	...	14	...	2	...	...	...	...	...	3	2	20	...	1	...	29	...	11	...	10	9	9	10	...	2	10	11	1	...	2	...	...	...	...	...
	Anglo-Indian ...	...	...	...	...	...	...	...	...	...	...	...	...	...	...	...	2	...	4	...	2	2	...	2	...	...	...	...	...	...	...	...	...	...	...	...
	Indian Christian ...	...	...	...	46	31	...	...	...	...	...	...	1	...	2	...	1	...	89	12	20	8	6	5	6	1	...	...	33	33	1	...	1	2	...	1

TABLE XVII.

TERRITORIAL DISTRIBUTION OF THE CHRISTIAN POPULATION BY SECT AND RACE.

Jammu and Kashmir State Census, 1911.

1. No Christian population has been returned in Udhampur District and Bhadarwah *Jagir*. The names of these administrative divisions, therefore, do not appear in this table.

2. The city totals are included in the totals of the districts to which they belong.

3. The figures shown under Lutheran denomination all relate to Moravians who exist chiefly in Laddakh District.

4. The table excludes one European female who returned herself as Bramho and one Anglo-Indian male who has become a Mohamedan.

TABLE XVII.

Territorial Distribution of the Christian Population by Sect and Race.

Jammu and Kashmir State Census, 1911.

District, Jagir or Ilaqa.	All Denominations.									Anglican Communion.									Baptist.									Congregationalist.								
	Total.			Distribution by race.						Total.			Distribution by race.						Total.			Distribution by race.						Total.			Distribution by race.					
				Europeans and allied races.		Anglo-Indians.		Indian Christians.					Europeans and allied races.		Anglo-Indians.		Indian Christians.					Europeans and allied races.		Anglo-Indians.		Indian Christians.					Europeans and allied races.		Anglo-Indians.		Indian Christians.	
	Persons.	Males.	Females.	Males.	Females.	Males.	Females.	Males.	Females.	Persons.	Males.	Females.	Males.	Females.	Males.	Females.	Males.	Females.	Persons.	Males.	Females.	Males.	Females.	Males.	Females.	Males.	Females.	Persons.	Males.	Females.	Males.	Females.	Males.	Females.	Males.	Females.
1	2	3	4	5	6	7	8	9	10	11	12	13	14	15	16	17	18	19	20	21	22	23	24	25	26	27	28	29	30	31	32	33	34	35	36	37
Total State ...	**975**	**618**	**357**	**134**	**116**	**9**	**7**	**475**	**234**	**194**	**101**	**93**	**87**	**84**	**4**	**2**	**10**	**7**	**3**	**1**	**2**	**1**	...	...	**2**	...	...	**9**	**3**	**6**	**3**	**5**	...	...	...	**1**
I.—Total Jammu Province (including *Jagirs*).	672	450	222	28	17	2	2	420	203	21	14	7	14	7	...	...	...	...	2	...	2	...	...	...	2	...	...	8	3	5	3	4	...	...	...	1
1. Jammu District (including city). ...	463	304	159	13	5	...	...	291	154	9	7	2	7	2	...	...	...	...	...	...	...	...	...	...	...	...	...	...	...	...	...	...	...	...	...	...
2. Jasrota District ...	170	128	42	...	...	...	...	128	42	...	...	...	...	...	...	...	...	...	...	...	...	...	...	...	...	...	...	...	...	...	...	...	...	...	...	...
3. Riasi ,, ...	1	1	...	1	...	...	...	...	...	...	...	...	...	...	...	...	...	...	...	...	...	...	...	...	...	...	...	...	...	...	...	...	...	...	...	...
4. Mirpur ,, ...	10	7	3	7	3	...	...	...	...	9	6	3	6	3	...	...	...	...	...	...	...	...	...	...	...	...	...	...	...	...	...	...	...	...	...	...
5. Punch *Ilaqa* ...	28	10	18	7	9	2	2	1	7	3	1	2	1	2	...	...	...	...	2	...	2	...	...	...	2	...	...	8	3	5	3	4	...	...	...	1
II.—Total Kashmir Province (including *Jagirs*).	218	118	100	89	87	5	4	24	9	158	75	83	63	74	2	2	10	7	1	1	...	1	...	...	...	...	...	1	...	1	...	1	...	...	...	...
6. Kashmir North (including Langet *Jagir*).	39	25	14	21	12	4	2	...	...	24	15	9	13	9	2	...	...	...	...	...	...	...	...	...	...	...	...	...	...	...	...	...	...	...	...	...
7. Kashmir South (including Srinagar city).	162	80	82	57	71	1	2	22	9	120	50	70	40	61	...	2	10	7	1	1	...	1	...	...	...	...	...	1	...	1	...	1	...	...	...	...
Total Kashmir Valley ...	*201*	*105*	*96*	*78*	*83*	*5*	*4*	*22*	*9*	*144*	*65*	*79*	*53*	*70*	*2*	*2*	*10*	*7*	*1*	*1*	...	*1*	...	...	...	...	...	*1*	...	*1*	...	*1*	...	...	...	...
8. Muzaffarabad District (*Wizarat Pahar*).	17	13	4	11	4	...	...	2	...	14	10	4	10	4	...	...	...	...	...	...	...	...	...	...	...	...	...	...	...	...	...	...	...	...	...	...
III.—Total Frontier Districts.	85	50	35	17	12	2	1	31	22	15	12	3	10	3	2	...	...	...	...	...	...	...	...	...	...	...	...	...	...	...	...	...	...	...	...	...
9. Laddakh District ...	63	32	31	3	9	...	...	29	22	2	1	1	1	1	...	...	...	...	...	...	...	...	...	...	...	...	...	...	...	...	...	...	...	...	...	...
10. Gilgit ,, ...	21	17	4	13	3	2	1	2	...	12	10	2	8	2	2	...	...	...	...	...	...	...	...	...	...	...	...	...	...	...	...	...	...	...	...	...
11. Frontier *Ilaqas* ...	1	1	...	1	...	...	...	...	...	1	1	...	1	...	...	...	...	...	...	...	...	...	...	...	...	...	...	...	...	...	...	...	...	...	...	...

TABLE XVII.

Territorial Distribution of the Christian Population by Sect and Race.

Jammu and Kashmir State Census, 1911.

District, Jagir or Ilaqa.	Lutheran. Total. Persons.	Males.	Females.	Distribution by race. Europeans and allied races. Males.	Females.	Anglo-Indians. Males.	Females.	Indian Christians. Males.	Females.
	38	39	40	41	42	43	44	45	46
Total State ...	62	32	30	3	8	...	...	29	22
I.—Total Jammu Province (including *Jagirs*).	...	...	...	...	...	...	...	...	...
1. Jammu District (including city).	...	...	...	...	...	...	...	...	...
2. Jasrota District ...	...	...	...	...	...	...	...	...	...
3. Riasi " ...	...	...	...	...	...	...	...	...	...
4. Mirpur " ...	...	...	...	...	...	...	...	...	...
5. Punch *Ilaqa* ...	...	...	...	...	...	...	...	...	...
II.—Total Kashmir Province (including *Jagirs*).	3	2	1	2	1	...	...	...	...
6. Kashmir North (including Langet *Jagir*).	3	2	1	2	1	...	...	...	...
7. Kashmir South (including Srinagar city).	...	...	...	...	...	...	...	...	...
Total Kashmir Valley ...	*3*	*2*	*1*	*2*	*1*	...	...	...	...
8. Muzaffarabad District (*Wizarat Pahar*).	...	...	...	...	...	...	...	...	...
III.—Total Frontier Districts.	59	30	29	1	7	...	...	29	22
9. Laddakh District ...	59	30	29	1	7	...	...	29	22
10. Gilgit " ...	...	...	...	...	...	...	...	...	...
11. Frontier *Ilaqas* ...	...	...	...	...	...	...	...	...	...

District, Jagir or Ilaqa.	Minor Protestant Denominations. Total. Persons.	Males.	Females.	Distribution by race. Europeans and allied races. Males.	Females.	Anglo-Indians. Males.	Females.	Indian Christians. Males.	Females.
	47	48	49	50	51	52	53	54	55
Total State ...	8	6	2	...	...	...	...	6	2
I.—Total Jammu Province (including *Jagirs*).	8	6	2	...	...	...	...	6	2
1. Jammu District (including city).	8	6	2	...	...	...	...	6	2
2. Jasrota District ...	...	...	...	...	...	...	...	...	...
3. Riasi " ...	...	...	...	...	...	...	...	...	...
4. Mirpur " ...	...	...	...	...	...	...	...	...	...
5. Punch *Ilaqa* ...	...	...	...	...	...	...	...	...	...
II.—Total Kashmir Province (including *Jagirs*).	...	...	...	...	...	...	...	...	...
6. Kashmir North (including Langet *Jagir*).	...	...	...	...	...	...	...	...	...
7. Kashmir South (including Srinagar city).	...	...	...	...	...	...	...	...	...
Total Kashmir Valley ...	...	...	...	...	...	...	...	...	...
8. Muzaffarabad District (*Wizarat Pahar*).	...	...	...	...	...	...	...	...	...
III.—Total Frontier Districts.	...	...	...	...	...	...	...	...	...
9. Laddakh District ...	...	...	...	...	...	...	...	...	...
10. Gilgit " ...	...	...	...	...	...	...	...	...	...
11. Frontier *Ilaqas* ...	...	...	...	...	...	...	...	...	...

District, Jagir or Ilaqa.	Presbyterian. Total. Persons.	Males.	Females.	Distribution by race. Europeans and allied races. Males.	Females.	Anglo-Indians. Males.	Females.	Indian Christians. Males.	Females.
	56	57	58	59	60	61	62	63	64
Total State ...	617	416	201	15	9	...	...	401	192
I.—Total Jammu Province (including *Jagirs*).	607	409	198	8	6	...	...	401	192
1. Jammu District (including city).	424	277	147	5	3	...	...	272	144
2. Jasrota District ...	170	128	42	...	...	...	...	128	42
3. Riasi " ...	1	1	...	1	...	...	...	...	...
4. Mirpur " ...	...	...	...	...	...	...	...	...	...
5. Punch *Ilaqa* ...	12	3	9	2	3	...	...	1	6
II.—Total Kashmir Province (including *Jagirs*).	10	7	3	7	3	...	...	...	...
6. Kashmir North (including Langet *Jagir*).	4	3	1	3	1	...	...	...	...
7. Kashmir South (including Srinagar city).	6	4	2	4	2	...	...	...	...
Total Kashmir Valley ...	*10*	*7*	*3*	*7*	*3*	...	...	...	...
8. Muzaffarabad District (*Wizarat Pahar*).	...	...	...	...	...	...	...	...	...
III.—Total Frontier Districts.	...	...	...	...	...	...	...	...	...
9. Laddakh District ...	...	...	...	...	...	...	...	...	...
10. Gilgit " ...	...	...	...	...	...	...	...	...	...
11. Frontier *Ilaqas* ...	...	...	...	...	...	...	...	...	...

District, Jagir or Ilaqa.	Protestants (Unsectarian or Sect not specified). Total. Persons.	Males.	Females.	Distribution by race. Europeans and allied races. Males.	Females.	Anglo-Indians. Males.	Females.	Indian Christians. Males.	Females.
	65	66	67	68	69	70	71	72	73
Total State ...	6	3	3	2	2	...	1	1	...
I.—Total Jammu Province (including *Jagirs*).	...	...	...	...	...	...	...	...	...
1. Jammu District (including city).	...	...	...	...	...	...	...	...	...
2. Jasrota District ...	...	...	...	...	...	...	...	...	...
3. Riasi " ...	...	...	...	...	...	...	...	...	...
4. Mirpur " ...	...	...	...	...	...	...	...	...	...
5. Punch *Ilaqa* ...	...	...	...	...	...	...	...	...	...
II.—Total Kashmir Province (including *Jagirs*).	3	2	1	1	1	...	...	1	...
6. Kashmir North (including Langet *Jagir*).	...	...	...	...	...	...	...	...	...
7. Kashmir South (including Srinagar city).	3	2	1	1	1	...	...	1	...
Total Kashmir Valley ...	*3*	*2*	*1*	*1*	*1*	...	...	*1*	...
8. Muzaffarabad District (*Wizarat Pahar*).	...	...	...	...	...	...	...	...	...
III.—Total Frontier Districts.	3	1	2	1	1	...	1	...	...
9. Laddakh District ...	2	1	1	1	1	...	...	...	...
10. Gilgit " ...	1	...	1	...	...	...	1	...	...
11. Frontier *Ilaqas* ...	...	...	...	...	...	...	...	...	...

TABLE XVII.

Territorial Distribution of the Christian Population by Sect and Race.

Jammu and Kashmir State Census, 1911.

District, Jagir or Ilaqa.	Roman Catholic.									Sect not returned.									Indefinite beliefs.								
	Total.			Distribution by race.						Total.			Distribution by race.						Total.			Distribution by race.					
				Europeans and allied races.		Anglo-Indians.		Indian Christians.					Europeans and allied races.		Anglo-Indians.		Indian Christians.					Europeans and allied races.		Anglo-Indians.		Indian Christians.	
	Persons.	Males.	Females.	Males.	Females.	Males.	Famales.	Males.	Females.	Persons.	Males.	Females.	Males.	Females.	Males.	Females.	Males.	Females.	Persons.	Males.	Females.	Males.	Females.	Males.	Females.	Males.	Females.
	74	75	76	77	78	79	80	81	82	83	84	85	86	87	88	89	90	91	92	93	94	95	96	97	98	99	100
Total State ...	**51**	**35**	**16**	**16**	**8**	**4**	...	**15**	**8**	**24**	**20**	**4**	**6**	...	**1**	**2**	**13**	**2**	**1**	**1**	...	...	..	...	...	**1**	...
I.—Total Jammu Province (including *Jagirs*).	26	18	8	3	...	2	...	13	8	...	...	...	...	...	...	...	...	...	...	...	...	...	...	...	...	...	...
1. Jammu District (including city).	22	14	8	1	...	...	...	13	8	...	...	...	...	...	...	...	...	...	...	...	...	...	...	...	...	...	...
2. Jasrota District ...	...	...	...	...	...	...	...	...	...	...	...	...	...	...	...	...	...	...	...	...	...	...	...	...	...	...	...
3. Riasi ,, ...	...	...	...	...	...	...	...	...	...	...	...	...	...	...	...	...	...	...	...	...	...	...	...	...	...	...	...
4. Mirpur ,, ...	1	1	...	1	...	...	...	...	...	...	...	...	...	...	...	...	...	...	...	...	...	...	...	...	...	...	...
5. Punch *Ilaqa* ...	3	3	...	1	...	2	...	...	...	...	...	...	...	...	...	...	...	...	...	...	...	...	...	...	...	...	...
II.—Total Kashmir Province (including *Jagirs*).	17	10	7	8	7	2	...	...	...	24	20	4	6	...	1	2	13	2	1	1	...	...	...	...	...	1	...
6. Kashmir North (including Langet *Jagir*).	4	3	1	2	1	1	...	...	...	4	2	2	1	...	1	2	...	...	...	...	...	...	...	...	...	...	...
7. Kashmir South (including Srinagar city).	13	7	6	6	6	1	...	...	...	17	15	2	4	...	...	...	11	2	1	1	...	...	...	...	...	1	...
Total Kashmir Valley ...	*17*	*10*	*7*	*8*	*7*	*2*	...	...	...	*21*	*17*	*4*	*5*	...	*1*	*2*	*11*	*2*	*1*	*1*	...	...	...	...	...	*1*	...
8. Muzaffarabad District (*Wizarat Pahar*).	...	...	...	...	...	...	...	...	...	3	3	...	1	...	...	...	2	...	...	...	...	...	...	...	...	...	...
III.—Total Frontier Districts.	8	7	1	5	1	...	...	2	...	...	...	...	...	...	...	...	...	...	...	...	...	...	...	...	...	...	...
9. Laddakh District ...	...	...	...	...	...	...	...	...	...	...	...	...	...	...	...	...	...	...	...	...	...	...	...	...	...	...	...
10. Gilgit ,, ...	8	7	1	5	1	...	...	2	...	...	...	...	...	...	...	...	...	...	...	...	...	...	...	...	...	...	...
11. Frontier *Ilaqas* ...	...	...	...	...	...	...	...	...	...	...	...	...	...	...	...	...	...	...	...	...	...	...	...	...	...	...	...

TABLE XVIII.

EUROPEANS AND ANGLO-INDIANS BY RACE AND AGE.

Jammu and Kashmir State Census, 1911.

1. This Table relates only to Europeans and Anglo-Indians, as no Armenians have been returned in this State.

2. The Districts of Jasrota and Udhampur and the Bhadarwah *Jagir* had no population of this class at the Final Census. Their names have therefore been left out.

3. The totals of the cities have separately been shown just below the districts in which they lie and totals of the entire district struck.

4. Of the total population of this class censused here, one European female gave her religion as Bramho and one Anglo-Indian male, Mohamedan. Both these units are included in this table, but in the tables dealing with religion they have been classed under the religions returned.

TABLE XVIII.

Europeans and Anglo-Indians by Race and Age.

Jammu and Kashmir State Census, 1911.

Districts, Jagir or Ilaqa.	Total. Total.	Total. Males.	Total. Females.	Europeans and Allied Races. British Subjects. All Ages. Total.	British Subjects. All Ages. Males.	British Subjects. All Ages. Females.	British Subjects. 0—12 Males.	British Subjects. 0—12 Females.	British Subjects. 12—15 Males.	British Subjects. 12—15 Females.	British Subjects. 15—30 Males.	British Subjects. 15—30 Females.	British Subjects. 30—50 Males.	British Subjects. 30—50 Females.	British Subjects. 50 & over. Males.	British Subjects. 50 & over. Females.	Others. All Ages. Total.	Others. All Ages. Males.	Others. All Ages. Females.	Others. 0—12 Males.	Others. 0—12 Females.	Others. 12—15 Males.	Others. 12—15 Females.	Others. 15—30 Males.	Others. 15—30 Females.	Others. 30—50 Males.	Others. 30—50 Females.	Others. 50 & over. Males.	Others. 50 & over. Females.	Anglo-Indians. All Ages. Total.	Anglo-Indians. All Ages. Males.	Anglo-Indians. All Ages. Females.	Anglo-Indians. 0—12 Males.	Anglo-Indians. 0—12 Females.	Anglo-Indians. 12—15 Males.	Anglo-Indians. 12—15 Females.	Anglo-Indians. 15—30 Males.	Anglo-Indians. 15—30 Females.	Anglo-Indians. 30—50 Males.	Anglo-Indians. 30—50 Females.	Anglo-Indians. 50 & over. Males.	Anglo-Indians. 50 & over. Females.
1	2	3	4	5	6	7	8	9	10	11	12	13	14	15	16	17	18	19	20	21	22	23	24	25	26	27	28	29	30	31	32	33	34	35	36	37	38	39	40	41	42	43
Total State ...	**268**	**144**	**124**	**226**	**124**	**102**	**23**	**16**	...	**3**	**25**	**24**	**58**	**41**	**18**	**18**	**25**	**10**	**15**	**1**	**3**	...	**1**	...	**5**	**7**	**5**	**2**	**1**	**17**	**10**	**7**	**1**	**1**	...	...	**6**	**2**	**3**	**4**	...	...
I.—Total Jammu Province (including *Jagirs*).	49	30	19	40	27	13	7	4	...	1	5	4	13	3	2	1	5	1	4	...	1	...	1	...	...	1	2	...	...	4	2	2	...	...	...	...	2	...	...	2	...	...
1. Jammu District ...	10	8	2	9	7	2	2	...	...	...	2	2	3	...	...	...	1	1	...	...	...	...	...	...	...	1	...	...	...	...	...	...	...	...	...	...	...	...	...	...	...	...
2. Jammu City ...	8	5	3	8	5	3	2	...	...	1	1	...	1	2	1	...	...	...	...	...	...	...	...	...	...	...	...	...	...	...	...	...	...	...	...	...	...	...	...	...	...	...
Total of Jammu District (including City).	18	13	5	17	12	5	4	...	...	1	3	2	4	2	1	...	1	1	...	...	...	...	...	...	...	1	...	...	...	...	...	...	...	...	...	...	...	...	...	...	...	...
3. Riasi District ...	1	1	...	1	1	...	...	...	...	...	...	...	1	...	...	...	...	...	...	...	...	...	...	...	...	...	...	...	...	...	...	...	...	...	...	...	...	...	...	...	...	...
4. Mirpur ,, ...	10	7	3	10	7	3	1	2	...	...	2	1	4	...	...	...	...	...	...	...	...	...	...	...	...	...	...	...	...	...	...	...	...	...	...	...	...	...	...	...	...	...
5. Punch *Ilaqa* ...	20	9	11	12	7	5	2	2	...	...	...	1	4	1	1	1	4	...	4	...	1	...	1	...	...	...	2	...	...	4	2	2	...	...	...	...	2	...	...	2	...	...
II.—Total Kashmir Province (including *Jagirs*).	187	95	92	164	82	82	14	10	...	2	18	19	34	34	16	17	13	7	6	1	...	...	...	...	4	4	1	2	1	10	6	4	1	1	...	...	2	2	3	1	...	...
6. Kashmir North (including Langet *Jagir*).	39	25	14	28	17	11	2	2	...	...	5	5	9	3	1	1	5	4	1	1	...	...	...	...	...	3	1	...	...	6	4	2	1	1	...	...	2	...	1	1	...	...
7. ,, South ...	39	21	18	36	19	17	4	3	...	1	2	2	7	7	6	4	3	2	1	...	...	...	...	...	...	1	...	1	1	...	...	...	...	...	...	...	...	...	...	...	...	...
8. Srinagar City ...	94	38	56	85	35	50	6	5	...	1	8	10	14	23	7	11	5	1	4	...	...	...	...	...	4	...	...	1	...	4	2	2	...	...	...	...	...	2	2	...	...	...
Total of Kashmir South (including City).	133	59	74	121	54	67	10	8	...	2	10	12	21	30	13	15	8	3	5	...	...	...	...	...	4	1	...	2	1	4	2	2	...	...	...	...	...	2	2	...	...	...
Total Kashmir Valley ...	*172*	*84*	*88*	*149*	*71*	*78*	*12*	*10*	...	*2*	*15*	*17*	*30*	*33*	*14*	*16*	*13*	*7*	*6*	*1*	...	...	...	...	*4*	*4*	*1*	*2*	*1*	*10*	*6*	*4*	*1*	*1*	...	...	*2*	*2*	*3*	*1*	...	...
9. Muzaffarabad District (*Wizarat Pahar*).	15	11	4	15	11	4	2	...	...	...	3	2	4	1	2	1	...	...	...	...	...	...	...	...	...	...	...	...	...	...	...	...	...	...	...	...	...	...	...	...	...	...
III.—Total Frontier Districts.	32	19	13	22	15	7	2	2	...	...	2	1	11	4	...	...	7	2	5	...	2	...	...	...	1	2	2	...	...	3	2	1	...	...	...	...	2	...	...	1	...	...
10. Laddakh District ...	12	3	9	5	1	4	...	2	...	...	...	...	1	2	...	...	7	2	5	...	2	...	...	...	1	2	2	...	...	...	...	...	...	...	...	...	...	...	...	...	...	...
11. Gilgit ,, ...	19	15	4	16	13	3	2	...	...	...	2	1	9	2	...	...	...	...	...	...	...	...	...	...	...	...	...	...	...	3	2	1	...	...	...	...	2	...	...	1	...	...
12. Frontier *Ilaqas* ...	1	1	...	1	1	...	...	...	...	...	...	...	1	...	...	...	...	...	...	...	...	...	...	...	...	...	...	...	...	...	...	...	...	...	...	...	...	...	...	...	...	...

PROVINCIAL TABLE I.

AREA AND POPULATION BY TEHSILS.

Jammu and Kashmir State Census, 1911.

Provincial—I
Area and Population
by Tehsils.

PROVINCIAL TABLE I.

AREA AND POPULATION BY TEHSILS.

Jammu and Kashmir State Census, 1911.

TEHSILS.	Area in square miles	Number of Towns.	Number of Villages	Number of occupied houses.	Population 1911. Persons.	Population 1911. Males.	Population 1911. Females.	Population 1901. (Both sexes).	Percentage of Variation. 1901-1911.	Percentage of Variation. 1891-1901.	No. of persons per square mile in 1911.	Uninhabited villages.	REMARKS.
1	2	3	4	5	6	7	8	9	10	11	12	13	14
Total State ...	84,432	61	8.865	553,124	3,158.126	1,674,367	1,483,759	2,905,578	+9	+14	37	178	
I—Total Jammu Province	12,439	28	4,525	310,172	1,597,865	846,790	751,075	1,516,450	+5	+5·68	128	108	
,, ,, District...	1,167	6	1,152	71.412	326,691	180,691	146,000	344.018	—5	+12	280	61	
Jammu city ...	*1¾*	*1*	...	*7,293*	*31,726*	*19,362*	*12,364*	*35,672*	*—12*	*+4*	...	...	
,, Tehsil ...	379¼	*1*	*310*	*19,302*	*85,577*	*47,944*	*37,633*	...	...	...	...	...	
Raj Kumar's Jagir in Jammu		..	*5*	*410*	*2,086*	*1,117*	*969*	...	...	...	...	...	
1. **Total Jammu Tehsil** ...	381	2	315	27,011	119,389	68,423	50,966	127,924	—7	...	313	27	Exludes Karlup.
2. Samba Tehsil ...	301	1	324	13,365	67,517	36,200	31,317	63,655	+6	...	224	15	
3. Sri Ranbirsinghpura ,, ...	159	1	297	15,405	68,061	37,416	30,645	78,856	—14	...	428	19	
4. Akhnur ,, ...	326	2	216	15,631	71,724	38,652	33,072	73,583	—3	...	220	...	
Total Jasrota District ...	989	4	571	31,837	151.802	81,375	70,427	154,213	—2	+2	153	14	
5. Kathua Tehsil ...	225	2	172	8,473	41,933	23,401	18,532	42,822	—2	...	186	9	Parol consists of 6 villages one of which is *bechiragh*, and Kathua of 3 villages.
6. Jasmirgarh ,, ...	185	1	262	9,155	44,530	24,107	20,423	42,364	+5	...	241	5	
7. Basohli ,, ...	579	1	137	14,259	65,339	33,867	31,472	69,027	—5	...	113	...	
Total Udhampur District	4.399	6	661	39,553	215,725	113,877	101,848	...	...	—12·2	49	2	
Udhampur Tehsil ...	*396*	*1*	*195*	*9,399*	*44,574*	*23,930*	*20,644*	...	...	...	*113*	*1*	
Chaneni Jagir ...	*93*	*1*	*45*	*2,166*	*10,589*	*5,674*	*4,915*	...	...	...	*114*	...	
8. **Total Udhampur Tehsil**	489	2	240	11,565	55,163	29,604	25,559	...	...	...	113	1	
9. Kishtwar Tehsil ...	2,823	1	153	7,011	48,778	25,859	22,919	...	...	...	17	...	
10. Ramban ,, ...	585	2	134	10.157	60,236	31,392	28,844	...	...	...	103	1	Includes Kund *Ilaqa* figures.
11. Ramnagar ,, ...	502	1	134	10,820	51,548	27,022	24,526	...	...	...	103	...	
Total Riasi District ...	1,875	4	652	37.341	206,809	109,026	97,783	...	...	...	110	6	
12. Riasi Tehsil ...	1,008	3	333	18,023	94,658	49,928	44,730	...	...	...	94	...	Includes Nandimarg figures.
13. Rampur Rajauri ,, ...	867	1	319	19,318	112,151	59,098	53,053	...	...	...	129	6	
Total Mirpur District ...	1,754	6	709	71,929	324,933	169.276	155,657	...	...	...	185	7	
14. Kotli Tehsil ...	598	1	224	20,019	96,121	49,665	46,456	...	...	...	161	...	
15. Mirpur ,, ...	391	2	293	23,199	98,119	50,968	47,151	...	...	...	251	5	
16. Bhimber ,, ...	765	3	192	28,711	130,693	68,643	62,050	...	...	...	171	2	
Bhadarwah *Jagir* ...	607	1	294	7,032	37,512	18,975	18,537	34,311	+9	...	62	17	
Karlup Ilaqa ...	*6*	...	*3*	*507*	*1,975*	*1,080*	*895*	...	...	...	*329*	...	
Thakiala Parao ...	*93*	...	*24*	*3,420*	*21,133*	*11,103*	*10,030*	...	...	...	*227*	...	
Punch Ilaqa ...	*1,549*	*1*	*459*	*47,091*	*311,285*	*161,387*	*149,898*	...	...	...	*201*	*1*	
Total Punch Ilaqa ...	1,648	1	486	51.018	334,393	173,570	160.823	304,488	+10	+13	203	1	
II–Total Kashmir Province	8,433	21	3,579	197.382	1,295,201	691,780	603,421	1,157,394	+12	+22	154	68	
,, ,, North...	3,553	8	1,376	68,115	460,786	244,637	216.149	...	...	...	130	21	
Uttarmachhipura Tehsil ...	*2,492*	*3*	*475*	*26,381*	*179,744*	*95,001*	*84,743*	...	...	...	*72*	*8*	
Langet Jagir ...	*185*	...	*77*	*3,134*	*20,865*	*11,068*	*9,797*	...	...	...	*113*	...	
17. **Total Uttarmachhipura**	2,677	3	552	29,515	200.609	106,069	94,540	...	...	...	75	8	
18. Baramula ...	416	3	348	18,458	120,399	63,982	56,417	...	...	...	289	7	
Sriparatapsinghpura	*460*	*2*	*473*	*19,789*	*137,540*	*73,375*	*64,165*	...	...	...	...	*6*	
Natipura		..	*3*	*353*	*2,238*	*1,211*	*1,027*	...	...	...	...	...	
19. **Total Sriparatap-singhpura**	460	2	476	20,142	139,778	74,586	65,192	...	...	...	304	6	
,, Kashmir South ...	2,806	10	1,395	102.232	639,210	342,835	296,375	...	...	...	228	36	Pampur consists of 3 villages Srinagar consists of 14 villages.
Tehsil Khas ...		*1*	*222*	*13,695*	*90,860*	*48,414*	*42,446*	...	...	...	...	*5*	
Srinagar city ...	*714*	*1*	...	*23,840*	*126,344*	*68,378*	*57,966*	...	...	...	...	...	
20. **Total Tehsil Khas** ...		2	222	37.535	217,204	116,792	100,412	...	...	...	304	5	
21. Awantipura Tehsil ...	454	2	387	19,523	128,170	69,192	58,978	...	...	...	282	10	
22. Kulgam ,, ...	586	2	458	20,044	132,061	70,213	61,848	...	...	...	225	8	
23. Anantnag ,, ...	1,052	4	328	25,130	161,775	86,638	75,137	...	...	...	154	13	
Total Kashmir Valley ...	*6,359*	*18*	*2,771*	*170,347*	*1,099,990*	*587,472*	*512,524*	*989,196*	*+11*	*+21·49*	*173*	*57*	
Total Muzaffarabad District	2,074	3	808	27,035	195,205	104,308	90,897	168,198	+16	+25	94	11	
24. Karnah Tehsil ...	1,017	1	104	5,084	41,492	21,737	19,755	35,628	+17	...	41	1	
25. Muzaffarabad ,, ...	547	1	429	14,642	94.295	50,653	43,642	82,542	+14	...	172	9	
26. Uri ,, ...	510	1	275	7,309	59,418	31.918	27,500	50,028	+19	...	116	1	
Total Frontier Province...	63,560	12	761	45,570	265,060	135,797	129,263	231,734	+14	46·02	4	2	
,, Laddakh District ...	45,762	3	465	33,604	186,656	93,220	93,436	...	...	...	4	2	
Laddakh Tehsil ...	*29,793*	*1*	*107*	*7,739*	*31,934*	*16,033*	*15,901*	...	...	...	*1*	*1*	
Mansar (village) ...	*55*	...	*1*	*34*	*190*	*111*	*79*	...	...	...	...	...	
27. **Total Laddakh Tehsil...**	29,848	1	108	7,773	32,124	16,144	15,980	...	...	...	1	1	
28. Skardu Tehsil ...	8,522	1	195	19,031	106,805	53,244	53,561	...	...	...	13	1	Skardu consisting of 2 villages.
29. Kargil ,, ...	7,392	1	162	6,800	47,727	23,832	23,895	...	...	...	6	...	
Total Gilgit District ...	3,118	2	80	3,558	23,969	13,299	10,670	...	...	...	8	...	
30. Gilgit Tehsil ...	1,535	1	45	2,458	15,675	9,108	6,567	...	...	...	10	...	
31. Astore ,, ...	1,583	1	35	1,100	8,294	4,191	4,103	...	...	...	5	...	
Total Frontier *Ilaqas* ...	14.680	7	216	8,408	54,435	29,278	25,157	...	...	...	4	...	
Chilas ...	2,800	1	88	2,198	12,508	6.908	5,600	...	...	...	4	...	
Nagar ...	1,600	1	30	2,390	13,347	7,148	6,199	...	...	...	8	...	
Hunza ...	3,900	1	33	1.712	10,126	5,457	4,669	...	...	...	3	...	
Punial ...	1,600	1	18	597	4,423	2,365	2,058	...	...	...	3	...	
Ishkoman ...	1,600	1	9	197	2,020	1,075	945	...	...	...	1	...	
Yasin ...	*1,200*	*1*	*19*	*655*	*6,316*	*3,291*	*3,019*	...	...	...	*5*	...	
Kuh ...	*480*	...	*11*	*245*	*2,064*	*1,166*	*898*	...	...	...	*4*	...	
Ghizar ...	*1.500*	*1*	*8*	*414*	*3,637*	*1,868*	*1,769*	...	...	...	*2*	...	
Total Yasin ...	3.180	2	38	1.314	12,011	6.325	5,638	...	...	...	4	...	

PROVINCIAL TABLE II.

POPULATION OF TEHSILS BY RELIGION AND EDUCATION.

Jammu and Kashmir State Census, 1911.

PROVINCIAL TABLE II.

Population of Tehsils by Religion and Education.

Jammu and Kashmir State Census, 1911.

TEHSIL.	Distribution by Religion.																		Number of Literate Persons.						Remarks.
	Hindu.		*Arya.*		*Bramho.*		*Sikh.*		*Jain.*		*Budh.*		*Zoroastrian.*		*Musalman.*		*Christian.*		*0—15.*		*15—20.*		*20 and over.*		
	Males.	Females.	Males.	Females.	Males.	Females.	Males.	Females.	Males.	Females.	Males.	Females.	Males.	Females.	Males.	Females.	Males.	Females.	Males.	Females.	Males.	Females.	Males.	Females.	
1	2	3	4	5	6	7	8	9	10	11	12	13	14	15	16	17	18	19	20	21	22	23	24	25	26
I—Total State ...	**372,089**	**317,253**	**593**	**454**	...	**1**	**17,038**	**14,515**	**191**	**154**	**18.281**	**18,231**	**22**	**9**	**1,265,535**	**1,132,785**	**618**	**357**	**5,101**	**299**	**5,952**	**236**	**52,198**	**1,150**	
II—Total Jammu Province (including *Jagirs*).	335,621	289,835	554	429	...	...	9,071	7,588	191	154	211	241	2	3	500,690	452,603	450	222	2,686	248	3,055	204	27,581	847	
Total Jammu District ...	108,196	87,274	310	294	...	...	1,722	1,434	181	153	...	...	2	3	69,976	56,683	304	159	1,118	144	1,245	119	9,774	417	
Jammu city ...	*12,032*	*7,740*	*87*	*45*	...	...	*414*	*281*	*181*	*153*	...	...	*2*	*3*	*6,552*	*4,066*	*94*	*70*	*530*	*98*	*548*	*68*	*4,028*	*291*	
Jammu Tehsil ...	*31,421*	*24,434*	*7*	*6*	...	...	*193*	*135*	...	...	...	...	...	...	*16,309*	*13,054*	*14*	*4*	*220*	*43*	*256*	*45*	*2,543*	*86*	
Rajkumar's Jagir (in Jammu) ...	*451*	*349*	...	...	...	...	...	...	...	...	...	...	...	...	*666*	*620*	...	...	*1*	...	*3*	...	*30*	*1*	
1. **Total Jammu Tehsil** ...	43,904	32,529	94	51	...	...	607	416	181	153	...	...	2	3	23,527	17,740	108	74	751	141	807	113	6,601	378	
2. Samba Tehsil ...	21,790	18,775	12	5	...	...	585	570	...	...	...	...	...	...	13,806	11,963	7	4	193	...	206	4	1,196	19	
3. Sri Ranbirsinghpura Tehsil ...	17,431	14,404	194	236	...	...	467	406	...	...	...	...	...	...	19,135	15,518	189	81	141	2	168	2	1,310	6	
4. Akhnur „ ...	25,071	21,566	10	2	...	...	63	42	...	...	...	...	...	...	13,508	11,462	...	...	33	1	64	...	667	14	
Total Jasrota District ...	61,994	54,273	45	27	...	...	58	50	...	...	4	7	...	...	19,146	16,028	128	42	308	5	318	8	3,138	63	
5. Kathua Tehsil ...	15,461	12,098	42	27	...	...	22	21	...	...	...	...	...	...	7,748	6,344	128	42	96	2	112	1	911	16	
6. Jasmirgarh „ ...	17,858	15,386	2	...	...	...	32	28	...	...	...	...	...	...	6,215	5,009	...	...	81	1	70	...	860	13	
7. Basohli „ ...	28,675	26,789	1	...	...	...	4	1	...	...	4	7	...	...	5,183	4,675	...	...	131	2	136	7	1,367	34	
Total Udhampur District...	68,786	61,962	12	5	...	...	61	67	2	1	205	234	...	...	44,811	39,579	...	...	228	12	262	12	3,963	55	
Udhampur Tehsil ...	*19,370*	*17,020*	*1*	...	...	...	*26*	*33*	...	...	...	...	...	...	*4,524*	*3,586*	...	...	*113*	*3*	*124*	*3*	*1,592*	*26*	
Chaneni Jagir ...	*4,838*	*4,388*	...	...	...	...	...	...	...	...	...	...	...	...	*836*	*527*	...	...	...	...	*20*	...	*279*	...	
8. **Total Udhampur Tehsil.**	24,217	21,408	1	...	...	...	26	38	...	...	...	...	...	...	5,360	4,113	...	...	113	3	144	3	1,871	26	
9. Kishtwar Tehsil ...	10,566	9,296	...	...	...	...	6	7	2	1	205	234	...	...	15,080	13,381	...	...	17	2	39	1	492	7	
10. Ramban * „ ...	9,514	9,002	9	5	...	...	25	15	...	...	...	...	...	...	21,844	19,822	...	...	15	1	26	2	510	7	
11. Ramnagar „ ...	24,489	22,256	2	...	...	...	4	7	...	...	...	...	...	...	2,527	2,263	...	...	83	6	53	6	1,090	15	
Total Riasi District ...	42,629	38,257	10	1	...	...	265	222	...	...	...	...	...	...	66,121	59,303	1	...	115	2	194	10	2,571	26	
12. Riasi Tehsil † ...	27,283	24,135	9	1	...	...	53	49	...	...	...	...	...	...	22,582	20,545	1	...	88	2	121	9	1,689	20	
13. Rampur Rajauri ...	15,346	14,122	1	...	...	...	212	173	...	...	...	...	...	...	43,539	38,758	...	...	27	...	73	1	882	6	
Total Mirpur District ...	30,956	26,231	140	85	...	...	1,779	1,377	8	...	...	...	...	...	136,386	127,961	7	3	538	65	616	39	4,909	201	
14. Kotli Tehsil ...	4,217	3,711	5	5	...	...	273	200	...	...	...	...	...	...	45,170	42,540	...	...	47	8	94	7	895	13	
15. Mirpur „ ...	3,728	2,532	86	55	...	...	826	669	...	...	...	...	...	...	46,321	43,892	7	3	254	49	288	24	2,124	142	
16. Bhimber „ ...	23,011	19,988	49	25	...	...	680	508	8	...	...	...	...	...	44,895	41,529	...	...	237	8	234	8	1,890	46	
Bhadarwah *Jagir* ...	11,375	11,556	...	...	...	...	...	...	...	...	1	...	...	...	7,599	6,981	...	...	37	2	56	3	682	18	
Karlup Ilaqa ...	*893*	*796*	...	...	...	...	...	...	...	...	...	...	...	...	*187*	*99*	...	...	*7*	...	*9*	...	*137*	...	
Thakiala Parao ...	*1,147*	*1,073*	*5*	*3*	...	...	*3*	...	...	...	...	...	...	...	*9,948*	*8,954*	...	...							
Punch Ilaqa ...	*9,645*	*8,413*	*32*	*14*	...	...	*5,183*	*4,438*	...	...	*1*	...	...	...	*146,516*	*137,015*	*10*	*18*	*335*	*18*	*355*	*13*	*2,407*	*67*	
Total Punch Ilaqa ...	11,685	10,282	37	17	...	...	5,186	4,438	...	...	1	...	...	...	156,651	146,068	10	18	342	18	364	13	2,544	67	
III—Total Kashmir Province (including *Jagirs*).	35,056	27,312	27	18	...	1	7,871	6,901	...	...	3	...	20	6	648,685	569,083	118	100	2,344	44	2,664	30	21,780	243	

* Includes Kund Ilaqa figures.

† Includes Nandimarg figures.

PROVINCIAL TABLE II.

Population of Tehsils by Religion and Education.

Jammu and Kashmir State Census, 1911.

Tehsil.	Distribution by Religion.																		Number of Literate Persons.						Remarks.
	Hindu.		*Arya.*		*Bramho.*		*Sikh.*		*Jain.*		*Budh.*		*Zoroastrian.*		*Musalman.*		*Christian.*		*0—15.*		*15—20.*		*20 and over.*		
	Males.	Females.	Males.	Females.	Males.	Females.	Males.	Females.	Males.	Females.	Males.	Females.	Males.	Females.	Males.	Females.	Males.	Females.	Males.	Females.	Males.	Females.	Males.	Females.	
1	2	3	4	5	6	7	8	9	10	11	12	13	14	15	16	17	18	19	20	21	22	23	24	25	26
Total Kashmir North ...	5,935	3,982	3	2	...	...	2,383	2,192	...	...	2	...	...	...	236,289	209,959	25	14	348	7	549	13	5,121	44	
Uttarmachhipura Tehsil ...	*2,090*	*1,426*	*3*	*2*	...	...	*897*	*834*	...	...	...	...	...	...	*92,002*	*82,477*	*9*	*4*	*153*	*4*	*227*	*5*	*1,984*	*24*	
Langet Jagir ...	*332*	*211*	...	...	...	...	...	...	...	...	...	...	...	...	*10,735*	*9,586*	*1*	...	*11*	...	*22*	...	*176*	...	
17. **Total Uttarmachhipura Tehsil.**	2,422	1,637	3	2	...	...	897	834	...	...	...	...	...	...	102,737	92,063	10	4	164	4	249	5	2,160	24	
18. Baramula " ...	2,158	1,489	...	...	...	...	748	616	...	...	2	...	...	...	61,060	54,302	14	10	140	3	187	7	1,849	19	
Sri Pratapsinghpura ...	*1,333*	*839*	...	...	...	...	*738*	*742*	...	...	...	...	...	...	*71,303*	*62,584*	*1*	...	*41*	...	*113*	*1*	*1,085*	*1*	
Nattipura ...	*22*	*17*	...	...	...	...	...	...	...	...	...	...	...	...	*1,189*	*1,010*	...	...	*3*	...	...	...	*27*	...	
19. **Total Sri Pratapsinghpura.**	1,355	856	...	...	...	...	738	742	...	...	...	...	...	...	72,492	63,594	1	...	44	...	113	1	1,112	1	
Total Kashmir South ...	26,298	21,456	24	16	...	1	1,448	1,138	...	...	...	...	20	6	314,965	273,676	80	82	1,786	27	1,877	12	14,359	129	
Tehsil Khas ...	*1,424*	*956*	...	...	...	...	*43*	*30*	...	...	...	...	...	...	*46,921*	*41,440*	*26*	*20*	*36*	*4*	*71*	...	*975*	*20*	
Srinagar city. ...	*15,696*	*13,043*	*24*	*16*	...	*1*	*316*	*170*	...	...	...	...	*20*	*6*	*52,271*	*44,670*	*51*	*60*	*1,385*	*21*	*1,199*	*9*	*7,909*	*86*	
20. **Total Tehsil Khas** ...	17,120	13,999	24	16	...	1	359	200	...	...	...	...	20	6	99,192	86,110	77	80	1,421	25	1,270	9	8,884	106	
21. Awantipura Tehsil ...	2,227	1,725	...	...	...	...	716	630	...	...	...	...	...	...	66,249	56,623	...	...	107	...	167	...	1,572	12	
22. Kulgam " ...	2,965	2,278	...	...	...	...	62	58	...	...	...	...	...	...	67,185	59,512	1	...	100	1	139	1	1,441	3	
23. Anantnag " ...	3,986	3,454	...	...	...	...	311	250	...	...	...	...	...	...	82,339	71,431	2	2	158	1	301	2	2,462	8	
Total Kashmir Valley ...	*32,233*	*25,438*	*27*	*18*	...	*1*	*3,831*	*3,330*	...	...	*2*	...	*20*	*6*	*551,254*	*483,635*	*105*	*96*	*2,134*	*34*	*2,426*	*25*	*19,480*	*173*	
Total Muzaffarabad District	2,823	1,874	...	...	...	...	4,040	3,571	...	...	1	...	...	...	97,431	85,448	13	4	210	10	238	5	2,300	70	
24. Karnah Tehsil ...	120	26	...	...	...	...	142	137	...	...	...	...	...	...	21,475	19,592	...	...	1	...	4	...	166	...	
25. Muzaffarabad " ...	1,917	1,398	...	...	...	...	2,836	2,549	...	...	1	...	...	...	45,893	39,691	6	4	149	10	174	5	1,364	55	
26. Uri " ...	786	450	...	...	...	...	1,062	885	...	...	...	...	...	...	30,063	26,165	7	...	60	...	60	...	770	15	
IV—Total Frontier Province.	1,412	106	12	7	...	...	96	26	...	...	18,067	17,990	...	...	116,160	111,099	50	35	71	7	233	2	2,837	60	
Total Laddakh District ...	358	49	11	7	...	...	33	8	...	...	18,067	17,990	...	...	74,719	75,351	32	31	52	2	177	2	2,128	52	
Laddakh Tehsil ...	*49*	*6*	...	...	...	...	*2*	*2*	...	...	*14,190*	*14,117*	...	...	*1,760*	*1,745*	*32*	*31*	*22*	*1*	*57*	...	*987*	*10*	
Mansar (village) ...	...	...	...	...	...	...	...	...	...	...	*111*	*79*	...	...	...	...	...	...	...	...	...	...	...	...	
27. **Total Laddakh Tehsil** ...	49	6	...	...	...	...	2	2	...	...	14,301	14,196	...	...	1,760	1,745	32	31	22	1	57	...	987	10	
28. Skardu Tehsil ...	180	15	...	...	...	...	12	2	...	...	16	...	...	...	53,036	53,544	...	...	9	...	32	1	458	1	
29. Kargil " ...	129	28	11	7	...	...	19	4	...	...	3,750	3,794	...	...	19,923	20,062	...	...	21	1	88	1	683	41	
Total Gilgit District ...	770	46	...	...	...	...	41	16	...	...	...	...	...	...	12,471	10,604	17	4	19	5	56	...	709	8	
30. Gilgit Tehsil ...	751	43	...	...	...	...	41	16	...	...	...	...	...	...	8,301	6,504	15	4	17	5	50	...	649	7	
31. Astore " ...	19	3	...	...	...	...	...	...	...	...	...	...	...	...	4,170	4,100	2	...	2	...	6	...	60	1	
Total Frontier Ilaqas ...	284	11	1	...	...	...	22	2	...	...	...	...	...	...	28,970	25,144	1	...	...	...	...	...	...	...	
Chilas ...	118	7	...	...	...	...	14	2	...	...	...	...	...	...	6,775	5,591	1	...	...	...	...	...	...	...	
Nagar ...	...	...	...	...	...	...	...	...	...	...	...	...	...	...	7,148	6,199	...	...	...	...	...	...	...	...	
Hunza ...	...	...	...	...	...	...	...	...	...	...	...	...	...	...	5,457	4,669	...	...	...	...	...	...	...	...	
Punial ...	3	2	...	...	...	...	6	...	...	...	...	...	...	...	2,356	2,056	...	...	...	...	...	...	...	...	
Ishkoman ...	...	...	...	...	...	...	...	...	...	...	...	...	...	...	1,075	945	...	...	...	...	...	...	...	...	
Yasin ...	...	...	...	...	...	...	...	...	...	...	...	...	...	...	*3,291*	*3,019*	...	...	...	...	...	...	...	...	
Kuh ...	*163*	*2*	*1*	...	...	...	...	...	...	...	...	...	...	...	*1,002*	*896*	...	...	...	...	...	...	...	...	
Ghizar ...	...	...	...	...	...	...	*2*	...	...	...	...	...	...	...	*1,806*	*1,769*	...	...	...	...	...	...	...	...	
Total Yasin ...	163	2	1	...	...	...	2	...	...	...	...	...	...	...	6,159	5,684	...	...	...	...	...	...	...	...	